PSYCHOTHERAPY
WITH
CHILDREN OF DIVORCE

Other Books by Richard A. Gardner

The Boys and Girls Book About Divorce
Therapeutic Communication with Children: The Mutual
    Storytelling Technique
Dr. Gardner's Stories About the Real World, Volume I
Dr. Gardner's Stories About the Real World, Volume II
Dr. Gardner's Fairy Tales for Today's Children
Understanding Children: A Parents Guide to Child Rearing
MBD: The Family Book About Minimal Brain Dysfunction
Psychotherapeutic Approaches to the Resistant Child
Dr. Gardner's Modern Fairy Tales
The Parents Book About Divorce
The Boys and Girls Book About One-Parent Families
The Objective Diagnosis of Minimal Brain Dysfunction
Dorothy and the Lizard of Oz
Dr. Gardner's Fables for Our Times
The Boys and Girls Book About Stepfamilies
Family Evaluation in Child Custody Litigation
Separation Anxiety Disorder: Psychodynamics and
    Psychotherapy
Child Custody Litigation: A Guide for Parents
    and Mental Health Professionals
The Psychotherapeutic Techniques of Richard A. Gardner
Hyperactivity, The So-Called Attention-Deficit Disorder, and
    The Group of MBD Syndromes
The Parental Alienation Syndrome and the Differentiation
    Between Fabricated and Genuine Child Sex Abuse
Psychotherapy with Adolescents
Family Evaluation in Child Custody Mediation,
    Arbitration, and Litigation
The Girls and Boys Book About Good and Bad Behavior
Sex Abuse Hysteria: Salem Witch Trials Revisited
Psychotherapy of Psychogenic Learning Disabilities

PSYCHOTHERAPY
WITH
CHILDREN OF DIVORCE

Richard A. Gardner, M.D.

JASON ARONSON INC.
Northvale, New Jersey
London

Library of Congress Cataloging-in-Publication Data

Gardner, Richard A.
    Psychotherapy with children of divorce / Richard A. Gardner. – Rev. ed.
      p.   cm.
    Includes bibliographical references.
    Includes index.
    ISBN 0-87668-564-5
    1. Children of divorced parents–Mental health. 2. Child psychotherapy. 3. Divorce–Psychological aspects. 4. Divorce therapy. I. Title.
    [DNLM: 1. Adaptation, Psychological–in infancy & childhood. 2. Divorce. 3. Parent-Child Relations. 4. Psychotherapy–in infancy & childhood   WS 350 G228pa]
RJ507.D59G37 1991
618.92′8914–dc20
DNLM/DLC
for Library of Congress   90-14477

Jason Aronson Inc. offers books and cassettes. For information and catalog write to Jason Aronson Inc., 230 Livingston Street, Northvale, New Jersey 07647.

To

my wife

Lee

and

our three children

Andrew, Nancy, and Julie

ACKNOWLEDGMENTS

It is to the children of divorce that I am most indebted. They have taught me most of what I know about their difficulties. If not for them this book could never have been written. Although their names have been replaced with pseudonyms, and identifying data altered, they and their parents have otherwise kindly granted me permission to report their experiences.

I am grateful to my publisher, Dr. Jason Aronson, for agreeing to publish this book before even the first word was written. As every author can appreciate, such confidence and reassurance can make a significant difference in one's motivation. In addition, I appreciate his permission to quote from the following previously published works of mine:

The Boys and Girls Book about Divorce. New York: Jason Aronson, Inc., 1970.

Therapeutic Communication with Children: The Mutual Storytelling Technique. New York: Jason Aronson, Inc., 1971.

The Mutual Storytelling Technique in the Treatment of Anger Inhibition Problems. *International Journal of Child Psychotherapy*, 1 (1): 34-64.

Understanding Children. New York: Jason Aronson, Inc., 1973.

Psychotherapeutic Approaches to the Resistant Child. New York: Jason
    Aronson, Inc., 1975.

My ever-loyal and dedicated secretary, Linda Gould, patiently and gra-
ciously undertook the formidable labor of typing the manuscript in its various renditions and tackled the even more painstaking task of transcribing
verbatim material from audio and video tapes. The accuracy of these transcriptions is a tribute to her fortitude.

I am grateful to four attorneys—Mr. John Finnerty, Mr. Arthur Kronen-
berg, the Honorable Sherman Lester, Judge, Superior Court of New Jersey,
and Dean Michael Sovern of the Columbia University Law School—for their
recommendations on many of the legal points discussed in Chapter 14. As the
reader will well appreciate on reading that chapter, their advising me does
not necessarily constitute an endorsement of all the views presented.

Lastly, I am grateful to my wife Lee. As a child psychiatrist she was able to
provide valuable assistance. And, as a most devoted mother, she has taught
me much that has enhanced my knowledge of how to relate to children—
observations that have served me well in this as in my other works.

CONTENTS

INTRODUCTION

One of the concomitants of the increasing divorce rate that we have witnessed in recent years in the United States, as well as in many other countries, is the rising percentage of divorces that involve children. Apparently, people are not staying together "for the sake of the children" as frequently as they did in the past. Accordingly, there has been an ever-growing population of children of divorce.

Although I do not believe that divorce per se necessitates a child's receiving psychotherapy, it certainly increases the likelihood of its being warranted. Most children exhibit great resiliency and marked tolerance to a variety of upsetting experiences, both acute and chronic. However, the stresses that often precede a divorce, the traumas of separation, and the conflicts that often beset the child afterward, can all contribute to the formation of psychopathology. It is not surprising, then, that most child therapists have at least a few such patients in their practice at any given time. In fact, such children probably comprise one of the larger groups of patients that therapists see.

Books for divorce parents abound, yet few are written for their children. Although I was able to find many articles in the psychiatric and psychological literature relating, either directly or indirectly, to the psychotherapy of such children, I could find no books specifically devoted to the subject. This volume was written to fill that gap.

Generally I work closely with parents when I treat a child. Because children's psychopathology is so intimately related to their parents' attitudes toward and involvements with them, working with a child alone makes the therapist's task much more difficult. Although separated and divorced parents present special problems with regard to such cooperation with the therapist, I still make every reasonable attempt to involve one or both of them in various ways in the child's therapy. This book well reflects this approach. Not only are Chapters 1 and 13 specifically devoted to the therapist's work with them (primarily at the guidance and counseling level), but the parents are very much present in the other chapters as well.

The bulk of this book, of course, is devoted to the techniques I utilize in treating these children. I have devoted myself to a detailed description of the psychodynamics of the various problems that these children exhibit. I describe as well the therapeutic approaches I use in the treatment of their difficulties. Some of these techniques are traditional; others are not so. In the latter group are some that I myself have devised and for the reader who is not familiar with them I have devoted Chapter 3 to their description. I appreciate that every therapist has his own style and that techniques that can be useful for one therapist may not be useful for another. I present here mine in the hope that some of what I have found useful may prove helpful to others as well. At times I provide general treatment approaches; however, I believe that specific examples provide the reader with the most meaningful information. Accordingly, a significant amount of the clinical material is verbatim—providing the reader, I believe, with the optimal kind of data for understanding the methods I use. However, theoretical discussion always complements such raw data. Throughout, the clinical data is presented in the form of isolated vignettes, demonstrating the particular points under discussion. However, such a book would be deficient, in my opinion, without a complete case study; this I have provided in Chapter 15.

Therapists who work with children are being increasingly asked to involve themselves in divorce litigation, especially in custody determinations. There is little in the literature on the subject and I have therefore devoted Chapter 14 to this important subject.

One cannot deal intensively over many years with such a painful, and often traumatic, subject without giving thought to some of the social and cultural factors that are contributing to one's patients' difficulties. Treating a patient is dealing with the final result of a series of unfortunate, and sometimes tragic, events. As a contribution, somewhat feeble I admit, to changing some of the social factors that have contributed to my patients' difficulties, I discuss in Chapter 14 and in the Concluding Comments some recommendations which, if they ultimately were to be utilized, might prevent or diminish the kinds of problems to which this book is devoted.

PSYCHOTHERAPY
WITH
CHILDREN OF DIVORCE

Chapter 1

ADVISING SEPARATING PARENTS

I believe that children of divorce are most likely to be effectively helped with their psychogenic difficulties if the therapist works closely with one and even both parents. Even though the parents may be separated, and even divorced, the likelihood of the child's being helped is significantly enhanced if both parents contribute to the child's therapy. There are a number of ways in which parents may involve themselves in the child's treatment.

In some cases one parent may absolutely refuse to involve himself in any way in the child's treatment. In such situations I generally advise the parent who is receptive to involvement to inform the nonreceptive parent that his or her failure to contribute makes it less likely that I will be able to help the child. However, I will not refuse to treat the child and my hope is that the uninvolved parent will ultimately appreciate that his or her contributions can be useful to me and will increase the likelihood that the child's therapy will be successful.

Sometimes the parents are willing to cooperate, but absolutely refuse to see me together. This is especially true around the time of the divorce, when the bitterness between the parents is most intense. I generally respect a parent's wish in this regard and I then see them separately. My experience has been, however, that around the time of separation most parents are willing to see me together even though there may be some discomfort. Sometimes the parents are so enraged during the joint session that it may not be very productive —other than providing the therapist with an opportunity to observe firsthand the nature of the hostilities that exist between the parents. More often the parental hostilities are not so bitter that useful work is precluded.

Parental contributions to the psychiatric disorders of children of divorce can be divided into two categories. One or both parents may be suffering with a significant psychiatric disorder and the child so exposed may develop psychiatric disturbances of his own. Or, a parent may be relatively free of psychiatric disturbance but may be handling the child in such a misguided fashion as to produce such disturbances. At times, of course, there is significant overlap. In general, in both cases, the parents are well meaning and are trying to do everything possible to protect the child from developing psychological difficulties.

It is beyond the scope of this book to discuss in depth the treatment of the many psychiatric disturbances that the parents of such children may exhibit. Rather, I will focus on those deleterious influences that result from parental misguidance. It is my hope that such guidance will help relieve and avert some of the psychiatric difficulties that result from such parental inexperience, naivete, and misguidance. Although my advice in this area may serve to mitigate and prevent some of the difficulties caused by parental psychiatric illness, I am well aware that I can play only a limited role in this regard because such disturbances usually require much more intensive approaches than mere information and guidance.

Advising Parents When Separation Impends

It is completely beyond the scope of this book to discuss marital counseling in general. There are, however, certain aspects of such counseling that I wish to focus on because they are of the utmost relevance to the welfare of the children of parents who are contemplating separation.

It is impossible for a therapist (or anyone else) to predict whether a couple contemplating separation will be better off married or divorced. The therapist does well, therefore, to maintain a strictly neutral position with regard to this question. In such situations his efforts should be directed toward providing the parents with a clarification of the issues involved and alleviating pathological behavior. If he is successful in this regard the parents will then be able to make healthier and more prudent choices. It is most important that, whatever decision they make, they have the feeling that it was truly made by one or both of them. If the decision turns out to be an unfortunate one they must feel that they have only themselves to blame and if their choice proves to have been a judicious one they have no one but themselves to thank.

A therapist who boasts of never having had a divorce in his practice is probably (either consciously or unconsciously) pressuring some patients into remaining married when they might have been better off divorced. On the other hand, the therapist with a high frequency of divorces might very well be encouraging divorce (again, either consciously or unconsciously) when attempts at working through the marital difficulties might have been preferable. Sometimes the therapist's own marital history may contribute to his applying such inappropriate pressures. If he has been divorced and there was a resultant improvement in his life situation, he may tend to overvalue separation as the best course of action when there is a marital conflict. On the other hand, if his own marriage is a satisfying one, he may tend to encourage attempts at working-through when separation might be more advisable. Lastly, the therapist who has never been married, his assets notwithstanding, is in a poor position to appreciate fully the problems and conflicts of marriage and does well, in my opinion, to involve himself in other therapeutic areas.

I am in agreement with Whitaker and Miller (1969), who hold that the ideal counseling situation is the one in which the partners are seen conjointly by a therapist who has had no previous experience with either. In this way he is most likely to be impartial from the outset. When a therapist sees only one of the spouses he hears only one side of the story; in conjoint counseling he can hear both sides (and the differences may be dramatic). Conjoint therapy also provides him with the opportunity to observe the couple's interactions. Even were he to see each partner separately he would not get as much information about each as the joint sessions can provide. I am not suggesting that he only see the partners together; in many situations seeing each separately as well can also be helpful. Another advantage of joint counseling is that if it results in a maintenance of the marital relationship, the partners have had a healthy experience in mutual inquiry that should serve them well in their future relationship. If, however, it results in their divorcing they should at least become clear about the reasons for their decision. Hopefully, what they have learned in their counseling will help them avoid another injudicious marriage.

In doing such counseling I do not hesitate to express my opinion regarding the appropriateness or inappropriateness of thoughts, feelings, and behavior. Although this may appear as if I am taking sides, it is not the side of the person so much that I am joining, but the side of health. In other words, I support salutary behavior, regardless of who exhibits it, and discourage pathological behavior, regardless of who manifests it. If the therapist is genuinely benevolent with regard to such confrontations and interpretations it is not likely that either party will consider him to be favoring the other even though in any particular session one partner may receive more criticism than the other.

In such counseling each partner may try to use the therapist as a tool in neurotic maneuvers. The therapist must be aware of such tendencies and strictly refuse to involve himself in such manipulations. For example, a wife may try to enlist the therapist's aid in pressuring her husband into spending more time at home when he has little motivation to do so. Or, a husband may try to enlist the therapist's assistance in getting his wife to remain in the marriage when she is strongly inclined to separate.

Even when the therapist is successful in maintaining a strictly neutral role, the partners may attribute to him motives that are genuinely not his. Usually these are projections of the patients and reflect their wishes that he manifest a particular attitude or behavioral pattern. For examle, a husband may conclude that the therapist's failure to condemn his wife for infidelity served to sanction it. And she too may consider this to be the case. A wife may interpret the therapist's neutrality as support for her decision to separate. Such a conclusion may arise from the need for support and encouragement to take such an anxiety-provoking step.

It is important for the therapist to appreciate that both parents are usually quite ambivalent regarding the divorce and they may waver between periods when one or both are quite sure that they will divorce to times when they may feel that they will be able to work things out. The therapist should appreciate that even when things are going badly it behooves him to refrain from encouraging either party to make the break. Each of the parents generally needs a period of desensitization to an impending divorce, and this takes time. He must show the greatest respect, therefore, for the parents' ambivalence, procrastination, and indecisiveness. They are all parts of the working-through process. It is also important to impress upon the parents (Schwartz, 1968) the notion that divorce is not necessarily the result of neurotic inability to adjust, but rather it can be a manifestation of a healthy attempt to rectify an unfortunate error.

It has been my experience that many couples divorce because they naively believe that their situation will be immeasurably improved in another marriage. They believe that the euphoria of romantic love should exist continuously and the failure of such intense feelings to persist is evidence of a deep deficiency in the relationship. I believe that such a view is a legacy of the chivalric tradition of the Frech Renaissance, has been perpetuated down the generations, and has enjoyed its widest popularity as a result of the ubiquitous mass media. I believe that a certain amount of romantic euphoria can enrich a relationship and counterbalance some of the pains and frustrations that are an inevitable part of marriage. However, the individual who feels that it is possible to maintain such feelings practically uninterruptedly throughout the course of a lifetime is doomed to disappointment. He will inevitably be disillusioned, no matter how many times he gets married. As with the narcotic that romantic love resembles, the individual will ultimately develop tolerance, will require more and more to get the same effect, and will ultimately find that it fails to provide euphoria at all.

Accordingly, I generally advise couples who are planning divorce to look carefully at those around them—especially those whom they consider to be enjoying "happy marriages." I suggest that they give special attention to those who have been divorced and remarried to see whether such couples have found the happiness that the separating couple anticipates in a remarriage. I recommend that they talk as intimately as possible with close friends and relatives who are willing to discuss their marriages and see if they can find anyone *in the real world* who even approaches the kind of happy marriage they are seeking. It is indeed amazing how few people do this and how many blindly believe they will be able to accomplish what no one off the movie screen has been able to achieve.

In addition, I try to help such parents appreciate that marriage invariably involves significant frustration and restriction—its gratifications notwithstanding. I ask them to try to weigh the disadvantages of the marriage against the misery they may suffer when separated and divorced. I suggest they talk carefully with friends and relatives who have been separated and divorced, and think seriously about whether they wish to suffer such pains and discomforts and whether their present pain is greater.

It is important for the therapist to direct the parents' attention to these considerations as part of the process of helping them weigh the pros and cons of the separation and divorce. It should not be part of an attempt to keep them together. To do so would be a terrible disservice and might contribute to their perpetuating a sick and extremely painful situation.

Weinstein (a lawyer) and Moskowitz (a psychiatrist) (1972) are a husband and wife team who have had extensive experience with predivorce counseling. Although they tend to emphasize the value of staying together, I believe their work is a significant contribution in that it serves to counterbalance what I observe to be a recent trend among counselors in which the divorce route is too frequently encouraged and the arguments for staying together are not given proper emphasis.

Family interviews can sometimes be helpful in such consultations. Younger children are not generally valuable sources of direct information; however, observing the parents with them can often provide useful data. Adolescents, on the other hand, if they are comfortable enough to provide their opinions and observations, can be a valuable source of information. On occasion, I have seen one or both of the parents of the couple anticipating separation. At times they are playing an important role in the decision. We never outgrow completely the influence of our parents and even after they die their wishes and thoughts enter our minds and influence our behavior. I believe that parents of couples anticipating separation are not utilized frequently enough in the counseling process. I believe that if this were to become more common practice the efficiency of the counseling experience would be enhanced. Of course, one should not go overboard with regard to family interviews and bringing in spouses' parents. There are many issues that are justifiably discussed alone—intimate issues that are of no direct concern to other parties.

When separation impends, individual therapy with married parents presents special problems. If therapeutic work with the one partner is successful, the changes may cause anxiety in the other. This is especially the case when the other is not in treatment. Therapy with one partner tends to unbalance and disrupt neurotic equilibria that may have served to keep the marriage intact. Sometimes the partner adapts and involves himself in healthier forms of interaction. The marriage then is maintained on a new and more secure foundation. On occasion, however, the partner may be unable to make such adjustments. He may then seek others with whom he can form his pathological involvements and gain his neurotic gratifications. Treatment in such cases may then contribute to the separation. There is no question that this is one of the dangers of therapy, and married people who enter into treatment should be apprised (at the appropriate time) of this possibility.

When a marital partner is in therapy the intimacy he or she shares with the therapist generally causes some feelings of alienation and jealousy in the other partner, and this can be divisive for a marital relationship and intensify marital difficulties. Whatever benefits the untreated marital partner may hope to derive from the spouse's therapy, he or she suffers a certain amount of invasion of privacy that generally results in some resentment toward the spouse and the therapist. If the therapist advises his patient not to discuss what goes on in the session with anyone, including the spouse, further feelings of alienation between the partners may be engendered. (To avoid this potentially divisive effect of therapy, I generally advise my married patients to discuss as openly and as freely as they wish any aspect of their therapy with anyone, spouse or non-spouse. I still respect their right to privacy, but believe that the more open communication there is between people, the less the likelihood of interpersonal and even intrapsychic difficulties.)

Many therapists believe that the ideal therapeutic program for a couple with marital problems is one in which each partner sees his own therapist. This view is especially common among classical Freudian psychoanalysts, who hold that the best way of resolving the intrapsychic conflicts that are contributing to a marital conflict is for each partner to work out his problems along with his own separate analyst. In addition, they believe that the development of a transference neurosis is compromised if the patient sees another therapist for counseling or if the patient's spouse were to come in for one or more joint interviews. I am in sharp disagreement with this position. A patient's transference is not necessarily diluted by seeing a second therapist for counseling. The pressure to form neurotic interactions with others is powerful and does not confine itself exclusively to one's own analyst. It is likely that the same pathological modes of interaction will reveal themselves with the counselor, as well as with a host of others whom the patient encounters. Many classical analysts will refuse to see a spouse along with a patient (or alone separately) even for one session, lest the closeness of the therapist's relationship with the patient be diluted. It does not speak well for such a relationship, in my opinion, if it can be jeopardized by a single meeting or even many meetings with a spouse. This is similar to a parent's saying that he only wants to have one child because if he has two he will have to reduce the amount of affection he can provide for each.

It is difficult, if not impossible, for a therapist to avoid siding with his patient in a marital conflict. I do not believe that a therapist can be so objective that he doesn't tend to be sympathetic with his patient's view. Hearing only one side of a story deprives him of the opportunity to get the kind of balanced and clear picture of the marital conflict that is necessary if he is to come to meaningful conclusions about it. Anyone who has involved himself in marital counseling quickly sees how differently the two partners can see the same situation. Furthermore the very nature of the therapeutic situation seduces the therapist into losing some of his objectivity with his patient and increases his tendency to side with his patient in a marital conflict. After all, the therapist cannot but be flattered that the patient has chosen him—over all the other people in the whole world—to confide in and share his innermost secrets. The therapist cannot but admire a person who shows such good judgment. And after the relationship has been established, and if the patient starts to consider the therapist the most sympathetic, empathetic, understanding, benevolent, and brilliant person he has ever had the good fortune to meet, the therapist's admiration and affection for the patient increases even further. We love most those who have the good sense to appreciate our assets. And we love even more those who enumerate these to us at length. Such affection on the therapist's part cannot but blind him to some, if not many, of his patient's defects—defects that are contributing to marital difficulties. Often this results in the therapist's developing totally unwarranted antagonisms toward the spouse.

This situation has caused, in my opinion, many divorces that should never have taken place. These are marriages that would have been saved, to the

mutual benefit of parents and children, if the therapists had seen both partners (not necessarily in joint counseling, and not necessarily with both parties
seeing the same therapist); just having had the opportunity to see the spouse
on occasion might have been enough to correct the therapist's distortions
that contributed to the marital difficulties. I believe that a therapist who refuses to meet with the spouse of a patient involved in a marital conflict is
acting in an unconscionable fashion. Although many are certainly well
meaning, I believe they are misguided in their rigidly subscribing to a theoretical principle that not only has not been conclusively validated, but has
strong and convincing arguments against it. Accordingly, if a husband is
paying for his wife's treatment and if her therapist absolutely refuses to see
him when a marital conflict is a primary problem, I advise him to refuse to
pay the therapist and insist that his wife choose a person with another view.
Otherwise, he may be paying a man to contribute to the further deterioration
of his relationship. I have no statistics on the subject, and it would be a difficult thing to demonstrate with certainty, but I am convinced that my view of
this situation is valid.

I believe that the ideal therapeutic program for a couple with marital
problems is one in which both parties can be seen by the same therapist, in
both individual and joint sessions. When, however, there is a significant
amount of material that each does not wish revealed to the other (whether
appropriately or not) then it is probably best for the two to be seen by separate therapists. A patient's therapy is compromised when the therapist has
relevant information which cannot be divulged. When the spouses have separate therapists there should be joint sessions as well. These are best conducted, in my opinion, by the two therapists alternating according to which
therapist would be preferable for focusing on a particular issue. The therapists should be free to communicate with one another and to reveal to one
another, at their discretion, what they consider to be indicated and constructive. Each should appreciate that he should not burden the other therapist
with information that he cannot reveal to his patient. Counseling by a third
party, although a viable alternative, is not as advisable as counseling by one
of the two therapists. There are enough potential contaminants with two
therapists involved (distortions, communications errors, rivalries); a third can
often compound these complications.

Another type of counseling experience that I have found useful as an adjunct to the individual work and as an alternative to seeing the couple alone,
is couples' group therapy. I have found three or four couples to be the optimal number for such a group. Two couples does not provide enough variety
of opinion and richness of interaction, and when one or more people are absent the group gets too small for efficient work. More than four couples
makes the group too large for each couple to get optimum opportunity for

airing their difficulties. The couples meet with me for an hour and a half, once a week, and then alternate after-group meetings at one another's homes where they have the opportunity to observe one another in their natural surroundings. The postgroup discussions are kept on the same therapeutic level and generally last two to four hours. In addition, the five or so hours of exposure increases the chances that people will relax and reveal themselves.

I wish to emphasize that I believe that therapy can be a very valuable experience for couples with marital difficulties. It may save many marriages and put them on a more secure foundation. It can help others, who are best off divorced, to do so in the least traumatic and most sane manner—and it can help those so separated make more judicious relationships in the future, both in and out of marriage. As described, however, there are certain therapeutic practices that can be deleterious to a marriage. If one is aware of these and avoids implementing them, then one can gain the advantages of the psychotherapeutic approach and need not expose one's patients to these potentially deleterious and divisive experiences.

On occasion, an individual may seek treatment because his spouse threatens separation unless he gets therapy. Because such a person's motivation for therapy comes from without, rather than from within, there is little likelihood that meaningful changes will occur. Unless a person is motivated to change things within himself because of inner pain he experiences over his problems, he is not likely to derive much benefit from a therapeutic experience. Such a person may come with the hope of altering those behavioral patterns that are alienating his spouse or he may wish to learn a way to manipulate the partner into remaining in the marriage. Again, with such intentions the therapy is most likely to fail.

Whether or not to stay together "for the sake of the children." Parents contemplating divorce generally will give consideration to staying together "for the sake of the children." They will generally recognize that their unhappy relationship may very well be deleterious to the children, but they fear that the alternative of divorce will even be more devastating. Accordingly, they may decide to remain together even though unhappy, in order to protect the children from the effects of a separation.

Despert (1953) was one of the earliest to emphasize the fact that divorce was not necessarily worse for the children than the maintenance of an unhappy marriage. The studies of Nye (1957) and Landis (1960) tend to substantiate Despert's position. Their studies suggest that there is less psychiatric disturbance in children from broken homes than in those from intact but unhappy homes. Gettleman and Markowitz (1974) emphasize how divorce can result in a cessation of the years of bickering that can be so detrimental to a child's psychological development. Nevertheless, one cannot predict which will be the better situation for any given child. Although the statistics may be on the side of separating, there are still children in separated and divorced homes who are worse off than they would have been had the parents remained together. Accordingly, it behooves the therapist to impress upon the parents what the overall odds are for a large number of children, but to impress upon them the fact that this may not necessarily apply to their own.

There are those who recommend that parents not consider the divorce's effects on the children in making their decision. They recommend that the parents make the decision as if the children were not being affected. They consider the children's welfare to be a contaminant to such decision making. My own belief is that the effects on the children should be one of the considerations, albeit minor. The major determinants should be whether or not the parents feel that there is enough pain in their relationship to warrant its being broken. However, in addition to considering the frustrations each will suffer following the separation and divorce, they should also take into account the effects of their decision on their children.

Sometimes parents will maintain that they are staying together for the sake of the children when in reality the relationship is being maintained for such other reasons as fear of the unknown, fear of criticism of relatives and friends, reluctance to suffer the financial pressures that the divorce will entail, fear of being alone, and fear of the increased responsibilities that will result from the divorce. Professions of concern for the children may often be only rationalizations to buttress various neurotic interactions. Sadomasochistic, overprotective, overdependent, symbiotic, and other pathological relationships may be serving as the basis for the marriage. The therapist should, insofar as it is possible, clarify these underlying issues for the couple while playing down the falsely benevolent considerations regarding the children's welfare. The therapist, however, must keep in mind the important advice of Arnstein (1962), who states, "Yet divorce is often a clean break which gives promise of a new and better life for all. Instead of looking back with regret and remorse, parents can look ahead and plan for a happier life for themselves and their young." Considering the new hope that a divorce may offer for both parents and children, it behooves the therapist to maintain the careful neutral attitude I have previously emphasized, providing all the while information, both pro and con, that will be of use to the parents in making their decision.

The percentage of divorces involving children appears to be increasing. In 1953, 45.5 percent of the divorces in the United States involved children; in 1958, the figure was 55.1 percent; and in 1963, the percentage was 61.1. Apparently the belief that marriage should be maintained "for the sake of the children" is losing its force (Plateris, 1967).

"Is there a critical age at which divorce is most deleterious to the child?"

The parent who asks this question is generally one who has read an article in which a person conversant with psychological theory describes such critical periods and advises parents who are contemplating divorce to wait until their child (or children) has passed the particular time in his development. I often consider the writers of such articles to be demonstrating quite well the mis-application and impractical implementation of psychological theory. Even if there were such critical periods, the likelihood that such advice would be useful for most families is quite small. If there is one child in the family then it might be possible for the parents to wait until the child has grown beyond the point when the divorce would be particularly traumatic. However, most families have two or more children. Accordingly, it is likely that after one child has passed the critical period, a younger child will be entering it. It is conceivable that parents who took such advice very seriously and decided to stay together until all the children had passed through the various critical periods might have to wait ten to fifteen years before getting a divorce.

Another reason why such advice is naive is that it fails to take into account other important considerations that are operative at the time when a couple is seriously contemplating divorce. It may have taken the couple many years to have reached the point at which they have finally decided to separate —the point at which the pain of their remaining together outweighs its advantages. To recommend that such parents maintain their relationship for months and even years is, in my opinion, giving priority to a speculated need of the child over an actual need of the parents. It may result in their suffering years of further hardship and misery. And the parent who does not follow the experts' advice in this regard may add an additional burden of guilt to that which he already suffers over the effects the divorce may have on his children. In addition, it is quite common that one or both have already become deeply involved with a third person. To suggest such a period of waiting may unnecessarily deprive the parties concerned of the opportunity for freer involvement in what could be a salutary and ego-enhancing relationship. There is probably no better way to assuage the pains, humiliations, and ego-debasements of a divorce than to find oneself with another person who considers one worthwhile and loving. The therapist should not be instrumental in depriving divorcing parents of this important compensatory experience.

Those who believe that there is such a critical period (or periods) often point to the oedipal phase as one of the child's most vulnerable. Neubauer (1960) and Westman (1972) are among those who believe that a father's leaving the home when a little girl is between the ages of three and five deprives her of a male figure at a time when she is most involved in forming the foundation for her future relationship with members of the opposite sex. The father's absenting himself during this period can contribute to the girl's developing various kinds of psychosexual difficulties. In addition, they hold that the little boy, during this period, is likely to consider his father's leaving to be the result of the boy's wishes that the father do so in order that the youngster may have unrivaled possession of his mother. Accordingly, he may develop distorted ideas about the power of his wishes and guilt over the fact that he has brought such a catastrophe upon his home. And such reactions are likely to foment various kinds of secondary neurotic symptoms designed to deal with these notions. An extension of this theory considers the youngster in the early- to mid-adolescent period also to be particularly vulnerable to psychological harm from parental separation. The theory holds that there is a reactivation of the infantile Oedipus complex in the postpubertal period with its upsurgence of genital-sexual excitation. Again, the father's leaving will deprive the girl of learning how to relate successfully to males, and the boy may develop the aforementioned magical thinking and guilt. In addition, many consider the adolescent period to be crucial for the boy's final male identification and his being deprived of a father at this time is particularly damaging.

Some claim that the couple should wait until the youngest child has started school. In this way, the mother will not be left with the burden of having to take care of many young children at home and will have greater opportunity for extra-domestic activities to compensate for the pains and frustrations associated with the divorce. Others advise parents not to separate at the time school starts because then the child is exposed to two separations simultaneously.

On the basis of my own experiences I am not convinced that there are *special* periods during which the child is *particularly* vulnerable to the effects of parental separation. Rather, I believe that from the day of birth the child is in need of both parents and that the removal of either will have a deleterious effect on his psychological development. Although the boy may not need his father during the first few months of life as a model for identification, he does so after that (possibly even until the time that the father dies). I do not see the three years to five years period or the adolescent period to be particularly crucial with regard to such identification; rather I envision the identification process as a continuum which tapers off in late adolescence and early adulthood. However, the process may continue to a lesser degree throughout the person's life. With regard to the little boy's interest in his mother, I believe that her role as the prototypical woman begins at birth and continues throughout life. Because she is the model upon which all other women are built and compared, her loss can result in significant distortions in the boy's relationship with females. The earlier the boy is deprived of his mother or his father, the longer he will suffer deprivation and the greater the likelihood that psychopathology will result.

With regard to the girl, I believe the same considerations hold. The earlier a girl is deprived of her father, the greater the likelihood she will have difficulties relating to men. Similarly, the earlier she is deprived of her mother, the greater the likelihood she will suffer not only problems in identification with females, but other difficulties as well—difficulties stemming from the generalized emotional deprivation entailed in the mother's loss. For both the boy and the girl I am in agreement that losses during the oedipal and adolescent period can be very detrimental; but I am not convinced that parental loss during these periods is more important than in other phases in bringing about an interference with the child's ability to grow up healthy and attain adult independence.

The only generalization with regard to this matter that I do believe holds is that the younger the child is when the loss occurs and the longer he is exposed to the loss, the greater will be the detrimental effects. However, I do not recommend that parents wait until the child or children get older so that they may be less affected by the separation. I do advise parents that I believe that the older the children at the time of separation the more opportunity they will have had for the beneficial effects of having two parents; however, I quickly add that they must consider the detrimental effects of the unhappy home on the children, as well as the many other factors of importance in making their decision. I suggest that they not consider the age of the children to be the most critical issue.

Predivorce shame and guilt. There are some parents who are quite ashamed to come for predivorce counseling. Generally they are people who have believed that only "crazy" people go to therapists and that if their friends were to learn of it they would be ridiculed. Although society has come a long way in recognizing that people with emotional problems are not suffering with a loathsome disorder, there is still much room for improvement in the attitude of many, if not most, people. Such parents need to be reassured that most of the people therapists see do not appear any different from anyone else and that their problems are not so grave that they are obvious to the world. Of course, there will be rare situations when the parents' difficulties are so deep that they are obvious to most around them and then, of course, such advice is not applicable. In addition, the parents can be helped to tolerate their embarrassment with the reassurance that their confidences will be held private and that the benefits that may accrue to them from such counseling would far outweigh any discomforts they may feel.

Most parents feel significantly guilty over a divorce. They appreciate that no matter how salutary the divorce decision may prove to be, the children are still going to suffer. Perhaps they will suffer less than they had in the unhappy home, but they will still experience certain deprivations. There is guilt not only over what has gone before, i.e., the detrimental effects of the parental conflict on the children, but over what is to come, i.e., the deleterious effects of living in a home without one of the parents. In fact, if a parent does not feel guilty over the divorce (all promises of a better life notwithstanding), I would consider this to reflect a deficiency in that parent's affection for the child and a lack of appreciation of the effects of the divorce on the child.

In counseling such parents I try to help them differentiate between two kinds of guilt. I use the analogy of the man who purchases an automobile and because of faulty manufacturing has an accident in which someone is injured. This man is treated quite differently by the courts from one who injures someone with his car in a premeditated fashion. The former is not considered a criminal whereas the latter is. Although the victim's pains and injuries may be identical, the drivers are in very different positions regarding the appropriateness of guilt. I try to help the parents appreciate that their marriage was a misguided one and that the suffering their mistake has brought to both themselves and their children was the result of their well-meaning but ill-advised union. I try to reassure them that to the best of my knowledge they have both tried very hard to do what they considered best for the children. (Of course, there are times, although rare, when this has not been the case and so such advice is not applicable.) I try to impress upon them that I view them as similar to the man driving the car with a factory defect. Although it may be true that the victim would not have been injured had the man not been driving the car at that time, it is also true that the driver was in no way at fault. Neither the driver nor the separating couple inflict pain through malicious intent.

I do not stop at that point, however. I try to impress upon the parents that what I have said will be far less effective in assuaging their guilt than their taking constructive action to interrupt a perpetuation of the unhealthy atmosphere to which they may have been exposing their children and to do everything possible to help their children "pick up the pieces" and make the best of a difficult situation. To the degree that they can actively contribute to the rectification of the children's situation, to that degree their guilt will be lessened. If they continue to embroil the children in their difficulties (if that has been the case), then they can expect them to continue suffering and they can thereby anticipate a perpetuation of their own guilt. I also advise them that my experience has been that many parents are so swept up in their antagonisms that they lose sight of the effects of the continuing hostility on their children. However, for most the fighting ultimately dies down and then they may first see how detrimental the unnecessary perpetuation of the hostilities has been. One could argue that I am providing such parents with unneccesarily harsh guilt evocation. I am in agreement that I am evoking guilt; but I am not in agreement that it is unwarranted. There are many individuals whose psychopathology relates to their deficiencies in guilt mechanisms—

with the result that many around them suffer needlessly. Fostering some guilt in many parents of divorce may not only be helpful to them in reducing their incessant conflicts, but can have a salutary effect on their children as well. Clearly, it is preferable to work with such parents and help them resolve their difficulties in a deeper and more meaningful manner; but even in such cases, judicious elicitation of guilt can be useful and of more immediate value.

Whitaker and Miller (1969) describe three common ways in which a spouse (more commonly the husband) may attempt to assuage his guilt over the divorce: 1) encourage (either overtly or covertly) the rejected spouse to take a lover, 2) facilitate the rejected spouse's return to a parent (or parents), and 3) provide a therapist. I too, have observed these guilt-alleviating maneuvers and would add a fourth: provide money. The therapist counseling divorcing couples should be aware that the guilt-alleviating motivation may be operative in such situations. Many need a lover in order to bridge the gap of loneliness that faces the individual getting a divorce. The single woman who absolutely refuses to involve herself with a married man may be depriving herself of an opportunity for marriage. Such a woman must appreciate that there are many men who can separate only if there is someone "waiting in the wings." The same holds true, of course, with married women anticipating divorce; however, as Hunt (1966) describes, such waiting third parties are less common for women than for men. When the leaving party has a lover he or she may encourage the partner to take on one as well in order to assuage his or her own guilt over the affair.

The party who returns to parents (usually the mother) is often doing so for very practical reasons: there is financial saving and grandparents are well suited to help take care of the children. However, dependency considerations are often quite important as well. The mature woman will generally find a return to her own home humiliating and infantilizing, and will be willing to suffer the privations of an independent existence rather than subject herself to the shame of "returning to the womb." Her husband, however, may encourage her returning to her parents not only because of the financial savings but to assuage his guilt over his "abandonment."

Many husbands (often previously unreceptive to their wives' going into therapy) will encourage such a decision around the time of the separation. Generally, such a husband's acquiescence is not particularly motivated by the desire to pay for his wife's gaining increased insight into her underlying psychological processes; rather it is a manifestation of his desire to lessen his guilt over leaving her. The husband may fear that his wife will "fall apart" and he hopes the psychiatrist will prevent the impending calamity to which he may consider himself a contributor. Others may hope that the therapist will substitute for them and thereby help fill the void for their wives. Wives themselves will often seek therapy for this reason and on occasion it is conscious. If this is the primary motive for such a wife's being in treatment, the likelihood that anything therapeutically beneficial will come out of the arrangement is quite small. Accordingly, the therapist should appreciate the presence of this element in such a patient's motivation for seeking treatment.

Although divorce imposes formidable economic hardships on the overwhelming majority of those who choose it, there are some who will use money in an attempt to assuage the guilt they feel over what they consider to have been an "abandonment" of their families. Of course, such a guilt-alleviating maneuver is most readily utilized by the wealthy. Alimony laws in most states are particularly well suited to assist such individuals. We are all familiar with the astronomical settlements, common among the rich, that enable the woman to "live in the life style to which she was previously accustomed." Their wives, too, can generally be counted upon to help such husbands assuage their guilt. But even poorer individuals may offer (or allow to be taken) more money than they can reasonably afford in order to lessen their guilt. Again, alimony laws and wives can generally be counted upon to comply with the neurotic offering.

There are some parents who will actually consult the children regarding *their* opinion as to whether or not the parents should get a divorce. The ostensible reason sometimes given for enlisting the children's opinion is that it is a sign of egalitarianism and democracy in the family. I am not a believer in such a democratic system, believing as I do that the judgment of children is not as good as that of most adults. In some of these situations the parents are essentially asking for the children's permission. The inquiry is approached with the hope that the children will provide it and thereby lessen the parents' guilt over breaking up the home. Others may be quite frightened of anyone's expressing anger to them—regardless of the age of the angry person or the appropriateness of the anger. Consulting the children about the divorce and asking permission is done in the hope that the children will not be angry. Such children may have long since learned of the parents' ultrasensitivity to angry responses on their parts and so they may comply with the parental wish that no anger be professed. The healthy parent recognizes the inevitability of angry responses on the part of the children over the divorce and has enough ego strength to tolerate such hostility.

A parent may not wish to tell the children about the reason for a divorce because of shame. Most commonly infidelity as the cause of the divorce is the reason which the parent is ashamed to disclose. However, other problems such as alcoholism, obsessive gambling, and drug addiction are common causes of divorce that are a source of great shame to the afflicted parent. In the latter cases the children are usually aware of the problem anyway. When infidelity is the cause they may or may not have become aware. Because I believe (as I will soon discuss in detail) that children should be given information about the *major issues* that brought about the separation (and I would consider infidelity to be in that category), the parent does the child a disservice when withholding such vital information.

Accordingly, I generally advise such a parent of the importance of providing his children with this kind of information. (I will detail below my various reasons for taking this position.) Although enumerating these reasons may make the parent more receptive to divulging the infidelity, it does not reduce the shame. To lessen this I generally try to help the parent appreciate that the word *infidelity* is in itself pejorative. Strictly speaking it refers to one's being unfaithful to a vow—with an implicit connotation of punishment from on high. (This is not to mention the additional punishment here on earth, from one's fellow men.) If the infidelity was the result of significant difficulties in the marital relationship and was an attempt to gain some solace and affection when there was little, if any, forthcoming at home, then I try to help the parent appreciate that the affair was human and almost predictable. If the faithful spouse exhibits condemning intolerance for the infidelity (especially when it was uncommon or unassociated with deep involvement) and if that spouse is unreceptive to attempting to work out any problems that may have contributed to such infidelity, then I try to impress upon the unfaithful spouse the inappropriateness of the other's attitudes. I try to impress upon the parent what I consider to be the unfortunate social, moral, and religious condemnation that is unfortunately the lot of the unfaithful. And I try to impress upon both parties the fact that the human being's desire for variety is ubiquitous and that marriage demands a degree of frustration tolerance of one's desires for variety greater than practically any other institution or situation. I try to impress upon the parents that some people are willing to accept the frustrations attendant on their inhibiting their desires for sexual variety because they are not willing to tolerate the repercussions of infidelity. Others choose to gratify these desires, to greater or lesser degrees.

My comments by no means cover the wide variety of those appropriate to such situations. In essence, I try to lessen shame to the point where the parent would be willing to divulge the fact of infidelity as a reason for the divorce. This is not to say that I suggest divulging unnecessarily the identity of the individual or individuals involved, nor details of the parents' sexual life—either with the spouse or with third parties. There may still be some shame left, and appropriately so because, whatever the circumstances, a trust has been broken. My aim is to lessen exaggerated and inappropriate shame to the point where the parent can, with minimal discomfort under the circumstances, provide his children with a proper degree of information concerning the reasons for the separation.

Advising Parents at the Time of the Separation

"When should the children be told about an impending separation?" Like many of the other questions dealt with in this book, there are no simple answers. On the one hand, telling a child long in advance may provide him with the opportunity to work through his reactions in a setting where the departing parent is still available to help him work them out. However, long periods of time between the announcement and the actual departure may serve to entrench the child's denial mechanisms. In addition, younger children are not appreciative of time passage with the accuracy of adults and so significant notice is of little value. Also, the long waiting period may prolong the children's agony.

On the other hand, giving extremely short notice does have the advantage of shortening the painful waiting period; it may, however, deprive the child of the opportunity to work through his reactions and to adjust adequately to the trauma.

Kliman (1968) is a proponent of long advance notice because it provides the child with an opportunity for expressing the angry feelings that inevitably arise during this period. I agree with him that it is better to express such anger when the parent is in the home than after he has left. After the parent's departure the child is more likely to utilize inappropriate mechanisms for anger expression, such as displacement and repression.

I generally advise parents to tell the children when a *definite* decision for separation has been made. I emphasize the word *definite* because it is cruel and psychologically deleterious to subject the children to the numerous decisions for separation that often precede the final one. Such cycles of dashed and raised-up hopes cannot but be psychologically deleterious to them. I recognize, however, that there may be times (hopefully not frequently) when the parents have made a definite decision to separate and then change their minds. The children must be told about the changed plans and will probably not suffer from one such cycle. The more frequent they become, however, the greater the likelihood that new traumas will be added to those to which the children have already been exposed. If the parents have decided upon a trial separation the child should be told this. Although this presents the danger of the back and forth situation, their not being told may result in new problems arising—problems which relate to loss of trust and the other effects of parental secretiveness and duplicity (which I will discuss in detail below).

There are some parents who tell the children at the last possible moment, ostensibly to shorten the children's agony as much as possible. My experience has been that in such cases it is more likely the parental agony that is of concern. With bags packed, the departing parent informs the children that he is leaving—and then rushes out of the house. Concern for the welfare of the children and "getting it over quickly" for their benefit is used as a rationalization to cover up parental cowardice, shame, and lack of concern for the children's need to work through the separation.

If the time between the actual decision to separate and the actual time of separation is long (many weeks, or even months) then one might wish to withhold the information until a few weeks prior to the separation. I believe this is a justifiable plan in that it protects the children from prolongation of their pain and yet provides them with an adequate opportunity for working through their reactions. Because of the range and variations in the capacity for humans to adjust to a trauma one cannot have any hard and fast rules regarding the optimum time between disclosure and departure. Giving practically no advance warning is clearly deleterious, as is the child's being party to every ambivalent decision. There is less danger, in my opinion, in the child's being told in advance and much to argue for it.

"Who should tell the children?" I am in agreement with Grollman (1969) that both parents should tell the children. Such an approach lessens the likelihood that one parent will try to make the other solely responsible. Although there certainly are divorces in which one of the partners is more responsible than the other for the deterioration of the marriage, the more common situation, in my experience, is that both partners have contributed (often through a dovetailing of their neurotic needs and interactions). Both parents' telling can serve to lessen the inevitable insecurities that befall children at such a time. Implicit in the fact that both parents are providing the painful information is the notion that, although soon to be separated, they will both be available to discuss the separation and divorce issues further. Having two parents available for consultation, support, and discussion is certainly better than one and can contribute (admittedly in only a small way) to the prevention of untoward psychological sequelae.

Sometimes a parent may not wish to be the one to tell the children and prefers that the other do so. At times the reluctant parent is ashamed of what may be revealed in such a conversation. Such parents are fearful of the children's probable angry response and cannot tolerate the hostility. Others may be so guilt-ridden over the impending separation that they cannot face their children's pained responses. Such a parent may request, and even try to coerce, the other parent into withholding vital information from the children. Generally, this is done in the service of withholding information that might be detrimental to the parent's image—both to himself and to his children.

I generally advise the parent who wishes to communicate the information to go ahead and do so. I recommend that he respect the partner's request to withhold information that should appropriately be withheld from the children, but that he not withhold information that is important for the children to have if they are to adjust optimally to the separation. As I maintain below, the main issues of the separation should be divulged to the children even if they involve such matters as infidelity. (One need not provide many specific details; rather, only those general issues that given the children a meaningful explanation of the causes of the separation.) The parent who withholds damaging information from the children (information that they should know if they are to deal optimally with the separation) in order to protect the image of the spouse is doing the children (and the spouse) a disservice. As I will discuss in detail below, such "protection" causes the child to lose trust in the parent who is withholding the vital information and confuses him about the parent whose liabilities are being covered up.

Sometimes a parent who wishes to provide more information complies with the withholding parent's demands from passive dependency on the spouse. Although recognizing the value of the disclosure, the parent is too fearful of invoking the anger of the partner to do what would be in the best interests of the children.

"How old should a child be before he is told that his parents are going to separate?" This question reminds me of a response made by an otolaryngology instructor of mine in medical school when asked the question: "How old should a baby be before one would provide him with a hearing aid?" His response: "If it were a breech delivery, I would wait until the head comes out." Although I would certainly not spend time giving a newborn infant, or one a few months old, a talk about a parent's impending separation from the home, I would allow the toddler access to such conversations with older children. Certainly by eight to nine months of age most babies differentiate their parents from strangers and, I believe, are significantly affected by a parent's departure from the home. There are many parents who will not tell preschoolers about an impending separation allegedly because "they're too young to understand." Such a position is often a rationalization for other avoidance maneuvers. If the child is old enough to recognize the existence of a parent he is old enough to be told (at whatever level of communication may have to be utilized) that that parent will no longer be living in the home. The fact that he may not be able to fully comprehend the import of what is being told to him is no justification for the message's not being sent. He is entitled to the message in the hope that it will be appreciated at some level, no matter how primitive. To withhold it from him is to create an environment of secretiveness that cannot but be psychologically detrimental (for reasons to be elaborated upon below).

"How should the children be told?" I believe that the best arrangement is one in which both parents sit down with all the children together and tell them about the impending separation. There are some who believe that the children are best told separately because their different age levels require ex-

planations of varying sophistication. Although I agree that separate explanations may very well be necessary, I see no reason why these cannot be provided in the presence of the other children. Although time may be lost in having to repeat the explanation in order to make it commensurate with the children's various levels of appreciation, there is much to be gained by the children's hearing the news together. They can gain a sense of closeness with one another that is not possible when they are told separately. And this sense of closeness is even more important at the time of impending parental separation. Being told separately invariably involves their "comparing notes." Intrinsic to separate discussion is an atmosphere of secretiveness and a distrusting attitude toward the parents. At this time the children can ill afford further compromises in their relationships with their parents. Telling them together avoids this drawback of the separate discussions. Another potential disadvantage of separate discussions is their structure. If the children are all in the home at the time, then they must be lined up (or at least wait their turn) while a sibling is in a closed room talking with the parents. Those outside cannot but feel distrustful toward the parents. If, however, the parents decide to tell each child when the others are not around, difficult logistics may be required. Even if this difficulty is overcome, the chances of A saying something to B before the parents do is great. (Children, like adults, are not famous for their abilities to keep secrets or withhold burning information.) This system, then, contains the risk of the child's being told by a sibling, rather than by a parent—a situation that is bound to undermine the child's confidence in the parents.

Many parents will hesitate to involve themselves in such discussions for fear that they will "break down" in front of their children. A parent may exclaim, "I just don't want them to see me crying; it will just make them even more upset." There are even professionals who advise parents to make sure that when they do tell the children they do so at a time when they are so composed that they will not show how upset they are—lest the children become upset as well.

I believe that such a position is naive and misguided. As I will discuss in greater detail, a healthy dealing with the divorce (for both parents and children) involves an experience analogous to the mourning period following death. During this time the individuals accustom themselves to the trauma, desensitize themselves to its pains, and work through their reactions to it. Vital to such accommodation is the expression of the various feelings that inevitably arise in such a situation. The parent must serve as a model for the child in fostering the expression of such emotional reactions. If the parent holds back his or her feelings the child is likely to as well, with the result that various pathological reactions to the separation may arise. Parents do

well then to express, in moderation, their emotional reactions to the separation. I am not suggesting that the parents begin telling the children about the
forthcoming separation at a time when they are overwhelmed with their feelings. It is preferable that they do so in an environment in which their feelings
are at a relatively low level; however, they should be accepting of the
apperance of stronger reactions and, appreciate that their expression *in front
of their children*, although painful, can be salutary for all concerned. I am
not suggesting either that wild hysterical outburstus are advisable. This
would be substituting one form of inappropriate handling of emotions with
another.

There are those who are hesitant to discuss with the children the reasons
for the divorce lest their bitter angry feelings toward the spouse be revealed.
They fear that such expression will undermine the child's respect for and relationship with the partner. First, I believe that the children are usually very
much aware of the angry feelings that exist between the parents. It is a rare
situation that the separation comes as an absolute surprise. In addition, if
there were no angry feelings then the child might wonder why the parents are
getting separated. Such repression can only serve as a model for the children
to repress their own anger and, as I will describe in detail in a later chapter,
such suppression is a common cause for pathological adaptations to the
divorce. In addition, as I will also soon discuss, the child who grows up in an
atmosphere in which he has been protected from criticisms of a parent may
develop unrealistic views about such a parent and this will interfere with his
identification process, as well as his ability to relate healthily to others.

"What should the children be told about the reasons for the divorce?" I
believe that some of the disturbances that children of divorced parents suffer
result from the fact that their parents, often with the best intentions and even
supported by professional authority, are not *appropriately* truthful about the
divorce to their children. I use the word *appropriately* because I do not believe that parents' lives should be an open book to their children. However,
parents have a tendency to hide from their children things which they have a
right to know, things which, if disclosed, would be psychologically beneficial.
Such information is usually withheld because the parents consider its divulgence to be psychologically deleterious to their children.

Children are far less fragile in this regard than most parents realize, and
they are much more capable of accepting painful realities than is generally
appreciated. What is more difficult for them to handle (and this is true for
adults as well) are the anxieties associated with ignorance and parental fur-
tiveness, for then fantasy runs free and their worst anticipations can neither
be confirmed nor refuted. Half-truths produce confusion and distrust whereas truth, albeit painful, engenders trust and gives the child the security of
knowing exactly what is happening to him. He is then in a better position to

handle situations effectively.

If the parents are being deceptive to the child regarding the reasons for the divorce (even though meaning well), the child will sense the parental duplicity. This will undermine his trust in his parents at a time when he is most in need of a trusting and secure relationship with them. An unnecessary burden is thereby added to those the child is already bearing. In addition, such duplicity creates a new burden for the parents. Generally, one lie must be built upon another in order to keep the system secure and to prevent its divulgence. If, for example, the child is told that the father is away on a business trip, new lies must be created to explain the failure of the father to return, and, as time goes on, these become even less credible. When the child does learn the truth (and he usually does at some point) he cannot but become disillusioned with those who have lied to him about such an important issue. Again, this occurs at a time when the child can ill afford such a compromise in an already deteriorated relationship with his parents. As Erikson has pointed out (1963), a child's basic trusting relationship with his parents is at the foundation of healthy personality development. Parental duplicity could predictably shake this foundation.

Accordingly, my general advice to parents regarding disclosure of the reasons for the divorce is that they follow the principle that if the child is old enough to ask a question he is old enough to receive an answer—commensurate with his level of appreciation and sophistication. The analogy to providing the child with information about sex holds well here. A four-year-old who asks his mother where babies come from might be told that the baby comes from "Mommy's belly." This answer will generally suffice at that age level. If the child asks how the baby started growing he is entitled to know something about the fertilization process. Generally, an answer such as "Daddy plants a seed in Mommy's belly" will suffice. However, if the child is sophisticated enough to ask the question, "How does the seed get in there?" he is entitled to some simple anatomic explanation such as "Daddy puts his penis in Mommy's vagina, and the seed comes out of his penis." Similarly, information about the divorce should be provided. Basic material should be given and questions should be answered as the child asks them.

As mentioned, I do not believe that the parents' lives should be an open book to the children. One can provide the child with the basic facts regarding the reasons for the divorce without necessarily divulging personal intimacies that are not the child's business. For example, if the parents are getting divorced because the mother is having an affair with another man and wishes to marry him, the children can be told, "Mommy doesn't love Daddy anymore. She loves another man and is going to marry him." If a frigidity problem is the cause of the breakdown of the marriage the child can be told, "Mommy doesn't like to hug and cuddle with Daddy very much and this

makes Daddy feel very bad. For a long time we have tried to solve the problem, but we can't. So we are getting divorced." A similar explanation will
generally suffice for a husband's impotency problem. A child, especially
when older, may ask questions about such intimacies that the parents might
justifiably not wish to answer. In such situations I generally suggest that the
parents respond in this vein: "There are certain things that Mommy and
Daddy consider personal and we do not consider it proper for us to discuss
these things with you. As you grow older you'll have more and more personal
things that you will not consider proper to talk about with us. We want you to
still ask all the questions that come to your mind. Most of them we will answer. However, if there is a question that we do not wish to answer we will tell
you so. We will not make believe we are answering it when we really aren't."
If the parent does not state directly that he is not answering a question, but
responds evasively or with a non-answer, he will discourage the child's further questioning and this will deprive the child of the benefits to be derived
from gaining accurate information.

More important than the information that the child gains from such questioning is the open atmosphere of communication that such interchanges
foster. Like the sexual questioning interchanges described above, the child
cannot generally fully comprehend all at once what is being told to him. Accordingly, he needs to repeat his questions over a period of time in order to
comprehend what is happening. The child must be given the feeling that his
questions will be welcomed at any time and that every attempt will be made
to answer them directly and honestly. He then gains trust and the security
that comes with accurate information. In addition, he gains the opportunity
to desensitize himself to the trauma. Repeated questioning and discussion is
vital to the working-through process and there is nothing that will more predictably squelch this important experience than parental duplicity and
evasiveness.

In providing the children information about the forthcoming separation it
is important for the parents to communicate *concrete* information, rather
than vague statements. For example, the child should be told exactly when
the father will leave and exactly where he is going to live. Very early they
should have the opportunity to see the place where the father is living so that
they can have a mental image of exactly where he is. This lessens abandonment anxieties. Detailed information should also be provided (if possible) regarding frequency of visitation and the settings in which they will occur. Such
information can also help the children feel more secure about a continuing
relationship with the parent who is leaving the home. If the mother and children are planning to move (to a smaller apartment or to the home of grandparents, for example) the children should be given as much detailed information as possible (when, where, etc.).

In providing information, however, it is important for the parents to appreciate that it is unwise to confront the children with too many facts at once. There are parents who will, in their desire to follow the above advise, dump a barrage of facts on the children and hope that they will be able to sort things out themselves. The children then become overwhelmed and confused and more may be lost than gained by the disclosures. It is for this reason that I generally suggest that the setting be one in which there is ample opportunity for open discussion. Information can then be provided in piecemeal fashion in accordance with the child's ability to comprehend and absorb it. In addition, the parent has the opportunity to use the child as a guide to determine how much should be given and at what pace.

There are times when it may be appropriate that the parent not provide a child with information regarding the reason for the divorce. For example, if the father has been involved in criminal behavior and if legal proceedings are underway, it may be detrimental to his position if the child were to learn the information and divulge it to others. Such a child might then justifiably be given only partial information. For example, he might be told, "Mommy doesn't love Daddy anymore and no longer wishes to live with him." The statement is true, as far as it goes, and so the child has not been told a lie. However, vital information has been omitted and so the truth has been compromised. Hopefully, as the child grows older and the disclosure no longer jeopardizes the father's legal position (most legal proceedings ultimately end) then the child can be given further information. There are times when identifying a third party involved in the divorce proceedings may be inappropriate and undesirable. For example, if the divorce is the result of a father's having an affair with a married woman and her husband is not aware that she is implicated, it is inappropriate to divulge this information to a child. The parents will probably have to respond differently to the child's questions regarding the identity of the third party in accordance with his age and level of sophistication. The younger child may have to be told: "We have answered all of your questions so far and were happy to do so. However, there are certain questions that we will not answer because they are too personal, and this is one of them. Right now we cannot tell you who this person is, but we may be able to do so in the future." An older child might be given more of the reasons that would justify the third party's identity not being revealed.

When the divorce is the result of one of the parent's suffering with a significant psychiatric disturbance, it is important for the nonsuffering parent to try to communicate to the children a sense of sympathy for the afflicted parent. For example, if a mother has decided that she can no longer tolerate her husband's alcoholism, in addition to telling the children about some of the indignities that she may have suffered because of the father's drinking, she should try to communicate to them the notion that the drinking is a psychi-

atric illness and cannot simply be cured by willpower. She would do well to
tell the children (if they don't know already) about how tolerant she has been
and about how much she has tried to be helpful. Although she should express
the resentments that she feels, she should also try to engender an attitude of
"he's more to be pitied than scorned."

The way in which deceiving a child about parental separation can have
devastating psychological effects on the child is well demonstrated in a case
described by Polatin and Philtine (1964). Rather than tell her three-year-old
daughter that her parents were separated, the mother informed the child that
her father had gone to work in another city and would not be returning to the
home. The child's first assumption was that she and her mother would soon
join the father. She repeatedly asked the mother, "When are we going to
Daddy?" As time passed, and such a visit did not materialize, the child began to assume that her father was dead and entered into a mourning period.
She stopped asking questions and began repeating to her dolls, "My Daddy's
dead. I'll never see him anymore." Although the mother appreciated that
there would inevitably be some contact with the father, she did not correct
the child's false assumption that the father had died.

Suddenly, one day, the father appeared. The little girl went into a state of
shock. She became apathetic, listless, and demonstrated no affection for him.
Whereas previously she had been gay and outgoing, she became withdrawn.
The experience was totally incomprehensible to the child—it was as if the
dead could come back to life. She protected herself from the anxieties of her
incomprehensible world by withdrawing into a state of apathy. It was only
through psychiatric treatment that the child was able to reverse the pathological state.

An experience from my own practice well demonstrates the possible deleterious effects of a parent's withholding vital information about a family
catastrophe from a child. Although in this case it involved the death of a
teen-age brother, the child's pathological reactions were similar to those that
could occur if a child were misled regarding the reasons for a parent's sudden
disappearance. In addition, the therapeutic approaches were similar to those
that I would utilize if a separation were similarly handled by a child's parents.

Ruth, a four-year-old girl, was referred because of phobic symptoms of six
month's duration. When Ruth was two, her brother Scott (then sixteen) was
stricken with leukemia. Scott survived for a year and a half, during which
time the mother's involvement with the boy left her little time for Ruth. The
child was not told that her brother's illness would be fatal, and at the time of
his death she was told that he had gone to heaven where he was very happy.
The family was South American, and the father had been temporarily
assigned to his firm's New York office. The family returned to their native

country for the burial. Unknown to the patient, her brother's body was in the cargo compartment of the airplane. Ruth did not attend the funeral. She was told that they had returned to South America to visit friends.

Upon returning to the United States, Ruth began exhibiting the symptoms which ultimately brought her to me. Whereas she had previously attended nursery school without hesitation, she now refused. When the doorbell rang, she became panicky and hid under the bed. She refused to visit the homes of friends. She seemed comfortable when close to both parents and would scream hysterically if they left. Upon their return to the United States, Ruth repeatedly asked questions about her brother, and she was told that he was happy in heaven with God. All of Scott's personal effects were destroyed with the exception of a few of his treasured possessions which were stored away lest the patient be upset by them. Within a week of their return, Ruth stopped asking questions.

It was quite clear that the phobic symptoms were directly related to the way the parents had handled Scott's death with Ruth. From her vantage point, people, without explanation, could suddenly disappear from the face of the earth. Every place is really dangerous because one knows nothing about the way in which such disappearances occur. It might be that people come to the door and take you away; or perhaps it happens at nursery school; or maybe neighbors do it. No place is really safe. Also, there's no point in trying to get a reasonable explanation from one's parents as to how it happens. They too cannot be trusted to be truthful. Ruth, without doubt, sensed her parents' duplicity.

I asked the parents what their genuine beliefs were concerning the dead brother's whereabouts. Both believed that there was no type of existence in the hereafter and although born Catholics they had no particular religious convictions. They felt that divulging their true feelings about their dead son would be psychologically deleterious to their daughter. I explained to them what I considered to be the source of their child's problems. I told them that I knew that they had always done what they considered to be in the child's best interests, but that they had made some errors. I suggested that they go home and tell Ruth exactly what had happened to their son—as simply and as accurately as possible. I advised them to tell her, as best they could, what their true beliefs were regarding his present state. I suggested also that they give her one of the brother's mementos and tell her that it would always be hers. They were most reluctant at first, but they finally gained some conviction that my suggestions might be valid.

I then explained to them the psychological importance of mourning and how their child had been deprived of this important experience. I told them that it was most likely that Ruth would ask the same questions over and over again, and that it was important that they patiently continue repeating

answers because this was a part of the mourning and working-through process. In addition, I suggested that they urge her to once again face the phobic
situations and each time reassure her that she, unlike Scott, would not be
taken away.

The parents were seen again one week later. They reported that my suggestions had been followed, and the child had responded well. She cried bitterly when told the details of the brother's death. As I had foretold, Ruth's
questions during the next few days were practically incessant. She was given a
picture of her brother which she carried around at all times. She showed it to
everyone she could and explained to them that it was her dead brother. She
then told how he had died and said that he was in the ground in her native
country.

There was a concomitant lessening of all her fears. By the time of the second visit she was again attending nursery school without difficulty; she no
longer cowered at the ring of the doorbell; she was visiting friends; and she
exhibited only mild anxiety when her parents went out at night. No further
sessions were schedules and the parents were advised to call me if they felt the
need for such, which they did not.

Another patient I once saw also demonstrates the deleterious effects of
withholding information about parental separation from a child and how its
revelation can have salutary effects. George came to treatment at the age of
seven because of a variety of behavioral disturbances. Although extremely
bright, he was doing very poorly in school. He was very agitated in the classroom, would not stay in his seat, and provoked other children. In the lunchroom he was messy and often threw much of his lunch on the floor. He was so
slow an eater that he was usually the last one to finish his lunch and had to
be coaxed in order to leave the lunchroom on time. He handed in sloppy
homework and at other times refused to do it entirely. He isolated himself
from other children and had no friends in the classroom.

At home, as well, his mother had difficulty with him. He was unruly and
unmanageable. He did not follow her instructions and refused to do even the
most minor household chores. At night, he had trouble sleeping and conse-
quently he was irritable and drowsy during the day.

The parents had been separated seven months at the time I first saw
George. The father, who was against his son's being brought to treatment
and who refused to see me, was described by the mother as being an extremely heavy drinker. Although their marriage was characteristically a difficult one in that there were frequent fights over the most minor issues, when
the father was inebriated the fighting would become extremely intense. The
mother states that the father would characteristically berate her in front of
George and would call her "crazy" and use other extremely derogatory
terms. The parents were involved in bitter litigation and there were prac-

tically daily telephone calls in which they would viciously castigate one another. In spite of these difficulties the mother agreed with the father that it would not be in George's best interests to divulge the drinking problem to him.

Early in treatment it became apparent that George was very much in the dark regarding the reason for his parents' separation. He was aware that they fought frequently, but sensed that other information was being withheld from him. In addition, it became apparent that George would spend long hours with his father discussing various fantasies. Often, these involved their building huge fantastic edifices that were totally beyond reality. They would discuss at length the various things they would do with these huge buildings, the people that would come and go, and the exciting adventures they would have. The more fantastic they became, the more George enjoyed these flights from reality. The withholding of information about alcoholism was really only part of a broader scheme in which the father fostered George's divorcing himself from the pains and discomforts of the real world.

I advised the mother not to respect the father's request that the alcoholism problem be withheld from George. She was convinced that such divulgence would be deleterious and I tried to help her appreciate that it was only one part of a broader problem in which George was being encouraged to remove himself from the stresses of reality. She did recognize the pathological aspects of the father-son flights into fantasy and her appreciation of this served to lessen her resistance to discussing the alcoholism problem. Following her revealing the drinking problem to George there was a definite reduction in his general level of tension. In my therapeutic work I not only reviewed with him the drinking problem, but discussed the broader problem of fantasy vs. reality. Within two months there was such a marked diminution of George's symptoms that therapy was discontinued. He began to perform extremely well in school, was getting along better with peers, and his general level of anxiety and agitation was markedly reduced. Although other issues were dealt with in George's treatment, the aforementioned experiences, I believe, contributed significantly to the alleviation of his difficulties.

When telling the child about the forthcoming separation, I generally advise parents to mention that they *did* love one another at the time of their marriage (if this was the case, and it generally is). This can provide the child with some security at a time when he is most likely to become quite insecure. Appreciating that he was a product of love—that he was born at a time when the parents wanted him and anticipated that they would be living together— can serve to enhance his feelings of self-worth at a time when they are most likely to be damaged. In the same context I also suggest that the parents try to impart to the child the notion that although they do not love one another anymore, this does not preclude each of them loving the child. The child must be helped to appreciate that in any triangle consisting of three individuals A, B, and C, that A and B may not love one another, but A and B can each love C. Conversely, C can love both A and B even though A and B do not love one another. Although this may seem an obvious statement, it may not be obvious to the child and he, more often than not, will conclude that if his parents don't love one another that he too may become unloved. This is not a totally irrational supposition. If Father, for example, can stop loving Mother, what is to stop him from discontinuing his love for his child? The child in a stable home may not consider the possibility that anyone is going to stop loving anybody.

I also advise the parents to communicate to the children that they realize now that their marriage had been a *mistake*. All too often children look upon their parents as perfect. Unfortunately, there are parents who perpetuate this delusion by withholding any information that would reveal deficiencies. Although such a practice generally stems from parental insecurity, it is usually rationalized as being in the best interests of the child to have a perfect image of his parents. Nothing could be farther from the truth. The child does best in an atmosphere where he comes to see his parents as having both assets and liabilities. Furthermore, he does well to learn which of their characteristics are in each of these categories. In this way he will grow up with realistic expectations from others and will be less likely to become disillusioned as each individual ultimately reveals defects. The parental deficiencies should be revealed in situations which are natural; contrived situations simply replace one form of neurotic behavior with another. Admitting the marriage to have been a mistake is one way in which the parents can provide their children with a healthy sense of their imperfection. Such disclosures can also lessen the likelihood of the child's becoming perfectionistic.

I generally recommend that the parents impress upon the children that the divorce was not the children's fault. As I will discuss in detail subsequently, children commonly develop the delusion that the divorce was due to their own misbehavior. Although such reassurance may not play a significant role in reducing their delusion of guilt, it may contribute somewhat to its alleviation and so should be communicated. When I discuss in detail the guilt reactions of children of divorce, I will elaborate on the more definitive approaches to the alleviation of this form of guilt.

The parents do well to encourage the children to ask as many questions as possible during their conversations. And although the issues are the ones that generally arise, the child should be encouraged to bring up any questions that are on his mind. The importance of such questions has already been emphasized and the reasons for eliciting them elaborated upon. Lastly, many children at this time have found helpful my *The Boys and Girls Book about Divorce* (1970, 1971). This book is written to be read by the child of divorce himself (or along with a parent) and in it are discussed the common problems that face such children. The issues raised can serve as points of departure for child-parent discussion. Such mutual inquiry and cooperative discussion can serve to reduce some of the parent-child schisms and other difficulties often brought about by divorce.

Advising Parents in the Early Postseparation Period

Should we tell the teacher? Those who argue against the teacher's being told hold that such divulgence is likely to add to the child's difficulties. With this knowledge, they fear, the teacher will tend to treat the child differently and make a "special case" out of him. Other believe that the teacher should not be told unless the child's reactions to the separation draw attention to him in the classroom and disrupt his work there. Only then, they hold, should the teacher be told so that her aid can be enlisted in dealing with the child's difficulties. McDermott (1968) believes that the teacher should be told in all cases because most children will react to the separation in such a way that their school work will be interfered with. Alerted in advance, the teacher will be in the best position to be helpful to the child and to contribute to the prevention of more serious psychological reactions.

I am in agreement with McDermott's position. I find it hard to imagine a child's not reacting strongly to parental separation even when the separation provides a respite from continual bickering and domestic unhappiness; a parent is still leaving the home—and this cannot but be traumatic. To wait until the child exhibits symptoms may deprive him of valuable early intervention—intervention that might reduce and even prevent the development of more serious reactions. When the teacher has been told about the separation she, possibly more than anyone else, can serve as a substitute for the departed person. Even if she is of opposite sex to the parent who has left, she can still serve as a second adult to compensate for the loss the child has suffered. She is with the child six or seven hours a day, five days a week, and is in an excellent position to provide support, reassurance, advice, etc. Furthermore, involving the child in classroom activities (especially pleasurable ones) can serve as an antidote to the child's suffering.

Those who would withhold the information from the teacher are not only depriving the child of important substitute gratifications but, in addition, are being naive. It is practically impossible to keep such an event from a child's teacher for a long period of time. Even if the child himself does not tell anyone about it, the word invariably gets around. Neighborhood children learn of the event and it soon spreads to classmates. Parental separation creates anxiety among peers. The other children cannot but become frightened that the same calamity will befall themselves if it can happen so close to home. Accordingly, the teacher is bound to learn of the separation. It is far better, therefore, for the parents to tell her themselves so that she can be in the best position to be of assistance.

That there may be some teachers who may handle the situation inappropriately does not justify, as a blanket policy, never telling the teacher. Some teachers whom the parents suspect might make a "priviliged character" out of the child might be discouraged from doing so by the parents discussing this with her beforehand and impressing upon her that singling the child out for special consideration, although well meaning, is not likely to help the child. My experience has been that most teachers are sympathetic and understanding, and even those who might tend to handle the situation inappropriately can be reasoned with in regard to this tendency.

Easing the child's difficulties during the immediate postseparation period. Following the departure of the parent, the remaining parent does well to keep open the lines of communication described previously. Hopefully, the child will continue asking questions and the parent will be receptive to discussing all issues that are raised. It is in this way that the child is most likely to avoid the development of untoward psychological reactions.

It can be helpful during this period for the child to actually see the departed parent's new living quarters. It provides the child with a concrete image of where the parent is and assuages fear of abandonment. The child should be provided with the address and telephone number of the new domicile. It is very important that frequent telephone calls occur during the first few weeks after the separation. But even after that, frequent telephone contact is desirable. If a child is old enough to make the calls himself he should be permitted to do so, within reason.

At this point children of the same sex as that of the departed parent may, in association with oedipal impulses, attempt to assume the role of the parent who has left. Accordingly, boys may try to take over the role of their father and girls of their mother. Generally, it is only when the parents comply with these tendencies (because of their own problems in this area) that difficulties may arise. If, after a father has left, a boy tries to assume his father's role in the family, the mother does well to permit only a reasonable degree of such identification. He will have added responsibilities and these should be impressed upon the boy. He will have to assume some of his father's obligations and to encourage the assumption of such responsibilities is appropriate. However, it is important for the mother not to encourage such identifications beyond the appropriate. Comments such as "Now that your father has left, you're going to be the man of the house" and "From now on you're going to be like my husband" suggest pathological tendencies on the mother's part and inordinate encouragement of the boy to assume the father's position. Similarly, it is appropriate to allow the boy some cuddling and short periods of resting together in mother's bed (as is appropriate, in my opinion, when the father is present). However, if a child begins sleeping in mother's bed throughout the night, on a continual basis, the likelihood that oedipal problems will arise is great. Both mother and son are entitled in such a situation to some compensatory affection, physical contact, and solace with one another. However, when such contact and involvement become intensified and prolonged, and when seductive elements are introduced, then the likelihood that pathological factors are operative is great. And what I have said about the relationship between a mother and son holds equally for a father and daughter when they are the ones who remain together following the separation.

Immediately following the separation there is likely to be a continuation of the same hostilities that brought about the separation in the first place. It is important to impress upon the parents that the longer these are perpetuated, the greater the likelihood the child will suffer untoward reactions to the divorce. During this period, frequent contact between the parents is necessary in order for them to work out the innumerable arrangements attendant on the separation. Generally, their hurt feelings and hostilities color practically every negotiation and transaction. Every attempt must be made to impress upon the parents the importance of their attempting to resolve their difficulties as soon as possible: the longer the hostilities continue, the greater the likelihood their children will become disturbed. I am not suggesting simple conscious suppression (which has some place here) but, more important, the encouragement of the parents to attempt to resolve their difficulties in a civilized and equitable fashion.

In addition, the parents must be helped to appreciate that considerable hostility on the children's part is a common reaction. They must be helped to handle such hostilities with a minimum of guilt evocation in the child. Their tolerance for anger on their children's part must be increased during this period and they must be helped to allow the child more acting out (within reasonable limits) than they generally would have permitted in the past. Not to do so is to foster the development of excessive guilt and repression and this sets the stage for the formation of psychopathological reactions. In addition, they must help the child direct his anger into constructive channels. In the chapter on the child's anger reactions I will discuss these issues in greater detail.

"We maintain a strict policy of never criticizing one another to the children." The rationale for this view is that it is important to the child's healthy psychological development that he have respect and admiration for each of his parents. Only virtues are to be discussed. The theory holds that if

too many of a parent's deficiencies are revealed to the child, that parent will not become an object of identification and the child's healthy psychological development will thereby be compromised.

I believe that such a position engenders distrust and confusion in the child. The child knows quite well that each of his parents believes the other to have serious personality flaws or why else would they have gotten separated? It's reasonable that a child whose parents speak only of the ex-partner's assets should ask, "If he was so great, why are you getting divorced?" Such a child already has enough trouble. He hardly needs the additional problem of a distrustful attitude toward his parents. Moreover, his picture of the praised person will necessarily be grossly distorted because he doesn't believe his primary source of information, and his fantasies can only be validated or refuted by his own, often primitive, observations.

The healthiest approach in such situations is to try to give the child as accurate a picture of his parents as is possible: their assets and liabilities, their strengths and weaknesses. Like all humans, his parents are not perfect. He should respect each of those areas that warrant respect, and hold in low opinion those qualities which are not worthy of admiration. If a parent's defects far outweigh his strengths, so be it. This is not a reflection on the child. The child may suffer from having no admirable figure with whom to identify, but is this worse than emulating a contrived person whose assets exist only in words—words the child cannot fully believe? Respect is earned; it cannot be obtained by fiat or duplicity. The child will usually see through facade.

The parent may ask "What should I do, tell him all the sordid details?" Obviously this would not be in the child's best interests either. There is a middle course. It may be difficult to follow; but there are some guidelines. Each parent in his relationship to the child must recognize that, whether he likes it or not, his behavior is judged by his child. It is the duty of each parent to help his children perceive such behavior accurately both in himself and in his ex-spouse. Since most divorced parents exhibit a notorious lack of objectivity when describing an ex-spouse's defects, they should be cautious and self-skeptical when doing so. However, some situations are obvious. When a father misses his visits, it indicates a lack of interest and should be labeled as such. When he exhibits genuine interest in the child's welfare, he shows his involvement, and it should be described in that way. When a mother leaves her child under the care of a seven-year-old, this is neglect, and it should be defined as such. When she deprives herself of a new dress to buy her children clothing, she is showing true concern, and her children should know it.

The details of the parental conflict, especially the "sordid" ones, most often are of little direct importance to the child. These are the private concerns of the parents, and the child should be told so. The child also has a right to certain privacies of his own, and these should be respected by the parents. The details of a parent's behavior toward him, no matter how contemptible, are *the child's business*. This must be faced by all concerned. These details should be discussed at a level comprehensible to the child and at a depth appropriate for his age. In such an atmosphere the child will know what to criticize and what to admire, what to love and what to dislike. He will then be far better prepared to handle those vicissitudes and paradoxes of life for which it is every parent's duty to prepare his child.

Time alone together. I consider the most potent preventive of psychological disturbance and one of the most effective antidotes to such disturbance to be the parent's spending varied periods of time alone together with each child. I usually recommend to all parents, regardless of whether their child is in therapy, that they set aside a time every day when they can be alone with the child without distraction or interruption. Each sibling should have his own time, from which the others are firmly excluded; and this time alone together should be cancelled only under unusual circumstances.

These periods are most effective when both parent and child are genuinely enjoying themselves. If the parent only *pretends* enjoyment in a game or activity, the child will sense the inevitable resentment of the parent's reluctant involvement, and the time spent together will thereby become a deleterious experience for the child. This time can also be profitably used for talking about one's feelings and for sharing the day's experiences—for finding solace, commiseration, and understanding and for relating anecdotes, achievements, and disappointments. It is during these moments of shared feeling and empathy that loving feelings flourish, and both the child and the parent become enriched by them. Such periods of time alone together can be most effective in assuaging the pain and frustration of children whose parents have just separated. These shared times together are even more vital during the postseparation period than at other times and can be extremely valuable in warding off postseparation pathological adaptations. I cannot recommend them strongly enough.

Chapter 2

DETERMINING WHETHER THERAPY IS INDICATED

Does Divorce Necessarily Cause Psychopathological Reactions in the Child?

One cannot meaningfully discuss the question of whether therapy is indicated for the child of divorce unless one is convinced that divorce can bring about psychopathological reactions in the child. *I believe that divorce per se does not necessarily produce psychopathology in the child. However, I also believe that the child of divorce is more likely to develop such reactions than the child who grows up in an intact, relatively secure home.* This whole book is based on this assumption; were I not to believe it, there would be no point in having written the book.

It is almost impossible to differentiate the effects on the child of the divorce itself from the effects of the various traumas he may have suffered both before and after parental separation. It is the exposure to a detrimental milieu over a period of time—rather than the acute trauma of the separation—that causes the child to develop untoward reactions. Of course, years of separation from a parent could be a chronic trauma; however, it need not be.

If the parent who lives away from the home maintains a good, consistent relationship with the child *and* relates reasonably to his former spouse, the child may be spared the development of pathological reactions to the divorce.

There are certain aspects of the divorce situation that make it likely that a child will develop psychological difficulties. Most will agree that a child needs an intimate relationship with both a male and female adult if he is to learn how to function adequately with others, both as a child and subsequently as an adult. He needs the same-sexed parent as a model for identification and he needs the opposite-sexed parent as a model for relating to others of the opposite sex. The child who is significantly deprived of one parent is more likely than the child who has good relationships with two parents to exhibit impairments in his psychological development and interpersonal relations. In addition, no parent can provide sustained affection. Children are inevitably frustrating and a source of resentment to a parent. Having a second parent available in the home lessens the chances that the child will suffer from the periods when he is rejected by a parent. As Bowlby (1951) has well demonstrated in his review of the literature on the subject, deprivation of parental affection is one of the most common and predictable causes of childhood psychopathology. And the child of divorce, having only one parent available in his home, is more likely to experience such deprivation. Lastly, it is not hard to see how the child of divorce will come to view human relationships as basically unstable. From his vantage point the significant individuals in one's life may suddenly abandon one forever. With such distrust of human relationships, it is likely that his involvements will tend to be tenuous and his psychological development unstable.

It is not surprising then that many studies (Glueck and Glueck, 1950; Gregory, 1965a and 1965b; Whitaker and Miller, 1969; McDermott, 1970; Morrison, 1974) find a greater incidence of psychiatric disorder in children from broken homes than in those from intact, stable homes. However, when one compares the incidence of psychiatric disturbance between children from broken homes and those from intact but unhappy homes there appears to be a higher incidence of psychopathology in children in the latter group (Nye, 1957; Landis, 1960). These findings suggest that parents who are miserable living together are not doing their children any favors by "staying together for the sake of the children." However, it is important for the therapist to appreciate that these are statistical studies—the findings describe large groups of children—and they include children who probably would have been worse off if their parents had separated—difficulties in the marriage notwithstanding. Accordingly, one cannot know what a particular child's reaction will be (Despert, 1953).

If these findings of a greater incidence of psychopathology in children of divorce were not valid; if children of divorce were not found to be a greater risk for the development of psychiatric disturbance, then one would have to reevaluate the assumption that a child's living with two parents is preferable to his living with one. The studies, therefore, indicate that such reevaluation is not warranted and that my assumption regarding the importance of a child's having two opposite-sexed individuals with whom to relate is supported.

As Mahler and Rabinovitch (1956) point out, there is no specific kind of pathology produced by marital discord. Similarly, there is no typical psychopathological reactions exhibited by children of divorce. Rather, there are a whole range of possible untoward reactions and it is the purpose of this book to discuss the manifestations, psychodynamics, and treatment of some of the more common ones.

Criteria for Recommending Treatment

Since divorce does not necessarily result in a child's needing treatment, what criteria should one utilize in deciding whether a child needs therapy? First, I believe it is important to emphasize that there is hardly a person who could not profit from therapy. All of us, no matter how stable, have some neurotic problems and inappropriate reactions. All of us could profit from a warm, accepting relationship with an objective and sensitive individual who is knowledgeable about human problems and receptive to discussing ours with us. How does one differentiate then those who *need* treatment from those who do not, since most could profit from it anyway?

In attempting to answer this question I will confine myself to issues relevant to children of divorce; however, some of the guidelines I will present are certainly applicable to others as well. Generally, most parents recognize that a child will develop acute reactions to the separation (such as depression, temper tantrums, and angry outbursts) that may be transient. Such children are usually not brought for consultation. If they are, one must try to determine whether the problems are truly acute. If the symptoms have originated at the time of the separation the child may not need treatment and the parents can be advised that the child's difficulties are likely to pass as he adjusts to the separation. However, they should also be told that if the problems do not diminish with time, a reevaluation is indicated. One cannot be very specific about the normal duration of such acute reactions. Generally, four to six weeks is a reasonable period for them to exist. When they persist (especially unabated) then therapy, or at least parental counseling, may be warranted. Sometimes, the initial reactions may be so severe that therapy or parental counseling is warranted during the acute reaction. More often such therapy will be of the supportive type with reassurances that the symptoms are likely to pass.

The child who needs therapy has generally exhibited difficulties for a significant period of time prior to the separation and whose symptoms have intensified as a result of it. There are children, however, whose symptoms date from the time of parental separation but have persisted for many months and even longer. In such situations, the parents are usually involving the child in various pathological maneuvers (using him as a spy, for example) or exposing him to constant traumas of a new kind (endless conflicts, for instance). They key principle then in determining whether treatment should be considered is the chronicity of the difficulties. Acute symptoms, especially those that arise in response to a particular trauma (such as parental separation), are not likely to require treatment. Rather, the child is likely to work out his reactions himself by natural reparative psychological processes. This is often accomplished through repeated questioning, normal working-through by preoccupation, and release of feelings through mourning and play fantasy. When these natural reparative processes become blocked, either through parental inhibition ("See how brave you can be," "Stop asking me so many questions") or through intrapsychic inhibitive processes already present in the child, then a therapeutic approach utilizing catharsis and desensitization may be indicated.

With regard to the chronic, nonreactive symptoms, there are a number of criteria I utilize in deciding whether treatment is indicated. One can, of course, determine whether the child is exhibiting any of the symptoms described in the standard nomenclature. Such symptoms as phobias, obsessions, and compulsions cause little difficulty for the therapist with regard to the question of whether therapy is warranted. Most often, in my experience, the patient does not present with such clear-cut symptoms. Rather, the child exhibits various kinds of behavioral difficulties (classroom disturbances, peer relationship problems) which exist to a certain degree in most children. One may recognize that the child is reacting to the separation, but he may be hard put to know whether his reactions are of such intensity that treatment is warranted. One of the important areas of inquiry that can help the therapist make his decision is school behavior. (Direct discussion with the teacher can be invaluable here.) Whereas in the home the child's behavior is normally disruptive and he is likely to periodically defy his parents, the healthy child is capable of inhibiting himself to a reasonable degree in the classroom. He well differentiates between school and home authorities and is able to refrain from expressing many things in school that he would guiltlessly reveal at home. The child without such controls is in psychological difficulty and is likely to warrant treatment.

Another important area of inquiry is peer relationships. Normally, a child will fight fiercely with siblings. A younger sibling makes a convenient scape-goat for one's pent-up hostilities, for he may not be able to effectively re-taliate and cannot remove himself totally from such maltreatment. One can-not exhibit such wanton cruelty to peers. They not only have the power to re-taliate but to reject and alienate. Accordingly, intense sibling fighting is a poor criterion on which to base the decision to treat a child; but poor peer re-lationships is a very good one. I particularly inquire into whether the child seeks peers and whether he is sought by them. If there is some impairment in either of these areas, I look into the reasons. A child with significant difficul-ties in his peer relationships generally needs therapy.

Uncooperative behavior in the home is generally a difficult criterion on which to decide whether treatment is indicated. Children normally balk at doing chores, keeping their rooms neat, getting up on time, going to sleep when they are asked, coming home when they are supposed to, etc. They generally take the path of least resistance, procrastinate as much as possible, and are happiest when their parents are "off their backs." Accordingly, dif-ficulties in these areas have to be quite severe before I will consider them valid reasons for therapy. If the child's refusal has a strong passive-aggressive element is also revealed in the consulting room, then it is more likely that I will suggest therapy.

Of course, one's own observations are extremely important in determining one's decision regarding therapy. But there are problems here as well. In his first session the child may be at his worst. The anxiety associated with his visit may be so great that he may appear to be much sicker than he really is. The failure to cooperate that often accompanies such anxiety may so frus-trate and anger the therapist that he may see the child as having worse prob-lems than actually exist. Accordingly, one does best to see a child a few times in those cases where one suspects that the child's problems appear worse be-cause of the strangeness of the situation. On the other hand, in the therapist's office the child may appear to be healthier than he really is. The child may do very well in the one-to-one relationship where he is getting all attention focused on him. Whereas in school, at home, and in his neighborhood, where he must suffer frustration and sharing, his difficulties may most blatantly exhibit themselves. It is therefore important to check one's observations with the parents to see how one's office observations compare with the parents'.

The therapist must recognize that parents who are referred from a school or other source may wish to deny that the child has difficulties. Although os-tensibly coming for a consultation, they may really be coming to confirm their opinion that the child is not in need of treatment. The parents who have recently separated may be especially prone to utilize the denial mechanism because of the guilt they may feel over their forthcoming divorce. If they can believe that the child doesn't need treatment then they will feel less guilty about the untoward effects of the divorce on the children.

Many children resist the idea of having treatment because they assume that it means that they are crazy or retarded. Or they fear the stigmatization they anticipate if others find out that they are going for therapy. The child of divorce may have an additional reason for refusing therapy. He may already feel shame over being the child of a divorced family and may not wish to voluntarily suffer the additional stigma of having to see a "shrink." On the other hand, there are children who may be very receptive to treatment. They may genuinely appreciate that therapy can be of help to them. The child of divorce may have an additional reason for seeking therapy. He may wish the therapist to assume the role of a surrogate parent in order to compensate him for the loss of his real parent. If this is one of the fringe benefits of therapy (to the degree that it can reasonably be accomplished in the therapeutic situation), fine; it should not, however, be a reason for recommending treatment. Treatment should be suggested for therapeutic, not primarily social, reasons; there are far less expensive ways for the child to get a parent surrogate. Of course, if therapy is indicated it is preferable that the child work with someone of the same sex as the departed parent, unless other considerations dictate otherwise. We can provide the child with this fringe benefit of treatment without making it the sole purpose of therapy.

Criteria for Not Recommending Treatment

As mentioned, children brought soon after the separation may not warrant treatment; their symptoms are part of the acute transient reaction to the trauma and may even be a manifestation of a healthy working-through response. For example, a child may become preoccupied with a TV story depicting a parental loss (either overtly or symbolically). He may become "hooked" on the story because it provides him with the opportunity to desensitize himself in piecemeal fashion to the trauma of his parents' separation. It is as if each time he repeats, talks about, or even playacts the story he reduces his pain. Even though the story may depict his situation allegorically and even though he may have no conscious awareness that the story relates to his own situation, it can help him work through the trauma. In fact, the symbolic representation may have been favored because it allows for desensitization without conscious awareness and its attendant anxiety. Such a child may not need therapy. All he may need is his parents' permission to indulge himself in his fantasies. In all likelihood the time he is so preoccupied will diminish daily and therapy will not be necessary. Of course, if the preoccupations continue unabated and they occupy a significant part of his life, then other factors are probably contributing and therapy would probably be indicated.

In addition, if the fantasies take on a more pathological character and demonstrate the utilization of various maladaptive defense mechanisms, then therapy should be considered.

Most parents recognize that a period of psychological instability is almost predictable after a separation and they generally do not seek therapy in the early postseparation period. Westman, Cline et al. (1970) found that only 3 of the 23 families of divorce that they studied sought treatment for the children within the first two years after the separation. The therapist should appreciate that some of those who do request consultation during the early period may be doing so not so much for their children as for themselves. As is so often the case in child therapy the parent will use the child as an "admission ticket" (Kanner, 1957) for his own treatment. Such a parent appreciates that the therapist will ask him about himself and recognizes that such a discussion may result in a recommendation that he consider treatment for himself. He has thereby provided himself with the opportunity to become familiar with the therapist without immediately having to directly discuss himself. He can also have a convenient excuse for not involving himself, if he has a change of heart, by claiming he has come only for the child. When it is clear that it is the parent, not the child, who is seeking and needs therapy, the child, of course, would not be treated.

There are parents who are very anxious about their children, and they may be quick to seek psychiatric consultation and even treatment for the most minor abnormalities. Often such parents have had extensive treatment themselves and may be quite "sophisticated" about psychoanalytic matters. And when a separation has occurred they may be certain that the child is going to develop problems that will require therapy. Even though the child has not exhibited any unusual reactions to the separation, they may request prophylactic treatment. Such treatment is, in my opinion, rarely effective in the absence of any significant problem. These children should not be treated, but an inquiry into the parental anxieties is certainly in order.

There are other children who are not really in need of therapy but who are brought because of the parents' need to assuage the guilt they may feel over the separation. Such children, of course, should not be treated. The indications for therapy are psychopathology, not parental guilt which needs to be assuaged. Of course, one should help such a parent deal with his guilt reaction more appropriately and realistically.

There are parents who are quite insecure and fear that following the separation they will not be able to rise to the challenge of bringing up the child alone. Such parents may seek therapy to insure that the child will not suffer from their own mismanagement. By putting the child in "good hands," they hope to avoid the deleterious effects of their assuming sole responsibility for the child. Again, the child may not need therapy and the parents' insecurities have to be focused upon. Sometimes such a parent will give the therapist a clue to the existence of this mechanism with such a comment as: "I want to put him in your hands, Doctor."

There are parents who project their own problems onto their children, see themselves as healthy and their children (or one particular child, singled out for this role) as being sick. It may be very difficult to convince such a parent that the child is not the one with the described problems. Typically, such a parent will seek another therapist who will treat the child. The parent may want to vicariously cure himself through the alleviation of the difficulties he sees in the child. Again, treatment not of the child but of the parent is indicated, but this is only possible if the parent can gain insight into what is happening.

In closing I wish to emphasize that I do not believe that divorce per se warrants a child's being in therapy. This is especially true if the child has a good relationship with the parent who does not live in the home. If the absent parent is uninvolved with the child or unavailable, there is a greater chance that the child will develop psychopathology. However, if the remaining parent makes efforts to provide such a child with surrogate relationships, then untoward psychological reactions may still be avoided. It is the primary purpose of this book to describe therapeutic approaches to those children who do require therapy because the aforementioned desiderata have not been satisfied; however, much that I will describe will be applicable to handling the normal child's untoward reactions that may not reach the intensity where treatment is warranted.

Chapter 3

SPECIAL THERAPEUTIC TECHNIQUES

In treating the psychological problems of children of divorce I utilize traditional techniques as well as certain innovations and modifications of my own. Although details of these methods have been published elsewhere (1971b, 1975), I will summarize some of these therapeutic approaches here because an appreciation of these methods will be helpful to the reader unfamiliar with them. Although the illustrative clinical vignettes presented in subsequent chapters will involve traditional approaches, they will demonstrate also my use of these alternative and sometimes preferable methods.

Work with Parents

A somewhat lengthy discussion of my views on confidentiality in child therapy is warranted if the reader is to appreciate fully the way in which I involve a child's parents in his treatment. First, I wish to emphasize that the views I express here regarding confidentiality in child therapy apply to children below the age of ten or eleven. What I will be discussing has absolutely no relevance to adolescent and adult therapy. I appreciate fully that teen-agers and adults require a confidential relationship with the therapist; in the treatment of children, however, I believe certain modifications of the traditional views regarding the importance of confidentiality to be justified.

I believe that child therapists have too readily accepted the adult model of psychotherapy (especially psychoanalysis) as applicable to work with children. I fully appreciate the numerous therapeutic techniques that have been devised specifically for children. However, much of the basic theoretical framework and therapeutic structure used in child therapy has been accepted indiscriminately from the adult model. The confidentiality issue is a case in point. Whereas adults may reveal many things to the therapist that should not be divulged, and whereas the adolescent needs to have such confidences respected as part of the developmental process, the average child (below the age of ten or eleven) has little in his life that realistically is unknown to the parents or should appropriately be kept secret from them. I am not saying that he is not entitled to his inner thoughts and his privacy, but when it comes to therapeutic considerations the advantages of their being revealed far outweigh, in my opinion, the disadvantages.

It is of interest that Freud (1909) in his famous analysis of Little Hans, the first child to be treated by psychoanalytic techniques, did not give any consideration to Hans's privacy. Having no guidelines regarding the application of the psychoanalytic method to the treatment of children, Freud decided to have the father treat the child himself under Freud's guidance. It would have been more consistent with Freud's previous pattern to have treated the child himself. From all possible alternative approaches, he chose to have the father serve as therapist. Freud clearly states his reasons for this dramatic departure: "No one else, in my opinion, could possibly have prevailed on the child to make such avowals; the special knowledge by means of which he was able to interpret the remarks made by his five-year-old son was indispensable and without it the technical difficulties in the way of conducting a psychoanalysis upon so young a child would have been insuperable." I think it unfortunate that most therapists have ignored this aspect of Little Hans's treatment. The psychodynamic theories that were considered by Freud to have been confirmed in Hans's treatment have become almost gospel, while the actual structure of the therapy—especially Freud's choice of the father as therapist and the attendant ignoring of Hans's privacy—is often completely ignored.

Although Freud was a strong proponent of confidentiality for his adult patients, there was no such consideration for Little Hans. His deepest and most humiliating secrets were to be directly revealed to his father, the person with whom one would think he would be most hesitant to discuss them. There is little evidence that Hans felt the need for confidentiality or that the therapy was an invasion of his privacy. There is little reason to believe that Hans's treatment was in any way compromised or otherwise interfered with by his being asked to reveal himself to his father. Even in Freud's one interview with Hans, the father was present. Yet, the more ardently and strictly the classical child analyst adheres to the Freudian theories, the less the likelihood he would have such an interview.

Most therapists, regardless of their therapeutic orientation, would not instruct a parent in the therapy of his own child. First, to be a therapist requires many years of exacting training and experience. Since the parent (with rare exception) has not had such training, he is ill equipped to conduct such therapy, and to teach him to treat his own child would be a disservice to the patient. In addition, the child's parent cannot have the objectivity which the therapist must have toward his patient if the therapy is to be successful. Yet Freud seems to have ignored these considerations. Irving Stone, in his recent novel about Freud (1971), states that Hans's father was one Max Graf, a graduate in jurisprudence, a doctor of music, and an editor. He was one of the members of Freud's weekly discussion group and therefore had some familiarity with psychoanalytic theory. Neither Freud nor Stone describe him as having had any previous experience as a therapist. But even if he had, Freud did not believe that he would be impaired enough by lack of objectivity to disqualify him as an effective therapist (which he apparently proved to be).

It is of interest that Melanie Klein, Anna Freud, and the child psychoanalysts who followed them—although basically accepting the Freudian theory (the differences between them notwithstanding)—did not generally utilize the parents in the treatment process. In fact, at the present time most classical child analysts, although they may get a history from the parents, confine their treatment exclusively to the child. They recognize that involvement with the parents may have therapeutic benefit; but the greater such involvement, the less they consider the treatment to be justifiably called psychoanalysis— which they consider to be the most definitive, reconstructive, and therapeutic form of therapy for those patients for whom it is the indicated treatment. Yet there is no question that Freud considered Hans to have been psychoanalyzed. A strange paradox.

Although I agree with Freud that parental involvement can be useful, I disagree with his statement that "no one else . . . could possibly have prevailed on the child to make such avowals." There was someone else who was probably even more knowledgeable than the father about the details of Hans's life: his mother. If the family were typical of other Viennese families at the turn of the century (and we have good reason to believe that it was), Hans's father probably had little to do with him. Although middle class mothers also delegated much of the child's care to nursemaids, they were still much more in contact with their children than were fathers. Perhaps Freud's choice of the father was a manifestation of male chauvinism characterized by a basic feeling that men were intrinsically better suited to this kind of work. We know that Hans's mother had previously been a patient of Freud's; perhaps this was a consideration. But such deliberations must be speculative. My main points are that Freud recognized the value of the parent as therapist and did not consider the divulgence of the child's privacy an important consideration. The reader interested in further elaboration of these aspects of Little Hans's case, as well as in my views regarding other facets of Little Hans's treatment, may wish to refer to my article (1972b).

For many years I myself practiced in the traditional way and saw my child patients alone, left the mother in the waiting room, and would only bring her in intermittently or would see her in separate sessions. Over the years I became increasingly dissatisfied with this method. If something were to come up in a session that I thought would be important for the mother to know, I would in the last few minutes of the session bring her in, give her a quick rundown on what had happened, and make some recommendations. I generally found that the mother would receive these recommendations with little conviction, because she had not been witness to the situation that brought them about and time did not often permit my elaborating on them. When I started to keep the mothers in the room I found that the child generally did not object and, in addition, the mother could carry my recommendations through with deeper conviction. Having directly observed the events that resulted in my suggestions and having had the time to discuss them with me in detail resulted in the mothers' more frequently and effectively carrying them out. I found also that very few children express a desire to see me alone. They have not read the books that we have that emphasize the importance of confidentiality and have no preconceived notion that therapy is supposed to be a private matter between the child and therapist.

Once in the room, the mother proved valuable in many other ways. The younger the child, the less likely he is able to recall events that have occurred since his last session. Knowledge of these is often vital to the understanding of many of the child's therapeutic productions. The mother proved to be a ready source of this important information. In analyzing the child's dreams, for example, I found the mother's assistance invaluable. She would often be able to tell me something about a dream element that made its meaning clear, whereas the child's associations to a dream often did not provide enough information for us to meaningfully analyze it. In understanding a child's self-created stories, the mother has also been useful. The understanding of such stories is vital to meaningful utilization of the Mutual Storytelling Technique (soon to be described); for without a valid understanding of the child's story the therapist is ill equipped to create a corre- sponding one of his own. The information given by the mother often provides just the added elements necessary for my creating a useful story.

From these experiences and considerations has evolved the following treatment structure I use for most children below the age of ten or eleven: The parent who brings the child generally stays in the room with the child and me throughout the session. A typical session begins with the child's being invited to discuss anything he wishes. Generally he talks about recent events. I try to gear him toward discussing material I consider therapeutically useful. The mother joins in as indicated. Sometimes the discussion may last five minutes; at other times it may last the whole session. When the point of low therapeutic return is reached the child and I then proceed to involve our- selves in a variety of other therapeutic activities, either traditional or non- traditional (some of the latter group will be described subsequently in this chapter). Sometimes it is the father who brings the child, sometimes both parents, and on occasion even a sibling or two join us. (Although the child's permission is asked regarding a sibling's joining us, the request is rarely re- fused. The siblings are often excited about coming because they have heard about the fun things that take place in my office; and the patient is often proud to show off his special opportunity to play these enjoyable games.) Generally, the parent stays with the child throughout the course of treatment. However, if the treatment is prolonged to the point where the child reaches the prepubertal period, the whole treatment pattern is changed. Not only is the parent not then present, but our involvement in the kinds of games to be discussed in this chapter (as well as in traditional play therapy) is discontin- ued. It is important for the reader to appreciate that I am not describing here *family therapy* (which, incidentally, I do when indicated—either as an ad- junct to a child's treatment or as a treatment program per se). The best name I can give for this treatment approach (admittedly cumbersome but never- theless well describing what I do) is: *individual child therapy with parental observation and intermittent participation.*

I do not wish to give the impression that I rigidly force this treatment pat- tern on all children. There are many children below the age of ten or eleven who should justifiably be treated alone. They are, however, in my opinion and experience, in the minority and the younger the patient the greater the bene- fits to be derived from active parental involvement. When I consider unfor- tunate is the traditional view (often rigidly held) that children automatically should be seen alone and that the parental presence must inevitably be a contaminant. I believe that the ideal approach should be a more flexible one in which the alternative of active parental involvement is seriously con- sidered. My experience has been that when one approaches therapy planning in this way most children will do best with parental involvement. There are, however, definite exceptions.

The child who is overdependent on his mother or the child who is overprotected by her (in severe form such relationships are often referred to as "symbiotic") needs a therapeutic experience separate from the mother. To see them together as the general therapeutic pattern may only entrench the problem. However, even in such cases an occasional joint session may be indicated to demonstrate more meaningfully the pathological pattern.

When the parent is borderline psychotic, or more overtly psychotic, and so poorly defended that he or she would not be able to tolerate the therapeutic revelations (even when symbolically expressed), parental participation is contraindicated. Exposure of such a parent to the child's therapy is not only inhumane but any benefits the child may derive from his treatment will be more than counterbalanced by the deleterious effects of the parent's psychiatric deterioration.

At times it may be necessary to keep the overbearing and intrusive parent out of the room. However, a child may also profit from occasional joint sessions in which such a parent's behavior is pointed out and discouraged and the child is encouraged to assert himself against it. When this is first done in the therapist's presence (with his implied protection of the child from the terrible consequences he anticipates will result from his self-assertion) it becomes easier for the child to express himself subsequently outside the office. Similarly, the child who is excessively fearful of expressing hostility to a parent may need the individual sessions if he is to express any hostility at all. However, with such children I try to reach a point at which the child becomes comfortable enough to express his anger directly to the parent, and this is more easily done first in the therapist's presence.

A rare but nevertheless very important situation in which the parent's presence is generally contraindicated is the one in which the parent is suffering with an incurable disease and is using denial and other related defense mechanisms as a way of dealing with his reactions to the illness. To expose such a parent to his child's attempts to work out his own feelings about the parental illness may not only be cruel to the parent but might also lessen the chance that the child will reveal his true feeling: he will probably appreciate (depending upon his age, intelligence, and sophistication) that his revelations may be deleterious to his parent.

One of the arguments often given for seeing the child alone is that the child needs to have a new special relationship formed with the therapist and that the presence of a third party compromises the formation of such a strong and deep involvement. I have not found this to be case in most situations. The presence of parents has not compromised my relationships with their children. One does not have to keep the child alone in a room in order to evolve a good relationship with him. All too often when the child is seen alone the child and therapist become "we" and the parents become "they." It's "us" *and* "them"; and this easily becomes "us" *vs.* "them." An artificial and unnecessary family schism may be created and this cannot but compromise the therapy. The child may find himself in the middle of a conflict regarding his loyalty—involvement with one person results in feelings of disloyalty to another. The child of divorce usually has enough loyalty problems already; he doesn't need a new one created by the therapeutic structure. With the parent in the room, however, such an antitherapeutic schism is less likely to occur. If the therapist is truly neutral, the child is likely to look upon him as someone who is deeply involved, or at least benevolently involved, with him and his parents.

Another benefit to be derived from this kind of approach is that it lessens the probability of the parents' removing their child from treatment because of their guilt over his illness. A parent generally feels guilty about bringing his child to a therapist (and the divorced parent even more so). He repeatedly asks himself: "What did I do wrong? Where did I fail? I love him so. I tried so hard and yet look what's happened." As I have described elsewhere (1969a, 1969b, and 1970a), such guilt is, in part, related to the attempt to control a situation in which one feels helpless. For control is intrinsically involved in the notion, "It's my fault." Although other factors may certainly be operative (such as unconscious hostility toward the child), the control factor, I believe, is the most common. Another way of alleviating such guilt is that of removing the child from therapy with the rationalization that he doesn't need it. It is as if the parent were saying: "There's nothing wrong with him. He doesn't need therapy. So I have nothing to feel guilty about." Such guilt, I believe, is more constructively and realistically alleviated by the parents' actively participating in the therapy. By assisting the therapist the parent directly counteracts the feelings of impotence that are at the basis of his guilt. Psychoanalysis of this and other factors in the parental guilt may be helpful —but understanding per se has limitations. It is only when analytic insight is translated into action that meaningful changes occur. And active parental participation provides the parent with just such an opportunity.

The parent will often feel rivalrous toward the therapist. In fact, such feelings are probably inevitable. The parents are asking the therapist to succeed in doing what they have failed at. They may observe their child to exhibit a respect for and admiration of the therapist that they do not ostensibly receive. If the child is seen alone, he may often speak to the therapist about things that he does not divulge to the parents. Such rivalrous feelings are inevitably picked up by the child and may produce a divided-loyalty conflict. If too painful for the parent, these feelings may result in the child's being removed from therapy. When the parent serves as an adjunct therapist, many of the cause of such antitherapeutic rivalry are obviated.

I believe that one of the reasons a therapist may hesitate to let parents observe his work is that he may be ashamed to have the parents see exactly what he is doing. If the parents are outside they may envision highly effective and therapeutic operations taking place between the child and therapist. If, however, the parents directly observe the therapist, they may become disillusioned. This is especially likely if he is engaging in what I consider low order therapeutic experiences: building models, playing checkers repeatedly, playing chess. The parent may justifiably complain and say something like "For this he had to become a doctor? For this I'm paying all this money?" But if the therapist is involved in higher order therapeutic activities (some of which I will discuss subsequently), he will have less to be ashamed of and will be more receptive to parental observation. However, even when engaging in the higher order therapeutic activities in which one is really doing effective and efficient therapy, the parent may still interpret what he sees as low order treatment or even consider the activities a waste of time and money. Accordingly, he may remove the child from treatment, which might not have happened had the parent been sitting out in the waiting room imagining all kinds of more sophisticated encounters. There is then, a potential drawback to having the parent present; but this disadvantage, in my opinion, is small compared to the many advantages. Each therapeutic procedure has its drawbacks and active parental participation is no exception.

A related advantage is that the parent's presence stimulates the therapist to do his best. Being observed all the time lessens the likelihood that he will lapse into slipshod and time-wasting activities with the child. This is even more true when the sessions are being tape recorded for home listening (a practice that I will soon elaborate upon).

There are therapists who take the position that they are the protector of the child against the indignities that he suffers at the hands of his parents. I think that this is an unrealistic position for him to take—because the family environment *among those who voluntarily bring their children for treatment* is rarely that deleterious. Even when the parents are divorced, it is one another they may have wished to hurt—not the child. The therapist does best to look upon the parents as people who have tried very hard at all times to do their best in spite of their problems; but things have gone wrong because they have been misguided or blinded or paralyzed by their psychiatric problems. The fact that they are coming to the therapist is a statement of their interest and affection for the child. Even if only one parent is coming, it is a statement of at least that parent's interest. Whatever problems the parents may have, scorn of them is totally antithetical to the treatment process. Parents will inevitably pick up the therapist's feelings toward them. If he is condescending, if he basically looks upon them as criminals who have perpetrated terrible acts upon the child or who have malevolently provided him with a detrimental environment, they will pick up these feelings and either remove the child from treatment or undermine it with their responding reactions.

One last comment on confidentiality. One day about six or seven years ago, when I was still using a tape recorder rather than videotape in connection with the Mutual Storytelling Technique, a nine-year-old girl came into the session with her own tape recorder and asked if it would be all right to tape what was going on between us so she could listen to it at home. I told her that it was not only agreeable to me, but that I was pleased that she wished to do so. In a subsequent session she told me how her parents liked to listen to the tapes at home with her (at that time her mother sat in the waiting room) and even her sisters. She had no feeling of divulgence of privacy whatsoever.

It was from this experience that I soon came to recommend to all patients (regardless of age) that they bring a cassette tape recorder to every session, tape record the *whole* session, and listen to the tape between sessions. The practice provides reiteration of the therapeutic messages and experiences, enhances the likelihood that what happens in therapy will become meaningful, and deepens the therapeutic relationship because of the extra experience with the therapist between sessions. For the cost of a cassette tape recorder and a few tapes (which can be used again many times over) the patient can get a much more intensive therapeutic experience. Sometimes patients will save tapes that are particularly meaningful and I have had a few fairly well-off patients who have saved the complete set of tapes from the whole course of treatment. Many of my child patients (especially the younger ones) play the tapes at home in front of siblings and other family members. The tapes' contents on occasion serve as a point of departure for family discussion and this contributes to the family atmosphere of open communication that I usually try to create for my patients. A father who rarely (if ever) comes to the sessions has an opportunity to hear what's going on. He thereby gets some idea of what he's paying his money for and, except when specifically contraindicated therapeutically (a rare situation), he's entitled to this. In addition. it keeps the father in touch with the therapist, makes him feel less a stranger, and thereby serves to improve the relationship between the two. The father whose only contact with the therapist is the monthly bill is not likely to involve himself meaningfully in his child's treatment. Listening to the tapes of the sessions can rectify significantly this kind of compromise of the child's therapy.

The clinical vignettes presented in subsequent chapters to illustrate the treatment approaches I use will provide a number of examples of the parent's usefulness in the child's sessions. The example I now present comes from the case of Jack, the boy whose treatment will be presented in detail in Chapter 15.

Clinical Example
A mother helps analyze a boy's dream.

Jack entered treatment about two years after his parents' separation. He was disruptive in school and at home. There was a basic organic deficit characterized by hyperactivity and impulsivity. Jack's father was most unreliable regarding his visits. When he was home he was frequently condescending to Jack, and the anger Jack felt in response to these indignities was being displaced onto siblings, peers, his mother, and his teacher.

Near the middle of his eighth month in treatment, during his fifty-fourth session, Jack spoke about his father's visit to the home that previous weekend. Although he tried to speak enthusiastically, it was quite clear that he was forcing the impression that the experience was pleasurable. Jack's mother, however, related how he had followed his father around all weekend "like a puppy dog." She stated that it was pathetic to see how Jack would not resign himself to his father's lack of interest. She described how whenever Jack would try to elicit his father's attention or interest he would be responded to with a "shut up" or "don't bother me." Jack became upset by what his mother said and denied its validity.

He then described two dreams. In the first he was in a hotel in Cooperstown, New York (the site of the National Baseball Museum). There he was trying to get onto a cable car of the kind they have in San Francisco. The patient could not figure out the meaning of the dream. He did describe, however, a pleasurable experience at Cooperstown with his mother and teen-age siblings a few weeks previously, but could provide no further associations. Jack's mother then offered further information. She described how the whole family had gone to San Francisco when Jack was about five and this had been one of the high points of his life. This occurred long before his father had left the home and Jack often referred to the experience with great pleasure. The meaning of the dream became clear: In response to the frustration that Jack had experienced with his father the previous weekend, Jack was dreaming of a return to happier days with his father in San Francisco. The more recent happy days with his mother in Cooperstown were marred by his longings to regain the joys of the San Francisco trip. (This longing was symbolized by his trying to board the cable car.) However, his lack of success in getting aboard reflected his appreciation, at some level, that his father could no longer provide the kinds of gratification he had given him in the past.

Had the mother not been in the room I would not have understood the meaning of this dream. Its analysis is a good example of the vital role that parents can play when they actively participate in the child's therapy. Both the mother and I agreed that the aforementioned interpretation was valid. When it was presented to Jack he agreed that it might be possible but he did not accept it with much conviction.

Jack then went on to relate his second dream. In it he was walking to school with a classmate and they were going to be late. There was a bus up ahead and Jack wanted to run and catch it. His friend, however, was resistive to the idea. The dream ended with neither boy reaching the bus. Rather, there is a confused discussion regarding whether they should have boarded it. Again, Jack was unable to ascertain the meaning of the dream and I could myself offer no specific suggestions. Jack's mother, however, stated that in her opinion buses symbolized Jack's father. When he had lived at home, Jack's father commuted into New York City and returned each day by bus to their suburban New Jersey home. Especially when he was younger, Jack would often ask if his father were on a passing bus. With this new information the dream became clear. It reflected Jack's ambivalence about joining his father. On the one hand, he desperately wanted to catch the bus; on the other hand, he did not anticipate acceptance by his father or gratifying experiences with him and so lagged behind. This is symbolized by the resistance of his friend (Jack's alter ego) to pursuing the bus.

As with the first dream, when Jack was offered the interpretation he passively accepted it, but I did not feel that I was "hitting home." However, I did have the feeling that there was some receptivity, that some seeds were planted, and subsequent experience bore this out. Had Jack's mother not been present these advances would have been much more slowly achieved. (The complete course of Jack's treatment will be presented in Chapter 15.)

The Mutual Storytelling Technique

Eliciting stories is a time-honored practice in child psychotherapy. From the stories children tell, the therapist is able to gain invaluable insights into the child's inner conflicts, frustrations, and defenses.

A child's stories are generally less difficult to analyze than dreams, free associations, and other productions of the adult. His fundamental difficulties are exhibited clearly to the therapist, with less of the obscurity, distortion, and misrepresentation that are characteristic of the adult's presentation. The essential problem for the child's therapist has been how to use his insights therapeutically.

The techniques described in the literature on child psychotherapy and psychoanalysis are, for the most part, attempts to solve this problem. Some are based on the assumption, borrowed from the adult psychoanalytic model, that making the unconscious conscious can itself be therapeutic. My own experience has revealed that few children are interested in gaining conscious awareness of their unconscious processes, let alone utilizing such insights therapeutically. Children do, however, enjoy both telling stories and listening to them. Since storytelling is one of the child's favorite modes of communication, I wondered whether communicating to him in the same mode might not be useful in child therapy. The efficacy of the storytelling approach for the imparting and transmission of values and insights is proved by the ancient and universal appeal of fable, myth, and legend.

It was from these observations and considerations that I developed the Mutual Storytelling Technique, a proposed solution to the question of how to utilize the child's stories therapeutically. In this method the child first tells a story; the therapist surmises its psychodynamic meaning and then tells one of his own. The therapist's story contains the same characters in a similar setting, but he introduces healthier adaptations and resolutions of the conflicts that have been exhibited in the child's story. Since he speaks in the child's own language, the therapist has a good chance of "being heard." One could almost say that here the therapist's interpretations bypass the conscious and are received directly by the unconscious. The child is not burdened with psychoanalytic interpretations which are alien to him. Direct, anxiety-provoking confrontations, so reminiscent of the child's experience with parents and teachers, are avoided. Lastly, the introduction of humor and drama enhances the child's interest and pleasure and, therefore, his receptivity. As a therapeutic tool, the method is useful for children who will tell stories, but who have little interest in analyzing them. It is not a therapy per se, but rather one technique in the therapist's armamentarium.

Basic mechanics of the method. Although drawings, dolls, puppets, and other toys are the modalities around which stories are traditionally told in child therapy, these often restrict the child's storytelling or channel it in highly specific directions. The tape recorder (either audio or video) does not have these disadvantages; with it, the visual field remains free from contaminating and distracting stimuli. Eliciting a story with it is like obtaining a dream on demand. The same method, however, can be employed—with some modifications—with dolls, blocks, drawings, and other traditional play therapy materials.

I begin by asking the child if he would like to be guest of honor on a make-believe television program on which stories are told. If he agrees—and few decline the honor—the recorder is turned on and I begin:

> Good morning, boys and girls, I'd like to welcome you once again to Dr. Gardner's "Make-up-a-Story Television Program." As you all know, we invite children to our program to see how good they are at making up stories. Naturally the more adventure or excitement a story has, the more interesting it is to the people who are watching at their television sets. Now, it's against the rules to tell stories about things you've read or have seen in the movies or on television, or about things that really happened to you or anyone you know.

Like all stories, your story should have a beginning, a middle, and an end. After you've made up a story, you'll tell us the moral of the story. We all know that every good story has a moral.

Then after you've told your story, Dr. Gardner will make up a story too. He'll try to tell one that's interesting and unusual, and then he'll tell the moral of his story.

And now, without further delay, let me introduce to you a boy (girl) who is with us today for the first time. Can you tell us your name, young man (woman)?

I then ask the child a series of brief questions that can be answered by single words or brief phrases, such as his age, address, school grade, and teacher. These "easy" questions diminish the child's anxiety and tend to make him less tense about the more unstructured themes involved in "making up a story." Anxiety is further lessened when he hears his own voice at this point by playback, something which most children enjoy. He is then told:

Now that we've heard a few things about you, we're all interested in hearing the story *you* have for us today.

At this point most children plunge right into their story, although some may feel the need for "time to think." I may offer this pause; if it is asked for by the child, it is readily granted. There are some children for whom this pause is not enough, but nevertheless still want to try. In such instances the child is told:

Some children, especially when it's their first time on this program, have a little trouble thinking of a story, but with some help from me they're able to do so. Most children don't realize that there are *millions* of stories in their heads they don't know about. And I know a way to help get out some of them. Would you like me to help you get out one of them?

Most children assent to this. I then continue:

Fine, here's how it works. I'll start the story and, when I point my finger at you, you say exactly what comes into your mind at that time. You'll then see how easy it is to make up a story. Okay. Let's start. Once upon a time—a long, long time ago—in a distant land—far, far away—there lived a—

I then point my finger, and it is a rare child who does not offer some fill-in word at this point. If the word is *dog*, for example, I then say, "And *that dog* —" and once again point to the patient. I follow the statement provided by the child with "And then—" or "The next thing that happened was—." Every statement the child makes is followed by some introductory connective and an indication to the child to supply the next statement—that and no more. The introduction of specific phrases or words would defeat the therapist's purpose of catalyzing the youngster's production of his *own* created material and of sustaining, as needed, its continuity.

This approach is sufficient to get most children over whatever hurdles there are for them in telling a story. If this is not enough, however, it is best to drop the activity in a completely casual and nonreproachful manner, such as: "Well, today doesn't seem to be your good day for storytelling. Perhaps we'll try again some other time."

While the child is engaged in telling his story, I jot down notes, which not only help in analyzing the child's story but also serve as a basis for my own. At the end of the child's story and his statement of its moral, I may ask questions about specific items in the story. The purpose here is to obtain additional details, which are often of help in understanding the story. Typical questions might be: Was the fish in your story a man or a lady? Why was the fox so mad at the goat? or Why did the bear do that? If the child hesitates to tell the moral of his story or indicates that there is none, I usually reply: "What, a story without a moral? Every good story has *some* lesson or moral!" The moral that this comment usually does succeed in eliciting from the child is often significantly revealing of the fundamental psychodynamics of the story.

For younger children the word *lesson* or *title* may be substituted for *moral*. Or the child might be asked: "What can we learn from your story?"

Then I usually say: "That was a very good (unusual, exciting) story." Or to the child who was hesitant: "And you thought you weren't very good at telling stories!"

I then turn off the tape recorder and prepare my story. Although the child's story is generally simpler to understand than the adult's dream, the analysis of both follows similar principles.

Fundamentals of story analysis. I first attempt to determine which figure or figures in the story represent the child himself, and which stand for significant people in his environment. It is important to appreciate that two or more figures may represent various facets of the *same* person's personality. There may, for example, be a "good dog" and a "bad cat" in the same story, which are best understood as conflicting forces within the same child. A horde of figures, all similar, may symbolize powerful elements in a single person. A hostile father, for example, may be represented by a stampede of bulls. Swarms of small creatures, such as insects, worms, or mice, often symbolize unacceptable repressed complexes. Malevolent figures can represent the child's own repressed hostility of a significant figure. Sometimes both of these mechanisms operate simultaneously. A threatening lion in one child's story stood for his hostile father, and he was made more frightening by the child's own hostility, repressed and projected onto the lion. This process is one of the reasons many children see their parents as actually more malevolent than they actually are.

Besides clarifying the symbolic significance of each figure, it is also important to get a general overall "feel" for the atmosphere and setting of the story. Is the ambience pleasant, neutral, or horrifying? Stories that take place in the frozen tundra or on isolated space stations suggest something very different from those which occur in the child's own home. The child's emotional reactions when telling the story are also of significance in understanding its meaning. An eleven-year-old child who tells me, in an emotionless tone, about the death fall of a mountain climber reveals not only his hostility but also his repression of his feelings. The atypical must be separated from the stereotyped, age-appropriate elements in the story. The former may be very revealing, whereas the latter rarely are. Battles between cowboys and Indians rarely give meaningful data, but when the chief sacrifices his son to Indian gods in a prayer for victory over the white man, something has been learned about the child's relationship with his father.

Lastly, the story may lend itself to a number of different psychodynamic interpretations. In selecting the theme that will be most pertinent for the child *at that particular time*, I am greatly assisted by the child's own "moral" or "title."

After asking myself what a healthier resolution or a more mature adaptation than the one used by the child would be, I create a story of my own. My story involves the same characters, setting, and initial situation as the child's story, but it has a more appropriate or salutary resolution of the most important conflicts. In creating my story, I attempt to provide the child with more *alternatives*. The communication that the child need not be enslaved by his neurotic behavior patterns is vital. Therapy must open new avenues not considered in the child's scheme of things. It must help the child become aware of the multiplicity of options which are available to replace the narrow self-defeating ones he has chosen. My moral or morals are an attempt to emphasize further the healthier adaptations I have included in my story. If, while I am telling my story, the child exhibits deep interest or reveals marked anxiety, which may manifest itself by jitteriness or hyperactivity, then I know that my story is "hitting home." Such clear-cut indications of how relevant one's story is are not, of course, always forthcoming.

After the moral to my story, I stop the recorder and ask the child whether he would like to hear and (when the videotape recorder is used) see the program. In my experience the child is interested in doing so about one-third of the time. Playing the program makes possible a second exposure to the messages that the therapist wishes to impart. If the child is not interested in listening to the tape, then we engage in other therapeutic activities.

The therapist's attitude has a subtle, but nevertheless significant, influence on the child's ability to tell a story. Ideally this attitude should be one of pleasurable anticipation that a story will be forthcoming and surprised disappointment when the child will not or cannot tell one. The child wants to be accepted by those who are meaningful to him, and, if a productive therapeutic relationship has been established, he will try to comply with what is expected of him.

Peer influence is also important. When the child gets the general feeling that storytelling is what everybody does when he visits the therapist, he is more likely to play the game. Lastly, and probably the most important factor in determining whether the child will involve himself, is his appreciation at some level that the therapist's communications are meaningful and useful to him. If the therapist's responding communications are frequently "on target," that is, if they are most often relevant to the child's problems and situation, the child is likely to become engrossed in the game. (I say *frequently* relevant because it is unreasonable to expect that the therapist will always accurately understand the child's story.)

Clinical Example
A boy afraid to reveal himself

George, an eight-and-a-half-year-old boy, was referred because of disinterest in his school work, shyness and general timidity. During the first month of treatment, George told this story:

> Once upon a time there was a man who explored caves and he was famous for exploring some things he found in caves of the cavemen and that the Indians marked on the walls. Once he went in a cave and some people wanted to come with him in case he got lost. He didn't want them to. He wanted all the money for himself. He got money for the things he found. He went in there and he got lost.
>
> The moral of the story is: don't be selfish. Let some other people share things with you. Share.
>
> *Therapist:* So the moral is to share?
> *Patient:* Yeah. Share more.
> *T:* You say he finally got lost. What happened to him?
> *P:* He never could get out. He kept walking around.

> *T:* What finally happened?
> *P:* He died in the cave.

I consider the underground caves to represent the child's unconscious. His exploration of these caves symbolizes his therapy, and he fears that such a dangerous journey to the unknown may have terrible consequences—death itself is not beyond possibility.

The people who offer to guide him represent the therapist. However, he is ambivalent about my joining him in this perilous underground excursion. At first, I am rejected—ostensibly because he would have to share with me the money he would earn from selling his findings. I believe this is a rationalization. George's real fear is that I will lead him to just those things he would rather not find. In addition, his rejection of me might reflect distrust. The boy's parents were divorced, his father was unreliable and at times excessively punitive. George's fear of therapy with me is probably related to his experiences with his father. The money issue is used to justify my not joining him in this adventure into the unknown. But without me the consequences might have been worse. Without my guidance he might become lost and even die. In the moral I do join him and protect him from the malevolent forces of the world, both internal and external.

With this interpretation of George's story, I related the following:

> Once upon a time there was a man and this man was a cave explorer and he was known far and wide for many interesting and unusual discoveries that he made in caves. He would explore the caves of ancient men and explore the caves of ancient Indians where he had discovered numerous drawings and relics from these olden days. He was known far wide for his discoveries.
>
> Now, once he came upon a very large and ancient cave and he said to his friends, "Although I have been hunting and trying to discover things in caves for many years, I'm quite frightened of going into this cave. I think I may get lost in there." And the friends said, "Oh, there's nothing to be afraid of in that cave." The man said, "Well, will you come with me?" And his friends said, "Okay, we'll come with you the first time and then you'll see that it isn't so dangerous and then you won't need us anymore."
>
> So they went into the cave with him the first time. Although there were some things in there that were kind of scary, he realized that they were right; that he didn't need them to accompany him because the things were not as scary as he had thought. Then he was able to go into this cave alone and he realized that what he originally thought was quite scary wasn't that dangerous.

And the lesson of this story is: sometimes you think something is scarier than it really is. If you try to do the thing you fear, you may find out that it isn't as scary as you thought it was originally. The end.

I attempted to convey the notion that in the early phases of treatment George might need my guidance, but that gradually he would be able to do more on his own. In addition, I tried to communicate the idea that his journey into the unconscious will not be as hazardous as he anticipates, but that he can only learn this by self-exposure. Finally, in my story I incorporated the idea that I am not a dangerous person to be alone with.

One week later, George told this story:

Once upon a time there was a man with airplanes—model airplanes and he wanted to make a model of this latest U.S. airplane. The government wouldn't let him because the other companies would find out how it was made. He took pictures when the government people weren't looking and then he made the model of the airplane. And then the other companies found out how the design was made and all that. And he got in big trouble and then the government had to make a new airplane so other companies wouldn't find out how to make it, because they didn't want them to find out how to make the plane. Then the guy who made the model got into a lot of trouble and they put him in jail.

The lesson of that story is: do not make anything that anybody doesn't want you to make anything or else you might get into trouble.

George's second story again reflects his fear that revealing himself will be followed by terrible consequences. The picture taking of the government's secret airplane is similar to the exploration of the underground cave of the previous week's story. Both reflect his fear of disclosing unconscious material. The utilization of the camera, X-ray machine, movie screen, and television set are common ways of representing self-confrontation both in children's stories and in adults' dreams.

In order to again lessen anxieties about therapeutic disclosures, I told this story:

Once upon a time there was a man who made model airplanes and the government made a new plane. It was a commercial flight plane and he wanted to make a model of it, but he thought, "Oh, they'd never give me permission for that. It's considered to be too much of a secret."

So one day he went to where they were testing the plane and he went to the edge of the landing field and he started to take pictures. And while he was taking pictures a man from the government came over and said,

"What are you doing?" He said, "I'm taking pictures." The government man said, "Well, why are you standing behind the hangar here and doing it in such a sly, secret way? Why are you hiding?" And he said, "Well, I thought that you wouldn't want me to take pictures." The man said, "Not at all. We are very proud of this plane. There's nothing secret about it. If you really want to take pictures, why don't you come right up to the hangar and take pictures both on the ground and while it's flying. We are very proud of what we did here and we'd like others to know about it, and any kind of publicity this plane gets we're happy to have." So the man did just that and he learned that many things that you think are to be kept secret are really not to be kept secret and are really better off openly discussed and exposed.

The moral of the story is that there are many things that you might think should be kept secret, but really don't have to be kept secret and you are really better off if you don't keep them secret.

As is clear, I attempted to impart to this boy the notion that things which he considers necessary to hide often need not be enshrouded in secrecy. Exposure, in fact, is often preferable to concealment. My story was another attempt to diminish George's early resistances.

A few weeks later, George told a third story which further revealed early treatment anxieties:

Once upon a time there was a man and he owned a company that made telephones. And that company made these mini-circuits for the telephones so that they would work better and so that the telephone wouldn't have to take up so much room. The men put the telephones in boxes with padding so that the mini-circuits wouldn't get broken or anything.

So once they sold a telephone to this person and it didn't work. So they complained to the company and the company found out that they didn't put padding in the box so a mini-circuit got broken. It was banging around inside. So they put in a new mini-circuit and they gave him his money back. He kept the broken telephone.

The moral of that story is that when you own a company you should make sure that things fit in a box so that they wouldn't get broken.

In this story the patient's feelings of fragility are revealed. George is essentially saying to me: "I'm too frail to withstand therapeutic confrontations. I'm too brittle to remain intact under the stress of treatment."

Accordingly, I told this story:

Once upon a time there was a man who owned a company and this company made mini-circuits for telephones. This man was a very finicky, fuddy-duddy, persnickety kind of fellow and he was constantly worried that the mini-circuits would get broken when shipped. He considered them to be very fragile and he was constantly worried about them. He insisted that the Shipping Department put a lot of padding into the boxes and as much padding that they would put in, when he would investigate it and inspect it, he would say, "Oh, no, not enough padding. Put another layer of padding."

Well, he began to notice that his company wasn't doing so well. They weren't making as much money as he would have liked and that began to upset him. So he brought an expert in—a man who looks into these things and tries to figure out why a company is losing money. And the man investigated the whole thing and he found out that the owner of the company was spending too much money on padding. He said to him, "Listen. These mini-circuits are very stable. They are not that fragile. They are not going to break that easily. You don't have to put much padding in here. In fact, they can go without any padding at all."

Well, the owner of the company was at first hesitant to accept that advice and he thought about it and he spoke to others. They said to him: "Listen, he's right. You're too concerned; you're too fearful. These things aren't that fragile. They're not gonna break that easily. I suggest that you listen to that man."

So he listened to him and at first he was scared because he was worried about those mini-circuits being sent without padding. But he did it and he sat at his phone waiting for the complaints to come in. He expected to have many complaints from people saying, "Hey, this mini-circuit is damaged." But to his surprise, there were no complaints.

And the he learned his lesson. He learned that sometimes things are not as fragile or as breakable or as easily destroyed as you might think. He realized that he was being too cautious.

Therapist: And the lesson of that story is what?

Patient: Well—that is—you just said it.

T: I want to hear you say it so I know you understand.

P: That things don't get broken so easily.

My essential message, of course, was that George wasn't easily damaged, that he could withstand more than he imagined, and that he was over-concerned with protecting himself. In the story "hard knocks" of reality are not as traumatic as the man anticipates.

Dramatization of the Therapeutic Communications

Just as the Mutual Storytelling Technique was developed from the observation that children naturally enjoy both telling and listening to stories, the idea of dramatizing them arose from the observation that children would often automatically (and at times without conscious awareness) gesticulate, impersonate, intone, and enact in other ways while telling their stories. I found that when I introduced such theatrics myself the child became more involved in my stories and receptive to their messages. Whereas originally I introduced the dramatic elements *en passant*, that is, in the process of telling my story (just as the children tended to do), I subsequently formalized the process by inviting the child to reenact our stories as plays following our telling them: "I've got a great idea! Let's make up plays about our stories. Who do you want to be? The wolf or the fox?" At times I would invite the mother and even siblings to join us. (We often face the problem of having a shortage of available actors.) We see here another way in which mothers can be useful in the child's treatment. (A little encouragement may be necessary at times to help some mothers overcome their "stage fright.") Of course, the therapist himself must be free enough to involve himself in the various antics that are required for a successful "performance." He must have the freedom to roll on the floor, imitate various animals, "ham it up," etc. He has to be able to be director, choreographer, writer, and actor—practically all at the same time. He may have to assume a number of different roles in the same play, and quickly shift from part to part. Such role shifts do not seem to bother most children nor reduce their involvement or enjoyment. Nor do they seem to be bothered by the therapist's "stage whispers," so often necessary to keep the play running smoothly.

The therapist who can create with the child such performances has a very valuable tool at his disposal. The enjoyment the child may derive from such plays can be immense. Accordingly, they can serve to entrench the child's involvement in treatment. In addition, such dramatizations enrich the therapeutic communications. One is not only transmitting the message verbally; rather one is adding a host of non-verbal stimuli (physical, kinesthetic, visual, tactile, and at times even olfactory and gustatory). Such multi-sensory exposure increases vastly the chances of the therapist's being heard and help immensely in his getting his messages to sink in.

There are some children, however, who are too inhibited, resistant or uncooperative to directly reveal themselves in the "Make-up-a-Story Television Program." I have found the games that I shall now describe to be effective in drawing this group of more resistive children into meaningful therapeutic involvement.

The Board of Objects Game

In this game (designed with Dr. Nathan Kritzberg) a board of sixty-four squares (a standard checker board serves well) or a larger board (100 squares) is used. In each square is placed a small toy figurine of the type readily purchased in most stores selling children's games and equipment (Figure 1). The figurines include family members, zoo animals, farm animals, small vehicles (police car, fire engine, ambulance, etc.), members of various occupations (doctor, nurse, policeman, etc.), and a wide assortment of other common objects (baby bottle, knife, gun, lipstick, trophy, lump of brown clay, etc.). A pair of dice is used in which one facet of each die is colored red. Lastly, there is a treasure chest filled with token reward chips.

The game begins with the child's throwing the dice. If a red facet lands face up (and this should occur once every three throws of the dice) the child can select any object from the board. If he can say anything at all about the object, he gets *one* reward chip. If he can tell a story about the object, he gets *two* reward chips. The therapist plays similarly and the winner is the one who has accumulated the most chips when the allotted time is over. If a person is lucky and both red facets land face up, the player can select two objects and get double rewards. He may tell one story in which both objects are included or he may tell two separate stories. When commenting on or telling a story about an object, it is preferable for the player to hold it and sometimes even move it about in accordance with what is going on in the story. The child will often do this spontaneously and the therapist should do so as well in appreciation of the enhanced efficacy of the dramatized communication. The therapist's various gestures, animal sounds, vocal imitations, accents, etc. can further involve the child and enhance his receptivity to the therapeutic messages. After being used, the figurine can be either replaced on the board or placed to one side, depending on the preference of the players.

Although the figurines are selected as to elicit fantasies covering a wide range of issues usually encountered in most children's therapy, their exact nature, form, and variety are not crucial. As mentioned, I believe that the pressure of unconscious material to be released in a form specifically meaningful for the child is far greater than the power of the facilitating stimulus to distort the projected material. Accordingly, the therapist need not be too concerned about his selection of objects in the event he wishes to make up such a game himself. The usual variety of such figurines found in most toy stores will serve well.

It is important that the therapist encourage an atmosphere in which conversations may take place about the comments made or stories told, rather than one in which there is fierce competition for the accumulation of chips.

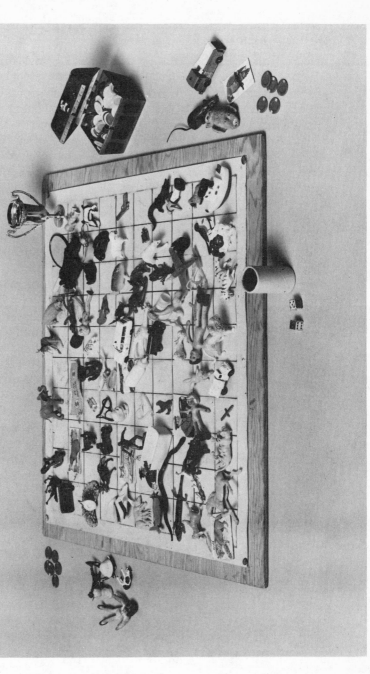

Figure 1

The therapist plays in accordance with the same rules to create stories of his own that are either specifically related to the comments or stories just related by the child or else relevant in other ways to the child's life and problems.

The game is a very attractive one and it is a rare child who does not respond in the affirmative when shown it and asked: "Would you like to play this game with me?" The child below five or six, who has not yet reached the point where he can meaningfully appreciate the rules and organization of standard board games, will still usually want to play. Some will enjoy throwing the dice until they get a red and will then choose an object. Such younger children may not be able to tell well-organized stories but may still provide meaningful, although fragmented, fantasies—especially because there is a reward chip that can be obtained for such revelations. The therapist must try to select from the disorganized fantasies those threads or patterns that are atypical, idiosyncratic, or pathological and then use these as the focus for his own responding comments. Often such younger children will be content to just play, fantasize, and collect chips without giving the therapist his turn. Generally, in such situations, I allow the child to tell a few stories—by which time I have gotten enough material to create one of my own. I then request my right to take my turn to tell stories (a request that is rarely refused) and use the opportunity to relate my responding messages, either in a story or nonstory allegory.

When the allotted time is up, the person with the most chips takes a prize from a conspicuously displayed box of "valuable prizes" (Figure 2).

The rules I have outlined are those I have found most useful. However, the therapist may wish to utilize his own variations and I too at times have modified the game (as in the description above of its use with younger children). I have found the game particularly useful with children at the kindergarten to second-grade level. At that age their reading ability is usually not great enough for them to play some of the more sophisticated games described in this chapter. Yet they do appreciate game structure and so generally become absorbed. At about the age of nine or ten, most children consider the game "babyish" and prefer the more advanced games described herein.

Bag Games

These three games (Figure 3) are attractive in that they appeal to the child's traditional enjoyment of the grab bag game, in which the child closes his eyes and pulls out an unknown object from a bag. In each, one reward chip is given for a simple response and two if the player can tell a story about what has been taken from the bag. The therapist enhances the child's

Figure 2

curiosity and enthusiasm by occasionally warning him not to peek and by exhibiting excitement himself when it is his own turn. The reward chips are contained in a treasure chest, which serves to further enhance their value. Again, the winner is the player who has accumulated the most chips at the end of the allotted time, and he selects a prize from the box of prizes (Figure 2).

The Bag of Toys Game. In a bag clearly labeled BAG OF TOYS are about forty to fifty figurines of the kind used in the *Board of Objects Game* (Figure 1). When putting his hand into the bag the child is warned against peeking ("Keep your eyes closed. Remember, it's against the rules of the game to peek"), and spending time feeling the objects is also discouraged ("No fair feeling. Just pick out one of the objects"). After the object has been selected and used as a focus for comment or story it is laid aside rather than returned to the bag. Again, the child will often add dramatic elements to his story and it behooves the therapist to do so as well.

The Bag of Things Game. In a bag clearly labeled BAG OF THINGS are forty to fifty objects that are less recognizable than those in the BAG OF TOYS (Figure 3). Whereas in *The Bag of Toys Game* the objects are readily identified (soldier, car, boy, fire truck, etc.), in *The Bag of Things Game* objects have been specifically selected because they are not clearly recognizable. Accordingly, the bag contains various kinds of creatures, monsters, wiggly things, a lump of clay, a few blocks, a plastic ring, an odd-looking sea shell, some strange looking robots, and assorted figurines that vaguely resemble people or animals. Because they are not clearly recognizable they tend to contaminate the child's fantasies less than toys in *The Bag of Toys Game*. Often the child tends to anthropomorphize the objects; but their amorphous quality allows their utilization for a wide variety of fantasies. In the course of play, used objects are laid aside and dramatizations are encouraged.

The Bag of Words Game. In a bag labeled BAG OF WORDS are approximately 400 words, each of which is printed with thick ink (a "Magic Marker" or "Flair" type pen will serve well) on a 2" X 3" card (Figure 3). Different-colored cards and inks can be used to make the game more attractive. Words have been chosen that are most likely to elicit comments and stories relevant to issues commonly focused on in therapy, e.g., *breast, anger, mother, father, boy, girl, foolish, doctor, love,* and *hate.* A full list of the words I have found most useful is given in Table 1; however, the reader is likely to think of a number of words on his own and may find some of my words less useful than I have found them. In accordance with the principle that the pressure of unconscious material is more powerful than the contaminating effect of the eliciting stimulus, the specific choice of words is not vital. Occasional cards provide the child with extra reward chips ("You get

Figure 3

two extra reward chips") and these increase the child's excitement while he plays. Used cards are laid aside and dramatizations are encouraged.

accident	birthday	children	doll
adult	birthday party	Christmas	dollar
afraid	black	cigarettes	draw
airplane	blame	circus	dream
allowance	blood	clay	dumb
alone	boast	clean	early
ambulance	boat	clothing	egg
anger	body	clown	enemy
animal	book	club	escape
annoy	bottle	cockroach	eyeglasses
ant	boy	compliment	fail
ape	brag	conduct	fall
apple	brat	cookie	famous
ashamed	breast	cop	fat
automobile	bowel movement	counselor	father
axe	boy	cow	fear
baby	boy scout	cowboy	feeling
baby-sitter	boyfriend	climb	fight
backside	brave	cripple	finger
bad	bread	crook	fire
bad habit	bug	cruel	fire engine
bad thoughts	build	cry	fireman
ball	bull	crybaby	fish
balloon	bully	cuddle	fix
bang	cake	curse	flour
bare	calf	dad	food
bath	camera	danger	fool
bathroom	camp	daughter	foolish
bathtub	camp director	dentist	forget
beat	candy	die	fox
beautiful	car	dinosaur	freak
beaver	care	dirty	friend
behavior	cat	dirty trick	frog
belly button	catch	dirty words	fun
best	cheat	discover	funny
bicycle	chewing gum	disgusting	game
big	chicken	doctor	garbage
bird	child	dog	garbageman

gift	job	model	playground
girl	joke	mom	please
girl friend	joy	money	poison
girl scout	judge	monkey	poke
God	kangaroo	monster	police car
good	kill	mother	policeman
grab	kind	mouse	polite
grade	king	mouth	pony
grandfather	kiss	mucus	poor
grandmother	knife	mud	present
grownup	lady	nag	president
gun	lamb	naked	pretty
hamster	large	nasty	praise
happy	late	naughty	pray
harm	laugh	new	prince
hate	lazy	nice	princess
healthy	leave	nightmare	principal
hear	letter	nipple	prize
heaven	lie	note	proud
hell	like	nurse	psychiatrist
hen	lion	old	psychologist
hide	lipstick	operation	punish
hit	little	operation	pupil
hole	lollipop	ostrich	queen
holiday	lonely	owl	quiet
homework	lose	paint	rat
honest	love	parent	refrigerator
hope	lucky	parrot	respect
horrible	mad	party	reward
horse	make	pass	rich
hospital	make-believe	pay	right
house	man	peacock	robber
hug	manners	penis	rotten
hungry	matches	pet	sad
hurt	mean	phoney	scaredy-cat
ice cream	medal	pick on	scarey
ill	medicine	picture	school
Indian	mess	pig	scold
insult	message	piggy bank	scoutmaster
invisible	milk	pill	scream
jail	mirror	plan	secret
jerk	mistake	play	secret plan

see
selfish
share
sheep
shoot
shout
shy
sick
silly
sissy
sister
skunk
sleep
slob
sloppy
sly
small
smart
smell
snail
snake
sneak
soap
soldier
son
song
sore loser
sorry
spanking
spear
spend

spider
spit
spoil
sport
steal
stick
stingy
stink
stone
story
strong
student
stupid
suck
surprise
sword
talk
teacher
teacher's pet
tease
teen-ager
telephone
television
temper tantrum
thank
therapist
thief
threaten
thumb
tickle
tiger

toilet
touch
tooth
toy
train
treat
tree
trick
tricycle
trip
truck
try
turtle
ugly
upset
vagina
vomit
water
weak
weep
whip
whisper
win
wish
wipe
wolf
warm
worry
worst
young
zoo

Scrabble for Juniors

Whereas in the standard game of adult *Scrabble** the players form their words with letter tiles on a blank playing board, in the child's version, *Scrabble for Juniors,** simple words are already printed on the board and the child attempts to cover the board letters with his own letter tiles (Figure 4). In the modification of the *Scrabble for Juniors* game devised by Dr.

*Manufactured by Selchow & Richter Co., Bay Shore, New York.

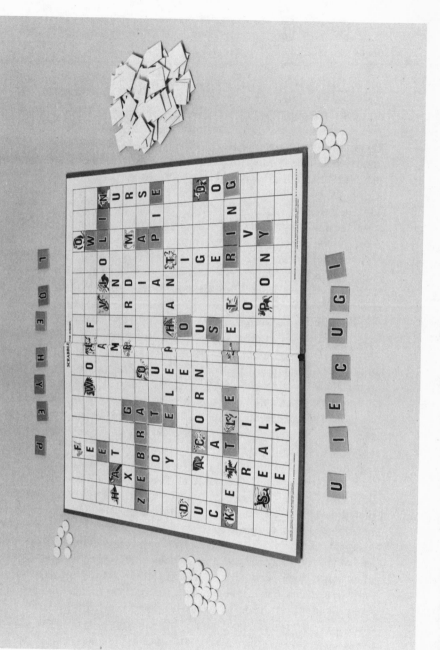

Figure 4

Nathan I. Kritzberg and myself, all the letter tiles are first placed face down along the side of the playing board. The patient and the therapist then each select seven letter tiles and place them face up in front of them. The game proceeds with each player in turn placing two letters over those on the board. The patient is advised to try to so place his letters that he will be working toward the completion of a word. The player who places the last letter necessary to finish a word (this need not be the final letter of the word, as letters do not have to be covered consecutively first to last) receives a reward chip. If the player can say anything about the word, he gets a second reward chip. And if he can tell an original story about the word, he gets two extra reward chips. (Accordingly, the maximum number of chips obtainable for completing a word is four.)

Generally, I try to let the patient be the first to complete a word in order to learn those issues that are uppermost in his mind at that time. This information enables me to relate more meaningful communications when my turn comes to comment on or tell a story about a word that I have completed. Because the players' letter tiles are placed face up, I can see what letters I can place on the board that would make it most likely for the patient to complete his word first. In addition, I may fail to complete a word that I am capable of and "by mistake" use the letter elsewhere. Although I, like most therapists, am a firm believer in being totally honest with my patients, there are times in child therapy when a little duplicity is justified because it serves the purpose of the child's treatment.

Sometimes the child will spot a particular word on the board and try to complete it because he is especially anxious to tell a story about it. In such situations the therapist can be fairly certain that the word has triggered significant associations. More often, however, the child's choice of a word depends upon the letters he happens to choose. In addition, most children tend to favor words on their side of the playing board. In spite of the drawbacks implicit in these determinants, my experience has been that the completed word will generally be used in the service of expressing those issues most pertinent to the child at that time.

Again, the winner is the player who has accumulated the most chips at the end of the allotted time. A slow pace is encouraged so that the words, comments, and stories can serve as a point of departure for discussion. Dramatizations are also encouraged during the course of play. The game is useful from the late first grade to about the fourth-to-fifth grade level. Older children find the words too "easy." My attempts to use the standard adult *Scrabble* game with these older children have not worked out well. They tend to get much too involved in the point values of the various letters and so swept up in the strongly competitive elements in the adult version that comments and storytelling tend to take a secondary role. Accordingly, I do not have adult *Scrabble* available in the office as one of the games the child can choose to play.

The Alphabet Soup Game

The Cambell's Alphabet Soup Game* is packaged in a container that closely resembles a very large can of Campbell's tomato soup (Figure 5). The container is quite attractive and therefore readily appeals to the child who is looking over toy shelves for a game to play. The equipment consists of a plastic bowl filled with plastic letters and two spoons. The modification that I have found most useful therapeutically is for the patient and the therapist each to scoop a spoonful of letters from the bowl and form a word with them. The patient (whom I generally allow to go first) gets a reward for having been able to form a word. If he can say anything at all about the word, he gets a second reward chip. And if he can tell a story about the word, he gets two extra reward chips. I then respond similarly to my word. The game can then proceed in a number of ways. One variation is for the players to attempt to form other words from the same batch of letters in order to obtain more reward chips. When the player is no longer able to, he can take a second scoop by "paying" two chips to the bank. These can be added to the original group of letters (the preferable alternative because there are then more letters with which to form words), or can serve as a replacement for them. Sometimes trading letters with one another adds to the enjoyment of the game. Or the two players can decide to trade their whole batch of letters with one another to see if they can form other words not previously used. Whatever the variations utilized (and I am sure the reader can devise his own) the basic principle holds that a player gets one reward chip for the word, a second for a comment, and two more for a story. Again, the winner is the player who has received the most reward chips at the end of the allotted time. He, of course, receives one of the Valuable Prizes from the previously described box of prizes.

The Talking, Feeling, and Doing Game

There are many children who, in spite of the various facilitating and seductive techniques that I have described, may still be unable or unwilling to express their underlying fantasies (whether in stories or less organized form) or to provide us with high-order material for meaningful therapeutic inter-

*Manufactured by Multiple Toymakers, a division of Minor Industries, 200 Fifth Avenue, New York, New York 10010.

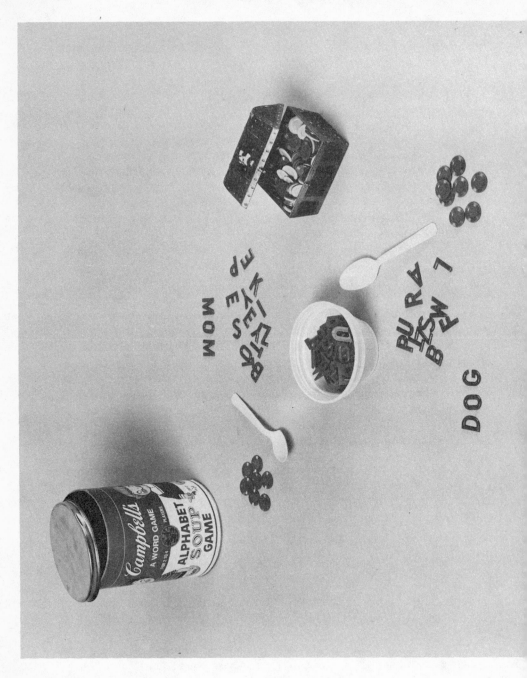

Figure 5

change. And there are others (also very common) who may involve themselves for short periods of time in such interchanges and then "clam up" or "cool off" with the result that a major part of the session is spent in low-efficiency or even therapeutically worthless activities. In an effort to draw such children into meaningful therapeutic involvement I have devised *The Talking, Feeling, and Doing Game*,* an instrument that I have found effective in engaging a significant segment of this previously unreachable group.

The Talking, Feeling, and Doing Game (Figure 6) is similar in appearance and format to many of the standard board games with which practically all children are familiar. The game begins with the child and therapist each placing their playing pieces at START. Each in turn throws the dice and moves his playing piece along a curved path of squares. Depending upon the color of the square on which the piece lands, the player selects a *Talking Card, Feeling Card,* or *Doing Card*. The questions or directions on the cards in each stack range from the very low anxiety-provoking (so that practically any child will be able to respond) to the moderately anxiety-provoking. If the child does respond (and the most liberal criteria are used—especially for the very inhibited child), he receives a token reward chip.

Some of the low-anxiety *Talking Cards* are: "What is your address?" "What present would you like to get for your next birthday?" "How old is your father?" "How tall are you?" "How old is your mother?" "How much do you weigh?" "What is your lucky number and why?" What is your telephone number?" "What kind of work does your father do?" Each of these questions can readily be answered by most children. The inevitable token reward fosters further involvement in the game.

Some typical moderate-anxiety *Talking Cards* are: "Make up a message for a Chinese fortune cookie." "Suppose two people are talking about you and they didn't know you were listening. What do you think you would hear them saying?" "Say something bad about your mother." "People are a mixture of both good and bad, that is, everyone has good and bad parts. Say something good about someone you don't like." "Of all the animals, which one is your favorite? Why?" "What things come into your mind when you can't fall asleep?" "Someone passes you a note. What does it say?" "What's the worst thing you can do to someone?" "If you could make yourself invisible, what would you do?" "A girl was the only one in the class not invited to a birthday party. Why do you think she wasn't invited?" "Make believe that you're looking into a crystal ball that can show your future. What do you see?" "Make believe a piece of paper just blew in the window. Something is written on it. Make up what is said on the paper." Most children, in my experience, will attempt to answer these questions. None are as anxiety-provoking as the free fantasy requested in the Mutual Storytelling Technique. If the child does not feel comfortable responding he is not pressured;

*Manufactured by Creative Therapeutics, 155 County Road, Cresskill, New Jersey 07626.

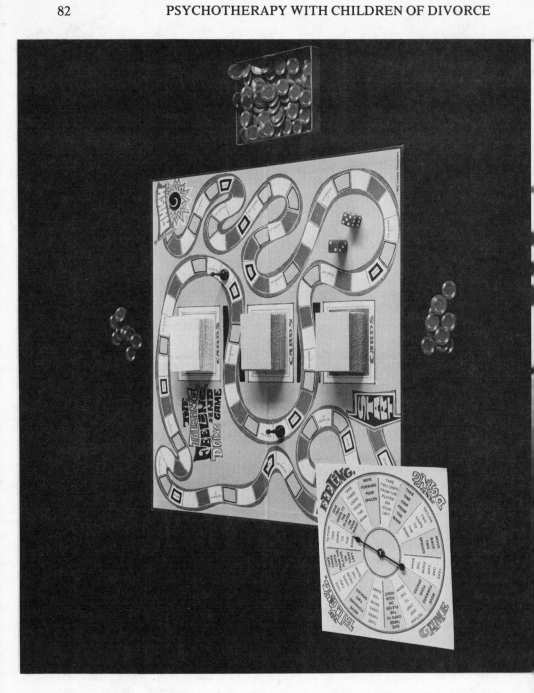

Figure 6

his only negative reinforcement is the failure to receive the reward chip. The therapist may, on occasion, pretend to be unable to respond in order to protect the child from feeling unworthy about his inability to answer. (I will elaborate below in greater detail on the therapist's responses.)

Some typical low-anxiety *Feeling Cards* are: "What food do you hate the most? Why?" "How do you feel when you stand close to someone whose breath smells because he hasn't brushed his teeth?" "How do you feel about taking baths or showers?" "How do you feel after you've made in the toilet?" "How do you feel when someone tickles you?" "How do you feel when someone hits you?" "What's something you could say that would make a person feel good?" "What do you think of someone who doesn't wipe himself after he goes to the bathroom?" "A boy got sick on the day of the class picnic and so he couldn't go. How did he feel?" "A boy was sent to his room for hitting his sister. How did he feel as he was sitting there alone? What was he thinking?" "On the last day of school a boy learned that he would have to repeat the same grade. What had happened? How did he feel?" "Tell about something you did that made you very proud." "What do you think about someone who picks his nose and then wipes the mucus on something?" "How do you feel while you're eating ice cream?"

Some typical moderate-anxiety *Feeling Cards* are: "All the girls in the class were invited to a birthday party except one. How did she feel? Why wasn't she invited?" "What's the worst thing a child can say to his mother?" "Everybody in the class was laughing at a boy. What had happened?" "A child has something on his mind that he's afraid to tell his father. What is it that he's scared to talk about?" "Everybody in the class was laughing at a girl. What had happened?" "How do you feel when you learn something bad about someone whom you love?" "What do you think about a boy who sometimes plays with his penis when he's alone?" "What do you think about a girl who sometimes plays with or rubs her vagina when she's alone?" "Tell about something you did that you are ashamed about." "A child is ashamed to tell his father about something. What is it?"

Some typical low-anxiety *Doing Cards* are: "Make believe you're blowing out the candles on your birthday cake." "With you finger draw a circle in the air." "Make a funny sound with your mouth. If you spit you don't get a chip." "Scream as loud as you can. How do the people feel who have had to listen to you?" "Stick your finger in your ear. You won't mind doing this if you have clean ears." "Stick your finger in your belly button. "Stick out your tongue at someone." "Make believe you're throwing a ball." "Nod your head, clap your hands, and stamp your feet—all at the same time." "Make believe you're doing a good thing." "Breathe in and out five times, without spitting. You do not get a chip if you spit. You do not get a chip if you breathe in anyone's face." "Make believe you're eating ice cream." "Dance around the room." "Hold your arms over your head and clap your hands."

Some typical moderate-anxiety *Doing Cards* are: "Make believe you're speaking to someone on the phone. Whom are you speaking to? What are you saying?" "Make believe you're opening a letter that has been written to you. What does it say?" "Make believe someone grabbed something of yours. Show what you would do." "Tell about something that makes you angry. Act out what you would do if that thing were happening right now." "Make believe you're having a bad dream. What's the dream about?" "Make believe you're picking up an envelope that you find while walking down the street. There's a note inside but no name on the front. You open it up. What does the note say?" "What is one of the stupidest things a person can do? Show someone doing that thing." "Make believe you're saying something nasty to someone. To whom are you talking? What are you saying?" "What is the most selfish thing you ever did? Make believe you're doing that thing now." "What is the most foolish or silly thing a person can do? Make believe you're doing that thing." "What is the bravest thing you ever did? Make believe you're doing that thing right now." "You're standing in line to buy something and a child pushes himself in front of you. Show what you would do." "You're standing in line to buy something and an adult pushes himself in front of you. Show what you would do." "Make believe you're doing a bad thing."

The child's responses are generally revealing of those psychological issues that are most meaningful to him at that time. The information so gained serves to guide the therapist in providing responses to his own cards that would be most pertinent to the patient. Of course, other information the therapist has about the patient contributes further to his ability to provide relevant and therapeutically beneficial responses.

Throughout the play any of the issues brought up by the cards can serve as a point of departure for discussion between the therapist and patient. It is preferable for the therapist to try to create an atmosphere of relaxation in order to encourage slow conversation rather than quick competition for the accumulation of reward chips. The therapist must use his discretion in deciding how much discussion is indicated for each patient. As is obvious, the *Talking Cards* tend to elicit responses of a cognitive nature, the *Feeling Cards* responses that are emotional, and the *Doing Cards* responses that require some action. In each case the first goal is to loosen up the child's inhibitions in these areas. The topics chosen cover the wide range of issues usually dealt with in most children's therapy. The cards are so designed that they can be read by most third graders. Late first and second graders will often enjoy trying to read the cards with the help of the therapist. And younger children (not old enough to read, but old enough to appreciate game structure) will enjoy the game with the therapist reading their cards to them. Because there are so many cards (100 in each stack), and because the general atmosphere is usually one of discussion over each card, there may be weeks (and even months) before the child may select the same card again. When that occurs he usually is at a different point in treatment, different issues may be meaningful, and he therefore generally provides different responses.

The winner is the person who has the most chips after both players have reached FINISH. The game is designed to take about thirty to forty-five minutes (this includes play and discussion). If less time is available, then play can proceed until the allotted time is up. The winner is the one who has accumulated the most chips when the designated time is over. The winner then gets a prize from the previously described box of prizes. Often the object chosen by the child is of psychological significance and a discussion of the choice and the child's comments about the object can be therapeutically useful. In addition, a few children have saved these prizes at home and started a collection. I believe that in these cases it represented a desire to maintain contact with me between sessions and served thereby to strengthen the therapeutic relationship.

It is important for the therapist to communicate to the child that it is perfectly acceptable not to respond to a card. The therapist himself may want to do this at times either because he may not feel it appropriate for him to reveal to the child certain personal material that is suggested by the card or because he wants to lessen any embarrassment the child may have over not being free enough to respond to a number of cards. On the other hand, one of the game's purposes is to provide the therapist with an opportunity to reveal personal things about himself to the degree that he considers it therapeutically indicated. All too often, therapists try to encourage children to reveal themselves, while themselves refraining from personal revelation. Not serving as good models themselves, they thereby lessen the likelihood of success in getting the child to reveal himself. It is not so much what the therapist reveals, but the process of his revealing that is therapeutic. Often the therapist may choose not to respond with self-revelatory material but rather to provide a response that is more directly relevant to the child's problems. No matter what kind of response the therapist chooses to give, his primary consideration should always be: "What response would be most therapeutic for this child?"

The path also contains squares that instruct the player to GO AHEAD and GO BACK varying numbers of spaces. If a player lands on a square marked SPIN, he spins a spinner which may provide him with extra tokens or instruct him to give up tokens (either from the bank or other player) or to go forward or backward a certain number of spaces. The spinner has proved particularly attractive to children and they generally become quite excited when they land on SPIN—even though there is a chance that they may lose chips or go backward. In addition, there are cards in each of the three stacks that instruct the player to take an extra turn or lose his next turn. All these elaborations, although they do not generally result in the elicitation of psychodynamic material, do add excitement to the game and thereby enhance the child's interest and involvement.

Although the game is primarily designed to draw out the inhibited child and to engage the uncooperative child, it can also be useful in the treatment of the child who is free to express himself. After a period of more revelatory therapeutic experience, such children usually need the less revealing (and thereby less anxiety-provoking) sort of therapeutic exposure that this game can provide.

Although primarily designed to be used in the one-to-one therapeutic situation, the game can be used in child group therapy as well (preferably for small groups of three to five children). When so utilized the therapist can use a child's response as a point of departure for group discussion. The game is particularly useful in child group therapy because it provides intrinsic structure in a situation that traditionally tends to become unstructured (the children tend to become playful, rambunctious, distracted, etc.). In addition, it facilitates discussion of problems in a setting in which such conversations are usually difficult to accomplish because of the reticence of most children to engage in them.

Generally, the material elicited with the Mutual Storytelling Technique is closer to pure dream and free fantasy than that revealed in *The Talking, Feeling, and Doing Game*. The "Make-up-a-Story Television Program" is so structured that there are no specific stimuli around which the stories are told. Traditional play materials such as dolls and puppets, although valuable and frequently effective catalysts for story elicitation, do contaminate the story and tend to draw the child's projections in specific directions. The cards in *The Talking, Feeling, and Doing Game* are similarly contaminating. However, I believe that the push of the unconscious material to be released in a form specific to the child's needs at that particular time is far stronger than the pull of the evoking stimulus and its power to significantly alter the projected material. Accordingly, the channeling of the projections is not, in my opinion, very significant.

My experience has been that the game is useful for children up to puberty. The adolescent usually finds the game "childish." This, I believe, is more related to the inhibitions that tend to befall youngsters during this period than to the fact that the game is beneath their level of maturity. Whether or not this is so, the adolescent generally does not wish to play the game (with the exception of those with significant problems such as borderline intelligence, minimal brain dysfunction, or psychosis) so that its use, effectively, ends at puberty.

Clinical Example
A boy torn between litigating parents.

Martin entered treatment at age seven because of poor school performance in spite of extremely high intelligence. He was sloppy in the classroom, would not do his homework, and was generally disruptive. Both in school and at home he was hyperactive and distractible; however, there was no organic basis for these symptoms. Rather, I considered them to be a manifestation of tension and anxiety. Martin's parents had separated about six months prior to his coming to treatment and there were many unexpressed feelings regarding his parents' separation and their continuing difficulties. Specifically, the parents were deeply embroiled in divorce litigation and this was clearly affecting Martin.

At the beginning of his third month of treatment, while playing *The Talking, Feeling, and Doing Game*, the following interchanges took place:

> *Therapist:* "What is one of the smartest things a person can do? Why?"
>
> I would say one of the smartest things a person can do is to think in advance what the consequences are . . . do you know what consequences mean?
>
> *Patient:* What?
>
> *T:* What will happen if he does something. In other words, when you're going to do something think in advance whether it's going to cause trouble or not or whether there's a possibility that what you are doing may cause trouble. And a smart person thinks in advance whether there's going to be trouble or not.
>
> *P:* Oh!
>
> *T:* And then he tries to avoid doing those things which might cause trouble. That's my opinion. What do you think?
>
> *P:* Okay.
>
> *T:* What do you think? Have a seat or else you won't be on television.
>
> *P:* You get a chip.

Martin was very attentive to what I was saying and I was quite sure that my message sunk in. However, his general level of activity was still quite high and at the end he moved away from the view of the television camera.

My comment was a general bit of advice which hopefully could serve Martin in many areas. I was particularly thinking about his school work where he did not appear to concern himself with the consequences of his disruptive behavior in the classroom.

When the patient took his next card the following conversation occurred:

Patient: "Name three things that could make a person happy."

Therapist: Hh hmm. Go ahead.

P: That someone should give them a great big kiss. That's one.

T: All right. Okay.

P: Number two. Someone could say, "I love you."

T: All right.

P: Number three. Someone could say or someone could um (pauses)

T: Go ahead

P: "You're a nice person."

T: Okay, so the three things are that someone would give a person a kiss, someone could say, "I love you," and someone could say, "You're a nice person"?

P: Yes.

T: Okay. Excuse me, could you stop kicking there please because that noise will come over the microphone and we won't be able to hear ourselves when we watch this on TV later.

P: Okay.

T: Okay. Now—you're still kicking. I have something to say about that. I would say that if a person wanted those things to happen to him, to be kissed, for someone to say, "I love you" and for someone to say, "You're a nice person," he has to work for that. Do you know what I mean?

P: Yeah.

T: He has to try to be nice so that people will love him and want to kiss him. Otherwise, they'll try to run away from him and go in the opposite direction.

P: Yeah.

T: So things like that don't just happen. Do you know that?

P: Right.

T: Okay.

Here, I tried to impress upon Martin the fact that his wishes would only come true if he were to behave in such a way that people would react in accordance with them. Like most children (and probably most adults as well) Martin wished to be loved without applying himself or developing ingratiating personality traits.

Again, Martin's hyperactivity revealed itself with his kicking noises. My comment attempted to communicate to him that he himself would suffer certain consequences over his kicking, namely, that the noises coming over the microphone would impair our watching the program that was being made of our playing the game.

Therapist: Okay, my card says, "What sport are you worst at?"
I think the sport I am worst at is basketball. I'm really a loser when it comes . . .

P (interrupts): Yeah, I'm not so good at basketball either.

T: Uh huh. What sport are you best at? What's the best one?

P: (doesn't answer)

T: Hmm? What's your best sport?

P: Well, my best sport is uh . . . mmm . . . (looking to his mother) what is my best sport?

T: You think of the answer.

P: Well, my best out of order I like best.

T: All right, what do you like best?

P: Oh, that's easy. That's easy. Bowling!

T: Uh huh. You like that the best?

P: Yes.

T: What's your highest score?

P: I never did bowl in a real bowling alley.

T: Uh huh. What kind of a bowling alley did you bowl in?

P: I have a toy bowling alley at home.

T: Uh huh. Oh, you like that very well?

P: Yes.

T: Okay.

P: And my friends think that Mrs. S. has a bowling alley where you bowl a little ball, and they have to hit the pins and then the pins go up.

T: Okay. Good. All right, I get a chip for my answer.

Most patients, regardless of age, tend to look upon the therapist as being extremely successful in all areas of functioning. Although this may be helpful in certain aspects of therapy, it can also be detrimental. To look upon the therapist as someone who is perfect, or almost perfect, may lower the patient's self-esteem because of the unfavorable comparison. Accordingly, when appropriate and when I believe it will be therapeutic, I admit deficiencies to my patients. Here, the card "What sport are you worst at?" provided me with just such an opportunity.

I then used the subject of one's ability at sports to ask the patient about the sport that he was best at. In this way I hoped to enhance his self-esteem by getting him to talk about something he did well.

The game then continued:

Therapist: Read it now.

Patient: "What is the most selfish thing you ever did? Make believe you're doing it."

Well, I don't know anything, but I'll do something.

T: Well, first say what it is and then you do it. What is the selfish thing?

P: Well, to grab things away from people.

T: For instance, what did you do . . . like what did you grab from somebody that was selfish?

P: Well, I don't know, but I'm just saying . . .

T (interrupts): No, you have to tell something that really happened.

P (getting agitated): Well, I don't know anything.

T: Okay, so you don't get a chip then.

P: Oh. Well, could I take another card?

T: Well, no, no. You have to try to think. Everybody once in a while does selfish things. No one's perfect.

P: I know.

T: So what selfish thing did you do?

P: I don't know.

T: I could think of something selfish you did.

P: What?

T: Should I help you?

P: Okay.

T: Your mother told me about it just before—before we started the game. Now what was the first thing she was upset about when she came into the office today?

P: I forget.

T: I'll give you a hint. It has something to do with a thing starting with the letter *c*.

P: I don't know.

T: The second letter is *a*.

P: The third letter?

T: r.

P: I don't . . .

T (interrupts): What's the word?

P: I don't know!

T: What's the word?

P: I don't know.

T: What does c-a-r spell?

P: Car.

T: Okay, the selfish thing has something to do with *car*.

P: Um.

T: What am I talking about?

P (exasperated): I don't know!

T: Ah, I think that you're—I can't believe that you don't remember after all that long talk that we had.

P: Oh, yes, broke the car and don't want to pay the money.

T: You broke the car. How did you break the car?

P: Well, I dented it or Philip dented it, but we were both just as responsible and I have to pay some money and I don't want to pay it.

T: What's going to happen?

P: I have to pay it!

T: All right, what was the selfish thing?

P: I didn't want to pay it, I guess.

T: That's selfish and what was the other selfish thing?

P: I don't know.

T: The other selfish thing was not thinking about the fact that this was a new car—one day old—a brand new car and you did not think about how your mother would feel if you dented it or scratched it or something like that.

P: Well, I didn't know it was going to happen.

T: Yeah, but you weren't careful. You weren't considerate of her property.

P: Oh.

T: Do you think that's selfish?

P: . . . (mumbles) . . .

T: Do you think not wanting to pay is selfish?

P: Well, no, I did want to keep my money.

T: Yeah, but you said you didn't want to pay.

P: Right.

T: Or at least pay part of it. Do you think that that is selfish?

P: Well, it cost $23.50. That's a lot of money.

T: Yeah, but that's only half of what it's going to cost. It's going to cost her $45.

P: Uh, um.

T: Hmm? Do you think it's selfish not to want to pay part of it?

P (in a low voice): No.

T: Okay, so you don't think that's selfish, so I guess if you don't think that's selfish then I guess you don't get a chip.

P (in low voice): I still want one.

T: Do you want to think of something else? Do you want to just skip your chance again?

P: No.

T: Okay. I guess we have a difference of opinion regarding whether that is selfish or not. See, my opinion is that there are two selfish things there. What are the two selfish things *I* think are in there?

P: That I wasn't considerate of the car and that I don't want to pay the money.

T: Right, but you don't think either one of those things is selfish?
P: No.
T: Okay, I guess we have a difference of opinion.

Prior to the session, the mother had complained bitterly that Martin and his friend Philip had jumped all over her new car and scratched it. As can be seen from the interchange, Martin did not wish to discuss this issue. His card gave me a good opportunity to go into it, but he resisted all the way in recognizing his mother's justification for resentment and requiring him to pay part of the expenses. (Philip's parents as well were being consulted regarding what obligation they and/or Philip were going to assume.) Because Martin did not agree that these were selfish things he did not get a reward chip. In discussing with a child an issue that we do not agree upon, I do not allow a conflict to develop. Rather, after two or three rounds in which each of us expresses himself, I will conclude the discussion with a comment such as, "I guess we have a difference of opinion. Let's go on." And this is what I did in this case. It is antitherapeutic to attempt to coerce a patient into accepting an interpretation. In such situations one usually gets statements of agreement but no real conviction that the therapist's position is valid.

The game then continued:

Therapist: "Make a funny sound with your mouth. If you spit you don't get a chip."
Hmmm. It's tough to try to do it without spitting. (makes funny loud sound)
Patient: You spitted.
T: I think that I spit.
P: Yeah.
T: Uck! I don't get a chip.
P (laughs): I could make a funny sound.
T: Do you think you can do it without spitting?
P: Hh hmmm.
T: If you can do it without spitting you get a chip. I'm going to see if you spit.
P: (makes funny sound)
T: That is a funny sound, right. Okay, you get a chip because you do it without spitting.

The game includes a number of cards that are designed to elicit humorous and enjoyable interchanges between the therapist and the patient. These are part of the seductive process mentioned in a previous chapter and are vital if the child's interest is to be maintained. In addition, in this particular card there is included a lesson in correct social behavior.

The game then continued:

> *Therapist:* "What's the best color eyes to have? Why?"
> Well, I don't think that there's any one color better than the other. I think that people are born with different color eyes and it really doesn't make any difference what color eyes you have, and one is neither better than the other. People are born different. What do you think?
> *Patient:* Well, I think that's right. I'll get you a chip.
> *T:* Okay. Why don't you sit in your chair because you're going to kick that wire. Here sit over here.
> *P:* Oh.
> *T:* Okay.

My response was designed to communicate the message that one should judge people on the basis of acquired attributes rather than innate characteristics. Those who are deficient in the former area may try to compensate by exaggerating the value of traits in the latter. Again, we see Martin's hyperactivity and my response.

We then continued:

> *Therapist:* Okay, you go now. What does your card say?
> *Patient:* "What's the worst thing a child can say to his mother?"
> Oh, that's easy. "You're stupid."
> *T:* Hh hmm. Can't you think of something worse?
> *P:* "I hate you."
> *T:* Hh hmm.
> *P:* "I hate you, stupid."
> *T:* Hh hmm. Did you ever have any thoughts like that about your mother?
> *P:* No.
> *T:* Never in your whole life?
> *P:* No, I don't!
> *T:* I can't imagine. I can't imagine in your whole life—in your *whole* life—how old are you now?
> *P:* Seven.
> *T:* In seven years you have never once thought that you hated your mother?
> *P:* No!
> *T:* Never once?
> *P:* Not that I hate her.
> *T:* What's the worst thought that you ever really had about her in your *whole* life of seven years?

P: I don't know, to tell you the truth.

Patient's Mother: I bet you thought I was stupid sometimes.

P: No.

P's M: Because I do stupid things.

P: Well, sometimes you do stupid things, but I never think you are stupid. But sometimes you've done a few stupid things.

T: But you never once had the thought that you hated your mother.

P: Noooo.

T: Never once? I don't think you really hate her all the time, but even once a little bit.

P: No.

T: Really? Okay. Because most kids on occasion, once in a while, when something happens they really get mad at their mother and they may say something like they hate her or they think it.

P: Oh.

T: You've never had that?

P: No.

T: What do you think about a child who would have such a thought?

P: Well, I think his mother would have done something that he really wouldn't have liked.

T: Right, that's true.

P: And it got him very very mad.

T: Right. Do you think that there's something wrong with a child who would have such a thought like that?

P: I don't know.

T: I agree with you that, you know, sometimes a mother will do something that will get a kid really angry and then he'll have that kind of thought.

P: Oh.

P's M: When he's gotten really angry he's barricaded himself in sometimes and pounded on the door and nailed himself in his room.

T: Hh hmm. When that happens do you hate your mother?

P: No.

T: Hh hmm. You don't. Okay. I was just wondering whether you had such thoughts because most kids do at times have thoughts like that.

P: Oh.

T: Even though they don't hate their mother all the time.

P: Oh.

T: But I find there's nothing wrong with that, you know, you have it once in a while.

P: Oh.

T: Okay, you get a chip.

P: Thanks.
T: Okay, now I go.

I used the card as an opportunity to enter into a discussion on the subject of inhibited anger—a subject that I considered to be particularly pertinent to Martin's difficulties. I felt that the anger he harbored toward his parents (especially because of their separation) was being displaced onto peers and his teacher. My attempt in this interchange was to help him get in touch with his angry feelings and to decrease his guilt over them so that he could express them more appropriately. He was listening intently to what I was saying, but it was clear that my ideas were somewhat alien to him. However, my experience has been that over a period of time such communications help a child become less repressed regarding his angry feelings.

The interchange in which I described some incredulity regarding Martin's never having had hateful thoughts toward his mother contains a term that I have found helpful in communicating with children. Specifically, the term "your whole life" is one that facilitates communicating with children at their own level. The expression of incredulity also served to help Martin become free in expressing any hateful feelings that he might have been aware of but was embarrassed to express.

Although the value of the mother's being present in the room has been emphasized throughout this book, here is an example of her presence serving somewhat as a contaminant. When I was requesting that Martin try to provide the answer to my question about the worst thought that he had ever had about his mother in his *whole* life, she provided a specific answer, namely, that he might have thought that she was stupid. I quickly went back to my question in order to pursue what I thought would be a more meaningful discussion. In spite of such occasional contaminations my experience has been that the advantages of having the mother in the room far outweigh its disadvantages.

The game then continued:

Therapist: Okay, my card says, "You're sitting on the beach and a bottle with a piece of paper washes up on shore. You take the paper out of the bottle. What does it say?"

It says here in this bottle, "I have run away from home because my mother thinks it's terrible for a child to be angry at her ever and I have mean parents. They don't know that it's perfectly all right for a child to get angry at a parent once in a while and they think it's terrible so I've run away. Please help me."

Patient: You get a chip.

T: I get a chip for that?

P: Yep.

T: What do you think happened to that kid?

P: Well, like someone might help him.

T: And what might they do?

P: Bring him back.

T: And say what?

P: And tell their parents not to be mean and talk to them and maybe get a psychiatrist like you.

T: Yeah, and what would the psychiatrist like me say to the parents?

P: Well, talk to them about being mean and something else.

T: And what would he say?

P: Oh, I can't tell you everything he'd say!

T: Right, but just what would be one—suppose you were the psychiatrist and let's say I was the guy who was bringing the kid and I would say and have the parents . . . first I would have that boy there . . . we got him back from that desert island and we got the parents and we say, "Sir, could you please say something to these parents to help their situation? What would you say to them?

P: Well, "Why are you always mean? You shouldn't always be mean."

T: Let's say I'm the father and . . .

P (interrupts): "You shouldn't always be mean."

T: What's mean? What have I done that's mean, Mr. Psychiatrist?

P: Well, I found . . . the man found this piece of paper . . .

T: Yeah.

P: . . . in the bottle. Read it.

T: Okay, and I'll read it. And it says here that my son is saying that I'm mean and wrong because I think that a child shouldn't be angry at his parents. What do you say about that?

P: Well, I think you should . . . (mumbles) . . .

T: You think what?

P: I think you should get a chip for that.

T: But we're playing this game where you are the psychiatrist and I'm the father and I'm saying, "I don't think it's right for a boy to be angry at his father." And what are you saying, Mr. Psychiatrist?

P: It's right for a boy to be angry at their parents once in a while.

T: You're saying that.

P: But not all the time, just once in a while.

T: Uh huh. All right. And suppose the father is doing something.

P: Doing what?

T: Let's suppose the father is doing something to make the child angry. Is it all right for him to be angry?

P: For him?

T: For the child to be angry?

P: Yes.

T: Uh huh. What should the child do when the father does something that makes him angry?

P: Just say that he's angry and say not to do it.

T: Hh hmm. Tell the father what he's angry about. Right. Okay. Let's go on.

At the beginning of this interchange I was not sure that I was getting through to Martin. However, as is clear, by the end he revealed that he understood what I was trying to say regarding anger and its expression.

Although I utilize traditional techniques in working with children of divorce, I have also found the methods described in this chapter to be particularly helpful in engaging such children. I have also found these methods useful in the treatment of children with many other kinds of psychiatric difficulties. The reader who is interested in more thorough discussions of these methods may wish to refer to my full-length texts (1971b, 1975).

Chapter 4

DENIAL

Denial is one of the most primitive of the defense mechanisms. What easier way is there to avoid suffering the untoward psychological reactions of a trauma than to deny its existence? The individual protects himself from such pain by blotting from conscious awareness the fact that the trauma exists. Generally, unconscious forces operate to bring about this state of psychological blindness. The family pattern, however, plays a significant role in determining whether the child of divorce will utilize this mechanism.

Parental Contributions to the Development of the Denial Mechanism in the Child

There are certain parental personality characteristics, modes of interaction, and ways of dealing with the child that may contribute to his utilizing the denial mechanism as a way of handling the separation trauma. (Although separation, on occasion, may not be a trauma in that it brings about a cessation of years of bickering, in most cases it is traumatic.) There are parents who believe that fighting in front of their children will necessarily be detrimental to them. I agree that continual fighting is certainly deleterious; occasional fighting, however, can have salutary effects on the child. It helps him appreciate that no one is perfect and that in every marriage there are times of dissension and friction. Such exposure makes it less likely that he will have unrealistic criteria for what constitutes a reasonably stable marriage and, therefore, lessens the likelihood that he will become disillusioned in a real relationship and possibly even divorce because of such disappointment. Parents who never fight in front of their children provide them with a continuous lesson in inappropriate suppression and repression of angry feelings. Although a fight may represent a failure in the parents' ability to settle their differences in a more civilized manner and to have dealt with the conflict at earlier stages of irritation, it should inevitably occur, at times, in the healthy marriage, because no one can handle all conflicts in an ideal and judicious way. This is the normal and expected environment in the relatively intact home. The parents who strictly enforce the rule of never fighting in front of their children may contribute to their becoming inhibited in expressing anger. Accordingly, they may contribute to the child's repressing his angry reactions to the divorce (reactions that are inevitable) and contribute thereby to his utilizing the denial mechanism. In this case, of the various cognitive and emotional reactions that are being denied, the angry reaction is the one repressed.

There are parents who are generally silent and noncommunicative people. The general atmosphere in the home is a quiet one and people may only communicate about matters that are essential to the proper functioning of the household. Such parents may be especially inhibited in expressing feelings. Accordingly, they will serve as models for such suppression and repression in their children. When a separation takes place they are not likely to communicate very much regarding details of what is going on, especially their emotional reactions. In such an atmosphere it is hard to imagine a child's not developing denial himself.

There are parents who will justify their not providing the children information about the separation with excuses such as: "The children are too young to understand," and "They're too young to have it affect them." Accordingly, the father may leave the home with absolutely nothing said to the children. If the youngsters do ask questions they are not answered, again with the rationalization that they are too young to understand. Such parents, of course, usually have other reasons for not communicating the separation to the children—for example, guilt and shame.

The denial mechanism is an extremely powerful one. The human being's ability to blind himself to the obvious is at times truly amazing. There are people who will take a few days to accept the fact that a loved one has indeed died. Many soldiers will enter combat with the delusion that others around them may be killed but that they somehow are immune. Similarly, there are parents who will actually separate and, amazingly, act then as if the separation had not taken place. Although living in separate domiciles, they will act as if nothing new has happened. Each goes about his or her business as if life will continue just as before. They will admit to the fact that they are living separately but deny that there are any other effects of the separation, either on themselves or the children. The children of such parents are likely to follow the parental pattern and deny that they have any untoward reactions. They, too, may continue living as if there were no changes.

Parents who actively encourage the child to suppress his emotional reactions to the divorce also contribute to the development of the denial mechanism. Comments such as "Be brave" and "Boys don't cry" foster suppression of emotions and contribute thereby to the development of the denial adaptation. When the child complies with such parental advice he is considered to have "taken it well." He is praised for his "maturity" and forbearance. Reacting stoically to a traumatic experience is a highly sanctioned quality in our culture. The woman who doesn't cry when her husband dies is said to have "taken it well." At the time of President Kennedy's assassination hardly a television announcer did not compliment the President's wife Jacqueline on her forbearance, and the people in high places serve as a model for the rest.

There are parents who, following the separation, will act as if the party who is no longer living in the home has never existed. When the absent parent has totally abandoned the family he still exists in memory and to deny this deprives the children of the opportunity to express their reactions and work them out. In addition, it contributes to the development of the denial mechanism. However, in the usual situation where the absent parent is very much involved, the utilization of this reaction by the remaining parent requires an even greater degree of denial of reality; yet it may be utilized and the children encouraged to react similarly. The remaining parent may strictly avoid any mention of the absent parent and act not only as if he doesn't now exist but also as if he had *never* existed. And the children, in order to remain in the good graces of the parent with whom they live, may react similarly.

Common Manifestations of the Denial Mechanism in the Child

There are children, however, who will exhibit denial without significant parental sanction, encouragement, or active contribution. Because it is such a primitive mechanism and so easily utilized it is not surprising that children may resort to it with facility. There are children who will react to the announcement of the separation with such calm that the departing parent may question his child's involvement and affection. Generally, such a reaction is not related to the absence of a feeling of loss. Rather, it may be a manifestation of the child's failure to appreciate time lapses, to his concretism ("If I don't see it happening, then it's not happening"), or his denial. Even after a parent has left and the remaining parent repeatedly invites the child to express his reactions, there may be none. Even though the child may be told that the departed parent is no longer going to be living in the home, the child may repeatedly ask when he or she is going to return. Each time, he questions as if he had never before been told the answer.

There are children who are told specifically the facts of the separation and who yet will speak and fantasize about the absent parent's returning. They will make such statements as: "Daddy's working late," "Daddy's on a business trip," "Daddy comes home very late, after I fall asleep. He leaves very early in the morning, before I wake up," "Mommy's coming home very soon," and "Mommy's living at grandma's house. Grandma told me."

The child may involve himself in play and fantasy that serves the function of restoring the absent parent. Trunnell (1968) describes the child fantasizing that he is involved in various activities with his father, e.g., driving in the car or sailing. Or, the child may play the role of the absent father in such games as "house." Although this is to a certain degree normal, the child of divorce may become obsessed with such a role. Of course, through identification with the absent father he hopes to regain him. On occasion, I have seen this mechanism operate following the death of a parent. A patient (and even adults exhibit this) may suddenly (it seems to appear overnight) take on many of the qualities of the absent parent: vocal intonations, gestures, personality characteristics, and even opinions. At times the transformation is almost uncanny.

The child may deny any concerns over the separation but may become very concerned over the welfare of another person or pet. Clearly, the child is displacing his worries over the well-being of the departed parent onto a substitute. Therefore, in addition to the mechanism of denial the child is utilizing displacement as well. Repression of hostility is also generally operative here. The child is angry at the parent who has left the home, is too guilty to express it overtly, and so transforms the wish that something will happen to the departed parent into fear that it will. If he is too guilty to express even that, the fear will be displaced onto a surrogate such as the remaining parent or a pet. The result is that the child, while obsessively concerned with the welfare of his hamster, appears to be oblivious to the fact that a parent has just left the household forever. This concomitant of the denial mechanism is often seen in patients suffering fatal diseases. When visited in the hospital they talk little about themselves but become excessively concerned over the most minor illnesses of their friends and relatives.

Sometimes the child's denial may relate to fear of and guilt over expressing anger. What appears to be denial is more a manifestation of inhibition in expressing the inevitable angry feelings that the separation has engendered in him. Often, such inhibitions are the result of parental attitudes toward the child's expressing hostile feelings.

At times, a child will fantasize that he is actually playing with the departed parent. This usually occurs at the age of from two to four years, the time when children most commonly develop imaginary friends. The child will talk to the invisible parent as if he or she were still there and will involve himself in prolonged games with the fantasized parent. In addition, he may exhibit many of the other behavioral patterns of involvement with the fantasized friend. Accordingly, he may express resentment when someone sits down in the chair previously occupied by the departed parent and loudly exclaim to someone who is seated in that chair: "Get out of that chair. You're sitting on my mother." When leaving home the child may cry out to the mother: "We forgot to take Daddy. He's still inside." The child may then return to the home and bring along the fantasized father. Crumley and Blumenthal (1973) found this to be a common reaction in the children of military fathers who are required to separate from their families for significant periods of time.

Idealization of the absent father, with an attendant denial of any deficiencies, is a common reaction. Westman (1970) describes such idealization and the development of idealistic fantasies about him. Freud and Burlingham (1944) observed a similar phenomenon among English children separated from their fathers during World War II.

Related to such idealization is the denial that an absent parent is disinterested. In the extreme, a child may still insist that the departed parent still loves him even though the latter has not been seen or heard from in many years. The notion is obviously related to the child's wish to avoid the painful realization that the absent parent no longer loves him. Sometimes, such denial will be fostered by the remaining parent, who may tell the child such things as: "Your father still loves you; he just can't show it." Although such a comment may be well-meaning on the part of the parent, it is misguided. The parent in such a situation is obviously trying to protect the child from the traumatic effects associated with the realization that a parent has abandoned and does not love him. Such a parent does better to confront the child with the painful reality and impress upon him that the deficiency lies in the abandoning parent, rather than in the child. Such a parent should help the child appreciate that there is something seriously wrong with a parent who cannot love his own child. In addition, he should also encourage the child to involve himself with others, both peers and adults, who will demonstrate that the child is still lovable. He must be helped to realize that although his own natural parent may not love him, it does not follow that no one else in the whole world could.

Therapeutic Approaches to Pathological Denial

The therapist must appreciate that the denial mechanism, although most often maladaptive, is created to produce a certain degree of psychological equilibrium. We all must utilize a certain amount of denial if we are to remain sane. Were we to clearly see every danger and emotionally react to all traumas, both present and potential, it is unlikely that we could preserve our sanity. All of us must build a psychological cement wall around ourselves in order to gain protection from the myriad painful stimuli that bombard us.

There are times when it is a disservice to a patient to attempt actively to remove the denial mechanism. The most obvious example of this is the dying patient. The patient with a fatal disease should not be told that her real concerns have nothing to do with her friends and relatives but are merely displacements of her concerns about herself. I am not suggesting that one routinely support denial mechanisms in a dying patient; rather, I am suggesting that they be respected. Some patients may wish to discuss their real feelings; others may not. (The therapist must proceed very cautiously and judiciously when dealing with such a problem.) Although the attempts to remove the denial mechanism in a dying patient may be inhumane, it is generally not cruel to attempt to do so in a child of divorce. The repercussions from such removal are not generally so detrimental.

Most often, the utilization of the denial mechanism by the child of divorce is maladaptive. Although he may be protecting himself from some psychological pain, the use of the mechanism most often is ill advised. Its maintenance interferes with healthier adaptations to the separation. Direct discussion of the child's utilization of this mechanism is generally anxiety provoking. The parents themselves may have tried to approach the problem head on, and failed. I have sometimes found useful the child's reading a children's story I have written, *Oliver and the Ostrich* (1972a), which deals in allegorical fashion with the denial mechanism. As all child therapists well appreciate, children will discuss their difficulties much more readily when talking about third parties, animals, and other symbols of themselves. Each situation must be approached in accordance with the particular factors that are contributing to the denial mechanism. If parental influences are contributing significantly, then the parents should be worked with. Trying to help a child reduce his use of the mechanism while the parents are actively fostering it is a most difficult, if not futile, endeavor.

My general approach to the underlying problems is to surmise what they are through history-taking, conversations with both the parents and the child on related matters, and analysis of dreams and stories. I then direct my therapeutic communications (either directly or allegorically, depending upon the child's tolerance) to the underlying issues. By providing reassurance and a resolution to these issues, the therapist may obviate the child's needs to utilize the denial mechanism. For example, a child may tell a story in which a dog's father runs away and the dog is left starving and can only get food by hunting for it in garbage cans. I will respond with a story in which the same dog fears that that will be his fate, and he even spends restless nights dreaming of himself searching for food in garbage cans. However, he is reassured by his older brother dog that they still have their mother, who then proves herself an adequate provider. In this way, I affirm that the absence of his father does not mean that the child is totally abandoned; he still has his mother. I do not deal directly with the denial mechanism but rather with the underlying factors that have contributed to its formation and perpetuation. Hopefully, when such a child is reassured that his mother will still take care of him, *and she proves to do so*, he will more readily accept the separation.

The verbatim clinical examples in this book, though demonstrating primarily my approaches to the underlying problems, will demonstrate as well my approach to the denying child. By demonstrating my treatment of the various problems that can underlie the denial mechanism, I will be providing the reader with methods for reducing the child's need for this adaptation. One must approach it circuitously and from below, so to speak, because like most symptoms it does not respond to a head-on approach.

Chapter 5

GRIEF AND DEPRESSION

In Freud's classic paper "Mourning and Melancholia" (1917) he differentiated between grief and depression. Both he saw as reactions to the loss of a loved person or other significant entity such as liberty, an ideal, etc. He referred to these treasured possessions as the love object. In grief, the individual is gradually able to give up the lost object and accommodates to the deprivation. The frustrations and anger the person feels over the loss is gradually dissipated as the individual acquires substitutive gratifications. In depression, the individual introjects the lost object and turns the rage he feels toward the object onto its internalized image. The rage is not only a reaction to the loss or "abandonment" but is a reflection, as well, of the ambivalence that exists toward it. The depressive's self-flagellation, then, is understood as hostility felt toward the loss object but directed against oneself. Although subsequent investigators have added to this basic formulation, most agree that there is a basic difference between the two states and that Freud's differentiating criteria have merit.

Grief

Although there are definite differences between the reactions a child may experience following a divorce and those he may suffer after the death of a parent, there are certain similarities as well. One such similarity is the occurrence of a grief reaction. A discussion of the grief reaction following the death of a loved one can be helpful in understanding the grief that a child may feel at the time of separation. Generally, after the death of a loved one the mourners become preoccupied with thoughts of the departed person. This preoccupation provides for a piecemeal desensitization to the trauma. Each time one thinks about the dead person the pain associated with his or her loss becomes a little more bearable. The phenomenon is similar to the kind of reaction soldiers may suffer in response to extremely traumatic combat conditions. In "shell shock" or the "combat neurosis" the individual relives in fantasy and dreams the battlefield trauma and may even hallucinate the shells falling around him. Although each repetition may be associated with terrible states of terror, there is a gradual diminution of the intensity and frequency of the panic states. Such repetition appears to be part of the natural process of accommodating to a trauma. Similarly, following a death the mourners may not only talk at length about the loved one, but may utilize various possessions of the departed person as a focus for such discussions. Objects that may have previously been of little significance now become treasured memorabilia. They not only provide a symbolic link with the departed person, but can serve as a focus for desensitizing preoccupations and discussions.

Although the child of divorce does not actually lose a parent, he may never again live with the departed parent and is likely to react grievously to the separation. In fact, considering the healthy purposes of the grief reaction, I would consider it pathological if a child who is old enough to appreciate what is occurring did not react with grief. However, in those rare situations where the child actually welcomes the separation because it promises a cessation of the misery he has been suffering, then the failure to have a grief reaction would of course not be pathological. Parents who inhibit the child in expressing his feelings by such comments as "Be brave" and "Big boys and girls don't cry" will generally squelch the child's natural expression of grief. Parents who will not cry and express other emotions of remorse and regret in front of the child—with the misguided belief that it is best to protect the child from such displays—serve as poor models for their child's expressing his grief. Parents who show little tolerance for the child's repetitious questioning may be depriving him of the reiterative discussion and preoccupation that is crucial if the grief reaction is to provide desensitization and catharsis. And, of course, parents who provide little or no information about separation further impede the child's profiting from a grievous response. The failure on the parents' part to appreciate and encourage grieving at this crucial time may cause the child to suppress and repress his reactions to the separation and this may contribute to his developing some of the untoward reactions described in this book.

Although the child of divorce may not need mementos of the departed parent (he still has the real person available), he should have the opportunity for frequent contact with the person who has left the home, either personally or via telephone. The parent should recognize as well that withdrawal into fantasy during this period need not represent an impending deterioration into psychosis; rather, it can serve as part of the grieving process and enable the child to work through his reactions to the separation. Play fantasy may serve similar purposes, either within or outside of the therapist's office.

Many observers, both lay and professional, are often struck by the lack of grief that some children appear to exhibit following the death of a parent. At funerals such children may not only appear unaffected by what has happened, but may exhibit a disturbing degree of normal play and rambunctiousness. Wolfenstein (1966) holds that children below the adolescent period are generally not capable of true mourning. Instead of gradually decathecting the lost object, there is an intensified cathexis with overt or covert denial of the irrevocability of the loss. The child is also likely to transfer the freed libido to an available substitute. Furman (1964) and Gauthier (1965), however, do describe mourning reactions in latency aged children. Deutsch (1937) considers the child's tendency to deny to be a common impediment to his developing a salutary grief reaction. Scharl (1961) and Shambaugh (1961) both consider the young child's tendency to regress in the face of painful affects to interfere with the development of a mourning reaction. On the basis of my own admittedly limited observations, I believe that there are some children who will exhibit the kind of mourning reactions we observe in adults; yet there are others who will use denial, regression, and other mechanisms to handle their reactions.

With divorce, an easily identifiable mourning reaction may, in my opinion, be even less frequent. First, I believe this is partly due to the fact that there is less of a loss. A parent's living elsewhere (even at a great distance) is a very different thing from a parent's being dead. Secondly, death is a sudden event —no matter how long anticipated. Separation, on the other hand, is the next step in a series of events that have slowly led up to it. It is rarely as shocking as death, therefore more easily accommodated to, and so less mourning is required to deal with it. When one adds to these factors the child's tendency to deny and regress, as well as parental mourning-impeding influences, it is not surprising that so few children mourn at the time of the separation. In spite of its infrequency, it does occur and I believe that it is preferable that it should. It behooves the therapist to encourage its development, because failure to do so may result in the child's developing pathological responses to the separation.

Depression

A state of depression in the child is generally characterized by: loss of appetite; diminished interest in and concentration on studies; general apathy; loss of enjoyment from play and peer relationships; helplessness; hopelessness; irrritability; self-deprecation; withdrawal; and, on occasion, suicidal preoccupation. The full-blown picture, of course, does not have to exist to justify the label—there are varying intensities to the syndrome. Because of their natural levity and *joie de vivre* (as well as the facility with which they can utilize primitive denial mechanisms) children tend not to become as readily depressed as adults in response to traumatic events. However, parental separation is a depressing event and children do become depressed in response.

In McDermott's studies (1968, 1970) of 116 children of divorced parents, about one-third were considered depressed. In some children the depression manifested itself overtly with self-destructive fantasies and behavior. In others it was covert and revealed itself through the child's accident-prone behavior and lack of concern for his safety. Some children alternated depressive states with hostile acting out—suggesting that when anger was internalized, depression occurred and that when it was acted out, the depression lifted. Other common manifestations of depression in McDermott's group included feelings of impotence and vulnerability, loss of the capacity to use play to work out reactions to the divorce, easily giving up and not trying, extreme boredom, failure to complete projects, regression, and inability to gain enjoyment. On the other hand, Morrison (1974) studied 127 children of divorce and could not find a significant difference between his group and a control group of children from intact homes with regard to symptoms of depression. I believe that children of divorce do become depressed and that the depression is most likely to occur during the first few weeks after the separation. The differences between McDermott and Morrison's findings may result from their having seen children after varying lengths of exposure to the parental separation.

In part, the depression of such children is reactive. The loss of a parent from the home *is* something to be depressed about. Accordingly, it is one of the expected reactions to the separation. If few or none of the other factors to be mentioned do not contribute to or entrench the depression, it should lift within a few weeks. The healthy human being is quite resilient—and children are especially so. If the depression persists, it is likely that other factors are contributing to its perpetuation.

If the child has not exhibited a healthy mourning experience, the pent-up feelings may contribute to a general feeling of discontent. Emotional cathar-sis is followed by feelings of psychological cleansing and even elation; where-as suppressed and repressed feelings continually press for release. The intra-psychic conflict so produced is emotionally draining and anxiety-provoking. Such states rob one of the capacity for enjoyment and contribute to depres-sion. In such situations the therapist does well to attempt to help the child have a mourning experience—even though belated. Sanctioning crying and demonstrating the value of the release of feelings can be helpful. Attempts should be made to alter parental attitudes (see above) that may have contrib-uted to the child's mourning inhibition.

Another factor that may contribute to a child's being depressed is parental depression, especially in the parent with whom the child lives. If the custodial parent welcomes the separation and sees it as an opportunity for a better life, it is likely that the child will take a more positive attitude toward it as well. If, however, the custodial parent becomes distraught and depressed and views it as the end of his or her life, then the child is likely to react similarly. In such cases the therapeutic work should be focused on the parent. Hopefully, an improvement in his or her attitude will contribute to a lessening of the child's depressive reaction.

Most agree with Freud that the loss of a love object is one of the most im-portant etiological factors in depressive reactions. And the child of divorce has certainly sustained such a loss. The healthy child is usually able to toler-ate such a loss because he generally has another parent who can help to make the deprivation more tolerable. In addition, he has the capacity to find sub-stitute gratifications with other adults. Accordingly, the depressions of such children are usually short-lived. If, however, the child has been overdepen-dent on the departed parent, the loss is felt much more acutely and the de-pression may become more severe. The feelings of helplessness may become profound as the child comes to fear that he cannot survive. Generally, such a child has been overprotected and made to feel that his very existence depends on his remaining close to such a parent. The therapeutic work must be oriented toward the child's coming to understand and experience that he has the wherewithal to function without the absent parent and that survival does not depend upon his or her continuous presence. In addition, if one has the opportunity, one can try to help the overprotective parent reduce his or her contribution to the child's problem.

Another factor that may contribute to a child's depression is his interpreting the parent's leaving as a rejection and abandonment of him, rather than of the remaining parent. He not only considers the parent's leaving as a statement that he is not loved, but in addition, that he is not lovable. He essentially follows this sequence of reasoning: "If he loved me, he would stay. His leaving means that he doesn't love me. If he doesn't love me, I am unlovable." The resultant feelings of self-loathing contribute to the child's depressive reaction. In working with such children I try to help them appreciate that in any triangle of three people, A, B, and C, A and B can dislike one another, but each can love C. I try to help the child see that his father still loves him, even though he no longer loves his mother; and that his mother still loves him, even though she no longer loves his father. In situations where there is indeed some deficiency in the absent parent's affection, I try to help the child appreciate that this does not mean that he is unlovable. I try to help him understand that the deficiency lies more in the parent than in him—that the parent who has little, if any, love for his own child is a defective person. If I can get the child to successfully gain affection from surrogates, this message is more likely to be incorporated as the child has living experiences that verify it.

Redirecting against himself the rage felt toward one or both parents is another element common to the child's depression. This mechanism occurs in children who are excessively fearful of expressing their anger. Generally, such children grow up in homes in which they have been made to feel guilty over their angry feelings—especially when felt toward parents and other loved ones. When the parents of a child with such "programming" separate, he finds himself in a particularly difficult situation. He can find little outlet for the anger that the separation inevitably produces, and he may direct it inward. Even without such a background the child of divorce is in a particularly difficult situation with regard to the expression of his anger. He may fear expressing anger toward the departed parent, lest he see even less of him; and he may fear directing it toward the custodial parent, lest he or she too will abandon him. In spite of this added danger of anger expression, most children do let it out. The child who is extremely guilty over hostile expression may find that there is only one safe target: himself. One best understands such a child's self-recrimination as hostility actually felt toward one of the parents but directed against the self. The fantasied introjection of the lost love object is facilitated by his or her departure. Identification with a lost loved one is one way of attempting to ease the pain of the loss. By utilizing a very primitive thinking process, the individual can delude himself into believing that there has been no loss at all—the departed person now resides safely within the self where he or she can be prevented from fleeing again. In addition, the self-derogation is a manifestation of the guilt the child feels over his hostility. The therapeutic approach to this aspect of a child's depression, is essentially that of treating anger inhibition problems. In Chapter 9 I will discuss in greater detail my approaches to such children. The therapeutic principles described there are applicable to the anger inhibitions of depressed children.

One cannot discuss depression without mentioning suicide. Suicide is rare in children below the age of 12. In addition, it is often difficult to differentiate in this young age group *bona fide* suicides from deaths resulting from specious attempts in which the child's poor judgment resulted in his inadvertently killing himself. A significant percentage of *bona fide* suicide attempts by children in this age group occur among those from broken homes. The despair and loneliness associated with feelings of being unloved and unwanted may be too much for the child to bear and he may take his life. A revenge element is often present. The child has the fantasy that the parents, whom the child sees as rejecting him, will be painfully guilty over the way they have maltreated him. He may fantasize being buried while the contrite parents cry out remorsefully how bad they feel about their neglect of the child and how they wish that they could once again have the chance to show their affection. But it is too late; they must live with their guilt. Sometimes there is a desire for death and rebirth into a happier life with truly loving parents. The child who considers the parental separation to have been his fault, that he has done bad things that brought about the separation, may try to kill off the bad parts of himself via the suicide attempt. Some feel so insecure and inadequate that they do not feel that they can survive without the loving care of both parents.

However, many suicide attempts in this age group (as is true in other age groups as well) are specious and manipulative. Mahler and Rabinovitch (1956) describe a five-year-old girl who, in a suicide attempt, swallowed a brooch that her father had given her. The attempt took place soon after her father informed her that he was going to leave the family. The swallowing of the brooch was not only a manipulative attempt to make the father guilty (and thereby return) but it also served to provide the child with a symbolic incorporation of her father, thereby magically restoring him to her own possession.

In closing I wish to emphasize that the treatment of such children is vital because depressed children are likely to become depressed adults and suicidal children (if they survive) are likely to become suicidal adults. And the broken home during childhood appears to be a most important contributing factor to the development of adult depression and suicide. Although some of the studies supporting this notion do not differentiate between parental death and separation, others such as that of Dorpat et al. (1965) make the distinction. They found that 50% of 114 patients who completed suicide and 64% of 121 patients who attempted unsuccessfully to commit suicide came from broken homes. In the completed suicide group the most common cause for the broken home was parental death, whereas in the attempted suicide group the most common cause was parental divorce.

Chapter 6

ABANDONMENT FEARS, ABANDONMENT, AND FLIGHT FROM THE HOME

Abandonment Fears

The child of divorce will often consider the departing parent to be abandoning him. Although continually reassured that this is not the case—that he is still loved very much—he tends to maintain this view. His world becomes a shaky place indeed. If one parent can leave the home, what is to prevent the remaining parent from doing so as well? The child living in an intact, relatively stable home is not concerned to a significant degree with a breakup of the home. For the child of divorce such an event is part of his scheme of things. The separation produces a general feeling of instability in all human relationships. It is almost as if no one can be trusted. If the custodial parent was the one who was instrumental in causing the departed parent to leave, what is to prevent his being similarly ejected from the household? The resulting insecurity and instability can indeed be frightening.

The parents' preoccupation with their conflicts prior to the separation and with the various legal and other details attendant on the separation may give them little time for or emotional investment in their children. Although the parents may still be in the house, the children already feel abandoned. And when a parent then leaves the home, further feelings of rejection are engendered. In addition, the new obligations that the custodial parent may then have to assume may result in the child's having even less time with the remaining parent than he had before.

The child may react with panic states in which there is sweating, palpitations, trembling, agitation, and an assortment of fears such as his getting sick with no one to care for him, and even of dying. Although the abandonment fear may contribute to such states, other factors are often operative. The child may harbor intense hostility toward one or both of the parents and his guilt over such hostility may result in his repressing his anger. When his rage presses for release, anxiety may result which compounds the fears he is already experiencing. Such a child not only needs the reassurances and the living experience that his fears of abandonment are unwarranted, but he has to be helped to feel less guilty over his hostility. In Chapter 9 I will discuss in detail the approaches I utilize to lessen such guilt.

A mother, for example, may have initiated the divorce proceedings because of certain activities of the father that she finds objectionable. From the child's vantage point the father has been forced to leave the house because he has been "bad." What is to stop her then from similarly forcing him to leave the house when he is bad (Sugar, 1970)? The child may come to appreciate that no matter how much love his mother may have for him, he has now become an added burden for her. Were she not to have had him her life would indeed have been much easier. The pressures of time, work, and money she must now suffer on his behalf are often formidable. Her awareness that having a child lessens her chances for remarriage must, at times, be painful. Thoughts about how much easier her life would be without the child are inevitable. These may even be verbalized by the mother; but even if not, the child senses them and reacts with fears that his mother may abandon him in order to lessen her burden (G. Gardner, 1956). Commonly, such a mother displaces the resentment she feels over her situation onto the child, and this further intensifies his fears of rejection and abandonment.

Following the separation, the child may wander around the house looking for the departed parent even though he has been repeatedly told that he or she will no longer be living in the home. He may search the closets, under the bed, or pathetically stand at the door awaiting his or her return. The father of a patient of mine moved to a foreign country and although he frequently wrote letters promising to visit his son, he rarely did. In an early session the child drew a picture of a boy on a beach chasing a butterfly. Although the child continued to try, he was never able to catch the butterfly—and there the story ended. One could not ask for a clearer and more poignant statement of a child's sense of abandonment and his futile attempts at reunion with a departed parent. In Chapter 5 I have mentioned the child described by Mahler and Rabinovitch (1956) who tried to incorporate symbolically the departed father by swallowing a gift brooch he had given her.

A child may cling excessively to the custodial parent. Separation anxieties may develop, and the child may refuse to visit friends or go to school. If such separation anxieties reach the point of panic, where for example a "school phobia" develops, then other factors are usually operative. Overprotective attitudes on the parent's part may be contributing (likely at the time of separation in order to assuage parental guilt) or the child's unconscious hostility toward the parent may be operative. By clinging to the parent he reassures himself that his hostile wishes have not been realized.

Some children, in order to win the affection of each of their parents, will say to each that which he knows will ingratiate him. Accordingly, when with the father he will side with him against the mother, refrain from saying positive things about her, and confine himself to those negatives that he knows his father wishes to hear. And he will involve himself similarly with his mother. In this way the child attempts to ensure that he is in the good graces of both parents and he may thereby avoid further rejection and abandonment. In therapy, such a child must be helped to see that his parents will ultimately come to realize that they have been "buttered up" and when this happens he may suffer even more rejection than he might have otherwise. In addition, he should be helped to see that he cannot feel good about himself lying in this way, and that the feelings of unworthiness so induced are adding unnecessarily to his difficulties. In short, he must be helped to appreciate that no one likes a liar: neither the people he lies to nor the liar himself.

Some children will try to lessen their feelings of abandonment by provoking punishment from one or both parents. They are willing to suffer the pain that such punishment entails for the reassurance that the parent is still very much there. What better way is there to confirm a parent's existence than to be struck or maltreated by him? Other factors, of course, may be operating in such behavior. The provocative behavior may serve as an outlet for the hostility the child feels over the separation. He may feel guilty over his anger and the punishment he elicits may help assuage such guilt. He may welcome the punishment as a way of strengthening his own superego controls. And such strengthening may be more necessary when a parent is absent.

When a mother, for example, moves back with her own parents following the separation the children are less likely to suffer with abandonment fears. Although they no longer live with their father, their two doting grandparents may make them feel that the trade wasn't really so bad. However, the situation usually isn't so simple. The grandparents often resent their new obligations. It is easy being doting grandparents when one visits the home of one's grandchildren. It is another story entirely having the children in one's home. Mother may be out working and the responsibilities of child care may be something the grandparents were glad to have behind them. Accordingly, the grandparents' resentment over their new obligations may cause the children to suffer further feelings of rejection and fears of abandonment. In addition, the mother who returns to the home of her parents may be a very dependent person. (I believe that a more mature mother would not choose this alternative, the obvious financial and other benefits of the arrangement notwithstanding.) Moving back with her parents only entrenches her dependency. Her children's observing her childish and immature relationship with her parents cannot but weaken their respect for and feelings of security with their mother. As a result the situation may produce even greater feelings of insecurity in the children (Sugar, 1970).

Psychotherapeutic Approaches to Abandonment Fears

First, I wish to emphasize that many abandonment fears reduce with time —without therapy being indicated. As the child has the living experience that his fears were unwarranted, that he still has good relationships with both parents, that they are still there in spite of the separation, his abandonment worries will generally lessen.

Cognitive distortions contribute to many of the child's abandonment fears. And it is one of the purposes of therapy to help the child correct such distortions. He must be helped to see that father, for example, has indeed abandoned *mother*, but not *him*, and that although father no longer wishes to have contact with mother, he very much wishes to see his children. He must be helped to appreciate that he still has *two* parents, and that if something happens to the custodial parent he can still live with the noncustodial. In addition, the parents should discuss with the child exactly which friends and relatives would be available to take care of him in the event that both parents could not. (All children, in my opinion, should be told who will be caring for them if their own parents die or become so incapacitated that they cannot care for them. For the child of divorce such information is even more important to impart.) In addition, if the situation warrants it, the therapist should discuss boarding schools and foster homes. The child's gaining the feeling that no matter what happens, there will be someone to take care of him is crucial in the therapy of such fears. Also, I have found helpful in this regard the child's reading (alone, or with me, or with his parents) the chapter "The Fear of Being Left Alone" in my *The Boys and Girls Book about Divorce* (1970b, 1971a). The following clinical examples demonstrate other

approaches I have found useful in the treatment of children with abandonment fears.

Clinical Example
A girl whose fighting parents neglect her.

Alice, a seven-and-a-half-year-old girl, was living with her mother and
stepfather when she first came for therapy. Her parents had divorced when
she was three and her mother remarried about a year prior to my initial visit
with her. The relationship between her mother and stepfather was extremely
stormy—there was frequent fighting—and the stepfather had little interest in
Alice. In addition, there was practically no contact with her natural father.

During her second session Alice told this story, her first in treatment:

Patient: Once there was a little girl and her name was Cindy and she
went out to play one day and she fell into the brook. She saw this deep,
deep brook and she was scared and she was tipping over and she fell into
it. So her mother was watching out the window while she was making the
dinner and she ran out the door. And she saw that her little girl had fell
in the brook. And she was crying—her mother—and Cindy.

Therapist: The mother was crying too?

P: Yes.

T: Uh huh.

P: Then the mother called the father and they both fighted over it
because the father thought why would a mother be so dumb to let Cindy
go near a brook? So they were both fighting for a long time until one day
Cindy got out of the brook and she made her mother and father make
up. So they made up and then Cindy fell into a sand trap. And then they
started fighting again. But this time Cindy didn't come out of the sand
trap. So the mother and father kept on fighting and fighting except the
mother decided to make up. And they made up.

The next time the mother saw the little girl and the little girl said that
she saw a horse. And the horse was galloping along, jumping over the
brook, and the little girl jumped over the brook also except she didn't
fall in and she jumped right onto the horse while the horse was galloping. Then they all got together and they were a family happy, but never
fighting again. And they all lived happily ever after.

T: And the lesson?

P: And the lesson was that if you think you shouldn't do something
that you think is fun and you get into trouble, then don't do it. But if you
think that you won't get into trouble or have an accident or something,

you can do it. Go ahead and do it. And that's what Cindy did. She thought that she wouldn't get into any trouble or anything so she just went along and did it.

T: But she did get into trouble.

P: Right.

T: You mean by falling into the brook?

P: Yeah.

T: I'm not clear. You gave a very complicated lesson. The lesson is what then now?

P: That if you think that something is going to happen to you by doing something that you want to do don't go ahead and do it.

T: I see. If you think it's going to be dangerous or something like that. Is that it?

P: Right.

T: I see. Okay. Now I have a question I want to ask you about your story. Do I understand that when Cindy fell into the brook the mother and father were so busy fighting between themselves that they kind of ignored the fact that she was in the brook? Was that it?

P: Yes.

T: Was it dangerous down in the brook?

P: Yes, because it was a very very deep brook.

T: So how did she get out?

P: There were rocks on the side of the brook and she happened to have sneakers on and she just climbed up.

T: Oh, so she got out herself. And the same thing with the sand trap.

P: Right.

T: She got out of that herself too?

P: Right.

T: And then the horse came along. And then he got her out of the brook again.

P: Right.

T: I see. Okay. Thank you very much. Now it's time for me to tell my story.

This story reveals definite healthy adaptations on Alice's part. Recognizing that her mother and stepfather are so involved in their fighting that they cannot be trusted to protect her from danger, she relies on her own resources. Both in the brook and in the sand trap she manages to save herself when her parents do not effectively heed her cries for help. In spite of this self-sufficiency, the patient still longs for some powerful figure to provide her with assistance. This is reasonable, considering her age. I considered the horse to represent me. I come along and bear the complete burden of saving her from danger.

The story also reveals Alice's attempts to affect a reconciliation between her parents and a cessation of their fighting. However, it also reflects her awareness that these attempts are somewhat futile. Their reconciliations are short-lived and her parents quickly resume their fighting.

With this understanding of Alice's story, I related mine:

Therapist: Once upon a time there was a girl and her name was Cindy. And one day she fell into a brook and it was a very deep brook. And her mother and father, instead of trying to get her out of the brook, they just kept fighting. And this made her very sad. And she said, "Well, I guess that's the way it is. I guess my mother and father are so involved in their own fighting that they don't care that much about me. So I'll have to get myself out of the brook myself." So she got out of the brook and the she tried to get her parents to make up, but they wouldn't make up. They are still fighting and she realized that trying to get her parents to make up was not going to do very much good because they just continued to fight.

Well, the next time she was playing in a sand trap and she fell into the sand trap. And once again her mother and father, instead of trying to help her get out of the sand trap, they just continued to fight. And she got out of the sand trap herself, and she thought to herself, "Wouldn't it be nice if I had a big horse so if I ever fell into things like this, the horse would just carry me away and then I wouldn't have any trouble."

Well, she said to her mother and father, "Could you buy me a horse?" And they said, "Sorry. We can't keep a horse around here. We have no barn. We're not set up for a horse. Besides, horses are very expensive to buy and they're very expensive to keep up. You can't have a horse."

Well, this made her kind of sad because she wanted a horse and she figured if she had a horse then the horse would be able to save her whenever she got into trouble. Well, she was quite sad and the next time this happened she saw a friend of hers. She fell into a sand trap again and a friend was playing there. And she said, "Hey, would you help me out?"

And her friend said, "Sure. But you have to help too." So the two of them together got her out of the sand trap. She didn't even bother calling her mother and father because she knew that they would always be fighting.

And she said, "You know, I'm very glad I met you."

And the girl said, "Why?"

She said, "Well, I need a friend. You see, my mother and father are fighting so much that they don't take care of me as well as I would like. But if I have a friend, then if I get into some trouble then my friend can help me."

The friend said, "Yes, I can help you, but you have to learn to help yourself too." And so the girl and the friend became very good friends and the girl realized that although she could count on her parents for certain things that there were other things she couldn't count on them for and that she would have to do these on her own. But it made her happy to know that she at least had a friend who could be helpful to her.

Patient: What was the lesson?

T: The lesson of that story is: that if your mother and father fight that much that they can't spend enough time or they don't want to spend enough time to help you when you're in danger you can do two things: You can learn to do these things on your own. And the other thing is you can get friends your own age who can be helpful to you as well. Those are the two lessons. Anything you want to say about that story?

P: No.

T: Did you like it?

P: Hh hmm.

T: What was the part you like the most?

P: The part when she found a friend and the friend said that you're going to have to learn to do these things on your own.

T: Hh hmm. Right. And you know that's true and also the girl learned to rely on friends as well, that parents aren't the only people in the world, that there were others who can be helpful to you as well.

P: Right.

T: Okay. Do you like playing this program?

P: Yeah.

T: Would you like to play it again sometime?

P: Hh hmm.

T: Let's say good-bye. Good-bye everybody.

P: Good-bye.

In my story I emphasized the healthy elements revealed in Alice's. I reinforced her salutary adaptation of relying on her own resources. In addition, my story introduces an alternative mode of adaptation, that is, reliance on peers. Although Alice could certainly not hope to get peers to fully compensate for the deficiencies of her parents, she certainly could look to them for some degree of substitute gratification. I specifically omitted the horse in my story because the question of Alice's remaining in treatment was very tenuous. Her natural father was unavailable to finance her treatment. Her stepfather was totally disinterested and unmotivated to spend money on her. And her mother's position did not allow her to finance the treatment either. To have introduced the horse as an active participant might have raised unrealistic hopes. This decision turned out to be a prudent one in that the parents did not follow through with my suggestion that further work with Alice was indicated. Further discussion revealed that it was not so much financial pressure but lack of motivation that was the main determinant in their discontinuing contact with me.

Clinical Example
A boy lost in the woods.

Kenneth, a ten-and-a-half-year-old boy whose parents had separated about six months prior to referral, told this story during his third week in treatment:

Patient: Once there was a boy named Bill. He went with his parents on a picnic and, um, his parents gave him permission to walk—go down—this is up in the mountains—this is all taking place.

Therapist: His parents gave him permission to what?

P: Go around and look in the woods.

T: Yeah.

P: So his brother and sister were down by the lake and since he loves forest creatures . . . (mumbles) . . .

T: Wait. His brother and sister did what now? Went down with him to the lake?

P: Yeah. And he was spying around and he saw some raccoon footprints.

T: Hh hmm.

P: And he being a very great lover of animals, um, followed them.

T: Yeah.

P: He kept on following them and following them, and following them until finally he saw that it was getting dark and it was getting cold. In the mountains it gets quite cold at night and he only had a thin jacket. And all of a sudden it was getting cold and it was getting really dark, and he couldn't follow the tracks back to the lake. And he started getting scared. He panicked and he went round and around in circles and circles for a few hours until he realized that he was going around in circles. Then he came back around and sat down and went to sleep. He could imagine his father and mother would go down to the sheriff's office and look for him. He would probably find his way back.

T: Yeah.

P: So he went to bed. And when he woke up he followed the tracks back and he walked back to the picnic grounds.

T: When he woke up he followed the tracks back. Yeah.

P: And he found the picnic grounds and he found his mother and father.

T: Hh hmm. I see. And that's the whole story?

P: Yeah.

> *T:* And the lesson of that story?
>
> *P:* There is none.
>
> *T:* Aw, come on. Usually there is a lesson to every story. What's the lesson of that story?
>
> *P:* Um, never follow a trail that isn't suited for the . . . (mumbles) . . .
>
> *T:* That isn't what?
>
> *P:* That isn't marked for the night.
>
> *T:* Okay. Now it's time for me to tell my story.

This story clearly reveals the patient's view that if abandoned by both parents, neither will seek him out. He will have to rely on his own resources in order to protect himself from abandonment and to reunite with his parents. In the story there is no mention made of the parents' attempting to find him and when he does return to the picnic grounds they do not appear to have left the picnic grounds in search of him. There are positive elements in this story in that it reveals that the patient is willing to assume responsibility for his own care in the face of the abandonment he suffers.

In actuality there was far less abandonment than this boy imagined. His mother, although working during the day in order to support the children, was quite devoted to them. The father, although suffering with significant psychological problems, also was deeply involved with the children.

This is the story I told in response:

> *Therapist:* Once upon a time there was a boy and he was out with his mother and his father on a picnic. And he decided that he was going to do some scouting around. Now he knew that his mother and father were not fully capable of finding him were he to get lost. Although they were good at many things, they were not good at finding him if he was lost, because they themselves had trouble finding their way about in the forest. But he knew that he could count on them somewhat, but he knew that he couldn't count on them completely. Anyway, he knew that at times he could count on them to help guide him through the forest, but he knew that at other times he would have trouble.
>
> So he decided to take a little can of paint and about every three or four hundred feet he would paint a little yellow spot on a tree so that he kind of made a trail for himself and would be able to find his way back. And in that circumstance he didn't get lost and if he got far away he had no trouble getting back. At other times he didn't have to take the can of paint because he knew that he could count on his parents when the forest was less dense and when there were standard markers and things like that.
>
> So the lesson of that story is: if you can't count on your parents to guide you at certain times you may have to guide yourself. At other times

when they can guide you then it's okay to count on them. The end. Anything you want to say?

Patient: Uh uh.

T: Okay. Any comments about that story?

P: Uh uh.

T: Okay.

The meaning of my story is clear. I essentially reiterate the patient's message and reinforce the healthy self-assertion exhibited in his story. Furthermore, I point out that his parents aren't totally abandoning him as his story would suggest. They can be counted upon to protect him at times; but at other times he will have to rely on his own resources.

Clinical Example
A sadistic murderer and a sleeping mother.

Tony, a ten-year-old boy with divorced parents, was brought to me because of poor school performance and hostile outbursts. His father lived in another part of the country and had little genuine interest in him, while his mother was more involved in dating than in spending time with her children. In the first session Tony told this story:

Patient: There was two boys, and one girl and a mother and a father, they went out in a car about five miles out of town, and they ran out of gas in the middle of the night. And they waited there for about an hour or two and then the man said, "I'm going to go back to town and get some more gas," and he walked back. He told the other people to go to sleep and after they went to sleep the sister woke up and she heard a scratching noise on the top of the roof and then she wondered what it was and she went back to sleep. And then she woke up and she heard it again. And a police was next to the car. And the police said, "Will you please get out and walk?" and she got out and walked. They said: "Whatever you do, don't look back." She kept on walking and walking walking.

Therapist: Where was the rest of the family?

P: They were still asleep. And when she got about one-half mile, she just had to look back and when she looked back she saw that the noise that was scratching on the roof was the biggest brother hanging on a tree with his bloody fingernails scratching on top of the roof.

T: So the big brother was hanging from a tree? Was he dead?

P: Yes.

T: Upside down? I see, and his bloody fingernails were scratching on the roof. Is that the whole story?

P: Uh-huh.

T: Who killed him?

P: That's supposed to be the mystery of the story.

T: Uh-huh.

P: But I could make somebody up.

T: Do that.

P: This monster and he had a big hook on his hand. There was nothing on that hand except the hook and he just takes the hook and he picked him up and he rammed it through his stomach and he took his shirt and he hanged it, and he took a rope and he hanged his feet from a tree. And then he jabbed a knife in his stomach and let him hang.

T: I see. Now what about the cop? Where does he fit into all of this?

P: All he was doing was just telling her to get out of the car.

T: Why did he tell her to walk away?

P: He was afraid that she would get hanged because of the man with the hook.

T: So he was trying to protect her. What about the other people in the car? What happened to them?

P: Well, they just were sleeping, I guess. The man with the hook never saw them.

T: What's the moral of that story—the lesson?

P: I guess it's to get gas before you leave town. That's the first time I've ever made up the moral of that story. I just made that one up.

T: Did you think of that story a lot?

P: Yes.

Although it was learned at the end that the story was not created *de novo* according to the rules of the television game, it is still rich in significant psychodynamic material. A repetitive fantasy is often a manifestation of powerful psychological forces, and I considered this one of equal value to the impromptu first story.

The monster represents Tony's father whom he saw as hostile because he had abandoned the patient. Before the divorce, the father had been cruel to him. The extent of the father's hostility is dramatically represented by the sadistic murder. Tony's mother is also seen as neglectful in protecting him from his father's rage—she sleeps during the murder. His sister, however, is singled out for protection from the father's wrath. She is not only spared but also ambivalently shielded from viewing the carnage. Running out of gas symbolizes the failure of both parents to provide those elements which are vital to the sustenance of the family.

With this understanding of Tony's story, I related the following:

Therapist: Once upon a time there was a family. This family consisted of a father, a mother, two brothers, and a sister. And one day while they were taking a trip, when they were about five miles out of town, they ran out of gas. And they sat around and waited awhile and then the father said, "You know, I think I'd better go back to town and get some gas. I don't think we're going to meet anybody here who is going to give us any." So the mother said, "Well, it's a dark night here and there might be a lot of scary things. I hear that there's a monster with a claw who is around here." And the father said, "Yes, I heard that, too, but you keep an eye open, Mother. You watch for him. This monster is not the kind of monster that can really hurt anyone if a big person is around to protect the children." At any rate, he went away and the children started to fall asleep and the mother started to fall asleep.

The mother fell lightly asleep and the boy was sort of sleeping too, but he knew that the monster was there too. And it was he who awakened and saw the monster outside the window. He immediately got up and said, "Mother, Mother, there's a monster out there," and the mother beat away the monster. She said, "Get out of here you filthy, ugly monster." And then the cops came and took the monster away to jail.

And the moral of that story is that if there's anything around you that is dangerous, speak up, cry out, and say something about it. Talk about it, ask for help, and that's the best way to get rid of those things.

In forming my story, I realized that it would be unrealistic to introduce any elements which would have encouraged Tony to try to change his father. The latter was geographically distant and too uninvolved emotionally to be expected to respond meaningfully to any overtures or complaints from the patient. Such encouragement would only have added to his frustration and rage. His mother, therefore, was his only hope. In Tony's story she sleeps, thereby exposing him to danger but, nevertheless, she is in the car with him. In my story he wakes her up and successfully enlists her aid. As I so often do, I attempted to get the child to actively participate in improving his own life situation.

Abandonment

As mentioned, most children consider themselves abandoned by the parent who leaves the home when separation takes place. In most cases this notion is false and the departing parent maintains an active interest in the children.

However, there are cases in which the term is appropriate. Either the parent cuts himself off from the children entirely, or his contacts are so infrequent and/or made with so little conviction that the children are essentially deprived of a meaningful relationship with him or her. It is to this problem of truly abandoned children (either abandoned in fact or psychologically so) that I direct my comments here.

First, I believe that a parent who so rejects his children is suffering a psychological disturbance. I believe that parental instincts are innate, and strong in the psychologically healthy individual. Like all other human functions, there is probably a wide range among individuals regarding the intensity of this instinct. But all, I believe, are born with it and those in whom it is either very weak or nonexistent are either repressing or suppressing the function. A parent with little or no overt expression of parental feeling will often rationalize the defect. Some believe that they just weren't born to be parents and having had children was a mistake. Others take the position that it's best for the children that they not have contact with them following the separation. "It's best that I make a clean break of it," they profess, or "Rather than see them once in a while, and raise their hopes and then disappoint them, it'll be better for them if I never see them at all." An extreme form of rationalization for rejecting children goes like this: "When one divorces, it's best for the departed parent and children to consider one another *dead*. Each must pick up the pieces and start life anew, without the other in any way impeding him." Although it is obvious how the children can be seen as impeding the adult in remaking his life, no explanation is given as to how continued contact with the adult is going to impede the children.

There are times when a parent, who was somewhat rejecting of the child prior to the separation, becomes so much more so afterwards that he or she can justifiably be placed in the category of parents discussed here. A father may suddenly become so swept up in his "freedom" that dating, traveling, and self-indulgence may result in his neglecting his children. A mother may become so burdened by her new responsibilities that she will have little time and conviction for affectionate involvement with her children; or the new resentments she now harbors may compromise significantly her maternal expression.

When abandonment occurs, it is common for the remaining parent to protect the child from what he or she considers to be the deleterious effects of revealing to the child the truth about the abandoning parent. Statements that are frequently utilized in the service of this goal include: "I guess he forgot. His memory was never very good," "He loves you inside; he just can't show it," and "He doesn't want to be mean; he can't help it." Parents who protect their children in this way are generally well-meaning. Often they are supported in this approach by professional authorities who espouse the view that the child's learning that a parent doesn't love him will cause psychological trauma. "Always reassure the child," they advise, "that the parent still loves him." Unfortunately, both the parents and professionals here are, in my opinion, misguided. The explanations provided the child cannot but confuse him. "What can this thing called love be all about," the child can only wonder, "if someone can love you and never (or rarely ever) show it?" I do not claim to have a firm definition of the word love; but the word does not, I believe, apply to a situation in which the so-called lover has practically no interest at all in being with the alleged loved one. Love is not love without reciprocity. Such communications are likely to contribute to the child's growing up with distortions about love that will interfere with his forming successful relations with others in the future. In addition, the child is likely to be somewhat incredulous of the parent who provides him with such rationalizations. He will often sense, at some level, the parent's lack of conviction when he or she presents them. Accordingly, they breed distrust of the remaining parent. The child has had enough distrust engendered in him already with the departure of one parent; he certainly doesn't need to develop distrust of the remaining parent—and such comments are likely to cause this to happen.

I believe that the child in such a situation should be told exactly what the situation is with regard to the absent parent's depth of involvement. If the parent's interest amounts to an average of one visit or greeting card a year, then the child should be told that the parent has little love for him but does think enough of him to extend himself to that degree. If there is no contact at all, then the child should be told that his parent does not love him. However, I would not simply stop with such an explanation. I would try to instill the notion that something is seriously wrong with a person who cannot love his own child. In a sense, he is more to be pitied than scorned. To be angry at such a parent is reasonable; but to pity him as well is also appropriate. Regarding the anger, the child should be helped to utilize his anger in the service of effecting a more meaningful relationship with the absent or deficient parent. If these efforts do not prove effective (and they most often fail with such parents), the child should be helped to appreciate that the angry feelings will best be dispelled by his gaining substitute gratifications from others. Regarding the pity, the child should be helped to gain a sense of pity for the parent because the latter is missing out on one of the most enriching experiences of life, namely, loving and rearing one's own child. In addition, I would try to help the child appreciate that just because his parent does not love him does not mean that he is unlovable. Others, both peer and adult, can love him both in the present and in the future. It behooves him, however, to seek such relationships in compensation for the deprivation he may be suffering over the loss of the parent. Lastly, if the child shows signs of trying to gain the affection of a parent who has proved himself incapable of providing such, he should be discouraged from such a futile pursuit. And telling the child that an unloving parent really loves him can contribute to such futile endeavors and is thereby another reason for not providing the child with such "protective" explanations. I not only recommend these approaches to parents in such a situation, but utilize them as well in my treatment of such children.

Of course, there are varying degrees of parental rejection and abandonment and only in extreme cases is there total separation between the child and the parent. The more common situation is the one in which the parent has varying degrees of contact with and interest in the child. It behooves the therapist to help the child gain as clear a picture as possible of the degree of involvement that his or her parent has. He or she should be helped to recognize that some degree of rejection is not the same as total abandonment. And such a child should also be helped to appreciate that ambivalence is normal and expected in all human relationships.

In the course of such a child's treatment I try to help him gain an appreciation of those behavioral patterns that he himself can look for to determine a parent's degree of affection. One criterion of parental affection is the frequency with which the parent wishes to be with the child. I help the child appreciate that parents have other duties and obligations; however, in spite of these, a loving parent will want to spend a significant amount of time with his children and will manage to do so. The parent who frequently finds excuses for not having such contacts (visitation limitations notwithstanding) may very well be somewhat defective in this area.

Another criterion the child can utilize to determine a parent's degree of affection is to determine how much the parent is willing to go out of his way in order to be of help to the child—especially when he is sick, injured, or suffering with other difficulties. I also encourage the child to observe how much pride the parent appears to have in the child's accomplishments and how much involvement the parent has in the things that interest him. If he observes the parent to be more often than not bored or involving himself in a forced manner, then it is likely that there is some deficiency in this area. I also suggest that the child try to determine how frequently the parent speaks favorably about the child to others. If the child never, or hardly ever, observes such conversations, it is likely that there is parental deficiency.

The child should also be encouraged to see how often the parent involves himself in *doing* mutually enjoyable things with the child. If this rarely occurs it suggests some deficiency in the parent.

I help the child appreciate that it is normal and expected that a parent will get angry at him from time to time and even a few times a day is within the normal range. However, if a parent is consistently grumpy and irritable with the child, then some deprivation is taking place.

The child should be encouraged to ascertain the amount of physical contact the parent desires to have with him. Parents who are somewhat compromised in this regard have little desire to have such contact. The younger the child the greater the likelihood that such physical contact will involve lying down in bed with the child from time to time, cuddling, tucking him in, wrestling, and allowing the child to come into the parent's bed on holidays and weekend mornings.

Clinical Example
A father who could do no wrong.

Amy, age ten, and her eight-year-old sister were seriously neglected by their father, who left the family two years prior to her coming for treatment. Her father often promised to visit, but rarely did so—often canceling appointments at the last minute or not showing up at all. Although she could count on a small Christmas present from him, he routinely ignored her birthday. Amy always accepted his excuses as valid, and denied that he was trying to use them to cover up any basic deficiencies in his affection for her and her sister. In Amy's eyes her father could do no wrong. But the anger she felt toward him was formidable and was a major contributing factor to her presenting complaints of rage outbursts (especially toward her mother with whom she lived), chronic irritability, and passive obstructionism. Her anger was often turned inward with resultant obsessive self-derogation and chronic feelings of worthlessness. Besides directing her anger toward her mother, she plagued her with requests that the parents reconcile, even though there was no evidence that either parent had any intention of getting together again.

Early in treatment, Amy told this story:

Patient: Um, my story is about one big bully and two little girls. Once upon a time there was a big bully named Big Bill and there were two little girls he always used to beat up. So one day the two little girls said, "We have to get away from Big Bill or else he will beat us up some more. I'm getting beat up so badly someday I might have to go to the hospital." So, there were also these two boys, also, who were the girls' friends and Big Bill got another bullying girl. So, of course, these children were much younger than Big Bill and his girlfriend.

Therapist: Wait, wait, Big Bill had one girlfriend?

P: Yeah, she was a bully too.

T: And the two girls had two boyfriends? Right?

P: But they were littler. So, um, it came that they had a big fight, Big Bill and his girlfriend and the two girls and the two boys who were gonna have. And the girls were terribly afraid but the boys said, "Don't worry, we'll try to protect you." So they started to fight. At first the small children were knocked down to the ground, but just then a boy sneaked up behind Big Bill and kicked him down. His leg was hurt so bad that he never (mumbles). But, the girl was still there.

T: Now wait. His leg was hurt so bad that he what?

P: His leg, but the girl was still there, and then a girl reached, went behind, and pinched her.

T: This is Big Bill's girlfriend?

P: Yeah, and so she went home too. So the two boys and the girls had won the fight.

So the moral of my story is: four people are better than two.

This story is typical of those told by children whose parents are divorced. The bully and his girlfriend are the patient's parents; the abused children are Amy and her sister (with two boys along as allies). By making her father a persecutor, Amy enjoys more involvement with him than she would were she to see him more truthfully as one who had abandoned her. In addition, Amy sees his rejection as active hostility—to which she adds her own projected anger. Her mother is seen as an ally of her father—gratifying thereby Amy's reconciliation fantasies. Her mother is seen as hostile for a number of reasons. Anger toward the father is displaced onto her mother (an available target). The mother's inability to meet the patient's insatiable demands (intensified by the absence of her father) is seen as hostility by the patient. The mother's refusal to remarry the father is seen as the mother's most hostile act. Lastly, much of Amy's own anger is projected onto her mother.

The story is one in which she simply vents the rage she feels toward her parents. She enjoys retribution for the injustices she sees herself to have suffered at their hands.

I told the following story in response:

Therapist: Once upon a time there was a big bully. His name was Big Bill. And, in this neighborhood there lived these two girls. It was a funny thing about these two girls, no matter how badly Big Bill treated them, they loved him. He would humiliate them; he would laugh at them; he would ignore them; he would make appointments and not keep them; and yet, no matter what he did these two girls would say, "Oh, we love Big Bill. He's such a wonderful person and everybody should love him like we do." People said, "Look at that, look at the mark you have on your face." They said, "Oh, that's just nothing, he was just playing." No matter what he did to them these poor, foolish girls just idolized him. They loved him and, of course, people began to laugh at them and said, "Isn't it foolish how these two girls worship that Big Bill? No matter how badly he treats them, they still walk around thinking he's wonderful."

But, there were times when these two girls were very sad and upset all the time. They asked people, "Why?" "Because you let Big Bill walk all over you and you don't want to see, really, what's going on. You don't express your feelings so it comes out in other ways. You don't let your real anger come out at Big Bill. You don't let your feelings come out, and so it happens later on in a different time and a different place and then you get depressed and upset or angry at other people and other things. It's really making your life miserable in other ways." Well, what do you think the girls thought after they were told that?

Patient: That they had been silly to let Big Bill beat them up and that they still worshipped him and they didn't worship him any more.

T: And they saw him as a human being after that—with both good and bad parts. When he was nice to them they enjoyed themselves with him and they respected him. But when he was not nice to them, they had nothing to do with him. They stayed away from him, and they found out that they were much less upset, angry, and depressed and things like that and the lesson of that story is what?

P: Look at everybody as a human being and nobody is perfect.

T: Right. What did you think of that story?

P: I thought it was very interesting.

In my story I tried to communicate a number of things. I attempted to help Amy appreciate that she was blinding herself to her father's neglect of her and that she was especially denying the angry feelings she felt toward him. I knew enough about her father to know that it was not likely that he would respond to Amy's expression of resentment with greater attentiveness or interest. However, I felt that such expression could be salutary for Amy in many ways. It would lessen her turning it inward toward herself, displacing it onto her mother, or projecting it onto others (especially her mother). By expressing it toward her father she would have the living experience of his failure to respond to her needs, and this hopefully would contribute to her giving up her neurotic quest for a benevolent, interested father as well as her obsession that her parents reconcile. My hope was that such messages would contribute to her gaining a more accurate view of her father, both his assets and liabilities. Hopefully, she would then be less likely to try to get from him what he was unable or unwilling to give her. Her father did, however, have some minimal involvement and my hope was that she would avail herself of the benefits to be gained (admittedly few) from her occasional contacts with him.

Clinical Example
A good God vs. a bad God.

Victor's mother divorced his father because of the latter's withdrawal and self-involvement. When physically at home he was rarely there psychologically. Following the divorce Victor saw little of his father, and when he did visit, the father had little meaningful involvement with Victor and his sister.

Victor was referred for treatment at the age of nine-and-a-half, about six months after his parents' separation. Victor refused to do his homework and bullied his classmates. He frequently stole from classmates and members of his family and would lie about his various forms of misbehavior.

During his third month of treatment he told this story:

Therapist: Good afternoon boys and girls, ladies and gentlemen. Today is Wednesday, the 4th of March, 1973.

Patient (interrupting): the 4th of March?

T: Excuse me, the 4th of April, 1973 and I'm happy to welcome you all to Dr. Gardner's Make-up-a-Story-Television Program. Our Guest today is having a little difficulty thinking of a story so I'm going to help him out and we'll start together. All right? Then I'll point to you and you'll say what comes into your mind at that point. All right?

P: Okay.

T: A long, long, long time ago . . . in a distant land . . . far, far, far away . . . way beyond the deserts . . . way beyond the oceans . . . way beyond the mountains . . . there lived a . . .

P: God.

T: A God. And this God . . .

P: And this God liked to help people.

T: Go ahead.

P: He liked to do—give them happiness and make them happy.

T: Hh hmm.

P: And one day this God met an evil God and this evil God didn't want the people to have these things.

T: Okay.

P: So this evil God took away these things.

T: All right.

P: And this nice God said, "Why are you doing this?"

The evil God said, "Because I am evil, and I like people to be sad."

"Well, I want them to be happy so give those things back." And these things were the happy God—the God that wanted the people to have the things and he said, "Give them back or I'll punish you."

And the evil God said, "You can't punish me."

The nice God did—did punish the evil God and there was no sign of the evil God again.

T: How did he punish him?

P: How did he punish him?

T: Hh hmm.

P: He put him down where he belonged—knocked him down there (pointing downward).

T: Where?

P: Down in the center of the earth.

T: Okay. Hh hmm. Now it's my chance to tell a story.

I considered the two Gods to represent two facets of Victor's father's personality: the good and the bad. The good, of course, symbolizes those personality traits that Victor finds admirable and benevolent; the bad represents those that Victor finds alienating. The story reveals Victor's desire that the undesirable and malevolent facets of his father's personality be totally obliterated. Then he would have an all-loving father instead of the father he considered rejecting and abandoning. Although Victor's father certainly did show interest in him, there was no question that there was some impairment of his ability to express affection to his son and, in addition, the separation was looked upon by Victor as a manifestation of his father's desire to abandon him. In a broader sense I considered the story to reflect Victor's desire that evil be totally expunged from the world and only goodness remain. With this understanding of Victor's story, I related mine:

> *Therapist:* Once upon a time there was a God and this God the people thought was a pretty good God because he used to do a lot of good things for the people. He would send rain, which would make the crops grow well, and he would make them pretty healthy and fairly happy.
>
> And one day along came another God and this God the people didn't like too much. In fact, they called him the evil God. And this evil God used to do things which bothered them. He would take the rain away so that the crops wouldn't grow and sometimes he would bring sickness, and the people got very angry and they said to the good God, "We would like you to get rid of that evil God."
>
> And the good God said, "Nope, I won't do that. The fact is that there are two of us. There's a good God and an evil God and both are in the world, and you're going to have to accept the fact that sometimes things are going to go well for you and sometimes things are not going to go so well, and that you cannot completely blot out or obliterate or get rid of the evil God, because he's there. And sometimes there will be droughts where there's no water and sometimes the crops won't grow and sometimes there will be sickness, and sometimes there won't be."
>
> Oh, the people were very upset about this. They were really upset. And they said, "You mean to say that the evil God is going to be with us?"
>
> He said, "Yep, that's the way the world is. The world has two Gods—a

good God and an evil God—and both are around, and sometimes things go well for you and sometimes things won't.''

Well, this made them quite miserable and they were very unhappy and they said to him, "Well, isn't there anything we can do about the evil God if we can't kill him off?''

And he said, "Well, the best advice I have for you is that you try to live so that you will be affected least by the evil God. In other words, I suggest that when you grow your crops you save some each year, put it aside in storage, so that when the rain stops and the evil God stops the rain, you'll have some stored food, so that you won't be hungry. And, in addition, let's say the evil God will make you sick. If you try to take care of yourself, eat properly, and treat illnesses in the early stages you won't be affected so much by it.'' He said, "That's what I suggest you do so that you can protect yourself somewhat against the evil God. You can try to avoid some of the problems that He'll cause you in life, but you can't avoid them completely. And other times you've just got to accept the fact that it's going to happen and that you can't get rid of the evil God so quickly. In fact, you can't get rid of him at all. He'll always be around to some extent and everybody suffers from him in different ways. Each person in their own life will be affected by him in some way or the other.'' The end.

Do you know what the lesson of that story is?

Patient: Uh, if there's an evil God you shouldn't just try and send it away. You should just try and live with it.

T: Okay, that's one lesson. Second lesson?

P: You should try and take care of yourself and if the rain stops you can have some food.

T: How do you get food if the rain stops?

P: Well, while the rain's still going you can grow the crops and put them in your storage, and when the rain stops you'll have food and you won't go hungry.

T: Right. So you can protect yourself against the "rainy days'' so to speak, you know. In this story the "rainy days'' are the droughts. (laughs) It's a little complicated, but at any rate you can protect yourself against hardship but you have to know that everybody in life has some and that you can't get rid of the evil God. The end.

Did you like that story?

P (Nods affirmatively.)

T: What part did you like?

P: Um, I liked the part where the evil God came in.

T: Where the evil God came in and what?

P: Then people didn't have any more crops but then the good God told them what they should do. (yawning)

T: Okay. Gettin' a little tired?

P: Hhmm.

T: Hhmm?

P: Yeah, a little bit.

T: Okay. Do you think this story has any relationship to you, to your life?

P: I'm not sure.

T: Well, think about your life. Tell me if you think there's any relationship between this story and things that may be going on in your life. You know, I said that in everybody's life there's some bad things that happened.

P: Yeah.

T: What about for you?

P: Bad things that happened to me? I get in trouble a lot.

T: Hh hmm. All right. Anything else?

P: Hhmm. Sometimes I lie.

T: What about like in this story these are things that happened from without—you know, from outside—nothing to do with the person. These are things which happened which he has no control over, like some people think that Gods do these things.

P: I don't think so.

T: Well, for instance, in this story some people get sick, other people their crops don't grow. Anything happen in your life that you had no control over? It just happened to you.

P: My sickness.

T: Anything else?

P: Sicknesses.

T: Anything else?

P: Um, mmm . . . mmm (shaking head negatively).

T: What about your parents' divorce? Would you put it in that category?

P: Yeah.

T: How would you put it in that category?

P: I couldn't control my parents.

T: You couldn't. Hh hmm. I think that—do you think that that's the kind of a thing that an evil God might do?

P: Hh hmm.

T: Hhmm?

P: Hh hmm.

T: So what does the story say about evil Gods? What does your story say about evil Gods?

P: They're mean and I don't like them.

T: In your story you want to get rid of them. Huh?

P: Hh hmm.

T: And what do I say in my story?

P: You should just try to live with them.

T: Anything else?

P: Hhmm. You can't control other things.

T: Well, what can you do about the divorce?

P: What can I do? I can just live with it.

T: Hh hmm. Anything else?

P: Nothing.

T: You can't change it.

P: No.

T: All right. What can you do about making yourself feel better?

P: Trying to forget about it.

T: All right. That's one thing. Are you still hooked on getting them together?

P: Mmmm . . . mmm

T: Hh hmm. Are you still thinking about it a lot?

P: No.

T: Hh hmm. What can you do to make yourself feel better about it?

P: Just forget about it.

T: All right. That's one thing. Anything else?

P: Uh, pretend they're not even divorced.

T: Pretend they're not divorced. How's that going to help?

P: Uh, well, like, um.

T: How does that help?

P: Well, when my father comes over, I can pretend that they're still together and I can be happy.

T: Hh hmm. Well, that's a dangerous business. I know it could be good in a little way to pretend that they're not divorced when he comes over, but what's bad about that, pretending they're not divorced?

P: But they are divorced.

T: What's bad about pretending that they are not?

P: Um, lying to yourself.

T: It's not looking at things. Blind to yourself, right? Anything else you can do?

P: Um . . . (pause) . . .

T: Well, how about involving yourself with other people so you don't feel bad about the fact that your father isn't around?

P: Yeah.

T: Okay. Do you want to watch this program?

P: Mmm.

T: Well, yes or no. What is "Mmm?"

P: Nah.

T: Nah. Do you want to play the other game we played last time?

P: Okay.

T: Okay.

In this story I attempted to help Victor see his father as a composite of both good and bad. Every child does best to see his parents as a mixture of both assets and liabilities; and this is especially important for the child of divorce because a parent's absence may make such a view difficult to form and hold. An absent father who sees the child only on weekends may spend so much time indulging him (often to assuage guilt) that the child sees little of the "bad" father who imposes restrictions, disciplines, etc. Or again, the child of divorce may wish to deny imperfections on the part of the absent parent or fear expressing his appreciation of such lest he see even less of the departed parent.

In this case I believed that Victor wished to repress completely his father's alienating qualities. His father was an aloof and somewhat distant man who had difficulty expressing affection toward his children and Victor had to come to terms with this. Denying this negative aspect of his father's person-ality was certainly not a healthy adaptation for Victor. In my story I not only suggest acceptance of this reality but, in addition, go further. Advising a patient simply to resign himself to an unpleasant situation is rarely effective. One must at the same time provide alternatives that can serve to compensate for the discarded mechanism. Here I advise Victor to avoid his father, if he could, when his father exhibited his malevolent characteristics and to seek and enjoy him all those times when his father could be more benevolent. In addition, I suggest that he provide himself with substitute gratifications to ensure that he would have some sources of pleasure when his father could not provide them. This is symbolically represented by the storage of crops grown during the rainy season in order to carry him through the droughts. My comment, "In this story the 'rainy days' are the droughts" was stated for my benefit and that of the patient's mother, who was present in the room during most of his sessions. I did not expect him to appreciate the humor but the re-mark was so apt that it was difficult to suppress it.

On another level, I considered Victor's story to reflect his feelings that his parents' divorce was an evil event and that the obliteration of evil in the world would prevent the occurrence of such tragedies in people's lives. My story was designed to introduce the notion that certain calamities are uncontrollable. As the post-story discussion reveals, the patient did appreciate my messages on the allegorical level. However, when I tried to directly translate these into the reality of his life he resisted appreciation of the import of my messages. Sometimes direct discussion of the relevance of the story to the patient's life can be therapeutically beneficial; at other times it produces anxieties and resistance and this was the case in this interchange.

Flight from the Home

At times, a child's fleeing from the home at the time of separation may be a way of coping with his fears of abandonment. His running away may enable him to fantasy himself the rejector rather than the one rejected. It is as if he were saying: "It is not I who have been abandoned; I am the abandoner. *I* decide if and when separation from my parents is to occur." He thereby gains a specious sense of control over a situation that is in fact beyond his power. In addition, the concern and attention that the runaway child gets may reassure him that he is still wanted, and this serves to lessen abandonment fears. This is especially the case when he is finally "found." The family's sighs of relief, thanking God that he is all right, etc. all make the child feel wanted. Even if he is punished for what he has done, the attention-getting purpose has been served. For with the punishment comes the reassurance that his absence has caused pain and that he really has been missed. In addition, running away provides the child with a false sense of ego-enhancement. It is not he who is the weak and impotent one who helplessly suffers rejection; he himself has the power to reject and his running away is a demonstration of this.

The child's running away from the home may be a hostile act that provides him with vengeful gratification. He may actually enjoy thinking about the grief his parents are suffering over his absence. It is as if the child were saying: "My father has hurt me by leaving the home; I'll hurt him in the same way." Alternatively, the child may project his own hostility onto his family and flee them because they are perceived as hostile to him (McDermott, 1970). Or, if the child considers his having been "bad" to be the cause of the separation, he may run away from home in order to avoid causing more trouble.

Fleeing the home is a dramatic act calculated to draw attention to the child. Accordingly it may serve as a cry for help. In the inevitable discussions that take place after the child's return, the assistance of a third party (minister, therapist, respected relative) may be enlisted. As the result of such third party intervention the child may gain help for himself, or he may fantasize the counselor's bringing about parental reconciliation. Or the child may believe that the guilt his act will engender in his parents will be so great that they will remain together in order to avoid further flights and other manifestations of the pains they have caused their child. The flight then can be a guilt-provoking device, designed to manipulate the parents into staying together.

Fleeing the home can serve to help the child deny the fact of the separation. If he is not home to observe a parent's absence, he can believe that the parent is still there. Or the child may be fleeing the general home atmosphere of loneliness and depression that the separation has caused. At times, the child will flee in order to find the departed parent and convince him to return. Sometimes the child may wish to live with the parent who has left the house and he runs from home in an attempt to rejoin him. There are times when identification with the departed parent appears to be operating. McDermott (1970) describes eleven children who ran away from home after visits from fathers who had previously left the family.

Parental sanctioning of the flight from the home is not uncommon. The mother, for example, may unconsciously (or even consciously) welcome the child's leaving because it lessens her burden. By the child's taking the initiative, she need not suffer the guilt she might experience if she herself actively encouraged or forced the child to leave. However, her passive compliance in such situations reveals her true intent. Some such parents will pack the child's valises and accompany them to the door after the first comment regarding his wish to go. Although the comment may have been made by the child as a test of the mother's affection (a reassurance he especially needs at the time of separation), she takes him literally as an excuse to get him out, and chooses to deny the obvious fact that he is really asking for reassurance that she still wants him to stay.

A child may go to the home of a friend where he may be welcomed. The friend's parents may commiserate with the child over the indignities he suffers in his own home and they may get the gratification of being his new protectors. I am very suspicious of the motives of such "good guys." Generally, their interest is less in the welfare of the child than in their competition with the runaway child's parents. Such people get easily "sucked in" and believe all the criticisms they are told about the child's parents in order to competitively enhance their own feelings of worth as parents. They may even go so far as to join in with the child in keeping his whereabouts a secret. It is rare that such behavior is justified. Most often, the appropriate thing for such parents to do is to refuse to harbor the child and to call his parents to pick him up. They should discourage the child from using flight as a way of dealing with a difficult situation; rather, they should encourage him to try to work the problems out with his parents. And the most appropriate thing for the "abandoned" parent to do is to call the "good samaritans," insist that the child be sent or brought back, and to threaten police and legal action if necessary. This is a true demonstration of affection; failure to do so serves the purposes of rejection. Deep down most runaway children want to be sought, their protestations to the contrary notwithstanding. It is the truly rejecting parent who does not comply with this covert wish and make every reasonable attempt to bring such children home.

Chapter 7

BLAME AND GUILT

Blame

Long before the parents' decision to separate is made, the child is introduced to the concept of *blame*. In their fighting the parents usually blame each other for the difficulties between them and so it is only natural that when the separation does take place the child tends to think along the lines of who was at fault. The problem is further compounded by the traditional legal system, which would only grant a divorce if one of the parties could demonstrate that he had been wronged by the other (who was considered to have exhibited such "reprehensible behavior" as adultery, mental cruelty, alcoholism, or drug addiction). Although no-fault divorce laws have evolved out of the recognition that both parties have usually contributed (often through psychological difficulties) to the deterioration of the relationship, the spouses themselves usually are quite strong in their opinions as to who was at fault. And when the couple needs to resort to adversary proceedings (whether to get divorced or to settle other conflicts such as those over alimony, support, and custody) the lawyers can be relied upon to intensify the problem of faultfinding. Lastly, the child is likely to look upon the parent who has initiated the separation proceedings to be the one who was at fault. He does not appreciate fully the often subtle contributions of both parents to the difficulties or that the party who first decides on separation may have done so only after years of tolerating terrible humiliations and indignities and may be in reality, the less culpable of the two partners.

The concept of there being one party to blame is the most likely one for the child to evolve himself even apart from parental influence. The child tends to think in the most simplistic terms and the younger he is, the less likely he is to appreciate the subtleties of joint contribution to the parental dissension. In addition, in their own conflicts, those below seven or eight tend to see one person (usually the other guy) at fault. It is rare for a young child to say, "I started it." His understanding of his own personal conflicts in terms of there being one guilty and one innocent party contributes to his considering his parents' altercations to be similarly derived.

In working with such children the therapist does well to impress upon the child the concept of joint contribution to many, if not most, conflicts between people. To make the discussions more meaningful, he does well to describe specific examples from the conflicts of the child's own parents. Such discussions, of course, are much more meaningful if the parents have provided the child with the basic reasons for the separation (in accordance with the principles described in Chapter 1). In addition, one does well to try to help the child appreciate the fact that there are varying degrees of control a parent may have over his own alienating behavior. Hopefully such discussions will result in the child's becoming more sympathetic to his parents' difficulties and less prone to blame either one of them. If a child's need to see one of his parents as perfect contributes to the problem, work with both this parent and the child may be indicated. Lastly, the child must be helped to appreciate that blame preoccupations are generally nonproductive and that he does better to direct his energies into more constructive ways of handling his reactions to the divorce.

Guilt

I use the word *guilt* to refer to the affect associated with a notion of wrongdoing. When an individual harbors thoughts or desires that are considered reprehensible by the significant figures in his milieu he is likely to feel guilty over them. And, if he acts them out he is likely to feel more guilty; in fact, the failure to experience such guilt would be a manifestation of malfunctioning within that milieu. Associated with the ideas of wrongdoing are feelings of worthlessness—as if the individual were saying to himself: "How terrible a person I am for what I have done." Generally, there is an anticipation of punishment in the guilt reaction, but this may not be clearly realized. The guilt reaction is inappropriate when it is exaggerated, when the consensus of significant individuals is that the act is not blameworthy, and when the individual fancies himself responsible for an event for which he was in no way responsible. Guilt reactions, especially those of the inappropriate type, are common among children of divorce.

Guilty children to whom responsibility is communicated. There are situations in which the child, in a sense, has played a role in the parental dissension. A parent, for example, may be unable to tolerate the demands and burdens of having a handicapped child and may wish to get out of the marriage in order to avoid such responsibilities. He may state this overtly or may provide other reasons for his withdrawal—excuses that serve to cover up his true motives. The healthy parent of a handicapped child inevitably has such thoughts at times, but is willing to assume the burdens of his upbringing because of his love for the child and does not act out his flight fantasies. The immature or irresponsible parent may do so.

The child of such a parent is likely to appreciate (even if not directly told) that his handicap was a major contributing factor in the parent's abandonment (a word that has more applicability to this situation than other types of parental separation). Accordingly, he will feel guilty and is likely to say: "If I wasn't so sick, my father (mother) wouldn't have left." Such a child must be helped to appreciate that the real fault lies with his parent rather than with himself, and that the healthy parent accepts the fact that a child may become ill, is willing to accept the responsibilities of its care, and does not abandon it. The child must be helped to appreciate that the defect lies in the parent. Venting of anger reactions on the child's part must also be encouraged; however, the child must be helped, as well, to resign himself to the rejection and obtain substitute gratifications so that there will be less anger generated. Also, engendering in the child a "he's-more-to-be-pitied-than-scorned" attitude can reduce anger and lessen the child's loss of self-esteem.

There are people who are not ready for parenthood or who may never be capable of such a role, and yet they have children. Such a parent may have a perfectly healthy child and yet may not be willing or capable of taking care of it. Such a parent's leaving is, in a sense, the child's fault—because had the child not been born, the marriage might have remained intact. And the child of such a parent is bound to recognize this and feel guilty. Such a child is best approached in a manner similar to that described for the handicapped child.

If a child learns that his conception was planned in an attempt to improve a faltering marriage and the "marital therapy" didn't work, he is likely to feel that the separation was his fault and that another child might have been more successful in keeping his parents together. If the child learns that his pregnancy was unplanned and that the burden of his upbringing was a contribution to parental dissatisfaction in the marriage, he is also likely to feel guilt over the separation. If the parents separate soon after the child is born because of the unwillingness on the part of a parent to assume parental responsibility, the child, when he gets older, is likely to surmise that his birth contributed to the breakup. There are situations in which parental differences over the raising of the children are a significant factor in the marital discord and this can result in the child's feeling that the separation was his fault. When a father complains bitterly that he is overwhelmed by the financial burdens of the household, then leaves, and does not fulfill his financial commitments to the family, the child is also likely to feel guilty.

In all these situations the separation has indeed taken place because of the parent's view that the child is in some way responsible for the marital breakup. Most often this is communicated to the child, either overtly or covertly. Sometimes such parents try to assuage the child's guilty reactions by trying to convince him that the separation is not his fault. But it is his fault in the sense that had he not been born the marriage might still be intact. In such cases, therefore, the child must be helped to see that such parental reassurances, although well-meaning, are specious. He must be helped to appreciate that the real fault lies with deficiencies not in himself but in the parent. In addition, concomitant anger and self-esteem problems should be dealt with as described in previous sections.

Guilt over disloyalty. Most children with separated or divorced parents have loyalty conflicts. Most youngsters are brought up with a deep sense of commitment to the members of their family, especially their parents. All children are supposed to love and respect their parents, and may even learn to feign or profess such attitudes if they do not in fact exist. Even when the marriage is faltering, both parents may continue to attempt to foster in the child (often without conviction) these attitudes toward the spouse. At this time, however, the child may not be required to take sides or express preferences. But when the separation occurs, the child may find himself in a situation where his loyalty is overtly tested, where he is required to make decisions and take actions that reveal, without question, his preferences. At such times a child's feelings of guilt may be profound—even to the point of paralyzing him from taking action or making decisions.

Some children take the side of whichever parent they are with at the time in order to avoid alienating that parent; but they will at the same time feel guilty over their disloyalty toward the absent parent. Generally, such children must be helped to avoid taking sides, even to the point of risking the alienation of a parent. If, however, the child is firmly convinced that one of his parents is indeed worthy of significant blame, and the therapist himself is of a similar view, then such a child must be helped to feel less guilty about his feelings of antagonism. He must be helped to see that his critical feelings about his parent are justifiable and that his guilt is unwarranted. He must be helped to see that love and respect must be earned, not demanded.

Some children will feel guilty for having a better time with their fathers on visiting days than with their mothers at home. They must be helped to appreciate that many children have better times on visiting days because there are fewer restrictions being placed upon them. Mother has to make them get up early, go to school, do chores and homework. Father, however, may not have to do such "dirty work" and often comes off as the "good guy." In addition to helping such children appreciate the normality of such reactions and preferences, such fathers should be helped, as well, to provide their children with more realistic visitation experiences. Providing the child with continual fun and games (often to assuage guilt) is not in his best interests. A more balanced experience—one that includes usual routines and occasional inevitable but not contrived frustration—provides the child with the healthiest experience and avoids the development of guilt feelings.

Visitation schedules may be rigidly defined in the separation agreement and divorce decree. Generally, the more specific these are the less flexibility and trust there has been between the parents. The child's needs for a visit of specific length at a particular time may not be consonant with what his parents have legally agreed upon. A child may feel guilty and disloyal if he does not wish to visit with a parent at a particular time, or to have a visit shorter than the allotted period. In such situations one should, of course, inquire into whether the parent is trying to provide reasonable visitation experiences. If not, then attempts should be made to rectify the situation. But even when this may be accomplished, the child may prefer an alternative arrangement, e.g., a shorter visit, bringing along a friend, or even a skipped visit (with advance notice to both parents, of course). And he must be helped to appreciate that such modifications and compromises of his visitations need not be a reflection of disloyalty: a piece of paper drawn up by his parents and their lawyers need not reflect *his* needs and wishes.

Clinical Example
A boy with a loyalty conflict.

Ten-year-old James's parents were separated and embroiled in bitter conflicts. His father had been flagrantly unfaithful to his mother and finally left the home to live with another woman. He was unreliable with regard to financial support of his family and this resulted in the mother's having to take on an increased work burden. In addition, he was unreliable regarding visitation and would often show up late and, at times, not at all. In session, however, James would not criticize his father and was quite evasive when discussing any subject that might result in his seeing his father at fault. Early in treatment he told this story:

> *Patient:* Once upon a time there was a little dog and he had a juicy favorite bone. The little dog loved it. He chewed on it for many hours. There was one strange thing about this little dog. He had a flea on him that was so strong that it could lift up the little dog. This flea loved to sit on top of the dog's back. He scratched the dog's back.
>
> One time there was this big dog trying to get the big bone from the little dog. The big dog thought that he could get the little dog into trouble and then he would leave the bone. So the big dog hit a man and took the stick that he hit the man with and gave it to the little dog so that people would think that the little dog did it. The flea grabbed the stick and threw it at the big dog who caught it. The dog chaser saw the big dog without dog tags. He took the big dog to the pound.
>
> The lesson of that story is: don't try to take things from people who are too small or you'll end up in trouble.

I considered this flea to represent James himself and the two dogs to symbolize his parents. However, I was not certain which dog represented James's mother and which his father. Accordingly, I asked him what the sexes were of the two dogs and he replied that they were both males. Since this response did not provide me with any further information helpful in understanding the meaning of this story, I decided that the little dog most likely represented James's mother and the big dog his father because James's mother was smaller than his father and the father was the one who most often instigated difficulties.

The story reveals James's realization that it is his father who is responsible for causing his mother's difficulties. It reveals, therefore, James's appreciation of the real situation; however, he cannot permit himself conscious awareness of this insight and so must depict it allegorically. Whereas in reality James did not have the courage to stand by his mother in her conflicts with the father lest he appear disloyal to his father, in the story James, as represented by the flea, actively sides with his mother and protects her from the father's plot. It is through his efforts that the culprit's plan is foiled and he ends up being removed by the authorities.

In addition, his story reveals an oedipal theme. The flea not only shares an intimate relationship with the mother dog (represented by his sitting on her back and loving to scratch it), but also by virtue of the flea's prowess (ability to lift up the dog).

It was with this understanding of James's story that I related mine:

Therapist: Once upon a time there were two dogs, a little dog and a big dog. In addition, there were two fleas, a young flea and a teenage flea. The two fleas were friendly with both dogs and they used to hop back and forth from one dog's back to the other. Sometimes they would stay with one dog and scratch its back and sometimes they would go to the other dog and scratch its back. Sometimes one flea would sit in one dog's back and sometimes the other flea would sit on the other dog's back. Then they would switch. Everybody seemed to be happy.

Then one day the two dogs began to fight and day after day they fought harder and harder. Although the big dog seemed to be starting all the trouble, the little flea was scared to take sides. Although he knew that the big dog was the real troublemaker, he was scared to say so because he feared that the big dog might hurt him or never have anything to do with him again. And so, whenever they fought, the little flea was very quiet.

One day the big dog took a stick and hit a man with it and then he gave the stick to the little dog and hoped that people would think that the little dog was the one that hit the man. The little flea wanted to throw the stick back at the big dog so that no one would think that the little dog started the trouble. But he was scared to do it because he was afraid that the big dog would not like him anymore. The big flea, however, told the little flea that he was making a mistake and that when two friends have a fight, the bravest thing to do is to say directly and out loud exactly who you think is right and who you think is wrong. He also told him that if he didn't do that he was not being loyal or friendly to the little dog and that he would be standing by and letting the little dog get into trouble when he didn't deserve it. The little flea realized that the big flea was right and so he picked up the stick and he threw it back at the big dog. The man who was hit with the stick saw the stick near the big dog and punished him for hitting him with it.

The big dog was mad at the flea for throwing the stick back. But both fleas told him that they had seen what had happened and that he was wrong for what he had done. They said that it was not nice of him to hit the man and then try to get the little dog blamed for it. The big dog began to think about what the fleas told him and after a while he realized that they were right. After that, each·time the big dog did something that the fleas didn't like they would tell him. Sometimes he would listen to them and change what he was doing; but other times he wouldn't. Sometimes he even got mad at them when they criticized him. However, most of the time he didn't. Most important of all, the two fleas felt very good about themselves when they spoke up and told what they were feeling. The little flea realized he had made a mistake by keeping quiet when he saw the big dog doing things that hurt the little dog. He realized that he was not being fair to the little dog in not defending her. He realized also that when he spoke up to the big dog he would sometimes get things changed.

The patient's story revealed that he could not consciously allow himself to take sides in his parents' conflicts; rather, he could do so only in symbolic fashion. My story goes one step further in that it specifies the value of taking sides and points out how misguided neutrality can be in such situations. The patient listened with interest and I felt sure that my message was sinking in. In subsequent months the patient gradually became freer to express his resentments toward his father and to deal with them more effectively and appropriately.

Guilt as a mechanism to gain control over the uncontrollable. One of the most common reactions of children of divorce, especially in the period around the time of separation, is the feeling that they were somehow the cause of their parents' difficulties—when there is absolutely no evidence that this was the case. The child may consider his having been "bad" to be the cause and he may promise his parents repeatedly that he will forever be "good." Any indiscretion or transgression, no matter how slight, may be seized upon as the cause, and the preoccupation may reach obsessive proportions. The child may even quote comments made by the parents to justify his conclusion. For example, he may interpret a father's saying to the mother "I can't stand being in this house any longer" to mean that he is the objectionable one, rather than she. The child may repeat the act(s) he considers to have caused the separation in order to strengthen his notion that it caused his parents' separation. The child may even *start* doing bad things in order to maintain this notion. McDermott (1970) describes a child who began to steal *after* the divorce and then claimed that his parents separated because of his stealing.

Although many factors may operate in the development of this delusion of guilt, the one that is most significant and frequent in my experience is the need to control the uncontrollable. Implicit in the statement "It's my fault" is the notion of control. The child feels helpless to change his parents' minds regarding the divorce decision. If, however, he can convince himself that he was the cause—that something he did brought about the decision to separate —it follows that there is something he can do to bring about a reversal of the decision. If he can delude himself into believing that his being bad caused his parents to separate, then all he need do is to be good and they will reconcile. This mechanism in the formation of the guilt reaction is quite common and yet it has not been given the attention it deserves in the psychiatric literature. I have described elsewhere its utilization in a wide variety of psychological phenomena (1969a, 1969b, 1970a). Although most often this type of guilt reaction arises without any direct influence from the parents or others, there are times when there may be an active parental contribution. For example, the family atmosphere may be one in which personal responsibility is always invoked to explain any incident, especially an unfortunate one. No matter how capricious the event and no matter how innocent the family members may have been in bringing it about, somehow someone is considered to have caused it. This tradition of finding out who was at fault can contribute to the child's looking to himself when parental separation occurs. Or a parent may actually consult a child regarding the divorce decision, even to the point of asking the child's permission (Sugar, 1970). Sometimes the child's permission is not really being sought; rather, the parent hopes that the child will approve so the parent can feel less guilty. In such cases the parent would generally have gone ahead with the decision, but without the child's approval would feel much more guilty about it. Others, however, may take the child's view into serious consideration and may even stay together because of the child's disapproval—so great is the parental guilt and fear of angering the child. In such cases the child's feelings of control are not delusional: he is *told* he has control and *in some cases may actually have it*. (The child who does indeed have the power to keep his parents together may develop a different kind of guilt: guilt over his being responsible for keeping his parents together in a state of misery.)

Reassuring such children that the divorce was in no way their fault is usually futile. Usually, the parents have attempted to reduce such preoccupations themselves, but to no avail. When one appreciates the mechanisms that underlie such guilt, the child's failure to respond to such reassurances become understandable. Although the therapist might also provide such a confrontation, he should do it as an introduction to the child's recognizing it as a false idea, inconsistent with reality. He must go beyond that point, however, and help the child appreciate that there are certain things in life that one *can* control and there are other things that one *cannot*—and parental divorce is in the latter category. The child must be helped to resign himself to this reality. However, the therapist should not stop there on that somewhat defeatist and depressing note. He must help the child recognize that he does have it within his power to *do* certain things that can help him lessen the pain of the separation. He has it within his power to gain substitute gratifications to compensate for the loss of his parent by involving himself more meaningfully with others, both peer and adult. When the child is able to accomplish this goal, a contributing element to the delusion will have been removed. And when the child has experiences in which he learns to differentiate the controllable from the uncontrollable, to change what he can, and not futilely to try changing what he cannot, then another element in this type of guilt reaction will have been reduced.

Clinical Example
A boy exhibiting self-blame delusions and parental guilt evocation.

Bruce was referred at the age of nine-and-a-half because of low frustration tolerance, moderate depression, power struggles with his parents, poor school performance, and impaired peer relationships. He had been adopted at six weeks of age and had a six-year-old sister who was also adopted. There were significant difficulties in the relationship between the parents: The mother was exhibitionistic and hysterical, whereas the father was obsessive. They had little sexual interest in one another and the mother passively complied with many of the father's irrational demands, especially those regarding the disciplining of Bruce. The father was excessively punitive and the mother often went along with his severe punishments, even though she did not fully approve of them.

After six months of therapy there was significant improvement in Bruce's difficulties; however, the problems between the parents became so grave that there was serious talk of divorce. Although Bruce ostensibly knew nothing about the parents' divorce deliberations, he told this story at that time:

> *Patient:* I can't think of a story.
>
> *Therapist:* Just sit and relax and I'll start and as soon as I point to you say what comes to your mind.
>
> Once upon a time . . . a long, long, long time ago . . . in a distant land . . . far, far, far away . . . way beyond the deserts . . . way beyond the mountains . . . way beyond the oceans . . . there lived a . . .
>
> *P:* Three bears. (Laughs)
>
> *T:* The Three Bears? A made-up story? Are you telling a made-up story?
>
> *P:* I just thought of that in the story.
>
> *T:* Okay. You can start off with the three bears if you want, but it has to be different from the regular three bears story.
>
> *P:* I don't even know about the three bears too much.
>
> *T:* Okay. Then you make up a story. And these three bears . . . Go ahead.
>
> *P:* Swam together.
>
> *T:* They swam together?
>
> *P:* Yeah.
>
> *T:* And they swam together. All right. There were these three bears and they swam together. Go ahead. Then what?
>
> *P:* All at once. They got, uh. The mother and father bear got a divorce.
>
> *T:* Excuse me a second. These three bears were a mother, a father,

and a what?

P: A baby bear.

T: Okay, there's a mother, a father, and a . . .

P (interrupts): And there's another one. I forgot there's four bears.

T: Four bears. Who was the fourth?

P: A brother.

T: And what was the baby? A boy or a girl?

P: A girl.

*T:*There was a baby girl and a big brother?

P: Yeah.

T: And then you said the mother and father got divorced?

P: Yeah.

T: All right. And then what happened?

P: Because the kids were always fighting.

T: Okay. Because the kids were fighting.

P: Now I don't know what to talk.

T: You don't know anything more to that story?

P: Hmm.

T: You just want to end it there?

P: Hmm. Not so good?

T: Hh hmm.

P: And then the kids were rotten all the time and then finally the big brother ran away so that he wouldn't get in trouble. He was always getting in trouble. So he ran away just for a little while so, you know, that they would think that, you know, he left a note that I will return in something—in so and so time—if you would be nice and get along.

T: Who was this note to? His mother and father?

P: Yeah. And get along. And so finally—'cause he was just spying on them to see if they would get along.

T: All right. So what happened?

P: And so then finally they got along. He was looking through like a little telescope so he could look in the window and see if they're getting along.

T: Hh hmm.

P: And so finally they get along and he comes home and then everybody is okay. And that's the end.

T: Okay. Now it's my chance to tell a story.

P: Yeah.

The bear family, of course, represents the patient's own family, and its constellation is identical to his in that there are, besides the parents, an older brother and a younger sister. In the story Bruce utilizes two maneuvers to bring about a reconciliation of his parents. First, he considers their impending separation to be due to the fact that "the kids were always fighting" and because "the kids were rotten all the time." The big brother bear then runs away in order to spare his parents further distress over his being bad. The implication here is that once he is removed from the scene things will be better between them. We see clearly here the child's concept of the divorce as an event that he caused by his fighting and as an event that he can prevent by discontinuing his disobedience. It is a good example of the development of a guilt delusion in the service of controlling the uncontrollable.

In addition, he attempts to bring about a reconciliation by evoking guilt in his parents. By running away he hopes that they will get along better. The implication here is that they would be so guilt-ridden over his running away that they would patch things up in order to get him to return. The story ends with the parents getting along once again. The implication is that his two maneuvers were successful in getting his parents to reconcile. With this understanding of Bruce's story, I related mine:

Therapist: Once upon a time there were four bears, a mother, a father, a baby sister, and a bigger brother. Now one day this mother and father told the children—of course, the baby girl couldn't understand too much—told the brother that things were very, very bad in their marriage and that they were thinking of getting a divorce. And he thought, "I know why they're getting a divorce. They're getting a divorce because I was bad." And so he said to the mother and father, "I know why you're getting a divorce. You're getting a divorce because I was bad."

And they said, "It had nothing to do with you. We're thinking of getting a divorce. We're not sure. We're thinking of getting a divorce because we don't like one another anymore. We're having troubles and problems between ourselves and it has nothing to do with you kids. And we are not getting divorced because of you."

Anyway, this boy didn't believe that. He felt that it was his fault and that they were getting a divorce because he was bad. And then he said, "I know what I'll do. I'll be very good." You see, he thought, "maybe if I'm very good and I don't do any more bad things maybe then they'll stay together." He said to them, "I promise to be very good."

And they said, "Well, we're glad you're going to be very good. It will certainly be nice if you're good, but that's not going to affect our decision. That's not going to make us decide one way or the other whether or not to get divorced."

And he said, "I don't believe it. I'll be good. You'll see you'll stay together."

Well, this boy was on his best behavior. He was on his best—it was very hard but he was trying very hard to be on his best behavior. Sometimes when he would be angry, and he would want to do things like hit his sister, or he would want to break something in the house, or he would want to run away to get his parents upset, he would stop and say, "I won't do that. I'm not going to do that. I'm going to be very good so that they'll stay together."

Well, he was on his best behavior and in spite of that the parents one day said to him, "We've decided to get a divorce."

And he said, "But I was very good."

And they said, "We know you were very good and it's very nice to see that you're so good, but that has nothing to do with the divorce." And they said to him, "You just want to try to control the divorce. There are certain things in life that you can't control and divorce is one of them."

Well, this got this boy very upset and he was very sad. And he was sitting in front of his house crying when . . . Do you want to hear more of this story?

Patient: Yeah.

T: Yeah. Well, all of a sudden a teen-ager passed and this teen-ager said, "What are you crying about?"

And he said, "I want my mother and father to get back together again."

And the teen-ager said, "You know, there are certain things in life you can't control."

And the kid said, "Hey, you know, that's just what my mother and father said to me. Those same words."

He said, "Well, it's true. You can't control that. That's their divorce."

He said, "What can I control?"

The teen-ager said, "Well you can control other things. You can make yourself feel better in other ways and do things with other people. But you can't control divorce."

Well, what do you think the boy did then?

P: Don't ask me.

T: Well, he began . . .

P (interrupts): probably climbed up a tree and acted like a monkey.

T: Climbed up a tree and acted like a monkey. Why did he do that?

P: So he would make his sister laugh because she was crying.

T: I see. She was crying about what?

P: Oh, somehow she learned that they were getting a divorce.

T: I see. What did the boy in my story learn? See if you could figure out the lesson in that story.

P: I don't . . . oh, some things you can't control in life.

T: Right. What is one of them?

P: Divorce?

T: Right, right.

P: Marriage.

T (smiling): Right. You can't control that. You can't control whether or not your parents get married or whether or not they get divorced. That's entirely out of your control.

Soon after that the boy thought of another way of getting his parents back together again. He thought that if he ran away then his parents would be so worried about him and so sorry that their fighting had caused him to run away that they would get back together again. So he ran away and sneaked back to the house with a telescope to see what was happening. What do you think he saw?

P: They stopped fighting?

T: No! Although they were sad and worried about the boy, they still continued to fight. And what do you think happened when he came back?

P: They were happy to see him?

T: Yes, they were very happy to see him; but they were also mad at him because he had worried them so much. Because they loved him so much—even though they no longer loved one another—they were very upset that he was gone.

He then asked them if they were still going to get a divorce. And what do you think they said?

P: I don't know.

T: They said that they were still going to get a divorce because they didn't love one another anymore. And although the boy felt sad about that he realized that running away hadn't worked, that his parents were still going to get a divorce. The end.

Anything you want to say about that story?

P: It was good. I liked it. Let's listen to it.

The reader should note that while telling my story I unconsciously got away from bears and began talking about boys. This commonly occurs and my experience has been that the child rarely corrects me with regard to this "error."

In my story I begin by emphasizing the point that there are certain things in life that one cannot control and divorce is one of them. I often use the teen-ager as the conveyor of my messages. I have found the teenager a valuable person to use for the communication of unpleasant messages. To most children the teen-ager is a more respectable authority than the adults and his words are taken more seriously. The patient listened receptively to what I was saying and at the end demonstrated his appreciation of my message. I did not think that Bruce appreciated the humor in his remarks regarding the fact that one not only cannot control a parent's divorcing, but cannot control their marrying either. (His mother, who was present in the room, did.)

I then focus on the guilt-evoking maneuver designed to effect parental reconciliation. Unlike the patient's story, in mine it doesn't work. The parents express their concern and love for the boy, but remain adamant with regard to their decision to divorce.

In my story I do, however, encourage the child's compensating for the loss of his parent by doing something that is very much under his control, namely, "doing things with other people." It is a general principle of psychotherapy that a patient will more readily give up a pathological adaptation if he is provided with an attractive and reasonable alternative—an alternative that may not have been entertained by him. Here I tried to introduce him to this compensatory alternative.

Self-blame as a denial of parental blame. A child may place the blame of the divorce on himself in order to deny parental fallibility. It makes a child feel more secure to see his parents as perfect. And if the parents have the need to present themselves as such (by never admitting defects, for example) then such tendencies on the child's part may be enhanced. A separation is a clear statement of deficiency in at least one parent (and generally both). The child with an inordinate need to maintain images of parental perfection may consider the defect to have been his rather than theirs and may dredge up a host of deficiencies to confirm this notion. Generally, the professed defects are similar in kind to those utilized to gain a specious sense of control over the uncontrollable ("I was bad." "My allowance is too big." "I fight too much with my sister."); however, here they serve to maintain the delusion of parental infallibility.

In working with such children, the therapist must determine whether the parents are contributing through their need to present themselves as perfect. If so, he must help them appreciate that they are doing their child a disservice and that they are lessening rather than enhancing their child's respect for them. They must be helped to recognize that maintaining a facade of perfection is a sign of weakness; and that the stronger and more mature person is willing to admit his faults. It should be pointed out to them that their child will ultimately realize what they are doing and will lose respect for them because of their duplicity and weakness. They should be encouraged to expose their deficiencies to their children to an appropriate degree—every personal flaw need not be disclosed—in a natural way. To have them do so in a planned and contrived way is not likely to work. Rather this should be done as situations arise (and they inevitably do in the course of living) that would warrant such revelations. And the divorce situation is one that can allow for such appropriate disclosures. The parents have to be helped to recognize as well that the child's viewing his parents as perfect will contribute to his developing interpersonal difficulties with others. Such a notion will produce inevitable disappointment and disillusionment with all others he may encounter, who will inevitably reveal their defects. In fact, this very factor might contribute to dissatisfaction in and even dissolution of his own marriage someday. In addition, such an image of his parents may result in his setting perfectionistic standards for himself. And this may result in continual dissatisfaction, as he can never live up to the impossibly high standards. Parents with very low feelings of self-worth may not be able to give up their need for such mechanisms, but most with time and patience on the therapist's part can do so.

In work with such children, the child has to be helped to become more comfortable with imperfection in significant adult figures. The therapist's revealing his own imperfections (again as such revelations may arise in the natural course of events, rather than in contrived fashion) can help the child accept adult imperfection in general. *The Talking, Feeling, and Doing Game*, described in Chapter 3, provides the therapist with many opportunities for such disclosures.

The child's need to see his parents as perfect may also stem from lack of confidence in his own abilities to cope with many situations he is in fact quite capable of handling. Accordingly, attempts to enhance self-confidence and competence is important in helping such children give up the delusion of parental perfection. In Chapter 11 I will discuss in detail some of the approaches I utilize to help enhance a child's self-esteem. In addition, the reader may wish to refer to the chapter in my *Therapeutic Communication with Children* (1971b) in which I discuss the use of the Mutual Storytelling Technique in helping children with self-esteem problems.

Guilt over hostility. A child's self-blame may relate to his guilt over expressing the hostility toward one or both parents that is generally engendered by the divorce. Except in those relatively uncommon situations in which the child welcomes the parents' separation, the parent who leaves the home is viewed by the child as an abandoner and this cannot but make the child angry. As mentioned, the child of divorce may fear expressing anger toward the parent who has left the home, lest he see even less of him; and he may fear expressing anger toward the parent with whom he lives, lest that parent leave him also. If the parents believe that a child's being angry at them is inappropriate, "wrong," or "bad" then the child is likely to become even more inhibited. Observing the parents' altercations and the destructive effects of their anger on one another can so frighten a child that he may become inhibited in expressing his anger. Guilt over such anger is operative in the aforementioned depressive reaction in which the child's anger toward the parent(s) is directed against himself. Oedipal factors may contribute to the child's guilt. A boy, for example, may wish (consciously or unconsciously) that his father leave in order that he be left with full possession of his mother. When the father indeed does leave, the boy may harbor the belief that he was responsible. (In Chapter 12 I will discuss in detail the oedipal problems of children of divorce.) Beres (1958) describes how the child of divorce views the parent who leaves the home not only as abandoning him but as doing so with hostile intent. Via the mechanism of identification with the aggressor, the child identifies with the hostile abandoning parent and considers himself equally reprehensible.

Intrinsic to this guilt feeling is an anticipation of punishment, which may or may not be clearly realized. Although the relationship between guilt alleviation and punishment is quite complex, punishment (even self-denigration and social alienation) can as a rule reduce guilt over real transgression; but it does not, however, reduce effectively most forms of neurotic guilt. Because neurotic guilt is not usually related to real transgressions (if it is, the reaction is exaggerated because of neurotic factors) it is not readily assuaged by punishment. Whatever the form of the guilt, the child who harbors it may try to lessen it via punishment. He may overtly or covertly encourage scapegoatism. He may become accident-prone. Or he may become disruptive and do just those "bad" things that will predictably get him punished. Crumley and Blumenthal (1973) found this mechanism to be quite common among the children of military men. Considering themselves responsible for their fathers' long absences they encouraged punishment in order to relieve their guilt.

A child may utilize masochistic maneuvers in order to lessen guilt. Often, this adaptation is fostered via identification with a masochistic parent. The divorce situation lends itself well to the gratification of masochistic needs. Although many factors operate in the formation of the masochistic character disorder (and it is beyond the scope of this book to discuss them) one element in masochistic behavior that is relevant here is the masochist's communication to those around him: "How noble I am to be able to suffer what others may not be able to endure." The divorce situation generally provides the masochist with a constant supply of indignities and frustrations over which he can loudly moan (and thereby get the esteem and admiration that he imagines his complaints gain for him). The child of such a parent may take on the masochistic adaptation for its guilt-alleviating value, but may also utilize it in a specious attempt to enhance his self-esteem.

Masochism can also be used to express hostility. Among other things the masochist says to his tormentor: "Look how you make me suffer. What a wretch you are." His attempt is to evoke guilt and its attendant feelings of self-loathing in the other. A child of divorce with a parent who utilizes this mechanism is likely to take it on as well. And the divorce situation is likely to supply such a parent and child with a wealth of issues that can easily be utilized for this type of gratification.

I will discuss in detail in Chapter 9 the approaches I use to reduce guilt over the hostility a child may feel over his parents' separation and divorce. In the therapy of the masochistic adaptation, the therapist must direct his attention to the particular elements that have contributed to it. When it is being used to express hostility, the child must be helped to appreciate how misguided and ineffective a method of anger release it is. He should be assisted in utilizing more effective methods—ones that will more predictably change those situations that are generating his anger in the first place. When the child is using masochistic maneuvers to enhance self-esteem, he must be helped to appreciate that most people do not admire the sufferer (as he would like to believe) and that deep down he does not even respect himself for trying to enhance his self-esteem in this way. He must be helped to bolster his feelings of self-worth in truly effective ways. In Chapter 11 I will discuss in detail how one may attempt to do this. Helping the child appreciate the futility of the masochistic adaptation in the parent from whom he may have learned it can also be useful. Most important, one must determine in each child the specific factors contributing to his utilization of the mechanism. One must then focus on the alleviation.

Concluding comment. In the early days of psychoanalysis, Freud considered neuroses to be the result of dammed-up feelings (usually sexual) in people who were excessively guilty over such impulses. One of the primary purposes of therapy was the reduction of guilt these patients harbored. The therapy relied heavily on the analyst's using his authority as a trusted and respected person to help the patient feel less guilty. Although the method was subtle it essentially got across to the patient the following message: "If I, an admired and respected psychoanalyst, say it is okay to have such feelings, you can be sure it is." Although things are far more complex (as Freud soon realized), this element is still present in most, if not all, analyses. (Many analysts will still not allow themselves to accept this because it places the analyst in such an unflatteringly grandiose and somewhat coercive position.)

This approach to the treatment of people with inordinate amounts of guilt is still useful in reducing certain uncomplicated forms of guilt in dependent and unsophisticated adults, as well as most children. In working with children who exhibit this simpler form of guilt (over anger, for example) I might say: "I've seen many children whose parents have separated and I cannot recall ever seeing one who wasn't angry about it." Here, by my letting the child know that everyone has this reaction he may become more comfortable expressing his feelings. Or I might say: "Your father and I have different opinions about whether or not it's all right for a child to think curse words about a parent. I believe every child has such thoughts at times. The wise child knows how to use his angry thoughts in a way that helps solve the problem that's making such words come into his mind." Hopefully, my relationship with the child will be such that my opinion here will become his, that he will become more accepting of his angry feelings, and hence less guilty over them. Of course, these comments to the child serve as mere points of departure for deeper and more extensive discussion with him. This aspect of the therapeutic approach to simple guilt and blame in children of divorce is utilized in the chapter "Who's to Blame?" in my *The Boys and Girls Book about Divorce* (1970b, 1971a). Here the power of the written word can be useful in assuaging this form of guilt reaction.

Chapter 8

IMMATURITY AND HYPERMATURITY

Immaturity

In response to a trauma, or to any situation in which a child's usual satisfactions are not adequately provided, it is common for him to regress to earlier developmental levels in the hope of regaining gratifications enjoyed previously. Or the child may remain fixated at the level he has reached in order to avoid taking on the newer demands attendant to higher levels of maturation. And parental separation is the kind of trauma that may result in such regression or fixation.

Regressive manifestations. Following the separation a child may start sucking his thumb again, using baby talk, and becoming in general more infantile and demanding. He may ask to be fed or to resume using his bottle. The fully toilet trained child may start soiling again or may ask his parent to wipe him when he goes to the bathroom. Morrison (1974) found enuresis to be twice as common in children of divorced homes than in children living in intact homes. The child may feign illness (stomachaches, headaches, nausea, etc.) in order to have an excuse to avoid the demands of school and to remain home and be put to bed and be pampered. Temper tantrums, irritability, and low frustration tolerance may be exhibited more frequently. The child may respond to the new responsibilities of living in a one-parent home by whining and complaining that he just cannot do the things asked of him. He may become clinging and refuse to go out and play or visit friends, when he had previously done so without difficulty. A younger child in the household will often provide a model for such regressive manifestations and makes their appearance more likely.

At times the child will parentify an older sibling or peer in a manner similar to that observed by Freud and Burlingham (1944a, 1944b) in war orphans and children separated from their parents by wartime conditions.

Parental contributions to the child's immaturity. Generally, such fixations and regressions are transient and clear up within a few weeks or months following the separation. When they persist, other factors are usually operative, the most common of which is parental overprotection and other forms of encouragement of the immature behavior. And the divorced parent is very likely to provide such encouragement as a result of the guilt he or she may feel over the split in the family. Overindulging a child is one of the most common ways to assuage such guilt. Visiting fathers, especially, are prone to do this. They, as the "abandoners," almost routinely feel guilty and are most likely to attempt to alleviate such guilt by providing the child with continual fun, games, and freedom from discipline during their limited visitation time. Because the father sees the children when he is not working, he has the time for these indulgences. The mother, however, cannot so readily provide such gratifications for the child if she is to most effectively run her household. Yet she may do so as well, her time limitations notwithstanding.

Either parent may see the separation as a threat to feelings of parental adequacy. The parent may therefore overindulge the child, thereby hoping to prove his or her competence. Or the parents may compete with one another over who can be the better parent, and the degree to which one can keep the child happy may be used as the measure of competence. Each parent may overindulge the child in order to win his affection away from the other, to gain an ally in the parental conflict. Such a child is being used as a vehicle to express parental hostility and is being bribed to serve as a pawn in the parents' battle.

A mother left with the children may try to lessen her feelings of abandonment and loneliness by keeping the children in a more dependent state than is warranted. She may have had past insecurities in relating to adults and the failure of her marriage may entrench these. Fearing further failures and rejections, she may become excessively involved with her children—captive companions who have already proved their deep affection for her. Such a mother may find excuses for the children's not playing in the street, visiting friends, and taking other steps to independence. Under the guise of concern for their welfare she provides herself with companionship and makes herself feel more useful. In the extreme, such children may develop neurotic inhibitions in school and social relationships because such involvements and successes, as steps toward independence, create feelings of disloyalty toward their mother. They may even remain in their homes when adults, never leaving the mother who "needs them so much."

A woman may feel that she has failed as a wife, but may try to compensate by proving herself successful as a mother. She may need to overdo this and become overindulgent. Or she may try to use a male child as a substitute for her lost husband. (It is far less common for a husband to do this with a daughter because his opportunities to find another woman are greater than his wife's to find another man—especially when she has custody of the children.) Such a mother may become seductive with the child, make comments about how he is now to be "the man of the house," make the boy her advisor and counselor, and reveal confidences to him. The oedipal problems that may result in such a boy will be discussed in Chapter 12.

The aforementioned reasons for a parent's becoming overprotective are a direct outgrowth of the divorce situation. Divorced parents, however, may excessively indulge their children for additional reasons which may or may not relate to the divorce. A parent may overindulge a child as a reaction formation to basic feelings of hostility toward it. Such a parent may resent the obligations, frustrations, and restrictions of parenthood and be too guilty over such feelings to allow them to come into conscious awareness. The overprotection serves to deny and repress these hostilities. This mechanism reveals itself most clearly in the parent who frequently anticipates harm befalling the child even when the situation does not warrant such concern and other parents do not envision danger in the same situation. Of course, the separated parent may have additional hostilities toward the child to deal with. For both parents the children cannot but place restrictions on their lives that they could very well do without. The children's very existence requires both parents to maintain a relationship with one another that they most often would have liked to completely sever, and they make each parent somewhat less attractive as a potential mate to others. These additional sources of potential resentment are likely to intensify the overprotective adaptation used to deny hostility.

Overindulgence of a child can be used in the service of vicariously gratifying parental dependencies. The parent, by projecting himself onto the child, can satisfy his own desire to be indulged. It is as if each time he is ministering to the child, he is ministering to himself. And the more gratification the child derives from such indulgence, the greater the parent's. A divorced parent may experience an intensification of such dependencies after the separation. This is especially true of a parent who has been abandoned.

A parent may try to compensate for feelings of inadequacy by trying to produce and rear a perfect child. Oversolicitous attitudes may develop in the service of this cause. Working on the premise that a perfect child is one who is always happy, the child's requests are rarely refused. The divorced parent may have even more reason to feel inadequate: the failure of a marriage cannot but lower one's self-esteem. Accordingly, this method of compensating for lowered feelings of self-worth is more likely to be utilized by the divorced parent.

The masochistic parent, who finds opportunities for suffering by making painful sacrifices for the child, may use overindulgence as a way of making such sacrifices. Another aspect of masochism pertinent to my discussion is the masochist's feeling that he is not basically of much use or value to others and that if he asks anything of others he will be rejected and abandoned. He believes that he will only be accepted by others if he relates on their terms. More specifically, he sees himself as capable of attracting only sadistic people —those who measure the affection of others by how much pain they are willing to suffer for the loved one. Accordingly, he operates on the principle: "The more pain I suffer on behalf of the one I love, the more I prove my affection." Therefore, he allows himself to be maltreated—to be used as a scapegoat, as an object for the release of hostility. And sacrificially giving to a child can provide just such gratification. The masochistically inclined parent who gets divorced may react to the separation by an intensification of the need for masochistic gratification. The wife, for example, married to a sadistic husband may have to find a new person to torture her after he leaves. And a child may be the most convenient person to serve as a substitute. And sacrificial giving (and its attendant overprotection) may be selected as the mode of gratifying this need.

A parent may overindulge a child in order to obtain vicarious gratifications that compensate for his own frustrations in life. The parent who raises a child in accordance with the principle "I want to give him everything I didn't have" can gain through the child some compensation for the disillusions and disappointments of his own life. Overprotection can enable such a parent to live through the child and compensate for his own privations. And the parent need not use the child to gratify past deprivations—present and even anticipated privations can be lessened via this mechanism. Making the child into everything the parent *wished to be but wasn't and will never be* can provide such a parent with solace for his disappointment with his own life. We all do this to some extent and it is healthy to a degree because it serves to provide a child with parental encouragement in his life's pursuits. However, when a parent's view of the ideal existence for a child is that he always gets what he wants, when he wants it, then parental overindulgence occurs and the child is likely to become overdependent. The divorced parent, having another reason for feeling deprived, may have an even greater need than the parent in a relatively stable marriage to utilize this compensatory mechanism.

A parent may keep a child at an immature level in order to protect himself against the lowered feelings of self-worth that would result if the child became his equal. Such insecure parents are essentially in competition with their children. They keep them down in order to maintain a specious sense of superiority. They frequently communicate to the child such messages as "You're not old enough to do this" and "You're not mature enough to handle that" in areas where the parents of their children's peers see no difficulties. The divorced parent is even more prone to feel insecure and may therefore be more likely to use this form of overprotection.

There are parents who overindulge a child because they cannot tolerate anger—regardless of the age of the person who exhibits it and regardless of its appropriateness. Such a parent may live by the principle "I must never do anything that will get another person angry at me." The best way to avoid the hostility of others is to avoid their being frustrated, that is, to do everything they want. When this principle is applied to such a person's child, the latter becomes overindulged and pampered. Since the child of divorce is likely to be angry and even more demanding than usual (at least around the time of separation), the likelihood of his being overindulged by such a parent becomes greater.

Therapeutic approaches to the immature child. Parental counseling is crucial to the treatment of most childrens' regressive and dependency problems because the parental contributions are often so significant. The parents should be helped to appreciate that regressive behavior following separation is common and normal. As Kliman (1968) suggests, the parents do well to allow intermittent gratification of such regressive cravings, especially in the period immediately following the separation. However, these indulgences should be gradually reduced, lest they become entrenched. The failure to allow such limited gratification of regressive tendencies during this period may result in the child's desiring to utilize them to an inordinate degree, and the foundation for pathological involvement in them will have been laid. Although this consideration must be kept in mind the parents should be advised regarding the discouragement of specific symptom perpetuation. For example, they should not comply with a child's request to stay home from school because of minor physical symptoms. Rather they should be advised to keep a child home from school only when there is bona fide evidence of physical disease. They should be encouraged to err on the side of sending a sick child to school and reassured that at the very worst he will be sent home, and that such an eventuality incurs essentially no risk or danger to the child.

The child who starts to wet should be asked to assist in the changing (and even cleaning) of his sheets. And the child who soils should also assist (to the degree appropriate to his age) in his cleaning himself and his underwear. Infantile demands should not be complied with and the child should not be allowed to manipulate his parents with temper tantrums. Baby talk should be discouraged by the parents' refusal to respond to communications made with infantile intonation. The child who wants to be fed should not be, even at the risk of his not eating (some parents may have to be reassured repeatedly that such a course will not result in the child's dying of starvation or developing a host of serious nutritional deficiencies). His request to have his bottle again might be complied with to a limited degree (in accordance with my previous statement about allowing for some indulgence in the regressive pattern). And appropriate disciplinary measures should be imposed on the child who shirks from his usual (and now new) responsibilities.

Most important, the therapist must determine the exact nature of the parental contributions (some of the more common of which have been discussed above). He then does well to direct his therapeutic approaches to the alleviation of these factors to the degree that he can. Although some mechanisms may be deep-seated (e.g. masochism) others (e.g. seductivity, using the child as confidant) may be reduced by counseling. But even when it is not possible for a parent to work out the underlying psychological problems that may be contributing to the overprotection, a certain amount of conscious control is usually still possible—so that the parental contributing factors may still be reduced.

With regard to my work with the child himself, I strictly avoid indulging any regressive manifestations that he may exhibit in my sessions with him. Above all, the therapist must not provide the child with the same neurotic responses the parents do. In addition, when my relationship with the child has been established and I know that he will be able to tolerate criticism, I will confront him with my negative reactions to his infantile behavior, e.g., "If you knew how you looked with your thumb in your mouth, I don't think that you'd do it." Such confrontations are made in the service of making the symptoms ego-alien (regressive symptoms, probably because of pleasure they afford the child, are often ego-syntonic). If this can be accomplished the child will more likely be motivated to remove them. In addition, an appreciation of the socially alienating effects of a form of behavior can contribute to a child's trying to gain conscious control over exhibiting a symptom. Although such suppression does not get to the underlying causes of a problem, it does, in my opinion, play a role in its treatment.

The primary focus in the therapy of regressive manifestations should of course be on underlying factors. Each case must be evaluated individually to determine what these specific factors are. A common cause of the child's regressing is his belief that the separation will deprive him entirely of his father. The child has to be reassured that this will not be the case (except, of course, in the rare situation when it is). However, the therapist has to help the child have *living experiences* demonstrating that his predictions are correct. Only then will the therapist's reassurances contribute to the reduction of the child's need to regress. The child must be helped to acquire substitute gratifications and to appreciate that separation need not result in the terrible deprivations he anticipates. To this end, more meaningful relationships with peers and other adults should be encouraged. Again, it is only when these are actually accomplished that the child will be able to lessen his need for the regressive adaptation.

Hypermaturity

When parents separate, the children are generally required to assume new responsibilities and obligations. Some regress in response to the new demands and others rise to the occasion and attain a new salutary maturity. There are others, however, whose new maturity is spurious. It has an exaggerated, misguided, or inappropriate quality that betokens a basic speciousness. It is to this pathological form of maturity, this hypermaturity, that I direct my attention here.

The child may manifest hypermaturity by becoming a caricature of an adult. He or she may take on adult mannerisms, and speech intonations and affectations. Large words and adult terminology may be utilized at every opportunity. The child may become paternalistic to other children and treat them in a condescending manner (much to the latter's alienation). Scolding, reprimanding, disciplining, and lecturing younger children may become quite common. At school the child may become teacher's helper (sometimes invited, sometimes not). The naive teacher may welcome the help and be delighted with the child; the classmates, however, may refer to the child as a "goody-goody" or "teacher's pet."

A number of factors may operate both singly and in combination to produce such behavior. At times there is parental sanction. The parents may be impressed with the child's adultlike behavior and even show him or her off to friends—thereby providing significant reinforcement to the pattern. A parent may use the child as a confidant, thereby encouraging premature acquisition of adult behavioral patterns. Seductive behavior and utilization of the child as a surrogate for the absent parent can also contribute to the child's developing the hypermaturity adaptation. The dependent parent may try to get the child to replace the absent parent, who served as protector, and may use various coercive methods (such as guilt evocation) to achieve this end.

Even without parental sanction, the child himself may assume the role. At times it serves to regain the lost parent by the process of incorporation and identification. Such an adaptation is seen most frequently following the death of a parent, but is also utilized by children after parental separation. The adaptation may be a way of compensating for the sense of impotence that the child may feel over the separation. Children are weak and helpless; they have no choice but to bear the rejections, abandonments, and other forms of maltreatment they may suffer at the hands of adults. By assuming adult status the child gains a delusional protection from such indignities. The child may view the separation as proof of the unreliability of adults; by becoming an adult himself—and self-reliant—he reduces such anxieties. Boys, especially, may acquire a new toughness in order to defend themselves against the sense of impotence that the separation causes in them.

The hypermaturity may be an attempt to regain the parent who has left the home. The girl may have learned that father left mother because she wasn't a good wife. Accordingly, she may try to surpass mother as a wife in order to attract father back to the household. Similarly the boy, learning that father was asked to leave the house because he wasn't a good husband, may use this as an excuse to gratify unresolved oedipal fantasies and become hypermature in the attempt to attract his mother. (I will discuss this in further detail in Chapter 12.) The children may understand that the separation took place because one or both of the parents was "bad." Accordingly, they may try to be very "good" in order to protect themselves from being ejected from the household. And assuming an adult role, in which the child behaves in an exemplary fashion, can provide protection against this eventuality.

In the clinical example presented below, the child exhibits what I consider primarily healthy forms of mature behavior in reaction to her father's leaving the home and her mother's psychiatric disturbance.

Clinical Example
Helen rises to the occasion admirably.

Helen initially came to treatment at the age of seven because of frequent nightmares, obsessions over losing things, and hypermature behavior. The parents had been divorced two years prior to my first seeing her, and the patient was living alone with her mother. The mother suffered with marked mood swings of elation and depression, which at times bordered on the psychotic. Helen was treated for one-and-a-half years with good results. She returned again at age ten with complaints of poor concentration, insomnia, and deterioration of her schoolwork. She was very bright and had always been among the highest in her class. During the six months prior to returning to treatment the mother had been hospitalized as a result of an attempted suicide. Subsequent to her discharge, she became agitated, went on buying sprees, and became sexually promiscuous. It was clear that she was suffering with a manic-depressive psychosis. Helen's second treatment experience lasted four months. This story was told during the second month:

Patient: On an Easter holiday a little girl named Julie went to her grandmother's house for the weekend and her grandmother lived in Florida. This little girl went there for a vacation just because she had never been to Florida before and her cousins were going to be there and she hadn't seen them in a long time. So while she was there—her grandmother lived right on the ocean—in the morning if she wanted to get up and go for a swim, if you had somebody watching you so nothing would happen, you could just get up and go. You wouldn't have to go to the beach or anything. It would be right in front of your house.

One morning Julie decided to go swimming and she got her cousins to go with her. She had two cousins. They were both girls, I guess. They all went swimming together and this happened practically every morning as a routine because they all liked swimming so much.

One morning one of Julie's cousins decided she should go swimming all alone because she wanted to go swimming and everybody else was asleep. They had been up late the night before trying to get something on the new television that they had gotten for Christmas. She didn't wake up anybody. She just went swimming and all of a sudden a big wave came and it knocked her over. Nothing serious happened to her and she thought it was nothing. But it was very rough and she wasn't very sure about staying out in the ocean or not. So she went on swimming and she got knocked over again. This time her head got hit against a rock on the bottom of the ocean and it began to bleed. She was conscious and she got up but she didn't want to tell anybody what had happened to her. So her sister, one of Julie's cousins, found out that she had hurt her head and so then she thought that she should tell some adult because something could have happened to her, but she didn't want to. She wasn't going to squeal on her own sister.

Finally Julie found out also and Julie felt that it would be more important to have her cousin healthy and everything than it would be to not tell anybody just because she didn't want anybody to know that she had gone swimming alone. So Julie did tell her grandmother and they went to a doctor and the doctor said the cousin was okay but it could have been a lot more serious if they hadn't done anything about it. Julie's cousin was mad at her for a while because she had told, but afterwards she realized herself that it's better to be healthy than it is to be, you know, than it is to try and hide something.

The moral of this story is: tell the truth and it will help you to stay healthy.

The cousin whose head got hit against a rock and who almost drowned represents the mother and her attempted suicide. That Helen depicts her as a peer is not surprising in that the mother, in her illness, was exhibiting many childish qualities. The patient was indeed assuming adult responsibilities in her relationship with her, and I would not have been surprised if the mother had appeared as the patient's child in the girl's stories. The cousin's request that no one be told about the accident relates to the patient's awareness, at some level, of her mother's wish to deny her illness. In fact, the mother, although in treatment, had practically no insight into the depth of her difficulties. Julie's mature decision not to honor the cousin's request for secrecy was a message to me that the patient was seeking my aid in handling her mother. Living alone with a mother who is intermittently psychotic is an overwhelming burden for any child and although this patient was doing admirably she still needed help. The story was a clear statement of this need.

Although she did not at first appreciate its significance, the girl was bright enough to analyze the story. We then directed our attention to ways in which she could more effectively handle the situation with her mother. In subsequent sessions, we spoke about what she could do about her mother's irresponsibility in caring for the home; her leaving the child alone for long periods of time; her bringing men into the house; and her excessive spending. The girl responded to these challenges with a degree of maturity and efficiency that was at times amazing.

Six weeks later, Helen told this story. Again, instead of telling a story in response, I analyzed her story with her. This time the analytic inquiry was recorded.

Patient: There was a girl named Linda and it was a rainy day and she was inside the house. It was too rainy to go outside so she decided to make something out of an old cardboard box and some paints and brushes and other things that she had. So she took the box and she cut four sides of it and she made like an old-fashioned dollhouse and it was very nice and she painted it. She decorated it and made furniture for it out of the remaining part of the box. When she was finished with that and finished admiring it, she decided to go over to her friend's house. She went over there and played a while and when she came back she saw her cat looking guiltily and the cat had by accident pushed down the house. It wasn't completely ruined but she had to repair a couple of parts of it and so she decided that since she was going to fix it up anyway she would add some more things to it and make it nice enough to give for a present to her mother. So she got some old clothes of hers and she made some curtains and tablecloths and such things for it. She put them in and she decorated it and instead of having it all covered so that you wouldn't be able to look in if you just passed by—you'd have to open up or look through the windows or lift up the roof or something. So she took some glass that had been broken before from a window when somebody had thrown a ball through by accident, and in just the right shape, so she made like a big glass window so you could see clear through. So now it was very dark and she had to get it out of the cat's reach so that she could save it for her mother's birthday. So she put it high on top of her closet and when her mother's birthday came she gave it to her. Her mother was very pleased with it.

The moral of the story is: if something terrible happens, don't feel badly enough so that you can't repair it again.

Therapist: That was a very good story, Helen. Now let me take a little time out to think about what it means. I have some idea what your story means, but I'd like to hear from you what you think it means. See if you can figure it out. Let's put this microphone in between us. It will pick up what both of us are saying. Now, let's just talk about it. What do you think?

P: I think the girl is me and the house is my mother, but I can't think what's left.

T: You think the girl is you and the house is your mother. If the house is your mother, what does it mean then?

P: That when she gets sick I repair her.

T: When she gets sick you repair her. What about that?

P: But I don't think that's the way I feel.

T: Now I'll tell you what I think the story means. I think you divide your mother into two parts there—the sick part of your mother and the healthy part of your mother.

P: What's the healthy part?

T: The healthy part of your mother is your mother as she appears and the sick part of your mother is the cat. And the house is your house. Here your house is very nice and then your mother gets sick and that kind of wrecks the house in a way. The sick part of your mother wrecks the house. Right? Disorganizes it, gets it all upset. Then you are put in the position of having to repair it again because your mother is too sick. Then you repair it and you hide the house from the sick part of your mother. You don't let the sick part of your mother destroy the house again, just like you—in the story you put the house . . .

P: But then I gave it to her.

T: You just hide it up in the closet so that the cat can't get to it.

P: I know, but who is the person I gave it to?

T: The healthy part of your mother. You preserved the house for the healthy part of your mother. You're watching that the sick part of your mother doesn't destroy things again. Aren't you?

P: Yeah.

T: Aren't you on the lookout for the sick parts of your mother?

P: I feel it's kind of fiction-like. It's not really realistic enough. I'm not on the lookout and I'm not like saving the house from her.

T: Aren't you on the lookout when you say that you'd better be careful she's "high [manic]."

P: I know but . . .

T: Don't you kind of see your mother as having two personalities, a sick and a healthy personality?

P: No.

T: Well, when she's high, isn't she different than when she's not high?

P: Yes. She's still the same person.

T: Yes, but she changes. Not that she's completely different, but she changes in a way. When she's sick her personality changes. Doesn't it?

P: Uh-huh.

T: When she's high her personality changes. She buys a lot of things. She also gets very depressed when she's sick. It's almost like two people. It's the same person but she has two different aspects to her personality.

P: Right.

T: It's the sick part that you've constantly got to watch out for. Right?

P: No. Cause if you—it's not really my job, but if I—like if somebody finds out that she's high fast enough she won't necessarily get lost.

T: Right, but you have to watch out for that.

P: I know, but in those aspects, you know; are you talking about high and low or are you talking about normal?

T: Normal and sick.

P: Oh, well. That's my job.

T: That's right. You keep your eye open for her if you see signs of sickness and I think the sick part of your mother is the cat, which can jump and do dangerous things and destroy the house. The healthy part of your mother is the normal mother whom you give the present to. The cat destroyed the house once—not completely—but it did a lot of damage—when it was your sick mother. Now, you're more cautious. You take the house and you put it up in the closet so that the cat can't get to it, which stands for your watching out that your mother—the sick part of your mother—isn't destructive again. And then in the story you're successful in doing that and then you and the healthy part of your mother enjoy the house.

P: All right. That's what the dream means but what does it mean in aspect to me. I mean what's actually happening?

T: In aspect to what? Well, it tells what did happen. Right? The cat destroyed the house—well almost destroyed the house. That means your mother when she was very sick almost destroyed the house.

P: The way I look at it.

T: Right. And now what this dream—it's not a dream really—what this story is saying is that you are going to be more cautious. You're watching carefully and you're going to protect the house from the sick part of her and it expresses the hope that you will be successful in avoiding the sick part of her and that you and she can enjoy the healthy part or good parts of the house together.

The story reveals how at times a patient's clinical improvement can be a step ahead of psychodynamic understanding. Helen was very much involved in looking for signs of her mother's decompensation and actively participated in keeping the household organized. In spite of our discussions regarding the details of these activities, she had difficulty analyzing the story when we came to the point of discussing her mother as sick. Helen wished to consciously deny this in spite of the fact that all her behavior indicated acute awareness of her mother's pathology. On further discussion she was able to appreciate the story's significance. Such analysis was helpful in further clarifying her role and, I believe, supported and mobilized her further in her tasks.

I might add here that I intermittently communicated with the mother's psychiatrist. We both felt that the situation, although a very difficult one, was not grave enough to warrant the mother's hospitalization. In spite of her difficulties, the mother was effectively working; she was meaningfully involved in her treatment; and there was no significant danger of suicide.

One week later, Helen reported this dream:

I was on a beach with my mother and father. Something bad was going on. There was a monster or a bad person there. It wasn't bad enough to get worried about. I don't know what he was supposed to do. I went swimming and nothing happened with the monster. Then we got into a beach jeep and went off.

Helen and I discussed the dream and concluded that the monster represents the sick part of her mother which the child is coming to see as less threatening as she develops the means to handle her. In addition, the presence of the monster does not interfere with her involving herself in her usual activities, which are symbolized in the dream by going swimming.

Later in the session, Helen told the following story:

Patient: There is a girl named Laurie and she went to a school in New York. She had a friend in her school that wasn't very smart and they had a test in grammar and Laurie got a very good mark, but her friend did not. Her friend got very upset about it and she made many resolutions that she would do better in the future. They were coming right up to spring vacation and she took practically all her books home and said that she was going to study a lot. Her friend's name was Stephanie.

So Laurie called Stephanie up during their vacation and asked her how much she had studied during the vacation. She hadn't done very much. Then she called her up towards the end and she still hadn't done very much, and when she came back to school she still hadn't done very much.

Laurie, instead of getting all upset about how her friend hadn't been trying, went out and had a good time anyway, but she was still a little concerned about how her friend ought to be doing better. So she let her friend know about this because she thought that if she didn't start working hard she might not pass the grade or anything. So her friend did start getting better marks until finally she was just as good and sometimes even better than Laurie.

The moral of this story is that if a friend of yours isn't doing well in something, try to help them as much as you can, but don't go overboard and get yourself all into the problem and concerned all about it. Just try to help as much as you can.

Therapist: Let's see if we can analyze this story. Do you have any ideas?

P: No.

T: You really do not have any ideas about this story? Not at all? Are you telling the truth?

P: I think I understand the moral.

T: What's your idea about the moral?

P: About the same thing that had to do with the dream.

T: All right. How so?

P: Well, instead of getting all upset about the monster and not going swimming; to be concerned about it a little bit, but still go swimming.

T: Does the story deal with the same thing?

P: I don't know. I really don't.

T: Well, let's say that you're Laurie. Who would your friend be?

P: Well, wait a minute. After spring vacation—you mean . . .

T: You see, you're Laurie and Stephanie is your mother and she's doing poorly in her tests means that she has some trouble with her health and you have to worry about her and you're concerned.

P: Oh, I understand.

T: Go ahead. Finish it.

P: I get concerned and I start telling her that she ought to start getting better and see a doctor or something and then she does get better.

T: Which is what's happening to your mother now. Isn't she kind of better?

P: Oh, yes.

T: So you bugged her awhile and she did get back in shape. Hmm?

P: What about the concern of me? I mean at the end, about not being concerned about the . . .

T: But at the end you say: "Laurie, instead of getting all upset about how her friend hadn't been trying, went out and had a good time anyway, but she was still a little concerned about how her friend ought to be doing better." So it's just like it was in your dream: you're concerned but not too much. I think it's the same thing as the dream. What do you think?

P: I think the dream was better.

T: In what way?

P: I don't know, except that it seems that I was more concerned in this one.

T: You're more concerned in this story. Well, the story tells about what you're feeling today.

P: And the dream?

T: The dream is telling you what was happening a few days ago—the day that you dreamed it.

P: Oh, can a dream tell what is happening on that day?

T: Mainly that day and the day or two before—about how you've been feeling about things.

P: So you think that's good too?

T: Yes, I think it's pretty good. It still shows some concern but there's an awareness that something has been done and things have gotten better. Okay.

P: Okay.

The dream and story are typical of the pre-termination phase of therapy. They reveal that major problems are close to being resolved. There is a realistic concern for her sick mother, but not the exaggerated involvement which would deprive her of her own gratifications. A healthy balance is being achieved. They also demonstrate how, in this stage of treatment, the therapist may use the story like a dream and directly analyze it rather than using it as the nucleus of his own story.

Two weeks later Helen related this dream:

Once there were two girls named Leslie and Joan. One weekend they went skating together in Central Park. Leslie was a fairly good skater but Joan wasn't. When Joan got on the ice she had to be careful. Leslie helped her. Leslie had a lot of fun but Joan didn't. As the day went on Joan got much better.

The moral of this story is: if at first you don't succeed, try, try again.

The story was analyzed with Helen in a manner similar to that previously described. She denied conscious awareness that it pertained to her situation with her mother. However, it was not difficult for her to recognize that Joan represented her sick mother and Leslie, the patient herself. Joan, like her mother, is "skating on ice." She is in a precarious life situation, "has to be careful," and requires Leslie's help. Leslie is capable of having fun, but Joan isn't—a clear reference to the mother's depression. The story ends with Joan's improvement—an accurate reflection of the clinical situation in which both the mother and the daughter were doing much better.

In the subsequent discussion we both agreed that the patient was ready to discontinue treatment.

Chapter 9

ANGER

The words *anger*, *hostility*, and *aggression* are often used interchangeably. Although there is some overlap in their meanings, there are also differences which should be made clear if discussion of these concepts is to be meaningful.

Anger often connotes an internal state, whereas *hostility* implies externally directed action. We speak of hostility between nations, but not of anger. The word *anger* can often convey a greater intensity of expression than the term *hostility*. One would more likely say "He was so angry that he felt his head would split" than "He was so hostile that he felt that his head would split." These distinctions, however, are minor; therefore, I use the terms synonymously.

Anger has two components: the psychological and the physiological. The former includes both angry thoughts and the affect, anger (the psychic component of the feeling). The physiological factor includes concomitant body reactions, such as changes in blood pressure, respiratory rate, and pulse rate. The physical constituent is certainly inherent, and identical responses can be seen and measured in many animals. Many higher animals appear to experience the psychic factor as well, and the tendency toward anthropomorphization often leads to the questionable assumption that they feel angry affect and even think angry thoughts.

Aggression can, on the one hand, be used in a complimentary sense when it means assertiveness: "This organization is looking for aggressive young men." On the other hand, when such aggression results in insensitivity to the feelings of others or when people are hurt, the word is definitely pejorative: "He's so aggressive, he doesn't care whom he pushes aside to get what he wants." At other times *aggression* is used as if it were synonymous with *anger* or *hostility*. Because of the confusion that this word sometimes creates, I try to avoid it and instead use *assertion* or *self-assertion* for desirable aggression, and otherwise use *anger* or *hostility*.

I believe that the capacity to react with anger is innate. This inborn physiological mechanism is activated by danger and enhances our efficiency in warding off and fighting threats to our well-being. We fight more efficiently when mobilized by a moderate amount of anger (too much anger may make us less effective); conversely, absence or inhibition of anger can compromise us significantly in dealing with threatening situations. Accordingly, anger has survival value. I believe also that the most predictable stimulus for evoking the anger response is frustration. Frustration occurs whenever we are thwarted (or believe we are being thwarted) from obtaining something we desire, regardless of whether it is vital to our survival. I would go so far as to say that frustration, if experienced long enough, will inevitably trigger the anger response. It is the purpose of anger, then, to enhance our efficiency in removing the noxious stimulus that frustrates us.

Sources of Anger in the Child of Divorce

The child of divorce has usually been exposed to an inordinate amount of frustrating experiences. The constant dissension between his parents prior to the separation deprives him of the calm and loving environment so necessary to psychological health. And following the separation he usually feels abandoned—and this cannot but make him feel angry. The divorce situation usually provides other sources of anger as well. The child may resent being different from his peers. They have two parents living in the household; he has only one. (This is especially true in areas—increasingly less common—where there are few divorced children.) The divorce generally causes each parent new frustrations and resentments, even though older ones may have been reduced or removed. The parent may still be so preoccupied with these that he or she has little benevolent affect available for the child. Resentments toward the spouse may be directed toward the child. A mother, for example, may repeatedly berate her son with such comments as "You remind me of your father" and "You're just like your father." She may use such identifications as justification for scapegoating him. The child is captive prey; he is too small to fight and too dependent to run. He therefore serves well as a target for parental hostility. And being so used is likely to engender reactive hostility in him. He may even take the parental "hint" and exhibit the very behavior the parent accuses him of manifesting. Such compliance may enable him to gain attention that he would otherwise not get.

The child may find a source of anger in the fact that his mother may have had to take on a job and is increasingly absent. The mother may resent her children for their very existence—lessening as they do her chances for re-marriage, restricting her dating, necessitating her having contact with their father, and providing her with new responsibilities she might prefer to do without. And the father too, to a lesser extent, may resent the children for these reasons as well. The child will sense these parental frustrations and react in kind. Social tradition (often incorporated into the legal) may have dictated the mother's assuming custody when the father would have been the preferable parent. Such a mother's resentment provides the child with yet another reason to be angry.

Neurotic Handling of Anger

I use the term neurotic to refer to those adaptations to the anger in which: 1) an intrapsychic conflict has arisen, 2) inappropriate mechanisms have been used in the attempt to resolve such conflict, and 3) the methods of reso-lution utilized do not involve gross breaks with reality, that is, are not psy-chotic. Generally such modes of adaptation result from the child's being guilty over or fearful of expressing his anger. He may have grown up in a home where he was taught (overtly or covertly) that expression of anger toward a parent is reprehensible. Or, observing the devastating effects of the expression of anger on each of his parents has inhibited him from reacting similarly. As mentioned, by its very nature the divorce situation is likely to inhibit the child in expressing his anger. One parent has already left the household; expressing resentment might result in his seeing even less of him. And he may fear exhibiting hostility toward the remaining parent, lest he or she leave as well.

In my discussion of these neurotic mechanisms I confine myself here to the *child of divorce* and the way in which maladaptive reactions to his *anger* may contribute to the formation of neurotic symptoms. In no way is my presenta-tion intended to be an exhaustive discussion of the many factors that con-tribute to such symptomatology.

Denial. One of the most common mechanisms that the child may utilize to deal with his hostility is to deny it. Most often this is unconscious—the child is really not aware that he is angry; although, at times, a child may be aware that he is but will be afraid to admit it to others. Powerful repressive forces are usually operative when this mechanism is used. It is probably the most primitive neurotic mechanism in that the individual deals with a danger (in this case an inner one, that is, one's own anger and its threatened eruption into conscious awareness) by simply making believe it is not there. It is not surprising that such a simplistic adaptation is attractive to the child and therefore one of the most commonly utilized by children.

When asked how he feels about some of the obviously anger-provoking situations attendant on the separation, the child may respond with a host of rationalizations designed to protect him from awareness of his anger. For example, one son of a physician stated, "My father can't come and see me because he'd have to leave his patients and some of them might die." Another patient, in response to my question regarding her feelings about her father's limited involvement since leaving the home, stated, "It doesn't bother me. I know he has to spend so much time working to send us money that he hasn't time to see us or call us."

Nightmares. All children experience occasional nightmares. The child of divorce is more likely to have nightmares and this relates, more than anything else, I believe, to repression of the hostility engendered by his parents' separation and his fear of becoming consciously aware of such anger. In the typical nightmare the child is fearful that a malevolent figure (a robber, a monster, etc.) will enter his room. Usually the intruder comes in from a window or closet or from under the bed. I believe that the interloper is the incarnation of the child's unacceptable angry impulses that have been relegated to the unconscious. At night, when other distracting stimuli are removed, the pent-up hostilities of the day, which continually press for expression, are attended to. Daytime activities such as sports, sibling fights, and television, which have provided some release of hostility, are no longer available. At night, residual hostility from unresolved daytime frustrations press for release. In the nightmare, the symbolic derivatives of the child's anger (the robber, etc.) press for expression into the child's conscious awareness (symbolized by the child's room). The greater the child's guilt over his anger, the more it will be repressed. The urgency for release becomes correspondingly greater, as does his fear of the anger symbols when they threaten to erupt into conscious awareness. Up to a point, the more guilt-ridden the child the more frightening the nightmare. When the guilt is extremely great, however, even the symbolic incarnations will be repressed, and the child will be "protected" from his nightmares—and this vehicle for release of anger will then no longer be available to him.

In addition, the malevolent figures can represent the child's hostility projected outward (they are outside his room), or they can symbolize hostile elements within significant figures (such as his parents). When the frightening figure threatens to abduct the child, then the dream may reflect separation anxieties. The nightmare, like all dreams, is rich in meaning, and many elements contributing to its formation are beyond the scope of this book to discuss in detail. Central to it, however, are the child's *own* repressed hostilities; and the fears the child experiences during the dream are most commonly of his *own* anger. It is for these reasons, I believe, that the child of divorce is likely to exhibit an increase in the frequency of his nightmares, especially around the time of the separation.

Tension and anxiety attacks. As the repressed anger strives for release, an intrapsychic conflict may be set up. The anger that has been relegated to the unconscious presses for expression and superego forces attempt to prevent the hostile thoughts and feelings from entering into conscious awareness. A chronic state of tension may thereby be set up which may manifest itself in a number of ways. The child may become hyperirritable, cry easily, and react in an exaggerated fashion to the most minor noxious stimuli. He may develop tics. Most commonly these are of the eyes (blinking) and the mouth (grimacing and puckering movements). When more severe, the head and shoulders may become involved and various vocal tics (grunting noises, frequent throat clearing) may appear. When the vocal tics become recognizable profanities (coprolalia), the term Gilles de la Tourette's syndrome is usually applied.

I am not in agreement with those who view most tics to have specific symbolic significance. For example, some hold that an eye-blinking tic may be a manifestation of the child's wish to avoid seeing unpleasant sights; or that a tic in which he jerks his head back represents the child's removal of his face from an imaginary hand that is slapping him for some transgression. These often appear to be attractive explanations and their validity may be hard to disprove. (This is true of most psychoanalytic explanations. One can attribute practically anything to anyone's unconscious and be secure in the knowledge that neither the patient nor anyone else can disprove it because it is *unconscious* and, by definition, not even known to the patient.) Although there may occasionally be a child in whom the tic may have specific symbolic significance, more often, I believe, it is merely one of the possible manifestations of a high level of tension. Each person's body has certain areas or organs that are more likely to respond to tension than others. Some react to tension with spasm of various parts of the gastrointestinal tract, others with palpitations, others with sweating, others with skeletal muscle spasm, etc. Alfred Adler referred to each of these sites as a *locus resistentiae minoris* (place of least resistance). He considered them inborn points or areas of weakness and did not give much credence to the theory that the organ was primarily selected because it lent itself well to symbolic expression of a particular psychological need. My own experience bears out Adler's views. Accordingly, I consider the child with tics to be a very tense child whose facial musculature is particularly sensitive to tension. In therapy I direct my attention to the underlying sources of such tension; only rarely have I found the search for a specific symbolic meaning to the tic to be therapeutically useful.

A related phenomenon is the anxiety attack. Generally this is seen in the child whose general level of tension is already quite high. In these episodes the child suddenly becomes extremely tense. There may be sweating, palpitations, shortness of breath, trembling, and fears that he may die. In severe forms the child may be thrown into a state of panic. The most common cause of such states in the child of divorce, in my opinion, is the threat of intense hostile feelings erupting into conscious awareness. Such a child is generally so guilt-ridden over his angry feelings that powerful repressive forces must operate to keep them out of conscious awareness. So repressed, they may build up; then, when they threaten eruption into conscious awareness, the child becomes overwhelmed with fear of the consequences of their expression.

Projection and phobias. The less direct contact we have with a person the greater the likelihood that we will harbor distortions about the individual. When parents separate the child is likely to develop distortions about the absent parent that would not otherwise have arisen. As Neubauer (1960) and Gregory (1965b) point out, the child of divorce is likely to either idealize or devalue the absent parent. The devaluation process is facilitated by the child's viewing the parent's leaving as a hostile act. The child is likely, then, to see such a parent as unduly punitive and may, generalizing from his "abandonment," anticipate similar treatment from others of the same sex. The child's considering the absent parent to be hostile may be further intensified by the projection of the child's own hostility. His guilt over his hostility may cause him to disown it and project it onto others. It is as if the child were saying: "It is not I who have these horrible hostile thoughts, it is he." The absent parent may then be seen as so hostile that the child expects to be injured or severely maltreated in other ways. With such anticipations the child may dread his contact with the parent and even become phobic with regard to him or her.

Phobic reactions regarding the parent (especially the absent one) may take other forms. The child may become excessively fearful that the parent may become sick or injured. Such concerns are reactions to the basic unconscious wish that harm befall the parent as an expression of the child's hostility. Guilt over such hostility contributes to the transformation of the wish into a fear. The child's basic image is essentially one of harm coming to the parent. By viewing the fantasy as one that he fears rather than as one that is desired, the child assuages his guilt while still gaining the gratification of the imagery. Another notion that contributes to such a phobia is the child's belief that his hostile thoughts per se have the power to harm. Such a child may need frequent proof and testimony that the parent is well in order to assure himself that his basic hostile wishes have not been realized. He may become so solicitous of the parent that he becomes an irritant. And separation anxieties may develop in the service of keeping the parent ever at the child's side. A school phobia would be one way in which these mechanisms might manifest themselves.

Sometimes the fear of harm from, or that of harm befalling, a parent is displaced onto an object or an animal. Freud's patient, little Hans (1909), utilized this mechanism. His fear that horses would bite him stemmed, in part, from his fear that his father would castrate him. And this anticipation of his father's hostility was intensified by Hans's projecting onto his father his own hostilities. Children today are more likely to use dogs for these purposes.

Compulsions. The development of compulsions and compulsive rituals is another way in which the child may deal with his anger. In the handwashing compulsion, for example, the child may consider his hands to be the potential tools for acting out his unconscious hostile thoughts and feelings. By compulsively cleaning them, he symbolically "keeps them clean" (that is, innocent of committed crimes) and washes off the "stains" of their potential or fantasied transgressions. A ten-year-old boy I once treated presented symptoms that demonstrated quite well the relationship between compulsive rituals and repressed hostility. Although his parents were not separated they were highly intellectualized people, very inhibited in expressing affection, and so were psychologically separated from one another and from him. The boy feared that if he knocked against an article of furniture (even accidentally) there would be the most terrible repercussions—the worst of which was that God would punish him by striking him dead with lightning. He especially feared hitting his foot against something because the possible punishments for that seemed to be worse than if the point of contact with the furniture were his hand or torso. Although he was ever cautious not to knock against anything he somehow would slip up at least a few times a day and "accidentally" hit against or even kick some household articles. He would then become very anxious, examine the furniture very carefully to be sure that it wasn't damaged, and run his finger over it a few times to be sure that it wasn't scratched or marred. Gradually the examination process developed into a specific ritual in which he had to rub his finger over the area exactly three times, after which he experienced some alleviation of his anxiety. In addition, he would look up toward heaven and beseech God not to punish him for what he had done. Gradually, his pleadings too became formulated into specific prayers that would reduce his anxiety if stated in a particular way.

I considered the furniture to represent the patient's parents and his knocking (and even worse, kicking) against them a symbolic expression of hostility toward them. The inspection for damages and scratches served to reassure the patient that he had not in fact harmed his parents. Ritualizing the examination further served to lessen such anxiety: prescribing a specific number of strokes shortened the examination period necessary to reassure him that harm had not been done. God, of course, represented the patient's parents (especially his father whom he saw as more punitive) and begging his forgiveness served to protect him from the punishment he anticipated for his transgressions. Again, ritualizing the prayer served to diminish the anxiety and provide him with a predictable (albeit magical) way of reducing it. It is clear that the patient's "accidents" were unconsciously planned and served as an outlet for his hostility. The rituals enabled him to assuage the guilt he felt over such expression. However, as is well known, "doing and undoing" (the psychiatric terminology for the aforementioned phenomena) is not the same as never having done anything at all. Because the patient felt he had to keep "doing" (giving vent to his hostility), he had to keep "undoing" (engaging in the guilt-alleviating rituals).

Generally, children who exhibit such symptoms (especially when they occupy a significant amount of time) are quite sick and one must consider the possibility of psychotic processes being present. (The aforementioned boy, however, was by no means psychotic, his rituals were not all-pervasive preoccupations, and he was helped by a therapeutic approach in accordance with the principles to be presented at the end of this chapter.)

Depression. As noted in Chapter 5, the child's repressing his hostility and directing it toward himself can contribute to his becoming depressed. When self-recriminations are present this mechanism becomes even more obvious. One does best to understand such criticisms as being displaced from a significant figure onto the child himself. If one follows the formula: substitute the word *father* or *mother* whenever the patient's name appears in a self-flagellatory statement, one will generally get a clearer understanding of what is going on in the child. When the child needs to assuage such guilt by inviting punishment, a masochistic element is introduced.

Therapeutic Approaches to Neurotic Handling of Anger

Introductory comments. As mentioned, I believe that the situation that is most likely to cause anger is one in which the individual experiences frustration over his inability to remove a noxious stimulus. Anger has survival value in that it enhances our efficiency in removing such an irritant. As long as the painful stimulus is present, anger will be provoked and even increased—resulting in ever more intense emotional reactions. The paradigms and discussion below summarize my concept of anger escalation which serves as a basis for my therapeutic approach.

Let us consider the situation in which a man gets a splinter in his finger. If he quickly removes the splinter (a noxious stimulant), he feels better.

> Noxious stimulus + Removal →
> Pleasurable relief of pain

If the splinter is too deep for him to remove with his fingernails, the man feels frustrated.

> Noxious stimulus + Inability to
> remove it→Frustration

The frustration serves to stimulate increased efforts to remove the noxious stimulus. He gets a pair of tweezers, takes out the splinter, and then feels all right.

> Frustration + Early removal of noxious stimulus→
> Pleasurable relief of pain + Cessation of frustration

If he cannot find a pair of tweezers, his frustration increases and he gets angry: "This god-damn splinter is painful. Where the hell's a pair of tweezers?"

> Frustration + Continual inability to
> remove noxious stimulus→Anger

So angered, he is mobilized to act further. He goes next door, borrows a pair of tweezers from his neighbor, and takes out the splinter.

> Anger + Removal of noxious stimulus→Pleasurable
> relief of pain + Cessation of anger

Suppose his neighbor has a pair of tweezers, but refuses to lend them. The pain and anger continue and now there are additional feelings of helplessness. His anger changes to rage—the feeling that comes with profound impotence over removal of a chronic noxious stimulus.

> Anger+Prolonged impotence in removing
> a noxious stimulus→Rage

The rage reaction has a purpose. It's a last-ditch stand. With it, irrational things are done which are in the service of removing the noxious stimulus, but which are often misguided. He rants and becomes abusive. Even if the neighbor then gives him a pair of tweezers, he suffers consequences, such as embarrassment and the need to make apologies. The anger reaction is coordinated and directed toward a specific goal. The rage reaction is more chaotic and is less likely to be effective. Even when it is, the slate is usually not then wiped clean. There are usually untoward side effects after its utilization.

Rage + Removal of noxious stimulus→Pleasurable
relief of pain + Untoward side effects

Fury is sometimes used to describe a degree of rage in which the inappropriate reaction reaches psychotic proportions, whereas rage is more typically neurotic. The enraged man with the splinter, who then rampages through his neighbor's house, attacking and possibly even killing his neighbor, would be considered to be in a fury. The rage has been so deranging that he has become psychotic.

Rage + Prolonged exposure to
noxious stimulus→Fury

Therapeutic efforts should be directed toward helping patients remove noxious stimuli at the earliest possible time. The sicker the patient, the greater the likelihood that he is not effectively dealing with noxious stimuli early enough and that he is harboring unexpressed anger, rage, and even fury.

Since life inevitably exposes us to noxious stimuli, anger is ubiquitous. However, the survival of society depends on a significant degree of anger inhibition. Over the millennia man has evolved various systems for protecting himself from those whose unbridled expression of anger would endanger him. The most widely efficacious system is guilt. It is very efficient because the individual deters himself from performing the hostile act and others need be less guarded. I have described elsewhere (Gardner, 1970a) the stages the child goes through in developing a sense of guilt. Briefly, in the first, the pain phase, the child is deterred from performing acts which are dangerous to himself and/or others by simple negative reinforcement. The two-year-old who runs into traffic will not be stopped from doing so again in the immediate future by a lecture on the dangers of automobiles. A strong reprimand (threatened loss of his mother's love), a not so gentel wrenching him from the street, or a smack on the backside is far more effective. He does not go into the street again because doing so has become associated with certain painful repercussions. It's as simple as that. Future consequences are too remote for his appreciation. In the next, the shame phase, the child deters himself from antisocial behavior because he fears suffering the displeasure (again, loss of love) of significant figures in his milieu. He envisions himself standing in the center of a circle of critical adults all crying out: "Shame on you." However, when these same significant individuals are no longer in the immediate vicinity, he cannot be relied upon to deter himself. This stage coincides with Erikson's (1963) second stage in which the primary life conflict to be resolved is that of "Autonomy vs. Shame." Erikson makes reference to the ashamed person's words to his observers: "God damn your eyes." At this stage the deterring forces are still externalized; one blushes in front of someone, not alone. In the final stage, the guilt phase, the inhibitions have been internalized. The child deters himself because he would despise himself were he to perform the unacceptable act. It's as if he said to himself: "How terrible a thing it would be were I to do that. How terrible a person I would be if I were to do that. I won't do that." As Piers and Singer describe it (1953), here the inner rather than the outer voice deters. This corresponds to Erikson's (1963) third stage, "Guilt vs. Initiative." Alone and unobserved, the child suffers the admonition of the internalized voices of authorities. Society can at last relax its vigil.

Since murder, the extreme expression of hostility, is such an irreversibly destructive act, society has had to utilize the most powerful mechanisms to prevent its unbridled expression. Religions have long been of service in providing ways to help man inhibit emotions and actions which are potentially dangerous to himself and others. Religious methods have relied heavily on the guilt mechanism. However helpful the guilt deterrent has been, I believe that it has been misapplied, misdirected, and used to excess. Since anger can lead to rage, then fury, and then murder, many religions have interdicted all the low milder forms of anger as a safety measure against the expression of the violent forms. The is somewhat like banning the use of fire because it can get out of hand, or prohibiting the production of electrical power because occasionally someone gets electrocuted. Fire and electricity are certainly useful and so is anger. It need not be lethal.

Anger must be harnessed and used to help deal with life's frustrations. Children must not be taught that there are good folk somewhere who are never angry. They must not be filled with guilt over the inevitable angry feelings they have.

The children I see in my practice are products of this heritage, and it is no surprise that problems around the expression of anger are common, if not the most common. More stories elicited in the Mutual Storytelling Technique center around the expression of anger than any other theme. Ames (1966) and Pitcher and Prelinger (1963) found anger to be the predominant theme in the stories they elicited from children.

Such findings are not surprising. The child is continually exposed to frustrations. He is bombarded with "Don't do this" and "Don't do that." It is no surprise, then, that he suffers many frustrations and resentments. He cannot overtly express them for fear of invoking even further criticism from his parents, especially if they believe that he should not be having any angry reactions to their restrictions. He can neither flee nor fight, and so he develops one or more adaptations. He denies and represses his anger (with the help of his minister and Sunday School teacher); he sublimates it (plays "war"); he displaces it (hits his brother); he releases it vicariously (watches horror stories on television); and he projects it ("It's his fault." "Kids always pick on me"). His dreams and fantasies symbolically allow release of his anger and are a powerful and effective form of substitute gratification because on one can stop him from them. They are things which he truly has all to himself.

Not all noxious stimuli are external, however. When the source of frustration, for example, is a low feeling of self-worth that a situation engenders in an individual, then expressing the anger externally is futile. If A feels worthless because B inappropriately deems him so, the problem will not be resolved by A getting B to change his opinion, but rather by A coming to appreciate that he is not necessarily what others consider him to be. These internal noxious stimuli are often more complex and difficult to remove than the external and may require intensive treatment if they are to be effectively dealt with. But the same principle still holds regarding their relationship to frustration and anger.

Children who handle their anger neurotically feel excessively guilty over their anger, repress it, and channel it into symptoms that are ostensibly good resolutions—but in fact are not. A child with compulsive rituals, for example, may have protected himself from the anticipated repercussions of expressing anger to his parents, but he must retain magical thinking processes (clearly maladaptive in a real world) to do so; these sap his energies in time-consuming and wasteful activities. The school-phobic child may enjoy the reassurance that his parent is still alive and has not been killed by his unconscious hostility, but he sacrifices his education for this relief from his tension.

We know relatively little about the reasons why an individual chooses a particular mechanism to deal with anger over which there is guilt. Why does one child project it and another repress it? Why does one child deny it and another direct it toward himself? Doubtless social influences and parental models play a role; but even in the same family one can observe different ways of dealing with unacceptable anger. As disparate as the neurotic symptoms may be that result from guilt over anger expression, the basic approach to these patients is quite similar. Specifically, I attempt to help the child to deal with those around him so that anger-evoking situations will be minimized. When he is successful there will be less anger for him to have to cope with. When he is not successful (as is inevitable since no one can be 100% efficient in avoiding anger-provoking situations), he will have learned to use his anger at the earliest possible time, in the most effective way, in order to alter or remove the noxious stimuli that he encounters. In the service of his being free to express his resentment, he must be helped to feel less guilty about his anger.

Work with parents. Work with parents is often helpful in treating such children. The parent may have very rigid and inhibited standards regarding anger expression and may have actively contributed to the child's guilt. They may believe that a child's harboring angry thoughts and feelings toward a parent is sinful, bad, abnormal, or otherwise unacceptable. And they may have overtly or covertly induced guilt in the child for such anger. I try to convince such parents that such views, although they have a long tradition, are not consistent with our present knowledge of what is best for the child psychologically. I attempt to help them appreciate that anger is a normal reaction to the frustrations that the child (like the rest of us) inevitably experiences in life. I try to help them appreciate that excessive guilt over anger can contribute to the formulation of symptoms and try specifically to help them understand how this occurred in their child. In such discussions the parents may fear that I am encouraging them to let their child run wild and turn into a little savage who goes about expressing his anger wherever and whenever he wants. They may even be supported in this notion by tales of other children who have gone to therapists who appeared to be suggesting such abandoned expression of anger. (Unfortunately there are some therapists who go this far, or almost so.) I try to reassure them that this is definitely not my goal—that this would be substituting one disease for another. Rather, my hope is that the child will find a healthy balance between too much and too little repression of his anger; and that at the present time he has too much and needs some loosening up—but not to the point of there being no suppression at all.

I try to help the parents differentiate between thoughts, feelings, and action. I try to help them appreciate that they do best by their child by assuaging any guilt he may feel over angry thoughts and feelings (which he has little power to control) and angry deeds (which he generally has the capacity to suppress). I advise them to use such comments as "We can see how angry are you over Daddy's leaving; but you can't go around the house breaking things." Such a comment sanctions the thoughts and feelings but prohibits acting them out. In such discussions the question of the child's cursing at his parents usually comes up. I generally advise the parents to reassure the child that they accept the fact that his anger at them may cause curse words to come into his mind. However, I suggest they add that at the present time a child's cursing his parents is socially unacceptable behavior, and that if he is angry at them he should use more polite words than those that come into his mind. I also advise them to help reduce the child's guilt by informing him that such words do have a use because they allow for a release of anger in a way that does not cause anyone physical harm. Present standards generally allow for their use in one's relationship with peers (especially when the other party uses them first) but not toward one's parents and other adults. For example, I suggest a parent might say, "I can see how angry you are that Mommy has to work; but I won't let you go around using such language to me. That kind of language is okay with your friends out on the street. What we have to do is figure out ways for you to be less angry about my working."

The parents have to be helped to appreciate that angry outbursts are especially common around the time of the separation and their tolerance for them has to be particularly high during this period. I do not suggest that *no* disciplinary measures at all be taken; rather, that they be used more sparingly during this period.

There are parents who cannot tolerate a child's anger because they operate in accordance with the dictum: "If someone is angry at me, regardless of the age of the person and the reasons for the anger, I must be at fault. I must be abominable." Accordingly, they may do everything to squelch a child's anger in order to protect themselves from what are to them such painful and fearful confrontations. The child may recognize his parent's intolerance for such anger expression on his part and may come to feel very guilty about his anger because of the devastating effect it has on his parent. Such a parent generally needs to be loved by everybody and cannot tolerate anyone's disapproval. Sometimes therapy may be necessary to help such a parent alter this view.

The child observing his parents being swept up in their hostilities and treating one another in a cruel and often inhumane fashion may become fearful of expressing his anger lest he cause similar suffering to others. If such parents can be helped to reduce their warfare, this contributing element to the child's guilt over his hostility may be reduced.

The parent may have to consider himself perfect, or at least attempt to present such a view of himself to his child. He may believe that it is against the child's best interests to see flaws in a parent and he will refrain from admitting or revealing any imperfections in the service of this goal. A child's anger at such a parent may be considered by the parent a sign of a defect in himself and so the child's expression of anger is strongly discouraged that the parent might maintain the image of perfection. Such a parent has to be helped to realize that he is doing his child a disservice: his child, if he comes to believe the ruse, will have unrealistic expectations of others, may come to believe that there are other perfect people as well, and will suffer inevitable disappointments and disillusionments as each adult he meets will ultimately reveal his imperfections. In addition, as he grows older he will in all likelihood come to appreciate the parent's duplicity and will then have real reason to lose respect for the parent. The parent should be helped to appreciate that his revealing his deficiencies in natural and uncontrived ways (as long as they are not extensive and frequently exhibited) will result in his child's *gaining* respect for him as he comes to appreciate that it is the strong rather than the weak person who has the courage to admit defects. If a parent can be convinced to alter his view and allow the child to express anger over a defect, he will reduce one of the elements contributing to the child's guilt.

In recent years we have experienced the popularization of what I consider a misguided application of psychological principles. Unfortunately used by many mental health workers, this approach encourages the child to express resentment and considers such expression the primary aim of therapy. "Once the hateful feelings are let out," we are told, "the loving feelings are then free to express themselves." And the method used to facilitate the release of the angry feelings is *labeling* them. Accordingly, the child of divorce whose father is late for his visits is told, "It must make you feel very angry that Daddy is late again." If the child agrees and expresses his resentment the method is deemed successful. Guilt has been assuaged by the parent's speaking the unspeakable and the child's expressing his anger drains the pool of repressed feelings that have caused him discomfort and even neurosis. I believe that a child who was in touch with his anger would respond indignantly to such a comment with a retort such as: "Of course I am. Wouldn't you be?" He would recognize the absurdity of that statement and its implicit condescension. If he were not consciously aware of his anger, it would not serve well to bring him in touch with it. (I will discuss in the next section the approaches I use to help such a child get in touch with repressed anger.)

Such an approach is in all probability a good first step for many children. It may lessen some guilt via the parent's mentioning the unmentionable. However, its fault lies in its incompleteness. It does not give proper attention to the primary purpose of anger: to remove a noxious stimulus. Although it may allow for temporary release of anger and alleviation of some tension it does nothing to bring about a change in the situation that caused the anger in the first place. Accordingly, the anger is likely to be continually generated because the provocative situation remains unchanged. It is a good first step but little will be acomplished if the child is not, in addition, encouraged to direct his feelings toward specific goals in order to accomplish something more than catharsis. For example, the child whose father is continually late for visits might be told: "Have you told your father how angry it makes you when he's late?" or "What do you think you can do while waiting for him so you won't be thinking all the time about when he's going to come?"

Comments such as these direct the child to use his anger constructively toward the goal of removing the conditions that originally generated the anger.

Parents have sometimes been helped by reading the chapter on anger in my book *Understanding Children* (1973a), in which I describe these and other approaches that they may use to lessen their child's guilt over anger expression.

Work with the child. Central to successful therapy with a child is the establishment of a good relationship with him. Without such a relationship the child is unlikely to take seriously the therapist's communications, identify with him, be motivated to suffer some of the frustrations often necessary to bring about therapeutic change, involve himself in salutary corrective emotional experiences, or enjoy the other therapeutic benefits that may be derived from the relationship. In my book *Psychotherapeutic Approaches to the Resistant Child* (1975) I discuss at length the various ways in which the child can gain therapeutically from his relationship with the therapist.

In helping children work through anger inhibition problems the therapist does well to serve as a model for anger expression himself. All too often therapists encourage their patients to express pent-up resentment and other suppressed feelings but strictly refrain from doing so themselves. Some even consider the presence of such feelings in the therapist toward the patient or any member of his family to be a manifestation of inappropriate or even neurotic reactions. Certainly the therapist may have such neurotic reactions; however, not all feelings in response to a patient or his family are necessarily inappropriate. The therapist is a human being. He also gets angry when frustrated, frightened when his safety is threatened, bored, anxious, etc. When the patient is doing things to induce or evoke such feelings in the therapist the latter does well to inform the patient of these reactions. Others may not be providing such feedback, and if they are it is generally not with such benevolent intent. The therapist who refuses such confrontations with his patient deprives him of a valuable aspect of treatment. Accordingly, in the treatment of anger inhibition problems the therapist does well to express his resentments if and when they arise in the course of the child's therapy. Such expression should not be contrived nor should situations artificially be set up which would be likely to provide the therapist with excuses for such expression. Rather, the therapist should be alert to opportunities for him to express resentments as they may arise in the natural course of the therapy. For example, the child who refuses to join with the therapist in cleaning up the toys near the end of the session might be told: "It gets me angry when I have to clean up these toys all by myself. If you don't help me, I won't let you play with these toys next time you come." The therapist here is not only serving as a model for expressing anger, but is demonstrating its use in preventing a recurrence of the anger-provoking situation. I have no hesitation using threats in my therapeutic work. Life is full of threats. If we don't pay our electric bills, our electricity is turned off. If we don't pay our telephone bills, our phones get disconnected. If we don't show up at work frequently enough, we most often get fired. In therapy as well the child must learn that there will be consequences for behavior that inconveniences others. Such exposures contribute to his gaining a more realistic view of life—and this is best accomplished through living experiences rather than simple talk.

In his encounters with the child's parents the therapist can serve as a model for self-assertion and the expression of resentment. It is in the area of making payments that the therapist most often has the opportunity to assert himself and express resentment. When working with an adult psychoanalytic patient one has the opportunity to delve into the reasons why he or she may be withholding payments or not living up to financial agreements with the therapist. Generally, we have no such relationship with the parents of our child patients. The resentments and jealousies that they often harbor toward the therapist are most conveniently expressed by laxness in meeting their financial obligations to him. Although the therapist may at times hesitate to make the child patient party to his difficulties with the parents regarding payment (lest he add to the child's concerns), there are times when it can be therapeutic for the child to be informed about such difficulties between the therapist and his parents. Such exposure can provide the child with the opportunity to observe his therapist expressing his resentments to the parents, and this may make it easier for the child to do so. Seeing that the repercussions of such expression are not devastating makes it easier for the child to act similarly. In addition, they give the child information about his parents that he may not previously have had. We all do best to have an accurate view of our parents, both their assets and their liabilities, and therapy can be helpful in providing this.

In addition to providing the child with various experiences that will help him more guiltlessly express his anger, the therapist should also impart to the child various communications that serve this end as well. Therapists vary regarding the methods they utilize in transmitting such messages. Some rely more on the verbal, others on the non-verbal. Some prefer secondary process, others primary process communications. Some prefer direct discussion, others rely heavily on play techniques. I prefer to use a variety of approaches and try to find those that best suit each child. In addition, I do not confine myself to a particular technique with any given child; rather, I use various combinations of methods that both the child and I are most comfortable with and enjoy at the given time. With regard to the transmission of such communications, I do not think that the modality of transmission is that crucial. What is important is that the message get through and each therapist utilize those modalities that work best for him. Accordingly, the reader should appreciate that in the discussion below I am not concerning myself with any particular therapeutic modality. Rather, I will be describing the various communications that I believe are important to impart to the child with problems in anger inhibition.

In accordance with the schema presenting the various stages of anger release, the child should be encouraged to express his resentment at the earliest possible stage so that his anger does not get suppressed, repressed, and built up internally. He should learn to become sensitive to angry thoughts when they first arise and be made aware of his tendency to make excuses that justify his not utilizing his anger appropriately. He should learn as well the physical sensations he experiences when he becomes angry, especially in the early phases. And he should be encouraged to assert himself and express his resentments at the earliest possible time in the service of altering the situation that is causing his resentments in the first place.

The child should not only be encouraged to try and rectify situations that cause irritation but to learn as well not to pursue lost causes. I often quote in this regard what I call Fields' Rule (after W. C. Fields, the comedian who allegedly first stated it): "If at first you don't succeed, try, try again. If after that, you still don't succeed, forget it! Don't make a big fool of yourself." (Actually, Fields is *really* alleged to have said: "If at first you don't succeed, try, try again. If after that, you still don't succeed, fuck it! Don't make a goddamn fool of yourself." However, for the purpose of my work with child patients, I recommend the expurgated version.) To encourage a child to persist in trying to achieve a goal that appears hopeless is antitherapeutic and even cruel. Rather, he should be encouraged to resign himself to failures and to redirect his attention to alternative pursuits that have a greater likelihood of success. For example, the child whose father shows little if any interest in him should be encouraged to try to improve his relationship with him and possibly effect a closer tie. If, however, after reasonable efforts the father proves himself to be unmotivated or incapable of a more intimate relationship, the child should be helped to resign himself to this unfortunate situation. He must be helped to see that just because his father has little if any love for him, this does not mean that he is unlovable. He must be helped to gain affection from others who are willing and capable of providing it. It is this combination of knowledge and experience that can make the therapeutic communications meaningful. The concept of the substitute gratification is important in helping a child resign himself to a failure. It is much easier to admit defeat in one area if one is simultaneously provided with reasonable hope of success in another.

As mentioned, anger arises when one is frustrated—when one cannot get something that he wants, or thinks he wants. One way to reduce anger is to appreciate that the thing one may want may not be a reasonable desire. If one can then stop craving that thing, one is less likely to be frustrated and hence angry. In my work with children I often refer to this principle as "changing your mind about the thing you want." A girl, for example, who wants her mother to stop dating is going to be continually angry as long as she persists in hoping that her mother will stop. If she can be helped to appreciate that her mother has the right to recreation, and is usually in better spirits upon her return, then the girl might give up or reduce her demands and thereby become less angry. (The oedipal rivalries and other factors that may contribute to such anger may make its alleviation more difficult than is implied in my example. Yet I have found this approach to be helpful as part of the working-through of problems of this sort.)

A related cognitive alteration that I have found useful is what I refer to as "changing your mind about the person you're angry at." The most common example of this is the child who has been brainwashed by one parent into believing that the other is the incarnation of all the evil that ever existed in the world. If therapy can help such a child correct some of these distortions, then he is less likely to be angry.

In the course of my work with such guilty children I try to help them differentiate between angry thoughts, angry feelings, and angry deeds. The three classes are discussed in detail, with my questioning the child throughout the discussion to be sure that he appreciates the distinctions. I try to impress upon him the fact that one has little control over the appearance of angry thoughts and feelings; whereas angry acts or deeds are very much under our control. I try to help the child recognize that angry thoughts and feelings are inevitable reactions to frustrations and that all people experience them. In addition, I try to convince the child that all people, at times, have the desire to perform angry acts and that most *do* act these out to a limited extent when the damage done is minimal; but that most *do not* when the inflicted damage would be great. My emphasis in such discussions is on the fact that these are the reactions and experiences of *most* people; this helps the child feel less guilty and atypical about his own anger reactions. One cannot evaluate the appropriateness of guilt without considering the relative prevalence of the particular guilt reaction. When a guilty person comes to appreciate that his own reactions are widespread he is likely to feel less guilty about them.

If a child's relationship with me is a good one and he has come to respect me as someone with wide experience in these matters and as someone whose word can be relied upon, he is more likely to be impressed by what I have to say. I have pointed out that the earliest analytic therapy (Breuer and Freud, 1895) relied heavily on the analyst's using his authority to lessen the patient's guilt. The analyst's saying that in his opinion there is nothing "bad" or "wrong" in a person's having certain thoughts or feelings seems to have helped these early patients feel less guilty. Despite later additions to the therapeutic approach, this basic technique still holds—even though the approbation may now be more subtly communicated. (A silent lack of disapprobation is just one of the ways that this can be very effectively accomplished.)

Magical thinking is especially prevalent during the period from three to five years, and many carry residua of such primitive cognition throughout their lives. (I am not referring here only to schizophrenics.) One such notion pertinent to this discussion is the idea that thoughts per se have the power to bring about real events. Simply stated, the very wish that something will happen can make it happen. Wish someone harm and it will come to pass. Wish someone dead and he will die. The failure to correct this distortion, or the maintenance of it beyond the age when the child should appreciate its absurdity, can contribute to a child's exaggerated guilt over angry expression. If he believes that his angry thoughts can actually harm the object of his hostility, he may become very wary of them indeed and frightened of expressing them. (Generally, words here are even more dangerous than thoughts.) It is one of the purposes of the therapy of such children to correct this distortion. In play stories, for example, I might say, "The dog was really angry at the cat, so angry that he wished that she would be killed. One night he wished very hard that the cat would be run over by a car. The next morning he went to see what had happened to the cat. But she was still alive! The next night he wished *even harder* (stated in strained voice). But still the cat stayed alive. And night after night and day after day—no matter how hard he wished the cat to die—she still stayed alive. No matter how hard he wished for the cat to be dead, she still stayed alive. His thoughts just couldn't harm her."

There are some children who are so repressed with regard to anger expression that they have little if any conscious awareness of angry thoughts and/or feelings. For example, the mother of a significantly repressed girl reported that the child waited three hours for her father to show up on visitation day and he never appeared. When the child was asked how she felt about her father's not showing up she replied, without any show of emotion, "He must have forgotten. Sometimes his memory isn't very good." The child was obviously guilty about expressing the angry feelings I knew she harbored and rationalized that her father had some kind of innate deficiency in memory that caused him to forget. One cannot get angry at a person with such an unfortunate handicap. To have tried to introduce this child to the psychoanalytic theory of forgetting would have been useless; her defenses were far too powerful for her to have been receptive to it at that point. I then continued, "I imagine you must have been very angry." Her reply: "No, he's just that way. He often does that. I'm used to it; it doesn't make me angry." Again the child rationalized in the service of denying her anger. At this point I replied,

"I cannot imagine that in all that time—in the three hours that you waited—that you didn't once, somewhere in the corner of your mind, have at least *one* angry thought about him. Some little angry feeling. I can't imagine someone in that situation not getting at least a little angry. I know that I myself would have been furious." My question was stated with an attitude of extreme incredulity. My hope was that I would make the admission of an angry reaction acceptable and the denial of it the atypical response. Although the child responded with further denials during that interchange, she subsequently allowed that she did occasionally get angry under similar circumstances. Such an approach is based on the assumption that even in the most severely repressed people, under enough provocation some of the anger does manage to erupt into conscious awareness. The patient, however, may be fearful of admitting this to the therapist—attributing to him the same kind of negative response as those who originally conditioned and contributed to the development of his or her guilt. The expression of this little spark of anger is strongly condoned by the therapist and the hiding of it emphatically discouraged. The patient is made to feel that its expression makes him or her like everyone else, and this can reduce fears of revealing it. Of course, the risk of such an approach is that the patient will feign such feelings in order to ingratiate himself with the therapist. However, this response has not been common in my experience.

As mentioned, the child of divorce is likely to have a distorted image of his parents, especially of the absent one. The diminished contact makes it likely that distortions will not be corrected by experience. Such negative distortions may be exaggerated even further by the child's projection of his own hostility onto the parent, i.e., he may consider the parent to be malevolent when this is not the case. He may thereby anticipate punishment and retribution when there is no reason for such expectations. Such distortions range in intensity from the mild to the paranoid. The milder they are the more likely they can be corrected by explanation and the child's having the *living experience* (through direct contact with the parent) that they are not valid. When they reach paranoid proportions their alleviation becomes much more difficult. Other elements that contribute have to be dealt with and in some cases they may never be worked out—paranoid symptoms, as most psychiatrists agree, being particularly resistive to psychotherapeutic approaches.

I have found the child's reading my *The Boys and Girls Book about Divorce* (1970b, 1971a), either alone or with me or a parent, to be particularly helpful in the therapy of anger inhibition problems. Many of the issues just discussed are dealt with in the book at a level understandable to most children. Not only does the printed word often have a power and credibility greater than the spoken, but the illustrations as well add to the efficacy of the messages and advice contained therein.

Clinical Example
A dragon that couldn't breathe fire

Roberta, a ten-and-a-half-year-old girl, was brought to therapy because of facial tics, nail biting, emotional inhibition, preoccupation with thoughts that she was inadequate, and impaired self-assertion. She was easily teased by friends and would not fight back. She poorly communicated her thoughts and feelings and became withdrawn and somber in situations that would arouse emotions—especially anger. At such times she might become aloof, tired, and would yawn frequently.

Her parents had been separated for about two years at the time of referral, but had not yet made a decision regarding either divorce or reconciliation. Each dated others and she frequently met the dates of her parents. They denied that this might have any untoward effects on her and took the position that this was the reality of their lives and she would have to adjust to it somehow.

Roberta told this story during her second month in treatment:

Patient: I don't know how to start it. Would you start it?

Therapist: Okay. Once upon a time . . . a long time ago . . . in a distant land . . . far away . . . there lived a . . .

P: dragon.

T: And this dragon . . .

P: His name was Ronald.

T: was named Ronald. Go ahead. And one day this dragon named Ronald . . .

P: went swimming.

T: went swimming. Yeah, go ahead.

P: And water got up his, um, thing that the fire comes out of his nose.

T: Yeah.

P: And he couldn't breathe fire anymore. And so he went to his doctor and he told the doctor that he couldn't breathe fire anymore and he didn't know why. And the doctor looked up in his nose and saw that there was water and he drained all the water and Ronald could shoot flames again.

T: Uh huh.

P: And he was happy forever after.

T: Okay. And the lesson of that story? (patient starts biting fingernails)

P: I don't know.

T: Hh hmm. Well, what do we learn from that story? What's the moral?

P (still biting fingernails): I don't know.

T: Can't think of any?

P: Nope.

T: Okay. Now it's my time to tell a story.

I considered the dragon to represent Roberta herself and its inability to breathe fire an expression of repressed hostility. The fire, with its potential for massive destruction, well lends itself to symbolizing anger. Similarly, water—as the most potent antagonist to fire—lends itself to the symbolization of those forces that squelch anger. The doctor's removing the water from the dragon's nose symbolizes Roberta's desire that the inhibitory forces be removed. However, such removal is done without any active participation on Roberta's part. She need only passively lie back and the doctor solves the problem for her. With this understanding of the patient's story, I related mine:

Therapist: Once upon a time there was a dragon and this dragon's name was Ronald. (patient still biting fingernails) And one day this dragon found that he couldn't shoot the flames out of his nose anymore and when he would try they wouldn't come out. Now on that very same day he happened to go swimming and some water did get up into his nose and he thought that this was the reason why he probably couldn't breathe (patient blinking, still biting fingernails) flames anymore.

So he went to a doctor and the doctor looked in his nose and the doctor said, "Well, that water that you described as being the cause of all of this is not there anymore. That water has dried out (blinking and still biting fingernails) and that isn't the reason why you can't shoot those flames out."

And the dragon said, "Well, what is it then?"

He said, "Well, I think that you're afraid to breathe fire anymore. I don't know what has happened to you but for some reason you are frightened. I see nothing physical about this. There's nothing . . . I think it's psychological. That's how I see it. You're probably afraid to breathe out those flames."

What do you think the dragon said?

Patient: "I'll try it. I'll like it."

T: Well, what do you think happened then?

P: He tried to blow fire and it worked.

T: Yeah. Well, actually what happened was it wasn't that easy. He was scared of letting out the fire. He had developed the idea that even if someone bothers you or if some enemy attacks you that to breathe out the flame is bad or wrong or nice people don't do that; (patient nonchalantly brushing off shoes with her hand) even in self-defense it's wrong for a dragon to breathe flame.

P: So why was he given the flame to begin with?

T: That's right. (patient inspecting sole of her shoe) He was a dragon who was given the flame to begin with and in spite of the fact that he was given the flame to begin with, he still had the idea that it was wrong to breathe it out. Now what do you think of that?

P (in bored fashion): I don't know.

T: Do you think it was a wise idea or not?

P: To not?

T: Pardon me.

P: What do you mean?

T: What do you think about the dragon's idea that even though he was born with the flame and the capacity to use it that he didn't?

P: Oh (yawning slightly), I don't think it was a good idea.

T: Hh hmm. Well, that's right. (patient playing with her necklace locket) It wasn't and what he did was he began to realize that he would have to start getting some practice in breathing out flames because he had gone for some time now being scared to breathe them out.

So when some other animal came along and bothered him or a person or another dragon (patient examining fingernails), he first let out a little bit of flame and realized that he did have the flame. And he was kind of scared. (patient biting fingernails) His knees were knocking and his teeth were chattering and he was very frightened at first. But he began to realize that each time he let out the flame it became easier and that he wasn't taken advantage of anymore. See, during the time when he wasn't breathing out his flame he was taken advantage of and people would do things to him because they knew that he wouldn't fight back, that he wouldn't let out his flame. (patient yawning while clapping her hand over her open mouth) But once he started to let out the flame he began to see that . . . Is this story bothering you? Is it boring you?

P (almost inaudibly): No.

T: Huh?

P: No.

T: Were you listening to it?

P: Yes.

T: Okay. (patient yawns again) At any rate, once he started to breathe it out he realized it wasn't so bad and he realized also that people would stop taking advantage of him.

And do you know what the lesson of that story is?

P: No.

T: Well, try to figure it out. What did this dragon learn?

P: That if you have something, if you are given something, you should use it even if you think it's wrong.

T: Uh huh. But did he change his mind about thinking that it was wrong?

P (playing with necklace locket while looking down at it): Hhmm. I think so.

T: How did he change his mind? What did he realize?

P: I don't know.

T: What did he come to realize?

P: That if you have something you should use it (sighs deeply, while stroking abdomen).

T: Hh hmm. And what was the purpose of the flame for him?

P (speaking through a yawn): To protect him.

T: Right. Okay. You don't seem to be too enthusiastic about this game. You seem kind of bored.

P: Hhmm.

T: Is that right?

P: Yeah.

T: Why are you bored?

P (smiling): I knew you'd say that. Um, because I am. No reason. I just am. (stroking stocking)

T: Hh hmm. Okay. Do you want to watch this?

P (in bored, condescending tune): I don't care.

T: Okay. Fine. Let's watch it then.

P: Is your clock right or is it a little fast?

T: No, that's the right time. (patient again looks down at her necklace locket and starts playing with it)

The written transcript cannot convey her attitude of extreme ennui as I got further along in the telling of my story. The patient sat back with a deadpan expression on her face and yawned profusely. At times she covered her mouth and at other times did not. Although her eyes remained open, I would not have been surprised had she closed them at any point. It was clear to me that her boredom served as a defense against her appreciating the true significance of my message, viz., that, although it may be anxiety-provoking, letting out one's resentment is far more adaptive and effective than suppressing it. Although she payed lip service to appreciating my moral and, ostensibly, gave the "correct" answers to my questions, it was clear that she was fighting against both herself and me in fully appreciating their significance.

The transcript does not convey an even more important phenomenon: the infectiousness of Roberta's ennui. Just as laughter and depression can be transmitted to others—others who have no reason themselves to be experiencing these emotions—Roberta's boredom brought about a moderate state of boredom within me. The transcript does not communicate the feeling of fatigue which I experienced near the latter third of my responding story nor can it communicate the inner pressure I had to place upon myself in order to push the conversation. I could not know how aware Roberta was of the effectiveness of this mechanism. It not only served to defend her from the anxiety elicited by the conversation, but essentially put a wet blanket on me, the transmitter of the anxiety-provoking material. It was an effective psychological smoke screen blown in my face and I don't think I could have gone on much longer with the interchange. It was not simply a feeling of being insulted by her yawns; it was more a feeling of overwhelming fatigue that gripped me. My attempts to focus on this defense mechanism were futile. Each time I broached the subject of her being bored, she denied that she was and I did not feel that pursuing this issue further would have been productive. The interchange closed with my feeling that I had not been successful in getting my message through, although I could not be sure. Her final comment about the clock going too fast (with the suggestion that the time had passed too quickly and that possibly she wanted more at some deep level) gave me a little hope that perhaps something had gotten through after all.

Clinical Example
Indirect expression of hostility.

Scott, a nine-and-a-half-year-old boy, became unruly in the classroom after his parents separated. He scapegoated children and was extremely provocative both with his peers and with his teacher. He was not able to express directly the rage he felt toward his father whom he considered to have abandoned him. About three months after the separation he told this story:

> *Patient:* Once there was a boy who had a dog. His father was allergic to dogs. One day he hid the dog so his father wouldn't be near the dog. But his father saw the dog so he had to get the dog out of there. His father said, "No more pets" because the boy did that.

This story reveals how the patient is unable to express directly the hostility he feels toward his father. Rather he expresses it passive-aggressively. The dog, to whom the father is known to be allergic, gets close to the father even though the boy (the patient) makes concerted attempts to prevent their coming in contact with one another. It is not by design that the boy exposes his father to the dog but rather by misjudgment. Although the story ends with the boy's being punished by losing the dog, he still accomplishes his goal of irritating the father. It appears that the punishment is worth the gratification of hurting his father. With this understanding of the patient's story, I told mine:

> *Therapist:* Once upon a time there was a boy and he had a dog. The father was doing things which bothered him very much but the boy found it very hard, if not impossible, to speak to his father about the things that were bothering him. One day he got an idea. He knew that his father was allergic to dogs and so he decided to have the dog jump on his father. When he did that, the father got angry and punished the boy by not allowing him to watch television for two days. Although the boy felt good about making his father's allergy get worse, he did nothing to solve the problem because he had not spoken to his father about the things that were bothering him.
>
> A few days later the boy decided to play another trick on his father. He knew how much it bothered his father when he would not take the dog out because then the dog would make in the house. When the father came home and saw that the dog made in the house he was very upset. It made the boy feel good to see how upset his father was. Once again, the boy was punished by not being able to watch television. This time, however, he couldn't watch for four days. Although he felt good when he saw his father so upset, what he did with the dog did nothing to solve the problem that he originally had with his father. Because he didn't talk about the things that were bothering him, he was still angry at his father and would get punished when he would let out his anger by letting the dog make in the house or letting the dog jump on his father, who was allergic to it.
>
> The moral of this story is: that if you are angry at somebody for something, talk to him about it. If you try to get back at him by doing things that bother him, you will be doing nothing to solve the problem. You will still be angry and he will be angry with you if you try to get back at him in ways that have nothing to do with the original problem.

The meaning of my story is obvious. The patient is discouraged from expressing his hostility through passive-aggressive maneuvers. In the story I point out how futile these are and how they do not solve difficulties in human relationships. Rather, I suggest direct discussion of the sources of irritation.

Clinical Example
A boy who feared he'd turn into a wild cannibal.

Ronald was referred at the age of eleven because of disruptive behavior in the classroom and disinterest in his school work. Although bright, he was doing poorly academically. His homework assignments were done in a slip-shod manner and he did not pay attention in class.

Ronald's parents had been divorced about two years prior to referral and his father was remarried. The mother had instituted divorce proceedings because she felt that her husband would not assume household responsibilities nor could she communicate with him. Although her husband was moderately successful in his legal practice, Ronald's mother considered him a failure at home. She described him as being disinterested in the children and procras-tinating to a pathological degree. My own observations of the father tended to confirm her view of him. He was an extremely obsessive man who could not make decisions and was markedly inhibited in expressing his feelings. He described his wife as being subject to hostile outbursts against him during which time she would berate him vociferously. She was, indeed, a somewhat labile person, but there was no question that her husband's passivity, lack of communication, and inhibition in the expression of feelings were chronic sources of provocation. Throughout most of Ronald's life he observed his parents fighting. Most often it was his mother screaming at his father in an attempt to get him to involve himself more in the family. At times, however, the father's defenses would break down and he would fly into wild outbursts of rage, during which time he would thrust his fist through windows and break down doors.

During his first week in treatment, Ronald told his story:

> *Therapist:* Ronald is having trouble thinking of a story, so I'll start. Once upon a time . . . a long, long time ago . . . in a distant land . . . far, far, far away . . . way beyond the mountains . . . way beyond the oceans . . . there lived a . . .
>
> *Patient:* . . . A wild man.
>
> *T:* A wild man. Good! Now, that's the beginning of your part of your story. Good. There lived a wild man and *this* wild man . . .
>
> *P:* . . . went around eating people.
>
> *T:* Okay. Good. Went around eating people. Okay. And one day this wild man . . .
>
> *P:* . . . tried to eat the fat man in the circus and couldn't do it.
>
> *T:* He tried to eat the fat man of the circus and couldn't do it and therefore what happened?
>
> *P:* He lived in a cave and he went back to his cave.
>
> *T:* Then he went back to his cave. Uh huh. Then what happened?
>
> *P:* Then the next day he tried even skinnier people and for a few weeks his people kept getting fatter and fatter, and then he tried eating the fat man in the circus again.
>
> *T* (interrupting): Excuse me. The next day he tried to eat skinnier people. What happened with them?

P: Well, he found that he *could* eat them.

T: He found he could eat the skinnier people.

P: Yes.

T: And then what happened?

P: Each day the people he ate kept getting fatter and fatter.

T: The people he ate. How did they get fatter? I mean, if he ate them how did they get fatter?

P: Like when he would eat fat people.

T: Yeah?

P: Like fatter people than he had eaten the day before.

T: Oh, each day he ate fatter and fatter people. Yeah.

P: And so after a long time—after a while—he decided he could—he would try to eat the fat man in the circus again and he did it.

T: And he did it!

P: Yeah.

T: He was able to. Okay.

P: And, well (long pause), one day this plane crashed and like it had a wild lady aboard and like she liked to eat people too, and like she could eat fat people and skinny people, just like the wild man could.

T: Hh hmm.

P: And so one day they met each other and got married and had little wild children.

T: Hh hmm. And then what happened? Is that the end?

P: No. (long pause) Yeah, I guess.

T: And what's the lesson of that story or the moral?

P: Uh . . . like if you keep trying to get things you might get it like when he was trying to eat the fat person, he kept trying to build up to where he could uh like when he could eat it . . . eat the fat person.

T: Okay, so the lesson is what?

P: Like if you keep trying for something you might get it.

T: So if you keep trying for something you might get it. Okay. All right. Now do you think that was a good thing to be able to try for, to be able to eat up people?

P (laughs): No.

T: Uh huh. I see. Okay. Now it's my chance. Okay?

P: All right.

This story is a clear statement of Ronald's view of his parents. He sees them both as cannibals, eating up all those around them. Of interest here is Ronald's choice of this primitive, oral-incorporative behavior as a way of expressing his feelings about his parents' hostility. Perhaps the choice of the mouth as the organ of hostile expression relates to the fact that his mother's mode of expressing her anger was primarily verbal where his father's was passive-aggressive, obstinate refusal to talk. One could speculate that his viewing his father as a voracious cannibal is a reflection of his desire that his father open his mouth and at the same time an appreciation of his father's basic underlying fear that were he to open his mouth violent, rather than innocuous, words would pour forth. Possibly, both the patient and his father, at some deep level, held the primitive belief that violent words are the equivalent of violent actions and that the mouth itself is a lethal weapon.

At another level the choice of the cannibalistic fantasy may relate to Ronald's feelings that he is being "eaten up alive" as he stands exposed to the barrage of hostilities interchanged between his parents. The story does not merely make reference to his past experiences but refers as well to his situation at the time of referral. The parents were still fighting about financial arrangements and visitations and Ronald was being actively brought into the conflict. He sees himself as turning into a cannibal himself ("And so one day they met each other and got married and had little wild children"). Although at times Ronald was "wild," e.g., when he exhibited disruptive behavior in the classroom, he most often expressed his hostility passive-aggressively—after the pattern of his father. Like his father, Ronald was verbally inhibited, probably as a protection against expressing his "wildness."

In addition to his parents' bickering, Ronald had another reason to be angry: his father was not too interested in seeing him. Although permitted twice weekly contacts (the father and his new wife still lived in the same small town), he only invited Ronald over once or twice a month. And even during these visits he spent little time with Ronald. Ronald was extremely afraid to express any resentment that he felt toward his father because of the latter's lack of interest, and the suppression and repression of such anger contributed, I believe, to his fear that he would become "wild."

With this understanding of the patient's story, I related mine:

Therapist: Once upon a time there was a wild man who used to try to eat up a lot of people and he married a wild woman. And they had some kids. Now my story is going to start with their kids. It's like a continuation of your story. Where your story stopped, mine begins.

Anyway, the kids of these parents became kind of upset because their parents seemed to be more interested in eating up other people than taking care of the kids. They were so involved in whether they could eat up thin people or fat people and trying to improve their record—trying to do better in eating up people. You know, they'd go from thin people to fatter people to very fat people, to fat people in the circus, and always trying to eat up all kinds of fat people. And this made the kids very unhappy. They were very sad and one kid said, "Look, this is really very bad. What are we going to do about this?"

And one kid said, "Look, let's talk to them. Maybe they'll stop trying to do it."

Well, they talked to them and it didn't help too much. It didn't help that much at all. They still went about their ways trying to eat up fat people. That didn't help.

So another kid said, "I know what I'll do. I'll play tricks on them. That will get 'em. That will show 'em. I'll get even. I'll do things that will bother them."

Another kid said, "I don't think that will help anything. That will just get them angry. That will just get them mad at us and then we may even see less of them then because that's not a way to do it by threatening them or forcing them or trying to hurt them."

And another kid said—what do you think another kid said as a suggestion?

Patient: I don't know.

T: He said, "Look, these are our parents. They're not perfect. They like to eat fat people; they're kind of wild in a way. Let's do this. Let's try to find our own friends and spend more time with our own friends and get our kicks there. And when our parents are not so involved in eating up these people and not so interested in that—you know, there are times when they're more interested in eating fat people; other times they're less interested. Then we'll spend time with them. So when they come back from the woods, from the jungle, trying to find fat people, and they have time at the end of those trips, then we'll spend some time with them. But while they're away we'll just make the best of what we can by spending time with other kids, young and old." And what do you think happened?

P: I don't know. They had more fun.

T: Yeah. They did that. They realized that there was no point in trying to get something that was impossible. Their parents were really not interested in changing that much. Their attempts to change them by talking hadn't really worked so they found that there was no point in trying that because it really wasn't going to work and they found that they were less angry when they would have fun in doing other things. The end.

Do you know what the lesson of that story is?

P: Uh, if you can't have fun with your parents have fun with friends.

T: Right. If someone won't give you the things that you want, try to find a substitute. Try to find it elsewhere. That's the end.

P: Hh hmm.

T: Do you like this game?

P: Yeah.

T: What was the part you liked the most?

P: I don't know.
T: Do you want to play it again sometime?
P: Yeah, I guess.
T: Okay. Good. Do you want to watch this a little bit?
P: All right.
T: Good.

In my story I first encourage the patient to talk to his father about his dissatisfactions. Recognizing, however, that there was not much likelihood that his efforts in this regard would be successful, I introduce the alternative that might be considered were his requests refused. I knew that the patient's mother could be brought to the point of reducing her angry involvement with her husband; but I knew that her husband's passive-aggressive mode of hostile expression was far less likely to be changed by any imploring on the patient's part. I considered it important to mention this alternative in order to help the patient assert himself more, but knew that it was equally important that I not raise his hopes too high regarding the success of this mode of reaction to his parents' difficulties.

The reaction of revenge, which the patient on occasion utilized through his disruptive behavior at home, is also entertained and then rejected because it would only worsen Ronald's relationship with his parents. I then introduced the substitute gratification adaptation that I believe so vital for these children to utilize. This is combined with a certain degree of resignation to a parent's difficulties. Ronald exhibited moderate interest in the story—in spite of his generally bored attitude toward the world around him—and this suggested that my message was being received. His readily providing a moral and his interest in viewing the program further confirmed that he was indeed receptive to the message I had communicated.

Acting Out of Anger

There are children who, instead of repressing their anger and possibly channeling it into neurotic symptoms, release it directly. When the hostile release is antisocial and unaccompanied by significant guilt it is said to be acted out. When such behavior is exhibited frequently in children below the pubertal period the term *behavior disorder* or *conduct disturbance* is used; in the adolescent period it is labeled *juvenile delinquency*; and in adults it is referred to as *psychopathy*. For simplicity of discussion I will refer to such behavior as delinquent or antisocial and will be referring to both children and adolescents unless otherwise specified. The relationship between breakup of the home and antisocial behavior in the child has been extensively studied (especially with regard to juvenile delinquency). Goode (1956) points out that the term "broken home" covers many possibilities: widowed; widowered; separated, father absent; separated, mother absent; divorced, father absent; divorced, mother absent; and both parents absent (from various combinations of death, divorce, and separation). Many studies clump all of these together under the rubric *broken home* and therefore do not provide meaningful data about the specific relationship between separation or divorce and delinquent behavior. Class bias also may contaminate such data. Delinquency is certainly recorded at a higher rate among the lower classes. This is partially related to the fact that middle and upper class families are likely to use money and influence to avoid the child's being prosecuted. In addition, divorce and separation occur more frequently in the lower classes. If delinquency is truly more prevalent among the lower classes (recording bias notwithstanding), then one has to consider the possibility that parental divorce or separation and delinquency are not related as cause and effect, but that both are linked with lower class life.

The Gluecks (1950) attempted to avoid the possible economic factor in trying to determine whether there is a relationship between the various types of broken home and juvenile delinquency by comparing the frequency of delinquent behavior in divorced, widowed, and separated homes with nondelinquent behavior in the same three groups *at the same economic level*. Of the delinquents studied, 8.7 percent had divorced parents, compared to 6.1 percent of the nondelinquents; the percentages for children who had lost one parent through death were, for delinquents and nondelinquents respectively, 18.3 and 13.4; but the significant statistic is that 12.4 percent of the delinquents had separated parents, compared to only 4.9 percent of nondelinquents. Apparently, parental separation is more likely to result in delinquent behavior than is parental death or divorce. The Gluecks (1952) go further and would consider the broken home as a sensitive indicator for predicting delinquency. Hunt (1966) points out that the Gluecks, although they studied homes in the same or similar neighborhoods, found that the physical and economic conditions in the broken homes were significantly worse than those in the intact homes and that these differences might have contributed to the different delinquency rates. Accordingly, confining oneself to studies within the same economic stratum may not be enough; one has to make detailed studies of the actual homes within each stratum if one is to determine with certainty if this factor is operative.

Gregory (1965a, 1965b) attempts to define more specifically the relationship between delinquent behavior and the various types of broken homes, while taking economic level into consideration. Divorce and separation were found more frequently correlated with delinquency than was the death of either or both parents. Other studies (Wylie and Degado, 1959; Short, 1966; Robins, 1966) appear to confirm that delinquent children are more likely than are nondelinquent children to come from homes broken by separation or divorce.

Such studies are countless and although one may be able to find flaws in many of them, it seems quite reasonable that there should be a relationship between breakup of the home by separation or divorce and delinquent behavior. After all, such children are being deprived and frustrated and it is reasonable to assume that some (if not many) of them will act out their anger. A sibling may be a convenient and safe scapegoat; or the parent with whom the child lives may become the focus, the absent parent not being so readily available. The parent who initiated the divorce proceedings may be selected as the target regardless of how justifiable the move and regardless of how little was his or her contribution to the difficulties. From the child's point of view *that* parent caused the separation and *that* parent should be blamed. The forms of acting-out behavior vary according to the child's age and level of sophistication. They range from primitive temper tantrums in the very young, through bullying peers, disruptive behavior in the home and classroom, cruelty to animals, fire-setting, defiance of authority, and on to a wide range of other types of antisocial behavior. I will discuss below some of the factors that contribute to the delinquency of children of divorce.

Superego lacunae. Johnson (1949, 1959) uses the term *lacunae* to refer to defects in the superego that could contribute to a delinquent's acting-out. These lacunae allow for guiltless expression of hostility. The superego is formed through parental and, to a lesser extent, social influences. It is from these that the child learns the dos and the don'ts, the rights and the wrongs. A number of authors (Keiser, 1953; Goode, 1956; Gregory, 1965a; Sugar, 1970) have pointed out that when one parent is absent from the home the child is less likely to have those exposures that produce a strong superego. It is probable that the loss of the father (rather than the mother) is especially conducive to the formation of a weak superego. Although many fathers are quite passive, uninvolved, and less available than the mother with regard to the child's upbringing, social forces may still impart to the child that the father is the severer disciplinarian. Many mothers will say, "Just wait until your father comes home and hears what you've done." And most teachers know that summoning a child's father to school implies that a more serious offense has been committed than when a mother is asked to come. Crumley and Blumenthal (1973) found an increase in antisocial acting-out among children of military fathers who were off on long tours of duty away from the home. Since the overwhelming majority of separations involve the absence of the father, the frequent development of superego deficiencies in children of divorce is not surprising. Gregory (1965b), however, concluded that although the loss of a father is more likely to contribute to delinquent behavior in boys, the loss of a mother is more crucial in the case of delinquent girls. Whether the father is more necessary than the mother to the child's superego formation, and whether there is a relationship between the sex of the absent parent and the sex of the delinquent child are questions which may not yet have been definitely answered. But most investigators do agree that a parent's absence is more likely to result in superego deficiencies than is the case when both parents are present.

In the intact home, when one parent is not on the scene, the other is generally available to teach, discipline, and impart those values that contribute to healthy superego development. When separation occurs and the custodial parent is temporarily absent, the child is more likely to be left with those who have less authority and hence less influence on superego development. And when the children are older, they are more likely to be left alone than children with two parents living in the home. Lastly (and by no means least) the participation of lawyers often contributes further to a weakening of the child's superego. Using the rationalization that justice must be done and that their clients must be protected from being taken advantage of, the lawyers are capable of turning otherwise sensitive and humane parents into gross psychopaths when it comes to their spouses. Epstein (1974) and Sopkin (1974) provide excellent examples of this tragic and unconscionable process. Observing their parents to behave with so little inner restraint contributes to the child's acting similarly.

Identification with acting-out parents. The child of divorce is often observer to some of the most cruel behavior that one individual can visit upon another. The parental hostilities frequently reach sadistic levels. There is often little place for honesty in their deliberations and the milieu becomes one of continual distrust. The most cruel things may be said with no holds barred on the use of profanity. Impulsive acting-out is common. The desire for vengeance may reach obsessive and even psychotic proportions. Sensitivity to the feelings of others may become totally lost. Power struggles become the only method of dealing with differences. And the parents may even physically harm one another, so vicious and violent becomes their rage. In such a milieu it is not surprising that the child is likely to react in kind. In Morrison's group (1974) 12.5% of the divorced fathers and 2.5% of the divorced mothers were diagnosed as sociopathic; none of the mothers and fathers in the never-divorced control group were so diagnosed. Sometimes a parent's leaving the home is a manifestation of psychopathy. Such a parent has little desire to fulfill his or her family obligations and has no guilt over abandoning spouse and children. Lastly, the child may not only develop psychopathic behavior via the simple mechanism of emulation of such a parent, but may do so as well through the mechanism of identification with the aggressor. Following the principle of "If you can't fight 'em, join 'em," he takes on the parental antisocial attitudes to be an ally rather than the target of the hostilities he not only observes but fears may be directed at him as well.

Parental sanction. Parental sanction (either conscious or unconscious) of a child's antisocial acting-out is common whenever a child exhibits antisocial behavior—both within and out of the divorce situation. A parent may not be able to act out his own hostilities because of internal inhibitions or the awareness of the consequences of doing so. The child lends himself well to the acting-out of such parental impulses. By doing so he may provide a parent with vicarious gratification, and may gain the parent's affection for his antisocial behavior. Lacking the judgment of the adult he may more readily engage in behavior that the adult would be wary of. Whereas in the intact household such parentally sanctioned acting-out is directed outside the home, in the divorced situation it is generally directed toward one spouse and encouraged by the other.

About half of the 425 divorcees studied by Goode (1956) wished to punish or remarry their husbands. The lingering feelings of hostility present in such women can most readily be acted out by their children. After all, the divorced parent usually has less contact with the former spouse than has the visiting child. Accordingly, the child often has greater opportunities to exhibit hostility directly to a parent than either one of them has to express anger toward the other. The child may become a readily available tool for the parentally sanctioned acting-out. He may willingly side with one parent against the other as a general pattern, or may switch sides and take the position of the parent he is with at the particular time. The ways in which children are used for this purpose are legion. The child may serve as an informer and provide information that could be devastating when litigation is taking place. One parent may encourage the child not to comply with the requests of the other, even in such small matters as which foods to eat and when to go to bed. A mother may "forget" to have the children ready for the father and they (even though old enough to appreciate the time and day) may also "fail to remember" to remind the mother about their appointment with the father. Or father may "forget" the time to return the children and they too may suffer similar memory lapses. Or the children may dawdle in preparing for their father's visit and Mother's sense of urgency for getting them ready on time may leave much to be desired. The children "get the message" from the mother and dawdle even more. The father may recognize that his bringing the children home early presents the mother with various restrictions and inconveniences. Their acting-up may serve as an excuse for the father's early return and they may do so in order to ingratiate themselves with him. The mother may encourage antisocial behavior in the children in order to hurt the husband by making him feel guilty: "Look at all the trouble you've caused by leaving. Look how upset they've become since you've gone."

At times the child may use the parent to act out his hostility. With each parent he relates all the indignities he suffers at the hands of the other. The parent he is with lends a most receptive ear, does not feel the need to gain corroboration, and acts out against the spouse. Such parents may become quite naive regarding what they will believe about the spouse, all in the service of having an excuse to hurt the partner.

Compensating for feelings of impotence. The child of divorce almost always feels insecure, especially around the time of separation. After all, his family—the most stabilizing force in his life—has fallen apart and this cannot but make him feel insecure. Angry feelings, especially when acted out, can provide the child with a specious sense of power. Although destroying furniture, for example, does not accomplish anything regarding the parental separation, it does provide a child with a sense of strength (as well as the relief of having let out some anger). Rage reactions are at times frightening to others and this can contribute to the notion that they are a measure of one's power. Such acting-out may also serve as a counterphobic measure. The child of separation is usually a frightened child, fearful of the many consequences of a parent's having left and fearful that the remaining parent may abandon him as well. He may utilize a variety of counterphobic maneuvers to deny such fear. He may, for example, climb in dangerous places, run across the street in front of traffic, or play with matches, just to prove to himself that he cannot be harmed.

The boy whose father has left the home may engage in delinquent acts in order to gain a feeling of masculinity to compensate for the loss of a male model. He may equate antisocial acting-out with masculinity, a view fostered to a significant degree by the public media. Living only with his mother (and in some situations with other females as well) may result in feelings that some of their femininity may wipe off on him and turn him into a "sissy." To avoid this he may gravitate toward "tough guys" and delinquents and become a willing member of their gang. A mother living alone with her son may try to compensate for her feelings of deficiency as a wife by becoming an exemplary mother. In the service of this goal she may try to make the boy well-disciplined and well-behaved. The child may react to such a mother with antisocial behavior, not only from the hostility that such pressures engender but because such acting-out serves to negate the weakness and femininity the boy sees to be an intrinsic part of the image his mother is trying to create.

Provoking punishment. A child may become delinquent in order to provoke punishment. This need not be done in the service of assuaging guilt; rather it may represent an attempt to gain an absent father's attention or even his return to the home. If the child becomes so unmanageable that his mother cannot handle him, she may resort to enlisting the father's aid in providing control. Although such involvement with the father may be painful, the child appears to feel that it is worth the price. In other words, if his choice is one of having no father at all or a father who reprimands, disciplines, and punishes, he chooses the latter alternative. In addition, there are times when the child wants the father's help in strengthening his superego development, and provocative behavior may well appear the only way to secure such help. Crumley and Blumenthal (1973) considered this factor operative in the acting-out of military children when their fathers were stationed on tours of duty distant from the home. By their delinquent behavior they hoped to get the father recalled, in part to provide external controls for the inner ones they felt to be weakening.

Testing and fears of intimacy. As mentioned, the child of divorce is very insecure. He lives with the fear that the parent who has left the home may abandon him even further and that the remaining parent may also leave him. One way for the child to gain reassurance that these calamities will not recur is through testing the parents' tolerance for his disobedient behavior. He works on the principle (central to masochism) that the more pain one will tolerate from another, the more one can demonstrate his or her affection. Although the provocations may result in punishment and various kinds of parental alienation, they do not generally result in the parents' further abandoning the child—and he is thereby reassured.

Another way of handling the anticipation of abandonment that results from the separation is for the child himself to become the initiator of rejection. His antisocial acts serve to keep people at a distance. He thereby becomes the one who controls the situation in which separation from another person has taken place, not the one who must passively suffer abandonment. In addition, such behavior protects him from intimate relationships. He has already been "burned" and wishes to protect himself from further disillusionment and disappointment in his relationships with others. And there is hardly a better way to do this than to provoke others with antisocial behavior.

Therapeutic Approaches to Acting-Out of Anger

Work with parents. Since the parental contribution to the child's antisocial acting-out may be formidable, counseling them is strongly indicated. However, such work is often impeded by the fact that because they have separated they have little desire to be with one another; yet the optimum therapeutic approach for the child's problems may warrant their having meetings (of varying degrees of frequency) together with the therapist. Although individual counseling with either alone can often prove useful, as is true in most marital conflicts, conjoint work can be invaluable. (I am referring to counseling here, not intensive therapy.) Whereas conjoint work with the parents of a child living in an intact home has as one of its goals the improvement of the marital relationship, conjoint counseling with parents who are separated cannot have this goal. Rather its aim should be for the parents to have the most civilized and humane relationship under the circumstances—one that will cause the least damage to themselves and their children. The situation may be so charged that this goal may be extremely difficult to achieve. And if lawyers are still involved and active litigation ensuing, it is just about impossible. If there is one thing that is antithetical to parents' conjoint counseling, it is adversary litigation. (I will discuss this in greater detail in Chapter 15.) For the child's sake, however, the therapist may have to attempt to work with such parents in the hope that some good may come of it. But he must recognize that lawyers may be advising the parents about what to reveal and what not to reveal, what to lie about and what to be truthful about. Although such legal counseling may make a mockery of the conjoint therapeutic interviews, the therapist may still have to go along with it in the hope that he may still somehow be helpful to the child.

Often such conjoint interviews may degenerate rapidly as each party uses it for the purpose of venting further rage or inflicting further pain on the partner. Whereas the therapist's goal is constructive, i.e., to explore ways of being helpful to the child, and although each parent may profess that that is his or her primary goals as well, each issue may quickly be used for the parent's own destructive purpose. To the degree the therapist can be successful in helping such parents reduce their hostilities, to that degree will he reduce certain elements contributing to the child's delinquent behavior. If the parents become less angry at one another, the child will be less angry and hence less likely to be delinquent. If they reduce their hostilities, the emulation factor will be reduced, i.e., two important models for the child's antisocial behavior will have been removed. If the parents can be helped to "fill" their superego lacunae the child, through identification, is likely to fill his as well. If the parents can be helped to spend less time fighting and more time with the child, he is less likely to be angry and hence less prone to act out hostility. In addition, having more time with them will obviate the need to gain their attention by provocative acts. Gaining more affection will make him more secure, less impotent, and so less needful of angry demonstrations as a way of gaining a sense of strength. If the parents can be helped to achieve a more intimate relationship with the child, he will be less likely to fear intimacy and push people away by antisocial behavior in order to protect himself from the tenderness that he sees to be dangerous. And if they are closer to him he will be less needful of provocative testing to see if they will still remain loyal and loving of him.

If the parents are actively sanctioning the child's antisocial behavior, either against outsiders or against one another, they should be helped to reduce this. If they are using the child as an informant, if they are being sucked into believing the child's criticisms of each other, if they are allowing themselves to be played one against the other, every attempt should be made to bring about a cessation of such involvement with the child. The parents have to be helped to appreciate that they are susceptible to becoming willing tools of the child in his desire to act out *his* anger toward them. Mother is seduced into acting out the child's hostility to father, and father is fooled into reacting similarly to mother. In addition, the parents may be contributing to the child's angry acting-out by not utilizing appropriate disciplinary measures. The therapist does well to explore this area as well and recommend more effective measures when indicated. (I have found useful in this regard the chapter "Reward, Discipline, and Punishment" in my book *Understanding Children* [1973].)

Sometimes the parents' rage that is contributing to the child's acting-out may be so great that the aforementioned type of counseling may not prove useful. The parent may appreciate intellectually, for example, that the continuation of hostilities is not only a waste of time and energy but detrimental to the child as well; and yet he or she may be helpless to refrain from perpetuating them. The parent may feel such a need for revenge that he may blind himself to the repercussions of his obsession with such gratification. In such cases individual therapy may be warranted, either with the child's therapist or another. When all parties are agreeable I prefer that the same therapist work with the child and one parent (especially the one with whom the child is living). However, if both parents warrant and are desirous of therapy it is generally not advisable that they work with the same therapist when separation and divorce has occurred. (Generally, the parents themselves recognize the dangers of such an arrangement and do not request it.)

Work with the child. The child with neurotic problems (both related and unrelated to anger) may be motivated to change himself because of the psychic pain he is suffering. The child who acts out his anger generally does not have inner pain and is thereby not particularly motivated to change himself. Accordingly, his main request may be that the therapist "get people off his back": teachers who "bug" him to finish his assignments, do his homework, and behave in class; parents who complain that he won't do household chores, stop fighting with his siblings, and come in the house when they call him; neighbors who complain that he bullies their children, etc. With such a child the seductive techniques described in Chapter 3 may be crucial if the child is to be engaged. But even more important is the therapist's establishing a good relationship with him. In the treatment of such children (possibly more than is true for any other disorder) the establishment of a good therapist-patient relationship is vital if the therapy is to be successful. And yet these may be the hardest children to engage. (Since it is beyond the scope of this book to discuss this vast and complex issue, the reader may wish to refer to my *Psychotherapeutic Approaches to the Resistant Child* (1975) for a detailed description of some of the methods I have found useful in engaging acting-out as well as other children who are difficult to involve in treatment.) It is in the context of such a relationship that the child has the best chance of strengthening his superego. It is only if the relationship is a good one that the child will identify with the therapist, take on his values, and incorporate his standards for socially acceptable behavior. And it is only when there is a good relationship that the child will respect what the therapist has to say and meaningfully learn from him.

As part of the therapeutic approach to such children, the therapist should try to help the child deal with anger-provoking situations at the earliest possible time so that there will be less anger to be acted out. The approaches here are similar to those described earlier in this chapter in my discussion of neurotic handling of anger. In both cases the child does well to learn how to avoid and reduce anger. In the neurotic there will then be less anger to channel into neurotic symptoms, and in the delinquent there will be less anger to act out.

Since peer pressure, support, and encouragement often contribute to a child's antisocial acting out, group therapy can sometimes be useful in the treatment of such children. This is especially true for adolescents. Whereas the child looks upon the therapist as someone of the adult generation (and therefore, like the parents, as someone to be somewhat distrusted), the views of a child's peers often have greater credibility for him. In addition, children are exquisitely sensitive to peer influence and the group can provide the child with the opportunity to hear such opinions in a protected situation, i.e., since the members of the group are not his friends or relatives he is safe from the social alienation that their negative opinions might result in if expressed in a social situation. My experience has been that most youngsters in a group will espouse and adhere to (with varying degrees of conviction) more conservative and traditional social standards than they might actually practice themselves. Although they do this, in part, to ingratiate themselves with the therapist, such professions are also motivated by the inner recognition of the value of such standards (usually imbued in earlier years); but only in the protected group environment will they allow themselves to admit their basic adherence to the traditional social norms. In school and neighborhood such compliance with traditional values may be met with much social criticism.

I have found direct discussion groups most valuable for the adolescents. Latency age children, in my experience, do not usually do well in discussion groups. Often their need for horseplay and their inability to sit still for long periods of time interfere with the smooth functioning of such groups and the therapist is often reduced to spending most of his time as a disciplinarian. I have found *The Talking, Feeling, and Doing Game* useful in providing the kind of structure that can involve latency children and makes group therapy with them a more meaningful experience. This is especially true when the group is small (three or four members).

In the groups I try to help the youngster acquire antidelinquent attitudes from his group peers. I encourage group support of the delinquent's attempts not to succumb to peer pressure to engage in antisocial behavior. I try to imbue the youngster with the important truth that it is often braver to defy dares and group pressure to join in antisocial activities than to involve oneself in them. I try to foster the notion that compliance is usually the weaker course, ostensible bravery in the activities notwithstanding.

Lastly, it is important for the therapist to appreciate that sublimation is an extremely common, harmless, and often socially constructive way for a person to express repressed hostility. Many youngsters I have seen who harbor deep-seated resentments over parental separation and divorce become very involved in sports. Not only does the competition provide a socially acceptable outlet for their anger, but the physical activity as well serves this purpose. Whatever drawbacks there may be to horror movies on TV and violence in films they do allow for vicarious hostile release. Accordingly, the therapist does well to recognize these outlets because they may be useful for the child of divorce, especially those who are prone to act out their hostile reactions.

Some children, especially in the early phases of therapy, may wish to rid themselves of their rage (which they sense as uncomfortable) by magic means. The example below describes how I may utilize the Mutual Storytelling Technique in helping such children deal more effectively with their anger.

Clinical Example
Magic removal of anger.

Joan, a ten-year-old girl whose parents were divorced, entered treatment because of outbursts of rage against her mother, a chronic attitude of surliness, obsessive self-derogation, and an antagonistic attitude toward teachers and peers. Early in treatment she told this story:

Patient: This story is about two orphan boys who were always wishing to be brothers and two orphan girls who were always wishing to be sisters. So one day a rich lady and her rich husband came over to adopt some children, but the boy couple and the girl couple did not like each other very much at all. Finally the rich lady and her husband made up their minds. They decided to adopt the two boys and the two girls so they became brothers and sisters.

Now they didn't like each other at all so they spent their time fighting.

Therapist: You mean the two brothers didn't like the two sisters? Is that it?

P: Yes, and the two sisters didn't like the two brothers. So they yelped and screamed, kicked and everything. So finally something had to be done. The rich woman said whoever could make her children stop fighting would get fifty dollars worth of gold coins.

Men and women from all around the world came. But one day a little bird came and the lady said, "What are you doing here little bird?" "I can make your children stop fighting," the bird said. So he went in where the children were fighting and he waved his wing around them. Suddenly they were all friendly together. So the bird received instead of fifty dollars worth of gold coins a gold nest.

So the people were very angry at this bird but they couldn't do anything about it. Birds from miles around came to see this nest. So the children stopped fighting and they all lived happily ever after.

I don't have a moral for my story.

T: You don't have a moral? Sure you have a moral—some lesson in that story.

P: Don't be jealous when you can't do anything about it.

T: Well how does that fit in with this story?

P: Well, the people were very jealous of the bird, but see they couldn't do anything about it—that the bird had made the two boys and the two girls friends. They wanted all the gold coins and everything, but they didn't get it so they couldn't do anything about it.

T: You mean people were jealous of the bird and the gold nest and everything else.

P: Yeah.

T: I see. Okay.

Joan's divorced father rarely visited her, and much of the anger she felt toward him was displaced to her mother. Without a father present, and with a mother at whom she was chronically enraged, this girl was left with a feeling of total abandonment.

The angry children represent Joan. However, I was not sure why she represented herself as two brothers and two sisters. She did have one sister with whom she constantly bickered. Perhaps the two sisters stand for the patient and her sister, while the two brothers represent boys she would like to have in her household for further companionship. The children are adopted by "a rich lady and her rich husband." With this device she goes from the emotionally impoverished home she sees herself to be living in to one where there is an abundance of affection which is symbolized by wealth.

The anger, by which Joan is plagued and sometimes paralyzed, is a disruptive element, even in her new home. This is magically removed by a special bird who waves his wing over the children. Although the children are now happy, the bird becomes the object of everyone's jealousy and anger because of the gold nest he receives for curing the children. The wealthy bird, I believe, is an alter ego of the patient. Its plight suggests that the patient feels that even if she got wealth, acquired affection, that is, there would still be those around her who would be critical of her. The bird's plight also implies that her pool of rage is so vast that she cannot see herself free from situations in which it is not present, either in herself or projected onto others.

With this understanding of Joan's story, I told this one:

Therapist: Once upon a time there was an orphanage and in this orphanage there lived two orphan boys who liked one another very much and they wanted to be brothers. In addition, there were two orphan girls who liked one another very much and they wanted to be sisters.

Well, one day a very rich lady came to the orphanage and she said that she was interested in getting four children—two boys and two girls—and what do you know, she chose the two friends that wanted to be brothers and the two friends that wanted to be sisters. So then they became brothers and sisters.

Well, as soon as they got home to the big mansion of the rich lady they started to fight. And they fought and they fought. This little rich old lady was kind of beside herself. She didn't know what to do. So finally she decided that she would give a reward of fifty dollars in gold coins to anybody who could figure out a way to stop these kids.

Well, people came from all over the land, making all kinds of suggestions, and they just didn't work. Nothing worked. Then a little bird came along and he said, "I think that I can make them stop fighting." So the little bird went in there and he waved his wings and you know what happened?

Patient: They stopped fighting?

T: No. They didn't stop fighting because the kids said to the bird, "What do you think that's suppose to do, bird?" The bird said, "These are magic wings and they are going to make you stop fighting." The kids all laughed. They said, "That's a riot, ha, ha. What are you, a nut, bird? Waving your wings is going to make us stop fighting? You must be cuckoo. That's how the cuckoo bird got his name because he thought that he could stop fighting by magic."

Well, then, in came the wise old owl. He looked the situation over and he said to these kids and the rich old lady, "I can't promise that I can help with this problem, but I will try." And the rich old lady said,

"Wonderful, wonderful, anything." The owl said, "Now you come around here, you kids, and tell me what it is exactly you are fighting about?" And then they started to talk about what they were fighting about. The boys said what they felt about the girls—the things they didn't like about the girls—and the girls told what things they didn't like about the boys. What things did the boys not like about the girls? What did they say?

P: That they were sissies?

T: And what did the girls say they didn't like about the boys?

P: That they were too rough.

T: Well whatever it was, the boys and the girls each aired their grievances. Do you know what "aired their grievances" mean? (Joan shakes her head no.) Each told what they felt was wrong with the other, and some of the things they were able to change and some they weren't. So after they did that they were all less angry at one another because they had changed certain things that were bothering them. And it was after that that they were far less angry at one another and they fought less frequently. And so the owl was given the fifty dollars in gold coin. And the people all appreciated and realized that he indeed deserved it because he had come forth with the wisest solution to the problem. And do you know what the morals of that story are? There are two morals that I can think of.

P: Don't be jealous when you know someone deserves it.

T: All right. That's one moral. I've got a couple more.

P: You can't stop fighting by magic.

T: Right, right. Magic doesn't solve problems. That's one moral. The other moral is that problems are solved by . . .

P: Intelligence.

T: Intelligence, by discussion, by communication, by talking to one another and trying to figure out what really are the things that bother you. That's how problems are solved and that's how people get less angry. The end. Anything you want to say about this story?

P: It was very meaningful.

T: In what way?

P: I don't know.

T: Why do you say it was meaningful?

P: It should be meaningful to me.

T: Is it meaningful to you?

P: Yes.

T: What part was meaningful to you?

P: About the owl and stuff, boys and girls—by talking.

T: Right. That's the best way. Okay?

Joan joined with me in ridiculing the bird who professed he could perform magic. I believe that my communication that there are no magical solutions to life's problems made more of an impact when presented in this manner than it would have if I had stated it categorically. The wise old owl—one of my more sneaky disguises—urges the children to look at the sources of their anger and to air them in a civilized fashion. Having utilized their anger in the service of removing sources of irritation, they feel less angry. In my story, no one is angry at or jealous of the owl. He justly deserves his reward.

The post-story discussion shows that the girl understood my messages. Joan's statement that the story was very meaningful to her was made with conviction. I believe that the humorous way in which a portion of my message was imparted contributed to her receptivity.

As mentioned, I do not consider conscious control of pathological behavior to be an inappropriate or low-order therapeutic modality. Certainly, working through underlying problems should be the main aim of a psychotherapeutic approach; however, conscious control also has a definite place in treatment. Once the child has the living experience that acting in a different way may be to his benefit, he may be more motivated to give up his symptoms and work them out. In addition, controlling the acting-out of the symptom may reduce the elements that are contributing to the symptom in the first place. For example, a child with feelings of low self-worth and few friends may hide the fact that his father has left the home. He may go to great lengths to avoid his friends' visiting his house lest they learn the truth about his father. He may make up stories about things that he has done with his father in order to keep the myth credible. He may not appreciate that the guilt he feels over his duplicity and the inner embarrassment he suffers over his efforts to hide the truth lower his self-esteem even further. In addition, when others learn the truth (as they inevitably will) he will suffer even further alienation. It behooves the therapist to help such a child appreciate that the mechanisms he is using to enhance his feelings of self-worth are in fact lowering it and that this kind of attempt to keep friends will probably result in his losing even more. This vicious spiral downward may be interrupted by the child's exerting conscious control over his lying. Telling the truth and having the living experience that he is judged for what he is and not what his father has done can be an ego-enhancing experience. And such enhancement may lessen his need even further to utilize maladaptive ego-enhancing maneuvers, whether lying or other types.

The child who is afraid to tell his divorced father that he is bored and resentful over being dragged along on business visits during visitation time has to be helped to consciously squelch his fear and express his anger to his father. Of course, this does not preclude inquiry into the factors that underlie his fears of self-assertion. If the child confines his conversations in treatment to his speculations about the consequences of such action the therapy will quickly become sterile. When he brings in material related to his living experiences associated with such assertion, then the discussions are likely to be more meaningful and his working out the problem more likely. And conscious control has to be utilized if the child is to enjoy the benefits of this aspect of his therapy.

With regard to antisocial acting-out, the child may be oblivious to the effects of his behavior on others. He may believe, for example, that others are admiring him for his prowess in bullying. It behooves the therapist to communicate to such a child that others are not really very impressed with someone who beats up younger children and that he, deep down, doesn't even respect himself for what he is doing. He may wish to blind himself to the repercussions of his behavior and live in the dream world that there will be none. Leonard, whose clinical material is presented below, was a good example of a boy with this attitude. He provoked and scapegoated others and was then surprised that they reacted in kind or rejected him. His parents, although separated, continually fought and Leonard acted out the anger he felt toward them. Rather than accept the fact of his provocations he saw himself as the innocent bystander who was picked upon by others without reason.

Clinical Example
The innocent bystander who always gets picked upon

Leonard entered treatment at the age of eight because of extensive provocative behavior. He had a reputation as a troublemaker throughout his neighborhood—so much so that parents prohibited their children from playing with him. He teased, poked, and hit other children and interfered with their play. At home he often thwarted his parents (especially his mother), and there were frequent power struggles over eating, dressing, etc. Leonard was basically angry at his parents for their feuding—especially when his discipline was used as the focus for their fighting. Much of his provocative behavior was consciously controllable; yet he invariably denied his initiation of and participation in his difficulties and always attributed his troubles to others.

While playing Scrabble for Juniors, the following interchange took place.

> *Therapist:* Leonard has completed the word *gate* for which he gets one reward chip. Now if you can say anything at all about the word *gate* . . .
> *Patient* (interrupts): . . . (mumbles) . . .
> *T:* What?
> *P:* Sentence?
> *T:* A sentence, right. You get a second one. Anything at all.
> *P:* We got a new gate in our backyard.

T: Who got a new gate?

P: I did.

T: Okay, take a second chip. Now if you can tell me a made-up story, completely made up from your own imagination, you can get two more chips—about the word *gate*.

P: Uh, all right, about a gate. Once we got a gate because dogs is bothering me and we had to get a gate because the dogs were bothering us a long time. And we—and we used our gate—when we used it so dogs didn't bother us. So last time when I came home from school a dog bit me on my side. So when he bit me I had to go get a tetanus shot. I got a tetanus shot. The doctor gave me a make-believe, um, let's see—gave me a shot . . .

T: Well, go ahead. Is this a make-believe story?

P: Yeah.

T: All right, then what?

P: The part of the dog—the part of the gate part isn't—is a make-believe story.

T: Is a make-believe story.

P: The part of the tetanus shot isn't.

T: All right, so the make-believe part is about a gate in order to pro-tect yourself from dogs.

P: Yes.

T: Okay, now what happens after that? Continue with that part.

P: Well, when he gave me—I was so happy I went out of that doctor's office before . . .

T (interrupts): Wait a minute, was that the real part?

P: Yeah.

T: I'm a little confused between the real part and the make-believe part of this story.

P: The gate part is the make-believe story and the part I'm telling now is make-believe.

T: Is make-believe too?

P: Yeah.

T: Okay, so how do you—all right, so even though there was a gate when you came home the dog still bit you.

P: Yes, because when I came out to play.

T: When you came out to play, all right. Then you got a tetanus shot. Then what happened?

P: Then we went home, but before I—before I got a chance to clean my side [from the bite] I was playing outside. I was so happy.

T: You were happy because?

P: Because I got one of those shots.

T: Okay, is that the end of the story?

P: Yes.

T: And the lesson of that story?

P: No lesson.

T: No lesson. Okay, you get two chips for that. All right, now it's my chance to tell a story.

P (handling his chips): Look at all these chips.

T: All right, now I can get two chips if I can tell a story.

P: Wait, I have to put more letters . . .

T (interrupts): After my story. It's my chance now to tell a story. Okay?

P: (nods affirmatively)

The story reflects well Leonard's attitude toward the world. He, an innocent party, is bitten by a dog. The gate is built to protect him from malicious dogs who bite without provocation. In addition, he is quickly and almost magically cured of the infection that might result from the bite. This, I believed, was a reflection of Leonard's wish that there be no significant repercussions from his antisocial behavior—regardless of who initiates it. With this understanding of the patient's story, I responded.

Therapist: Now if I can tell a story about the word *gate*, I can get two reward chips. Okay. Here I go.

Once upon a time there was a boy and the dogs in the neighborhood didn't like him and the reason they didn't like him was that when he would go out into the street he would do things, like he would pull the dogs' tails or he would poke them with sticks.

Anyway, he went to his father and he said, "Would you please build a gate in order to protect me from all those dogs who are constantly trying to bite me and pick on me and things like that?"

And his father said, "I'm not going to build a gate because you'd go outside that gate and you'd still bother the dogs. If I know you, you'd bother the dogs and jump over that gate and then they wouldn't be able to get back at you or they might even jump over the gate too. See, the problem is not going to be solved by a gate. The problem is going to be solved by your stopping with this stuff, with pulling dogs' tails and poking them with sticks."

Well, the boy was very mad at his father because his father wouldn't get a gate, so he went out one day and he was poking a dog and the dog bit him. Then he had to go to a doctor and then he had to get a tetanus shot. And he was very unhappy about that. He came home crying, "I want you to get a gate!"

And the father said, "I'm still not going to get a gate. I hope you've learned a lesson with this bite and I hope you're not going to poke those dogs. If you poke those dogs and you pull their tails, then they are going to bite you and that's all there is to it." So what do you think happened?

P: Um, he didn't poke the dogs anymore.

T: Well, what happened was that it took him a long time to learn that lesson. He still was angry at his father for not getting the gate, but gradually he realized that his father was right, that the gate wasn't going to solve any problems. That wasn't the answer, because once he went outside the gate he'd still be in the same situation with the dogs. So he gradually stopped poking those dogs and then they gradually stopped biting him. In fact, what happened was that then they became friendly with him as he gradually stopped poking the dogs and pulling their tails, and then he never spoke about a gate again. The end.

Okay, I get two chips for that.

My story appeals to one aspect of Leonard's difficulties, namely, his denial of his own participation in bringing about his troubles in his relationships with his peers. The story directs itself to this aspect of his problems; it does not focus on the underlying sources of his anger. There was little that Leonard could do directly about his parents' conflicts (I was working with them on this) and so it would have been difficult to create a story that involved him in such efforts. In addition, Leonard's story did not, I believe, touch as directly on that problem as it did on his seeing himself as helpless to protect himself from malicious peers. I appealed to self-recognition of his contribution and conscious control of his acting-out. Hopefully he, like the boy in the story, would then enjoy a better relationship with those around him. There would then be less anger to act out and the vicious cycle would be interrupted.
act out and the vicious cycle would be interrupted.

Another example of a situation in which a child wished to act out his anger and profited from my apprising him of the fact that there would be repercussions for his behavior occurred with a ten-year-old boy whom I will call Sam. During session one day Sam expressed great disappointment over the fact that his father, who was living in a foreign country, had once again written a letter informing him that a promised visit would not be realized. Again the letter contained a promise of a future visit at a specific time, but Sam had been disappointed so often before that he was inwardly enraged. However, instead of expressing the anger he felt toward his father he lashed out at others, especially his classmates. In our session, after I had made a double jump in a game of checkers, he suddenly came around to my side of the table and with an enraged expression shook his fist in front of me in such a way that I was quite sure he was going to strike me in the face. I firmly stated:

"Sam, office therapy is for people who can control their actions. You can say anything at all here; but you cannot harm me or destroy my property. If you cannot stop yourself from doing such things we'll have to talk about your stopping therapy." Sam dropped his fist and we began to talk about whom he was *really* angry at. I do not believe that anything is accomplished therapeutically when the therapist merely allows himself to be a target for the patient's hostility. The patient must be helped to direct his hostility toward the appropriate people in the most constructive and civilized manner possible. In essence, I let Sam know that his behavior would have consequences. Obviously, had I not had a good relationship with Sam at the time of this experience he would not have been deterred by my threats. If there was no relationship to lose there would have been no reason for him not to use me as an outlet for the hostility he felt toward his father.

The clinical examples presented below demonstrates a number of the approaches I utilize in the therapy of youngsters who act out their anger.

Clinical Example
The Indian who started a fire.

Mike entered treatment at seven-and-a-half because of disruptive behavior in the classroom and lack of cooperation with his teacher. Although very bright, his slipshod attitudes and lack of interest in his studies resulted in poor academic performance. His parents were divorced and he lived with his mother. With both parents he was recalcitrant and frequently entered into power struggles over the most minor issues. During his third month of treatment, while playing *Scrabble for Juniors*, this interchange took place:

> *Therapist:* Mike completed a word. What word?
> *Patient: Indian.*
> *T:* Okay, you get one red chip for that. Now if you say anything about the word *Indian* or tell a story; it doesn't matter which one you do first. You can either tell a story or say something.
> *P:* Um, well, once an Indian started a fire.
> *T:* An Indian started a fire. Okay, you get a chip for that. Now if you can tell a story; this is a completely made up story, you know.
> *P:* Once upon a time there was an Indian. He lived all alone and he was scared to make a little campfire. He didn't know how to hunt. He didn't know how to make anything as a weapon. And once he got killed by a tiger who came around his camp.
> *T:* Is that the whole story?
> *P:* Hh hmm.
> *T:* Okay, what's the lesson of that story?

P: Um, if you don't know how to defend yourself or anything, try to find somebody to help you.

T: Hh hmm. Okay. You get two chips for that.

I understood the statement "once an Indian started a fire" to symbolize Mike's anger. I believed that Mike's acting-out at home and school was related to the anger he felt toward his parents for their divorce. The story, however, then proceeds along different lines. The Indian is "scared to make a little campfire." I considered this to reflect Mike's fears of expressing his anger, his acting-out notwithstanding. He then goes on to describe the consequences of the Indian's fears of learning those things that are important for Indians to learn. Because he did not know how to make campfires, hunt, and make weapons he got killed by a tiger. On the one hand, Mike was driven to act out his anger; on the other hand, he was bright enough to appreciate that his obstructionistic refusal to learn was compromising his acquisition of the knowledge and skills necessary to function adequately in society and protect himself from the dangers of the world. The fear of making fires, then, is best understood as a reflection of Mike's awareness of the consequences of his acting-out. The story reveals then some therapeutic advance and an incorporation of previously communicated messages of mine.

With this understanding of Mike's statement and story, I responded:

Therapist: Now if I can say anything about an Indian or tell a story I can get chips too. Right?

P: (nods affirmatively)

T: All right. First I'm going to tell a story. Once upon a time there was an Indian and when this Indian was a boy there were certain things that were happening in his life that made him very angry, things that were going on in his family—his mother and his father and even other relatives. He was really mad about these things. Well, instead of telling the people what he was mad about, instead of doing that, what he would do would be to refuse to learn the things that were important for Indians to learn. Like when they were teaching the Indians to make fires, he said, "I'm not going to learn how to make fires," because he knew that that bugged his mother and father and his relatives. So when they taught the Indian boys how to hunt, he wouldn't learn how to hunt. When they'd give him a bow and arrow and they'd ask him to shoot it, you know, he wouldn't learn how to do it so that the arrow didn't shoot right, or when they were teaching him to use guns—not guns—knives and spears and things like that, he just wouldn't learn. These were useful things for him to learn but it was more important for him to hurt his mother and father by not learning because he was mad at them. And so what happened was that as he got older and the other Indians became very good at these things—building fires and hunting—and he wasn't very good at these things at all. And he began to become very ashamed.

Well, one day he was going through the woods and some wild animal came up and started to attack him. He ran away and climbed up a tree, and the animal was at the bottom of the tree trying to get him. And it was really a scary situation and he really didn't know how to defend himself. He couldn't use any weapons. Fortunately for him some of the other guys happened to be passing by and they heard the noise, and they heard the screaming, and they heard the animal and everything. And they came and scared away the animal and they fought him off. And then this Indian came down. He was quite embarrassed in front of all of his friends because they were his age and they were very good at these things. And he then realized that he had been making a big mistake in not learning how to do these things.

But he spoke to his older brother about it and he told his older brother that he really wanted to learn how to do these things, but he had a conflict in his mind. Do you know what I mean by conflict?

P: (shakes his head *no*)

T: Well, he had mixed feelings. If he did these things then he would have no way of showing anger to his parents or getting even with them. Do you understand what I mean?

P: Hh hmm.

T: Because they wanted him to learn how to do these things. So what do you think he did?

P: He learned anyway. If he wants to get angry with his folks it's all right for him, but then when he gets older he won't know how to do the things and then he'll be making trouble just for himself.

T: Right, but what about the angry feelings he had toward his folks?

P: I don't know too.

T: Well, he was still angry at his folks. Right?

P: Uh huh.

T: And wasn't he showing the anger by not learning how to build fires and things?

P: No.

T: Yes he was. That's how it happens in my story. He was hurting them. When they said, "Build a fire. Learn how to build a fire. Learn how to use a bow and arrow," he wouldn't do it because he knew it made them upset. That's how he showed his anger. Do you understand what I am saying?

P: Yeah.

T: Repeat it so I am sure that you know what I mean.

P: When they told him to learn how to build a fire he was angry at them and everything. He didn't do it to show them that he was angry.

T: And how did that get back to them? By not learning how to build a fire. How did that hurt them?

P: Because they really wanted him to do it so when he gets older he'll be able to defend himself and how to do things on his own.

T: Right. And now when he decided that it was important that he learn how to do these things, what did he do with the anger that he felt toward his parents? He had no way of . . .

P (interrupts): Push away.

T: What?

P: He threw it away.

T: What away?

P: His anger.

T: No. You can't do that. It doesn't work that way. What he did was that he spoke to his parents about the things that were bothering him, you know. He showed it. He told them directly what it was that was bugging him, and he had never mentioned that before. He just showed his anger by not doing the work. You understand? By not learning how to build fires and learning how to hunt. And when he spoke to them about it what do you think happened?

P: They forgive him?

T: Well, they didn't forgive him. They—actually that's one of the things that did happen, however. He thought that they would be very angry at him and he found out that they weren't as angry, but they were also able to do some of the things that he wanted and change some of the things. Do you understand that?

P: Uh huh.

T: Now you tell me what I said so I'm sure you understand.

P: He was—uh, it's hard to say.

T: Well, what did he do? What did he do to his parents?

P: He told them about it, so it wouldn't be on his mind anymore.

T: Right, right. Were they able to control some of the things?

P: Yes.

T: Was he scared that they would be very angry at him for telling them how angry he was?

P: Yes.

T: Did they punish him or do terrible things to him that he feared that they would do?

P: No.

T: Right, right. He was scared to talk to them at first, but he found out that when he did that they didn't do the terrible things he thought.

P: Like my father said if I lied to him about something, like he says, "Did you take any of my quarters (mumbled) from me?"

T: His quarters did you say?

P: Quarters, yeah.

T: Yeah.

P: Like this is, you know, an example, and I say "no" and he says, "I'm going to spank you. Well, then I say, "Will you hit me if I tell you the truth?" And he says, "I will hit you if you don't tell the truth, and if you do tell the truth I won't hit you." Like I told him if I told him the truth about the quarter, if I didn't steal it, he wouldn't spank me because I admit it to him.

T: Right, right. But did he punish you for stealing?

P: Well, no, this is just an example.

T: Well, do you think a kid should be punished for stealing?

P: Yeah, just like robbers. They have to be punished.

T: Right, right. But if you confess to it then you usually get less of a punishment. But if you lie about it then you should get an additional punishment or a worse punishment because then you are doing two things wrong. You are stealing and then you're lying. Right?

P: Right.

T: You're stealing and then you're lying. All right, let me ask you. Can you figure out what the lessons of my story are?

P: Do what your parents say no matter how angry and how you feel?

T: No, that's not a lesson. Nope. No, that's not a lesson. See if you can figure out another lesson.

P: I can't think.

T: Well, what should you do if you are angry at your parents?

P: Admit it. Say you are.

T: Right! Tell it to them. What should you not do if you are angry at your parents?

P: Hide it.

T: And show it in what ways?

P: That you really mean it?

T: What was the way the Indian boy in my story showed his anger?

P: Um, he did bad things to show it.

T: What bad things?

P: Like not learning how to make a fire and not learning how to defend himself.

T: Right. And who got hurt by his not doing that?

P: Him.

T: Right, right! So he learned that by speaking to your parents about the things that you're angry at sometimes you can change things and also he found that they weren't going to do terrible things to him for telling them how angry he was, and he learned that if you are going to show the anger by not learning that you're going to hurt yourself more than them. Anything you want to say about that story?

P: No.

T: Okay, do I get two chips for that?

P: (nods affirmatively)

T: Okay. Now I can get one more chip if I can say something about the word *Indian*.

P: All right.

T: I would say: the Indian learned that if you're angry at your parents you should tell them about it so that you can try to change things and you should not try to hurt them by not learning because if you do that you'll hurt yourself more than you'll hurt them. The end.

In my story and discussion I tried to take the patient one step beyond his. Whereas Mike's story reveals an appreciation of the self-defeating aspects of his antisocial acting-out, mine not only emphasizes these but encourages him to express his anger directly so that the likelihood of its being displaced and acted out is reduced. Although there was some question as to whether my messages were "getting through" in the earlier phases of the interchange, I was convinced at the end that my communications were being accurately perceived and Mike's comments, I believe, confirm this.

Clinical Example
"By far, the worst kid in the class."

Ralph entered treatment at the age of nine because of a severe behavior disorder. He was uniformly defiant of all authority, would answer his teachers with such expressions as "Up yours" and "Screw you," and would tell his school principal to "Fuck off." He was extremely disruptive in the classroom, bullied other children, tripped them, yelled out at will, and spent more time out of the classroom (as a disciplinary measure) than in it. His teacher described him as "by far, the worst kid in the class." His parents were divorced and with each of them he was similarly antagonistic, especially with his mother. His frustration tolerance was practically nil, and he operated on the principle that he was entitled to do whatever he wanted, whenever he wanted to. When thwarted he reacted with surprised indignation—with an attitude of "How dare you try to thwart me or try to stop me from doing what I wish?" In short, he wanted there to be absolutely no repercussions from his acting-out; he wanted to be allowed to totally indulge himself in expressing his rage. He wished to blind himself totally to the pains and discomforts he was inflicting on others and resented any attempts to help him appreciate what he was doing both to himself and others.

During my first session he left the room after five minutes when I broached the subject of why he was coming to see me. A week later, his father did manage to get him to return and I decided to avoid any mention of his presenting complaints at that point; rather my primary aim was to establish a good relationship with him (if possible) and once that was established I would try to help him more directly with his difficulties. During his third session, when I asked him if he would like to play "Dr. Gardner's Make-up-a-Story Television Program," he replied that he would do so, but only if we changed the name to "Ralph's Make-up-a-Story Television Program." I readily agreed and we proceeded:

> *Therapist:* Good morning boys and girls, ladies and gentlemen. Today is Friday, the 24th of January, 1975 and I'm happy to welcome you once again to "Ralph's Make-up-a-Story Television Program." It's my pleasure to tell you that our guest today is Ralph. Now let me tell you how this program works. Okay?
>
> *Patient:* Hh hmm.
>
> *T:* On this program we invite boys and girls down to see how good they are at making up stories. Now it's against the rules of the program to tell any stories about anything that really happened to you or anyone you know. The story must be completely made up from your own imagination. It can't be from anything that you've read in books, anything that you've seen on television or in the newspapers, magazines, or heard on the radio. It can't be about anyone you know. Naturally, the more interesting the story is the more enjoyable it will be to watch on television. Then when you finish telling your story you tell the moral of that story, the lesson you can learn from that story. Then when you finish your story I will tell a story and I'll tell the lesson or moral of my story. Okay, here he is for the first time on this program, Ralph with his own original made-up story.
>
> *P:* Ooh, now I gotta start thinking.
>
> *T:* You're on the air.
>
> *P:* A kid bought a rubber duck.
>
> *T:* A kid bought a rubber duck. Go ahead.
>
> *P:* A yellow one.
>
> *T:* Go ahead. You just tell the story. Don't worry about me.
>
> *P:* And so the rubber duck started . . . (mumbles) . . .
>
> *T* (interrupts): Pardon me?
>
> *P:* And the rubber duck squeaked all the time, even when he was in bed. He didn't know what was in the rubber duck so he ripped it open and he saw a . . . (mumbles) . . .

T (interrupts): He saw a what? Squeaker?

P: Squeaker—and I don't know how to make up a story.

T: Go ahead. That's an excellent start. A story has a beginning, a middle, and an end. That's a very good beginning of a story.

P: So then he took out the squeaker and he put it back together.

T: So he took out the squeaker . . .

P (interrupts): . . . and he put it back together and it still squooked, so he opened it up again and he took everything out. And it still squooked—squeaked—and then it turned blue. And then he took out a blue squeaker, then he took out a yellow squeaker, and each time he took it out it was a different color squeaker. The color changed on um what was started to be the yellow um rubber duck. I can't think of anything more.

T: Go ahead. You're telling a very good story.

P: And then the rubber duck walked far away onto the George Washington Bridge, and it jumped off it and swam into the Hudson River and swam back to its house—but he couldn't find it.

T: Hh hmm.

P: And so then he followed the rubber duck after he found it. And so the rubber duck fell . . .

T (interrupts): Then the boy found the rubber duck and what happened?

P: It fell and it squeezed again. And he thought he had made it stop squeezing.

T: You mean squeaking.

P: Squeaking. Everybody was looking at him and then it started jumping and running to the George Washington Bridge again, and the boy couldn't find what was so big about the George Washington Bridge and in the water and so he looked in the water. He saw someone—a rubber duck squeaking waiting for him and then he jumped in and he swam ashore and that's the end.

T: And he got the rubber duck?

P: No!

T: What happened?

P: The other rubber duck was in the water . . .

T (interrupts): Wait a minute—the other. You mean—wait a minute. There are two rubber ducks here?

P: See, he saw another rubber duck and he jumped in after he saw the duck.

T: Oh, you mean he was looking for the original one?

P: No, they were both together!

T: Excuse me, I'm a little confused here. I don't remember the point where the second rubber duck suddenly came into the story.

P: As soon as they both went to the George Washington Bridge.

T: They both. Who's they both?

P: The boy and the one rubber duck. And the first time when he jumped into the George Washington Bridge.

T: Jumped into—you mean jumped into the water?

P: Yeah, he saw a rubber duck and then he jumped out. See? And now he's going back to see that rubber duck and they're going in the rubber duck house.

T: Excuse me, I'm very confused. Do you understand? (looking to patient's father)

Patient's Father: Was there a rubber duck in the water?

P: Yeah.

T: I don't understand about the relationship between the first and the second rubber duck.

P's F: When he jumped into the water the first time there was another rubber duck in the water?

P: Yeah, and then he came out.

Patient's Mother: Who was in the water, the rubber duck or the boy?

P: The rubber duck! No, the rubber duck!

P's F: The second time the boy went in also.

P: He watched!

P's F: Oh, he watched.

T (interrupts): Okay, I have an idea.

P's F: In other words, there was a girl rubber duck and a boy rubber duck.

T: Wait a minute. He didn't say that. Please don't introduce new things, please.

P's F: Okay.

T: I think you ought to go back in the story because we're all confused about this. Now let's go back . . .

P (interrupts with annoyance): Oh brother!

T: Come on. It's a good story.

P: I can't make no story; I forgot it!

T: Well, then, I think you were doing very well, but now we're all confused about this.

P: I don't want to do it again.

T: Okay, you want to quit playing this game? We'll just turn it off and do something else.

P (annoyed): Okay, I start with another story.

T: Okay, then you want to make up a different story?

P: Wait, wait. I know how to find out. Uh, this is all on there. Right? (pointing to videotape recorder).

T: It's all on there.

P: So when we listen to this you'll hear the whole story.

T: No, no. Listen. I'm telling you how the program works. The program works that you've got to tell a story.

P: I don't like it.

T: Then we'll quit the program. We'll do something else. If you don't follow the rules of the program then you don't watch it. The rules of the program are that you have to make up a story.

P (angrily): Well, that's the only story that I can think of! And I don't remember anymore.

T: You have not given us a story that we can understand.

P (impatiently): Oh, then I'll just make up any story. A boy went to bed and never woke up!

T: Well, I think . . .

P (interrupts): The moral of the story is: Don't go to bed.

T: I think we'd better quit this story.

P: Well, I don't want to 'cause you don't understand it.

T: Well, then we'll just not watch this and we'll do something else.

P: Well, if you quit then I'll quit on any other game.

T: Then that's up to you, but if you're going to play this game you play it right like any game. If you play a game like Monopoly you're not going to . . .

P (interrupts angrily): Look man!

T (continues talking): If you're not going to play by the rules I don't play the game.

P (interrupts again): Wait man! Wait a second! Um, I hate to tell you something.

T: Hh hmm.

P: Then how come you wrote down the story?

T: I started to write down and then in the middle of the story I got kind of confused. I don't think your parents are any clearer on it than I am.

P: All right, then I'll continue from the middle of the story.

T (approvingly): Okay, that's a *very good idea.*

P: Where are we?

T: You can go back to any point. The point that I got confused with is that we had this duck who had these . . .

P (interrupts): Squeakers.

T: He had these squeakers in there and he still was squeaking and each time the boy opened him up there was still another squeaker in there. At that point I was following you all the way, and then suddenly I got kind of confused. If you want to go back to that point just go on.

P: Then the duck went away, ran away.

T: The duck ran away, okay. I'm going to cross out all this other stuff (points to some of his notes) because it's kind of garbage and I can't understand it.

P: And he ran away and he um (pauses)

T: The duck ran away. Go ahead.

P: And he went to the George Washington Bridge and then jumped in.

T: Okay, and he jumped into the Hudson. Why did he do that?

P: Because he saw another squeaking duck.

T: He saw in the water another squeaking duck?

P: Yeah, his brother.

T: Okay.

P: And so . . .

T (interrupts): Okay, now wait now. Slow up. He saw a second . . .

P (interrupts): And so then he had to go back.

T (interrupts): Hold it. Wait. This time I want to be sure that I get it right so I'm going to slow you down and I'm going to write it down so I get it clear. (proceeds to write) He saw a second squeaking duck there and it was his brother. Then what did he do when he saw that duck?

P: He went back on the water into the George Washington Bridge, back to . . .

T (interrupts): Stop, stop, stop, stop, stop! We've got two ducks now. We've got his brother in the water and we've got the duck on the bridge seeing his brother down there. Now at that point what happened?

P: He goes back.

T: Who? Which duck? Let's call duck #1 the guy with the squeak and duck #2 the brother. Okay?

P (nods approvingly): Duck #1 squeaked went back.

T: The squeaker goes back. He leaves his brother in the water? Huh?

P: Uh hum.

T: Okay, let me write this down. His brother is in the water . . .

P (continues): And when he goes tell his owner and when he finds someone . . .

T (interrupts): Wait a minute. He goes and tells his owner what?

P: Where his brother is. Then he follows him and on the way . . .

T (interrupts): Wait a minute. Who's he?

P: The brother—the big brother—the human being.

T: Oh, the boy.

P: The boy. And the boy comes and he falls down on the George Washington Bridge.

T: Wait a minute. The boy comes now. We've got the boy, the squeaking duck on the bridge, and the brother down in the water?

P (speaking quickly): The squeaking duck falls . . .

T (interrupts): Slow up boy. Slow up.

P: The squeaking duck falls down on the George Washington Bridge.

T: The squeaking duck falls on the bridge or off the bridge?

P: Down on the bridge.

T: He just, as he's walking, he falls.

P: Uh huh.

T: Okay, now let me get this—slow up now. The brother and the squeaking duck go back to the George Washington Bridge and the squeaking duck falls on the bridge. Okay, then what happened?

P: Then he goes to the side . . .

T (interrupts): Who's he?

P: The duck takes a . . .

T (interrupts): The squeaking duck?

P: Hh hmm. He takes a swan dive into the water.

T: The squeaking duck goes into the water. Go ahead. Then what?

P: He sees his brother.

T: To see his brother.

P: Uh hmm.

T: Yeah, go ahead.

P: Who has a house in the water.

T: Hh hmm. Go ahead.

P: They come out of the water back to the owner. They go home.

T: Both of them now?

P: Hh hmm. With the brother—I mean the boy. And then they—and then that—and then that's the end.

T: That's the end. Okay. The lesson of that story?

P: The lesson? When you buy a duck make sure it doesn't have five squeakers in it.

T: Now, let's see (writes) when you buy a duck . . .

P (interrupts): A rubber duck.

T (continuing to write): Make sure it doesn't have five squeaks. Now a couple of questions. Did the boy finally get all the squeaks out of the duck?

P: Mmm. No, because um—because see he finally learned that all, that it was all, then he put in another squeaker, only when it squeaked.

T: I'm a little confused. Say that again.

P (pressing imaginary duck): Only when you go like this it will squeak when you press him in.

T: It still did squeak. And was there still a squeaker in there?

P: No.

T: Oh, and how did it squeak then?

P: He made a thing that made it squeak when you pressed it.

T: What's the thing?

P: A little air hole and when you press it it squeaks.

T: Oh, I see. A squeak with an air hole. Now did the boy like the squeaking or not?

P: Yes.

T: He did! So why did he take the squeakers out then?

P: Because he didn't like him never stopping.

T: Oh, they would squeak all the time. He just wanted him to squeak when he wanted the duck to squeak.

P (nods approvingly): Uh huh.

T (writes): Squeak—time—so now he wanted him to squeak only when he wanted.

P: Yeah.

T: Uh huh. I see.

P: Are we done?

T: I have to understand your story. Let me tell you that when you tell a story you go on and on and you don't particularly care whether the people who are listening can understand it, which doesn't make for much of a story, if a person can't understand it. I think that when I tell my story if I just ramble on without your understanding it I don't think you'd enjoy it very much. Now I have another question with regard to the brother here. Was the brother a squeaker?

P: No, he was regular.

T: He was regular. Which means what?

P: He was a real—he was just—the boy didn't have to fix him. He was regular. He only squeaked when he wanted him to.

T: He squeaked when the boy wanted him to?

P: Hh hmm.

T: Uh huh. Okay. Good.

Many of the patient's alienating qualities are clearly revealed in this interchange. His lack of cooperation throughout is obvious. The only way I was able to get him to cooperate was to threaten him (softly but firmly) that if he didn't follow the rules of the game and tell a reasonably coherent story, that he would not have the opportunity to watch himself on television. I took a very matter-of-fact attitude, had no strong feelings that I *had* to get him to tell a story, and would have readily discontinued the game if he did not cooperate. The word *threat* is a no-no word in my vocabulary. We are surrounded by threats. If we don't pay our electric bill, our electricity is turned off. If we don't do our jobs, we ultimately get fired. And Ralph had to learn that his behavior has repercussions—repercussions that will cause him some personal discomfort. In addition, my not being under pressure to get him to reveal himself through a story was also vital to my success here. Had Ralph for one second sensed that I *needed* to get him to tell a story, he would have seized upon the opportunity to gain the gratification of thwarting me. When a therapist is in a position where he *needs* the patient to do something, he seriously compromises his efficacy as a therapist.

Ralph's primary intent here was to get through telling his story as quickly as possible so he could see himself on television. He did not concern himself with whether his story was understandable to his listeners, nor did he want to suffer the inconvenience of providing us with an explanation. I firmly refused to let him indulge himself in this lack of concern for our frustration. If he was not going to clarify, he would not be allowed to see himself on television. Ralph's parents and teachers were trying to change his behavior with long explanations, bribing, and pleading. I felt that he needed firmness backed by reasonable clout (not physical, but psychological). Although giving me a hard time all the way, Ralph ultimately cooperated—confirming my belief that he was basically looking for such firm guidance, his ostensible resistance notwithstanding.

As indicated in the transcript, Ralph's mother and father were present while we were playing the storytelling game. We see here an example of how a parent's attempt to help can backfire. In his attempt to understand Ralph's story, the father introduced new material (about boy and girl rubber ducks) and thereby risked contaminating the story. I quickly pointed out this error to him, and I believe he understood. (Fortunately Ralph did not incorporate the father's contaminants into his story.) This danger of the parents' presence is far outweighed, in my opinion, by the advantages of their being in the room. No therapeutic approach or technique is without its disadvantages and active parental participation is no exception.

Although I never was able to fully understand the part of the story involving the George Washington Bridge and the second duck, I did believe that I understood the beginning and the end sections regarding the duck and its squeaking. I had no strong need, however, to push Ralph in an attempt to clarify the central section. I had enough material for what I considered a good responding story and so decided to quit while I was ahead. The squeaking duck, I believe, symbolizes autonomy on the part of others whom Ralph encounters in life. They squeak when they want, even though Ralph is irritated by it. In an attempt to control those who so annoy him, Ralph rips open the rubber duck and removes the squeaker. But each time he does this, another squeaker appears and the animal goes on squeaking. Finally Ralph manages to remove all the squeakers and inserts a new device (an air hole type squeaker) that is totally under *his* control, that is, the duck squeaks only when Ralph presses it. Otherwise it is powerless to squeak. Ralph thereby satisfies his desire to totally dominate those around him, to make them his puppets, and control completely their talking (and by implication their actions). The fantasy, of course, related to Ralph's clinical behavior in which he wanted his own way in every possible situation, and resented strongly anyone who thwarted him in satisfying any of his whims. And the one area in which he most wanted to be indulged was that of his antisocial acting-out. His anger was tremendous and he wanted total indulgence in being permitted to express it.

I believe that the fantasy has another meaning as well. As the transcript conveys, Ralph was agitated, anxious, talkative, and impulsive. These qualities are well represented by the ever-squeaking duck. Ralph would like to be able to gain control over the duck (the projection of himself) and the story reveals his success in achieving this goal. Accordingly, there is a healthy element in this fantasy. Although these two explanations deal with separate issues, they do not preclude one another. One of the beauties of dream and fantasy is that they can serve to satisfy many needs simultaneously. We are rarely as clever as our patients' processes of fantasy formation and would ask too much of ourselves if we were to try to create stories that deal simultaneously with two or more themes in as efficient a manner as our patients. Accordingly, I decided (as I usually do) to create a story around only one of the themes. I chose the first because it was the one that was causing Ralph the most immediate difficulty with those around him. Our interchange continued:

> *Therapist:* Now it's my chance to tell a story. Okay.
>
> *Patient:* (mumbles something)
>
> *T:* You don't want to hear my story?
>
> *P:* All right.
>
> *T:* Okay. You know, I'm not going to tell—if you don't want to hear my story I'm not going to tell it. I don't tell stories unless you want to hear it.
>
> *P* (interrupts): Okay, what's your story?
>
> *T* (continuing): And if you're going to sit there and yawn and jump up and down I'll stop. That's all.
>
> *P:* What's your story?
>
> *T:* Now the way it works is that my story has the same characters or animals but different things happen to them. That's how it works in my story.
>
> Once upon a time there was a boy and he had two ducks and these ducks, like all ducks, squeaked. They had voice boxes. They were real ducks.
>
> *P:* Hh hmm.

T: They had voice boxes and they squeaked. And this boy said to the first duck, "Stop that squeaking. You'll squeak only when I want you to squeak."

And the first duck said, "No, no. You're not my boss. At times I will listen to you—like if you think that I'm squeaking in the middle of the night and waking you up and I think it's right that you should tell me to stop, or if I'm squeaking and you're watching television or something and it's bothering you then I'll stop. But I'm not your slave. I'm not going to go around just stopping when you tell me to stop."

Well, the boy got very angry and he said, "I want you to *stop* squeaking when I tell you and you'll *start* squeaking when I tell you. I'm your boss and I'm going to tell you when to squeak."

And the duck said, "No, I won't follow your orders. I won't listen to you. I will squeak when I want to. However, I will respect your desires, your needs, and your right that I keep quiet at times."

Well, this got the boy so mad that he said, "I know what I'm going to do. I'm going to rip out your voice box. That's what I'm going to do." So he took the duck and he ripped out the duck's voice box in his throat. What do you think happened to the duck?

P: He couldn't talk.

T (solemnly): He died.

P (surprised and disappointed): Oh.

T: The *duck died*! The boy had the idea that you could rip out a duck's voice box and then he would still remain alive. Possibly a very trained surgeon might be able to perform such an operation and still keep the duck alive, but this boy was not a trained surgeon and the *duck died*. And actually this boy was very sad. The duck was a very good pet of this boy. He liked him very much and he was quite sad, but you can't bring a dead duck back to life.

Well, he had one duck left, and he had a problem there because to this other duck he said, "What about you, buster? Are you going to squeak when you want?"

He said, "Yeah."

The boy didn't know what to do. He knew that if he took out the duck's voice box and ripped it out that that duck would die, too. And yet if the duck was around he knew that he couldn't control that duck— that that duck insisted upon squeaking when he wanted to squeak. However, he, like the brother, said, "I will listen at times when you request my not squeaking. If you're doing something that warrants my keeping quiet I will respect that request, but I will not always stop squeaking just because you say so." What do you think the boy did?

P: Ripped out his voice box.

T: No. The boy was wise. He knew that if he did that he'd have a second dead duck and he'd have no pet and no friend.

P: So he just did it that way.

T: What way?

P: He let the duck squeak.

T: He realized the duck was right. He realized that you can't go around telling people what to do whenever you want them to do it and that the best way to get along with people is to at times do what they want and at times they'll do what you want.

P (interrupts): All right, is that the moral or the end?

T: And what do you think the lesson of my story is then? What can one learn from this story?

P: It's your story.

T: Yeah, I know, but I want to see if you're smart enough to figure it out.

P: I want you to do it.

T: You can't figure it out?

P: I don't know. Don't take a duck's voice box out. All right?

T: And if you do what will happen to the duck?

P: He'll die. All right?

T: Right. And the second lesson is . . .

P (interrupts): Now can I watch television?

T: Just let me finish my story and then we can watch it. No, it's not polite. You have to let me finish my story. I let you finish yours. The second lesson of my story is that if you think that you can go around controlling everybody they will not take it. They will not accept it and you'll be very lonely. You'll have no friends. People don't want to be bossed around all the time and if you want to get along with people sometimes you have to do things that they want and sometimes they'll do things that you want. The end.

Anything you want to say?

P: No.

T: Okay, now we can watch it.

The meaning of my story is obvious. I attempted to help Ralph appreciate that total control over other people's actions is an impossibility. However, if he makes reasonable requests, many will comply with them; but if his demands are irrational, he will not be able to get them satisfied.

There was no question that Ralph was much more cooperative and involved with me as the story progressed. Although still quite anxious to see the television program, he was so engrossed in my story that there were minimal interruptions and distractions. Besides providing therapeutic communications, the experience was salutary for Ralph in other ways. It provided me with an opportunity for dealing with Ralph's antisocial behavior in a way more effective than that used by his teachers and parents. His parents' observing my ways of handling Ralph provided them with hints for dealing with him at home. (This is another one of the benefits of having the parents in the room. Telling them how to handle a patient and *demonstrating* it in the natural course of one's experiences are two very different things.) Also there was a more subtle, but nevertheless definite, deepening of our relationship and strengthening of rapport during this and similar interchanges. Ralph respected me for not allowing myself to be manipulated by him. He wanted controls on his antisocial acting-out and I was helping him gain them. In addition, I basically found Ralph likable—in spite of his antisocial behavior. His rebellious behavior against authority was never physically destructive. Although telling a principal to fuck off is certainly not one of the milder ways of acting out, it is not one of the more destructive types either. Within a few sessions Ralph had calmed down considerably. Although tranquilizers were prescribed, I believe that interchanges such as the one presented here were the most important factors in bringing about these salutary changes.

Chapter 10

RECONCILIATION PREOCCUPATIONS

The usual reaction of most children to the announcement of their parents' separation is to plead that they not separate. Except in the rare situation when the child has been so traumatized by the departing spouse that he welcomes the separation, children would generally prefer to live with the pains, frustrations, and discomforts of their parents' dissension than to be deprived of one of them. Generally, it is the parents who are suffering much more than the children. The child by nature is very narcissistic (he doesn't differ very much from adults in this regard) and is not generally affected by arguments that Mommy or Daddy cannot stand the pain anymore and will be happier living out of the home. Nor can he project himself too well into the future and believe that he may be better off when his parents are separated.

The children's pleas that the parents not separate can be one of the most guilt-provoking experiences a divorcing parent may have to suffer and there are many who remain together in order to avoid such guilt. Separating parents have to be helped to appreciate that their guilt is healthy and predictable and an inevitable concomitant of their decision. In fact, were a parent not to feel guilty in such a situation I would consider it a manifestation of some deficiency in his relationship with his children. After all, he has contributed to his children's unhappiness (even though he has not wished to do so). Whether the spouses remain together or separate, the children are likely to suffer. And even though the divorce may result in their suffering less, they are still being deprived of the more desirable atmosphere of a two-parent home (the most preferable of arrangements, in my opinion—the present popularity of alternative life styles notwithstanding). Therapy can do little, therefore, to assuage this component of parental guilt. The parents can, however, be told that the most effective way to reduce this guilt is to do everything that will prevent and alleviate unnecessary suffering on the part of the children. They should be helped to appreciate also that the children's pleas are proof of their affection; that were they not preoccupied with a reconciliation it would reflect a deficiency in their relationship with the departing parent.

Normally such preoccupations diminish with time as the children become used to their new life style and become resigned to the fact of the divorce. However, there are children who persist for many months, and even years, in trying to get their parents to reconcile even though they have been repeatedly told that there is no chance whatsoever of the parents' remarrying. There are children who will entertain fantasies of their parents' reuniting even after one or both have remarried. When such preoccupations persist beyond the usual time for their disappearance, other factors are usually operative—factors that go beyond the mere fact of divorce and the natural desire to resume what the child considers a happier state of affairs.

Causes of Reconciliation Preoccupations

Malevolent ties between the parents. Probably the most common reason for the persistence of reconciliation preoccupations in the child is the failure of the parents to become *psychologically* divorced. Although they may be *legally* divorced, and even remarried to others, they may still maintain a psychological tie that can be quite strong. The persistence of such ties (even though subtle and disguised) is the most powerful contributing factor to continuing reconciliation fantasies in the child. The most common manifestation of such a tie is the maintenance of hostilities. Arguments over alimony, support, visitation, etc. can persist for years. And lawyers and the courts can be relied upon to contribute to this prolongation. Although a hostile relationship is ostensibly one that should offer the child little hope for reconciliation, it actually provides much more than the parental relationship in which matters have been settled and there is little, if any, residual hostility. The child appreciates, at some level, that a hostile relationship is much deeper than one with little or no emotional involvement. In the malevolent relationship, the ex-spouses expend significant time and energy in being involved with one another (either directly or through their lawyers). In such a milieu fantasies of the parents being together (albeit malevolently) are frequently evoked; whereas when the parents have essentially settled their differences such fantasies of "togetherness" are less likely to occur. The child of the hostile parents appreciates, at some level, that his parents still need one another —even if the need is for sado-masochistic gratification (and divorce provides one of the best opportunities for such satisfactions for those with the propensity). Sensing their continuing needs for one another cannot but engender hopes that his parents will once again live together. Half of the 425 divorcées studied by Goode (1956) wanted to punish or remarry their ex-husbands— another confirmation of the ancient appreciation that love and hate are much closer to one another than to no involvement at all.

The child may actually foment difficulties between the parents and help perpetuate their fighting out of the appreciation that any contact between them is more likely to bring about a reconciliation than their having no contact at all. And the parents may actively comply with the child's machinations to bring about such involvements between them. Each may be selectively credulous of the child's negative and provocative comments about the other, whereas in other areas they would be judiciously cautious regarding their belief in what the child says.

An even more subtle form of interaction may contribute to the perpetuation of the child's reconciliation fantasies. The parents may decide that any type of friendly and civil involvement on their parts may engender in the child reconciliation fantasies. Accordingly, they may strictly refrain from any contact in front of the child and reduce their other communications to an absolute minimum (even less than would be naturally indicated and desired). In most cases, such an arrangement is only ostensibly made for the benefit of the child. Usually, it is a rationalization for the parents to protect themselves from acting out on or giving in to their residual attraction for one another. The facade of coolness and aloofness is a defense against strong needs for involvement. As is often the case, malevolence is used as a device to protect the individual from benevolence. In such a situation, the energy utilized in maintaining "distance" is greater than that expended if there were the usual and necessary contacts. And the amount of mental imagery involving the ex-spouse is greater than in those who have more relaxed attitudes toward one another. As is often the case, the mental life of the parent becomes the mental life of the children. They too become involved in the strict adherence to the rules and regulations of the distance keeping operations and they thereby get involved in this tie, which is only speciously a non-tie.

Benevolent ties between the parents. The frequency with which separated and divorced people maintain benevolent ties with one another is hard to ascertain. Not only does embarrassment often lead such individuals to hide their involvements, but legal factors play a significant role. Many states will not recognize a period of separation to be valid if there has been a resumption of sexual contact during the period. In other words, the individuals may have to start counting the days of separation all over again if they wish to qualify for a divorce. Ten percent of the divorced couples studied by Westman, Cline et al. (1970) admitted to having had sexual relations with one another after the divorce. If ten percent of those interviewed in this study admitted such involvement, the likelihood is that it was higher. Although the child is generally not exposed to such sexual involvement, he is generally aware of the continued benevolent involvement out of which such sexual contacts take place. Seeing his parents still getting along well together cannot but stimulate fantasies of reconciliation.

With greater receptivity on society's part to varying life styles, the "on the fence" arrangement is becoming more widespread. People go on for years never making a final decision. The departing spouse comes back and forth, never being able to decide what to do. One father, for example, may spend two or three nights a week at the home; another stays for a few days or weeks, departs, only to return again for another stint. In such situations the child cannot but have persistent reconciliation fantasies. The children may add to the frequency of the visits and contacts by structuring situations that encourage or provide the parents with excuses for such involvements. They may, for example, insist that both parents be present at every possible school function, birthday party, etc. Even the aid of grandparents and other relatives who support a reconciliation may be enlisted.

And just as the children may try to find excuses to promote their parents having contact with one another, the parents themselves may use similar tactics. Mother may call Father for advice on inconsequential matters or to tell him about something cute the child did that day. Father too may find justification for contacting Mother about trivial things that pertain to the children. Each parent here is using concern for the child as a rationalization for involvement with the spouse. And such involvements perpetuate reconciliation fantasies in the child.

Just as artificial aloofness may be used to disguise deep attraction, false friendliness may be used to hide hostility. The parents may present facades of friendliness with the rationalization that showing their deep rage is bad for the children. When they do come together one can feel the coolness of the atmosphere but their words and gestures are ever so polite. Generally, the children are not fooled; they appreciate (albeit vaguely at times) that there is still a lot going on between their parents. Again, the situation contributes to the perpetuation of reconciliation fantasies because the basic continuation of the hostilities is present.

A common parental contribution to reconciliation preoccupations in a child is such fantasies on the part of a parent. A mother who persists in her hopes that she may ultimately be reunited with her husband makes it extremely difficult, if not impossible, for her children to resign themselves to his departure. Even if she refrains from verbalizing her hopes the children somehow sense them. Her statements to the children that Father is never returning cannot be made with any credible degree of conviction. The feeling of longing that is conveyed when she speaks of her husband will also convey her true feelings. And her taking every opportunity to resume contact will also belie her true feelings.

Factors within the child. When the departed parent offers the child much more gratification than does the custodial parent, reconciliation preoccupations are likely to persist. There was a time, not too long ago, when the court was required to give a mother custody unless gross and extreme negligence could be definitely established. Only if the mother were a prostitute, drug addict, or severe alcoholic, or if she exhibited other forms of severe neglect could the father hope to gain custody of the children. (Even then prolonged litigation was often necessary.) The assumption was that the female was innately superior to the male in performing parental functions. Accordingly, many children were forced to remain with mothers who were far less equipped to take care of them than were their fathers. Fortunately, in recent years the courts have come to appreciate that femininity is not necessarily to be equated with parental capacity; as a result, although the percentage is still quite small, many more fathers are now being granted custody, and this contributing factor to reconciliation preoccupations is therefore becoming less common.

The child who is excessively guilty over unconscious hostility toward the departed parent may become obsessed with his returning to the home. He may be preoccupied with the latter's welfare, fear frequently that he is sick or injured, and seek the continual reassurance of his well-being that his return to the home can provide. There may be associated separation anxieties which make the termination of each visitation especially difficult. As noted in Chapter 9, such concerns are related to the child's belief that his unconscious anger will result in his parent's actually being harmed; such fears can only be assuaged by the parent's continual presence.

The child whose guilt over his parents' separation is a manifestation of the need to control an uncontrollable situation (as discussed in Chapter 7) may also manifest preoccupations with his parents' reuniting. He may be preoccupied with notions that the divorce took place because he was "bad," and conversely, that they will reconcile if he is "good."

Oedipal problems may contribute to a child's obsession with parental reconciliation. A boy, for example, living with a dating mother may find the seemingly endless flow of men in and out of his mother's life an unbearable burden. He had enough trouble dealing with the jealousy he felt toward his father for the intimacies he shared with his mother. Now it appears that practically every man in the world—with the exception of himself—has such opportunities. Preoccupations with his parents' remarrying may be his only way of stemming the tide of these unwanted strangers. Similarly a girl, even though living with her mother, may learn of her father's dating and develop similar reactions. Toward the parents of the same sex as well, the child may develop jealousies over dating and see reconciliation as the only hope for reducing such feelings of rivalry. For example, a girl may be jealous over all the attentions her mother is receiving and long for the time when only one man demonstrated these.

I can best introduce my next point anecdotally. Skinner, in his classical operant conditioning experiments in which a hungry rat is taught to press a bar in order to obtain a pellet of food, differentiates between the strength of such conditioning when the reinforcement is given *periodically* as opposed to when it is given *aperiodically*. For example, let us imagine an experiment in which three rats in three separate cages each receive a total of 100 pellets in the conditioning process. The first is given a pellet after *each* press of the bar. Then no further pellets are given. Let us say that after x number of presses the rat returns to the random frequency of bar presses present before reinforcement was instituted. In other words, the rat, no longer gaining pellets, stops pressing the bar more than he normally would in his chance encounters with it as he roams the cage. The response is then said to have been extinguished. If the second rat is also conditioned with a total of 100 pellets, but each one of his is given only after *five* bar presses, i.e. on the fifth press after four unrewarded presses, it may take 5x, 10x, 15x or even more bar presses before the rat returns to his previously random frequency of bar presses. Having expected unrewarded presses, he has become accustomed to them and expects most of his presses to be unrewarded. Accordingly, it takes him a much longer time to become deconditioned. Let us now consider a third rat who is rewarded aperiodically. Sometimes he may receive two pellets in a row, or three pellets out of five presses, and at other times he may go fifty or a hundred presses before being rewarded. His tolerance for unrewarded presses is far greater than that of the other two rats and the extinction of his conditioning may take significantly longer. In fact, he may require 100x or 200x or even more presses before returning to his random frequency. He may never give up and may even continue pressing until he drops from exhaustion —so powerful is the aperiodically conditioned response.

I believe that a child whose parent provides him with little affection, but who still gives some in an unpredictable way is likely to foster the kind of response exhibited by the third rat. The child of such a parent may become obsessed with parental reunion in the service of his gaining affection from the lost parent. He just never seems to give up trying to extract affection from a parent who appears to have little (but not *no*) capacity to provide it. He may spend his whole life in this futile quest and others can only wonder why he never gives up, never seems to be able to see the obvious. Such a child is, of course, particularly difficult to treat.

Some children live in areas where divorce is either very uncommon (increasingly rare) or where the child of divorce is stigmatized (also becoming rare). Such children may try to hide the fact that their parents are separated and may avoid having friends to their homes, lest the secret be divulged. In the service of avoiding such disclosure they may become preoccupied with reconciliation.

As part of the process of adjusting to parental separation the child does well to provide himself with substitutive relationships, both adult and peer. In this way he can partly compensate for the loneliness and deprivations of his parents' separation. The child who fails to do this, whatever the reasons, is more likely to develop preoccupations regarding the departed parent's returning. Of course, reconciliation obsessions per se can interfere with the development of such relationships and a vicious cycle is thereby set up.

Therapeutic Approaches

Since the parental factors in a child's reconciliation obsession may be formidable, everything must be done to reduce them. However, the therapist is usually in a difficult position to accomplish this. Separated and divorced parents generally prefer to have as little to do with one another as possible. Accordingly, they are generally not going to be receptive to counseling, even for the benefit of their children. Those who are maintaining their relationship via hostile integration may agree to counseling, but usually use it as a platform for expressing grievances rather than cooperatively trying to reduce the hostilities. And when lawyers are still on the scene such counseling may make a mockery of the therapy as each party withholds that which might compromise his or her legal position. For these reasons I have had little direct experience with joint counseling of separated or divorced parents. Working with one of the parents is more common, while the other parent may or may not be seeing another therapist. On occasion, I have been able to counsel both parents in a constructive way, but such situations have been rare. The more successful one is in reducing pathological interaction between the parents the greater the chances of alleviating the child's reconciliation obsession. On occasion, however, the malevolent interaction of the parents has been so deep and fierce that I have had to inform them that I am working against insurmountable odds—that it is unlikely, if not impossible, for me to help the child as long as their hostilities are maintained at such a pitch.

The child burdened with social stigmatization must be helped to appreciate that the problem lies with those who stigmatize rather than with himself. And the child who tries to hide the fact of divorce must be helped to appreciate that he is adding new and unnecessary burdens to those he already has to bear.

The examples below are typical interchanges directed toward the alleviation of reconciliation preoccupations.

Clinical Example
Discouraging a mother's dating.

Marcia entered treatment at the age of ten because of angry outbursts and a surly attitude toward just about everyone. Her parents were divorced and she saw little of her father, who was predictably unreliable regarding visitation and following through on promises. During the few weeks prior to the interchange presented below, I pointed out to Marcia's mother that although she complained bitterly about her loneliness and frustrations, she was not actively doing those things that would increase the likelihood that she would meet another man. Her response was to make minimal and ambivalent efforts to meet men. Marcia was aware of my discussions with her mother. It was during this period that she related this story while playing "Dr. Gardner's Make-up-a-Story Television Program."

Patient: Hello, ladies and gentlemen, this story is about two birds and a very mean one. One bird was a lady and one was a man and they were in love with each other and wanted to get married, but the bullying bird warned the lady . . .

Therapist: Wait a minute, does the bully make a third one?

P: Yeah, there are three birds.

T: Well, is the bully a man or a lady?

P: The bully is a man, and the bully also wanted to marry the lady bird. So there were many, many fights about who would get her for the wife. Now the bully would try more and more tricks to see if he could get the girl bird but one day they were—the man bird and the girl bird were flying away and the bully flew up and bumped into the man bird and knocked him on the ground. The girl bird was very surprised and just then the bully got her and tied her up with ropes and took her to his nest. So, um, the boy bird was very hurt, was hurt very much, and tried to get up but then at the bully bird's nest the girl bird was tied and held prisoner. "I will drop you in the river if you don't marry me," the bully bird said to the girl. So the poor girl was really deeply—was deeply sad about the loss of her real boyfriend and she had no choice.

But meanwhile the boy bird was getting up now and was off to rescue the girl bird. He flew a long way, and he knew where the bully bird's nest was, and just as the bully bird was trying to fly with her in the river, he knocked the bully bird down and the girl bird flew down on the land but not in the river. So they had a terrific fight and finally the boy bird won and the bully bird was all beat up. He limped away and the girl bird and the boy bird flew off together. Soon they were married and they all lived happily ever after. And, the bully bird got another girl and married her because she was a bully too. But she never ever saw the boy bird and the girl bird again.

The moral of this story is, um, what's the moral of the story? Um, um, the moral of the story is: don't try to take somebody's else's joy away or you'll be sorry. That's the moral of my story.

Although the story could be interpreted as an example of Marcia's trying to enhance her self-esteem by getting two men to fight for her affection, I believe that there is a more meaningful interpretation considering that her mother was making her first attempts to date at the time the story was told. The lady bird—first referred to as a lady, but then as a girl—represents the patient's mother, the man bird stands for her father, and the bully bird symbolizes her mother's prospective suitor. The loving relationship between the man and lady bird reveals Marcia's denial of her parents' schism and her wish that they be reconciled. By making the bully bird a coercive intruder, she can deny her parents' dislike for one another as well as her mother's active interest in finding a substitute for her father. All would be well if it weren't for some interloper who disrupts their blissful relationship. The story ends with her unrealistic wishes gratified: her parents are reconciled and suitors are removed from the picture.

Stories such as this are typical of children whose parents are divorced. In response, I told this one:

Therapist: Once upon a time there was a lady bird and she felt very sad because she used to see other lady birds who would have men birds who would follow after them and want to marry them. And, she would even see some lady birds have two men fighting over them. But, this lady bird was very lonely; she not only didn't have two men fighting over her, she didn't even have one man who wanted her, so she was very lonely.

One day she was speaking to another friend and the friend said to her, "Why are you so lonely? Why are you so sad?" And she said, "I'm sad because I don't have any men fighting over me or I don't even have any men who want to be with me." So the friend said, "Well, are you doing anything about it?" She said, "What am I to do, they just don't come around?" She said, "Well, don't you go to the places where the men are, don't you go out?" And she said, "No." So she said, "Well, how do you expect to meet men if you don't go where the action is, as they say? You'll never meet a man unless you go where they are. You've got to put yourself out. You've got to be there at the same time and same place when they're there. That's the only way you're going to meet them. You can't expect them to find you if you don't put yourself in the position where they are going to meet you."

Well, the lonely lady thought about what she had been told and realized that her friend had given her good advice so she began to join clubs and organizations which men joined and gradually she began to meet men and she finally ended up marrying someone.

And do you know what the lesson in that story is?

Patient: Um, let's see, don't, um, if you want to be with somebody, go where they are.

T: Uh-huh, you just can't sit on your backside and expect it to happen. Tell me something, what about your mother, does she go out and try to be where the men are and try to meet people?

P: Um, yeah.

T: Are you sure? Where, where does she go?

P: Well, she goes to dances and everything.

T: When? When does she go? When was the last time?

P: Oh, she goes all different times.

T: When? When was the last time she went out like that?

P: I don't know because sometimes she doesn't tell me.

T: How do you know she goes to dances and everything?

P: Because, because sometimes she does tell me and, um—

T: When was the last time she went to a dance?

P: The last time I know of is, um, the Jack and Jill, no, that's not the last time. I don't know, it was Friday, I don't know which Friday though.

T: Was it a long time ago or recently?

P: Probably, recently.

T: Do you think that your mother is doing as much as she could to get married again?

P: No.

T: Why do you say that?

P: Well, she could go away and try to find one. There aren't any intelligent, handsome men around here.

T: Where could she go?

P: She could go for a trip around the world or something.

T: Yes, but that costs a lot of money, doesn't it?

P: I suppose—

    T: Well, what else do you think she could do?
    P: I don't know. Let's do something else.
    T: Okay.

In my story the possibility of a reconciliation between the man and lady bird is not even discussed. To consider it—even to deny it—could have raised Marcia's hopes far more than my not mentioning it at all. The divorce is a *fait accompli.* The advice regarding loneliness is really presented for both the patient and her mother. Marcia handled her frustration and loneliness by outbursts of rage; the mother by depression and complaints. Both passively sat back, hoping for better days, the patient by her parents' remarriage; the mother by vague fantasies of someone pursuing her. Neither was actively seeking realistic substitutes for the lost father. In my story they are advised that passively living in a dream world isn't going to accomplish very much. It is only through active planning and realistic effort that alternative gratifications can be realized.

In my post-story discussion I attempted, through the discussion of the mother's efforts to find someone else, to encourage Marcia to seek her own substitutes. However, my efforts were not too successful—Marcia did not have enough interest to pursue the topic meaningfully.

Clinical Example
Finding substitutes for the departed parent.

Paul entered treatment at the age of seven because of disruptive behavior in the classroom, sloppy attitudes toward his school work, isolation from other children, and difficulty falling asleep at night. His parents had separated about six months previously and were still deeply involved in litigation over financial settlements and visitation. Paul was extremely bright and although his school performance was poor, he could read quite well, even though he was in the middle of the first grade.

During his second month of treatment the following interchange took place while playing *The Alphabet Soup Game:*

    Therapist: All right. Our guest has completed the word *ring* for which he gets a coin from the treasure chest. All right, do you want to say anything about the word ring? If you do, you can get one more.
    Patient: Well, once a boy gave a girl a ring.
    T: Okay, that gets a chip.
    P: One of those kinds of rings that you wear on your finger.
    T: Right. Okay, now do you want to tell a story? You can get two more.

P: Yeah.

T: Okay.

P: Well, once upon a time there was a little girl and she had a boy-friend and later they got—in a few years they got married and the boy gave—well, they got engaged. The boy gave the girl a ring and the girl gave the boy a ring, and then they got married and they lived happily.

T: That's the whole story? That's a very short story. Hh hmm. Okay. Do you want to add a little bit more? I don't know how much of a story that is that it should really deserve two chip credits. That isn't very much of a story. See if you can add a little bit more to it.

P: Well, after they were married they had a nice time, but then once they went down to an old, old . . . (mumbles) . . .

T: They went to where?

P: An old, old river.

T: They went to an old river?

P: Yeah, on sightseeing—on a sightseeing trip, rather. I said it too slow.

T: Old river on a sightseeing trip, yes.

P: And then when they got there there was a pretty little bridge, and the girl fell in. It was a deep—she didn't know how to swim. The man knew how to swim very well. The man jumped right in after her. (makes splashing sound.

T: Hh hmm.

P: And then the man grabbed her up on her back—grabbed her up on his back, rather, and then he swammed ashore. And then in that river they took a little walk down by some rocks, and then they had a boat ride in that river. And then they went home and they lived happily.

T: Hh hmm.

P: Until their days were over.

T: Until their days were over.

P: Yes.

T: Hh hmm. Sounds like an ending of a story I know.

P: What?

T: They lived happily to the end of their days?

P: Yes.

T: Now what story was that? Oh, they lived together to the end of their days.

P: Yes.

T: Yes, what story is that?

P: Oh, like in the "Princess and the Three Tasks." [a story in one of the author's children's books (1974a)]

T: Right. Did you notice in my stories they never end with "they lived happily ever after?" Did you know that?

P: They always?

T: None of my stories have that ending.

P: Never?

T: Never! Not in my stories. Other stories have it, but none of my stories have that ending, "They lived happily ever after."

P: Oh.

T: Do you know why?

P: Why?

T: Because no one lives happily ever after.

P: How do you know?

T: Because everybody's life is a mixture of happy things and unhappy things. Nobody is happy all the time.

P: Yeah. I know.

T: So that's why I don't end a story with "they lived happily ever after" because my stories are real world stories. Right?

P: Yup.

T: So that doesn't happen in my stories. Okay, so you get two chips for that story. What colors do you want? Take your own colors.

P (chooses yellow chips): Yellow.

In the story, as originally presented, a boy and girl meet, the boy gives the girl a ring, "and then they got married and they lived happily." That was the whole story. I considered it to reflect the patient's desire that his parents' marriage would not have ended in separation; rather, they continue to live happily. However, in order to elicit more information in the hope that it could either confirm or refute my initial supposition, I encouraged Paul to elaborate on the story. Such encouragement was helped by my wondering out loud whether or not such a short story really deserved two chips.

With this encouragement he described how the girl fell in a river while they were in a boat on a sightseeing trip. The man rescues her and then they both go home and live happily. I considered this elaboration to confirm my initial supposition. In reality it was Paul's mother who had left his father and in this story it is the girl who leaves the boy by falling out of the boat in which they are both traveling. The boy's rescuing the girl symbolizes Paul's desire that his parents reconcile.

The patient's ending his story with "they lived happily" was reminiscent of the type of closing statement I make in the fairy tales that I have written for children (1974a). The stories do not end with "and they lived happily ever after." Rather, they end with such statements as "and they lived together until the end of their days." I used this as a point of departure for a discussion in which I communicated the message: "everybody's life is a mixture of happy things and unhappy things. Nobody is happy all the time." Such appreciation can help lessen the child of divorce's burden and, in addition, provide him with realistic expectations about the future. Hopefully, such an attitude might lessen the likelihood of his becoming divorced in the future.

A few minutes later I completed the word *Dad* and the following interchange took place:

> *Therapist:* My word is *Dad* and for the word *Dad* I get one chip. If I can say something about the word *Dad* I get two chips. Okay?
>
> *Patient* (interrupts): Dr. Gardner.
>
> *T:* Yes.
>
> *P:* Is your TV on?
>
> *T:* Oh, yeah, yeah. It's taking our picture. Okay, for my first chip I'll say, "Dads are not perfect. They're a mixture of good and bad."
>
> *P:* Right.
>
> *T:* Right. Okay, that's a second chip. Now if I can tell a story including the word Dad I get a third chip. All right?
>
> *P:* Mmm.
>
> *T:* Once upon a time there was a boy. Let's make it a girl.
>
> *P:* Okay.
>
> *T:* And this girl had a Mom and a Dad and they were happy for a while and they enjoyed being with one another. But one day the Mom said that she did not want to live with the Dad anymore.
>
> *P:* Oh?
>
> *T:* And she just wanted to separate and this made the boy feel very sad and he wanted . . .
>
> *P* (interrupts): the girl, you mean.
>
> *T:* The girl, excuse me. I'm very sorry. This made the girl feel very sad and made her want to get her mother and father together again. And she said to the father, "Go after her! Get her back! Bring her back!"
>
> And the Dad said to her, "Nope. We've had a lot of trouble in our marriage and maybe it's better."
>
> She said, "Well, get her back for me. I want the two of you to stay together."
>
> And the Dad said, "I know it hurts you very much and it hurts me very much that we're not going to all live together as one family, but I'm so miserable and she's so miserable that it's probably better that we not remain married."
>
> And he kept trying to get his father to get his mother back—to go after her—but the Dad just refused and the Mom refused. And so after a while what do you think happened?

P: So they got a divorce.

T: Right. Now while the boy was very sad . . .

P (interrupts): The girl.

T: Excuse me, I'm sorry. While the girl was very sad she stopped doing her school work and she stopped playing with her friends and that was really unfortunate because then she added to her problems. If she had done her school work and played more with her friends she would have felt better about the fact that her mother and father were getting separated. But she gradually realized that she couldn't get them back together and she also realized that not playing with her friends and fouling up in school were just making her problems worse because then she was even sadder.

P: That's kind of in one of your books.

T: Is one of my books like that?

P: Yeah.

T: I don't—what . . .

P (interrupts): Something like that in one of your books.

T: Yeah, which book was that?

P: The Boys and Girls Book about Divorce]1970b, 1971a].

T: Hh hmm. And what do I say in there that's like that?

P: You should play more with friends . . .

T (interrupts): Hh hmm. When what?

P: They're having a divorce.

T: Right. What do you think of that advice?

P: It's pretty good.

T: Good. Have you tried it out?

P: Well, I do feel better about it.

T: Hh hmm. What was the main thing that made you feel better about it?

P: Oh, well, it really helped me a lot.

T: How did it help you? In what way?

P: Well, in your books and the way you tell people—the way you give advice—and so forth.

T: Yes, what advice? You see I give a lot of advice in those books. Which advice was most helpful to you?

P: Well, I couldn't say which. It was all very good advice.

T: Hh hmm. I see. Nothing—no special bit of advice?

P: No, everything was very special.

T: Hh hmm. Okay. Now let's—we have to stop this game now. Let's count up and see who wins.

I first used my opportunity to make a single statement about the word *Dad* by commenting on the fact that Dads are a mixture of both assets and liabilities. This is important to communicate to all children; however, children of divorce—exposed as they often are to extreme parental derogation of one another—need to have this point especially emphasized.

In my story, when the Mom and Dad get divorced, they do not reconcile. The child's repeated requests that they do so are to no avail. However, rather than leave her frustrated and unhappy I suggest that she compensate for her loss by involving herself with others. The patient immediately recognized the advice as being similar to that which is found in my *The Boys and Girls Book about Divorce*.

Clinical Example
"If I steal their money, they won't have enough to get divorced."

John began treatment at age seven-and-a-half because of behavior problems both at home and in school. He was disruptive in the classroom, often stared into space, and frequently refused to do his homework. At home he was recalcitrant and entered into power struggles over the most minor requests. His parents had been separated for two years at the time of referral, but could not decide whether to get divorced. During his second month of treatment, while playing *Scrabble for Juniors*, the following interchange took place:

Therapist: I completed the word *house* for which I get one red chip. Now if I can tell a story about the word *house* I can get two more. Okay?

Patient: (nods affirmatively)

T: Once upon a time there was a boy and he decided that he wanted to be a builder of houses when he grew up and he thought that that would be really great to construct houses. So in high school . . .

P (interrupts): Is this your story?

T: Yes, this is my story. So when he went to high school he went to a trade school where they taught people construction and unfortunately instead of paying attention in the class his mind would wander off into space. He would daydream. When the teacher would ask them to do homework, you know, house plans and things like that, drawings of houses, he would just kind of goof off. When they would take the class out to show them how to build houses he really wouldn't pay too much attention and, as a result, when he got out of school he didn't really know too much about how to build houses.

Well, when he got his first job after about a week the man said to him, "Listen, it's very clear to me that you don't know too much about

building houses. If you don't shape up I'm going to have to fire you."
Well, that didn't bother him too much because he just continued to go
along and make believe that there would be no consequences. You know
what consequences mean?

P: Uh huh.

T: What does consequences mean?

P: Make believe that, you know, there's nobody around to give them
any punishment or anything.

T: Yeah, there'd be no trouble. So, to his amazement, a week later the
boss said, "I'm very sorry, but I'm going to have to fire you. You're
really not up to this job. You don't know how to do it." Anyhow, that
happened two or three times and then he finally got the message. So
what he had to do was that he then had to go back to school and this
time pay much more money because the first time when you go to regular school which the community has, you know, you get that free. But
after you're out you can't go back to high school and get it free so he had
to learn to do this and then when he learned and he tried much harder
then he was able to keep a job and he was able to be a good construction
man.

And the lesson of that story is: you don't learn something by just sitting around and daydreaming, and if you don't learn your job well no
one is going to keep you. The end.

So I get two for that and then I get one more if I can say something
about the word *house*. The man did not learn how to build houses and so
they didn't keep him on the job as a construction man.

As mentioned, one of John's problems was that he did not attend to his
schoolwork, stared into space during his lessons, and seemed to be oblivious
to the consequences of his failure to learn. I used the word *house* as an
opportunity to impart a message about the consequences of laxness. The approach is admittedly superficial, but it is part of the treatment of such problems. Although I recognized that John's school difficulties stemmed in part
from his parents' separation, I was not directing my attention to this underlying issue in the story I chose to tell. It was in John's responding story that
his parents were brought in.

Therapist: Now you can get two if you can tell a story. You can get one
if you say something about the word *house*.

Patient: Okay, I want to say something about the word *house* first.
The house fell down.

T: Okay, you get a chip for that. Go ahead. Now if you can tell a story
about a house you get two more.

P: Once upon a time there was a mommy, a daddy, and a kid living in a house. And the mommy and the daddy always argued a lot and they decided they had to get divorced but they didn't have enough money. So they made up they got money and they were saving it up and as they were saving it up there still wasn't enough after a few years because the little kid he would always take it and hide it in his socks.

And one day ten years later the parents were wondering about what happened to all that money. And they asked their kid if he knows where the money is. And he said, "Yeah, I know. It's in my socks."

And they said, "Why? We wanted to get divorced." "I was saving it up for you," he said. But he was lying to them. He wanted to keep it and as the months had been going along he was taking some of that money and buying bubblegum and everything. And then he gave the money back and there was only like a few dollars back.

T: Hh hmm. So what happened then?

P: So his parents asked him if he had spended any. "Yeah," he says. "Yeah, and it's all in my tummy because he bought a lot of sweet stuff and he ate it all up. So they said that all that money had gone to waste in his tummy like.

T: Hh hmm.

P: Just like when you throw money away in the woods, they say, "it's down the drain" or something.

T: Right, right. So what happened then?

P: And his parents really got angry at him and they punished him. They always locked this—they always put it in a safe place where he didn't know where it was.

T: All right. So what finally happened?

P: That's it.

T: Okay. What's the lesson?

P: The lesson of that story is: if you steal admit it. Don't lie about it.

T: Okay. That's certainly a good lesson. You get two chips for that story; however, I would like to ask you a couple of questions about that story. As I understand it, am I correct in this that the boy stole the money from his parents so that they wouldn't have enough money to get a divorce? Is that it? Do I understand that correctly?

P: Yeah, kind of. No, no. He just wanted to buy things of his own.

T: Yeah, but you were saying that the parents were saving up money in order to get divorced. Didn't you say that?

P: Yup.

T: Well, why did they have to save up money to get divorced?

P: Because they didn't have enough money.

T: Why do you need extra money when you get divorced?

P: Well, I thought you needed money to pay the people to use the place where you're going to get divorced.

T: To pay the people who get you divorced?

P: Yes.

T: You mean people like the lawyers?

P: Yeah.

T: Any other reason why you need extra money if people get divorced?

P: Like say you are going to use a church or something. Maybe you'd have to pay the person in order to—if you were going to use a temple you'd pay the rabbi or something.

Patient's Mother (laughing): You'd cater it.

T (laughs): For a divorce too? Any other reasons why people would need extra money?

P: No.

T: Well, okay, as you see it they need extra money to get divorced. So by his stealing the money was he trying to prevent them from getting divorced?

P: No.

T: He wasn't. He was just stealing the money . . .

P (interrupts): Because he wanted it all his own and he wanted to buy things.

T: I understand. But you said in your story that as a result of the fact that they had less money after ten years they still weren't divorced. Did I understand that correctly?

P: Right.

T: So didn't his stealing the money prevent them from getting divorced?

P: Yeah, but he didn't mean to.

T: Oh, he wasn't thinking about it.

P: He wasn't thinking about it. He was just thinking about himself and the money.

T: But it just happened to have that effect as well.

P: Right.

T: Hh hmm. Well, what do you think about a boy—let's not take the boy in your story—say a boy who decides that he's going to try to stop his parents from getting divorced? What do you think about that idea?

P: Well, what I would do is I would take the money from them and I'd hide it until they gave up, but I wouldn't spend it. I would give it back to them.

T: When you say "until they gave up" what do you mean?

P: I mean after they, you know, had it all settled and everything and since they didn't have enough money—they couldn't just get enough—they'd try living together again.

T: Oh, I see, so if you had a plan like that you would keep the money. You wouldn't spend it.

P: I'd keep it until they gave up trying to get divorced.

T: Do you think that can work?

P: Maybe.

T: Well, I'll tell you my opinion on that subject. Do you want to hear my opinion?

P: Yeah.

T: I think that would be a bad idea.

P: I know.

T: Why?

P: Because if they really want to get divorced they should get it.

T: Yeah. Right. And it's not likely that that would happen, that you'd be able to steal so much money that they couldn't get divorced. So if a boy is sad about his parents' getting divorced would you agree with me that it's a good idea probably to realize that he can't stop it? Huh?

P: Um, well, he could stop it.

T: How?

P: By just avoiding taking the money.

T: Yeah, but could he stop his parents from getting divorced?

P: Getting divorced. Well, instead of, you know, say they are having an argument or something, just stay out of it. That would help them.

T: Okay, but do you think you could really stop them from getting a divorce if they really wanted to?

P: Well, no.

T: Right.

P: I don't think there is any way.

T: Well, what could the boy do to make himself feel better if his parents do get divorced?

P: Help them around the house and make them happy.

T: Right. He can help make them happier cooperating more. That's one thing. And what about the feelings of loneliness that he may feel because one of his parents isn't living in the house anymore? What could he do about that?

P: What do you mean?

T: Well, often when a child's parents get divorced he gets kind of lonely because one the parents isn't living in the house. Right?

P: Hh hmm.

T: So what could he do?

P: I don't know.

T: What would you do? What do you do when that happens? For instance, like you're living with your mother, right?

P: Right.

T: Now what do you do when you feel lonely for your father?

P: Well, maybe I'd call him up. I'd pretend he's there.

T: You can pretend he's there.

P: Maybe that helps.

T: Well, I don't like make-believe things—real things.

P: I'd call him up.

T: Hh hmm.

P: Or ask him to come over for dinner or something.

T: And that happens sometimes?

P: Sometimes, yes.

T: Or you can go out with him. Right?

P: Hh hmm.

T: And suppose he's not around. What else could you do?

P: Just think about him.

T: Okay, that helps a bit. What about spending time with other people, like friends and things like that.

P: Oh, yeah, well sometimes don't think about it.

T: Uh huh.

P: And sometimes the feelings go away.

T: Do you know what that's called when you can't have your father when you get someone else?

P: What?

T: That's called a *substitute*, like you know in school.

P: Like in school when the teacher is sick you have a substitute teacher to take her place.

T: A substitute teacher. Right. Well, you can have a substitute person sometimes when your father is not around, substitutes of both your own age and even older people. Okay, very good. So we have to stop here. Let's turn this off. Let's count up the chips. Okay, I have three, six, seven. How many do you have?

P: Three, six, seven.

T: It's a tie score.

P: Yup.

T: Okay, good game.

The story is a good example of the kinds of reconciliation fantasies harbored by children of divorce. Recognizing that the divorce process can be a very costly one, John attempts to prevent it by depriving his parents of the funds necessary for its accomplishment. Although the patient describes the boy's primary purpose in stealing the money to be his love of candy, he did allow that it had the incidental effect of preventing his parents from getting a divorce. In the subsequent discussion about "another boy" he too attempts to prevent his parents' divorce by stealing money, although he hides the funds rather than squandering them on goodies. In the discussion to follow I tried to emphasize the futility of such a maneuver, the value of resigning oneself to the inevitable, and the value of finding substitute gratifications to compensate for the deprivations attendant on parental separation.

Chapter 11

SELF-ESTEEM

I believe that deprivation of parental affection is the primary cause of most forms of psychopathology in children (and by extension, in adults) and that the low self-esteem that generally results from such deprivation is the central problem being dealt with in most psychogenic disturbances. I appreciate that symptoms are quite complex and that many factors operate in their formation and perpetuation. However, I also believe that the attempt to compensate for feelings of low self-worth plays a crucial role in the origin and maintenance of such symptomatology. The child who boasts does so, in part, to bolster a lagging self-esteem. The child who refuses to apply himself to his academic work fears, among other things, that his deficits will thereby be exposed. The child who runs away from home hopes to find more loving (and thereby more ego-enhancing) parents or to evoke enough guilt and fear in his parents to stimulate them to provide him with more affection (and hence, enhanced feelings of self-worth). We repress from conscious awareness thoughts and feelings over which we are guilty in order to protect ourselves from the low self-esteem attendant to our conscious awareness of them. The examples are legion. And it is not stretching a point, or oversimplifying, to say that the self-esteem problem is central to the formation of psychogenic pathology, the multiplicity of other contributing factors notwithstanding.

In this chapter I will confine myself to those self-esteem problems commonly seen in children of divorce. The reader who is interested in a more general discussion of my views on the origin and treatment of self-esteem problems should refer to the chapters on this topic in two of my previous books (1971b, 1973a).

Parental Factors Contributing to a Child's Low Self-Esteem

The child of divorce, more than the child living in an intact home, is likely to be deprived of parental love. Certainly, most departing parents are deeply involved with their children and regret the pains and frustrations that the separation is causing them. In spite of formidable attempts on the departing parent's part to reassure the child that he is still loved, the child is still likely to consider himself to have been abandoned. He generally goes further and assumes that he has been rejected because he is unlovable. The child judges his own self-worth by what his parents' views of him are. (It is only later, when he goes into other homes, attends school, and broadens his experiences that he utilizes other criteria—both external and internal—for determining his self-worth.) If he believes that a parent does not love him, he concludes that he is unlovable. Such a child has to be helped to appreciate that he may be distorting, that he may have a "wrong idea," that his parent's leaving the house has not been due to the fact that he is unlovable.

The separation and the inevitable feelings of insecurity it produces in the child (important people can abandon one at any time; home stability is fragile at best) make the child feel small and vulnerable. An important source of protection and guidance is no longer so readily available. Such feelings of insecurity, lack of protection, and helplessness cannot but lower the child's self-esteem.

Information from both parents helps the child gain a sense of what he is really like and the knowledge of his assets contributes to his feelings of high self-worth. With one parent gone, he is deprived of one source of potentially esteem-enhancing information. Hopefully, the therapist can serve to some degree to compensate the child for this deprivation.

When the child takes sides with one parent in the parental conflict, he risks alienating the other. The loss of affection that his disloyalty (feigned or real) may result in cannot but lower his feelings of self-worth. If he subscribes to the view that the "good" child is one who is loved by both parents, then his alienation of one will make him "bad" and hence loathesome (G. Gardner, 1956).

When, indeed, the departing parent has little, if any, love for the child then a more shattering blow will have been dealt to the child's self-esteem. Such a child has to be helped to see that the deficiency lies within the parent, not within himself. The child may interpret an absent father's failure to pay his alimony to be a reflection of his own worthlessness. It is as if he were saying to himself: "If I was worth anything, he'd send the money. I'm not worth paying for." Again, the child has to be helped to appreciate the distortions that are operating here in lowering his sense of self-worth.

The child may identify with the rejected parent and assume that the parent who has left has little if any affection for the whole family, not just the parent who has been left behind. In the situation, for example, in which a father has left the home, the child may assume that because Mother is not acceptable to Father the children are not acceptable to him either. Such a child has to be helped to clearly differentiate between himself and his mother. Particular focus should be placed on the specific qualities in the mother that the father claims are the sources of his alienation. The child has to be helped to gain clarification as to whether the mother does indeed exhibit these qualities or whether the father is distorting. If the traits do exist, the child has to be helped to determine whether he possesses them also. If so—and this is unusual—he should be helped to change: not in order to effect a reconciliation (by then it would usually be inappropriate and futile) but to avoid alienating others. The same considerations hold for the situation in which a mother, for example, rejects a father and he is the one who leaves the house. The child, by identification, may assume he is similarly rejectable and is likely to be forced out of the house.

Divorce usually places new burdens on each of the parents. Mother is now all alone in caring for the day-to-day needs of the children. Except for those who are wealthy, divorce creates economic hardship. Mother would be much more available and attractive to most other men were it not for the children. The mother's career goals may also be compromised by the children. Father, too, may see the visitations as a source of restriction on his life. Even if the parents do not verbalize these frustrations and resentments, the children are likely to sense them. And feeling oneself a burden on one's parents cannot but contribute to a child's feelings of low self-worth.

The child may be used as a scapegoat. A mother, for example, may take out on the child the resentments she feels toward her husband. Being used as the target of hostility cannot but make the child feel loathesome.

In Chapter 8 I have discussed some of the elements in the divorce situation that may contribute to a parent's becoming overprotective. The child of such a parent is likely to become immature and regressed. Whatever gratifications he may derive from such regression, the child is likely to feel shame as well.

A parent may attempt to use the child as a substitute for the spouse who is no longer available. A mother, for example, may tell her son that he is now "man of the house" and although she generally does not go so far as to use the boy for overt sexual satisfaction, she may be overly solicitous and seductive and thereby gain some measure of sexual satisfaction. The anxieties and frustrations so produced in the boy cannot but be ego-debasing (as are all feelings of frustration and tension). Or she may use the child as a confidant and ask him to advise her in matters that he is totally ill-equipped to provide advice on. Believing that he should be able to serve his mother in this regard, and observing his failure to do so, produces feelings of inadequacy.

Situational Factors Contributing to a Child's Low Self-Esteem

If parents separate soon after a child is born, the child, when he becomes old enough to appreciate this, may believe that his birth somehow brought about the separation. "If I had not been born," he reasons, "they might still be together. They wanted one another—that's why they got married—but they didn't want me. When I was born, they became so unhappy that they got divorced." The notion may have its roots in the need to gain control over an uncontrollable situation as discussed in Chapter 7, and the therapeutic approaches to this delusion have been there described. If the child learns that he was conceived in an attempt to save a faltering marriage and his birth was not successful in accomplishing this, he may reason that another, better, child might have been successful. The sense of failure attendant to this notion cannot but lower a child's feelings of self-worth.

The economic privations that a divorce often causes may play a role in lowering a child's self-esteem. This is especially true when the divorce results in a significant lowering of the family's life style. Although material possessions do not, I believe, play a significant role in determining one's self-esteem, they do have an effect. It is much harder for a poor man to feel good about himself than one who has a reasonable degree of material comfort. As Tevye says in *Fiddler on the Roof*, in introduction to his song "If I Were a Rich Man": "Dear God, you made many, many poor people. I realize, of course, that it's no shame to be poor. But it's no great honor either."

If the child lives in a community where there are few children from divorced homes he may feel very different from others and less worthy than those living in intact homes. If, in addition, he is stigmatized because of his parents' divorce, he may feel even less worthwhile. Such a child must be helped to appreciate that the divorce situation in no way warrants a person's being laughed at or ridiculed—that it has nothing to do with sin or being bad. He has had bad luck; but he has done nothing to justify his being taunted or rejected. He has to be helped to appreciate that he is not necessarily what others say he is (a message that has to be communicated frequently to many adults in treatment as well).

A particularly difficult situation is the one in which a child is stigmatized because of a parent's bad reputation. For example, the child of a notoriously alcoholic father may suffer significant ridicule himself. As difficult as it may be, it is important to try to help such a child appreciate that his stigmatization is totally inappropriate and cruel. He has to be helped to appreciate that he in no way contributed to his father's socially alienating behavior and therefore is in no way to blame. He has had the *misfortune* of having a father who has disgraced himself by his behavior, but the child only adds to his burden if he takes the disgrace onto himself as well. Society does not punish a son for the crimes of his father nor one person for the crimes of another. Similarly, he should not be punished for the misdeeds of his father. He must be helped to view those who ridicule him as having significant distortions in their own thinking. It is *they* rather than *he* who should be ashamed of themselves. Lastly, he must be helped to appreciate that in spite of occasional taunts, he will ultimately be judged by the kind of person *he is*, not what his *father is*. If he is fun to be with, considerate of others, and exhibits other admirable and desirable traits, he will be liked and sought—his parent's deficiencies notwithstanding.

Factors in the Child that Contribute to Low Self-Esteem

Although many of the neurotic reactions that the child may have to parental separation arise in an attempt to enhance feelings of self-worth, they generally lower the child's self-esteem even further. Intrinsic to guilt is a feeling of self-loathing. If a child tries to lessen guilt over hostility to a parent, for example, he may turn the hostility inward and become depressed. Although spared the guilt and the anticipated repercussions of his expressing his anger, the depression and associated recrimination result in an even greater loss of self-esteem. The child who projects his anger may also spare himself the lowered self-esteem associated with awareness of his hostility, but he then suffers with esteem-lowering fears of those upon whom he has projected his hostility. The child who holds in and suppresses resentment, who does not assert himself in the service of dealing with anger-provoking situations, suffers with the dissatisfaction with himself that is inevitably associated with pent-up resentments. Although regression may provide certain pleasures, the child cannot but feel ashamed over his immaturity and fearful that peers will learn of his childish behavior. Shame and fear compromise significantly one's feelings of self-worth. The therapeutic approaches to these and other esteem-lowering neurotic adaptations are described in particular discussions of each of these neurotic manifestations, i.e., in the chapters on guilt, depression, immaturity, anger, etc.

The child may try to hide the separation from his friends. Although protected thereby from their anticipated ridicule, he suffers with the lowered feelings of self-worth attendant to his fears of disclosure and the inner shame associated with the knowledge of what he is doing. And when his secret is revealed (as it inevitably comes to be) he suffers even more shame and social alienation than if he had disclosed the separation in the first place.

The child who plays one parent against the other in an attempt to win favor may suffer guilt and feelings of disloyalty over his duplicity—and these feelings will generally lower his feelings of self-worth. On the other hand, the child who does not report back to one parent information about the other when requested to do so, may also feel disloyal and unworthy.

Additional Therapeutic Approaches

Because symptom formation is so intimately associated with specious attempts to enhance a lagging self-esteem, anything the therapist can do to genuinely increase a child's sense of self-worth can be therapeutic. In fact, one can consider the *genuine* enhancement of self-esteem to be the universal antidote to psychogenic symptoms. I emphasize the word *genuine* here because it is common for therapists to attempt to raise children's self-esteem by specious methods such as bestowing undeserved praise, flattery, patronizing compliments, and artificial affection. Compliments not actually associated with specific accomplishments can be ego-debasing rather than ego-enhancing. To say to a child, "Aren't you a nice girl," or "What a fine boy you are," makes most children squirm. They recognize the artificiality of the compliments; they appreciate that they are being "buttered up"; and they sense that these particular comments are being utilized because the praiser cannot think of more meaningful ones, i.e., praises based on specific accomplishments. To say, however, "Boy, this cake you baked is really good!" or "You play the piano beautifully," or "What a swat! You hit the ball right over the fence," makes a child stand a few inches taller.

Of all the approaches to enhancing self-esteem there is none so important, in my opinion, as the gaining of competence. One cannot feel good about oneself if one cannot focus on specific areas of talent, skill, knowledge, etc. about which to feel good. Therapy, whatever other goals it may have, must include helping the individual gain competence in important areas of living —especially those in which the individual has exhibited deficiency. Therapy must help the patient more effectively handle himself in the course of his daily activities. It must help him relate more satisfactorily and gratifyingly to people. It must teach the techniques of competent involvement. It must help the individual become aware of areas in which he tends to act inappropriately, and to teach him both by word and experience the ways in which he can avoid repetition of self-defeating behavior. Strupp (1975) is a strong proponent of this view and considers what he calls "lessons in constructive living" to be central to psychotherapeutic change. One cannot really feel good about oneself unless one has something specific and concrete to feel good about. Otherwise the sense of self-esteem is delusional and cannot really produce a feeling of stability. And the individual is then almost doomed to resort to the utilization of specious ego-enhancing maneuvers and will end up even worse than he was before.

Feeling that one is genuinely needed by at least one or two people is also crucial to one's self-respect. I cannot imagine anyone's really respecting himself if no one needs him for anything. One of the important criteria I utilize in determining whether a depressed person is suicidal is whether he believes that no one in the whole world will miss him if he were dead. Although children are, for the most part, dependent on their parents and need their parents far more than their parents need them, the child must still feel that his loss would be painful for his parents if he is to have a healthy sense of self-worth. Recognizing that he has the power to make his parents laugh, to give them warm inner feelings, and to contribute to their pleasure in having a *family*, contributes to his feelings of self-worth. The child of divorce is bound to question the need his parents have for him. In some cases there may be significant deficiencies on the part of one or even both parents in their need for a child. His sensing that he is now an increased burden to his parents (for the reasons already given) may further lessen his feelings of being needed and useful. In fact, his main feeling may be that they want to dispose of him, which is, unfortunately, sometimes the case. The therapist can communicate to the child that he finds the child useful. When the therapist actually enjoys being with the child, when he has fun with the child in the course of the therapeutic experiences, the child will gain a sense of pride and self-importance. It is as if he says to himself, "I have the capacity to give him pleasure. With me he can have fun. I am therefore a worthwhile person." Accordingly, the therapist does well to try to select therapeutic activities that are enjoyable to both the child and himself and to refrain from engaging in activities that he himself finds boring. His resentment when engaged in the latter will be picked up by the child and the patient will not only be deprived of the benefits of the therapist's pleasure but will have an anti-therapeutic exposure instead that will be ego-debasing. (The techniques described in Chapter 3 have proved useful for me in providing the child with enjoyable therapeutic activities that I too have gained pleasure from as well. This is an important element in their efficacy.)

A common source of lowered self-respect in child patients is the notion that they are the only ones in the world who have the abominable thoughts and feelings that they harbor within themselves. Parents often confirm such suspicions and deepen thereby the child's detestation of himself. It behooves the therapist to reassure such a child that he has seen many children and that most, if not all, have similar thoughts and feelings. When appropriate, he should inform the child that he (the therapist) has had and still has (if this is the case) similar ideas and emotional reactions. Such comments can contribute to the child's feeling less loathesome as he comes to appreciate that he is not so unique or atypical. In addition, the therapist's revealing (when appropriate) deficiencies of his own can help the child feel less loathesome about his defects. As mentioned in Chapter 3, *The Talking, Feeling, and Doing Game* can provide the therapist with opportunities for such revelations in an uncontrived way in the natural course of the therapeutic interchange.

When a patient tells me, "I feel terrible. I'm no good," I will often ask if he is doing something that may contribute to such feelings. Often, after some thought, I get an affirmative answer (admittedly, more commonly from the adult than the child). The child may be cheating, stealing, or lying. The child of divorce may be spying on one parent for the other, or playing one parent against the other. In such situations I generally tell the child (if he has anything approaching normal superego development): "As long as you continue doing that, you're going to feel lousy about yourself. It's hard for me to imagine anyone's feeling good about himself when he does such things. I think that when you stop doing that you'll see that you'll feel much better about yourself."

A child in therapy may believe that he is crazy and this may contribute to feelings of self-loathing. Some children may not even verbalize this; yet the burden lies heavily upon them. It is important for the therapist to be aware that the child may be silent about this ego-debasing preoccupation, and it behooves him to bring it up if he suspects that it is contributing to the child's sense of low self-worth. It is in the first few interviews particularly that the child may harbor such notions. I usually approach the issue in this way when I sense that it may be operating: "Many kids think that just because they're coming here, it means that they're crazy. Have you had any such thoughts?" If the child admits that he has, I will try to draw him out about their exact nature and discuss with him his specific ideas and distortions. With most children, somewhere in the discussion, I will say something along these lines: "Although I don't know you too well, I know you well enough to be able to say that you are *definitely not crazy*. Yes, it's true that you do have some problems and that you need to see me, but this doesn't mean that you're crazy. In fact, most of the kids I see do not look any different from others in their classes or neighborhoods. They're kids, like you, with a few problems in a few things. They don't have so many problems that anyone would call them crazy." There is, however, an occasional child who *is* psychotic. To such a child I will generally say: "Yes, you do have a lot of problems and sometimes you do things that some people would call crazy. I think that that's a cruel word and I don't use it here. There's something wrong with somebody who calls someone else that. What we have to do is try to help you stop doing and saying those things that get you to be called crazy."

The divorce situation can provide the child with esteem-enhancing experiences if he can rise to the occasion and avail himself of them. The extra responsibilities which the child of divorce is often asked to assume can provide him with an increased sense of competence. In addition, I urge many parents to join community organizations for divorced people. (The most well-known of these family-oriented organizations is Parents Without Partners.) There are many potential therapeutic benefits to be derived for children from such membership. The organization provides the child with opportunities to be with many other children of divorce, lessening thereby his feelings of being unique and different. There, he can form relationships with surrogate parents of opposite sex to the one who has departed from his household. For older children discussion groups can be beneficial. The sense of belonging to a special club, the feeling of communality, and the recreational activities can be therapeutic as well.

In the examples below, I present some clinical vignettes that demonstrate some of the aforementioned therapeutic approaches.

Clinical Example
A girl with an unpredictable and rejecting father.

Julie, a ten-year-old girl, entered treatment because of a chronic surly attitude, outbursts of rage and generalized antagonism toward authority. Her parents were divorced and her father, who lived in a city about 200 miles away, was unreliable regarding visits and only rarely showed any interest in her. Julie, however, denied his rejection and continued to hope that more involvement would be forthcoming. During her second session she told this story:

> *Patient:* Hello, everybody.
> *Therapist:* Hi.
> *P:* This story is the story of a ghost and a maniac. Well, once upon a time there was a girl ghost and a boy maniac. So the maniac was really in love with the girl ghost but he had never told anybody that. One day he asked to marry the girl ghost. The girl ghost was very pretty and beautiful but she also had another lover. So one day she and her other lover were out on a date and they got annoyed at each other. So the girl ghost said, "I don't love you anymore." So she quickly ran, uh, stomped away angrily. Of course, the lover was very disappointed to lose his beautiful

girl, but that's the way it goes.

So the maniac was walking out, and the girl ghost said, "Oh, hello, is that you again?" And he said, "Yes, lovely. Will you please come on a walk with me?" "It would be my pleasure," the girl ghost said. So they each went out on a walk. Now the maniac was very ugly, but the girl ghost didn't think of his ugliness at all compared to his manners. So finally she got to like him very much and they were always going out on dates. One day the maniac bought her an engagement ring. "So," he said, "would you like to marry me?" "With pleasure," she said. So they invited some of their friends to their wedding.

Now the jealous lover had heard that she was getting married to someone else. He had to stop the wedding; so the wedding procession was now beginning when the other lover got there. "Stop the wedding," he screamed and in horror everybody turned around. He had a big witch with him. "Ha, ha, ha," the witch laughed, "I see that the girl ghost will not accept my brother. Well, I'll cast a, I'll cast a spell on everyone of you if you do not marry my brother." Well, the girl goes—

T: Wait, wait a moment, I'm a little confused. The jealous lover came and he wanted who, he wanted—the witch was his sister, is that it?

P: Ya.

T: Oh, and she said, "You've gotta marry my brother."

P: Well, so everybody was so unhappy, especially the girl ghost. She didn't want to marry the lover because she, she wasn't in love with him anymore; but, of course, she didn't want to be turned into anything terrible. The girl and the ugly maniac kissed each other goodbye and the girl ghost went over to the witch. "Well, have you made up your mind little twinky toes?" asked the witch meanly. "Yes," the girl ghost said sadly; so, unfortunately, they had to be married.

Well, later when they were married and living in a house the ugly maniac came, and he took the girl ghost away with him and they both ran away. Now then, by then, the girl ghost had forgotten all about the ugly maniac, so when he came she screamed in terror and when he asked her, she said, "I don't want to marry you, you are too ugly," but he was very kind, and she was having a lot of trouble with her ugly, mean old husband. So she ran away with him and they were each married. She didn't care about his ugliness anymore, and they all lived happily ever after.

The moral is it doesn't matter how ugly a person is; it's their manners and the way they feel about you.

T: Okay. Thank you very much. That was an excellent story. Now it's time for me to tell my story.

Julie depicts herself as a ghost—as dead, inhuman, having no substance, and unreal. Her feelings of worthlessness are profound. She feels that only the lowest creatures could possibly be interested in her. One of her suitors is an ugly maniac and the other, the brother of a witch, is described at the end of her story as ugly and mean. In the story, she gains some ego-enhancement by getting the two men to fight over her.

Her feelings of inadequacy were in part related to her father's rejection of her. She adhered to the dicta, "If he doesn't love me, I am unlovable," and "If he has left me, there must be something terribly wrong with me." The story also reveals her feelings that all men are basically ugly, cruel, and un-loving, like her father. In the story she regains her lost father; it is better to have an ugly man than no man at all. The ugly monster, however, has "good manners," in other words, he provides her with the tenderness and devotion her father deprives her of.

This is the story I told in response:

Therapist: Once upon a time there was a girl ghost and there was a man whom she liked very much. He was a nice-looking man and she wanted to marry him very much and he first showed interest in her for a little while. And, then, one day they had a big fight, and he said, "You are very ugly and I never want to see you again." And he walked off and she felt very bad and she began to cry, and then a friend of hers came along and the friend said, "Why are you crying?" And she said, "Because I'm ugly." He said, "What do you mean because you're ugly?" She said, "Well, my boyfriend left me, and he said I'm ugly." The friend said, "There are two things wrong with your thinking: 1) just because somebody calls you ugly doesn't mean you're ugly and 2) just because somebody leaves you doesn't mean you're ugly." And she said, "You mean that?" And he said, "Yes," and she said, "Yeah, but you know my boyfriend is a pretty smart guy and he really knows a lot." And he said, "Yeah, he may know a lot but he's out in left field when he calls you ugly. I can tell you that you're not ugly and if you think you're ugly because he calls you ugly that means that there is something wrong with you."

Well, with that she began thinking and she realized that just because somebody leaves you, it doesn't make you ugly, and just because somebody calls you ugly, it doesn't make you ugly. So she found someone else who was very nice, she grew up, and she lived happily ever after. Do you know what the moral of that story is?

Patient: No.

T: My story has two morals: if someone calls you ugly it doesn't mean you are ugly, and the other moral is if somebody leaves you, it doesn't mean you're no good. Those are the two morals of my story. What do you think of that?

P: I think it's a very nice story.

T: What's the part you liked the most?

P: Um—I liked that when the boyfriend—he told her the truth about herself.

T: I see. Okay.

In my story I tried to get Julie to question two basic premises which contributed to her low self-esteem, one of the more common problems suffered by children of divorced parents. They assume that they have been abandoned because they have been bad or because they are in some way unlovable. Correction of such distortions is an important part of the treatment of these children. One must emphasize to them that the divorce is the result of the parents rejecting each other (or at least one parent rejecting the other), but that rejection of the child was in no way involved. Also, in order to help the child compensate for the loss, one must reiterate that there are many others with whom one can form gratifying relationships, both in the present and in the future.

Three weeks later, Julie told this story:

Patient: Good afternoon, ladies, and gentlemen, this story is about a little girl and her talking doll. Once upon a time there was a little girl named Alice, and she had a secret because she had a talking doll who was her friend and could really walk and play. This doll was really alive. So one day the talking doll was lost. Alice burst into tears and she had to find her. Alice lived in this big spooky house so she went up to the attic where there were all different things around. She looked into all the trunks and suitcases but she couldn't find her talking doll anywhere. So, soon she saw her dog just chewing up something. Uh, she wondered if it was her talking doll or not. No, it was just the talking doll's dress. So she ran and asked the dog where was the talking doll. Now this dog could talk, too, so he said, "I think the talking doll went out to get something to eat but I don't know really 'cause that's where she usually goes."

So Alice ran out of the house to all the restaurants around the neighborhood. At one, right sitting on the table there was the talking doll, feasting and feasting. So, Alice said, "Hold on Elizabeth"—that was the talking doll's name. So, Elizabeth went back. "I'm sorry if I scared you, but I was very, very hungry and the cook is not at home now she went to do some shopping." "Oh, that's all right, Elizabeth, I'm very glad to have you back." So they all, they went—

Therapist: Hold on a second, is it that I'm sorry that I scared you by going away, but the cook wasn't there and I was hungry?

P: Yeah.

T: Okay.

P: So they went back into the house and then they had even more because the talking doll had that much time to feast before Alice found her, so Alice thanked the dog very much because he's the one that had really found the talking doll.

T: Did you say that the rest had more to eat? Is that it? Because the talking doll—

P: Yeah, didn't have that much time to feast because Alice, um, found her.

T: Oh, in other words, so that there was more food left for the rest.

P: Yeah.

T: Okay.

P: And, so, they played games and danced and then the cook came back and it was dinner time and she cooked a delicious stew for everybody. Then when Alice went to bed she whispered, "Oh, Elizabeth, I'm so glad to have you back."

The moral of this story is: Don't—now let's see what's the moral of this story—um, um—don't look places where you know you can't find somebody. There's my moral.

T: How does that apply to this story?

P: Well, because Alice really knew that she couldn't, um, find the doll in the attic and everything, but the dog knew where she was. The dog usually knew where Elizabeth goes, so that's why that's the moral.

T: I see. Okay. Thank you. Well, that was a very good story.

P: Thank you.

Alice is the patient and Elizabeth, the talking doll, her alter ego. The cook, the provider of food (love), symbolizes the patient's mother. Sometimes she is home and sometimes she is not, that is, her love is not always available. When she is not there to provide affection, Julie—in the form of the doll Elizabeth —seeks food outside the home. The restaurant, I believe, represents the father who, indeed, lived in another city. The hunt for food is her quest for affection. The moral, "Don't look places where you know you can't find somebody," refers to her quest for love. It has healthy elements in that Julie is learning from messages imparted in previous stories not to persist futilely in trying to extract love from someone who is not able to provide it. She is beginning to seek love elsewhere when it is not forthcoming. The restaurant, however, is a distorted symbol for the father in that it implies continuous availability of food. Julie sees her mother as giving affection only intermittently, and her father as continually so—a gross reversal.

With this symbolic reversal in mind, I told my story:

Therapist: Now it's time for me to tell my story. Once upon a time there was a little girl named Alice and she had a secret. She had a talking doll named Elizabeth and this talking doll was her friend and she and Elizabeth would talk about everything when they were alone. Now, in this house they had a cook and once in a while they would go out and eat in a restaurant and Elizabeth and Alice always used to argue as to who made better food, the restaurant or the cook, and they could never figure it out. Now, sometimes when the cook would make a meal Alice would say, "This meal is very good," and Elizabeth would say, "Uch, terrible. Ooh, this food is terrible. Feh!" Anyway, then sometimes the cook would make a meal and it was Alice who would say, "Wow, is this food really good." And it was Elizabeth who would say, "Ich, how could you like that? It was disgusting." And, when they had gone up to the restaurant, it was the same thing. Sometimes Alice would like the food, sometimes Elizabeth would like the food. Sometimes Alice would hate the food, sometimes Elizabeth would hate the food. So, they began to learn that no cook, be it the restaurant cook or the cook in the house, is perfect. That sometimes they make good food and sometimes they make bad food. But they decided to see who made the best food more often and they kept score and they watched carefully and they tried to see— and who do you think they finally concluded made the best food more often, not that that person made the best food all the time but had a higher percentage of times when the food was good? Who do you think it was—the cook or the restaurant?

Patient: The cook.

T: Why do you say that?

P: Um—because, um, the cook could make their favorite foods all the time so that it would be good but the restaurant only had a menu of different things sometimes.

T: Right, that's what I thought too. Besides, home cooking is usually better than restaurant cooking. You know in really home cooking, the cook can put in all the best kinds of things and tries to please the family because the family are the cook's loved ones that she often has a greater desire to make good food for. So Alice and the dog gradually realized that the cook could be counted on more often than the restaurant to make good food, although once in a while the cook would make a poor meal, but more often the restaurant would make a poor meal and you know what the morals of that, that story has a couple of morals, you know what those morals are?

P: Ummm—

T: Well, the morals are: nobody is prefect, everybody has their good and their bad parts like this cook. She wasn't perfect; she had times when she would cook good meals and other times when she would cook bad meals. And the second moral is: when you have a choice between two people, both of whom are not perfect, you try to spend more time with the one who will or has more to offer you and in this case it was the cook. She wasn't perfect, but she did give them more than the restaurant. But, once in a while they would go to the restaurant too. The end. What did you think of that story?

P: Very nice.

T: What was the part about it you liked the most?

P: Um, when they found who was nearest perfect, who was the nearest to being perfect, not perfect, because nobody could be perfect.

T: Uh, huh, right, okay.

In my story, I helped Julie gain a more accurate picture of her parents regarding their relative abilities to give her affection. This is an important goal of practically every child's therapy; but in the treatment of children whose parents are divorced, it is even more vital. Such children often have a more distorted view of their parents than those whose parents are together. There are a number of reasons for this. The divorced parents, in their antagonism, communicate to the child either overtly or covertly many criticisms of each other that are not valid. The child's fear of alienating his parents may cause him to repress his awareness of their deficiencies. An absent parent, who mainly provides recreation when visiting, is not in a situation conducive to the exposure of defects. Acquiring an accurate picture of the parents—especially regarding their abilities to give love—can help the child avoid frustration and neurotic reactions which stem from vain attempts to secure affection from an individual beyond his capacity to provide it.

During Julie's fourth month of treatment she told this story:

Patient: This story is about two different watermelons. Each of the watermelons knew that the watermelons that the farmer chose and sold to a person were the finest so they each argued about who or which one the farmer would pick. Soon it came time for the farmer to pick his crops, and he went to the watermelons first. "Shush," said the first one, "I can hear the farmer. Of course, he's going to pick me cause I'm so ripe and fresh. I don't have many seeds in me either." So the other watermelon also wanted to be picked by the farmer and the other watermelon was really ugly but you never know how somebody is inside. He was very ugly but he was good inside.

So the farmer soon came and looked at the watermelons. He looked at the first one who smiled boastfully at him. "Pick me," he whispered. So the ugly watermelon didn't say anything—just stood still like a good watermelon should. So the farmer knew which one to pick. He took the ugly one out of the ground and went back to the farmhouse. So the boastful watermelon was very angry because he hadn't been picked because he thought that he was was the finest.

The moral of my story is: Don't brag before you know what's going to happen.

Therapist: Anything else in your moral?

P: Uh.

T: What about the ugly watermelon? Can you say anything about it?

P: Well, I think that he was happy that he was picked and he used to think that he was very ugly, but now he knew that he wasn't. But he was clean inside and the other watermelon was mean and everything like that.

T: I see. You mean the one that looked nice was really mean?

P: Yeah.

The ugly watermelon is, of course, the patient, who considers herself homely and compensates for this deficiency by depicting her alterego as modest. The story has positive elements in that it reveals her appreciation that boasting is an alienating personality characteristic and that modesty can be an asset. Although boasting was not one of Julie's vices, modesty was certainly not one of her virtues. She was loud-mouthed and grumbled chronically. Accordingly, I told this story:

Therapist: Once upon a time there were two watermelons and they were in a patch. Each year at harvest time the farmer would come and he would pick the best watermelon. These watermelons were twins and they both looked quite good. Inside they were both quite good also. They were both quite friendly and happy inside and good people and outside they both were quite beautiful. But there was one difference. The second watermelon, in spite of the fact that it was very beautiful, at times for reasons unknown to the farmer, would snarl up its face; it would growl and complain. It was really good inside and a very friendly and nice person inside, but outside it was constantly complaining. It would constantly say, "Ah, the sun's too hot," or "There's not enough water around here," or "It's crowded around here with all these vegetables," or "It's so cold at night," or this complaint and that complaint, or "The forest around here isn't rich enough in food and all the animals come around here and they sit on me and they bother me."

Well, the other watermelon wasn't one of these growling snarling complainers. Anyway, when the farmer came to choose which of the two watermelons he wished to take, which one do you think he chose?

Patient: The first one?

T: Why?

P: Although they looked alike the first one was better inside and had a kinder heart.

T: They both had kind hearts.

P: Well, the first one didn't complain and was satisfied.

T: And the second one was the complainer. He kind of bugged and irritated the farmer. He said, "Number Two, I know that you have as good a heart as Number One, but you are constantly bothering me with your constant complaints. For that reason, although your heart is as good as the other watermelon and you are as pretty as Number One, you bother me—you bug me—and for that reason I am going to choose Number One." Well, that year the second watermelon learned a lesson and then it made a resolution never to do that again. When the watermelon stopped it got a lot of friends. Although it never won the prize, it still lived fairly happily since it learned from its mistakes.

And the moral of that story is that people do judge you on your appearance. You may be good inside but if you are going to walk around and snarl all the time, people are not going to take to you. The end.

What do you think about that story?

P: It was interesting.

T: Do you think it had anything to do with you?

P: No!

T: Not in the least?

P: No!

T: You are not like any of the watermelons in my story?

P: No!

T: I thought there might be a slight resemblance?

P: No!

T: Okay. The end.

In my story I attempted to direct Julie's attention to personality qualities which are more pertinent to her own problems. You may be "good" inside, but if you are obnoxious on the outside you are going to miss out on many of the gratifications and rewards which the world has to offer. As the post-story discussion reveals, the patient would not admit that the story had anything to do with her. Such denial, however, did not necessarily mean that my message had not reached her. She was actively interested in my story and I had the feeling that at some level it had had an impact. Insisting that the child verbalize "insight" can often be anti-therapeutic. The child may consider admission of his defects a humiliation. It is not necessary to "rub his nose in them" or insist upon testimonials. If he alters his behavior in a salutary direction, this is real proof that the therapist has been heard.

Clinical Example
Nick, the braggart.

Nick, an eleven-year-old boy was referred because of marked disinterest in his schoolwork, recalcitrant behavior at home, lying, petty stealing, and insomnia. He was a "wise guy" and his relationships with peers was poor. His mother had decided to divorce his father a few weeks prior to his first visit. His father, a salesman, was of limited intelligence. His compensatory braggadocio engendered in his wife an attitude of chronic irritation and scorn.

During his second month of treatment, Nick told this story:

Patient: Today I'm going to tell a story about me, myself, and I.
Therapist: Okay.
P: There was one boy named me—that was Robert Smith. There was another boy in Italy named Roberto Smitho and another person in Germany, I mean in France, named Roberto de Smith. Now, funny thing about it was that we were all born at the same time and we all look alike.

One day Roberto de Smith from France came to America. By some accident I was waiting for my grandmother, and he came off the ship and we saw each other and we looked exactly alike. Now, I walked up to him and said, "What's your name?" He said, "Roberto de Smith." And he said, "What's your name?" So I said, "Well, my name is Robert Smith." I said, "I think we're look-alikes." So I was talking to him and my grandmother came off the ship, and I told her about my experience with this boy and since he was there alone, I invited him to come to my house.

A couple of day later my father was coming off an airplane from Italy and I met another boy that looked like me. And you know who that is. That's Roberto Smitho. But the same thing happened. Now he's living in my house. So he's wearing my clothes also and we have to work in the street and we're working in the street together one day—so one of my friends saw us three and he didn't know what to do. He said, "Which of you are Smith?" We all raised our hands because all of our names were Smith. Roberto Smitho thought he said Smitho. Smith, you know, American. I thought he said my name, and Roberto de Smith from France thought he said his name. And this guy, my friend, didn't know what to do! "Which of you three live on 135 E. 134th St., Apt. 10C?" We all raised our hands 'cause all of them were living at my house. So my friend didn't know what to do. So I stood up and explained to him that I had these foreign friends over and he started to laugh like anything.

Now, then they all flew back together and I felt lonely because I didn't have any more double.

So the moral to the story is: to have doubles are much better than to have none.

T: Why is that?

P: Well, you have more friends because, you know, each person likes somebody else and you see him and say, "Oh, yeah, I remember you," and you have a whole list of different friends. Each will like to do different things and everybody will like you. Thank you.

T: Wait a moment. I'm a little bit confused. What were some of the advantages of having these two friends there?

P: Well, Roberto Smitho liked to play baseball and I liked to go swimming and water skiing and all that water stuff, and Roberto de Smith liked to play football. Each of us did something else at the same time.

P: Everybody liked me because I did—like one person would say, "Oh, you swim beautifully," or say to me, "Oh, you're a beautiful football player . . .

T: Oh, I see. In other words, people didn't know that there were three of you.

P: Right!

T: Oh, I see. So that . . .

P: Only that one friend of mine.

T: So then you could fool people into thinking you were a great all-round person. I see. Now I get it. Okay.

P: And also let's say if Roberto Smitho was better in history and there was a history test that day, I'd let him go to school instead of me.

T: I see.

P: Thank you ladies and gentlemen. And now Dr. Gardner will tell his. So hold on until Dr. Gardner gets ready to think of his. Please tell us the name of the story?

T: This is a story called "The Three Boys."

P: Now don't forget at the end you must tell us the moral of your story and I'll be asking you questions.

T: Okay, you can. Now remember that my story can have many things that are similar to your story, but invariably at some point it gets different.

The story reveals Nick's tendency to utilize deceitful maneuvers to bolster his lagging self-esteem. He does not feel well-liked by peers. His refusal to share, to respect the rights of others, and his excessive clowning alienated other children. In the story Nick compensates for this deficiency by taking for himself the admiration and respect earned by his alter egos. They do the work and he gets the praise. Roberto de Smith plays football and Nick is told: "Oh, you're a beautiful football player." Roberto Smitho takes the history test and Nick gets the good grade. He manifests no guilt or embarrassment over his duplicity but rather prides himself on his cleverness.

I told this story in response:

> *Therapist:* Once upon a boy there was a time.
>
> *Patient:* (laughs)
>
> *T:* Once upon a boy there was a time!
>
> *P:* Now let's begin with the story.
>
> *T:* This boy's name was John Smith and John Smith felt very bad about himself. He wasn't a very good sport. He wasn't very good in athletics and he wasn't very good in school. He had a couple of subjects that he was okay in, but for the most part he wasn't real good. Are you listening to my story? What are you mumbling there? All right. Anyway, he sometimes thought about the fact that there might be in a country like Germany another kid named Johann Schmidt and he thought maybe he'd have the same name as him. And he thought that there might be in France a boy whose name was Jean Smithe.
>
> *P:* (laughs and mumbles something)
>
> *T:* Well, anyway, one day while he was waiting for someone at the dock there showed up . . .
>
> *P:* Where?
>
> *T:* At the dock and there he sees this kid who looks just like him and they go over and they start talking to each other and sure enough it's Johann Schmidt, and he takes him home to his house.
>
> *P:* Rats!
>
> *T:* And then his father is traveling in France and his father meets this boy named Jean Smithe and he brought this boy home. So these three boys stay at John's house.
>
> *P:* (keeps mumbling in background)
>
> *T:* And John thought of a good idea. "I think it will be a good idea— I know that these kids have certain talents and abilities that I don't have —I think I'm going to pass them off as me and everybody will like me." Stop the mumbling. If you want to continue playing this game you'll have to stop mumbling. Anyway, the boys thought that was a great idea too. So what happened was sometimes when the kids would call up and

say, "Hey, John, you want to go out and play football?" he'd say, "Sure." And he sent out Johann Schmidt who was a very good football player, but there was poor John sitting home alone, very lonely, and not getting any of the fun of playing football because Johann was out playing. Johann would come home and say, "Boy, that was really great! What a game . . .

P: Did the kids know there were three?

T: No. He didn't let anybody know that there were . . .

P: Well, doesn't he know how to swim or anything . . .

T: Yeah. But the thing is that he wanted everybody to think that he was a good all-around sport.

P: Yeah, but that's what he was doing by having them . . .

T: Yeah, but then he was home alone. He wasn't having the fun of playing football because Johann was out playing football. Now, of course, John was a good swimmer so when they called to go swimming, John would go himself, but when they called for someone to play basketball, he would send out Jean.

P: (still mumbling things)

T: So he was quite lonely. In fact, when he was out swimming, Jean and Johann would have to stay home and they were quite lonely and would have to play in the house because they didn't want anybody to find out their secret. So, although the boys thought at first that this would be a good idea, after a while they realized it wasn't so hot because the other guys had to walk around keeping a secret all the time fearful of discovery. You know, they didn't have much fun doing these things.

P: Wouldn't they all have accents?

T: These boys in their countries learned pretty good English. In your story what happened to them? Did they have accents in your story?

P: I believe they did.

T: Well, one day one boy who was playing with Johann said, "You know, you speak a little funny today. You speak with a slight German accent." And Johann said, "No, I don't!" He said, "John doesn't speak that way. You sound a little German." He replied, "I'm not German." He said, "You don't even say German like an American. You sound like a German." Anyway, the boy began to suspect and after that when they were playing with Jean, they realized that Jean spoke with a little French accent.

P: Oh.

T: And then they began to get wiser and they said, "We think there's something fishy." The next evening they went up to the house when the boys didn't expect them, and there they saw the three of them. Well, following that, poor John, everybody said, "Well, what kind of liar are you?

Gee whiz. What kind of liar are you? You tried to put something over on us."

P: (mumbles some words) Yeah, yeah, yeah.

T: And, of course, the two boys felt bad too, and they went back to their native lands.

P: Yeah, yeah, yeah.

T: And poor John was very embarrassed and then he realized that it really wasn't a good thing to try to fool everybody. So what finally happened was he decided that although he might not be a star football player, it was possible for him to be a passable football player, get the pleasure of playing football, and be honest with your friends.

P: Right, right, right.

T: And my story has two morals. Do you know what the morals of my story are? See if you can figure them out.

P: I don't know.

T: Come on. Figure out the morals.

P: I don't know.

T: One of the morals of my story is that the main fun from doing something comes from doing it yourself.

P (with accent): You're joking.

T: And the second . . .

P: (blows into microphone)

T: If people find out you're a liar, they will not like you.

P: That's true, true, true, true, true, true, true. Thank you very much Dr. Gardner. Dr. Gardner, I'd like to ask you a question.

T: Yes, please.

P: Well, why didn't the two children at home want to go out somewhere else; you know, like some kids would be playing baseball, some kids—

T: They were afraid to be seen in the streets, two at a time. If one kid would come and say, "Hi there John." Let's say the real John was out playing football and Johann was walking in the street and some kid says, "Hey, I'm confused. I thought I just left you at the park. What are you doing out here? How could that be?" So he'd suspect not realizing that he would be seeing Johann. So once you start something like that you've got to cover yourself up if you want it to go through. They had to lie a lot, sneak, and it made them very uncomfortable.

P: I see. Thank you Dr. Gardner.

My story emphasized the virtue-is-its-own-reward theme in an attempt to encourage Nick to consider non-psychopathic methods of bolstering his self-esteem. Johann has fun while playing football; and Jean while playing basketball. The stay-at-homers lose out on these gratifications. Another drawback of the scheme is that they all suffer fears of discovery which are ego-debasing. When the devious plan is finally revealed, they all endure the humiliations one must inevitably experience on being so exposed.

As was often true while playing the storytelling game, Nick would present a facade of mere superficial interest; a devil-may-care attitude with which he attempted to conceal his genuine involvement. He would mumble, tap, hum, and engage in other distractions although he was, for the most part, very much with me as his post-story questions show. When told to stop his distracting noises, he would usually do so (at least temporarily). When I was able to keep these irritations at a tolerable level, he'd gradually stop the horseplay as his absorption in the storytelling deepened. This is what happened here: by the end of my story the clowning had stopped and he was definitely immersed in the game.

His comments at the end reveal his resistance to my communications. He tries to present a plan by which the two boys hiding at home could still enjoy the gratifications of sports by sneaking out and playing elsewhere. In order to discourage this subterfuge—its purpose to fill loopholes in the scheme rather than to abandon it—I pointed out its impracticality and, more important, its drawback of producing further feelings of self-loathing: "They had to lie a lot, sneak, and it made them feel very uncomfortable."

Chapter 12

SEX IDENTIFICATION AND THE OEDIPUS COMPLEX

Growing up in a household with only one parent is likely to deprive the child of the psychological benefits to be derived from the two-parent household. The boy's relationship with his mother and the girl's with her father are the prototypes of their future relationships with the opposite sex. In addition, the same-sexed parent serves as the most important model for the child's own sex role. Although most single parents are aware of the importance of the child's having a good relationship with the absent parent, even the best efforts to accomplish this do not usually provide the child with the full benefits of the relationship. Living with someone in the same home is very different from visitation—love, interest, proper guidance, etc. notwithstanding. In this chapter I will focus on two possible sources of difficulty that may arise in the divorce situation, namely, sex identification and oedipal problems.

The Freudian Theory of the Oedipus Complex

Toward the end of the third year of life, Freud believed that the primary source of sexual gratification shifted from the oral and anal regions to the genitals. Important areas of sexual interest in this, the phallic phase, which lasts until the age of five or six, are said to be voyeuristic and exhibitionistic, as well as urethral-erotic. In the phallic phase, sexual interest is said to be strong and is primarily directed toward one's own genitals and expressed through masturbation, whereas in the genital phase, which begins at puberty, the sexual focus becomes externally directed.

During the phallic phase, Freud believed, both normal and pathological children *universally* develop what he called the Oedipus complex. The term *oedipal* was derived from Oedipus, the hero of the Greek tragedy *Oedipus Rex*, written by Sophocles about 430 B.C. In the play, Oedipus through a series of fateful events, actually consummates the oedipal act; namely, he kills his father and has sexual intercourse with his mother. The term *complex* refers to a constellation of thoughts and feelings centering on a particular theme. Briefly, then, the child with an Oedipus complex manifests a genital-sexual attraction to the parent of the opposite sex and an associated feeling of envy and hostility toward the parent of the same sex. The urges are considered to be genital-sexual, although not necessarily specifically associated with heterosexual intercourse as the primary source of genital gratification. Oedipal fantasies, according to the classical Freudian school, may include a variety of misconceptions regarding the exact nature of the parents' sexual life: the child may fantasize that the parents get pleasure by looking at one another's genitals; by engaging in oral-genital contact; by rubbing themselves against each other; or by going to the toilet together. Included also are fantasies of marriage and the desire to give the mother babies or to bear the father's children. In each case, the child fantasizes himself or herself in the role of the rival parent. In addition, the boy may fear that his hostility toward his father will result in the latter's retaliation, especially by castration, and this produces what Freud called castration anxiety.

Freud considered the Oedipus complex to be part of normal human psychosexual development and regarded the failure to resolve or come to terms with it to be the central element in the etiology of all neuroses.

His explanation for the development of the Oedipus complex in the male was far simpler than in the female. The boy's possessive love of his mother and murderous rage toward the father is a natural extension of the loving relationship the mother has always provided him. The resolution of the Oedipus complex involves resigning himself to the fact that he cannot totally possess his mother—a resignation made easier by his fear of castration by the father. Observing the female's absence of a penis confirms for him that his own penis can be removed. In addition, through identification with his father, the boy incorporates the latter's dictates against incest and patricide. Such "identification with the aggressor," further assists him in repressing his oedipal impulses. He develops a contempt for all who could have slept with his mother, be it himself, his father, or anyone else; the "mother-fucker" is considered most loathesome. Lastly, Freud (1924) considered biological maturation to be operative as well: "The time has come for its [the oedipus complex's] dissolution, just as the milk-teeth fall out when the permanent ones begin to press forward."

For the girl, things are more complicated. When she first observes that the little boy has a penis, she considers herself to have been deprived of a most valuable organ. Her mother, who bore her this way, is blamed, and the little girl turns to her father for love. (Because the mother also lacks this invaluable part, the girl's respect for her markedly diminishes.) The father, as the possessor of a penis, is looked upon as a more likely source of gratifying the little girl's desire to have one herself; and through fantasied sexual intercourse with the father, the female child hopes to incorporate a penis. The adult female, by bearing a male child, can satisfy her desire to produce a penis of her own. Even if the baby is a female, it can still symbolically represent the longed-for penis. Other factors that contribute to the transfer relate to the girl's anger toward her mother. The mother becomes an object of hostility because she inhibits the little girl's masturbation and because she refuses to give up her affection for the father in order to devote herself totally to the child.

In the female's oedipal resolution too, the child resigns herself to the fact that her mother's love for her father is such that she can never have him completely to herself. Rebuffed by her father, she renounces and represses her oedipal wishes. Since her father will not provide her with the penis she so desperately wants, getting one symbolically through childbearing is the best she can hope for, and she must turn eventually to other men for this purpose.

My Concept of the Oedipus Complex

First, I believe that there is a biological sexual instinct that attracts every human being to members of the opposite sex. From birth to puberty this drive is not particularly strong because during this period the child is not capable of fulfilling the drive's primary purpose of procreation. Although weak and poorly formulated during the pre-pubertal period, it nevertheless exhibits itself through behavior that I consider manifestations of *oedipal interest*. The normal child may speak on occasion of marrying the parent of the opposite sex and getting rid of his rival. These comments may even have a mildly sexual component, such as "and then we'll sleep in bed together." Instinctive impulses for territorial prerogatives may also be operative here. But I do not believe that psychologically healthy children have the desire in this period for genital-sexual experiences with the parent, nor do I believe that their sexually tinged comments are associated with strong sexual-genital urges. Rather, what the healthy child may on occasion want is a little more affection and attention, undiluted by the rival.

In a setting where the child is not receiving the affection, nurture, support, interest, guidance, protection, and generalized physical gratifications (such as stroking, warmth, and rocking) that are his due, he may, in his frustration, become obsessed with obtaining such satisfactions and develop the kinds of sexual urges, preoccupations, and fantasies that Freud referred to as oedipal. The instinctive sexual urges, which are normally mild and relatively dormant, have the *potential* for intensive expression even as early as birth. Getting little gratification from his parents, the child may develop a host of fantasies in which the frustrated love is requited and the rival is removed. Such fantasies follow the principle that the more one is deprived, the more one craves and the more jealous one becomes of those who have what one desires. Such manifestations can appropriately be called *oedipal problems* in the classical sense. Thus, the foundation for the development of neurosis is formed not, as Freud would say, through the failure to resolve successfully one's sexual frustrations regarding the parent of the opposite sex, but through the failure to come to terms with the more basic deprivations the child is suffering.

Whereas Freud considered the sexual preoccupation to arise in the child automatically, I believe that this mode of adaptation to parental deprivation is only one of many possible adjustments and that family and cultural factors play an important role in determining which one is chosen. Parental seduction is only one factor that tends to foster the oedipal adaptation. This seduction need not be overtly physical; it can arise through verbal provocations and titillating exposures. Without parental seduction the child is less likely to involve himself in a sexual adaptation to parental deprivation and is more likely to utilize nonoedipal mechanisms. Seduction enhances the likelihood, but is not essential to the development, of oedipal difficulties. (I have seen oedipal problems arise without parental seduction.)

I also believe that family and cultural factors that tend to foster the child's rivalry with the same-sexed parent can also be instrumental in bringing about the complex. I agree with Fromm (1948) that the authoritarian father in a patriarchal household may be a contributing factor in the formation of the Oedipus complex in the boy and with Sullivan (1953), who postulates that the parent's stricter attitude toward the same-sexed child fosters oedipal rivalry. Once again, however, I have seen children utilize the oedipal mechanism in the absence of significant rivalry-engendering behavior by the parents.

The classical paradigm of sexual attraction to the opposite-sexed parent and hostility toward the same-sexed seems to me an oversimplification of what one observes clinically. Most often there is great ambivalence toward both parents. The boy with a depriving yet seductive mother has good reason to be angry. He is deprived of basic affection and provided with seduction as a substitute. Clinically the anger may be revealed directly, but more commonly it is handled by a variety of defense mechanisms that repress or displace it or allow for its discharge in symbolic fashion. If any of the anger remains in conscious awareness, the child may become fearful of his mother's retaliation. To protect himself, his avowals of love may increase since they serve to deny his basic anger. Or his hostile impulses may take the form of his fearing that his mother will die, and this too may be handled by obsessive concern for her welfare. A variety of other possible mechanisms as well may come into play to assist the child in handling his basic ambivalence. A boy may still harbor, in addition to his rivalrous hostility toward his father, deep-seated loving feelings and dependent longings toward him. The hostility may cause anxiety that he may lose the father. And this may result in obsessive protestations of affection. Anyone who has observed what is sometimes referred to as a childhood "oedipal panic," whether in the boy or in the girl, will readily confirm that intense feelings of love, hate, and fear regarding *both* parents dominate the clinical picture.

The Unresolved Oedipus Complex as a Source of Psychological Disturbance

Neuroses, most would agree, are the result of many factors acting in various combinations: cultural, social, familial, psychological, and biological. For Freud, the psychobiological (especially the psychosexual) factors were crucial and he considered the unresolved Oedipus complex to be at the root of all neuroses. In my opinion, whatever cultural, social, and biological factors may be operative in the etiology of neurotic symptoms, parental—and especially maternal—deprivation is essential to their formation. All neurotic symptoms are in part an attempt to cope with this basic deprivation; and the way in which the child chooses to adapt is determined by biological, cultural, social, and familial influences. One deprived child becomes overdependent, an adaptation elicited and perpetuated by his overprotective mother. Another reacts by withdrawing, an adjustment with which his neglectful parents are comfortable. Another discharges in sports the hostility he feels toward his rejecters—sports being, in addition, an activity of premium value in his milieu. Another takes drugs or becomes a juvenile delinquent because that's how kids on *his* block adapt. Another uses his symptoms to enjoy compensatory attention. And so it goes. One could cover the gamut of psychogenic symptoms and find the common element of deprivation in each of them. I am fully aware that symptoms are most complex and many factors contribute to their formation, but the adaptation to emotional abandonment is central and omnipresent. The well-loved child is generally relatively free of psychopathology.

I use the term *oedipal* then to refer to those mechanisms by which the child, in the attempt to compensate for early emotional deprivation, obsessively craves for and tries to gain the affection of the opposite-sexed parent. Oedipal problems are likely to arise in a situation of parental seduction or paternal authoritarianism, but they can appear in other family settings as well.

The range of psychological reactions to parental rejection is broad; and many, if not most, contain elements of more than one stage of psychosexual development. Rarely does one see purely oral, anal, or phallic phase symptomatology. When the predominant theme appears to involve obsessive attempts to gain the love of the opposite-sexed parent or excessive rivalry with the same-sexed parent, then one can conveniently apply the term *oedipal*. The homosexual, whose obsessive "love" of males is often, among other things, a thinly disguised attempt to deny an underlying hatred of men and who fears women because they too closely resemble his forbidden, seductive mother, could, because his difficulties fundamentally reflect the oedipal paradigm, be considered to have oedipal problems. When a patient's adjustment to the privation involves, for example, compulsive eating, the term *oedipal* is not usually used even though the food may be a symbolic representation of the mother's love. The more remote the overt symptom is from the themes of mother-love and father-hate (or vice-versa), the less likely it will be labeled oedipal. However, if the compulsive eater (who is considered to be suffering with "oral" difficulties) has a dependent, thinly disguised sexual relationship with his mother, his problems would more likely be considered oedipal.

Thus, the term *oedipal* is misleading because it purports to describe a symptom complex that rarely, if ever, exists in pure form. Most often, if not always, there are elements of other stages of psychosexual development. In addition, to use the term *oedipal* is equivalent to naming pneumonia "cough" or encephalitis "headache." Just as cough and headache are the superficial manifestations of the more general underlying diseases, pneumonia and encephalitis, so the Oedipus complex is only one possible symptomatic manifestation of a whole class of symptom complexes resulting from the basic disorder of parental deprivation. Also, the term is restrictive because it tends to focus undue attention on the sexual elements in the adaptation while disregarding the more important nonsexual aspects. It suggests that the primary problem is sexual, which it is not.

My comments on the Oedipus complex here in no way constitute a total theory. Nor do I wish to suggest that parental deprivation of love can successfully explain all oedipal problems or indeed all neuroses. There is still much in this field that requires reexamination and clarification. My intent is merely directed to correcting widespread distortions and making Freud's basic concept more directly applicable to contemporary society.

The Resolution of the Oedipus Complex

The normal child, according to Freud, resolves his Oedipus complex by the age of five-and-a-half to six. He then enters a six-year period of sexual quiescence—the latency period—which terminates at puberty. There is, indeed, little sexual interest in this period but not, I believe, because of repression of oedipal drives and resolution of the Oedipus complex, but rather because, as I have described, there is relatively little genital-sexual urge to be repressed in the first place. It is not until puberty, with physiological genital maturation, that sexual urges of adult intensity are normally present. The child has the potential to exhibit such interest and achieve such gratification, but to do so would be, in my opinion, pathological.

In spite of this low level of sexual activity during this period, there is probably more sexual interest and fantasy than in the preceding phases of life, not less as Freud indicates. Because of the child's greater experiences with those outside his home, he is more likely to have encountered arousing sexual stimuli.

The word *resolution* is generally used to refer to the cure or dissolution of the Oedipus complex, but I prefer to use the term *alleviation* because oedipal involvements and interests are never completely resolved. At best oedipal problems can be alleviated. My therapeutic approach to oedipal difficulties reflects my concept of the Oedipus complex itself: the problems to be alleviated are not the result of parental sexual seduction but rather of more generalized emotional deprivation. Therefore, I consider the improvement in the parent-child relationship crucial to the alleviation of oedipal problems in the child. The boy who has obtained little gratification from his mother may become fixated in the effort to secure it. His entire life may be devoted to this futile pursuit. It is as though he reasoned that there is no point in moving on to seek satisfaction from others. If his own mother does not provide him with enough affection, how can he expect strangers to offer it? A therapeutic attempt is therefore made to improve his relationship with his mother so that he will obtain some of the gratifications that are his due in childhood. Gratification at this time will make him more confident about his ability to obtain similar satisfactions from others in the future. The same rationale holds for my attempts to improve the girl's relationship with her father. The father plays a significant role in the girl's development of a healthy sense of femininity, and the girl who lacks a salutary paternal experience is likely to develop pathological oedipal adjustments.

To accomplish an improvement in the parent-child relationship, the child must come to terms with the fact that there are problems in his involvement with his parents that have to be worked on. I attempt to help the child change those elements in his behavior that might be contributing to the difficulties. I try to help him gain a more accurate picture of his parents, their assets and their liabilities, the areas in which they can provide him with meaningful gratifications and those in which they cannot. He is helped to accept the fact that he cannot completely possess either of his parents and that the affection and attention of each of them must be *shared* with other members of the family. This sharing concept is an important one to impart. The child must be helped to appreciate that no one can possess another person completely: his father shares Mother with the children; his mother shares the father with the children; and he has no choice but to share his mother with his father and siblings. In the context of sharing, however, *he must be reassured that, although he may not get as much as he might want, he will still get something*.

He is encouraged to seek satisfactions from his parents in the areas in which they are genuinely capable of providing them and at such times as they can be provided. And he is encouraged to pursue elsewhere those gratifications that his parents are incapable of giving him. Deeper involvement with peers is encouraged to help him compensate, and he is consoled with the hope that as he grows older he will be increasingly able and free to enjoy meaningful relationships with others. For boys, identifications with assertive men are fostered so that their future chances of obtaining a desirable mate are enhanced. Identification with a male therapist, teacher, camp counselor, or scoutmaster can be helpful in this regard. Identifications and behavioral attitudes that will increase the likelihood of the girl's attracting a mate in the future are also fostered.

Whereas for Freud the resolution of oedipal conflicts comes out of fear of castration, resignation, and natural biological processes, in my approach the child is given something in compensation for his loss and is, therefore, more likely to give up the obsession. The child with oedipal problems has not pursued these alternatives on his own and must be helped to do so. I cannot imagine true resolution without such substitutes.

Attempts are also made to diminish the guilt the child may feel over his sexual or hostile thoughts and feelings and to correct misconceptions that contribute to such guilt. He is repeatedly told, for example, that his impulses in these areas are shared by most, if not all, children. He is reassured that hostile thoughts, as such, cannot harm. He is encouraged to use his anger constructively to bring about a reduction in his frustrations and resentments. I try to encourage his entry into situations where he may have the living experience that the expression of anger does not generally result in the dire consequences he anticipates. Little direct attention is given to penis envy, masturbation, castration anxiety, child-bearing, and sexuality in general. Even when the child's symptoms are overtly sexual, emphasis on the relatively non-sexual approaches I have described is more therapeutically effective. As I have said, the sexual is most often a symbolic representation of more basic non-sexual problems that are more directly dealt with in my approach.

In addition, I work closely with the parents and attempt to correct any misguided approaches to the child that might be contributing to the schism in their relationship with him. If the parents are motivated for, or receptive to, psychiatric treatment for themselves, I help them arrange for it, either with me or with another therapist. If, from such therapy, they can provide the child with more affection, there will be a greater likelihood of his alleviating his oedipal problems.

Regarding the resolution of oedipal conflicts, one final point should be made. The term *resolution* implies a final working through, a complete solution, a coming to peace with one's Oedipus complex. I think that the more one has been deprived, the less the likelihood that one can fully resolve his reactions to early deprivations. All patients, I believe, regardless of their pathology and the length and success of their treatment, never completely give up the attempt to get one more drop of milk from the empty breast. Often, the breast has been far more freely flowing than the patient realizes. The child ill appreciates the efforts of his parents and the time and energy involved in his upbringing. He more often recalls the frustrations and deprivations. The child's hypercritical attitude toward his parents is further intensified by his projection of his own hostilities onto them. Because of this projection he perceives them as far more malevolent than they really are. Even when he becomes a parent himself, after he has had the opportunity to view the parent-child relationship from another vantage point, he tends to maintain and preserve his own childhood distortions.

What about the so-called normal people (whoever they are and whatever that means); those out there whom therapists never see; those whose life adjustments are good? My guess is that they too never completely cease trying to please their mothers and fathers and gain their approbation. In their minds' eye, even when they are old and *their* parents have long since died, thoughts like "My mother would have been proud of me for this" or "I'm glad my father wasn't alive when that happened; he would have never forgiven me" still persist. For the first five years of life, children endlessly seek their parents' approval, and for the next ten to fifteen they are still significantly dependent on it. I do not believe that such "programming" can ever be completely erased.

Sex Identification

To begin, there are obvious differences between the sexes that are undeniable. Let us refer to these, for the sake of this discussion, as the *primary sexual functions*. In the female this function is childbearing and breast-feeding. Although the female may choose not to bear a child herself or not to breast-feed the one she does give birth to, she cannot relegate these activities to the male. The male's primary sexual function is that of fertilization. He cannot transfer this function to the female. So much for the obvious and irrefutable.

Now to the speculative. I believe that there exists within each woman a *maternal instinct* that is part of the primary sexual function. I believe it to be innate and psychobiological; that is, it has both psychological and biological components. It includes the physical urge to copulate in order to conceive. That the female, if healthy, will want to have sexual intercourse without the goal of conception in no way weakens my argument. The primary biological purpose of copulation is fertilization not orgasm. Bearing the child within her and having the physical capacity to nourish the child from her own body contributes to the formation of a kind of psychological tie with the child that the male cannot fully develop. I believe all women to be born with this capacity, which, like many other physiological functions, varies in intensity in different people. When there is little or no expression of the maternal instinct, repressive psychological factors are operative; even the most mannish lesbian, somewhere deep down, wants to be a mother.

I believe also that the male has a *paternal instinct*, which is also psychobiological. It includes a biological desire to copulate and thereby bring about the birth of a child. Again, that he may want to have sexual intercourse without fatherhood as a goal does not in itself refute my point; he still has within him the deep-seated urge to have children at some time in his life. In addition, I believe that there is a psychological tie that the healthy man develops with the child he has fathered—even when it only exists *in utero*. This interest in its welfare is a manifestation of his paternal instinct. These urges, which go beyond the procreative, manifest themselves in his desire to provide the mother and child with food, clothing, and shelter and to master whatever technical skills are necessary in his society to achieve this end. Being physically strong enables him to perform many of these functions more efficiently than the female—and this was especially true before the invention of machinery.

Speaking teleologically, these inborn maternal and paternal instincts serve the purpose of perpetuation of the species. In the service of this goal, they include not only the urge to participate in the reproductive process but also the innate desire to rear the child so that he or she can become a functioning member of society and thereby further ensure the survival of mankind.

Each sex, in addition to the primary sexual function, has the innate capacity and the desire to gain gratifications in the other's primary area. For the sake of this discussion, I will call these the *secondary sexual functions*. The female, as a secondary and ancillary interest, has the desire to involve

herself in the traditionally masculine activities and to enjoy the many satisfactions they can offer. These, of course, vary from age to age and society to
society and run the gamut from the most ancient traditionally masculine
pursuits, like hunting and building shelter, to modern professions and skills.
The male likewise has deep-seated instinctive urges to involve himself in the
details of his child's care that have been traditionally the mother's function.

*Each sex has been denied the opportunity to obtain gratifications in its
area of secondary sexual functioning.* The examples of discrimination against
women are legion. However, men have been subjected to a similar, but more
subtle, form of prejudice. They have been enslaved by the tradition (more of
their own making, than of women's) that it is unmasculine to involve oneself
in the particulars of child rearing. Hugging and cuddling one's baby, feeding
it, cleaning it when it wets and soils, dressing it, and so on are activities that
men have been led to believe are unmanly and engaged in only by the weak
and effeminate. The goal we should strive toward (and we have made definite
headway in recent years) is that women be given opportunities to gain gratifications in traditionally male areas. This will necessitate not only great flexibility on the part of social institutions to accommodate her childbearing and
child-rearing involvements but also an alteration of social attitudes regarding
the male's involvement with his children. Such changes have to be laid down
in the earliest years of life, both in the home and in the schools, if they are to
be meaningful. The ideal is not, I believe, a 50-50 split—half the time the
mother is with the children and half the time the father—as many Women's
Liberationists propose. Rather, I believe, that when the children are in their
earliest years they do best with the greatest amount of time being given by the
mother, who, as I have said, is instinctively more involved with and capable of
caring for them during this period. This is not to say that the father should
not be around. Every encouragement should be given him and every opportunity provided him to satisfy his paternal needs without embarrassment or
the fear that he will compromise his masculinity. As the child grows older,
mothers should be given more and more time and opportunity to satisfy their
interests in their secondary area of functioning.

In line with this view, I do not agree with those parents who try to minimize
sexual differences in their children in order to prepare them for a future
world that will allegedly not recognize such differences. I do not believe that
boys and girls in childhood should be dressed alike. (That teen-agers are
doing so in the mid-1970's is not, in my opinion, significantly affecting their
sexual orientation. By that time sexual identity is pretty well established and
will not be significantly altered by such a superficial thing as clothing.) Nor
do I believe that boys should be given dolls and girls trucks *as primary presents for important occasions*, such as birthdays and Christmas. I do believe,
however, that such presents might be given in an ancillary fashion, or on less

important occasions, to strengthen interest in each sex's secondary area of functioning. In the traditional game of house, the girl should still be encouraged to play the role of "mother" and the boy that of "father." However, I would also encourage the "father" to come home from work early a couple of days a week or to give over his Saturdays to take care of the children while mother is out taking courses or working at something she is interested in. These are the kinds of identifications that I believe are healthiest for parents to foster and it is on this concept of maleness and femaleness that my ensuing discussion is based.

The child of divorce has limited contacts with the parent who lives away from the home, and if this parent is of the same sex, the child will be deprived of opportunities for identification. One must consider, however, not only the frequency of contacts but their quality as well if one is to accurately assess a parent's value as a model for identification. As Gettleman and Markowitz (1974) emphasize, a same-sexed parent living in the home can be a poorer model for identification than one who lives elsewhere. Also, the identification process takes place primarily during the first three to four years of life. If the separation takes place after the child has reached this age (commonly the case) then the child may not suffer significant problems related to the failure to form an adequate sexual identification. Derogation of the absent parent by the parent with whom the child lives may interfere with the identification process (Kliman, 1968). A boy, for example, whose father is constantly criticized by his mother (with whom he lives) is less likely to look upon his father as a model for emulation.

One of the ways in which all children strengthen their identifications with their parents is through play and play fantasy. Playing house is one of the most common ways in which this process takes place. Accordingly, even in the intact home when a father is away at work, his son may play that he is doing his father's work in order to entrench his masculine identity. When separation occurs, the child may still utilize this mechanism for identification. However, like all substitutive methods of gratification, it is never as good as the real thing and there are limitations on the extent to which substitution can serve before one begins to suffer the effects of the original deprivation.

A mechanism that the child of divorce may utilize to compensate for the loss of the same-sexed parent is that of accomplishing a very rapid identification with him. This process is sometimes seen in both children and adults after the death of a parent or other loved one. In an attempt to compensate for the loss, the child may incorporate many aspects of the deceased person's personality—often almost overnight. To many observers the effects are almost uncanny. It is as though the individual were saying: "He is gone, I cannot have him. However, I will become like him. In this way I will have some of his qualities ever with me." In some cases it appears as if the individual were saying, "I will *be* him. In that way there will be no loss at all"—so complete appears to be the identification. Similarly, the child of divorce may utilize this process to deal with the parental loss. However, since it has delusional and fantasized elements, and since the identification has occurred almost instantaneously, it does not have the depth of the more natural and slowly developing process. Accordingly, the behavioral patterns so acquired are less adaptive. In addition, since there has been less discrimination in the formation of such identifications (the child has incorporated the whole bag, so to speak) more maladaptive patterns are likely to be taken in.

No discussion of sexual identification would be complete without mention of the child's identification with a homosexual parent. One would think that the son of a homosexual father, for example, would be more likely to be homosexual than the son of a heterosexual father. To the best of my knowledge this does not appear to be the case, i.e., the prevalence of homosexuality among sons of homosexual males does not appear to be higher than among sons of heterosexual males. (I know of no good statistical studies on the subject. The statement is made on the basis of my own experiences as well as those with greater experience in this area such as Bieber [1974].) I believe that this somewhat surprising observation is not difficult to explain. On the one hand there are, I believe, some boys who *do* become homosexual because of identification with their homosexual fathers. However, the most important factor in bringing about a homosexual orientation is brutal and rejecting treatment by a father. Since most homosexual fathers do not treat their sons this way, the population of homosexual fathers shows a lower statistical incidence of brutality than does the population of heterosexual fathers. Rather, the homosexual father generally tends to be very solicitous toward his children, gratifying his "maternal" cravings in a very tender and affectionate way. Accordingly, the "homosexuogenic" identification factor in the population of homosexual fathers seems to be counterbalanced by the "anti-homosexuogenic" factor of parental benevolence. And so the studies of large groups would probably not reveal a significant difference in the frequency of homosexuality in the sons of homosexuals as compared to heterosexuals. But this should not lead us to conclude that a father's homosexuality *in a given case* may not be a factor conducive to his son's becoming one. It is his probable absence of cruelty to his son that will protect the boy from a homosexual orientation and will counterbalance the identification factors that would contribute to the child's becoming homosexual.

Parental Factors Contributing to Oedipal Problems in Children of Divorce

Parental separation during the child's oedipal phase. Many therapists (for example, Neubauer, 1960; Westman, 1972) believe that when separation occurs during the oedipal period the child is particularly vulnerable to the development of problems related to the failure to resolve the Oedipus complex. Without a father fully available to identify with, the boy is not likely to incorporate paternal dictates that contribute to the repression of his sexual desires toward his mother. He may interpret his father's leaving as the fulfillment of his wishes that he do so, i.e., he may consider himself to have been the victor in the oedipal rivalry. The girl is deprived of her model man, and so is likely to develop difficulties in her relationships with men, both present and future.

I believe that every period of childhood presents its own special problems for the child when a separation occurs. Each developmental level has its own needs and is subject to its own particular frustrations. I do not believe that the oedipal period is the one in which the child is *most* sensitive to the loss of a parent. Rather, I believe that the younger a child is at the time of separation, and the longer he lives without two parents, the more deprivation he will suffer and the greater will be the likelihood of psychopathology.

Using the child as a parental surrogate. Some parents may deal with the frustrations they experience over the loss of a spouse by attempting to get their child to serve as a substitute. A mother, for example, may tell her son, "You're the man of the house now that daddy's gone." Although such a boy may find the comment anxiety provoking because he does not feel equipped to assume the awesome responsibilities that such a position entails, he also finds it gratifying because it suggests that he can satisfy cravings for fuller possession of his mother. Oedipal resolution is thereby made more difficult, especially if the boy has a prolonged experience in which he becomes the mother's confidant and is frequently required to assume many responsibilities that his father ordinarily would have. A girl, similarly, may be encouraged to take her mother's place by her father—with similar repercussions.

When the parent becomes sexually seductive with the child, the chances of oedipal problems arising become even greater. I am not referring here to actual overt sexual experiences with the child—these are rare—but to such common forms of titillation and subtle seductivity as undressing seductively in front of older children, titillating embracing and stroking, and frequent talk about sex and nudity. The parent may be seductive because it can provide an outlet for sexual cravings. This may be especially true for the mother who may have few opportunities for sexual gratification. Having failed in a marriage (even though the father's difficulties may have been the more significant in bringing about the separation) will generally make her insecure in her relationships with other men, and this may contribute to her choosing her son—someone who has already proved his loyalty and affection.

A parent may be seductive with the opposite-sexed child, not so much for sexual release but as a manifestation of feelings of rivalry with the spouse. The seduction, then, is part of a broader campaign to win the child away from the spouse. It becomes a vengeful and hostile maneuver. Feeling insecure as a marital partner, the parent may try to prove himself extremely effective as a parent. And seduction may be utilized to enhance the child's affection—and thereby the parent's self-esteem.

The seductive parent builds up the child's hopes for more intense gratifications—which are generally not forthcoming. The frustrations and resentments so engendered may produce attitudes of distrust toward all members of the opposite sex and can contribute not only to difficulties in oedipal resolution but in the child's future relationships with the opposite sex. (I will discuss such problems in greater detail later in this chapter.)

Parental dating. The child living in an intact home need resign himself only to the fact that one person, and only one person, has prerogatives with the opposite-sexed parent that he does not enjoy. Most psychoanalysts agree that such resignation does not come easily for many people and is a central problem in many neurotic problems. The child who lives with a dating parent has a much more difficult time resolving his Oedipus complex. A boy living with a dating mother—especially one who meets a large number of transient dates in her home—is likely to conclude that just about every man in the world shares intimacies with his mother in ways that he does not. Such an atmosphere cannot but produce in him resentments toward both his mother and the men who date her. If a series of such men sleep over at the house (even though the child has no opportunity to observe sexual activity) such feelings may be even more intensified. And the sexual excitation that such encounters on the mother's part may produce in him can cause added frustration and resentment. A girl living with a dating father, or whose father exposes her to numerous girl friends during visitation, is likely to react similarly.

It is common in such situations for a child to become very antagonistic to both the parent and the date and to utilize various maneuvers to prevent the dating or alienate the date. Last-minute temper tantrums, crying spells, "sickness" (often associated with vomiting, soiling, diarrhea and other dramatic manifestations of illness), fierce sibling fighting, and sudden homework crises may be utilized in the service of preventing the parent from going out. Or the child may be overtly hostile to the date in an effort to dissuade him from returning. Recognizing that questions that have proved to be embarrassing to both mother and her friend may have alienating value the child may inquire, "Are you going to be my new daddy?" or even more provocatively may ask, "Are you going to sleep over here like some of the other men do?" A child may say to a mother: "Daddy's going to be angry at you when he finds out what you're doing." And another may inquire of a father, "Does mommy know that a lady is going to sleep over here tonight?" Sometimes the hostility the child feels toward the absent parent may be displaced onto a date.

Generally, I advise parents not to expose their children to each new date; rather they should be met outside the home. When, however, a parent has formed a meaningful relationship with a new person then, I believe, the children should meet him. Although such contacts are likely to generate oedipal rivalries, they can also provide the child with many benefits that can potentially outweigh the discomforts and frustrations of having this new person on the scene. Ideally, the new person can serve to compensate the child for some of the deprivations he suffers over the absence of one of his parents—and this benefit cannot be underestimated. In addition, the child can be helped to appreciate that this new relationship makes the parent with whom he lives a happier person and this cannot but affect his own sense of well-being. When mother is frustrated and grouchy he is likely to suffer as well; on the other hand, when mother is in a good frame of mind, she will involve herself more benevolently with her children.

An adolescent girl whose mother has a whole string of affairs and who communicates this to her daughter, either overtly or covertly, is likely to react similarly herself as she models herself after her mother. She comes to subscribe to the view that the greater the number of men one can attract, the more attractive one is. The youngster thereby is likely to fail to gain appreciation of the value of more continual and deeper relationships. In addition, her awareness of her mother's activities can be very titillating, as she is stimulated to fantasize exactly what her mother is doing, and this can contribute to her desire to gain similar gratifications herself. Her oedipal rivalry with her mother may cause her to compete with her. Such competition may be confined to boys of her own age, but at times she may seek older men and even her mother's lovers. She may be more seductive with her mother's boy friends than with her father—the latter being viewed (generally correctly so) as less sexually available. Resolution of the Oedipus complex in such girls is very difficult; they are so stimulated to gain gratification with a series of older men that there is little desire to have one peer as the primary, if not exclusive, source of satisfaction.

Factors in the Child of Divorce that Contribute to Oedipal Problems

Magic fulfillment of oedipal wishes. In the vast majority of cases of separation it is the father who leaves the home, leaving the mother with the children. Such a situation is likely to evoke many fantasies, especially in boys, that relate to the Oedipus complex. It is the boy's wish that he win his mother away from his father and gain total possession of her. To achieve this end the boy will fantasize his father's leaving and, at times, even dying. Often the fantasies take the form of fears rather than wishes; but in either case they accomplish the same end, namely, removal of the rival for the mother's affection. When the father leaves it is likely that the boy will consider the departure to have been caused by his wishes. The same phenomenon is seen when a father dies. Meiss (1952) describes a five-year-old boy who, following the death of his father, believed that the death was the fulfillment of the child's oedipal wishes. He was preoccupied with fears that his father would return to castrate him in revenge. In fact, the father was a very kindly man; but the oedipal fantasies were so powerful that this reality was lost sight of. Boys whose fathers have separated will also feel guilty over their wishes that the father depart and may anticipate punishment and retaliation from the father. They may entertain fantasies of restitution or punishment in order to assuage their guilt or mollify the father. Westman (1972) describes a five-year-old boy who stated: "Will daddy come home if I cut off my penis?" In the less common situation when it is the mother who has left the home, the female children may entertain similar fantasies.

As part of the treatment of such children it is important to emphasize that thoughts cannot per se bring about events. In a story told to such a child I might say: "And the little boy wished very, very hard that his father would leave the house so that he could be all alone with his mother. But no matter how hard he wished, the father still stayed. The thoughts just couldn't make the thing happen." I might, with play dolls, have the child and I both wish that a particular male doll will remove itself from the play house by our wishing that it do so. We both wish very hard and then observe that the doll continues to remain where it was—no matter how hard we wish it to move. The story might then continue: "Then one day the father decided to leave and he said to the boy, 'I'm leaving because your mother and I don't love one another anymore. I decided to leave. It has nothing to do with your thoughts. Your thoughts and wishes can't make me leave. I decided by myself.' " I might play similar games or tell similar stories about a girl who wishes her mother to be hit by a car and in spite of her wishing very hard, no accident occurs. But even when it does I am careful to reiterate that the wish and the event are unrelated as cause and effect. Of course, other factors contribute to such fantasies, e.g., guilt, control, and hostility, and the therapeutic approaches to these elements have been discussed elsewhere.

Parental reactions to oedipal fantasies. A boy may fantasize that his mother has forced his father out of the house in compliance with his wishes that she do so. Or the child may believe that mother herself wanted father out of the house so that she could live all alone with her son. Such fantasies usually stem from the projection onto the mother of the child's own wishes for full possession of her. In other words, he assumes that she too wanted to get rid of the father for the purpose of living alone with her son, and he interprets the father's departure as the result of the mother's desire to reject him in favor of her son.

A girl may believe that her mother knew of her designs on her father and forced him out of the house in order to thwart the liaison. She may fantasize that the mother knew of her desires that father and daughter force mother out of the house so that she could have her father all to herself, and consider the father's leaving to be the result of her mother's attempt to foil the plot. Or she may suspect that her mother, aware of these designs on the father and plans for rejection of her, has forced the father out of the house in retaliation (Arnstein, 1962).

Oedipal factors contribute to each parent's finding a willing ally in the opposite-sexed child. A son, for example, may not basically agree that his father is the scoundrel the mother considers him to be, but may blind himself to his father's assets as a way of satisfying oedipal cravings for his mother. A girl may side with her father against the mother for similar reasons. Boys tend to be more rambunctious and aggressive than girls and are more frequently punished for such behavior. McDermott (1968) suspects that some boys may consider the father's leaving the home to be a result of the mother's banishing him for his masculine aggression. Whether greater aggressiveness in boys is innate or socially induced, there is little question that it is more common than in girls. I believe, therefore, that male displays of oedipal rivalry tends to be more common than female, and I suspect that it is usually stronger. There is another important reason for my holding this view. The mother is generally the one who provides many more gratifications for the child than the father. All other things being equal, if a child has to be deprived of one parent from the earliest years of life, I believe that he would be much better off psychologically living with his mother. The boy has more reason than the girl to develop oedipal rivalries. He wants possession of the more valuable of the two parents, while the girl's longings for the father are diluted more by her ties with her mother. In other words, if the boy were to satisfy his oedipal cravings he would gain the more important parental figure. If the girl were to satisfy hers, she would lose the more important parent —so she is less likely to crave her father so strongly or wish so quickly to get rid of her mother.

Pathological Sequelae of Unalleviated Oedipal Problems in Children of Divorce

Literally thousands of books have been written on the psychological problems that can stem from unresolved or unalleviated oedipal problems. Here, I confine myself to those factors that exist in the child of divorce's situation that are particularly conducive to the development of oedipal problems.

Identification problems. Mahler and Rabinovitch (1956) present a number of reasons why oedipal resolution is more difficult for the boy when there is marital discord (and by extension, when there is separation or divorce). When the father is absent or less readily available, there is less opportunity for a boy to identify with him and in the process incorporate the father's prohibitions regarding his wife. Such identification is important if the boy is to renounce his erotic claims on his mother. It is not only his absence or relative unavailability that interferes with the identification process. It is more difficult for a boy to emulate and identify with a person whom his mother (his first and most important love object) intensely dislikes. It is as if he asks himself: "If she says he's no good, how worthwhile a person can he be?" And such a view interferes with the boy's using him as a model. In addition, it is hard for the boy to identify with someone who is hostile to his mother.

In the absence of the father a boy may take on feminine traits. These may become part of a homosexual orientation (to be discussed below); but the two need not necessarily go together, i.e., not all effeminate boys are homosexual and not all homosexual boys are effeminate—although there is some correlation between the two. Sometimes a boy may try to deny his effeminate orientation by hypermasculinity. As is true of most, if not all, reaction formations the disguise does not work completely and the underlying problem that is being covered up will usually reveal itself in subtle ways. Accordingly, the basic passivity and feelings of weakness that often accompany such an orientation are sensed by others and the youngster does not utilize the most effective and efficient methods for dealing with life's problems. On occasion, a girl will identify with her separated (but not totally absent) father in the attempt to gain affection from a somewhat deficient mother with whom she lives. Observing her mother to continually crave for father she hopes to gain mother's affection by such identification. Neubauer (1960) describes such an identification on the part of a girl, and in this case it was sanctioned by the father who had originally wanted her to be a boy.

Pathological attitudes toward the mother. Having been deprived of a father, the child of divorce is likely to develop abnormally strong dependencies on the mother, the only remaining parent. Having been "abandoned" by one parent, the child hangs on tenaciously to the one he still has. A boy, for example, may remain excessively involved with his mother, become a "momma's boy," and in extreme cases never marry. Those who do marry may still be so involved with their mothers that marital problems arise. Such dependencies may (but not necessarily) be associated with homosexual problems, overt or latent. In other words, not all momma's boys are homosexual and not all male homosexuals are momma's boys, but there is some correlation between the two. A girl, too, may exhibit such dependencies and may never marry, using as her excuse her "loyalty" to her mother.

The child living alone with a mother may become excessively fearful of expressing hostility toward her. Having already lost a parent, the child fears losing the second—and he or she will refrain from any behavior that might alienate the mother or cause her to be rejecting. Such an adaptation is especially common in homes where the child is made to feel guilty over the inevitable resentments toward parents that arise in the normal course of living—whether in the intact or divorced home. Accordingly, oedipal feelings of rivalry and hostility tend to get repressed, guilt results, and the working-through of oedipal reactions is impeded.

Pathological attitudes toward the father and other men. As Forrest (1966) well describes, the female needs a male in her home in order to learn how to relate to men, both actively and passively. She has to learn what men are all about as well as learn about herself—especially about the kind of woman she is—via male comments and feedback. A girl growing up without a father is likely to be deprived of these experiences, so important for her healthy psychological development. Hetherington (1973) describes girls who have been brought up without fathers to be more anxious and uncomfortable in the presence of men. Such girls tend to look upon men as strange. They do not know about men; what to like and what to dislike; what to do and what not to do when with them. They may find quite early that making themselves sexually available is likely to result in attentions that they otherwise might not have enjoyed, and this may become their only way of involving themselves. Such an adaptation may be intensified by the intense longing for male affection that may have existed for years. While as a child such a girl was unable to attract male surrogates, she now finds that—almost like magic—she now has a way of gaining their enthusiastic interest. And when she can gain sexual pleasure herself in the process, her temptations to involve herself in this way may be so great that she may blind herself to the untoward effects of making herself freely available to a large number of men. The absence of a father may interfere with the girl's superego development and make such lack of inhibition in sexual expression even more likely. Keiser (1953) describes such an adolescent girl whose parents were divorced when she was four. She had overt sexual fantasies about her father (whom she rarely saw) and actively vied with her mother for her lovers.

Having been rejected by her father, a girl may develop a strong dislike for and distrust of all men. Anger and distrust may become her primary reactions to all men, and these attitudes may interfere significantly with her ability to enter into meaningful and rewarding relationships with them. She may anticipate that all men will, like her father, ultimately abandon her. Sometimes her own hostility will be projected onto the male and this will add to her fear and anticipation of rejection. Such girls may never marry; or, if they do, marital problems are likely.

As described in Chapter 10, the intermittently rejecting father may induce in his children a pathological craving for his affection. Like the aperiodically reinforced rats in Skinner's experiments, they never give up trying to gain affection from him. The daughter of such a father may become most attracted to men who only rarely provide her with gratification and will be willing to suffer many humiliations in the hope of receiving the rare satisfaction. The pattern may become so deeply entrenched that she will spurn those who consistently treat her benevolently. It seems as if being maltreated by a man is the kind of relationship she is most familiar with and willing to involve herself in; she basically distrusts any other kind—professions to the contrary notwithstanding. In addition, it seems that such women have so deeply associated love with pain that they cannot imagine that one can exist without the other. These elements contribute to the masochistic relationships that they form.

Homosexuality. Although I consider it possible that there are those whose homosexuality is the result of biological variation, I consider the overwhelming majority of homosexuals to be suffering with a form of psychopathology. I believe that homosexuality, as the primary sexual orientation for those who have reasonable opportunities for heterosexual experience, is a manifestation of psychiatric disturbance. I agree with Bieber (1962) that it is more likely to occur in homes where a child has been deprived of a loving and affectionate parent—and such is the situation for the child of divorce. Many factors contribute to a homosexual orientation. I will focus here on those that are likely to be seen when parents are living apart.

The boy living alone with a mother is likely to be deprived of the intimate association with his father that is most conducive to his identifying with him. In addition, living with his mother makes it more likely that feminine identifications will take place. These two factors may contribute to a homosexual orientation. In addition, if his mother is seductive he may come to see women as tantalizers and rejectors—and this may contribute to his turning to men for his sexual gratification. The absence of a father, or a father's providing only intermittent gratification, may result in the son's developing a lifelong quest to gain affection from a male; this may become a significant element in his becoming homosexual. The maltreatment that homosexual males have often experienced at the hands of their fathers is well known. The sons of such men basically hate their fathers and their surrogates. However, they deny their anger and deal with it by reaction formation. Their obsessive "love" for a male is basically an attempt to deny their underlying hatred.

The girl growing up in a home without a father is likely to develop a homosexual orientation as well. Having been abandoned by her model man while her mother has remained loyal to her may contribute to her distrusting all men and seeking the more predictably satisfying female as her love object. Men become strangers; women are familiar. If such a girl receives little affection from her mother, and if her mother appears to be continually seeking her father's return, she may take on a male identification in the hope of gaining mother's love. It is as though she were saying to herself: "My mother does not love females. She does love males; look how she still craves my father. If I become a male, maybe then she'll love me. I'm here; my father is not. I have a better chance than he of getting her love. All I need do is be male." In addition, when the mother too is rejecting, the girl may develop a hatred of her that is dealt with by reaction formation—similar to that described for the male homosexual. Accordingly, she may also become obsessed with her "love" for females as a method of denying her basic hatred.

Clinical Example
"Jack and the Beanstalk is the worst book I ever read."

Albert entered treatment at the age of seven because of disruptive behavior in the classroom and inattentiveness to his schoolwork. Although of high intelligence, he was doing only mediocre work because of these difficulties. Albert's parents had been separated for two years when he entered treatment; he lived with his mother. The parents were very ambivalent about whether they wanted to divorce. There were no siblings, his mother feeling that she had so much trouble handling one child she could not consider having a second. At home he entered into power struggles with his mother and reacted similarly to his father during visitation.

While playing *The Talking, Feeling, and Doing Game* this interchange took place:

> *Patient* (reading from card): "What is the worst book you ever heard or read? Why?" Um, *Jack and the Beanstalk*.
> *Therapist:* Why is that the worst book?
> *P:* Because he meets the giant and the giant . . . (mumbles) . . .
> *T* (interrupts): Wait a minute, because he does what?
> *P:* He meets the giant.
> *T:* And the giant?

P: Tries to kill him.

T: Uh huh. Okay. Tell me more about that story. What in particular is so bad about that story?

P: Um, when the giant came down he went *bam* right into the ground!

T: All right. I see. But tell me something. Why did the giant want to try to kill Jack?

P: Because he didn't want him trespassing on his property.

T: Okay, so who started the trouble?

P: Jack.

T: Uh huh. What do you think of that? Huh?

P: I get a chip.

T: You get your chip all right. Take a chip. What do you think of that? So the giant tried to kill Jack but Jack started the trouble. Huh?

P: Well, when Jack was going into the castle to see what happened the giant came out.

T: What was Jack doing up in the castle?

P: He was looking around.

T: What was he looking for? Put your chips down. You'll make noise on the microphone. What was he looking for?

P: He wanted to see if there was any money. He was going to steal the money that he [the giant] had.

T: Ah hah! So he was going to steal the giant's money.

P: Yeah.

T: All right.

P: So his family wouldn't be poor.

T: Uh huh. Who was in the family?

P: Jack and his mother.

T: Uh huh. I see. So do you think that the giant was right in being a little angry?

P: No.

T: Why? Jack was coming up to steal his money.

P: No, first he didn't know about it and then Jack went into the castle and the giant wanted to eat him at first. And, so, he went up and he was looking around.

T (interrupts): Well, what was he doing up in the castle in the first place?

P: First, he was looking around. Then he met the giant's wife and he hid in the oven, and the giant smelled his flesh. But the giant went away and then Jack came out again and he saw the giant counting his money and when the giant went to sleep he tried stealing it. And the giant caught him taking the golden eggs—with the goose that makes golden eggs—and he started chasing him down.

T: I see. But what was Jack's original purpose for going up there in the first place?

P: Because it was a beanstalk he found and he climbed up to find out. He was curious.

T: He was curious. I see.

P: That's the end up there.

T: He didn't go up there to get money originally?

P: Well, when he saw the money he wanted to because his family was poor.

T: I see. Do you think—who was it that started the trouble then?

P: I'd say the giant because Jack didn't really want to hurt anybody or yell at them.

T: But he wanted to steal money.

P: Well, no, he didn't know that there was a giant there, but when he saw the money he wanted to steal it because he knew that his family was poor.

T: Okay.

P: He did start a little trouble but the giant did too.

T: But who was the first one to start the trouble?

P: Jack.

T: What should Jack have done?

P: Wait until he goes out.

T: And then steal the money?

P: Yeah!

T: Oh, don't you think . . .

Mother (interrupts): How would you feel if you were the giant? Supposing you were the giant and a little fellow came snooping around your house?

P: Oh, well the guy was killed anyway.

T: Who started the trouble?

P: Jack.

T: And what should Jack have done really? What would have been a better thing to do?

P: Uh, what?

T: What would have been a better thing for Jack to do?

P: I don't know.

T: Here he is living alone with his mother and he's poor.

P: Right!

T: What can he do?

P: Well . . .

T (interrupts): Other than steal money from the giant.

P: Nothing else.

T: That's the only solution to his problem?

P: Uh humm.

T: You can't think of any other solution other than stealing money?

P: Yes.

T: Come on! If a man is poor, he can only steal money? That's the only thing he can do? No other alternatives?

P: He was a boy. His mother didn't have a job.

T: So what did he do?

P: I don't know.

T: Think about it.

P: Let himself die?

T: Well, that's one possibility. I think there are better ones though. Here he is this boy with his mother and he's running out of money. Are you saying there are only two possibilities? He can kill someone and steal someone's money or he can let himself die. Are there any other possibilities?

P: No, I cannot think of any.

T: Think. Think hard.

P: I give up.

T: Come on now. What does a person do when he doesn't have money?

P: Go hunting for animals?

T: Okay, so he gets food on his own.

P: I know but he didn't have anything. They didn't have . . . (mumbles) . . .

T: They didn't have what?

P: Guns!

T: Okay, if he doesn't have a gun then what else can he do?

P: Um, I don't . . .

T (interrupting): What does a person do when he doesn't have money, other than steal?

P: He goes to work.

T: Right!

P (shouts): I know, but how can he get work? He needs money to get his job?

T: You don't need money to get a job.

P: Don't you, Mom? Besides they lived like right in the woods almost.

T: So, if he can go out into the woods to go up to the giant's place in the sky, why can't he go out into the woods and get a job?

P: He didn't know there was a giant at the end of the beanstalk.

T: No, no, but he was out of the woods. Right? He met the man with the cow. Remember that he traded the cow for the beans?

P: Yeah.

T: So he was out of the woods.

P: No—oh, yeah.

T: So what could he have done?

*P:*He could have got a job, but he was a boy!

*T:*Well, boys can't earn as much as men but . . .

P (interrupts): All right!

T: Huh? So he gets a job.

P: It's your turn.

T: So what's the final . . .

P (interrupts): I'm bored with this.

T (laughs): You are bored with this. All right, but we both agreed that he could have gone out and worked.

P: Yeah. (reaches over and tries to take some of the therapist's reward chips)

T: Are you trying to steal my chips?

P: Hh hmmmm.

T: Earn your own chips, fellow. I earned these chips. They're mine and you've got yours.

P (returning chips): All right.

T: Okay. All right then. So let's go on.

Up until the nineteenth century the overwhelming majority of fairy tales were not written down; rather they were handed down by word of mouth from generation to generation. The modifications were countless, each relater altering the story at his or her whim. Accordingly, each story came to be a potpourri of many fragments without significant internal consistency. It wasn't until the nineteenth century that people like Hans Christian Andersen and the Grimm brothers recorded them. However, the renditions that they chose to transcribe cannot be considered to represent the only or even typical versions. Since then there has been greater consistency with regard to the transmission of many of the tales, but the variations are still quite numerous. For these reasons most of the stories do not lend themselves to simple or unified psychoanalytic interpretation—even though their universal appeal reflects their deep psychological import. Anyone trying to analyze even one of them soon finds himself dealing with many disparate and often contradictory themes, reflecting the varying psychological needs of the multiple authors who have contributed over the centuries to the story.

Jack and the Beanstalk, however, is one of the few fairy tales that appears to have certain consistent themes that are maintained throughout the story. Of all the fairy tales that I know of, it probably has the most pure oedipal theme. In the most common version, the story begins with Jack's living alone with his mother—his father having died. At the outset, then, Jack has already satisfied his oedipal longings: his father is dead and he has total possession of his mother. There aren't even any brothers or sisters described who might vie with Jack for his mother's affection. He has her all to himself. However, we soon learn that everything is not going so well. Supporting a mother in the style to which she has become accustomed requires a certain amount of financial wherewithal which Jack does not have available. It is to the acquisition of such funds that the story primarily directs its attention. As the family gets even more desperate, Jack's mother sends him to town to sell their cow. In the famous exchange, Jack trades the valuable animal for a bag of beans which, he is promised, will grow stalks that will reach to heaven. Although an ostensibly stupid deal, for which Jack's mother is justifiably enraged, the beans soon prove to be "really magical" and the stalk sprouts—quickly shooting up into the clouds. The trade essentially serves as a way for Jack to reach the sought-after treasures in heaven. It is, therefore, a *deus ex machina*, a contrivance that allows the real purpose of the story to be realized.

Jack then climbs into the clouds. He finds a land up there, travels awhile, and soon comes to the home of the giant—who, of course, represents Jack's father. He is in the sky, that is, in heaven—where good people go when they die. Interestingly, he is one of those rare individuals who has been able to "take it with him," that is, he has with him all his earthly possessions and treasures. The story essentially deals with Jack's attempts to acquire his father's material wealth—without bringing back his father in the process. Most fathers, when they die, are considerate enough of their sons to leave their wealth behind; Jack's father has not been particularly decent about this. It is also of interest that Jack finds a willing assistant in a little old lady who lives in the giant's castle and exhibits a surprising disloyalty to the giant. She, of course, is Jack's mother again, serving as his accomplice in his plots against his father. The gratifications of oedipal wishes often require the assistance of an adult because of the child's immaturity and relative impotence in accomplishing his designs on his own.

First, Jack is successful in stealing the giant's gold. The gold, as a treasured possession of the giant, also represents Jack's mother. In addition, it provides him with the means to ensure his mother's remaining with him. He returns to earth and once again lives in grand style with his mother. However, Jack and his mother have no other visible means of support and so, as their resources dwindle, the spectre of poverty soon looms once again over them.

Jack then goes up the stalk again and steals from the giant a more consistent form of funds: the goose that lays the golden eggs. Not only does the goose provide an inexhaustable supply of gold to keep Jack and his mother financially solvent indefinitely, but additional psychological gratifications are provided by the goose as well. The goose, the layer of eggs, serves well as a symbol for Jack's mother. This kind of repetition, seen frequently in dreams and myth, serve to intensify and entrench a particular psychological need. Although Jack already has his mother-wife down on earth; and although he has her once again in heaven in the form of the old lady accomplice; and although he has acquired her again, during his first escapade in heaven, in the symbolic form of gold; Jack wins mother still again from his father—this time in the form of the goose. Actually, each mother symbol serves a different purpose. The mother on earth serves as wife, caretaker of his home, and provider of food. (We are given no hint as to whether the union has also been "consummated" in the physical-sexual realm—at a level, of course, appropriate to Jack's stage of psycho-sexual development.) The mother in heaven serves as his accomplice in stealing father's treasures. The gold, as mother symbol, is a valuable possession as well as a potential provider of nutriment. And the goose that lays the golden eggs is the all-giving provider as well as the child-bearing mother. The endless supply of golden eggs well symbolizes the breast that continually gives forth milk. And the golden eggs, the issue of the goose, well symbolize Jack himself: mother's "golden boy."

Although one would think that Jack would now be content, he is not. (What in the world is it that the boy still lacks?) He once again goes up to heaven and steals the giant's golden harp. The harp—curvaceous, capable of producing euphoric music, and an instrument that one fingers and plays upon—well lends itself to symbolizing a female. (And who else should it be but Jack's mother?) But this time the sexual elements are more obvious. Now that that's been taken care of, there is no longer any reason for the giant's existence. Jack has acquired all he needs to satisfy indefinitely all (and I mean all) his oedipal fantasies. Accordingly, as Jack flees with his final acquisition, the giant follows him and is killed when Jack chops down the beanstalk while the pursuing giant is still on it. (Desires to castrate the giant are also symbolically gratified here.) Jack then returns home and presumably lives happily ever after. What more could any boy want?

In spite of the traditional popularity of the story, Albert considered it the *worst* story he had ever read—because the giant tried to kill Jack. I considered this to reflect Albert's desire that there be no repercussions for the gratifications of his own oedipal fantasies. The story that the child considers to be the "worst" that he has ever read may really be the "best" (psychologically speaking), but guilt may require his denying the gratifications the story provides. This I believed to be the case with Albert. He was, in fact, living alone with his mother since his parents had separated, and he had no siblings to compete with for his mother's affection. At some deep level his oedipal fantasies were being realized. His only wish now was that his father not retaliate like the giant for what was done to him.

The discussion quickly revealed that Albert chose to deny the fact that it was Jack, not the giant, who had started all the trouble—that the reason the giant tried to kill Jack was that Jack had stolen his possessions. This gross distortion of the story indicates that powerful psychological factors were at work—factors that served Albert's need to deny his own role in his difficulties with his father. Albert's father, unlike the giant in the story, was still very much around. In fact the parents, after two years of separation, were still undecided as to whether to get divorced, still had strong feelings for one another, and even had intercourse on occasion. Although living with his mother, Jack could not conclude that he had totally won his mother away from his father. I felt that the anger that Albert was expressing in his clinical symptoms stemmed, in part, from the desire to cover up the fear he had over his father's anticipated retaliation for Albert's having taken possession of his mother. In addition, I considered some of Albert's anger to relate to his frustration over not having been completely successful in satisfying his oedipal desires, because his father, although out of the house, was still very much on the scene. (This need not preclude his being angry also over his father's leaving. We can be angry about each of two opposing and contradictory sources of irritation.)

In my comments and discussion, I focused on two issues. First, I corrected Albert's distortion regarding whether it was Jack or the giant who started the trouble. My main intent here was to help Albert appreciate that in his altercations with his father he was playing a provocative role and was thereby responsible for some of the pains he suffered in his relationship with him. I was not concerned as much about the question of who is most responsible for father-son oedipal rivalry as I was in pointing out Albert's role in perpetuating the hostilities.

Having gotten that point straight (I hope), I focused on an issue that is central to successful alleviation of oedipal difficulties, namely, the child's gaining substitute gratifications, both in the present and in the future. The child must be helped to appreciate that he has it within his power, in the present, to gain some of the gratifications that his father enjoys. In helping Albert appreciate that boys can work and earn money—they need not steal it —I was essentially saying to him that if he applies himself he can gain some female affection (as symbolized by money, the valuable possession) on his own. I agreed with him that boys can't earn as much as men and, by implication, that boys have to be satisfied with less when it comes to the possession of women and money. But such resignation is necessary to healthy oedipal resolution.

It was fascinating how, after my making this statement, the patient, for the first time in the course of his therapy, reached over and tried to take some of my reward chips. He thereby acted out his oedipal fantasies the same way

Jack did; and the timing of this acting-out was Albert's way of saying to me: "I don't care what you said, I want to steal my mother from my father. I won't work for my own money. I won't accept a substitute." With this understanding of Jack's act I responded, somewhat firmly: "Earn your own chips, fellow, I earned these chips. They're mine and you've got yours." In essence I was reiterating the message so crucial for the child to accept if he is to resolve his oedipal conflict. Albert returned my chips, accepting on the concrete level that he cannot have what is mine, and that he'll have to earn his own. On the symbolic level my hope was that he heard my deeper message, namely, that both his father and I still retain control over our possessions (money and women) but that he has it within his power to earn his own.

Clinical Example
Oedipus complex alleviation and self-esteem.

I first saw Scott at the age of seven-and-a-half, when he was referred because of difficulties in school. He picked on other children and was frequently scapegoated. He was disruptive in the classroom and did not attend to his homework. There was some evidence for an underlying neurological problem in that he experienced altered states of consciousness associated with a definitely abnormal electroencephalogram (localized spike discharges) and problems in fine motor coordination and visual memory. In addition, I considered psychogenic difficulties to be present and these primarily related to problems that the parents were having. Scott's father, a well-known businessman in the community, was an emotionally isolated individual who was impaired in his ability to express affection for his wife and children. Over the next year I saw Scott intermittently, during which time there was a definite improvement in the presenting symptoms.

I saw Scott again at age nine-and-a-half, two months after his parents had separated. Scott's mother felt that she could no longer tolerate her husband's self-involvement and removal from the family. Although her husband had been in therapy, she felt that he was not committed to it and that he was not profiting from it. Following the separation Scott became progressively more upset. He refused to do his work in school and fought often with his classmates. He began to lie frequently and occasionally stole from his siblings and peers. He exhibited a chronically surly attitude that alienated most who came in contact with him. During the third month after he returned to therapy Scott told this story:

> *Patient:* Once there was a sun. And this sun like to shine upon everything. He felt gay every time he did. And one day the rain went where he was and tried to block him off, but he tried to push it away. You see, he

didn't want this rain coming to where he could have fun, and have sunlight. So then the rain poured on the sun and the sun just faded away and the sun was sad. And so the rain came down and the sun was unhappy and that was it. Then the sun tried to make up for it but then . . .

Therapist (interrupting): Wait a minute. What finally happened? The rain poured on the sun and the sun . . .

P (interrupting): faded away.

T: The sun faded away or the rain faded away?

P: The sun.

T: The sun faded away. You mean he lost all his power of light.

P: Yeah.

T: Yeah.

P: So then he tried to get back but he couldn't because he had no light and he had to stay that way forever. The end.

T: Hh hmm. I see.

P: And he didn't have any friends either.

T: Who didn't have any friends?

P: The sun did have friends. People. The people liked the sunshine.

T: Uh huh. I see. All right. Now I'm not clear on the very end. You said the sun had friends?

P: Yes.

T: Even though the . . .

P (interrupting): Yeah, people . . . because people like the sun to shine on them.

T: Yeah, but you said the sun faded away. It didn't have any light anymore. Didn't you say that?

P: Yeah.

T: Yeah, but after he had no light and heat they still . . .

P (interrupting): Oh, after he had no light he had no more friends.

T: Okay. I see. Now what's the message in that story?

P: Oh, I'll have to think up a lesson.

T: Try to think. What can we learn from that story?

P: You learn that if you're someone else and someone else decides that you're at someplace they shouldn't just go butting in and then fade them away and then just barge in like that.

T: Why did the rain do that? Why did the rain fade away the sun?

P: Because the rain drops rained on the sun and it burned out all the sun's . . .

T (interrupting): But why? Why did the rain do this to the sun?

P: Because the rain was jealous of the sun because he had a . . . (mumbles) . . .

T: Wait a minute. The rain was jealous of the sun because the sun had what?

P: A nice big town.

T: Town?

P: Town.

T: A city, you mean?

P: Yeah.

T: What do you mean the sun had a big town? Do you mean that the sun owned the city?

P: No. He had this particular city that he just found and he wanted to put some sunlight on it.

T: Oh, and why didn't the rain want him to put sunlight on it?

P: Because he was jealous and . . .

T (interrupting): Jealous of what?

P: The sun. And he [the rain] was evil and so then he wanted to rain up the city.

T: He was evil. He was just plain evil.

P: Yeah.

T: But what was he jealous of?

P: He was jealous of other people if they were better than him or if they had a bigger spot than him.

T: Hh hmm. The rain was. I see, because the sun was all over. I see. So then he put him out. Uh huh. I see. Okay, now it's my chance to tell a story.

The story contains interesting symbols. Both the sun and the rain are consistently referred to as "he." We are told that the sun was admired by all the people in the city and that the rain was jealous of the admiration that the sun enjoyed. Accordingly, I felt that the sun most reasonably represented Scott's father and that the rain symbolized Scott himself. Scott's father did enjoy a good reputation in his community and the story reveals Scott's jealousy over this. He expresses his jealous rivalry by completely obliterating the sun's power and the latter thereby loses the affection of all the townspeople.

The story certainly has definite oedipal components and describes, in a classical manner, a son's rivalry with his father. In addition, I was sure that the anger that Scott felt toward his father for abandoning him (as is so often the case, the father's leaving at the time of separation is seen by the children as an abandonment) was being expressed in this story. Robbing his father of all his power and prestige is certainly a most potent and effective retaliatory device. Lastly, I considered the story to reveal Scott's impaired sense of self-worth and his attempt to compensate by lowering his father to what he saw as his own level. There had always been some impairment in Scott's father's ability to demonstrate affection and this was interpreted by Scott to mean that he himself was unlovable. The separation further entrenched these feelings of low self-worth.

Of the many themes suggested by the story I decided to focus on the self-esteem element. I felt that by concentrating on this element I would at the same time be dealing, at some level, with the oedipal and anger issues that were also suggested by the story. Enhancing self-esteem cannot but assuage oedipal difficulties and reduce problems around anger. Accordingly, I told this story:

> *Therapist:* Once upon a time there was rain, and this rain was traveling along and he saw this sun. And this sun was shining over a city. And he got kind of jealous and he said, "Gee, look at that sun, that big guy up there in the sky. He shines over this whole city and really the people admire him for this and I'd like to get rid of that guy. Everybody seems to be liking him. He has a lot of friends. If I can come along with my rain and wash out his heat and his light . . .
>
> *Patient* (interrupting): power.
>
> *T:* and his power then I'll be happy." So he started to come toward the town and try to wet the sun and to squelch the sun's heat and light.
>
> Well, as he was getting close all of a sudden some clouds came along and the clouds said, "Where are you going? Where are you going, rain?"
>
> He said, "I'm going to blot out that sun. I don't like him. I'm jealous of all his power and his heat and his light."
>
> wet him a little bit and possibly squelch a few of the flames and the heat that comes out of him, but you know he's a bigger guy and you're really not going to wash out all that sun's power and heat and light. You're certainly not that strong, but even if you were—even if you could do that —what would that gain you?"
>
> He said, "Well, I don't know. I'm just jealous of his power. I'm jealous of his heat."
>
> The cloud said, "Well, let's say you had all that water and you could make the sun stop giving off heat and light. What then?
>
> He said, "Well, then the townspeople wouldn't like him anymore and they wouldn't get that sun and light."
>
> The cloud said, "Where would that leave you?" Let's say that happened. Where would that leave you? Would that leave you with a better position?
>
> He thought about it and he said, "Well, I wouldn't feel so bad with him around."
>
> Then the cloud said, "Well, look, you think you're going to feel better about yourself by making him look worse and if you think that's a way to build up your self-confidence you're making a mistake. You will find that that's not going to work. It's not going to work at all. You don't

build up your self-confidence by knocking other people down and it's just not going to work."

So what do you think happened?

P: He didn't blot out the sun.

T: Yeah. First of all, he couldn't even if he tried, but then he realized that the clouds were right—that you don't make yourself feel better by trying to knock the other guy down. What you do is to try to build yourself up. What do you think the rain could have done to build himself up to make himself feel better?

P: Just forget about it.

T: Well, the rain can do a few things. What power does rain have? Like sun has power to give sunshine.

P: Rain has the water to let plants grow.

T: Uh huh! That's right. So what did the rain do then? What could the rain do?

P: Let plants grow.

T: Okay. And how did he feel about himself—how did the rain feel about himself causing all the plants to grow?

P: Good.

T: Hh hmm. Now what's the lesson of that story?

P: Well, you shouldn't just blot out the sun if you think he should be darn sure because . . .

T (interrupting): You shouldn't blot out the sun. What's that?

P: Because the sun has more powers than you and you can't blot out all those things—light and heat.

T: Okay. That's one lesson. What's another lesson?

P: The other lesson is: If you really think about it, you know, you will have some importance to you too.

T: Hh hmm! What about gaining importance by making the other fellow—knocking him down and making him weak or taking away his power? Does that work?

P: No.

T: Why not?

P: Because that just leaves you in a dead end.

T: Right, but what is the way to make yourself feel important?

P: Try and build up more.

T: Right. Do your own thing. Do something that you're made to do. The sun feels good about himself, you know, giving off sunshine and the rain made himself feel better about himself by giving off the rain by helping crops grow and giving people water. Okay? Do you like that story?

P: Yeah.

T: What's the part you like the most?
P: Hhhmm. The one where the clouds talk to him.
T: Hh hmm. And what did they say?
P: They said you shouldn't blot out the sun.
T: And what did they say he should do?
P: He should just think about it and do his own thing.
T: Right. Okay. Good-bye everybody.

The messages in my story are fairly obvious. I point out to the patient that his father is, first of all, far too big an opponent for him to realistically subdue. More important, however, I emphasize that he would not gain anything were he to rob his father of all his powers. I then point out what measures the patient can take to enhance his feelings of self-worth. This is a vital maneuver in all therapy. It is not enough to discourage the utilization of defense mechanisms; one must also provide alternative modes of adaptation that not only replace the mechanisms but do so to the patient's benefit. I tried to communicate the ancient and ubiquitous truth that genuine self-esteem can only come through the acquisition of meaningful competence. This is what Plato was referring to when he spoke of a man's "virtue" and this is what youngsters today are talking about (whether they appreciate it or not) when they talk about "doing one's own thing."

The quickness with which the patient answered my questions and involved himself in the story confirmed my belief that my messages were truly received. During the following week the mother reported an improvement in his school performance. In addition, he was much easier to handle at home.

Chapter 13

ADVISING PARENTS SUBSEQUENT TO THE SEPARATION AND DIVORCE

Just as one of the important determinants of whether a separation will cause psychopathology in the child is the extent of preseparation psychological trauma, an important determinant of the child's developing postseparation psychological difficulties is the parents' interaction with both the child and one another following the breakup of the marriage. The more pathological these interactions, the greater the likelihood of the child's developing maladaptive reactions.

Although my discussions in previous chapters on the treatment of the child's pathological reactions has included the kinds of advice I would provide parents, I present here advice that has not been covered elsewhere to a significant degree—especially that which has prophylactic value in helping the parents avoid the development of pathological reactions in their children.

The parents should be helped to appreciate the value of maintaining open lines of communication with the child as a potent preventive of the child's developing untoward psychological reactions to the separation. Many distortions can thereby be rectified—distortions that may be contributing significantly to the child's undesirable behavior. All too often parents hide the truth from their children with the misguided belief that many divulgences would be deleterious. As mentioned, such withholding will often result in the child's harboring many fears that are unwarranted and can produce distrust of the parent at a time when the child can least afford such a compromise in the parent-child relationship. The parents have to be helped to be patient regarding the child's repeated questioning about the separation and to appreciate that such reiteration is part of the healthy desensitization and working-through process. They have to be helped to appreciate, as well, that such questions by the child may extend over a period of years because as he matures he becomes ever more appreciative of the many factors that may have operated in bringing about the separation. When younger he was not sophisticated enough to ask certain questions and he should not be deprived of the answers just because the inquiries take place months, or even years, after the event. (Again, I wish to emphasize that I am not suggesting that the parents' lives should be an open book to the child; rather, I am only stating that he has the right to information that is pertinent to him because the failure to provide such can contribute to the formation of pathological reactions.)

Probably the most valuable preventive of the child's developing untoward reactions to the separation is each parent's spending time alone with each of the children separately. For the custodial parents such times should occur every day, and for the parent who lives away, every day of visitation. During such periods the parent and child do well to involve themselves in mutually gratifying experiences: talking about personal matters, reading, playing games, listening to music, etc. Such times should have the highest priority for both. Such experiences deepen the relationship between the two and thereby serve to protect the child from the various kinds of difficulties that arise from impairments in the parent-child relationship. And for the divorced parent, providing such experiences is even more vital, because of the greater likelihood that the child will suffer from psychological difficulties.

Two Common Myths

"Never criticize your ex-spouse to your child." This is among the most common bits of advice given to separated parents, and even professionals often profess it enthusiastically. It is based on the assumption that the child is less likely to respect, emulate, and identify with a parent who is so criticized. Even though one may harbor intense feelings of hatred toward the ex-spouse (the usual case, especially in the period immediately following the separation), one is advised to strictly refrain from expressing such feelings to, or in front of, the child. Only assets are to be mentioned.

Although well meaning, this advice is, I believe, misguided. All of us, whether or not our parents are divorced, do well to get as accurate a picture as possible of our parents—both their assets and their liabilities. Children tend to incorporate and accept their parents in toto. They operate on the principle: "If it's good enough for them, it's good enough for me." They swallow the whole bag, so to speak. Accordingly, they indiscriminately identify with many qualities that are maladaptive. Hopefully, as we grow older we learn to accept those qualities that are healthy and reject those that are not.

In a healthy home each parent can be a source of information for the child regarding qualities of the other that are undesirable for him to acquire. Ideally, such information should be imparted in a benevolent fashion, e.g., "Your father thinks that just because a person is black he is less worthy than others. I don't agree with his thinking," "Your mother thinks that something terrible will happen to you if you don't eat everything she gives you. I don't agree with her." In addition, the parent does well to admit his own defects to the child in appropriate situations, e.g., "I'm afraid to swim. I know there's nothing to be afraid of. I just can't help it. However, I hope that you'll learn to swim because I can see that it can be a lot of fun." In such an environment the child is likely to grow up having real expectations from people and not suffer significant disappointment when they reveal their deficiencies.

Divorced parents as well owe their children this information. To deprive the child of it not only contributes to his developing difficulties in his interpersonal relationships but produces distrust of the parent who withholds this vital information. Hearing nothing but good things about his father the child can only wonder: "If he's so great, why have you divorced him?" The divorce is likely to have engendered feelings of distrust already; withholding information adds unnecessary distrust at a time when the child can least afford this additional burden. Admittedly, separated parents may be the least objective persons to provide such information. The rage that often exists at that time is often blinding, and distortions and exaggerations may be extreme. In spite of these impairments to accurate communication, I still advise separated parents to impart to their children what kinds of people they consider their spouses to be—communicating their opinions with regard to their assets *as well as* their liabilities. Often this is best done in a situation when the parent is actually exhibiting behavior that confirms the opinion. Other times it is best transmitted during quiet discussion. It is only during periods of rage that the parent is well advised to distrust his judgment. (In work with the children, as well, I advise them to be somewhat incredulous of criticisms made while a parent is enraged.) I also advise parents when criticizing their former spouses to preface criticisms with terms like, "In my opinion," and "As I see it." In this way they communicate to the child the notion that what they are saying may not be completely accurate.

There are parents who ostensibly subscribe to the dictum of never criticizing the spouse to the child, but subtly communicate their profound condemnation. Sugar (1970) describes a number of these subversions quite well. For example, when a child asks a mother about the reasons for the divorce and she tells him to ask his father, the child is likely to conclude that the truth is so bad that it cannot be told by a nice lady like his mother. The father who says, "I would not want to say anything *against* your mother," gets across the message that there are terrible things about the mother, but that he is just too much of a good-guy to tell everyone about them. The mother who says, "I'm not going to say anything that will make you think less of your father," is clearly implying that there are a number of disparaging things she knows about the father but is just not verbalizing. Because the details are not provided, the child is likely to imagine the defects to be far worse than they really are. When asking a child if he wants to see his father, a mother may say, "Do you *really* want to see your father?" and in this way also communicates to the child her basic loathing for her ex-husband. And the parent who continually prides himself on how strictly he refrains from criticizing the ex-spouse provides the child with a barrage of criticisms and food for thought about the other parent's despicable behavior.

Parents often ask what they can do when the ex-spouse continually disparages them and bombards the child with lies about them. I generally advise such parents that their best defense against such vilification is to provide the child with the living experience that he is not what the ex-spouse describes him to be. I try to impress upon the parent that if he is loving and concerned the child will ultimately come to appreciate this (even though at times confused by the critical, contradictory messages). I discourage the parent from questioning the child about what particular criticisms were made and attempting to correct them one by one. Such an endeavor is usually futile (the child cannot remember them all and they may be endless) and, in addition, the parent's defensiveness may contribute to the child's disbelief of the refutations. Lastly, with regard to the parent who involves himself in such continual disparagement of the ex-spouse, I generally try to help him see how much harm he is doing his child. I try to get him to appreciate that his hostility toward his ex-spouse is so great that he is blinding himself to the repercussions on his child of his trying to gain vengeance in this way. I also try to get him to appreciate that his child will (if he does not already) respect him less for involving himself in such a campaign. Of course, if therapeutic work with such a parent is possible, then one can go into the factors that underlie such behavior and one is then more likely to bring about its discontinuation.

In working with parents regarding this problem (as well as many others to be discussed in the chapter) I try to help them reach the kind of relationship that often exists between countries who basically harbor great antagonism toward one another, but find it in their mutual interests to maintain civilized relations. And in the divorce situation the children as well can benefit when the hostile parties so conduct themselves.

"Always reassure him that his father (mother) still loves him." This is another common bit of advice to divorced parents (often provided by professional authorities) that is well meaning but misguided. The advice is most often suggested in those situations when it is least applicable, namely, in situations where the absent parent has little, if any, contact with his children. The father, for example, who has not been heard from in eight years is said to still love his children "but just can't show it." The mother who has disappeared for a similar period is described as "keeping her love inside." Those who provide children with these patently absurd excuses do so because they believe that if the child were to be told the truth he would be psychologically devastated.

The child who is provided with such excuses cannot but become confused about what love is if one can love someone and yet never exhibit any evidence of it. Although I do not claim to have a firm definition of love, I believe that reciprocity is somehow involved. And such confusion can contribute to the child's having difficulty in forming loving relationships both in the present and future. In addition, the child is likely to sense the absurdity of the comment and the duplicity of the parent who makes it. Accordingly, he may become distrustful of his only remaining parent—not a very happy thing to happen to a child of divorce.

It would be cruel, however, to tell such an abandoned child simply that the absent parent doesn't love him and leave it at that. The child has to be helped to appreciate that this does not mean that he is unlovable. He has to be helped to appreciate that the defect lies in the absent parent rather than in himself—that there is something seriously wrong with someone who cannot love his own child. He has to be helped to gain gratifications from others in compensation for the deprivations he may experience over the loss of his parent. Telling the child that the abandoned parent still loves him is not going to provide any feeling that he is really loved. He has to have the *living experience* that there are indeed others with whom he can have affectionate and loving relationships. Only then can he really be convinced that the defect does not lie within himself. The child also has to be helped to become comfortable with the angry feelings he will probably have over his rejection. He has to be helped also to appreciate that such anger is natural and attempts should be made to assuage any guilt the child may feel because of it. However, as discussed in Chapter 9, mere expression of anger serves little purpose. The anger will truly disappear only when, through the gaining of substitutive gratifications, the situation is so changed that the anger is no longer generated.

For the child who is not completely abandoned, but whose absent parent has little meaningful contact, a similar approach should be utilized. Here the child has to be helped to try to gain greater contact with the absent parent. If this fails after reasonable attempts, he must be helped to resign himself to the reality of the situation and discouraged from trying to extract more affection than the absent parent is willing to or capable of providing, e.g., one visit a year, two postcards a year, a Christmas present a year, etc. Again, the child has to be encouraged to find substitute gratifications elsewhere so that he does not suffer significant frustration and lingering resentments. All of this information should be imparted to parents and detailed help given them in implementing it. In addition, the same principles should be followed in the therapeutic approach to children whose difficulties have been intensified by this well-intentioned but ill-advised attempt to lessen their pain.

Visitation

Visitation and the divorce decree. In the preparation of the separation agreement and the divorce decree, arrangements are usually made for the absent parent's visitation with the children. It is well to advise parents that stipulated visitation times are quite unnatural and do not generally coincide with the needs and desires of the parties concerned. Accordingly, the more flexible the schedule, the greater the likelihood the visitation experiences will be gratifying. Such flexibility presupposes a certain amount of trust and cooperation between the parents. Sadly, these preconditions are often not present, and the greater the degree of distrust and antagonism the lengthier and more detailed the schedules become.

Like any other transaction or negotiation between the warring partners, the visitation arrangements can be used as a weapon. After all, the children are the parents' most prized possessions. What better way to wreak vengeance on a partner than to deprive him, to the degree possible, of his children. Often a parent will demand more visitation time than he or she really wants or can practically handle. The purpose here may be to use the demand as a bargaining tool in the conflict over alimony and support payments. The parent knows in advance that he will reduce his visitation requests if the spouse will grant concessions in the financial area. The therapist's attempts to get such parents to appreciate that they are causing their children psychological damage by so using them may be futile, so blinded are they by their rage. And their lawyers can often be counted upon to support the parents in these sick transactions with the rationalization that they are only protecting their clients' interests. What the lawyers are generally referring to when they talk of their clients' interests is money. They are not concerning themselves with the welfare of the children, although they will invariably pay lip service to their deep commitment to this consideration.

Other neurotic factors may also be operative in the visitation requests and negotiations. A mother, for example, may be so enraged at her husband that she will believe that any contact he may have with the children will be dele-terious to them. As a result, the children may be deprived of optimum visita-tion experiences and thereby suffer. At times a parent may demand far more visitation than is reasonable in order to assuage guilt over the separation. A father, for example, who never took particular interest in the children, sud-denly becomes deeply involved with them at the time of separation. The chil-dren may see more of him after he leaves the house than they did when he was living at home. Such enthusiasm is usually short-lived—based as it is on guilt rather than genuine affection. However, because it exhibits itself at the time when separation and divorce agreements are being drafted, it may result in the children's being deprived of some of the beneficial time they could have been spending with their mothers.

In order to prevent such utilization of children, Goldstein (1973), in an otherwise excellent book, has recommended that the custodial parent be granted full control over visitation arrangements. I believe that this is dan-gerous advice. It is like placing lethal weapons in the hands of children or incompetents. An enraged parent, at his or her whim, may unilaterally decide to cut the children off completely from the ex-spouse for reasons that may be quite frivolous. The children then will be deprived of all the benefits to be de-rived from contact with the other parent. When a parent wants to see the children and they wish to see him or her, it is rare that a third party (whether spouse or court) is justified in interfering with their getting together. It is only in very unusual circumstances that such interference can be in the children's and the parent's best interests.

Previsit games. Neurotic use of the visitation does not stop at the signing of the divorce decree. There are various ways in which the parent can use the visitation to express hostility toward the ex-spouse. Passive-aggressive maneuvers are among the most common. Father, for example, may be late or even "forget" entirely to pick up the children. And mother's arrangements (like a date, for example) may then have to be cancelled. Mother, similarly, may take a very "relaxed" attitude about having the children ready, may have "forgotten" that this was the day for the father to get them, and thereby foul up his plans as well. The actual appearance of the father may provide the mother with an opportunity to let off a little steam and she may even look forward to his coming because of the neurotic gratification she can derive upon his appearance.

A mother may be excessively fearful of a father and inappropriately antici-pate his harming the children. Such fears may be transmitted to the children, thereby compromising the gratifications they can derive from the visit. Ex-spouses tend to exaggerate the detrimental effects of each other's behavior on the children. Only in cases of gross negligence or danger should restrictions be placed on the visitation. Removing the children because of minor deleterious exposures deprives them of the growth experience of dealing with the unpleasant and may rob them of the benefits to be derived from contact with the visiting parent. If they wish to see one another, then the advantages probably outweigh the disadvantages.

Sugar (1970) points out how the custodial parent can undermine the child in his desire to see the visiting parent with comments such as: "You *want* to visit your father?" and "You don't *really* want to go visit with your father again on Sunday?" Or the parent may offer alternatives to the child's visiting that may not have entered his or her mind and in this way discourage the child from making plans with the ex-spouse.

A mother may have residual or persistent affectionate feelings for her ex-husband and welcome his coming to pick up the children as an opportunity for further contact. Father, too, may linger for similar reasons. Although separation and divorce usually hurt the esteem of both parties, the non-custodial parent usually suffers an additional blow to his feelings of self-worth. Most healthy fathers gain a sense of importance as head of a household. Whatever drawbacks there may be to having the responsibilities of being the "breadwinner," there is a sense of pride and accomplishment that can also be derived from the position. Being admired and emulated by the members of one's family can be a great source of ego gratification. The separated father may feel this loss acutely and does well to make every attempt to compensate for this deprivation and its attendant lowering of his self-esteem (Polatin and Philtine, 1974). Three ways in which the father can regain his sense of self-worth in this area are: 1) spending as much time as is reasonable and possible with his children, 2) involving himself in a second family, and 3) finding other esteem-enhancing activities.

A common and most insidious practice is that of the mother's refusing to let the father visit with the children because of nonpayment or late payment of alimony and support. Although this tactic may work, it effectively punishes the children for the actions of their father. There is probably no more blatant example of the child's being used as a pawn in the parental conflict. Although it may be hard to convince her, such a mother should be helped to appreciate that the loss of money is small (no matter how great the amount) compared to the psychological toll such a practice can have on her children. She has to be helped to appreciate that there are times when it is more prudent to admit that one has been defeated, than to win a victory that may be injurious to her children. Although vengeance may be sweet, in this case it cannot but be soured by the harm caused the children. In war, both sides are generally the losers—and divorce wars are no exception.

The visit. One of the common problems that custodial parents frequently complain of is the visiting parent's lateness, last minute cancellations, or failure to show up for the visits. It is important to impress upon the visiting parent the value of predictability and reliability with regard to the visitation. Divorce has undermined the children's stability already; there is no need to add to their difficulties by irresponsibility regarding the visitation appointments. One must try to impress upon such parents the importance of advance planning and how salutary it can be for the child. If a father has to miss an appointment he does well to inform the children well in advance of the cancellation. Many such parents seem to be oblivious to the fact that building up the children's hopes and then disappointing them at the last minute can be devastating.

As mentioned, the ideal visitation program is one in which there is the greatest flexibility. Separation and divorce decree stipulations can never take into account all the needs and desires of the mother, father, and children at any particular time. Most often specific times are designated. However, the parents do well to use these merely as guidelines. If the children do not wish to visit on a certain day they should not be forced to (beyond the occasional prodding that most children need for their own good). Similarly, a father who visits a particular day out of guilt or obligation would probably do best to select another day. When the father and children get together and basically do not wish to do so at that time, it is likely that the resentments so engendered will lessen the pleasure that they can derive from the experience.

Separation and divorce decrees most often clump all the children together when defining the times of visitation. Such a practice does not take into consideration the individual differences of the children and their separate desires at a given time. In accordance with the aforementioned principle of flexibility, I believe that it can be to the children's benefit to be split up with regard to visitations. Not only does this practice avoid the resentment caused by forced visiting, but it allows each of the children more individual attention from the parent who is being visited. Some hold that such a practice can increase sibling rivalries. This has not been my experience. In fact, because it provides each child with more individual attention, there is less to be rivalrous about. Furthermore, separating children is just about the most foolproof way of preventing their fighting. It is only when one child is preferentially selected to visit more frequently that sibling rivalries are likely to be increased.

When the father picks up the children, and they are in a good mood, he will tend to interpret this to mean that they are happy to leave their mother, who treats them so badly, and come to him where they will receive love and affection. The mother will tend to interpret the smiling faces to mean that they are looking forward to the indulgence and spoiling that the father will provide them in order to "buy their love." If they are unhappy, the father understands this to be the result of the maltreatment they have received at their mother's hands. The mother sees their unhappiness as the result of the dread they feel over the visit with the father and their anticipation of the horrible things that happen when they are with him. And the therapist working with one of these parents may be hard put to know where fantasy ends and the truth begins. Even when he has the opportunity to meet with both parents, the truth may be very difficult to ascertain.

As every father who spends a significant amount of time alone with his children knows (whether in the divorced or intact family situation), things can get tedious at times. Adults are adults and children are children, and there is just so much child's play and childishness that an adult can tolerate. Accordingly, a father does well at times to allow his children to bring along friends and child relatives. Such joiners take some of the pressures off the father. The only danger of this practice is that the father will too frequently allow the visitors to take over his obligations.

The question is sometimes raised as to whether it is bad practice for the visiting parent to spend any (and even all) of his visiting time in the original home. Such visits are said to protect the child from the anxieties produced by being taken out of the home and having to adjust to a new environment. First, I believe it is important to emphasize to those who make such an inquiry that far more important than the place where the visits occur is the nature of the relationship between the parties. The quality of the activities that the visiting parent and the children partake in, and the enrichment they derive from them, is far more important than the place where they take place. The other consideration, of course, is the receptivity of the custodial partner with regard to the ex-spouse's returning to the home. If such visits occur routinely then I would wonder about the reasons for the divorce. Most divorced people wish to see as little as possible of their former spouses. Having him or her frequently back in the home suggests that there is still a significant ongoing relationship and that the visiting parent is not just being accommodated so that the visits might take place in a familiar atmosphere with a minimal of anxiety-producing change.

One of the most common problems that arises over visitation results from the contrast between the child's experiences during his visits outside the home (usually with his father) and those he has with the custodial parent (usually the mother). With father he has fun, plays games, visits enjoyable places, and may have few obligations to assume. With mother, on the other hand, it's getting up early, going to school, and doing homework and household chores. Father may feel quite guilty about his having left the home and may try to assuage his guilt by continually providing the children with good times. In addition, he may hesitate to properly discipline lest the children get even angrier at him. Sometimes the father provides endless entertainment in order to avoid more direct contact with his children in a natural and human way. The father may contribute even further to this state of affairs because of rivalrous feelings toward the mother or from the appreciation that it can serve as a way of hurting her. The children may even come to the conclusion that if they were to live with the father permanently that this would be the kind of life they would lead all the time. In such a situation the father gets to be the "good-guy" and the mother acquires the epithet of the "meanie."

Such fathers have to be helped to appreciate that they are doing their children a disservice. They have to be helped to see that the best kind of atmosphere they can provide their children is one that most closely approximates the original home—especially with regard to the balance between pleasant and unpleasant activities. Such indulgence of the children creates in them unreal attitudes toward life and makes it more difficult for mother, teacher, and others to get them to learn the restraint that is necessary if one is to be a self-sufficient, mature adult. In addition, such fathers have to be helped to appreciate how detrimental it is to the children to be used as a pawn in the parental conflict. The children have enough trouble already; they should not have to suffer the additional burden of divided loyalties. Sometimes longer periods of visitation can be an effective antidote to such indulgence. Endless entertainment can be exhausting and produce financial strains in all but the wealthy.

There are other fathers, however, who do just the opposite. They give little thought to the nature of the activities they provide the child and delude themselves into believing that merely being together is enough. Accordingly, they may drag the child along on business visits, seat the child at an office desk for hours on end to amuse himself as best he can, or prop him up in front of the television set for as long as the child will tolerate. The child may resent being so neglected but may be fearful of expressing his anger, lest he see even less of his father. Such children have to be helped to assert themselves in order to bring about a cessation of such a deplorable practice; and such fathers have to be helped to see how neglectful they are.

Ideally, both the father and children should decide together exactly what activities they will have together. Attempts should be made to select those that will not cause significant boredom or resentment in either. Each, however, must be willing to make certain compromises—as is true in the planning of activities in the intact home as well. In addition, such fathers should be encouraged to participate in some of the "dirty work" such as getting their children to do homework and chores. Otherwise they are neglecting their children by depriving them of real life experiences, experiences that will help them optimally adjust to a world in which there is both pleasure and pain.

Postvisit problems. A common complaint that mothers have when the children return from their visits with the father is that they are unmanageable and unkempt. Twenty-five percent of the 425 divorced women studied by Goode (1956) considered the children harder to handle after returning from a visit with their father. (Two percent found the children easier to handle.) Often the father's relaxed attitude and indulgence makes it harder for them to readjust to the more rigorous demands of the mother's household. With school, discipline, housekeeping, etc. the mother may have to run a tighter ship. The father may interpret the children's restlessness on returning to the mother as proof that he is the better parent and that the children are unhappy about having to live once again with their mother, the Ogre. The child who cries on returning to the mother is understood by the father as doing so because he doesn't want to leave him. The mother considers the child to be crying because of the maltreatment he has been exposed to.

On the other hand, when the children return in a happy frame of mind, the mother tends to interpret this as a sign that they are glad to get rid of their father and return to the warmth and friendliness of her home. The father usually considers their happy mood to be a reflection of the good treatment they have received from him.

The natural history of visitation. As time passes, visitation by the departed parent tends to diminish. It is in the early phases following the divorce that the guilt is the greatest and the need to assuage it through frequent contacts with the children most strong. As time goes on the visits become more of a drain, especially if the parent has the need to make them a continual source of fun and games for the children. The visits occupy considerable time and are often costly. As time passes many fathers generally want to use their free time and money more for dating and other recreational purposes than for their children. As the children grow older, they generally want to spend more time with their friends—as they would in the intact household.

Remarriage of a parent can have a significant effect on visitation. When the father was single, the children may have had little competition for his time. When he is remarried and has children of his own (or children from his new wife's former marriage) he cannot provide the children from his first marriage with as much attention. The father's new wife may have professed great interest in and affection for his children prior to her marriage; but afterwards such feelings may diminish considerably. Sensing themselves outsiders in the new home, they may become less desirous of visiting. A remarried mother who has custody of the children may also be less desirous of her former husband's visiting the home. His periodic reappearance may compromise somewhat her relationship with her new husband. When single, she had a greater need to get the children "off her hands." Now that she is remarried she may feel them less of a burden.

There are situations in which a parent is deprived of the right or opportunity to visit and may still wish to. For example, a father may have moved so far away that frequent visiting is impractical and financially impossible. On occasion, a misguided or punitive judge may prevent a father from seeing his children at a frequency that is appropriate or desired by him. Sometimes an angry and vengeful mother will so poison her children against their father that they will not only refuse to see him but will vociferously berate him, call the police, etc. when he comes to the home. Generally, I advise the parent in such a situation to continue, in a reasonable way, to maintain contact with the children. Letters, presents sent by mail, and telephone calls can often serve well here. Sending messages through friends and relatives can also be useful. Knowing that father is still out there, thinking of them, and trying to maintain contact with them can be salutary. If the parent has the desire to maintain contact with his children he should use every reasonable means to do this. To comply with the children's and other's requests that he suppress these desires can deprive father and children of an important psychological bond.

Money

Money is one of the issues that obsesses many divorced parents both around the time of the separation and subsequent to it. Divorce is an expensive proposition and the specter of contributing to the upkeep of two homes may be the major reason why there aren't more divorces than there are. Most therapists appreciate that it is inappropriate for them to involve themselves in the details of who gets how much and why. Generally we are wise enough to know not only that such deliberations are not within our realm, but also that we do not want to get involved in the mind-boggling and petty disputes that such decisions entail. Besides the realistic reasons why money is of such concern to separated parents, there are many psychological ones as well. Money has great symbolic value to many, if not most, patients in therapy. Because it can readily be used as a vehicle for expressing love and hostility (in accordance with whether one gives it or withholds it), it readily lends itself to a variety of psychological symbolizations. And, as a treasured possession of each of the separated parents, it ranks with the children as an object that quickly gets embroiled in the parents' conflicts.

Probably one of the most common complaints made by divorced mothers is that their husbands are not sending the money provided for in the divorce decree. The percentage of husbands who consistently, over many years, live up to their alimony and support commitments is, I believe, quite small. The withholding of such payments not only provides the husband with more financial flexibility, but can serve as a very potent weapon for the expression of hostility toward the ex-wife. When one adds to this the fact that the courts are relatively impotent to enforce this aspect of the divorce decree, one can see how tempting it is for husbands to renege on this obligation. The court's weakness stems from the fact that its two most common forms of punishment, namely, fines and incarceration, if imposed make it less likely that the wife will get what she requests and is usually entitled to. In addition, if a wife resorts to a lawyer to help her acquire the funds, she may lose more money than she gains because of the legal costs.

I try to help such mothers make reasonable attempts to get what they are entitled to. When this fails, I discourage them strongly from pursuing the matter further. I try to help them appreciate that the emotional drain on them (and often the children) entailed in maintaining the hostilities cannot be counted in dollars. I try to help them use their energies in ways that will more predictably enable them to acquire funds. Above all, I try to help them appreciate that the conflict over funds may last years, and even then prove futile. If there is a pathological vengeance element involved ("I just can't sit and let him get the satisfaction"), I try to help such a mother appreciate that even if she wins after years of struggle, she still loses because of the psychological drain on herself and usually the children. When working with husbands who so renege, I try to help them appreciate that the rationalizations they invoke to justify their not paying are usually unjustified and that for extra financial security they are jeopardizing their children's psychological welfare.

The mother whose husband defaults is often tempted to seek revenge and/or attempt to get him to pay by withholding the children from visitation. As mentioned, I strongly discourage this because of the detrimental effects it can have on the children. The financial privations they suffer because of their father's withholding payments is punishment enough. It only adds to their difficulties if they are prevented from continuing their relationship with their father. Admittedly, such a father has already proved himself to be deficient via his failure to live up to his financial commitments toward his family. However, this deficiency, as grave as it may be, does not make him totally worthless as a father nor incapable of providing his children with some healthy experiences in his contact with them.

The number of complaints that each parent may have about the other's handling of money is endless. Mother complains that father's financial commitment to his new wife and children is greater than to her and their children. Father accuses mother of using support money to buy things for herself, to the neglect of the children. Mother denounces father for sending support checks to the child, in the child's name—thereby compromising her authority. Often the therapist will feel as impotent as the patient to effect a change in these practices because it is the other party, not one's patient, who is engaging in them. The best one can do then is to help the patient give up the neurotic contributions of his own that are perpetuating the marital conflict.

Dating and Remarriage Considerations as They Relate to the Children

A mother will often ask about the advisability of having dates meet her at home. Some feel that not to do so is secretive; on the other hand, they feel uncomfortable about the child's meeting each new date. Generally, I advise mothers not to expose their children to every new date. As discussed in Chapter 12, the boy in an intact home has trouble enough coming to terms with the fact that his mother shares certain intimacies with his father that he does not enjoy. The boy with a divorced mother who is dating has many other rivals as well—each of whom seems to have certain advantages over him with regard to having an intimate relationship with his mother. There is no need for a mother to accentuate this problem by having her son meet every new date. The same considerations hold true for a girl's meeting her father's dates. In addition, if the child looks forward to the parent's remarrying in order to compensate for the loss of a parent, each new date may raise his hopes unnecessarily. And the child who dreads the thought of parental remarriage is being provided with needless exposure to the object of his concerns. Accordingly, I generally suggest that parents meet transient dates outside of the home and only introduce the children to friends with whom an ongoing relationship has already been established. These people need not be potential marriage partners. What the parent should try to avoid is exposing the children to the seemingly endless parade. That is the situation that is likely to produce the greatest amount of difficulty for the children.

Some parents may hide all dates, transients as well as those with whom they may become deeply involved, in order to avoid the hostile reactions they know their children will have to the new person. Such hiding is not in the children's best interests. It is neurotic to comply with another person's neurotic demands. Such compliance only entrenches such children's manipulations and deprives them of the growth experience of dealing with something they find unpleasant. Such a parent is probably afraid of anyone's anger—regardless of the age of the person who is angry and the appropriateness of the anger—and has to be helped to look into the basic fears that are being covered up by this rationalization.

Another common question relates to the effects on the child of an opposite-sexed friend staying overnight in bed with the parent (without, of course, the child's observing or overhearing sexual activity). In accordance with what I have said about dating, if such experiences occur with a large number of different friends then the effects can be quite detrimental. However, if such intimacy is reserved for deep, ongoing relationships, I see no reason why the child should develop untoward reactions. It is the parade that is the dangerous thing, in my opinion, not sexual intercourse performed out of the child's presence or awareness.

Occasionally parents (usually custodial mothers) will seriously consider marrying people they are not sure about, because they feel it would be good for the children to have a father or mother figure living in the home. Just as I generally discourage parents who are considering divorce from staying together "for the sake of the children," I similarly discourage single parents from remarrying for their sake. I am not suggesting that the children's needs be totally ignored in such deliberations; rather, I am suggesting that they not be given highest priority. One marries and divorces primarily for oneself, not for one's children. Although I believe strongly that children do best in a situation in which mother and father figures are present, this does not mean that *any* mother or *any* father figure will do. One must consider who these people are and the nature of the relationship between the parents as well as that between parents and children. The mother who is ambivalent about remarriage, but who is considering it for the children's sake, must take into consideration the fact that a poor relationship with her new husband is likely to have untoward effects on the children. In addition, she must consider his relationship with the children as well if she is to be able to make any decisions as to whether a remarriage will be in the children's best interests.

Occasionally a single parent will wonder about remarriage to someone who seems suitable and desirable in every way except for the fact that the person does not seem to have a good relationship with the children. One should try to help such a parent ascertain whether the difficulties are the result of deficiencies in the potential spouse or are the result of distortions or difficulties in the children. In the former case the parent should try to determine whether such defects are confined to children or whether they are manifestations of broader deficiencies in human relationships. If it is only a defect with regard to children then the parent should be clear about this deficiency beforehand and recognize that it will be one of the drawbacks of the marriage. If there is a broader problem in human relationships then the parent might do well to get a clearer picture of the potential spouse before making a definite decision. (Some joint counseling might be useful here.) If it is the children's problems that are compromising the relationship, then it is inappropriate not to remarry for this reason. It is not in their best interests psychologically to comply with inappropriate or neurotic demands on their part; to do so would only enhance their maladaptive behavior.

A discussion of parental remarriage would not be complete if it omitted mention of one of the single parent's greatest dangers, namely, marrying again for the same neurotic reasons that brought about the first marriage. Bergler (1948) considers this highly likely in those who have not received proper treatment—especially treatment directed to the alleviation and cure of those neurotic factors that specifically caused the marriage to fail. He states: "Since the neurotic is unconsciously always on the lookout for his complementary type, the chances of finding happiness in the second marriage are exactly zero. . . . The second, third, and nth marriages are but repetitions of the previous experience." Monahan's study (1958) tends to confirm Bergler's somewhat pessimistic prognosis for remarriages. He found that second marriages were twice as likely to end in divorce as first marriages and that the risk for a third marriage was even greater. He found that if both spouses had been divorced two or more times the probability of that particular marriage failing was five times greater than for a first marriage. Accordingly, the therapist does well to warn parents of their tendency to find someone who will complement their own neurotic patterns. He should try to help them appreciate that in spite of their resolution to seek someone entirely different this time, powerful unconscious forces will cause them to draw toward someone with whom they can involve themselves in the same old neurotic pattern. I generally advise such parents, when contemplating remarriage, to seek counseling (either alone or jointly) if they sense any difficulties in the new relationship. Such advice, unfortunately, often goes unheeded and I have seen a number of remarriages which were uncannily similar to the previous ones—often with the same tragic consequences.

Assorted Warnings

A common error that separated parents make (especially in the early phase) is to use the child as a source of information about the ex-spouse. It is natural for a parent to be curious about what the former partner is doing (especially with regard to dating and spending money) and the child can be an excellent source of information. Frequently this information is used in litigation. Often parents are so compelled to extract such information from their children that they blind themselves to the deleterious effects on the child of his allowing himself to be used as an informer. He cannot but be ashamed of himself for his disloyalty, yet he provides the information so as not to alienate the inquirer. Such a parent may also deny the loss of respect he himself suffers from the child's vantage point, because basically the parent is not handling himself in a respectable manner.

In working with such children I try to discourage them from involving themselves with their parents in this way and try to get them to be self-assertive enough to refuse to answer each parent's questions about the other. In addition, I will often say: "No one respects a spy or a tattletale—neither the people he spies for nor the spy himself. The people whom he spies for know that he can't be trusted with a secret. And the spy can't like himself because he knows that what he's doing is wrong because it hurts other people." I also point out to the child that his spying is contributing to the continuation of his parents' fighting. And I suggest that parents also use this approach if one or both are motivated to discontinue this shameful game.

Commonly each parent will try to get the child to be an ally in the parental conflict. As is true in all wars, the more people one has on one's side, the greater the chances of victory. Many children, from fear of appearing disloyal, will take the side of the parent they are with at the time. Such a response causes the child to think less of himself because of his dishonesty. In addition, he lives with the fear that his duplicity will be revealed (which it most often is) and then he will suffer the alienation of those who have learned of it. Others, however, do consistently side with a particular parent against the other, may blind themselves to positive qualities in the parent to whom they are antagonistic, and thereby compromise what could have been a richer and more rewarding relationship.

Again, I generally advise children to try to assert themselves and refuse to take sides. This does not mean, however, that they should refuse to gain information about each parent. Getting information and taking action are two very different things. Although the discrimination between the two may be difficult (and the younger the child, the more so), one should attempt to help the child make it. He has to be helped to decide whether the information he has warrants his taking action or not. For example, he has to be helped to see the difference between fighting his own battles and fighting a parent's. If, for example, his father gambles, then both child and mother suffer unnecessary privations. Such a child should be encouraged to tell his father how much the gambling bothers him in the hope such assertion will play some role in rectifying the situation. On the other hand, if his father dislikes his mother but loves him, the child does himself and his father a disservice if he joins forces with his mother against his father. He has to be helped to appreciate that by doing so both he and his father lose out on the gratifications to be gained from a loving relationship. In addition, I try to help the child appreciate that his parents' comments about one another (especially when made in anger) may not be completely trustworthy. Accordingly, I try to help him form his own opinions about each *on the basis of his own observations*.

Some children will take advantage of the parental hostilities to their own ends. When with the mother they will try to ingratiate themselves with her by saying critical things about the father in order to gain special favors, privileges, or presents. And they may act similarly when with the father. Divorced parents are particularly susceptible to this maneuver because they so relish hearing critical things about one another. Whereas they would usually be incredulous of many of the absurd things the child might communicate in other areas, when it comes to critical information about the ex-spouse they may exhibit amazing gullibility.

When working with such children I try to appeal to the lowered sense of self-worth they must somewhere feel over their duplicity. In addition, I try to help them see that they are causing themselves to suffer unnecessary fears of disclosure. With the parents I try to help them interrupt the game by alerting them to its occurrence and pointing out their credulity. Some parents quickly catch on to what has been happening and can discontinue their involvement. Others are so angry that they cannot avoid getting "sucked in" and so are continually manipulated by the child—an unfortunate situation for both.

Helping the Child with Peer Problems

In years past the child of divorce often suffered significant social stigmatization. Generally, this (like other forms of prejudice) originated with parents and was transmitted through the children. Because of the ubiquity of divorce in recent years there is hardly a classroom or neighborhood where there aren't at least a few children from divorced homes. Accordingly, such children are less subject to ridicule and social alienation. However, as Gettleman and Markowitz (1974) point out, there are certain situations in which the child of divorce may still be treated differently from those in an intact home. For example, a child who visits his father on weekends may be freely invited to other children's homes, but parents may be reluctant to allow their children to visit in the home of the divorced father. He may be considered less capable than a woman of caring for the children, or the mothers may want to keep their distance from him lest the relationship take on sexual overtones.

Although social factors causing the child of divorce to feel different from and less worthy than others have been reduced, internal factors have not. Although the proponents of society's giving greater acceptability to alternate life styles may see nothing wrong with a child's living with only one parent, children do not seem to be strong adherents to this cause. The child of divorce sees others who have two parents living in the home. He has only one and compares himself unfavorably with those he considers more fortunate. Such feelings may become intensified by the "understanding" and "sympathetic" attitudes of his peers. In order to assuage their own anxieties over this misfortune occurring to them (it now becomes "close to home" for them), they may become oversolicitous of the child of divorce (especially in the period just following the separation). By reassuring them, they are really attempting to reassure themselves. And their questions about how he is dealing with the problem derive less from the desire to help the child of divorce handle his problems than from the need to provide themselves with information about how to deal with this calamity should it befall them. In addition, parents of the child's friends may be solicitous out of pity and overprotective in an attempt to provide the child with compensations for the privations he may be suffering. Such attitudes on the part of his peers and their parents cannot but make the child of divorce feel different, inferior, and somewhat defective.

In response the child may harbor deep feelings of shame and try to hide the fact of the separation. He may go to great lengths to keep the secret. Many will stop inviting children to their homes and find excuses for turning away those who do come—lest the father's absence be detected by the visitors. As mentioned, such a response only increases feelings of self loathing and adds unnecessary fears of disclosure. Parents are well advised to help children appreciate that they are adding to their burden by dealing with the separation in this way. If the parents themselves are ashamed of the separation then it is most likely, if not inevitable, that this will be transmitted to the child and only add to the humiliation he already feels. Such parents are in no position to help the child with his shame; they have to be helped to work out their own problem in this area first.

New enlightenment about divorce notwithstanding, there are still some children who are taunted because of it. I generally advise parents of children who are so treated to help them appreciate that the defect really lies in those who laugh at them. In addition, such children have to be helped to recognize that they are not necessarily what others claim them to be. Another reassurance that can help relates to the proverbial "sticks and stones" saying, namely, that taunts cannot really harm. Most important, the child has to be helped to appreciate that he will ultimately be judged on the basis of the kind of person he actually is. If he gets along with other people, is nice to be with, and respected, other children will want to be with him—regardless of the marital status of his parents.

Having been "abandoned" by a parent, the child of divorce is more likely to be distrustful of his relationships with others, adults and peers alike. Verbal reassurances do not work very well in reducing such distrust. Only living experience that people can still be reliable is likely to reduce this distrust. And it is the absent parent's involvement here that is most crucial. If he or she continues to maintain meaningful involvement, then such distrust is likely to be reduced; if not, then it will probably persist and even increase. In such cases, it is only through meaningful and prolonged substitutive relationships that the distrust can be dispelled and it behooves the parents to encourage and facilitate such relationships.

On occasion, the divorce will have occurred because of significant socially alienating behavior by a parent, e.g., drug addiction, chronic alcoholism, or prostitution. When these problems become known to the community (as they often do) then the child may be subjected to terrible ridicule and even mockery. It is very difficult to help a child rise above such derision and appreciate that there is something wrong with a person who would blame a child for the behavior of a parent. But this is central to the approach to such a problem. In addition, such a child has to be helped to appreciate that if he is basically friendly and fun to be with, that he should ultimately be accepted by most for what *he* is and not for what his *parent* is or was.

Boarding Schools

I believe that the healthy parent wants to live with his child—at least until the teen-age period—and will suffer some pain and frustration upon being separated from him or her. Accordingly, I believe that a parent who voluntarily sends a child below the age of puberty to live elsewhere, when there is a reasonable possibility of his living at home, manifests some deficiency in his or her parental capacity. And sending a child (from here on, unless stated otherwise, I am referring to children below the pubertal period) to boarding school is, until proven otherwise, a sign of such parental defect. Such parents typically utilize such rationalizations as: "It's better for him to be away from all the conflict," "Private schools are the only places where one can get a really good education," and "Our home is split up; there they have good mother and father substitutes, all in the same place." When "family tradition" is used as the reason for sending young children off to boarding school, then the *family tradition*, I believe, is one of neglect and disinterest in children. The fact that sending children as young as four years of age off to boarding school is common practice in England does not, in my opinion, make the practice any less pathological. When cholera becomes epidemic it's still a disease.

When separated parents send their children to boarding school they routinely reassure them they are not being sent away because they aren't loved. And professional authorities strongly urge such parents to emphasize this fact. But the children know better. They know the truth. They know they are being sent off because neither parent wishes to assume responsibility for their care. They know that their parents want them out of the way. Accordingly, such reassurances are in most cases hypocritical. The child knows the parents' deficiency; lying about it only causes further distrust. Such parents would do far better for both themselves and their children if they would openly admit that they are deficient as parents and that they are sending the children away in the hope that others may be able to do a better job. With such an approach they would at least be avoiding the distrust that results when they try to cover up their real reasons for sending the children away.

At times a child may consider his being sent off to boarding school a punishment. It is not hard to see why this occurs. It is a painful experience just like punishment. In addition, the ultimate punishment for all children is loss of parental affection; and being sent away to boarding school is most often just that. Furthermore, as described in Chapter 7, such notions may serve the child's need to gain control over an uncontrollable situation. Being sent away in punishment for some transgression is less anxiety provoking than being rejected at the whim of others. Accordingly, reassuring the child that he isn't being sent away as punishment for misbehavior is futile. (Again, many professionals advise parents to provide such reassurances.) Rather, the child has to come to appreciate that he is being sent away because of deficiencies in his parents. He has not generally been particularly "bad." What has been bad is his luck. He has to be helped to accept his parents for what they are; to enjoy what he can from his relationships with them; and to look elsewhere for the gratifications that they are unable and/or unwilling to provide. In addition, when the delusion of control is present, the child has to be helped to differentiate between those things he has control over and those he does not. He must learn to give up on foolhardy quests and direct his attention to pursuits in which there is a greater likelihood of success. These approaches are not only useful in the psychotherapy of such children, but can be used as well by those parents who have the ego strength to utilize them themselves with their children.

There are children who prefer the boarding school because they are thereby removed from the strife and misery of their home life. But anyone who believes that these children are better off than those in intact homes (and even intact homes with a moderate amount of dissension) is misguided. These children are just expressing preference for the better of two detrimental alternatives. Even the child who requests to go is not generally asking to leave a relatively warm and loving home; rather, he sees the boarding school environment as exposing him to less trauma.

As mentioned, the comments above are relevant to children below the pubertal period. The adolescent is in an entirely different situation. His being sent off to boarding school is not necessarily a psychologically detrimental experience and does not necessarily mean that he is being rejected by his parents. If such a child has gained the benefits of good parenting from one or both parents (either in a divorced or intact home) the boarding school experience can be enriching and maturing. But even in this period, the parents do well to keep up frequent contact with the youngster via mail, telephone, and visits.

Clubs and Organizations

In recent years many clubs and organizations have been formed specifically for divorced parents and their children. Probably the most well known of these is Parents Without Partners* which has hundreds of chapters in the United States, Canada, and various other countries. Although many parents join in order to meet potential candidates for remarriage, the organization provides a host of activities that are of value to divorced parents and their children. Most chapters (and they seem to be everywhere) have various family

*Headquarters: 7910 Woodmont Ave., Washington, D.C. 20014.

activities, outings, picnics, etc. which enable children to have close contact with opposite-sexed parent surrogates. Discussion groups and lectures provide the members with valuable information that can be helpful to themselves and their children. Adolescent discussion groups and recreational groups for children help these youngsters feel less different and provide them with opportunities to work out some of the special problems that children of divorce often have. Because these activities have definite therapeutic benefit I often suggest that divorced parents join PWP or a similar organization.

An organization that can be useful for boys who live alone with their mothers is Big Brothers of America.* Men volunteer to spend time with boys who are fatherless or whose fathers are not frequently available to them. Strong father-son type relationships are often formed and can serve such boys to compensate for their paternal deprivation. Big Sisters International provides similar opportunities for fatherless girls and for those who need a mother surrogate.**

In addition, I generally recommend that the children join various clubs that are likely to provide them with parental surrogates. Boy scouts, Girl Scouts, Cub Scouts, Brownies, Little League, Y's, summer camps, and various organized recreational activities can provide such adults for these children.

Stepparents

Children's reactions to stepparents. In legend, story, and fairy tale stepmothers have traditionally been wicked. And in real life, as well, stepmothers are rarely depicted as benevolent. So deeply ingrained is the stepmother's bad reputation that the name itself is almost intrinsically pejorative and many jokes capitalize on this. I believe that one of the reasons for this tradition relates to the fact that a stepmother is a convenient person upon whom a child can displace hostility felt toward his or her natural mother which cannot be expressed. When the natural mother has died, her children may still harbor feelings of resentment toward her for having "abandoned" them—in spite of their awareness that to do so was not her wish. Obviously, such hostility cannot be expressed overtly, or often even covertly. A stepmother, as a maternal figure who is very much alive and available, may serve as an ideal target. And when a natural mother is alive, guilt over and fear of her loss and rejection may prevent a child from directly expressing anger to her. Again, a stepmother may serve well as a substitute.

The reader who accepts this hypothesis may wonder why stepfathers have not equally served as targets for displaced hostility. I believe that children have traditionally been less fearful of expressing resentment to their mother

*Headquarters: 220 Suburban Station Building, Philadelphia, Pa. 19103.
**Headquarters: 224 Suburban Station Building, Philadelphia, Pa. 19103.

than to their fathers. Fathers are usually bigger and more physically powerful and are therefore riskier persons upon whom to vent anger. Because they generally spend less time with children than mothers, they are less exposed to children's misbehavior, less desensitized to it and, therefore, less tolerant of it. Because mothers spend more time with children than fathers they are forced to discipline them more. Receiving more punishment from the mother makes it more likely that children will resent her, have more experience expressing their anger to her, and be more comfortable doing so. Mothers may even become the repository of hostility felt toward fathers. This, too, contributes to the stepmother's becoming the scapegoat, thereby preserving the good name of the father (and even the stepfather).

Natural mothers, almost predictably, are rivalrous with their children's stepmother. And stepmothers are not famous for their benevolence toward their husbands' former wives. A stepmother, in order to ingratiate herself with her husband, may try very hard to form a good relationship with his children. It is rare for a natural mother to respond positively to these overtures. The children are thereby placed in a conflictual situation. With their loyalties divided between their mother and stepmother, they usually side with their mother—the one with whom they usually have the deeper and more important relationship. Accordingly, their affection for their stepmother is compromised and she is seen as less loving than she may really be. One could argue that a really mature and healthy mother would appreciate that a stepmother can provide her children with many gratifications in compensation for the deprivations they have suffered because of the divorce and that three loving adults are better than two. I myself have not met such women and I believe that the therapist who presents such an ideal to these natural mothers may cause them unnecessary guilt as they fail to live up to what is probably an unrealistic and unattainable goal.

In counseling stepmothers I try to help them appreciate that the "cards may be stacked against them" with regard to their forming a loving relationship with their stepchildren. Even when the natural mother has totally abandoned the children, the stepmother may find herself the butt of displaced hostility. She must be helped not to take all such anger personally. Hopefully, if she is genuinely affectionate the children will come to appreciate her and develop a warm, meaningful, and even loving relationship with her.

Stepfathers, too, may be used as targets for hostility that children may feel toward their natural fathers, but the other elements that contribute to difficulties with stepmothers do not seem to operate with such intensity in children's relationships with their stepfathers. Men, in my experience, do not seem to be as jealous and possessive as women with regard to the children's developing affectionate relationships with others. I believe that this is partly related to the closer relationship that the mother, as the bearer of the children, has with her offspring. I suspect, but I am not certain, that the female is innately more oriented toward child rearing. But social factors are very important here as well. A society which does not provide the female with opportunities for meaningful gratification in areas other than childbearing and child rearing is likely to produce women who jealously covet their children— their primary source of ego-enhancement. In such a society men, having extradomestic sources of ego-enhancement in their careers, are less dependent on their children to give their lives meaning and less jealous of those who share their children's affection.

There are other factors as well that may contribute to difficulties in the relationships between children and their stepparents. We all experience some anxiety in new relationships, and children, being less competent to handle them, even more so. Children of divorce will usually be even more hesitant than the child from an intact home to involve himself deeply with a strange adult. Having "lost" one important adult already, he anticipates a recurrence of the "abandonment" and is likely to need time to "warm up." Adults should be advised to take these factors into consideration. Coming on too strongly and overwhelming the child may make it even more difficult for him or her to get involved.

Oedipal factors can contribute to difficulties in the children's relationships with their stepparents. Incest taboos are hard to maintain even in the intact household. Children in the oedipal period are often quite overt about their physical desires toward the opposite-sexed parent. Although such desires may not be specifically for heterosexual intercourse, they do include various other kinds of heterosexual activities, e.g., erotic play with the opposite-sexed parent and the observation of undressing and toilet functions. The adolescent's sexual development can be a source of sexual stimulation to the parent. The youngster's attraction to the parents, then, become even harder for them to handle, intensified as they are by the parental stimulation (often thinly disguised by such mechanisms as reaction formation and hostility). With stepparents the incest taboo is usually less strong on the part of both the children and the adults. Accordingly, the situation becomes much "hotter." In addition, the child, before separation, may have resigned himself to the fact that the parental dyad is sacrosanct. When the parents break up, and a newcomer replaces one of the parents, the child is less likely to view the marital relationship as inviolable. A boy living with a mother may consider the arrangement a fulfillment of oedipal fantasies. The appearance of a stepfather on the scene robs him of the total possession of his mother that he considered himself to have had. Accordingly, the oedipal rivalry and hostility may become very intense. And a girl living with her divorced father may have similar reactions to her new stepmother. Prior to the separation the child had to come to terms with *one* rival for the affection of the opposite-sexed parent.

Now that one has been displaced, a second has suddenly appeared on the scene. It is as if after David subdues Goliath, a second giant suddenly appears from behind a mountain. And the child may wonder how many more giants there are behind it.

I have limited myself to describing factors in the homes of remarried parents that may contribute to and intensify basic oedipal problems. The number of ways in which these difficulties become translated into clinical difficulties is great. They cover a wide range of neurotic and, at times, even psychotic adaptations and are beyond the scope of this book. I have, however, described a few of these in Chapter 12.

All of the aforementioned factors may contribute, in varying degree, to children's impairments in their relationships with stepparents. Such children may feel guilty over their resentments and believe that there are other good, upstanding children who harbor no such hostilities. Parents should be advised that such negative reactions are the norm and only require treatment when they become extreme or symptomatic. If the parents themselves believe that the child should be capable of unadulterated benevolence toward the stepparent, then they are placing an unnecessary burden upon their child and contributing thereby to his guilt. They should be advised to reassure the child that his hostile feelings are normal and inevitable and that, hopefully, as time goes on there will be more loving feelings appearing as well.

Stepparents' reactions to children. Because of the many factors interfering with the development of positive feelings in children toward a stepparent, the latter is likely to be slowed down in his forming loving feelings toward the children. Genuine love must involve reciprocity. If the object of our affection shows little inclination to respond, our ardor cannot but diminish. There are, however, factors present in the stepparents—factors independent of the children—that contribute as well to difficulties in their relationships with the children.

First, it is unreasonable to expect a stepparent to have as much affection for a stepchild as he or she would have for a natural child. We are more likely to develop a strong psychological bond with a child derived from our "own flesh and blood" than with a child born of other parents. Parents who believe that they should be just as loving toward their stepchildren as they are toward their own children are placing an unnecessary burden upon themselves and will inevitably feel guilty about not living up to this unrealistic standard. I am not saying that it is not *possible* for a stepparent to love a stepchild as much as his own; I am only saying that it is entirely reasonable that he may not. There are parents who, although they do feel a preference, consider that it would be harmful to the stepchildren if they were to reveal this to them. "They're all the same to me," they profess, "sometimes I forget which ones are mine, which ones theirs, and which ones ours." I find such "forgetfulness" incredible and so, I believe, do the children involved. Such a parent would do better to communicate with the children, at the proper time and in the appropriate situation, comments along these lines: "Yes, I do love my own children more than I love you. I do feel great affection for you children and I hope that as time goes on I will feel even more. The more loving things we do for one another, the more our love should grow. And that's the same with my children as well. When they're lovable, I love them more. When they're not, I love them less." The last statement should be included to let the children know that love must be worked at—one must earn it—whether one is a natural child or a stepchild.

As mentioned, the stepparent is well advised to take it slow with the stepchildren and let the relationship grow. Overwhelming them with hugs, kisses, luscious praise, gifts, etc. is bound to turn them off and retard, if not squelch, the development of healthy, affectionate relationships.

A stepparent should be aware that he probably harbors some misconceptions about a child's natural parent. A stepmother, for example, may have spent countless hours listening to her husband describe the various indignities he has suffered at the hands of his former wife. Naturally, she will tend to side with her husband. If he is still trying to wreak vengeance on his former wife or maintain other forms of hostile interaction, she is bound to become his ally in the battle. In such an atmosphere it is not likely that she will be able to form a good relationship with the stepchildren because of their ties with the natural mother. This is just another example of the detrimental effects of postmarital warfare and another reason why it behooves the therapist to do everything possible to bring about a truce.

A common problem causing difficulties between stepparents and stepchildren relates to the marked differences between premarital fantasy and postmarital fact. A woman with no children of her own, when involved with a man with children whom she wishes to marry, may entertain unrealistic fantasies about how wonderful life will be with him and his children. In her enthusiasm to get married she may unconsciously underestimate the problems that will beset her after she has achieved her goal. Or she may feign affection for the children out of the recognition that such displays of endearment to them will make her more attractive to her would-be husband. After marriage, and the lessening of romantic euphoria that inevitably occurs when one lives together with a *real* human being, the bride may become oppressed with the new burden she has taken on. Other women ease into the role of motherhood and gradually become accustomed to its frustrations. Having it thrust upon her cannot but produce feelings of being trapped and overwhelmed. Disillusioned and frustrated, such a stepmother becomes resentful and will focus her resentment on the children, whom she will consider the basic cause of her difficulties. Even in situations in which the children live with their mother and visit on weekends, the stepmother is likely to grow resentful. Instead of spending time alone on weekends with her husband, he is either off with his children or they're underfoot in the house. And such anger toward the children is inevitably sensed by them and results in a further deterioration of the relationship between them and their stepmother.

Disciplining the stepchildren often presents special problems for a stepparent. A stepmother may be hesitant to be as firm with her stepchildren as she otherwise might be—lest she alienate her husband. If she has children of her own who are in the home, they will immediately recognize the preferential status being granted their stepsiblings and will become resentful both of their mother and the "privileged characters." Such a woman is doing her husband no favors. By leaving the heavy disciplining to him, he becomes the "bad-guy" and she the "good-guy"—reputations that cannot but interfere with the children's developing healthy relationships with both her and her husband. A stepfather, also, may get sucked into a stepchild's ploy: "You can't punish me; you're not my real father." Stepparents should be advised that the best thing they can do for their children and themselves is to utilize the same disciplinary measures that they ordinarily would use with their own children. Children want and need proper and humane discipline—their protestations to the contrary notwithstanding. There is nothing in the relationship between stepparent and stepchild that warrants the children's being deprived of healthy guidance and discipline.

Because a stepparent is not the natural parent there is a danger that he or she will be less committed to the child's upbringing. In such a setting, for example, the child may be deprived of the parental reinforcement of educational pursuits that plays such an important role in the child's motivation in school. On the positive side, the stepparent is less likely to have the exaggerated commitment to the child's growth and development that can impair him in other ways.

Mention has been made of a stepparent's hesitation to properly discipline his or her stepchildren and the intensification of sibling rivalry that can result from this practice. A stepparent's hostility toward the stepchildren can be transmitted to his or her natural children and this can significantly increase sibling rivalry problems. At times, a stepparent may use the natural children to act out the hostility felt toward the stepchildren. This can be accomplished, for example, by not appropriately disciplining the natural children when they bully the stepchildren. The natural children appreciate the parental sanction for their scapegoating—even though never verbalized.

A common problem is the question of what a child should call a stepparent. First, it is important to help stepparents appreciate that it is the basic relationship between the stepparent and stepchild that is important, not the names they use to address one another. Also, they should be dissuaded from trying to force the child to use a name that he is not comfortable with. Often this is done to provide an appearance of intimacy and closeness for a relationship that may be somewhat deficient. Such coercion only makes the relationship worse.

The child's using terms like *Mom* or *Dad* can be confusing in that one may not know whether the child is referring to the natural parent or to the stepparent. In addition, if the natural parent has anything approaching a healthy relationship with the child, he or she will generally object to the child's using these terms with the stepparent. And the child himself will generally feel some disloyalty when doing so. As mentioned, the special relationship that most often exists between a child and a natural parent cannot so easily be formed with a stepparent. The use of the terms *Mom* and *Dad*, then, is often contrived and thereby to be avoided. When, however, the child's relationship with the natural parent is either very bad or nonexistent, and if he has the genuine desire to use these terms with the stepparent, then I can see no objection to their being used. In the more common situation, where the child still has a meaningful relationship with the natural parent, many children will use some combination of *Mom, Ma, Dad,* or *Pa* and the stepparent's first name. Others will just address the stepparent by his or her first name. Some stepparents are comfortable with this, others not. Just as the stepparents should respect the child's wishes regarding which terms he wishes to use when addressing them, the child should respect theirs as well.

Child therapists are occasionally consulted on questions related to adoption. A natural father, for example, may ask if he should give his daughter up for adoption by the stepfather. He may claim that he still loves his child and wants to maintain a good relationship with her, but she feels awkward in school and with peers because she has a last name different from that of her half-siblings, mother, and stepfather. If such a father's claim of deep involvement proves to be specious and he is using the child's request as an excuse to give the responsibilities of his daughter's upbringing over to her stepfather, then I would generally suggest that the adoption process proceed. However, if the father's claims are valid and he wishes to remain the legal father but is considering giving up his daughter because he believes that it may be in her best interests to do so, I generally dissuade him from allowing her to be adopted by the stepfather. In such a case it is likely that the adoption will be psychologically traumatic to the child and the benefits of having the same last name as others in her household will be outweighed by the rejection implicit in the adoption.

There is, however, a compromise that can be recommended in this situation that is most often workable, namely, that the child use the last name of the stepfather but legally retain the last name of the natural father. Most schools, in my experience, will go along with a parent's request for this.

When the youngster grows older he or she can then decide which last name to use. Switching back to the legal name becomes easier then, because the youngster is no longer so deeply identified with the family. Or he or she can then legally change the last name to that of the stepfather—without having to be legally adopted by him.

Another question concerning adoption is occasionally asked of the therapist. A boy, for example, is totally abandoned by his natural mother in infancy. The natural father soon remarries, the stepmother adopts the infant, and he is brought up with no distinction made between him and his stepsiblings. Having no memory of her, and still having no contact with her, the only mother he knows is his stepmother. The question asked is whether this boy should be told the truth about his natural mother. My inclination is to answer yes. My main reason for saying this is that should the child ever learn his true origins he cannot but be resentful of his father and stepmother for having withheld such important information. And the shock of such a disclosure could result in lifelong distrust of them. The argument that the boy will probably never find out is not convincing. In such a situation there are usually dozens of people who know the story and the likelihood is greater that either they or their children, by design or error, will divulge the truth. It is almost impossible to rely on dozens of people to maintain a conspiracy of silence. If one could be one hundred percent certain that the child would never find out, then I might agree that no good purpose would be served by the child's knowing. Since this is rarely if ever the case, the child, in my opinion, should be told. And I would tell the child when he is first able to appreciate such things—generally between three and five years of age. This is the same period in which children adopted in the more traditional fashion should be told of their origins.

As is obvious, the stepparent-stepchild relationship has many things working against its success that are intrinsic to the new family situation. However, if these difficulties can be avoided or overcome (and they can in many cases) the child is likely to derive many benefits from the new relationship. Most important, the presence of a stepparent provides the child with a "second chance" to either live in or experience an intact home. And it is the absence of such a home that is at the root of many of the problems that children of divorce develop.

Grandparents

Just as in-laws can play a significant role in a couple's decision to marry, they can also contribute to a couple's marital difficulties, and even be one of the causes of the divorce. A wife may complain, for example, that her husband is still a child in his relationship with his parents. A husband may displace onto his in-laws hostilities that he harbors toward his own parents—thereby causing a loyalty conflict in his wife that may play a significant role in their marital difficulties. Often in-laws feel their son- or daughter-in-law as a disappointment because he or she does not live up to the image they had of what their son- or daughter-in-law would be like. And their son or daughter's involvement with his or her spouse may be reduced in response to such parental attitudes. Each set of in-laws may side with their own son or daughter, thereby intensifying marital difficulties. And in-laws may play a significant role in helping a son or daughter decide either to dissolve or maintain an unhappy marriage.

When a family is intact, it is quite common for the two sets of grandparents to compete with one another for the affection of the grandchildren. When this is kept within reasonable bounds, the children may benefit because it can provide them with much affection and a deep sense of family belonging. When, however, the children are subjected to questions as to which grandparents they like best or are asked to take sides in any conflicts that may be present, then, of course, such "affection" is significantly diluted. When divorce occurs the grandparents may take sides as well—thereby polarizing the grandchildren's parents even more and contributing to the multiple problems that beset children who are placed in the middle of such conflicts. If the grandparents can rise above the feuding of their children, both they and their grandchildren can enjoy the benefits of their continued good relationship.

A divorced mother with children may return to live with her parents. Often financial considerations make this a reasonable and possibly the best decision. If the mother has to work, it is often better for the children to be taken care of by their grandparents who, as familiar figures, may make excellent parental surrogates (especially in the case of the grandfather as a substitute for the absent father). In addition, grandparents usually love the children more deeply than would a housekeeper. However, there are a number of drawbacks to such an arrangement that parents should be apprised of before making such a decision. Although the grandparents can enjoy an unadulterated and joyful relationship with their grandchildren when they visit on Sundays, living with the children is an entirely different story. It is easy to be overwhelmed by the grandchildren's cuteness, brightness, cleverness, etc. when one doesn't have to change the diapers, get up in the middle of the night, break up sibling bickering, etc. When the kids move in, the joys of grandparenthood soon diminish. In addition, the grandparents have got to be somewhat resentful of the new obligations that they now have to assume. They've been through the whole child rearing bit; and they've looked forward to a little more relaxation in their old age. Now they suddenly find themselves having to go through the whole scene again. And such resentment can contribute to dissension between the grandparents and their daughter and can be displaced onto the children. Or the unhappiness the mother feels in such a situation may make her less loving as a mother to the children.

Another problem that may arise in such a situation relates to the mother's dependency on her parents. A more mature mother is likely to be willing to suffer many deprivations and inconveniences rather than move back with her parents. A more dependent and immature mother may more readily choose the alternative of living once again with her parents. In the latter situation the children will soon appreciate that their mother is really still a child in her relationship with her parents. Their respect for her will thereby be diminished as will their confidence in her as a protector and source of guidance. They may look then to their grandparents as their true sources of strength—a situation that is quite detrimental to their relationship with their mother. Sugar (1970) points out how the children in such a situation may consider themselves to have suffered two losses: 1) their father from the household and 2) their mother to their grandparents.

Another potential source of difficulty in such an arrangement is that the mother and grandmother may become quite competitive with one another over who "knows best" how to take care of the children. The children may then be subjected to very different schools of thought regarding their upbringing and can become quite confused and divided in their loyalties. Or the grandmother may be quite ambivalent about disciplining the children, considering this to be the role of their mother. Part of her motivation for taking this position may be to avoid their having any reason for being angry at her. In this way she enjoys the reputation of the all-loving, all-giving good grandma and her daughter is looked upon as the family witch—again, not a situation conducive to the children's having a good healthy relationship with their mother, or their grandmother.

At times many, if not all, of these potential drawbacks to the mother's returning to the home of her parents may not exist and the children may derive deep gratifications from the arrangement. It is important for the reader to appreciate (if he hasn't already) that much of what I have said about mothers who return to the homes of their parents is only applicable to Western culture in the last hundred or two hundred years. Previously, and in many parts of the world today, people could not enjoy the luxury of separate homes, or even rooms, for each new married couple, and extended families were the rule. Divorce or abandonment by a parent in such an arrangement was probably far less traumatic than it is for a child in twentieth century Western culture. In the extended family arrangement the child has many familiar surrogates —people with whom he has lived all his life—who can take over the parental role. And grandparents today have the potential to provide the child with similar satisfactions. People are living longer than they ever have and elderly people find themselves ever more useless in a society that is not basically designed to utilize optimally their talents, skills, and experience. For many grandparents the presence of the grandchildren in their home can provide them with a "new lease on life," and a new sense of meaning to their existence.

Lastly, I generally try to impress upon separated parents that they do their children a terrible disservice by drawing their grandparents into their conflict or by allowing them to polarize them further. Ideally, parents should be able to see the grandparents as important sources of emotional gratification for their children and as people who, possibly more than anyone else, have the interest and capacity to provide their children with love and affection—the latter being the most effective preventive of and antidote to the untoward psychological effects of the divorce.

Alternate Life Styles

I believe that the recent trend toward greater social acceptability for divorced parents is healthy both for themselves and for their children. Such parents and their children have enough trouble already; they do not need the additional, unnecessary burden of being looked upon as freaks and made social outcasts. Gettleman and Markowitz (1974) provide many examples of how prejudices against the divorced (sometimes overt, often subtle) are deeply entrenched in mental health practice, the courts, the churches, and the mass media. In an attempt to counteract some of these unfortunate biases, some have gone to the opposite extreme and extolled single parenthood as being superior to the married type. I believe that this notion substitutes one form of pathological thinking for another. I believe that monogamous marriage—all its restrictions, frustrations, and difficulties notwithstanding—is the best arrangement for a child's healthy psychological development. A child, regardless of sex, needs intimate involvement with a mother *and* a father. It behooves the single parent to do everything possible to provide his or her children with substitutes for the absent parent. The parent who claims that he or she can be both "mother and father" is dealing in self-delusion. I am deeply sympathetic with the woman who, advancing in years and seeing little prospect of getting married, decides to have a child out of wedlock. However, if she believes that her children will do just as well without a father figure, she is, in my opinion, deluding herself. Such a woman does well to actively involve her children with father surrogates as much as possible.

Divorced people, having already been "burned," are often (but unfortunately, not always) more circumspect with regard to marrying again. Recently, many more are living together on a trial basis in order to be sure that they are "right" for each other. I believe that the increasing social acceptance of this practice is healthy, in that it helps people avoid disastrous remarriages. One problem that often concerns such people is the effect of such a relationship on the children. They are often particularly worried about criticisms their children may be exposed to from peers. Sometimes such parents will advise their children to tell others that they are married or they instruct them to avoid answering questions about the nature of the relationship between the two adults living in the house.

I believe that the most important factor in protecting children from any detrimental effects of such a relationship is the parents' conviction that what they are doing is right for them and ultimately in the best interests of their children. If they are not ashamed of what they are doing, then it is less likely that their children will be. But if they try to hide the fact, and even worse, if they try to use their children as allies in the various cover-up maneuvers, they are likely to increase their children's shame and provide them with additional and unnecessary psychological conflicts. The best they can do is to take an attitude as matter-of-fact as possible and to help their children view as idiosyncratic anyone who criticizes them for what their parents are doing. The parents should be advised, as well, to impress upon the children the fact that the most important thing that will ultimately determine their friendships will be their own behavior, not that of their parents. If they are friendly, considerate of others, and enjoyable to be with, they are most likely to have friends —regardless of the exact marital status of their parents. Lastly, I wish to emphasize that I do not believe that one or even two such arrangements need cause a child psychological difficulties, oedipal or otherwise. However, if there are a series of such relationships, then, I believe, the child is likely to develop untoward psychological reactions. Then oedipal difficulties (as described in Chapter 12) are likely to develop, as well as others that stem from the child's rising expectations and disillusionments and the unpredictability of the situation.

In recent years many married men (and to a lesser extent, women), who are bisexual and/or homosexual, have "come out of the closet," announced their homosexuality, and divorced in order no longer to live in what they consider a sham and hypocritical arrangement. Many problems may arise for the children of these parents, especially when such a parent encourages (either overtly or covertly) the child's attaining a homosexual orientation or when such a parent involves himself and the children actively in meeting and socializing with homosexual people (though not commonly with overt sexual exposure). In Chapters 12 and 14 I discuss these problems in greater detail and include therein the advice I would impart to parents in such situations.

Many more types of intermediate situation are now becoming prevalent. Regardless of whether or not the parents have a divorce decree, many people still maintain various kinds of contacts and involvements with former spouses. Some will spend two or three days a week with the family and live elsewhere the rest of the week. Some children live in the father's house half the time and in the mother's the other half; this is best done when both homes are in the same school district so that there is little disruption of schooling. I know of a situation in which the family owns a three-story town house. The father lives on the top level, the children on the middle, and the mother on the lower. The parents are divorced and the children have free access to both parents. The parents do not appear to mind (so they say) each other's dating. Future experience and research will enable us to ascertain the effects of these and other alternative arrangements on the psychological lives of the children involved.

Chapter 14

THE THERAPIST
AND CHILD CUSTODY
LITIGATION

Historical Considerations

In this chapter I discuss the adversary system, especially as it applies to divorce/custody conflicts. I trace the history of the system as it has been applied at various times to the resolution of divorce/custody conflicts and describe how changing attitudes regarding parental preference have played an important role in the judiciary's position regarding which parent would be the preferable one for raising the children. With such background the reader will be in a better position to understand where we are today and what are the desirable directions for the future.

The Adversary System

Determining whether or not a person accused of committing a criminal act is guilty or innocent is a problem that has confounded mankind since the dawn of civilization. Finding successful methods of determination is crucial for the survival of civilized societies. Many methods have been devised to assist those involved in making such important determinations. Criteria that have been utilized have not always been the most humane and judicious. Historically, people on a lower level of the social hierarchy were more likely to have been presumed guilty (and this situation, unfortunately, still prevails today). In fact, people of noble rank have often been considered immune from procedures designed to determine whether or not an accused is guilty or innocent. Commonly the decision was made by the ruler of the group, often unilaterally. The use of torture as a method of extracting confessions is an ancient tradition that, unfortunately, is still used in parts of the world today. Signs from the heavens, the association of the crime with certain natural events, and a wide variety of magical and preposterous tests have been utilized.

One system that has evolved in Western society has been the adversary system. This involves both the accuser and the accused presenting to a presumably impartial third party (or group) the arguments that support each one's position. The group may be a judge, a tribunal, or a jury. Each side is allowed to withhold, to a reasonable degree, that information which would weaken its position if divulged, and each is encouraged to present in full detail that information which supports its contention. Out of this conflict of presentations the impartial party(ies) is allegedly in the best position to determine who is telling the "truth." No one claims that the adversary system is perfect; but its proponents hold that it is the best we have and that the likelihood of the accused being treated fairly is greater with the adversary system than with any other system yet devised. I am not convinced that this is the case. I am certainly not convinced that it is the best system for determining who is a better parent, and I am not even convinced that it is the best system to determine whether or not an accused individual has indeed committed a crime. I will have more to say about these issues subsequently.

The Adversary System as Applied
to Divorce/Custody Litigation

Until recently (the 1960s and 1970s, in the United States), the adversary system was the main one utilized in divorce cases. This was consistent with the concept that the kinds of indignities complained of in divorce conflicts were minor crimes called *torts* (Latin: wrongs). Once viewed as crimes, divorce conflicts were justifiably considered in the context of adversary proceedings. Divorce laws in most states were predicated on concepts of guilt and innocence, that is, within the context of punishment and restitution. The divorce was granted only when the complainant or petitioner proved that he or she had been wronged or injured by the defendant or respondent. In most states the acceptable grounds for divorce were very narrowly defined and, depending upon the state, included such behavior as mental cruelty, adultery, abandonment, habitual drunkenness, nonsupport, and drug addiction. The law would punish the offending party by granting the divorce to the successful complainant.

If the court found that both the husband and the wife were guilty of marital wrongs, a divorce was not granted. If *both* parties, for instance, had involved themselves in adulterous behavior, they could not get a divorce. Therefore, in such situations, the parties often agreed to alter the truth in a way that would result in their obtaining a divorce. Often this would require one party to take public blame — court records in such cases are usually public. Frequently one party would agree to be the adultress or the adulterer, or the one who had inflicted mental cruelty on the other. "Witnesses" were brought in (usually friends who were willing to lie in court) to testify in support of the various allegations, and everyone agreed to go through the little theatrical performance. Even the judge knew that the play was necessary to perform if he was to have grounds to grant the divorce. All appreciated the cooperation of the witnesses, and there was practically no danger of their being prosecuted for their perjury. Although such proceedings rarely made headlines in the newspapers, the records were available for public scrutiny and distribution. The knowledge of this possibility became an additional burden to the person who, because of the greater desire for the divorce, was willing to be considered guilty, while allowing the spouse to be considered innocent. In addition, there were possible untoward psychological sequelae resulting from the acceptance of the blame, and this could contribute to residual problems following the divorce.

In recent years there has been greater appreciation by state legislatures of the fact that the traditional grounds for divorce are not simply wrongs perpetrated by one party against the other, but that both parties have usually contributed to the marital breakdown. In addition, the kinds of behavior complained of by the petitioner came to be viewed less as crimes and more as personality differences, aberrations, and/or psychopathology.

With such realizations came the appreciation that adversary proceedings were not well suited to deal with such conflicts. Accordingly, an ever-growing number of states have changed their laws regarding the grounds for divorce and the ways in which people can dissolve their marriages. These new statutes are generally referred to as *no fault divorce laws*. They provide much more liberal criteria for the granting of a divorce. For example, if both parties agree to the divorce their living apart for a prescribed period may be all that is necessary. (And the period may be shorter if no children are involved.) One does not have the problem of designating a guilty and an innocent party. Some states will grant a divorce on the basis of "incompatibility." The term may not be defined any further, and it may be quite easy for the couple to demonstrate that they are incompatible. The latest phase of such liberalization enables some individuals to divorce entirely without legal assistance. In California, a state that has often been at the forefront of such liberalization, a couple can now obtain a divorce via mail and the payment of a small fee, if they have no children and there is no conflict over property.

The passage of no-fault divorce laws has been, without question, a significant step forward. By removing it from adversary proceedings, divorce is more readily, less traumatically, and usually less expensively obtained. However, many no-fault divorce laws require the agreement of *both* parties to satisfy the new liberal criteria. Divorce can rarely be obtained unilaterally. If one party does not agree, then adversary proceedings are necessary if the person desiring the divorce is to have any hope of getting it. In addition, the new laws have not altered the necessity of resorting to adversary proceedings when there is conflict over such issues as visitation, support, alimony, and custody. Although no-fault divorce laws have reduced considerably the frequency of courtroom conflicts over divorce, litigation over custody is not only very much with us, but for reasons to be described soon, is on the increase. And the adversary system — a system designed to determine whether an accused individual has committed a criminal act — is being used to determine which of two parents would better serve as custodian for their children.

The Basic Ways in Which Protracted Custody Litigation Cause Psychiatric Disturbances

Custody litigation is one of the more severe forms of psychological stress. Its potential for causing psychiatric disturbance is quite high. And prolonged custody litigation is even more likely to cause such disorders in both parents and children. When psychological disturbance was not previously present, litigation will predictably result in the development of such. When psychological disorder has already been present (often the case for parents who choose to litigate), litigation will invariably bring about an intensification of symptoms. Most therapists whose patients have been involved in such litigation have observed such deterioration. I, personally, have seen people embroiled in such conflicts develop neurotic and even psychotic symptomatology — symptoms that I considered to be the direct result of the stresses of their divorce litigation. I have seen suicide attempts, alcohol and drug abuse, psychotic breaks, and heart attacks which I considered directly attributable to the psychological trauma of protracted divorce and/or custody litigation.

Adversary litigation, especially when protracted, is predictably going to produce a variety of mental and emotional reactions that will be quite strong and, in some cases, they will become chronic. The anger, frustration, sense of impotence, fears, and a variety of other thoughts and feelings that arise in this situation are likely to result in the development of a variety of psychological symptoms. When I use the term *psychological symptoms,* I refer to maladaptive and inappropriate ways of dealing with the problems of life with which we are all confronted. Healthy human beings utilize judicious solutions to these problems. A person with psychiatric disturbance uses maladaptive and inappropriate ways of dealing with life's problems. The strong thoughts and feelings that are generated in the course of protracted litigation are likely to result in an individual using injudicious and inappropriate solutions to problems, both related and unrelated to the litigation. Although the symptomatic solution may appear initially to be the most efficacious, it generally results in more trouble rather than less for the patient. What we refer to as psychodynamics are basically the pathways and processes by which these misguided solutions produce symptoms. In short, there are three steps in the process: (1) the basic problems of life, (2) the maladaptive and inappropriate solutions (generally referred to as the psychodynamics), and (3) the symptoms. First I will focus on the specific ways in which protracted custody litigation causes people to use maladaptive solutions to life's problems—both related and unrelated to the litigation. In the subsequent two sections I will discuss how these maladaptive solutions manifest themselves in psychiatric symptoms in parents and children.

Anger and Adversary Litigation

Anger has survival value in that it enhances our capacity to deal with irritations and dangers. We fight harder and more effectively when we are angry. Anger builds up when there is frustration and helplessness, and it is reduced when the irritants are removed. However, when the noxious stimulus remains, the anger persists as well and may even be increased—resulting in even stronger emotional reactions. When there is a prolonged sense of impotence over the failure to remove a noxious stimulus, rage results. The difference between rage and anger is that anger is generally rational, but in the state of rage irrational things are done in the service of removing the noxious stimulus. In mild irritation and anger one can still focus on the irritant and make reasonable attempts to remove it. However, with prolonged frustration and the rage that results, the anger reaction will not be coordinated and directed toward a specific goal. Rather, the reaction will be more chaotic and therefore less likely to be effective. Even when rage is effective in removing the irritant, there are untoward side effects after its utilization. There are still "pieces to be picked up." The term *fury* is sometimes used to describe a degree of rage that is so great that the inappropriate reaction reaches insane proportions. In rage, the reaction, although inappropriate, would still not generally be considered crazy. In the state of fury, one may even commit murder, so deranging is the rage. Protracted litigation is likely to turn frustration into irritation, irritation into anger, anger into rage, and rage into fury.

People involved in custody litigation are fighting. They are fighting for their most treasured possessions—their children. The stakes are extremely high. Litigation over money, property, and other matters associated with the divorce produce strong feelings of resentment and anger. However, they are less likely to result in reactions of rage and fury than are conflicts over the children. Children are the extensions of ourselves, our hopes for the future, and thereby closely tied up with our own identities. Fighting for them is almost like fighting for ourselves. The two may become indistinguishable, and the fight becomes a "fight for life."

The adversary system, which professes to help parents resolve their differences, is likely to intensify the hostilities that it claims it is designed to reduce. It provides the litigants with ammunition that they may not have realized they possessed. It contributes to an ever-increasing vicious cycle of vengeance—so much so that the litigation may bring about greater psychological damage than the pains and grief of the marriage that originally brought about the divorce. Although some attorneys are genuinely appreciative of the vicious effects of protracted litigation and recognize the terrible psychological trauma that may result from adversary proceedings, other attorneys are not. For the latter, the name of the game is to "win." They believe their reputations rest on their capacity to win and they fear that if they appear to be moderate and conciliatory they will lose clients. Lawyers recognize that the more protracted the litigation the more money they are going to earn. In addition, they may lose perspective once they are swept up in battle, so intent are they on "winning." Weiss (1975) states the problem well:

It is possible for lawyers to negotiate too hard. In pursuit of the best possible agreement for their clients, some lawyers seem to worsen the post-marital relationship of their clients and the clients' spouses. They may, for example, actively discourage a client from talking with his or her spouse for fear that the client will inadvertently weaken his or her negotiating position, or will in thoughtless generosity make concessions without obtaining anything in return. Or they may take positions more extreme than their client desires in order eventually to achieve an advantageous compromise, but by so doing anger the client's spouse and further alienate the spouse from the client. Some separated individuals reported that until negotiations were at an end, their relationship with their spouse became progressively worse.

Gettelman and Markowitz (1974) provide a good example of the problem:

For many divorcing couples, their biggest headaches begin after they retain their respective attorneys. Recently we talked with the ex-wife of a famous and wealthy stage actor. It had taken her three years to obtain a divorce in California, which is one of the more progressive states! In her words, "Once the lawyers smelled money, they acted in cahoots to bleed us and draw out the proceedings." Although their separation had started out amicably, they grew to loathe each other; she believed that both his lawyers and her own successfully manipulated her and her husband into feeling victimized by each other.

Nizer, in his book *My Life in Court* (1968), states: "All litigations evoke intense feelings of animosity, revenge and retribution. Some of them may be fought ruthlessly. But none of them, even in their most aggravated form, can equal the sheer, unadulterated venom of a matrimonial contest." I would add to this the following sentence: "And of all the forms of marital litigation, the most vicious and venomous by far is custody litigation!" The stakes are higher than in any other form of courtroom conflict in that here the parents' most treasured possessions—the children—are at stake. Conflicts over money and property pale in comparison to the ruthlessness with which parents will fight over the children.

Sopkin (1974) describes in dramatic terms how sordid and sadistic such litigation can be. He focuses particularly on the role of attorneys in intensifying and prolonging such conflicts. In his article "The Roughest Divorce Lawyers in Town" (although the "town" referred to by Sopkin is New York City, the legal techniques described are ubiquitous and by no means confined to that city), he describes a brand of attorney often referred to in the field as a "bomber." Sopkin quotes one such bomber (Raoul Lionel Felder, a New York City divorce attorney) as saying: "If it comes to a fight, it is the lawyer's function using all ethical, legal and moral means to bring his adversary to his knees as fast as possible. Naturally, within this framework the lawyer must go for the "soft spots." The kinds of antics that such lawyers utilize and promulgate are indeed hair-raising. One husband is advised to hire a gigolo to seduce his wife into a setting where a band of private detectives are engaged to serve as witnesses. Another husband is advised to get his English-born wife deported because she is not yet a citizen.

Elsewhere Sopkin states: "Getting a lawyer out of his office is expensive, but to crank up a bomber, pump him full of righteous indignation, and ship him down to the matrimonial courts can be terribly expensive — running from fifteen, twenty, or twenty-five thousand dollars. . . . Bombers are in business to accommodate hate. . . . But the incontrovertible fact remains that if there is big-time money at stake, or serious custody questions at stake, or you want to leave your husband/wife with nothing but a little scorched earth, get a bomber." Although Sopkin's examples are not typical, they are not rare either. In litigation "winning" is the name of the game. The lawyer with the reputation for being "a softie" is not going to have many clients. Although more human and less pugilistic attorneys certainly exist, even their "fighting instincts" often come to the fore when they are caught up in adversary proceedings. Although the more sensitive may even then not be willing to stoop to the levels of the bombers, they still are likely to utilize all kinds of deceptive maneuvers to "win" for their clients.

The criticisms of the adversary system as applied to divorce and custody proceedings come not only from mental health professionals, but from some lawyers and judges as well. One attorney, Glieberman, in his book *Confessions of a Divorce Lawyer* (1975) states:

> I made sure that each client I handled — whatever else he or she thought about me — came away feeling two things. One, I was thorough as hell. Two, I was out to win. Frankly the second was easy. I love to argue and win. . . .
>
> If a divorce was what someone wanted then my client and I became a team, did everything in our power, not just to win but to win big. . . .
>
> There's only one rule on divorce settlements: If you represent the wife, get as much as possible. If you represent the husband, give away as little as possible. . . .
>
> Now, as I walk through the outer door of my office heading for the courtroom, I know that I'm walking to a case where there will be no compromises, no conciliations, no good feelings to balance the bad. This will be an all-out confrontation, a real tooth and nail fight. I'll love it. . . .
>
> Now finally we're here. And it's a real circus. The other side has two accountants, a tax lawyer, three expert witnesses and a defendant; our side has one accountant, a comptroller, no tax lawyer because I've become an expert at that, and seven expert witnesses.

A judge, Forer (1975), criticizes the legal profession's own Code of Professional Responsibility — a criticism which is most relevant to divorce and custody litigation:

A lawyer is licensed by the government and is under a sworn duty to uphold and defend the law and the Constitution of the United States. Despite the license and the oath, the role of the lawyer is by definition and by law amoral. . . . He must press the position of his client even though it is contrary to the public good, popular opinion and widely accepted standards of behavior. Canon 7 of the Code of Professional Responsibility promulgated by the American Bar Association declares in part, "The duty of a lawyer, both to his client and to the legal system is to represent his client zealously within the bounds of the law." In other words, the skilled judgment of the lawyer that his client's case is spurious or without merit is irrelevant. The lawyer must, therefore, be a Hessian, a mercenary, available for hire to do the bidding of whoever pays him. . . . If the client wishes to sue or contest a claim, the lawyer must either zealously pursue his client's interest or withdraw from the case. If Lawyer A withdraws, Lawyer B will accept the case and the fee.

Another judge, Lindsley (1980), is critical of the utilization of the adversary system in custody disputes. He states:

The adversary process, historically effective in resolving disputes between litigants over contracts, torts, business matters, and criminal charges, where objective evidentiary facts have probative significance, is not suited to the resolution of most relations problems. In family disputes, the evidence that we would find most meaningful is more likely to consist of subtle, subjective, human relations factors best identified and discerned by psychologists and behaviorists who do not approach the inquiry as antagonists. When you add the concept of "fault" as the necessary basis for deciding questions relating to the family, *I think it is fair to say that no other process is more likely to rip husband, wife, father, mother, and child apart so thoroughly and bitterly* (italics mine).

A highly respected judge who has concerned himself deeply with mental health issues, Bazelon (1974), holds that the adversary system is not necessarily detrimental to clients. Its ultimate aim, he states, is to gain knowledge and resolve differences. It attempts to resolve differences through the opposition of opposing positions. Its ultimate aim is resolution, and the cross-examination process is one of the important ways in which information is gained. I am in agreement with Bazelon regarding the methods and aims of the adversary system. I am not, however, in agreement with his statement regarding the risk of detriment to clients. His statement that the adversary system is "not necessarily" detrimental implies little risk for the development of psychopathology. My experience has been that in divorce and especially custody cases the risk for the development of psychopathology is extremely high. Bazelon's position is idealistic in that he does not make reference to the sly tricks, duplicity, courtroom antics, and sneaky maneuvers that lawyers will often utilize in order to win. He makes no mention of attorneys' attempts to unreasonably discredit the experts, cast aspersions on their characters, and try to make them look silly or stupid.

Although Judge Bazelon's view is that of the majority of jurists today, there are dissenters among the judiciary. One of the most outspoken critics of the use of the adversary system in solving custody disputes is Judge Byron F. Lindsley who states (1976):

> The adversary process, historically effective in resolving disputes between litigants where evidentiary facts have probative significance, is not properly suited to the resolution of most family relations problems. . . . Where there are children and the parties cannot or will not recognize the impact of the disintegration of the marriage upon the children, where they fail to perceive their primary responsibilities as parents—i.e., custody and visitation—we make it possible for parents to carry out that struggle by the old, adversary, fault-finding, condemnation approach. . . . This kind of battle is destructive to the welfare, best interests, and emotional health of their children.

I fully appreciate that many attorneys begin their involvement with divorcing litigants by attempting to calm them down and bring about some compromises in their demands. However, when such efforts fail, many get swept up in the conflict and join their clients in trying to win the battle and punish the spouse. (And taking the children away is one predictable way of implementing such punishment.) The training of lawyers primes them for such encounters. Therapists, because of their orientation toward understanding and reducing hostility, are less likely to rise so quickly to a patient's cry for battle and lust for vengeance. Accordingly, lawyers are often criticized for inflaming their clients, adding to their hostility, and thereby worsening divorcing spouses' difficulties. A common retort to this criticism is: "We're only doing what our clients ask us to do." Such lawyers claim that they are just the innocent tools of their clients and that their obligation is to respond to their clients' wishes even though such advocacy may be detrimental to the client, the spouse, and the children.

I believe that this response is a rationalization. I believe that lawyers have greater freedom to disengage themselves from a client's destructive behavior than they profess. I believe that financial considerations often contribute to their going along with the client. (I fully recognize that there are physicians, as well, who recommend unnecessary medical treatment. For both professions the practice is unconscionable.) There are attorneys who discourage their clients from litigating in court with the professed reason that it may be psychologically damaging. This may only be a coverup. In actuality they appreciate that they may reduce their income per hour if they go to court — because only the wealthiest clients can afford the formidable expense of protracted courtroom litigation. To the wealthy client, the latter consideration does not often serve as a deterrent for the lawyer, and the psychological considerations are then often ignored.

There are many couples who, at the time of the separation, make a serious attempt to avoid psychologically debilitating litigation. Having observed the deterioration of friends and relatives who have undergone prolonged litigation, they genuinely want to make every attempt to avoid such unnecessary and traumatic sequelae to their divorce. Unfortunately, many such well-meaning couples, in spite of every attempt to avoid such a catastrophe, gradually descend into the same kind of psychologically devastating experience. An important contributing element to such unfortunate deterioration relates to the anger and rage engendered by their having involved themselves in protracted adversary proceedings. The system fosters sadism. The aim of simply *winning* often degenerates into one in which each side is bent on depleting the other of funds, producing psychological deterioration, or even destroying the other party. The result, however, is most often a Pyrrhic victory in which both sides lose, even though one may ostensibly be the winner.

The expression of anger tends to feed on itself. The notion that anger merely needs to be dissipated and then the individual is free from it is probably an oversimplification. The fact that some expression of anger is necessary and that its release can produce some feeling of catharsis is certainly the case. However, it appears that another phenomenon may also be operative, especially when anger is great. Here the expression of anger does not result in its dissipation but rather in its intensification. When a person starts to "roll" with anger, more anger may be generated. It appears to have an existence of its own. An extreme example of this is the murderer who stabs the victim to death with a knife thrust into the heart. Although the victim is now dead, the murderer continues to stab the victim repeatedly. Obviously, there are no further useful purposes for such anger release. In less dramatic ways individuals, once angry, tend to perpetuate the process. And protracted divorce litigation is an excellent demonstration of this phenomenon. The fight intensifies and rolls on for months and even years, having a life of its own, almost independent from the original issues that began the litigation in the first place.

A common result of parents being swept up in such litigation is that they blind themselves to the stupidity of what they are doing. A father, for example, may be so blinded by his rage that he fails to appreciate that he is giving far more money to his attorney (and possibly his wife's, in that he may be paying her lawyer as well) than he would have given to his wife had he agreed to her original request at the outset. The depletion of funds to his wife not only compromises her psychological stability but that of his children as well in that the more psychologically and/or financially debilitated she is the more impaired will be the children's upbringing. One mother, who lived in a large house with the children, made every attempt to increase her husband's bills as much as possible. She turned on the heating system to maximum capacity and, simultaneously, turned on every air conditioning unit in the house. And both systems would operate simultaneously, sometimes up to 24 hours a day. Every electrical outlet was used to maximum capacity at the same time, to the point where the house was blazing with light for weeks at a time, especially on vacations. All this was done with the knowledge and support of her lawyer! Every form of destructive act known to mankind has been perpetrated by one parent upon the other in the course of custody litigation—and even murder is not unknown (I myself had such a case recently).

Impotent Rage

Rage, when expressed, is certainly devastating. But released rage is probably less devastating to the individual than rage that cannot be expressed. The sense of inner turmoil, lowered self-worth, and impotence that results from unexpressed anger contributes significantly to the development of certain types of psychological disturbance. At every step in the separation-divorce process the client may suffer such reactions to bottled-up rage.

The returned and unreturned telephone calls. A lawyer is engaged who asks for a retainer that may represent the person's only savings. Already there is a loss of a sense of security as the money is turned over. From the outset there is commonly frustration. Telephone calls are unanswered. The lawyer's secretary informs the client that the attorney is not available at that time, the usual explanation being that he or she is "in conference" or "in court." And each time the client calls the same excuse is given. It almost appears that the attorney is never free to talk on the telephone, and this increases significantly the client's frustration. My experience has been that only a small percentage of attorneys actually return telephone calls. The client continues calling and the secretary keeps putting him or her off. And she is only doing her job, which is to protect the attorney from the barrage of frustrated and irate spouses. By this point the client wishes to discharge the attorney and seek the services of another. However, he or she is trapped. The attorney is not likely to release the retainer, or most of it, and there is no money left to engage the services of another lawyer. The impotent rage so generated contributes significantly to the development of psychiatric disorders.

Just one of the lawyer's hundred cases. The client may not be aware of the fact that the attorney may be handling simultaneously up to 150 cases. This number is not unusual for a highly sought-after divorce attorney. The author finds about ten cases his absolute maximum when serving as an impartial examiner in custody litigation. No human being can possibly do justice to many more at the same time. And when one talks about handling 100 or more divorce cases simultaneously one enters into the world of grandiose delusions. A common practice for attorneys in such situations is to let all communications pile up in the client's file and respond only to subpoenas, court dates, and other compelling communications.

The attorney's lack of conviction for the client's position. Another source of difficulty is the fact that attorneys are taught, as early as law school, that a good lawyer should be able to represent his or her client adequately even though there may be no commitment to the client's cause. Attorneys are taught that the client deserves representation and that the lawyer's personal feelings about the justification of the client's position should not, in many cases, be given serious consideration. It is naive on the part of the legal system to assume that lawyers who represent clients without conviction for their client's position are going to work as assiduously as the ones who have conviction for the client's cause. The client in such cases may come to recognize the lawyer's lack of involvement in the case. The attorney, who presents him- or herself as the client's advisor, protector, and advocate, may soon be viewed by the client as an enemy, so slipshod and feeble are the attorney's efforts. However, the clients are not in any position to extract themselves by that time. This too produces a sense of impotent rage.

In most law schools the students are required to involve themselves in "moot court" experiences in which they are assigned positions in a case. The assignment is generally made on a chance basis and has nothing to do with the student's own conviction on a particular matter. In fact, it is often considered preferable that the assignment be made in such a way that the student must argue in support of the position for which he or she has less conviction. On other occasions, the student may be asked to present arguments for both sides. I am in full agreement that such experiences can be educationally beneficial. We can learn from and become more flexible by being required to view a situation from the opposite vantage point. However, I believe that those attorneys are naive who hold that one can argue just as effectively without conviction as one can if one has bona fide commitment to the client's cause. Noncommitted attorneys are going to do a less effective job in most cases. Accordingly, their clients are coming into the courtroom in a weakened position. Most attorneys are not likely to turn away a client whose position they secretly do not support, and it would be very difficult for a parent to find one who is going to admit openly that he or she basically doesn't support the client's position. This is another reason for my recommending that parents, if they possibly can, avoid the adversary system in settling custody disputes.

Therapists, in contrast, generally work in accordance with the principle that if they have no conviction of what they are doing with their patients, the chances of success in the treatment are likely to be reduced. For example, if the therapist's feelings for a patient are not strong, if the relationship is not a good one, or if the therapist is not convinced that the patient's goals in therapy are valid, the likelihood for the patient's being helped is small. Without such conviction the therapy becomes boring and sterile—with little chance of anything constructive coming out of it.

I was once in a situation where I had good reason to believe that an attorney was basically not supporting his client, and that such lack of conviction contributed to his poor performance in the courtroom. In this particular case I was supportive of the mother's position and, although an impartial, I was treated as an advocate in the courtroom (the usual situation). Early in the trial the guardian *ad litem* (an attorney representing the children's interests) suggested that I, as the impartial, be invited into the courtroom to observe the testimony of a psychiatrist who had been brought in as an advocate for the father's side. The father's attorney agreed to this. I was a little surprised when I learned of this because I did not see what he had to gain by my having direct opportunity to observe his client's expert. I thought that there would be more to lose than gain for this attorney because it would be likely to provide me with more "ammunition" for the mother.

When the father's advocate expert testified, I took notes and, as was expected, observed the attorney providing him with ample time to elaborate on his various points. (This is standard procedure when questioning an expert who supports one's position.) When I took the stand, I was first questioned by the mother's attorney, the attorney whose position I supported. He, in turn, gave me great flexibility with regard to my opportunities for answering his questions. Then, the father's attorney began to question me. To my amazement, he allowed me to elaborate on points on which I disagreed with him. He persistently gave me this opportunity and I, of course, took advantage of it.

During a break in the proceedings, the judge asked the father's lawyer, "Why are you letting Gardner talk so much?" I believe this was an inappropriate statement for the judge to have made, but it confirms how atypical and seemingly inexplicable the father's attorney's examination of me was. The lawyer shrugged his shoulders, said nothing, and on my return to the stand continued to allow me great flexibility in my answers. I had every reason to believe that he was a bright man and "knew better." I had no doubt that he did not routinely proceed in this way. I believe that this attorney's apparently inexplicable behavior was most likely motivated by the desire (either conscious or unconscious) that his client, the father, *lose* custody because of his recognition that the mother was the preferable parent for these children at that time. He "went through the motions" of supporting his client, but did so in such a way that he basically helped the other side win the case.

An attorney, Watson (1969), encourages lawyers to refuse to support a client's attempt to gain custody when the attorney does not consider the client to be the preferable parent. The suggestion is made from ethical considerations and the recognition that the attorney doesn't do as well with the client for whose position he or she does not have conviction. This is a noble attitude on Watson's part. Unfortunately, far too few lawyers will subscribe to this advice and most succumb to the more practical consideration that if they do not support their client's position they will lose him or her and the attendant fee (which in divorce cases may not be inconsequential). Being represented by an attorney who is basically helping the other side produces feelings of rage. And being "locked in" with such an attorney inevitably produces even more rage. The problem may be compounded by the fact that the attorney may not even be aware of the fact that he or she is operating on an inefficient level because of his or her lack of conviction, and the client may not even appreciate the fact that he or she is being poorly represented. This lack of realization on the part of the client and/or attorney does not negate the net effect of the client's weakness in the litigation and the sense of helplessness and frustration such weakness engenders.

Calculated stalling and court delays. In custody litigation, as is true for many other forms of litigation, time is on the side of one of the parties. Stalling then becomes a practical advantage for that person. Most recognize that time is on the side of the parent with whom the children are residing, regardless of whether or not that parent would ultimately prove to be the preferable one. The ways in which the stalling can be accomplished are myriad. Telephone calls to the stalling attorney are unanswered. Letters are not answered. It may take months for a father's letter to get to the mother via the intermediary attorneys. Then the response may take a few months to be received. By this time not only have many distortions crept in but the original issue that brought about the letter in the first place has been surpassed hundreds of times over by many more immediate problems. And the cost of these letters (sometimes running to a few hundred dollars per letter) also produces a sense of impotence and anger. The side who gains by procrastination is ever providing reasons for delay such as sickness, vacations, and obligations that take priority. It is no surprise then that many cases may go on for years, increasing thereby the sense of impotent anger. When all is prepared for courtroom litigation and everything is in order, one may find a six-to-nine months' wait for the next available court date (a common situation). This only prolongs the agony and the sense of helplessness.

Courtroom frustration. And when the court date finally arrives, the client may recognize that his or her attorney is ill prepared. As mentioned, with one hundred cases or so it is not likely that the attorney has given more than the most superficial attention to the client's case. On a number of occasions I have observed directly attorneys ruffling through their notes while waiting for the judge to be seated. It was apparent that they knew very little about the case. And when the client who observes this is paying in the neighborhood of $150 to $200 an hour for the attorney's services (a not uncommon fee), the anger and impotence can be formidable.

On the witness stand, each side observes the other making statements — under oath — that the other party is convinced are lies. The structure of adversary proceedings is such that there is absolutely nothing that the observing spouse can say at that point. The listener must sit silently in the courtroom and squelch very strong impulses to scream out his or her thoughts and feelings. Each recognizes that the result would be the judge ordering immediate silence and even threatening to have the disrupting party removed (physically if necessary) from the courtroom. And if one attorney tries to bring out in subsequent examination that such-and-such was a blatant lie, one may still not be successful. There may be dozens of such issues; and the time that it takes to cover all of them would be impossibly long, and the expense to do so would be prohibitive. Accordingly, only a small fraction of all of each party's desired responses are ever brought to the attention of the judge. This too increases the clients' sense of impotent rage.

The capriciousness and common injudiciousness of the final decision. Last, when the case draws to a close, one has very little security that true justice may be done. If the client is poor, the judge may hear only an insignificant fraction of all the pertinent information. There are cases in which the total presentation of data to the judge may comprise about ten minutes. The judge's job is to churn out as many cases as possible. Obviously, under such circumstances, the likelihood of there being any relationship between what would be in the best interests of the children and what the judge decides is purely coincidental. If, however, the client is wealthy and can afford a trial of weeks in duration, there still may be little relationship between what the judge finally orders and what is in the children's best interests. The amount of information presented to the judge may be mind boggling; even the most brilliant judges with the most comprehensive memories could not possibly absorb and process effectively all the information. The adversary method of data presentation — one in which there is selective withholding of information that might compromise each side's position — is also likely to obfuscate. The system allows for nit-picking, digression into irrelevancies, and the belaboring of minor points. This too lessens the likelihood that a judicious decision may finally be made. Even after all this time and expense, the final ruling may be injudicious. And this may result in feelings of impotence and rage that go on for months — or years — after the decision has been made.

Communication Impairments

Many difficulties in life arise because of improper communication between parties. Although the adversary system presents itself as a time-honored method for obtaining "the truth," the system is structured to increase the likelihood of impaired communication, predictably causing unnecessary and additional distress to clients. We are all familiar with the childhood game called *Telephone* in which a message is whispered down a line of children, from one to the next. The fun of the game rests on the assumption that the message that originates with the first child is not likely to be the same one received by the youngster at the end of the line. The game is a good demonstration of the kind of problem that arises when two clients communicate only through their lawyers. Not only is there a significant time lag between the initiation of one parent's complaint and the final response, but the distortions that creep in along the way are inevitably a source of significant frustration.

The adversary system engenders poor communication in another way. People get the feeling that whatever they say, whether verbally or in written form, may be used against them. And so communication may be reduced to a standstill. Weiss (1975) quotes a divorcing parent:

> The lawyers got involved and we had that situation where we are told not to talk to each other and there was a lot of mistrust. And it got to be impossible. Like I was afraid anything I said would be used against me. Our communi-

cation just stopped completely. I said, "God, I just can't believe that it has come to this where we have known each other for ten years and we can't say anything at all to each other." There was so much bitterness and so much anger and so much mistrust.

The adversary system also encourages lying. The less ethical lawyers will directly encourage fabrications; but even the most ethical attorneys are known to overtly or covertly communicate to their clients that they do not wish to be given certain information. This is just another kind of duplicity and is no less reprehensible. A lie of omission is no less a lie than a lie of commission. Many in the legal profession do not appear to appreciate this obvious fact. As early as law school, students are taught to strictly withhold from disclosure to the court any information that might compromise their client's position. This teaches duplicity at the earliest level. Well-seasoned lawyers have become expert liars, so much so that they may not even appreciate that they have become living lies. And in the course of protracted litigation the client may be tutored in the same skills. The atmosphere of distrust that is created in the clients cannot but contribute to the development of psychiatric disturbance.

Some attorneys will strongly suspect that their client is indeed in the weaker position in custody litigation, but will in subtle ways encourage the client not to reveal compromising information because it may weaken his or her position. In short, these lawyers are encouraging their clients to lie to them (lies of omission rather than lies of commission). They will not ask questions that may place the client in the position of revealing information that may be detrimental to his or her claim. Or the attorney may overtly encourage the client not to disclose any information that might compromise his or her position—so that the lawyer will not be placed in an ethically conflictual situation. A kind of tacit agreement is made between the lawyer and the client that certain things will not be revealed. Such a conspiracy of silence may be necessary for the maintenance of the lawyer-client relationship. In this way the lawyer rationalizes that he or she is being ethical, avoids lying to the court, and cannot be considered to be encouraging perjury on the client's part or otherwise permitting a fraud to be perpetrated on the court. And not incidentally, such a conspiracy of silence may be necessary if the lawyer is to keep the client and the attendant fee.

The adversary system is based on the assumption that one of the best ways to learn the "truth" is to have each client present his or her position before an impartial body (generally a judge, jury, or tribunal). Lies of *commission* are illegal, but they are still common. Although perjury is a criminal offense, action against a parent who perjures him- or herself in a divorce case is rare. Lies of *omission,* however, are encouraged and built into the system. In fact, there are situations in which it is illegal to introduce certain evidence, so much so that its introduction might result in a mistrial. Although attorneys who are in strong support of the system do not consider it perfect, they consider it the best that we have. I am not in agreement. In fact, it is a source of amazement to me that at this relatively late date in the evolution of modern civilized society, this notion still prevails. I am astonished that its obvious deficiencies have not been fully appreciated. I do not believe that the adversary system is the best we have, either for criminal cases or divorce cases. In fact, it may be one of the worst we have, even for criminal cases, for which it was originally designed.

One of my reasons for making such a strong statement is that the system strictly prevents the accused and the accuser from direct confrontation with one another in the courtroom. It thereby deprives itself of a valuable source of information. If the accused had the opportunity to confront directly his or her accuser, it is far more likely that the questions posed would be on point and revealing. Filtered through attorneys and the restrictions of courtroom examination and cross examination, spontaneity and direct interchange are lost. Responses are prepared, often with weeks and even months intervening between the posing of the question and the response. I believe that there is nothing like an eyeball-to-eyeball confrontation for bringing out duplicity, fabrication, and distortions. The stuttering, flushing, tension, and slips of the tongue that are likely to occur under such circumstances can be important in revealing what "the truth" really is. No matter how brilliant the attorneys and the judges, no matter how encyclopedic their knowledge of the law, the fact remains that none of them were at the scene of the alleged crime or the event under consideration. The involved parties at least allege that they were, and in many cases they actually were at the scene. More than anyone else, they have detailed recollections of what really went on. If the events did not indeed occur, this is much more likely to be revealed under circumstances of direct discussion and confrontation between the parties. Admittedly, in some inflammatory situations the parties may have to be protected from one another and even separated physically. But occasional use of these preventive measures should not be a reason for abandoning this valuable source of information.

This holds true for divorce and custody conflict as well. The adversary system strictly prohibits such interchanges in the courtroom, depriving itself of valuable information and lessening the likelihood that the true facts will be brought out. This obfuscation produces further frustration and confusion for the parents and increases the likelihood that an injudicious ruling will be made by the court. The communication problems not only cause tension and grief in their own right but may result in an injudicious decision by the court. This cannot but add to the stresses and contribute to the development of psychopathology.

The Dehumanizing Effects of Adversary Litigation

Protracted adversary litigation is an extremely dehumanizing process. The attorneys are out to win. Their concern with technical and legal issues is often so deep that they lose sight of the human factors involved. Their concern with whether something is legal or illegal often blinds them to more important moral and ethical issues. The following vignette demonstrates the point well.

Two clients have appointments to see an attorney. The first is a man. He has never previously been married and is presently married to a woman who has been divorced and who has two children. She has custody of the two children. He comes to the attorney to ask his advice regarding the advisability of adopting his stepchildren. The attorney strongly discourages him from doing so, informing him that if this marriage ends in a divorce, and if he has adopted the children, then he will have the obligation to provide for their support. However, if he does not adopt them, he will have no obligations for their support after a divorce. In this case, the attorney strongly dissuades the client from going ahead with the plans for adoption.

The next client to see the same attorney is a woman. She has been divorced, has two children, and is now married for the second time to a man who has never been married before. She has custody of the children. She has come to the attorney to ask his advice about her new husband adopting the children. He advises her to proceed as rapidly as possible with the adoption plans. He tells her that once her new husband has adopted the children, he will be obligated to support them, even if this marriage ends in divorce. Furthermore, he warns her that if her new husband does not adopt the children, he will have no obligation at all to provide for their support if they are divorced at some future date.

In each case the attorney is protecting his client's best interests. At no point in his advice to these clients is there any consideration for the welfare of the children. His primary consideration is the pocketbook of his clients. The decision as to whether or not to adopt should be based on a variety of considerations including the financial and the psychological effects on the parties concerned. Parenting is far more a psychological than a monetary phenomenon. The feelings and attitudes of the adoptive father, the reactions of the children (especially with regard to their feelings about being adopted and how this will affect their relationship with their natural father as well as their stepfather), and the reactions of the mother should all be taken into consideration. Although this lawyer may receive an A+ from his professor in law school, he gets an F− from me. He failed abysmally to consider the human factors in each case. Psychological reactions cannot be evaluated quantitatively with money. But they are definite entities which if ignored are likely to cause psychological difficulties.

There are many attorneys who have been litigating in custody cases for so many years that they are totally insensitive to the pain and suffering they are causing both their own clients and those of their adversaries. They pride themselves on their capacity as excellent tacticians and skilled litigators. They perfunctorily mouth their commitment to what is in the best interests of the children as a maneuver in their stratagems. They manipulate, fabricate, and exaggerate to preposterous degrees the deficiencies of their adversaries' clients and appear totally insensitive to the denigration and extreme financial privation they are promulgating. They appear to be pitiless in their attempts to wreak havoc on the other party. The end result is epitomized by Sanford Berger (1980), a Cleveland attorney, in a Writ of Certiorari submitted to the Supreme Court of the United States of America on behalf of a divorced client's request for protection from cruel and unusual punishment (associated with penalties suffered in divorce litigation), as guaranteed by the Eighth Amendment of the United States Constitution stated:

> In all that is decent . . . in all that is just, the framers of our Constitution could never have intended that the "enjoyment of life" meant that if divorce came, it was to be attended by throwing the unfortunates and their children into a judicial arena, with lawyers as their seconds, and have them tear and verbally slash at each other in a trial by emotional conflict that may go on in perpetuity. We have been humane enough to outlaw cock-fights, dogfights and bullfights; and yet, we do nothing about the barbarism of divorce fighting, and trying to find ways to end it. We concern ourselves with cruelty to animals, and rightfully so, but we are unconcerned about the forced and intentionally perpetrated cruelty inflicted upon the emotionally distressed involved in divorce. We abhor police beating confessions out of alleged criminals, and yet we cheer and encourage lawyers to emotionally beat up and abuse two innocent people and their children, because their marriage has floundered. Somewhere along the line our sense of values, decency, humanism and justice went off the track.

The process debases all of the participants: the clients, the attorneys, and even the judges. It dehumanizes and such dehumanization cannot but contribute to the development of psychological disturbances in both parents and children. In the next two sections I will describe specifically how the processes described in this section bring about a variety of psychological disturbances in both parents and children.

The Most Common Forms of Psychiatric Disturbance Produced in Parents by Protracted Litigation

In the previous section I discussed the kinds of stresses and frustrations that protracted custody litigation causes in the litigants. At this point I will describe some of the more common symptoms that result from these detrimental exposures. Protracted custody litigation will predictably bring about psychopathology in parents who have not exhibited significant symptomatology previously and will predictably intensify such symptoms when present at the outset. People with characterological and neurotic problems may start exhibiting the symptoms of borderline disorders and even psychosis.

Depression

A common way of dividing depressive symptomatology is into the *endogenous* and *exogenous*. Endogenous depression refers to depressive symptomatology that arises from within. Generally, genetic predispositions are considered to be present, but internal psychological factors are also operative. Exogenous depressions are generally considered to be the result of external stresses. Psychiatrists tend to be divided with regard to the role of these various factors. In the 1940s and 1950s, primarily under the influence of psychoanalysis, most forms of depression were generally viewed as arising from internal psychological conflicts. The genetic predisposition was considered to be minimal if not entirely absent. External factors were also considered to be important. In recent years, with the increasing popularity of the purely biological explanation, many psychiatrists view depressions as resulting from genetic, metabolic, and biochemical abnormalities and do not pay much attention to the internal psychological factors and/or the external stresses. The primary treatment modality is antidepressant medication. It is this examiner's opinion that the present shift is unfortunate. I believe that there may be some genetic predisposition to depression, but it is small. I believe that the primary reasons for most types of depression relate to external stresses and internal psychological factors. The discussion here is based on this assumption.

I recognize that I am in the minority on this subject among my colleagues in the field of psychiatry. I have given serious consideration to new developments in the field that rely heavily on the primary biological etiology, and I hold that the weight of the evidence still supports the position that depressions of the kind we are discussing here are best understood as manifestations of internal psychological and environmental processes. I am not referring here to bipolar-character (formerly manic-depressive) psychosis, in which the evidence for a biological-genetic predisposition is strong. I am referring to the much more common types of depression, of which the depressive reactions to divorce and custody litigation are good examples.

With regard to the exogenous factor, parents involved in custody litigation have much to be depressed about. The stresses and strains attendant to such litigation would be likely to depress anyone. Absorbed and swept up in the details of litigation, there is little time for pleasure and healthy pursuits—common antidotes to depressed feelings. Depressing things are happening practically every day. The prospect for immediate alleviation of the depressing irritants is small. The whole scene is a bleak one. The indignities one is suffering at the hands of one's spouse also contribute to the depression as does the sense of impotent rage. The communication impediments produce even further feelings of frustration and depression.

In addition to the exogenous factors, complex internal psychological mechanisms are also often operative. One of the factors that contribute to depression is inhibition in the expression of anger. The anger becomes turned inward and directed toward oneself. Even individuals who do not have anger inhibition problems find themselves inhibited in the expression of their anger in association with litigation. As mentioned, one cannot scream out in the courtroom. In fact, one must "shut up" completely. The best one can do is to whisper into an attorney's ear at a time when one might like to leap across the courtroom and strangle the individual on the stand or beat him or her into admitting the truth. The inhibition of such rage is likely to produce depressed feelings. Furthermore, individuals who are inhibited in the expression of anger may develop self-flagellatory symptomatology. They constantly castigate themselves with comments such as "I'm stupid to have done that," "What a wretch I am," and "What a fool I've been." The person may justify such self-recrimination by dwelling on past indiscretions that may have long since been forgotten. These are trivial and do not warrant the degree of self-denigration that the individual exhibits. Errors and minor indiscretions become exaggerated into heinous crimes.

A further contributing factor to depression is guilt. By guilt I mean an individual's feeling of low self-worth experienced following thoughts, feelings, and acts which the individual has learned are unacceptable to significant figures in his or her environment. In essence, the guilty person is saying: "How terrible a person I am for what I have thought, felt, or done." Custody litigation is likely to encourage individuals to perpetrate upon others, indignities that would have been impossible to conceive of prior to the onset of the legal proceedings. The resultant guilty feelings can contribute to depression. Over a period of time, however, under the influence of attorneys, the guilty feelings are likely to be reduced. Certainly, the attorneys themselves would be useless if they were to be concerned too much with guilt. In fact, I would go further and state that feelings of guilt and being a successful divorce attorney do not go hand in hand. Attorneys who are too concerned about the damage they are doing to the spouses of their clients, and even to their own clients, will probably starve (at least as divorce lawyers). Like bombardiers who must place distance between their airplanes and the people below who are being killed, divorce attorneys must desensitize themselves to the horrendous psychological traumas they are causing their clients.

Another factor that may contribute to guilt relates to the identification of the spouse with a mother or father. Spouses generally are psychologically symbolic of one's own parent of the opposite sex. Children are often taught to feel guilty about the expression of hostility toward a parent: "How can you do this to your mother?" and "What a terrible thing to say to your father." Any situation that engenders significant degrees of hostility toward a spouse may rekindle such childhood guilt feelings. And adversary litigation is just this kind of situation. This guilt is different from the aforementioned guilt which is related to present-day hostilities and sadistic behavior toward another person. Rather, it has its derivatives in earlier childhood guilt, and it, too, can contribute to depressed feelings.

The chronic feeling of dissatisfaction that is likely to occur during protracted litigation is another factor that contributes to depression. The individual continually fears that he or she is losing. There is an ongoing quest for more and more and the constant feeling that one is getting less and less. And the attorneys are ever pointing out how much the other side is getting away with. These feelings of dissatisfaction also contribute to depression.

People who are prone to become depressed are often those with three sets of aspirations that must be maintained if they are to feel worthy. When these goals are not maintained, they tend to react with depressed feelings. The three goals are: (1) the wish to be loved and respected, (2) the wish to be strong, superior, and secure, and (3) the wish to be good and loving rather than hateful and destructive. Protracted custody litigation is likely to compromise significantly a person's capacity to reach all three of these goals. In such litigation one is generally despised and hated; rather than feeling strong, superior, and secure, the individual is likely to feel weak and impotent; and rather than viewing oneself as loving and good, the likelihood is that one is going to involve oneself in hateful and destructive endeavors. In other words, adversary litigation produces just the opposite of what the depression-prone person aspires to and is therefore likely to bring about depressed feelings.

People who are depression prone are likely to regress to infantile states of helplessness, and this is likely to take place in stressful situations when they do not feel they have the capacity to cope. At such times, depressed patients become clinging and demand support and protection from those around them. Adversary litigation is just the kind of stress that is likely to produce regression and helplessness in the depression-prone person.

People who react in an exaggerated fashion to severe loss are also prone to become depressed. The loss of a spouse is clearly in this category. And when the lost person becomes hostile (as is more likely in adversary litigation), the sense of abandonment is even greater and the likelihood of depression even stronger. When one adds to this the threatened loss of one's children, those who love one more than anyone else in the world, the likelihood of a depressive reaction becomes even greater.

The fight-flight reactions are of survival value. When confronted with a danger, organisms at all levels either fight or flee. This is an essential mechanism for survival. Some individuals are more likely to fight when confronted with a danger and others to flee. It is probable that both genetic and environmental factors contribute to the pattern that will be selected. The healthy individual is capable of making a judicious decision regarding which mechanism to bring into operation when confronted with a threat. I view many depression-prone individuals as people who are fearful of invoking either of these survival mechanisms, that is, they are too frightened to fight because they do not view themselves as having effective weapons, and they fear flight because they do not consider themselves capable of surviving independently. They need protectors at their side—not only to protect them from the threats of others but to provide for them because they do not feel themselves capable of providing for themselves. They become immobile and paralyzed in a neutral position. They neither fight nor flee. In their immobility they protect themselves from the untoward consequences they anticipate if they were to surge forward and fight the threat. In addition, their immobilization insures their being protected and taken care of by their protectors. Of course, the "success" of the depressive maneuver requires the attendance of caretaking individuals who will provide the indulgence and protection the depressive person requests, demands, or elicits. Without such individuals the reaction may not be utilized. Well-meaning figures in the depressive person's environment are often drawn into the game, not realizing that their indulgence is a disservice. They may consider themselves loving, sacrificial, giving, and devoted. Although some of those qualities are without doubt present, they often fail to appreciate that the same maneuvers are perpetuating the depressive symptomatology.

Protracted adversary litigation is likely to involve years of fighting. The battle is indeed a bloody one and the chances of winning unpredictable because of the capriciousness of the courts. It may thereby intensify dependent cravings for support and protection because of the feeling that if one loses (the coin can land on either side) one will be stripped of much support. The situation, then, increases significantly the likelihood that depression-prone individuals will become clinically depressed, even to a significant degree.

In the extreme, depressed people lose their appetite, become increasingly withdrawn, suffer with profound feelings of hopelessness and helplessness, are constantly flagellating themselves and may, on occasion, commit suicide. The self-punitive action may serve to assuage guilt and relieve the painful depressed feeling. Some depressed patients view the suicide as a method of wreaking vengeance against those who have been rejecting of and hostile toward them. Protracted adversary litigation increases one's desire to wreak vengeance and in some the likelihood of suicide being used as a form of retaliation.

Paranoia

The term paranoia refers to a psychiatric disorder in which the individual persistently harbors delusions of persecution. The term delusion refers to a false belief that is generally not held by the majority of other individuals in the same environment. The paranoid person harbors delusions of persecution that are not corrected by confrontation with reality. There is a persistent and unalterable quality to paranoid delusions, and they are often supported by complex reasoning processes. Because the fundamental assumptions upon which the entire structure is based are false, the whole system is basically illogical. Differentiation should be made between the paranoid personality disorder and the paranoid psychosis. Individuals with paranoid personality patterns are generally not considered psychotic; those with a paranoid psychosis are. The paranoid personality pattern precedes the psychosis and predisposes the individual to the development of the psychotic disorder.

People with paranoid personalities tend to be suspicious, stubborn, distrustful, secretive, obstinate, and resentful of authority. They are often humorless and exquisitely sensitive to criticism. They tend to "build mountains out of molehills" and anticipate rejection and other malevolent treatment at every turn. They tend to project onto others their own unacceptable personality qualities and view others as egotistical, derogatory, querulous, and embittered. Paranoid people appear to walk around with a "chip-on-the-shoulder" attitude and are quick to enter into arguments. They have a strong need to demonstrate power and when placed in a position of authority may become petty tyrants. Such individuals have difficulty recognizing, let alone admitting, their faults and deficiencies. They are experts at detecting the most miniscule evidences of rejections and disparagements in the comments and behaviors of others and then exaggerating the pain and humiliation they allegedly suffer.

All the aforementioned personality traits, although deep-seated, do not necessarily mean that the individual is psychotic. In spite of the paranoid person's rigidity, there is still some flexibility and there is still the possibility of correcting a distortion with reason and confrontation with reality. In short, although people with paranoid personalities may go through life believing that everyone is antagonistic to them, they are still healthy enough to change their opinions when the evidence strongly indicates that the suspicion was unwarranted.

People with paranoid delusions at the psychotic level are not capable of such flexibility. They are not likely to change their minds even when confronted with the most compelling evidence. Those who attempt to refute the delusions tend to be viewed as liars and as falsifying their data. The paranoid delusion becomes fixed, rigid, and unalterable. Paranoids are often ingenious in their capacity to reinterpret data that does not support their delusion(s). This point is well demonstrated by the old anecdote about the paranoid who tells his psychiatrist that he is dead. The psychiatrist asks him, "Can a dead man bleed?" After the patient responds in the negative, the psychiatrist then pricks the patient's finger and expresses a few drops of blood. To this the paranoid patient replies, "Gee, that's the first time I've ever seen a dead man bleed." And this is typical of the paranoid delusion. One just "can't win" if one tries to use logic to get the patient to alter his or her opinion. Furthermore, the delusions may become the guiding themes of the patient's life and become all-consuming obsessions. There may be little mental activity left for other purposes, and this may interfere significantly with the individual's functioning in life. The paranoid preoccupations impair judgment and discretion, and this obviously compromises the individual's capacity to function.

Protracted litigation is likely to intensify paranoid traits in individuals with a paranoid personality as well as contribute to the progression into paranoid psychosis. I would go further and say that even individuals without paranoid personalities may start developing along that continuum as a result of protracted litigation. The reasons for this are well epitomized by the old witticism: "You're not paranoid, they really *are* against you."

Furthermore, there are some individuals in whom the paranoid personality patterns have been a contributory factor in bringing about the marital separation. The ongoing litigation, then, contributes to an intensification of the very problems that have brought about the separation and divorce in the first place.

It is not difficult to see a direct relationship between the development and intensification of paranoid symptomatology and the adversary system. Paranoids are distrustful people. Litigation engenders even further distrust—there are indeed an attorney and a former spouse who *are* secretly plotting against the individual. Without specific information regarding exactly what the schemes are, even the healthiest person is bound to suspect malevolent elements that may not be present. The paranoid, of course, is inevitably going to view the plotting as even more dangerous—intensifying the paranoia. Paranoid people are stubborn and obstinate. Litigation encourages obstructionism as one of the stratagems of the battle. In custody litigation, especially, it is usually to the advantage of the custodial parent to prolong the proceedings. That parent usually recognizes that the longer the children remain with him or her, the greater the likelihood they will express their preference for the custodial parent and the greater the likelihood the judge will support the children's request to stay where they are. Paranoids tend to exaggerate and "build mountains out of molehills." Adversary litigation does this routinely, and hours may be spent on miniscule points in the various affidavits and certifications as well as in the courtroom. Paranoids are characteristically argumentative and hostile. Litigation is also argumentative and hostile and cannot but intensify such traits. Paranoids are often meticulous and obsessively precise in their dealings with others, especially in situations where they suspect foul play. The legal system again encourages such an approach in human interactions. Paranoids need to demonstrate their superiority. In adversary litigation the name of the game is to "win." What better way to demonstrate superiority than to be the victor in protracted litigation.

Paranoids tend to involve themselves in endless bickering. Protracted litigation is essentially the same process. Paranoids tend to blame others for their own dissatisfactions and deficiencies. In the adversary system one studiously avoids revealing any of one's own weaknesses and continually attempts to expose every defect of the other party that may be responsible for the difficulties. It thereby supports and perpetuates these destructive personality traits. Paranoids are masters of detecting slights and minor disparagements in the comments and behavior of others. In adversary litigation one's antennae are ever out for manifestations of such slights in order to justify one's position. Paranoid individuals tend to become spiteful and vindictive. Adversary litigation provides an excellent vehicle for the release and expression of such vengeful tendencies. It thereby intensifies them. Paranoid individuals will often suspect that others are prying in their private affairs in order to use such information malevolently. In protracted litigation there may actually be such attempts. Detectives are hired to surreptitiously collect information and such spying cannot but increase paranoid tendencies. Each party is encouraged by his or her attorney to collect any and all information that can be useful in compromising the other side's position. And such information is often gained secretively.

Tape recordings are not uncommon. Although it is generally illegal to tape record a conversation between two parties—both of whom are unaware that they are being recorded—it is legal to tape record a conversation between oneself and another party, without the other party's being informed beforehand that such a recording is being made. Although judges vary with regard to the admissibility of such recordings in court, they are commonly made in the hope that the evidence will be judged admissible. But even if not, such tapes are legal to make. Accountants may be brought in, against one's will, to review one's financial records and business practices. Investigations by probation officers and even police records may be brought in. Mail may be tampered with. At the trial information gatherers whose existence was not even known may suddenly appear to provide testimony. All of these practices are commonplace and all of them intensify paranoia.

A common form of paranoia is the litigious type. These are people who are quick to litigate and sue. Every new litigation brings spin-off suits, further controversies, and new grievances. Each time the individual does not receive satisfaction (the usual reaction), there are new feelings of injustice. There are people who spend their lives in such litigation. Unfortunately, law is a field which attracts many paranoid personality types and even paranoid psychotics. It is not difficult to understand why, considering the similarities between the kind of thinking that goes on in the mind of the paranoid and the procedures followed in the litigious process. The team of a paranoid client and a paranoid lawyer is not rare. Pity the poor spouse who has to deal with such a combination. The attorney and the client jointly build up, strengthen, and intensify the client's delusional system. Some judges are familiar with this phenomenon and can bring about an end to the litigation. However, judges themselves are often drawn from the ranks of the attorneys, and thus they have their share of paranoids. Such judges may not have insight into what is going on in front of them, namely, a paranoid client being supported by a paranoid lawyer. When one adds to this combination a paranoid judge, not only may the litigation go on for years but the damage done to all parties concerned may be formidable and irreversible. And if the litigation is in the custody realm, the children are likely to suffer terribly.

People with a paranoid personality disturbance are likely to become inordinately jealous regarding a spouse's infidelity—even to the point of delusion. Transient encounters, with little if any sexual import, tend to be interpreted as manifestations of the spouse's infidelity. When a paranoid personality progresses into a full-blown paranoid psychosis, delusions of infidelity then appear. In such situations, there may be absolutely no evidence for infidelity, and yet the individual persists in the firm belief that the partner has been sexually unfaithful. If divorce proceedings ensue and the paranoid party brings the alleged infidelity to the attention of an attorney, he or she may then consider it obligatory to pursue the matter further with inquiries, depositions, the hiring of detectives, certifications, cross-examinations, and so on. The attorney's taking the matter seriously (and, in such an attorney's defense, it may behoove him or her to do so) only strengthens the delusion. When the alleged infidelity is introduced as support for the client's belief that this infidelity damages the accused spouse's parental capacity, the custody proceedings are further complicated. The children's relationship with the so-called unfaithful parent may then become compromised, and this adds to *their* psychological trauma.

In short, the attorneys in the adversary process, sometimes acting in good faith, contribute to the perpetuation of a paranoid person's pathology and its detrimental intrusion into the lives of the spouse and the children. In past years a single act of infidelity, even one unknown to the children, might not only put a person in an extremely disadvantageous position with regard to divorce litigation, but might be used as a reason for considering that parent *totally incapable* of taking care of the children. In addition, this standard applied much more often to women than to men, a bias often incorporated into state statutes. Fortunately, in recent years, especially in the larger cities, courts have not placed great weight on marital infidelity as a factor in deciding custodial capacity. Certainly this is the case regarding post-separation liaisons. It is only when the children are exposed to a parade of such partners and/or when they are exposed to actual sexual encounters that parental capacity is questioned.

Many paranoid individuals exhibit grandiosity. This serves as a form of compensation for feelings of profound inadequacy. People with paranoid personalities tend to consider themselves superior to others. The lower the feelings of self-worth the more the likelihood this compensatory mechanism will prevail. When this progresses into a paranoid psychosis, the individual may develop delusions that he or she is actually some famous historical figure such as Napoleon, the president of the United States, Christ, or even

God. In adversary litigation each side attempts to denigrate the other as much as possible. The more faults in the other individual one can bring out, the greater the likelihood one will be successful in the litigation. The more parental defects in the other parent one can expose in custody litigation the greater the likelihood one will gain custody. Such onslaughts on the self-worth of an individual are likely to increase the tendency to utilize compensatory mechanisms such as grandiosity. It can also serve to shift paranoid personality disorders into a grossly paranoid delusional system.

People with paranoid personality disorders basically feel weak and impotent. Part of their paranoid system provides them with a specious sense of power. They are likely to condemn most vociferously those who make them feel weak and helpless. When the person is not too disturbed, such factors may contribute to socially beneficial endeavors. They become the leaders of causes, support the weak and the helpless, and try to improve their sense of dignity and control. When the individual's paranoid personality disorder deteriorates into a paranoid psychosis, delusions may develop in which the individual feels he or she has control that is not present in reality. Believing that one is Napoleon, Christ, the president of the United States, or God provides the person with a feeling of control over millions of people, if not the world. The greater the insults to one's feelings of control and power, the greater the likelihood the individual will develop compensatory grandiose control mechanisms. Protracted litigation inevitably produces feelings of impotence. The adversary system necessarily produces such feelings, even in the most stable. Accordingly, it is likely to foster paranoid compensatory control mechanisms. And this can contribute to the development of protective control mechanisms in which such individuals are constantly defending themselves against those who would make them feel impotent. Such people may build walls around their homes, have watchdogs, hire bodyguards if they can afford it, and set up various kinds of defensive systems.

Another factor operative in the paranoid system is that of shame. Shame refers to the feeling of low self-worth that one experiences when significant figures in the environment demonstrate disapproval of one's thoughts, feelings, or behavior. Shame is taught in the early phases of child development as a method that parents use to discipline children. "Shame on you" and "You should be ashamed of yourself" are standard disciplinary measures. (I am not commenting on the judiciousness of these measures, but only describing the phenomenon.) Shame develops earlier than guilt. In shame the deterrent to unacceptable behavior is the feeling that significant individuals will surround one with pointing fingers and say, "Shame on you." In guilt the inhibitions are internalized and the critical forces work from within. One only blushes with shame in the presence of another; one can feel guilt when all alone (Gardner 1970). People with paranoid personality disorders are particularly sensitive to situations in which they may feel shame. Suffering already with profound feelings of low self-worth, they cannot tolerate further damage to their self-esteem by public criticism of deficiencies. In such situations they are more likely to develop protective mechanisms in which they consider themselves to be persecuted and are likely to take action against those who would so expose them. This is a common element in the violent destructive behavior of paranoids. Competent psychiatrists appreciate that it is dangerous to expose people with paranoid personality disorders to public statements of their deficiencies. And the legal system does just this. Most often divorce and custody courts are open to the public, and when the individuals involved are well known the details of their cases may be followed by the newspapers and public media. This is a very risky business for paranoids. With the deterioration that may ensue, the whole family is likely to suffer.

Paranoid individuals project their own unacceptable hostility onto others. This is a central mechanism to the paranoid process. They consider themselves good and even holy people, free from sin and malevolence. These unacceptable impulses are projected out onto others. Their marriages are traditionally tumultuous because of their tendency to project their own hostilities onto their spouses and view them as malevolent. In the course of litigation this mechanism is fostered and entrenched by the attorneys' attempts to substantiate and "prove" the malevolence of the spouse. The children thereby suffer as the deficiencies and the so-called malevolence of the spouse are elaborated upon in detail and brought to their attention.

Rationalization is another mechanism almost invariably utilized to a significant degree by paranoids. Rationalization refers to the tendency to provide excuses for unacceptable behavior that does not involve any deficiencies in the person him- or herself. It is a process designed to maintain self-respect and prevent feelings of shame and guilt — feelings that would be experienced if one were to allow oneself to recognize one's true and basic motivations. Paranoids in particular are always blaming others in their interpersonal difficulties. Adversary litigation promulgates this process in a highly orchestrated way. The other party's contribution to the interpersonal difficulties are studiously delineated, whereas the client's own contribution(s) is strictly removed from presentation to the court. The system thereby strengthens rationalization and entrenches paranoia.

Post-Traumatic Stress Disorder

When discussing post-traumatic stress disorders, the psychiatric literature generally describes these reactions in association with such catastrophes as floods, tornadoes, military combat, severe automobile accidents, plane crashes, volcanic eruptions, rape, and concentration-camp existence. It is not common to include protracted litigation on the list, but there is no question that it can be equal in its magnitude to the aforementioned and produce the same kinds of untoward psychological reactions. The disorder results when an individual who is exposed to a terrifying catastrophe or to prolonged or repeated threats is so overwhelmed that he or she feels that protection against annihilation, mutilation, and even death is unlikely. Individuals exposed to such traumas are flooded with thoughts and feelings that they feel they cannot cope with effectively. This may result in a state of helplessness and collapse in which the individual feels completely impotent. It may end in trance-like states and total removal from meaningful social involvement.

Withdrawal into a trance-like state is only the extreme reaction. More common but typical responses include recurrent and intrusive recollections of the traumatic event, including recurrent dreams. The individual may suddenly act or feel as if the traumatic event was reoccurring. In such states all the mental and emotional reactions attendant to such reoccurrence will be relived. There is often an associated removal from involvement in the daily activities of the world as one is swept up in the thoughts, feelings, and events associated with the trauma. There is an obsession to talk about and think about it at every opportunity. There is an impaired capacity for pleasure and relaxation. The individual may be excessively alert to any kind of trauma and exhibit exaggerated startle reactions to the most minor unpleasant stimuli. Sleep, eating, and sexual interest may be impaired. There may be trouble concentrating and there may be an exaggerated reaction to any situation that reminds the person of the trauma.

Individuals who are inhibited in expressing hostility are more likely to develop post-traumatic stress disorders than those who are more comfortable with expressing their anger. If one is to be successful in litigation, one has to be comfortable with the expression of hostility. With the encouragement of their attorneys, many individuals are brought to the point of feeling comfortable with false allegations and even perjury. The affidavits that one reads in association with divorce and custody litigation are replete with allegations of the most sordid and sadistic nature. Often the attorneys will exaggerate minor indignities and turn them into campaigns of vilification. If one is to "win," one has to be comfortable with such hyperbole. People who are excessively guilty over the utilization of this kind of "ammunition" are more likely to develop post-traumatic stress disorders. The adversary system increases the likelihood of the development of this disorder in such individuals.

Individuals who develop post-traumatic stress disorders are more likely to have come from broken homes or unstable environments. Protracted litigation is likely to produce just this kind of family background. Although divorce by definition breaks up a home, there can still be some stabilizing forces operative after the separation. Under ideal circumstances the individuals might still be able to gain some support and gratification from one another. This is possible when the divorce is amicable. Furthermore, the children can also serve as stabilizing and unifying influences, the divorce notwithstanding. Although this is certainly a compromised kind of home stability, it is still a kind of stabilization. The children know that if one parent were to become incapacitated or die, the other parent would still be available to provide parenting. And this can be a source of security for each parent as well. The knowledge that the other parent can also provide adequate parenting if necessary may be very reassuring. Adversary litigation diminishes the likelihood that these remaining stabilizing elements will be present. Many parents, at the time of the separation decision, will vow that they will not allow their situation to deteriorate like it has for many of their friends and relatives. Unfortunately, adversary litigation reduces the likelihood that such noble goals will be realized; thus it increases the likelihood of the development of instability that predisposes to the post-traumatic stress disorder.

Another factor that contributes to post-traumatic stress reactions is the disorganizing effect of fear. Franklin Delano Roosevelt was cognizant of this fact when he stated: "The only thing we have to fear is fear itself." (I do not know if this statement was original with him.) Fear is a normal reaction to a threatening situation. It has survival value in that individuals who flee earlier and more quickly are more likely to avoid life-threatening dangers than those who do not have a sensitive and quick flight response. We flee more effectively when we are frightened. But this refers to known dangers from which a direct line of flight is obvious. In adversary litigation there is much greater uncertainty regarding what one has to fear because the outcome is far less predictable. This increases the likelihood that the fear reaction will become intensified and disorganized. This interferes with logical thinking and reasonable self-protection. In such an agitated state the individual is likely to make injudicious decisions. In short, exaggerated fear and disorganization, common manifestations of the post-traumatic stress disorder, are likely to exhibit themselves in protracted adversary litigation, much to the detriment of the parents and the children.

In such a state of disorganization and intensified fear, the individual may exhibit any of a number of symptoms: chronic tension, tremulousness, an ongoing state of apprehension, weeping, depression, dizziness, urinary frequency, insomnia, nausea, vomiting, diarrhea, and emotional outbursts. In extreme cases the individual exhibits psychotic symptomatology such as delusions and hallucinations in which the traumatic event is relived as if it were actually occurring. A common example of this phenomenon is the combat reaction in which the soldier hallucinates battlefield conditions, including bombing, tank attacks, and so on. The individual actually believes that he is still in combat and behaves accordingly. He may run in terror and hide as if his life were indeed in danger at the moment. These states may alternate with periods of "freezing" similar to catatonic withdrawal.

The reliving of the traumatic event serves a definite purpose in the post-traumatic stress disorder. It provides for systematic desensitization to the trauma. It is as if each time the person relives the trauma it becomes ever more bearable. The same process is operative in mourning wherein the individual repeatedly thinks and talks about the recently departed person. Personal items of the deceased take on new meaning and many of these become treasured memorabilia. Most societies set aside a prescribed period for mourning, during which time other activities are given much lower priority. This increases the likelihood that the bereaved will be free to involve themselves in the mourning process and desensitize themselves to the trauma.

In the post-traumatic stress disorders, the individual similarly brings about such desensitization via the reliving of the traumatic event. If the doctor had a pill that could remove these repetitive thoughts, prescribing it would probably be a disservice to the patient. Cessation of the desensitization process would probably interfere with the normal, healthy adjustment to the trauma. It is no surprise, then, that people who are involved in protracted litigation become obsessed with the events associated with the trial, and months and even years later are still obsessed with its details. Such preoccupation interferes with optimum involvement in other aspects of life and deprives the individual of the richness of experience that life has to offer. The *longer* the litigation, the *greater* the likelihood of the development of the post-traumatic stress disorder.

Months and even years after the formal cessation of the litigation, the individual may still be reliving the divorce and courtroom experience and exhibiting, to a lesser degree, many of the aforementioned symptoms. The longer the litigation and the greater its stresses, the greater the likelihood the individual will exhibit residual symptoms. The situation is similar to that of Vietnam veterans and concentration-camp victims examined years after the termination of their ordeals. A high percentage have been found to still exhibit such symptoms as frequent nightmares related to the trauma, low frustration tolerance, a high level of tension, difficulty relaxing, and impaired intimacy with others. Just as the reiteration, nightmares, and obsessive preoccupation serve to help the individual desensitize him- or herself to the psychological trauma while it is occurring, these residual symptoms reflect an ongoing need to work through the trauma. It is as if each time the individual talks about or thinks about the traumatic event, it becomes a little more bearable. In some cases of divorce/custody litigation, the trauma is so formidable that the mere cessation of the litigation is not enough; individuals may need years of further accommodation and desensitization. Again, I am not referring here specifically to the traumas of the divorce per se, but rather to the additional traumas that result from ongoing litigation.

A factor in the fear of forming new relationships following a separation relates to the distrust caused by the divorce and the further distrust engendered by the tactics utilized by the spouse under the influence of his or her attorney. Many people involved in such litigation comment on how vicious and cruel the former spouse had become during the course of litigation — so much so that the initial pains and indignities that resulted in the separation appear mild in comparison. With such an experience the individual reasonably is cautious regarding new intimacies and this may extend for years. In the extreme, a kind of "psychic numbing" is produced that impairs significantly the development of new relationships. The individual lives in continuous fear of reoccurrence of the same trauma.

Alcohol and Drug Abuse

It is not surprising that protracted custody litigation is likely to produce alcohol and drug abuse in the predisposed and intensifies such symptoms in those already so addicted. Many of the factors in ongoing litigation that contribute to alcohol abuse are relevant to drug abuse as well; however, there are some differences worthy of discussion.

Alcohol abuse. Samuel Johnson said: "In the bottle, discontent seeks for comfort, cowardice for courage, and bashfulness for confidence." Individuals who are involved in ongoing litigation have much to be uncomfortable about and alcohol can provide comfort. They need courage; alcohol also impairs judgment and can thereby induce a feeling of courage. If they are shy or bashful they are not likely to "win." Alcohol provides the feeling of self-confidence that increases the likelihood of "victory." Furthermore, alcohol provides relief from continuing emotional stress. Therefore, it becomes a quite attractive way of dealing with the stresses attendant to protracted litigation.

Alcohol provides pleasure. The more vicious the litigation, the more depressed and unhappy the individual will be and the greater the likelihood that he or she will resort to some agent that will produce a sense of well-being and even euphoria. Alcohol facilitates social contacts. The more protracted the litigation, the more alienated one will be from one's spouse, and the greater the likelihood one will want to resort to an agent that enhances the likelihood of meaningful social contacts elsewhere. And if custody litigation is involved, there is the likelihood that one will be alienated from one's children, increasing thereby the need to establish other relationships. Alcohol alleviates pain; it is a kind of analgesic. And the pain can be either physical or psychological. Protracted litigation is an extremely painful experience and it thereby increases the likelihood that individuals who are involved in it will abuse alcohol. Alcohol is a tranquilizer; it reduces tension and anxiety. Protracted litigation is inevitably anxiety provoking and fraught with tensions.

Alcoholism is more common in those who have suffered separation from significant figures. Although divorce and separation per se involve a separation, ongoing litigation enhances the likelihood of an even severer kind of alienation from a former spouse. There are many separated and divorced people who still have cordial relationships with one another, will cooperate in the care of their children, and can provide each other with a variety of gratifications — their divorced state notwithstanding. In fact, such support and gratifications may even take place when each of the divorced parents has remarried. I am not recommending ongoing intimate relationships, but only meaningful cooperation and communication regarding the children and other matters of mutual interest. Protracted litigation reduces the likelihood of such cooperation and thereby increases the chances of alcoholism.

A common situation that contributes to the development of alcoholism in women who are housewives is the prospect of the so-called "empty nest syndrome." As their children grow older, they find little in their lives to provide the ego enhancement that came from child rearing. They thereby become risks for the development of alcoholism. When still married, they may continue to have meaningful involvements with their husbands and loving relationships with their grown children and subsequently their grandchildren. With the divorce, however, this network of healthy stabilizing involvements may be reduced significantly. If the divorce has been filled with animosity and alienation of both the ex-spouse and the children, the likelihood of these women becoming alcoholic is even greater.

Many individuals with alcoholic problems are extremely dependent. Often the dependency is on a spouse. Divorce increases the likelihood that such a dependent tie with be broken. And if a divorce is fraught with animosity, there will be even less opportunity for dependent gratifications. A woman alcoholic, for example, whose husband divorces her because of her drinking may still derive some dependent gratifications from her former husband. Not only is he providing her with food, clothing, and shelter, but he may even provide her with psychiatric care and benevolent interest motivated by sympathy. If, however, they have involved themselves in protracted litigation, it is not likely that she will receive such ongoing support and this is likely to increase her alcoholism.

Many alcoholics are basically very guilt-ridden people. They may have been brought up in homes in which very stringent values (religious or otherwise) have been inculcated. Hostile and sexual feelings especially have to be repressed if they are to conform with the standards of their environment. When there is a threatened eruption into conscious awareness of their unconscious strivings in these areas, they become excessively guilty. Alcohol may serve to alleviate the painful feelings associated with such guilt. In guilt one feels bad about oneself; with alcohol one feels good. Alcohol serves as an antidote to guilt feelings. In protracted litigation, many more angry feelings have to be mobilized if one hopes to "win." (The reader will note that I persistently put the word *win* in quotations because no one really wins in protracted litigation. It is at best a Pyrrhic victory.) The guilt evoked in the course of such litigation, then, increases the likelihood that the individual will drink.

In our society drinking is often associated with the "macho image." The men depicted in alcohol advertisements in newspapers and television are invariably well built, powerful, well in control of a situation, and competent. In these advertisements one never sees weak and inadequate individuals drinking. Yet it is the latter group that are typically the ones who drink the most. Like smoking, alcohol has been associated with masculinity in the public eye. A man in the throes of divorce may suffer a certain amount of ego debasement, especially if it was his wife who initiated the separation. Drinking, then, can serve to compensate in fantasy for this impaired loss of masculinity.

Alcohol is a sedative and can induce sleep. Sleep is an ancient method of withdrawal from the unpleasant. The more stressful the divorce, the greater the likelihood that the alcoholic-prone individual will resort to this form of sedation. Again, protracted litigation is certainly going to increase this likelihood.

I will not discuss in detail here some of the derivative effects of alcoholism. These relate not only to its effects on the body (especially the liver and the brain), but its increasing the likelihood of vehicular accidents, crime (in the predisposed), and suicide. Alcohol abuse also increases the chances of personality deterioration, work failure, and psychotic decompensation. The latter includes such disorders as acute hallucinosis, alcoholic paranoia, and Korsakoff's psychosis (a psychotic deterioration associated with organic brain deterioration). All of these disorders, sadly, are more likely to develop in those unfortunate alcoholics who become involved in protracted litigation.

Drug abuse. Drug abuse often begins in adolescence (and occasionally in the preadolescent period). It is less likely to be present in the middle-aged and the elderly. Accordingly, divorcing parents are less likely to suffer with drug abuse problems than their teenaged children. Although less frequently seen in middle age and although less common than alcoholism, it is still a problem in the divorcing, especially those who expose themselves to the stresses of ongoing litigation.

Individuals who use addicting drugs are primarily motivated by the wish to induce and perpetuate an intensely satisfying state of personal existence, even at the risk of physical and mental deterioration. The people who are most prone to resort to the use of drugs are those whose lives are fraught with frustration and grief. Any situation that increases these feelings is likely to enhance the desire of addiction-prone individuals to utilize drugs. Extended divorce litigation is just the kind of a stress that such individuals might deal with by the use of drugs.

Individuals who take drugs are often immature and have few healthy resources to help them tolerate stress. The sense of impotency associated with this failure to have acquired adequate coping skills is likely to be enhanced during protracted litigation, thereby increasing the tendency to use drugs. Drug addicts are often dependent on maternal figures and often the suppliers are viewed as such psychologically. In fact, a supplier is sometimes referred to as "mother." Accordingly, a man who is addicted to drugs may suffer more from the loss of his wife (his surrogate mother) than one who does not have this fixation. If the rejection by his wife is intensified by adversary litigation, the loss is intensified and the likelihood of drug addiction even greater.

Many addicted individuals are basically sexually inhibited. When sexual desires arise, significant anxiety is produced. Narcotics not only reduce the tensions and anxieties associated with emerging sexual impulses, but suppress these desires and serve as a substitute for them as well. Marital separation may result in a reduced availability for sexual gratification, increased likelihood of sexual arousal, and an increased need for drugs to deal with these feelings.

Addicted personalities generally have little frustration tolerance. They want immediate gratification of their needs, such as is the case for young infants and younger children. Delayed gratification is very much out of their scheme of things—they "want what they want when they want it." Protracted litigation provides an atmosphere which is predictably going to frustrate addiction-prone individuals even more. The attorneys delay, often by design, and the courts are notoriously slow. Therefore, for addiction-prone individuals, addiction becomes more likely. Some of the people who resort to drugs are neurotic individuals who are under treatment for symptoms such as anxiety, obsessive compulsivity, and psychosomatic symptoms. They may have been provided medication by their physicians. With rare exception, such medication is in the tranquilizer category, but some of these have addictive potential as well and under the stresses of ongoing litigation they may become more addicted to their tranquilizers.

Tension and Anxiety

Protracted litigation produces a significant amount of tension. And a variety of symptoms may arise that attempt to reduce the tension. Anxiety, which is related to tension, is also likely to increase. In anxiety the individual is not consciously aware of any threat, but there is a general state of heightened tension. At times the anxiety erupts into *anxiety attacks* or *panic attacks*. The individual suffers with palpitations, shortness of breath, sweating, and a feeling of impending doom. Psychoanalytic theory holds that anxiety attacks are the result of the threat of eruption into conscious awareness of unconscious thoughts and feelings about which the individual feels guilty. Generally, these relate to hostility and sexual drives. More biologically oriented psychiatrists are dubious about the psychoanalytic explanation and consider panic attacks to be more a biological phenomenon, not unlike a seizure. The fear-flight reaction is necessary to survival and individuals with a very high threshold for the triggering of this reaction may not have survived as well during our evolution as those whose fear-flight mechanisms were brought into play more readily. It is reasonable to assume that there are some individuals whose threshold is extremely low, and in whom the most innocuous stimuli will trigger the reaction. The anxiety attack may then be viewed as a manifestation of such ultrasensitivity of the fear-flight mechanisms. Perhaps it is a combination of this *and* the psychological factor that is operative in many patients.

People undergoing litigation are more likely to suffer an increase in the frequency of anxiety attacks. If repressed hostility and/or sexual urges are contributing factors, then the situation is likely to bring about an increased threat of eruption of such feelings. Litigation engenders anger as well as sexual deprivation, and the more alienated the spouse the greater the likelihood of the emergence of these feelings. Protracted litigation invariably engenders a significant amount of hostility. Individuals who are inordinately guilty over the expression of anger are likely to be made anxious over the emergence of their anger and this may increase their anxiety attacks.

The anger of people with anxiety neurosis often relates to the frustration of dependency gratifications. The greater the antagonism of a spouse on whom the individual was dependent, the greater the anger and the greater the likelihood of anxiety attacks. And protracted litigation is likely to frustrate such dependency gratifications. Many patients (especially women) may try to use their attorneys as a substitute person for the gratification of their strong dependency needs. Most often they experience further frustration here in that the lawyer is not likely to satisfy more than an infinitesimal fraction of such patients' demands. (It is a rare divorce attorney who has not had some experience with such individuals.)

Individuals who are prone to have anxiety attacks not only have stringent consciences with regard to sexual and hostile feelings but are generally overconscientious people. They often feel that they must live up to the highest standards and are extremely critical of themselves when they fail to do so. Involving themselves in protracted litigation may result in great guilt over the degraded forms of behavior they find themselves resorting to. And this may result in feelings of depression, sleeplessness, irritability, restlessness, weeping outbursts, and feelings of inferiority and inadequacy.

Somatoform Disorders

The term *somatoform disorder* refers to a wide variety of symptoms suggestive of physical disease. However, there is no evidence of physical disorder after thorough physical examination and laboratory testing. In the absence of any organic or structural abnormality, the symptoms are considered to be psychological in origin. Of the various somatoform disorders, the ones I will focus on here are the *somatization disorder* and the *psychogenic pain disorder*.

In the *somatization disorder* the individual has frequent complaints about a variety of distressing symptoms. The symptoms run the whole gamut of physical symptoms. They may be cardiopulmonary, gastrointestinal, neurological, respiratory, and so on. The individual becomes preoccupied with these physical symptoms. The preoccupation may reach obsessive proportions. The complaints are associated with great tension and fear of horrible physical disease. Patients with this disorder typically travel from doctor to doctor, always complaining about the failure of the previous physician to have cured them. They tend to overmedicate to the point of becoming drug abusers. Many are often subjected to unnecessary surgical procedures.

In many of these patients the physical symptoms are manifestations of generalized tension and anxiety. Most individuals have some weak point, an organ or system of organs that tends to react inordinately to stressful situations. Under tension some individuals may vomit, others have diarrhea. Some develop palpitations and others high blood pressure. Others sweat, have headaches, or suffer with muscle spasms. The selected organ is often one in which there is a neurophysiological predisposition on a genetic basis. The symptoms may serve other purposes. Dependent individuals, who travel from physician to physician, may gratify their needs for the kind of attention that a child would obtain from a parent. In others the visits to the physicians fill up the emptiness of their lives. A middle-aged woman, for example, whose children are grown and whose husband has little interest or involvement with her, may spend her days in physicians' offices focusing on her various symptoms. Such preoccupations divert her attention away from the real problems: her no longer being needed by either her children or her husband. If such a woman gets divorced there may be an even further increase in her symptomatology. And if she involves herself in ongoing litigation, the further alienation of her husband is likely to increase her symptoms even more. She becomes even more tense, symptoms increase, and she develops an even greater need for attention.

People who develop somatic forms of symptomatology are likely to have certain personality characteristics. They are narcissistic and prone to self-display and dramatization. They need immediate gratification of their wishes, but avoid effort to gain their goals. They are often self-engrossed and offended by trifles. They are extremely dependent and bid for sympathy and for attention to their symptoms. They overreact to painful stimuli. They tend to rule and dominate their environment by being sick and try to control others through pity and guilt. When alienated from a spouse, such individuals may try to utilize these symptoms even more frequently in order to gain gratifications. The stresses of protracted litigation are likely to intensify even further the need to utilize this method of involving other people.

Somatoform pain disorder is a related problem in which the patient exaggerates the pain and discomfort associated with a known physical illness. The complaining envelops the individual's life and is, in part, an attempt to evoke social responses. Low back pain, gastrointestinal distress, tinnitus, or other common sources of genuine physical discomfort may become exaggerated and all encompassing. This problem is often seen in dependent individuals who use the pain to invite solace, protection, and indulgence. It often stems from childhood experiences with an overprotective mother. The deprivations associated with protracted litigation are likely to increase the utilization of such symptoms.

Personality Disorders

Whereas patients suffering with *neuroses* and *psychoses* exhibit symptoms that may be viewed as undesirable by the patient (especially the neuroses), the term *personality disorder* refers to a class of psychiatric disturbances in which the individual's personality structure and pattern itself is the manifestation of the psychiatric disorder. Most often, the person exhibiting such symptomatology does not consider him- or herself to have psychiatric problems. Rather, they view themselves as *normal* individuals who have a particular personality pattern which they may recognize as being somewhat different from others but not a pattern that they would want to change. Protracted litigation may bring about an intensification of such disorders.

Explosive personality. Individuals with this type of personality disorder exhibit low frustration tolerance. They react in an exaggerated fashion to relatively slight irritating stimuli. Between the outbursts they may appear normal. Their relationships with other people, however, are quite labile and fluctuating because of their poorly controlled outbursts of hostility and anxiety. They are people who are said to have a "low boiling point." They are like volcanoes ready to erupt. In their outbursts they may become destructive, abusive, and assaultive. They are quick to quarrel and slow to simmer down. During the outbursts their judgment is usually impaired significantly.

Individuals with this kind of disorder are generally immature. They are very dependent on others and utilize the adult equivalent of temper tantrums to manipulate others into submitting to their wills. They view these rage outbursts as manifestations of strength, when in reality they are thinly disguised attempts to compensate for inward feelings of weakness. The presence of this disorder may very well have been one of the reasons for the divorce. Divorce proceedings are likely to intensify it, and the longer the divorce proceedings, the greater the likelihood of deterioration — that is, an increase in the frequency, duration, and magnitude of the outbursts.

Avoidant personality disorder. Although people with this disorder tend to withdraw from meaningful social involvement, they do not do so to the extent that they can justifiably be referred to as *schizoid* or *schizophrenic.* However, they are certainly on the continuum toward the development of these more serious disturbances. These individuals are excessively sensitive to social situations and frequently expect to be humiliated and rejected. Their withdrawal comes from an attempt to protect themselves from such alienation. They generally have low feelings of self-worth and are less able to tolerate the inevitable slights and rejections that we all experience in life.

Distrust from the anticipation of malevolence from others contributes to the development of the avoidant personality disorder. The symptomatology is likely to intensify in situations which actually result in malevolence directed toward the individual. Predictably, the animosity engendered by protracted divorce proceedings is likely to intensify this disorder. The distrust that these patients already have is multiplied many times over as they become exposed to more horrendous indignities. If the litigation extends long enough the intensification may be irreversible.

Antisocial personality disorder. These individuals are also referred to as having *psychopathic personalities* ("psychopaths") or *sociopathic personalities* ("sociopaths"). Individuals with this disorder are unable to form significant attachments, although they may feign such loyalty to others. They have little capacity to put themselves in other people's positions and are generally incapable of expressing sympathy and empathy. They have no sense of social responsibility, although they may verbally describe correct and socially appropriate behavior. They have practically no sense of guilt or remorse over the harm they inflict on others. By *guilt* I refer to an inner feeling of lowered self-worth that occurs when an individual has thoughts, feelings, or has committed acts that he or she has learned in childhood are "wrong" or "bad." The development of guilt is necessary for the survival of a civilized society. If the overwhelming majority of people in a society do not exhibit guilt mechanisms, they will not deter themselves from exhibiting antisocial behavior and the group may not survive. This internal type of guilt should be differentiated from the guilt being referred to by the judge who says to the person on trial, "How do you plead, guilty or innocent?" The word *guilt* here is not being used to refer to any internal psychological process but simply to the question of whether or not the individual did indeed commit the crime he or she is alleged to have perpetrated. Psychopaths know about this kind of guilt and generally will avoid committing inappropriate and antisocial acts from the recognition that, if caught, they might suffer some punishment from society. However, they cannot be relied upon to restrain themselves from committing these acts when there is no threat of divulgence. Psychopaths are exploitive and predatory, and the main deterrent to their exploitation of others is the anticipation of immediate punishment. They have little genuine conviction for adhering to or complying with social codes or ethical standards.

Individuals with this kind of personality disorder may be excellent candidates for ongoing divorce and/or custody litigation. They have little guilt or remorse over the pains they inflict upon their spouses. They may often team up with attorneys who have similar traits (a certain amount of insensitivity to the feelings of others is a basic requirement for success as a divorce litigator), and the combination may cause a significant amount of psychological destruction. It is common to find an intensification of this kind of psychiatric disorder in those patients who are predisposed to it.

Although the intensification does not generally result in particular discomfort for the psychopath, it may result in severe stress for the psychopath's victim, in this case the unfortunate husband or wife whose psychopathic spouse feels absolutely no guilt over the pains and humiliations being inflicted on the former partner. The adversary system feeds into the hands of such people and is thereby the cause of much psychological damage to the other parties involved.

Dependent personality disorder. Individuals with this disturbance tend to be passive in their relationships with others and relate most intensively to those who will assume responsibilities for them. They do not feel capable of making their own decisions and continually rely on others. They lack self-confidence and see themselves as helpless and often stupid. They generally have not developed significant competence in any area and are ill-equipped to function on their own. Essentially they are children who have never grown up. In the face of stress they tend to regress even further with excessive dependency on others. The disorder is more common in women who, in traditional homes, are often programmed to assume such a role.

Patients with this disorder tend to regress in the face of stress. They become infantile and clinging and try to extract what they can from those around them who may be willing to indulge them. Litigation is the kind of stress that is likely to intensify this disorder. These are the women who, without strong economic reason, go back to their parents' homes upon the breakup of their marriages. They then resume functioning as children and may even get their mothers to take care of their own children on an ongoing basis. In short, they join their children to be taken care of by their mothers. The dependency may have been a factor contributing to the dissolution of the marriage. The more stressful the divorce litigation, the greater the likelihood of such regression.

Concluding Comments

In this section I have described what I consider to be the most common forms of psychiatric disorder caused in parents by protracted custody litigation. I have not exhausted all the possibilities. Nor have I described in as much detail as I might have the wide variety of symptoms that can exhibit themselves in each of the categories discussed. My aim has been to impress upon the reader how psychologically devastating can be the various disorders that are likely to arise, and my main hope has been that such descriptions will result in the readers' thinking again about entering into litigation, especially custody litigation. Parents who exhibit these symptoms are likely to be compromised significantly in their parenting capacities. And this surely will cause their children to suffer additional psychological trauma.

The Most Common Forms of Psychiatric Disturbance Produced in Children by Prolonged Custody Litigation

Although divorce does not necessarily cause children to develop psychiatric disturbances, it increases the risk for the formation of such symptoms. Elsewhere (Gardner 1977, 1979), I have described many of the ways in which the divorce situation brings about untoward psychological reactions in children. Wallerstein and Kelly (1980) have also described in detail the ways in which divorce results in childhood psychopathology. There are a wide variety of disorders that may result from divorce. Here I will discuss specific types of psychiatric disorder that are likely to develop when a child has been embroiled in and/or exposed to prolonged custody litigation.

Antisocial Behavior

Children of divorce are likely to become angry at being deprived of a parent who is often viewed as an abandoner. Furthermore, the parental fighting deprives them of optimum attention and care, and this too produces resentment. People who involve themselves in prolonged custody litigation are going to produce even more anger in their children because the aforementioned deprivation and frustrations are likely to be even greater. One way in which these children are likely to express their resentment is through antisocial acting out. The term *acting out* refers to the reaction in which the anger is expressed directly and overtly in the form of antisocial behavior. Some children are too guilty or inhibited to express overtly their resentment. These children may develop a variety of symptoms in which the anger is dealt with symbolically. These disorders are referred to as anger inhibition problems. Here I will focus on the acting out of anger and in the next section on anger inhibition problems.

When the acting out occurs in childhood the term *conduct disorder* is often utilized. The child exhibits little sensitivity to the feelings of those toward whom the anger is directed and who suffer as a result of the antisocial behavior. They may become physically violent against individuals and/or their property with little guilt or remorse. Destruction of property, vandalism, firesetting, and assault are seen. Lying and stealing are also common. There are chronic violations of the general rules of society, both at home and at school. They may be truant and generally defy all attempts on the part of their parents to provide structure and discipline in the home. They are often a menace in the classroom, disrespecting the teacher's authority and interfering with the classroom routine. They refuse to cooperate in their studies, do not do homework, and are generally defiant of all authority.

In adolescence these youngsters are generally referred to as *juvenile delinquents,* during which time, in addition to the aforementioned symptoms, they may then involve themselves in additional forms of antisocial behavior such as drunkenness, reckless driving, substance abuse, and indiscriminate sex. Furthermore, the amount of damage they are capable of doing is increased because of their relatively advanced age. Then, when these youngsters enter into adult life, the persistence of this pattern warrants their being referred to as *psychopaths* or *sociopaths.* It is important for the reader to differentiate between the terms *psychopathology* and *psychopath.* These are often used interchangeably by the general public, but they have entirely different meanings. Psychopathology is synonymous with psychiatric disorder. It basically means disease of the mind. Psychopathy, however, has a very specific meaning. Psychopathy is one kind of psychopathology. Typically, psychopaths are individuals who suffer little, if any, guilt or remorse over the commission of antisocial acts. Inner inhibitory processes do not deter them from committing antisocial acts; rather, it is only when external threats and punishments are imminent that they will restrain themselves. Children exposed to ongoing custody litigation are being exposed to influences that may contribute to the development of such disturbance in adult life. Then, even more sophisticated forms of antisocial behavior may be utilized, which may result in their being apprehended by the police, and even sent to jail.

There are certain aspects of the child's involvement with parents who are litigating for custody that increase the likelihood that these symptoms will develop. The child of divorce is often an observer to some of the most cruel forms of behavior that one parent can inflict upon another. The parental hostilities often reach sadistic levels. Whereas the parents may be perfectly respectable and civilized in their relationships with others, in the area of divorce litigation they may descend to the most primitive levels of animal behavior. There is little place for honesty in their deliberations and such dishonesty will generally be fostered by their attorneys. The most cruel things may be said with no restrictions. Impulsive acting out on their part is common, acting out in which they may inflict physical harm on one another. The desire for vengeance may reach obsessive and even psychotic proportions. Sensitivity to the feelings of the spouse may be totally lost, with little guilt or remorse over the damage that is being done to the other party. Viciousness and violence may become the norm. Parents who are psychopathic themselves, or predisposed to such behavior, are more likely to embroil themselves in such vicious litigation than those who are not. But even the more civilized and healthier may degenerate in this way under the guidance and supervision of their attorneys. And when the litigation involves custody, the stakes are even higher and the violence even more formidable. The most treasured possessions, the children, are at stake and no holds may be barred in such a battle.

Children model themselves after their parents and emulate their behavior. When parents exhibit the kinds of hostilities just described, it is quite likely that their children will exhibit similar behavior. One factor is simply that of identification and the psychological incorporation of the parental behavioral patterns. Another factor is generally referred to as the *identification with the aggressor* principle. Stated simply, it is the mechanism of "If you can't fight 'em, join 'em." Observing the damage done by the stronger parent against the weaker, the child may identify with the stronger parent in order to become his or her ally against the weaker. Such children then protect themselves from being the target of the same traumas and indignities. On a number of occasions parents who have been litigating over the custody of their children have come to me to provide therapy for the children because of complaints by the school and people in the neighborhood that the children are acting out antisocially. Their view of the therapy is that they will drop the child at my doorstep, I will treat him or her once or twice a week for 45 minutes, and then ultimately "cure" the child of these psychopathic tendencies. They will often tell me that they do not wish to be in the same room with one another because of the hostility that will ensue and that I should not get involved in their problems. Such a request is ludicrous. There is absolutely no chance of my helping such a child. No matter what input I could provide during those sessions, no matter how skilled a therapeutic approach I might utilize, following each session the child is being thrown into the same cauldron of rage that he or she left for the session. It is simpleminded and even grandiose on the part of the therapist to think that he or she can help a child under these circumstances. And it is naive of the parents to think that this can be accomplished. Accordingly, I inform such parents at the outset that there is no possible way I can help the child without active involvement on their part, an involvement in which the goal will be to reduce their animosity and help them resolve their problems (not bring about reconciliation, just reduce their fighting and anger). Some parents appreciate the judiciousness of this approach and are willing to participate in such a therapeutic program.

Others are so blinded by their rage that they cannot appreciate the reasonableness of this approach and seek therapy elsewhere. Unfortunately, they do not have great difficulty finding therapists who will treat such children on their terms. It is a therapeutic approach that is doomed and is a waste of time and money.

The emulation and identification factor is only one that results in antisocial behavior in children whose parents are litigating for custody. Another relates to the active utilization of the child as a weapon in the hostilities. In such cases a parent may be actively teaching the child to act out. For example, a mother calls her separated husband to enlist his aid in the disciplining of their two boys who are living with her. They do not respect her authority but she knows, from previous experiences, that they will be more receptive to their father's disciplinary measures and threats. When she calls him on the phone and pleads with him to speak to them he replies, "They're all yours, baby. Since you asked me to leave, don't ask me to be of any help to you." This father is so bent on vengeance that he is blinding himself to the fact that he is depriving his children of important parental guidance. His desire to hurt his wife is so great that he cannot allow himself to see the detrimental effects on his children of their being utilized in this way as weapons in the parental conflict.

I once saw a boy whose father requested that he make a tape recording of his mother's conversations with her man friend. He did so, turned the tape over to his father, who then gave the tape to his attorney. Although there was some question as to whether or not the tape was admissible as evidence in the custody conflict, the boy's behavior here was obviously reprehensible and is a good example of the ways in which parents involved in custody litigation may encourage their children's antisocial acting out.

Divorce hostilities have much in common with warfare. Each side collects its ammunition and gains as many allies as possible. And the attorneys are often the ones who orchestrate the stratagems of the battle. There is one important difference, however, between traditional wars and divorce wars. In traditional wars one posts guards around one's borders in order to protect oneself from the infiltration of spies and saboteurs. In divorce wars potential spies and saboteurs (the children) are allowed free access to both territories. In fact, they are often welcome to cross borders and are greeted with open arms, hugs, kisses, and presents. They thereby allow themselves to be utilized for "inside jobs." Sometimes this is active on the child's part, but sometimes not. Younger children, especially, may be useful spies without their even being aware of the fact that they are serving in this capacity. A mother may ask a reasonable question such as, "How was your weekend with your father?" and be provided with vital information that may be useful in her custody litigation without the child's being aware of the fact that he or she is providing such. In fact, even mothers who may not be actively attempting to acquire such information may find that the normal and healthy inquiry about what went on during the visitation is likely to provide some important ammunition. One could almost say that one cannot avoid it. A boy, for example, may tell his mother about the large diamond his father bought his new woman friend. His main intent may simply be to express to his mother the excitement he felt over seeing such a "big diamond." "It's the biggest diamond I ever saw in my whole life." Such a mother may immediately report this to her attorney as evidence that her husband's financial situation is far better than he claims. A father, for example, picks up his son for a weekend visitation. In the car he asks a simple and innocuous question, "So how was your week, Jimmy?" One cannot deny that this is a reasonable enough question, even when not motivated to gain information about the mother.

The boy replies, "Things are really great in the house now since Mike moved in." To which the father replies, "Mike. Who's Mike?" Son: "Oh, Mike, he's Mommie's new friend. He's really a great guy. Because he doesn't work, he's home every afternoon when I get home from school and so he can play baseball and basketball with me. He's really taught me a lot about using a bat."

There is no father who is so saintlike that he is able to receive this kind of information with equanimity. He is likely to report the existence of this "gigolo" to his attorney and immediately take steps to protect himself from being exploited as well as demonstrate that his wife is unfit to have custody of the children.

Because of their innocence, gullibility, and poor judgment, children are likely to perform antisocial acts that the parent may be too judicious to engage in. One parent actively encouraged the children to break objects in the home of the other. I was convinced in this case that this parent, even if allowed entry into the home of the former spouse, would not have overtly destroyed her former husband's property. The children, in order to ingratiate themselves to their mother, acted out her wishes here. She taught the children how to steal and destroy property surreptitiously and then taught them how to lie about what they had done. She provided them with alibis which, of course, were not believed for one moment by the father. She then taught the children to complain about his constantly accusing them of stealing and lying and used this as a justification for the courts considering her to be the preferable parent. Unfortunately, her attorney, hearing only her side of the story (which did not include the coaching sessions), accepted his client's rendition as valid and listed the father's accusations as one of his defects. This is a good example of the ways in which attorneys do significant damage by involving themselves in a system which studiously and strictly prevents them from hearing directly the other side's position.

One father actively encouraged his child to provoke the mother at every opportunity. He went through the course of the day's events and tutored the child in obstructionistic behavior. He told the child what words to say when refusing to comply with the mother's requests that the child eat, dress, turn off the television, and even do homework. So vengeful was this father that he had to blind himself to the fact that he was contributing to the development of psychopathic behavior in this child, as well as compromising significantly the child's educational process. The child's naiveté and poor judgment, as well as his great desire to ingratiate himself to his father, resulted in his complying with these most vicious and insidious requests.

There are subtle ways in which parents may foster the antisocial behavior. A mother, for example, may "forget" to have the children ready for the father and they (even though old enough to appreciate the fact that an appointment has been made) may also "forget" to remind the mother of their appointment with their father. By so forgetting they ingratiate themselves to their mother and serve thereby as weapons in her attempts to thwart and frustrate the father. Or a mother may say such things as "I know you have a lot of homework today, perhaps you shouldn't see your father. You don't want to fail your test, do you?" Or the children may dawdle in preparing for their father's visit and the mother's sense of urgency for getting them ready on time leaves much to be desired. The children may "get the message" from the mother and dawdle even more. A father may appreciate that his bringing the children home early may present the mother with various restrictions and inconveniences. Or, his "forgetting" to pick them up at the assigned visitation time may compromise her dating.

When a parent is denigrated by another parent, the denigrated parent becomes a less respected authority. Such deprecation is common in divorce and even more common when there is custody litigation. It behooves the parent to point out as many flaws as can be found in the other if one is to hope for success in the litigation. Children invariably pick up such criticisms and are likely to believe them, no matter how outlandish. Without respect the child is less likely to identify with the parent's values and morals, and this contributes to antisocial behavior. Without respect and admiration the child is less likely to comply with the parental demands and is more likely to flaunt that parent's authority. The denigration of the parent also reduces the child's sense of security with that parent. A parent who is not admired and respected is not viewed as a reliable protector and advisor. This loss of security produces feelings of frustration and resentment and this can contribute as well to antisocial behavior. And custody litigation is likely to compromise the parent's reputation in this way and bring about this kind of antisocial acting out.

Some children act out their anger in passive-aggressive ways. Rather than being overtly defiant, they are covertly defiant. They are slow and obstructionistic. They profess compliance but actually do just the opposite. By their recalcitrance they recognize that they are producing frustration and resentment in the parent who is trying to get them to move along more quickly. However, their professions of compliance are designed to protect them from any guilt or retaliatory punishment because they can say that they are "really trying." And they may gain support for this maneuver by the other parent who is secretly gleeful over the frustration they are causing the spouse.

Protracted custody litigation results in the children's being neglected. The parents are so swept up in their hostilities that they do not give proper time and attention to the children. The emotional deprivation that results is a source of frustration and anger in the youngsters. In response they may act out antisocially as an attention-getting device. Most children, if confronted with the choice of being either totally ignored or punished, will choose the latter. The antisocial behavior, then, serves to provide them with some kind of compensation for their feelings of deprivation in that it produces the attention that they are not otherwise receiving. In addition, it serves as a vehicle for the acting out of the anger they feel over the deprivation. And in custody litigation the deprivation is bound to be formidable because the litigation is so absorbing to both parents. In fact, it may obsess them and be the most common thought on their minds.

Anger Inhibition Problems

When the term *neurosis* is used it generally refers to a type of psychological problem in which there is an internal conflict, the resolution of which is represented by the symptom. As mentioned, the symptomatic adaptation to a problem is often considered to be the best; in actuality, it often turns out to be an extremely injudicious choice—with the individual ending up worse off than he or she would have been had more appropriate solutions been utilized. The earliest neurotic conflicts studied by Freud were sexual inhibition problems in women. Such women might present with a symptom of paralysis of the legs. Freud interpreted the symptom to represent an attempt to resolve a conflict between the patient's biological desire to engage in sexual activities and her excessively rigid conscience which dictated that such activities were wrong and/or sinful. By developing a symptom the sexual energies, according to Freud, were channeled into the legs and the symptom served to protect the young woman from sexual encounters because of the "paralysis." Sexual inhibition problems are not frequently seen these days, primarily as a result of the recent "sexual revolution" in which people have become much more comfortable with their sexual feelings.

Anger inhibition problems, however, are very much with us. Society cannot allow free expression of resentment. There must be some inhibitions taught children if we are to live together in a civilized society with a reasonable degree of security and the knowledge that individuals are not going to wantonly harm us with a high degree of predictability. Certainly, external threats of punishment can serve to deter individuals from freely expressing anger. However—and this was probably a more recent development—the internalized inhibitory mechanisms are generally preferable in that the social authorities can relax their vigil because individuals can generally be relied upon to inhibit themselves from acting out their anger. When the inhibitory mechanisms become too punitive, too excessive, then the background is set for the development of neurotic symptoms, the purpose of which is to deal with the bottled-up anger.

Many factors in the divorce conflict may contribute to a child's developing anger inhibition problems. The child is exposed to the expression of formidable hostility between the parents. This is likely to be quite frightening. Children in this situation may fear that if they were to express such anger themselves they may be the object of similar retaliations. The children may be quite angry over the fact that the parents' involvement in their conflicts is so absorbing that the children are neglected. However, they may fear that if they express this resentment there will be even further neglect and/or rejection. Another factor that may contribute to the development of anger inhibition problems in children of divorce is the child's fear of expressing any resentment toward the parent who has left the home, reasoning that he or she may be subjected to even further abandonment. The parent who leaves the home is generally viewed as an abandoner, no matter how justifiable the departure. The child may then fear that any resentment expressed over this rejection will result in even greater deprivation from the departed parent. And the child may even fear expressing resentment toward the remaining parent, lest *that* parent abandon him or her as well. After all, one parent has already proven him- or herself to be an abandoner. Abandonment is now very much in the child's scheme of things. What is to prevent the remaining parent from abandoning the child as well?

When the parents litigate, these fears of anger expression may become even greater. When lawyers, judges, psychiatrists, and psychologists are brought in, the fight escalates even further. The child can only imagine the worst things happening when these "heavy guns" are brought into the action. Summonses are issued, subpoenas are brought to the home by sheriffs, police may appear on the scene, and threats of fine and even jail are heard. All these experiences frighten these children even more, and they may deal with the anger they feel in such a setting by repression and suppression of their hostility.

Denial. One of the most common mechanisms that the child may utilize to deal with hostility is to deny it. Most often this is unconscious — the child is really not aware that he or she is angry — although, at times, a child may be aware of the anger but be afraid to admit it to others. Powerful repressive forces are usually operative when this mechanism is used. It is probably the most primitive neurotic mechanism: the individual deals with a danger (in this case an inner one, that is, one's own anger and its threatened eruption into conscious awareness) by simply making believe it is not there. It is not surprising that such a simplistic adaptation is attractive to the child and therefore one of the most commonly utilized by children. Children who are inhibited in this regard are often brought up in homes in which one or both parents exhibit similar problems. The parents thereby serve as models for their children's dealing with anger in this manner.

The child who is embroiled in custody litigation is likely to be quite angry. There is emotional deprivation, forced interviews with psychiatrists, psychologists, lawyers, and judges. The child may be asked to take sides, and this too produces resentment because of the fear of the loss of affection of a parent whose position is not supported. When children are asked how they feel about some of the obviously anger-provoking experiences that they have had in association with the litigation, they may respond with a host of rationalizations designed to protect themselves from awareness of their anger. One son of a physician stated, "My father can't come and see me because he'd have to leave his patients and some of them might die." Another patient, in response to my question regarding her feelings about her father's limited involvement since leaving the home, stated, "It doesn't bother me. I know he has to spend so much time working to send us money that he hasn't time to see us or call us." A boy whose parents were swept up in extremely vicious custody litigation was quite angry over the fact that his father was lying about the degree of involvement he claimed he had during the course of the child's upbringing. The child knew that this was a fabrication designed to enhance his father's position in the custody litigation. The boy wanted to live with his mother, but denied any conscious angry feelings over what his father was doing. When asked how he felt about what his father was saying he replied, "It really doesn't make me angry because I know that he's lying because he loves me so." When I pointed out to him that these lies might result in his being placed by the court in his father's home he replied, "I'm sure that won't happen. The judge will know better." When I then informed him that even judges are not infallible and that they sometimes make mistakes, the boy replied, "I don't think this judge will make a mistake. He's a good judge." By insisting that the judge would ultimately rule that he could stay with his mother, the boy protected himself from eruption into conscious awareness of the angry feelings attendant to the recognition that he might be placed with his father because of the latter's lies.

Nightmares. All children experience occasional nightmares. The child whose parents are involved in custody litigation is more likely to have nightmares and this relates, more than anything else, to repression of the hostility engendered by the parents' litigation and the fear of becoming consciously aware of such anger. In the typical nightmare the child is fearful that a malevolent figure (a robber, a monster, etc.) will enter his or her room. Usually the intruder comes in from a window or closet or from under the bed. I believe that the interloper is the incarnation of the child's unacceptable angry thoughts and feelings that have been relegated to the unconscious. At night, when distracting stimuli are removed, the pent-up hostilities of the day, which continually press for expression, are attended to. Daytime activities such as sports, sibling fights, and television, which have provided some release of hostility, are no longer available. At night, residual hostility from unresolved daytime frustrations press for release. In the nightmare, the symbolic derivates of the child's anger (the robber, etc.) press for expression into the child's conscious awareness (symbolized by the child's room). The greater the child's guilt over anger, the more it will be repressed. The urgency for release becomes correspondingly greater, as does his or her fear of the anger symbols when they threaten to erupt into conscious awareness. Up to a point, the more guilt-ridden the child the more frightening the nightmare. When the guilt is extremely great, however, even the symbolic representations will be repressed, and the child will be "protected" from his or her nightmares—and this vehicle for release of anger will then no longer be available.

The malevolent figures may represent the child's hostility projected outward (they are outside his room) or they can symbolize hostile elements within significant figures (such as the parents). When the frightening figure threatens to abduct the child, then the dream may reflect separation anxieties or the desire to be with the abducting parent. The nightmare, like all dreams, is rich in meaning, and the many elements contributing to its formation are beyond the scope of this chapter to discuss in detail. Central to it, however, are the child's *own* repressed hostilities. The fears the child experiences during the dream are most commonly of his *own* anger. It is for these reasons, I believe that the child embroiled in or exposed to ongoing custody litigation is likely to exhibit an increase in the frequency of nightmares. Elsewhere (1986, 1988) I describe in great detail my views on the origin of nightmares as well as a wide variety of other dream phenomena.

Tension. As repressed anger strives for release, an internal psychological conflict may be set up. The anger that has been relegated to the unconscious presses for expression, but guilt prevents the hostile thoughts and feelings from entering into conscious awareness. A chronic state of tension may thereby be set up which may manifest itself in a number of ways. The child may become hyperirritable, cry easily, and react in an exaggerated fashion to the most minor irritants. The child may develop tics. Most commonly these are of the eyes (blinking) and the mouth (grimacing and puckering movements). When more severe, the head and shoulders may become involved, and various tics (grunting noises, frequent throat clearing) may appear.

I am not in agreement with those who view most tics to have specific symbolic significance. For example, some hold that an eye-blinking tic may be a manifestation of a child's wish to avoid seeing unpleasant sights, or that a tic in which the child jerks the head back represents removal of the face from an imaginary hand that is slapping him or her for some transgression. These are attractive explanations to some psychoanalysts and their validity may be hard to disprove. (This is true of most psychoanalytic explanations. One can attribute practically anything to anyone's unconscious and be secure in the knowledge that neither the patient nor anyone else can disprove it because it is *unconscious* and, by definition, not even known to the patient.) Although there may occasionally be a child in whom the tic may have specific symbolic significance, more often, I believe, it is merely one of the many possible manifestations of a high level of tension. Each person's body has certain areas or organs that are more likely to respond to tension than others. Some react to tension with spasm of various parts of the gastrointestinal tract, others with palpitations, others with sweating, others with skeletal muscle spasm, and so on. Alfred Adler referred to each of these sites as a *locus resistentiae minoris* (place of least resistance). He considered them inborn points or areas of weakness and did not give much credence to the theory that the organ was primarily selected because it lent itself well to symbolic expression of a particular psychological need. My own experience bears out Adler's views. I consider the child with tics to be a very tense child whose facial musculature is particularly sensitive to tension. In therapy I direct my attention to the underlying sources of such tension; only rarely have I found the search for a specific symbolic meaning to the tic to be therapeutically useful.

A discussion of tics would not be complete without some mention of *Gille de la Tourette's syndrome.* By definition, this disorder (commonly referred to merely as *Tourette's syndrome*) consists of multiple tics combined with coprolalia (the compulsive uttering of profanities). Whereas a number of years ago Tourette's syndrome was generally viewed to be rare, it has received increasing attention in recent years. When Gille de la Tourette first described the disorder in the late 19th century, he considered it to be a manifestation of a neurological lesion. He was not, however, able to locate the exact place in the brain where the disorder presumably arose. In the 1940s to 1960s, primarily under the influence of psychoanalysis, the disorder came to be viewed by many psychiatrists as a psychological disturbance. The coprolalia was considered to relate to anger inhibition in that the child was viewed as being too inhibited to overtly express resentment and did so compulsively via the verbal tics. By claiming helplessness over these utterances, the child did not have to feel guilty.

In more recent years, with the shift of the pendulum back to biological explanations for various psychological phenomena, many psychiatrists consider Tourette's syndrome to be a purely biological disturbance. The coprolalia is not considered to have anything to do with anger inhibition. Rather, it is just one manifestation of the poor control of impulses that these children exhibit in both the motor and the verbal areas. Although the site of lesion has yet to be determined, the general consensus is that the disorder is related to weaknesses in cerebral inhibitory mechanisms. The tics represent impairment in those cerebral mechanisms that inhibit motor movement and the coprolalia is believed to be the result of a weakness in those brain mechanisms that suppress socially unacceptable verbalizations. With the recent increasing attention to the disorder, there has been a widespread increase in the diagnosis of the disorder. At the present time the definition has been extended to include children with multiple tics *without* coprolalia necessarily being present. In fact, some "experts" on the disorder will even view occasional tics as the early signs of incipient Tourette's syndrome. I believe that things have gone much too far here. I do believe that Tourette's disorder, as originally defined, is rare and that it probably does have a strong neurological contribution. But the overwhelming majority of children who have tics are suffering because of some inborn biological tendency to express tension via motor spasm, and the primary etiological factors are environmental. Children exposed to ongoing custody litigation may very well develop tics. To quickly diagnose them as being in the early phases of Tourette's syndrome may result in losing sight of the fact that they are reacting to family problems. It may also result in their being treated with very powerful medications that may produce lethargy, impaired concentration in school, and other toxic side effects. All this is a terrible disservice to these children.

The skeletal muscles are only one area that can respond when there is tension. There are certainly other places of least resistance (again to use Adler's term). Some children's gastrointestinal tracts will respond with diarrhea, constipation, nausea, or vomiting. Others develop palpitations, shortness of breath, or increased blood pressure. Others respond with sweating. Some exhibit spasm of the bronchiolar musculature and develop asthmatic symptoms. For some, the bladder is a weak organ and they become bedwetters. Others may soil as a manifestation of their tension. Still others may stutter. Although many consider stuttering to be psychogenic, I believe it has a high biological "loading." The articulatory apparatus is a very recent development on the evolutionary scale and has complex representation on both sides of the brain. Although language (the ability to understand the meaning of a symbol) is primarily a left brain function for most people, speech (the articulation of spoken language) is bilaterally represented. It is reasonable to assume that with such sophisticated and complex mechanisms imbalances may take place which produce speech impairments. The same tensions may manifest themselves in irritability, low frustration tolerance, and temper outbursts in response to minimal irritations. And all these manifestations of increased tension are likely to be seen in children involved in custody litigation. It is one of the most tension-evoking experiences a child can suffer.

Anxiety attacks. As mentioned in my discussion of adult anxieties, I believe that there are some individuals in whom the anxiety attack may be viewed as a seizure-like phenomenon. It represents a low threshold for the discharge of certain neurological stimuli. For others, complex psychological factors are operative. And, of course, both factors can be operative. Generally, anxiety attacks are seen in children whose general level of tension is already quite high. In these episodes the child suddenly becomes extremely tense. There may be sweating, palpitations, shortness of breath, trembling, and fears of death. In severe forms the child may be thrown into a state of panic. In children exposed to ongoing custody litigation there are certainly psychological factors that may very well contribute. There may be a threat of eruption into conscious awareness of hostile feelings. These children may be so guilt-ridden over their angry feelings that powerful repressive forces must operate to keep them out of conscious awareness. So repressed, these feelings build up and then threaten eruption into conscious awareness. The child then becomes overwhelmed with the fear of the consequences of their expression and the anxiety is a concomitant of such fear.

Some children develop a specific type of anxiety reaction referred to as the *separation anxiety disorder*. These children become increasingly panic-stricken at the prospect of going to school — hence the earlier name *school phobia*. They are often very dependent and immature children who are overprotected by their parents, usually their mothers. Such mothers generally communicate to the children the following message: "The world is a dangerous place, calamity can befall you at any point, and it is only I who can protect you from catastrophe. Accordingly, always stay by my side and all will be well with you. If however you stray, terrible things will happen." A trauma such as a separation or a divorce can exacerbate this disorder because it is associated with a threatened separation from a parent. Although it is the father who usually leaves the household, removal of a parent is now very much in the child's scheme of things. It is as if the child reasoned: "If my father can now leave, why can't my mother? Marital relationships are flimsy and weak and parents can abandon children quite easily." And, when the parents are litigating for custody, there is even greater reason for the child to develop this disorder in that he or she may be wrested away from a parent upon whom he or she is quite dependent. This cannot but be extremely anxiety provoking.

Another factor that contributes to the development of the separation anxiety disorder is anger inhibition. The mothers of these children are quite ambivalent about them. On the one hand, they are deeply involved with their children and get many gratifications (both healthy and neurotic) from their upbringing. On the other hand, another part of them wishes to get rid of the child because they basically resent the obligations of child rearing. This resentment may represent itself in hostile wishes and thoughts, destructive impulses, and even desires that the child be dead. It is not that the parent really wishes the child all these terrible calamities, only that the primitive mind thinks along these lines. Such hostility reflects itself in the anticipation of danger associated with the overprotection. The mother is always viewing the child to be at risk for being hit by a car, drowning, acquiring serious illnesses, and so on. Visual imagery here belies the underlying hostility. However, because of guilt over these unacceptable impulses, the mother becomes overprotective to insure that the calamities do not befall the child. The child develops the same pattern and is always fearing that something terrible will happen to the mother. Here too there is the mechanism of anger toward the mother and clinging dependency on her in order to assure him- or herself that the angry thoughts and feelings have not been realized. The child's basic anger comes from the resentment engendered by the mother's overprotectiveness and the restrictions that it places on the child's life. Elsewhere (1985) I describe these mechanisms in greater detail. Protracted custody litigation increases the child's anger and increases the likelihood that the aforementioned mechanisms will be utilized. There are other factors operative in the development of the separation anxiety disorder. I have only mentioned here those that are likely to be affected by ongoing custody litigation.

Projection and phobias. The less direct contact we have with a person the greater the likelihood that we will harbor distortions about the individual. When parents separate, the child is likely to develop distortions about the absent parent that would not otherwise have arisen. The child views the parent's leaving as a hostile act. The child is likely, then, to see such a parent as unduly punitive and may, generalizing from the "abandonment," anticipate similar treatment from others of the same sex. The child's considering the absent parent to be hostile may be further intensified by the projection of the child's own hostility. Guilt over hostility may cause the child to disown it and project it onto others. It is as if the child were saying: "It is not I who have these horrible hostile thoughts, it is he(she)." The absent parent may then be seen as so hostile that the child expects to be injured or severely maltreated in other ways. With such anticipations the child may dread contact with the parent and even become phobic with regard to him or her.

Phobic reactions regarding the parent (especially the absent one) may take other forms. The child may become excessively fearful that the parent may become sick or injured. Such concerns are reactions to the basic unconscious wish that harm befall the parent as an expression of the child's hostility. Guilt over such hostility contributes to the transformation of the wish into a fear. The child's basic image is one of harm befalling the parent. By viewing the event in the fantasy as one that is feared, rather than as one that is desired, the child assuages guilt while still gaining the gratification of the imagery.

Another notion that contributes to such a phobia is the child's belief that hostile thoughts per se have the power to harm. Such a child may need frequent proof and testimony that the parent is well—to provide assurance that his or her basic hostile wishes have not been realized. The child may become so solicitous of the parent that he or she becomes an irritant. In protracted custody litigation there may be reduced contact with a parent, and this increases the likelihood of the aforementioned distortions arising. In addition, the anger evoked by such litigation facilitates the child's viewing the parent as being hostile to him or her, even though the hostility is directed toward the former spouse.

Compulsions. Although compulsions may have a strong neurophysiological loading (and the recent efficacy of certain antidepressants in reducing them lends confirmation to this), I still hold that the psychogenic contribution is important. The development of compulsions and compulsive rituals is another way in which a child may deal with anger. In the handwashing compulsion, for example, the child may consider the hands to be the potential tools for acting out unconscious hostile thoughts and feelings. By compulsively cleaning them, the child symbolically "keeps them clean" (that is, innocent of committed crimes) and washes off the "stains" of their potential or fantasied transgressions. A ten-year-old boy I once treated presented symptoms that demonstrated quite well the relationship between compulsive rituals and repressed hostility. Although his parents were not separated they were highly intellectualized people, very inhibited in expressing affection, and so were psychologically separated from one another and from him. The boy feared that if he knocked against an article of furniture (even accidentally) there would be the most terrible repercussions—the worst of which was that God would punish him by striking him dead with lightning. He especially feared hitting his foot against something because the possible punishments for that seemed to be worse than if the point of contact with the furniture were his hand or torso. Although he was always cautious not to knock against anything, he somehow would slip up at least a few times a day and "accidentally" hit against or even kick some household articles. He would then become very anxious, examine the furniture very carefully to be sure that it wasn't damaged, and run his finger over it a few times to be sure that it wasn't scratched or marred. Gradually the examination process developed into a specific ritual in which he had to rub his finger over the area exactly three times, after which he experienced some alleviation of his fears. In addition, he would look up toward heaven and beseech God not to punish him for what he had done. Gradually, his pleadings too became formulated into specific prayers that would reduce his fears if stated in a particular way, for example, "Please Oh Lord, do not punish me for the terrible thing I have done."

I considered the furniture to represent the patient's parents and his knocking (and even worse, kicking) against them a symbolic expression of hostility toward them. The inspection for damages and scratches served to reassure the patient that he had not in fact harmed his parents. Ritualizing the examination further served to lessen such fears: prescribing a specific number of strokes shortened the examination period necessary to reassure him that harm had not been done. God, of course, represented the patient's parents (especially his father whom he saw as more punitive) and begging his forgiveness served to protect him from the punishment he anticipated for his transgressions. Again, ritualizing the prayer served to diminish the fear and provided him with a predictable (albeit magical) way of reducing it. It was clear that the patient's "accidents" were unconsciously planned and served as an outlet for his hostility. The rituals enabled him to assuage the guilt he felt over such expression. However, as is well known, "doing and undoing" (the psychiatric terminology for the aforementioned phenomenon) is not the same as never having done anything at all. Because the patient felt he had to keep "doing" (giving vent to his hostility), he had to keep "undoing" (engaging in guilt-alleviating rituals).

This boy's parents were not separated. However, they were isolated individuals and psychologically removed from both him and one another. His symptoms are described here because they demonstrate well the way in which repressed and inhibited hostility can bring about a compulsion, a form of neurotic symptomatology. Similar alienation between spouses and children is likely to occur in ongoing custody litigation. Thus, it increases the risk for the development of compulsions in children who are prone to utilize such mechanisms for dealing with anger that they are guilty about expressing.

Depression. The child whose parents are litigating for custody has much to be depressed about. As mentioned previously, it is reasonable that an exogenous depressive reaction will form. There is also an anger-inhibition element in such depression in that the guilt over hostility may result in the anger being directed toward the child him- or herself and this can contribute to the depression. When self-recriminations are present this mechanism becomes even more obvious. One does best to understand such criticisms as being displaced from a significant figure onto the child himself. If one follows the formula "substitute the word *father* or *mother* wherever the patient's name appears in a self-flagellatory statement," one will generally get a clearer understanding of what is going on in the child. When the child needs to assuage guilt by inviting punishment, a masochistic element is introduced.

Concluding comments. It is important for the reader to appreciate that the differentiation between anger inhibition problems and anger acting-out problems may sometimes be vague. Although it may initially seem paradoxical, there are individuals who can exhibit both disorders simultaneously, or at least manifestations of both disorders in the same individual at different times. I recall once seeing an eight-year-old boy whose parents brought him to me because the school threatened to expel him unless he went into treatment immediately. His teachers and the principal described him as one of the most difficult children they had seen in years. The term they most frequently used to describe him was that he was "obnoxious." He defied his teachers' authority and gained sadistic pleasure in frustrating them. He openly used profanities toward them in the classroom and provoked other children into acting out similarly. He disrupted the lessons and would often bully classmates, even during the class lessons. He absolutely refused to cooperate in classroom assignments, and doing homework was entirely out of the question. In the classroom he would often throw spitballs and fly paper airplanes. When the teacher sent him to the principal's office he would laugh at her condescendingly and boast about the fact that the principal, as well, had no control over him. And, in the principal's office, he behaved similarly.

The patient's parents were separated and involved in one of the most vicious custody litigations I have seen. They were completely obsessed with their hatred of one another, to the point where they spoke of little else. The patient and his six-year-old brother were living with their mother and were constantly exhibiting similar disruptive behavior in the home. Interestingly, the father denied ever observing a significant degree of antisocial behavior during visitations. He could not deny that the patient was indeed as disruptive and arrogant as described because he believed that what the teachers were telling him was valid. In addition, when he would call the home, he would hear the patient and his brother cursing at their mother and provoking her over the telephone. However, when the patient visited with his father he was a "model child." In fact, on those occasions (relatively rare) when the father would bring him to visit with friends and relatives they would invariably ask him to come again with the patient because he served as such a wonderful model for their children, so well behaved was he!

The father was a caterer and most of his work had to take place on weekends. During visitations he would generally bring the child to accompany him at various weddings, Bar Mitzvahs, and other catered affairs. The boy spent long hours sitting in the kitchen, talking with the kitchen help, while his father was occupied elsewhere. He would sometimes spend as much as 14 hours straight following his father around to the various affairs that he was catering.

My understanding of the situation was this. The boy was basically angry at his father, but was afraid to express such anger for fear he would see even less of his father. He viewed the father as the "abandoner" because it was he who initiated the separation. Recognizing that his father was basically less committed to him and his brother than his mother, he feared that if he were to express resentment toward his father he might see even less of him than he already did. Accordingly, he was on his best behavior when with his father and, considering the formidable amount of hostility that we know existed within this child, it is reasonable to say that on visitations he exhibited an anger inhibition problem. However, I believe that the boy felt much more secure venting his hostility on his mother, teachers, and the principal. He recognized that his mother was a safe target in that she had proven herself loyal to him and was not likely to abandon him for utilizing her in this manner. It certainly enabled him to discharge his hostility in a way in which there were no significant repercussions. As far as displacement of hostility onto his teachers and his principal, these individuals also lent themselves well to serving as targets. As far as he was concerned, he would not have been unhappy had he never returned to school again. He had no commitment to the educational process and did not project himself into the future and appreciate the consequences of his recalcitrance in the classroom. In his relationship with his mother, teachers, and principal he exhibited an anger acting-out problem and in this particular case these symptoms were deeply entrenched by vicious custody litigation.

Disloyalty Problems

One of the more common problems that confront children of divorce relates to loyalty. Parents are children's most treasured possessions. The loss of a parent can be one of the most devastating traumas that can afflict a child. Whereas prior to the separation, divorce may be a theoretical phenomenon — something that happens only to other children in one's class and neighborhood — following the separation it is indeed a reality. A child feels abandoned by the parent who has departed from the home. The parent is viewed as having been disloyal. Most children, if they had their say with regard to whether or not their parents should divorce, would vote that they remain together. They have little if any sympathy for the grief and suffering the unhappy marriage has brought to their parents. Their general position to their departing parent is: "If you really loved us, you would stay and put up with whatever pain you claim you are suffering." They may not, however, be able to express the resentment they feel over such parental disloyalty, fearing they may see even less of the departed parent.

It is extremely common for each parent to attempt to bring the children in on his or her side in the separation and divorce conflict. The children often recognize that refusal to cooperate in this regard may result in alienation of one or both parents. A common way for children to deal with these pressures is to say to each parent what they believe that parent wants to hear at that particular moment. This is particularly so with regard to agreeing with criticisms of the other parent. Children will either remain silent with regard to refuting such criticisms or actively join in or even add a few of their own. In this way the children hope to ensure that they will remain in the good graces of each parent and not be subjected to the rejection and alienation they anticipate would be their lot if they were to take the position of the other side.

This adaptation is so common that examiners should assume that it is taking place in custody litigation. Examiners who do not appreciate this are likely to contribute to the psychological damage that results from such litigation. The children's comments predictably intensify the hostilities as each parent quotes the child's statements in defense of his or her own position. When with mother, a child may consistently tell her how much she is the preferred parent in the litigation — and with father the same tale is told. Each parent then quotes the child's statements to the attorneys, these become incorporated into the various affidavits and certifications, refutations and allegations of fabrication ensue, and the litigation heats up. My experience has been that it is often quite difficult to convince the parents (and even their attorneys) that the children are lying. The parents are so desirous of proving that they are "right" that they lose judgment with regard to this extremely common phenomenon. And often their attorneys, who should know better, support the parental delusion because of their commitment to their client's position, regardless of how weak it may be.

I recall one 14-year-old boy who told his father how miserable he was living in his mother's home, and he spent each visit describing in detail the indignities he suffered at her hands. This finally reached the point where the father began to litigate for custody of the boy. Although the mother claimed that the boy was telling her that he wanted to remain living with her, the father ignored her statements and assumed that she was lying. A few months later, I was brought in by the court as an impartial examiner and, in a joint session with the father, the boy admitted that he really did not wish to live with his father but was only saying so in order to ingratiate himself to him. By this time the father had spent almost $10,000. Although he was 14, his desire to ingratiate himself to each parent was so great that he blinded himself to the consequences of his duplicity. It is important to appreciate that children are naive in this regard, and their capacity to project themselves into the future and appreciate the consequences of their behavior is seriously impaired — and the younger the child the more valid is this principle. Children live for the moment and say whatever will get them immediate gratification, regardless of how much trouble their fabrications cause their parents. And lawyers earn their living from the litigation that ensues from these fabrications, and psychiatrists, as well, are paid to "pick up the pieces."

Lawyers, mental health professionals, and judges who interview children who are embroiled in custody litigation, in accordance with the aforementioned principles, should take into consideration who the child is with when statements are made about parental preference. Examiners who do not take this into consideration are likely to make erroneous recommendations. Accordingly, the children must be seen with each parent alone and with both parents together. It is in a family conference, especially, that such tendencies are likely to be "smoked out." It is not simply the people who are in the same room with the children who will influence what they say; even those outside in the waiting room will have an effect. If mother brings a child for a custody evaluation, it is likely that the child will support her position, recognizing that she is in the waiting room and that she is most likely to have access to the most recent statement on parental preference. Judges should appreciate this when interviewing children in their chambers. They do well to have both parents sitting in the courtroom during their interviews. Otherwise, the parent with whom the child last spent time may have a significant influence on parental preference. For example, if a child spent an enjoyable weekend with father, the child may fear father's alienation if the mother is named as the preferred parent. The parent who brings the child to the interview has an opportunity for last minute programming, and this too must be considered by the interviewer.

Children who lie to each parent for the purpose of gaining favor do not generally feel particularly guilty about their disloyalty. The benefits they derive from their fabrications appear to outweigh any discomfort they may feel over guilt. However, there are some children who do indeed feel guilty over their lying, and this contributes to feelings of lowered self-worth and depression. Others fear disclosure of their lying, and they will studiously avoid situations in which the parents can compare notes. And the parents themselves may support such avoidance of opportunity because they themselves do not wish to risk disclosure of the fact that they are being "buttered up." In custody evaluations in which I serve as impartial examiner, I insist upon the right to require joint interviews among the various concerned parties. And this, of course, invariably involves interviews in which both parents and the children are present together. It is in such interviews that the children's fabrications are most likely to reveal themselves. In fact, on a number of occasions, I have seen children panic and run out of the room because the "jig is finally up." Although such scenes are often psychologically traumatic for a child, they can often have therapeutic benefit in that they provide the child with the realization that he or she cannot get away with such ongoing lying indefinitely. In addition, they may provide the parents with an eye-opening experience regarding the child's fabrications.

In conclusion, we can see how the litigious process and loyalty conflicts interface with one another. Children's loyalty conflicts are likely to increase the probability of litigation. The litigious process, by the enforced separation that is often attendant to it, is likely to intensify loyalty conflicts. There is thereby an upward spiraling of the children's problems and an associated entrenchment of their psychiatric disturbances.

The Parental Alienation Syndrome

Introduction

Therapists who treat families involved in custody disputes should be familiar with the etiology, pathogenesis, and manifestations of a disorder which I have referred to as the *parental alienation syndrome*. The evaluator who is not familiar with this disturbance will be compromised in conducting an adequate custody evaluation. In fact, a lack of familiarity with this disorder may result in the examiner's taking at face value the children's comments — with the result that an injudicious and even psychologically detrimental recommendation may be made. Accordingly, I devote a section of the chapter to a discussion of this disorder before proceeding with the chapter on the interviews with the children.

Prior to the early 1980s, I certainly saw children whom I considered to have been brainwashed by one parent against the other. However, since that period I have seen — with ever increasing frequency — a disorder that I rarely saw previously. This disorder arose primarily in children who had been involved in protracted custody litigation. It is now so common that I see manifestations of it in about 90 percent of children who have been involved in custody conflicts. Because of its increasing frequency and the fact that a typical picture is observed — different from simple brainwashing — I believe a special designation is warranted. Accordingly, I have termed this disorder the *parental alienation syndrome.*

I have introduced this term to refer to a disturbance in which children are preoccupied with deprecation and criticism of a parent — denigration that is unjustified and/or exaggerated. The notion that such children are merely "brainwashed" is narrow. The term *brainwashing* implies that one parent is systematically and consciously programming the child to denigrate the other. The concept of the parental alienation syndrome includes the brainwashing component, but is much more comprehensive. It includes not only conscious but subconscious and unconscious factors within the programming parent that contribute to the child's alienation from the other. Furthermore (and this is extremely important), it includes factors that arise within the child — independent of the parental contributions — that play a role in the development of the syndrome. In addition, situational factors may contribute, i.e., factors that exist in the family and the environment that may play a role in bringing about the disorder.

There are two important reasons for the recent dramatic increase in the prevalence of this syndrome. First, since the mid-to-late 1970s, courts have generally taken the position that the tender years presumption (that mothers are intrinsically superior to fathers as parents) is sexist and that custodial determinations should be made on criteria relating directly to parenting capacity, independent of a parent's sex. This concept became known as the *best interests of the child presumption.* Second, in the late 1970s and early 1980s the joint custodial arrangement became increasingly popular. The notion that one parent be designated the *sole* custodian and the other the *visitor* was considered inegalitarian; joint custody promised a more equal division of time with the children and of decision-making powers. Both of these developments have had the effect of making children's custodial arrangements far more unpredictable and precarious. As a result, parents are more frequently brainwashing their children in order to ensure "victory" in custody/visitation litigation. And the children themselves have joined forces with the preferred parent in order to preserve what they consider to be the most desirable arrangement, without the appreciation that in some cases primary custody by the denigrated parent might be in their best interests.

These changes have placed women at a disadvantage in custody disputes. Under the tender years presumption, mothers were secure in the knowledge that fathers had to prove compellingly significant deficiencies in their wives' parenting capacity before they could even hope to wrest custody of the children. Under the best interests of the child presumption, especially when the sex-blind doctrine was used in its implementation, mothers' positions became less secure. And, with the subsequent popularization of the joint custodial concept, their positions became even more precarious. Accordingly, mothers have been more likely than fathers to attempt to alienate their children against fathers in order to strengthen their position in custody/visitation conflicts. And, for reasons to be elaborated upon, children have been supporting their mothers much more than their fathers, providing thereby their own contributions to the parental alienation syndrome.

Because of this clinically observed difference, namely, that mothers are more likely than fathers to be the alienators ("brain-washers"), I will, for simplicity of presentation, refer more frequently to the mother as the preferred or "loved" parent and the father as the rejected or the "hated" parent. I place the words *loved* and *hated* in quotes because there is still much love for the so-called hated parent and much hostility toward the allegedly loved one. This does not preclude my observation that on occasion (in about 10 percent of cases) it is the father who is the preferred parent and the mother the despised one. It would be an error for the reader to conclude that the designation of the mother as the preferred parent and the father as the hated one represents sexist bias on my part. Rather, it is merely a reflection of my own observations and experiences as well as others who work in the field. It also would be an error for the reader to conclude that my belief that mothers, more often than fathers, are the active contributors to the brainwashing components necessarily implies condemnation of these women. Actually, as I will discuss later, I am in sympathy with most of these mothers and believe that they have been "shortchanged" by the aforementioned recent developments.

In this section I will first describe the most common manifestations of the parental alienation syndrome. I will then describe the factors that I consider to be operative in bringing about the disorder. I divide such contributing factors into four categories: (1) brainwashing (conscious programming), (2) subconscious and unconscious programming, (3) the child's contributions, and (4) situational factors. I will then discuss approaches to the prevention and treatment of this disorder.

The Manifestations of the Parental Alienation Syndrome

Typically the child is obsessed with "hatred" of a parent. (As mentioned, the word *hatred* is placed in quotes because, as will be discussed, there are still many tender and loving feelings felt toward the allegedly despised parent that are not permitted expression.) These children speak of the parent with every vilification and profanity in their vocabulary—without embarrassment or guilt. The denigration of the parent often has the quality of a litany. After only minimal prompting by a lawyer, judge, probation officer, mental health professional, or other person involved in the litigation, the record will be turned on and a command performance provided. Not only is there a rehearsed quality to the speech, but one often hears phraseology that is not commonly used by the child. Many expressions are identical to those used by the "loved" parent. (Again, the word *loved* is placed in quotations because hostility toward that parent may similarly be unexpressed.) Typical examples: "He harasses us." "He sexually molested me." "His new girlfriend is a whore."

Even years after they have taken place, the child may justify the alienation with memories of minor altercations experienced in the relationship with the hated parent. These are usually trivial and are experiences that most children quickly forget, e.g., "He always used to speak very loud when he told me to brush my teeth." "He used to tell me to get his things a lot." "She used to say to me 'Don't interrupt.' " "He used to make a lot of noise when he chewed at the table." When these children are asked to give more compelling reasons for the hatred, they are unable to provide them. Frequently, the loved parent will agree with the child that these professed reasons justify the ongoing animosity.

The professions of hatred are most intense when the children and the loved parent are in the presence of the alienated one. However, when the child is alone with the allegedly hated parent, he or she may exhibit anything from hatred, to neutrality, to expressions of affection. When these children are alone with the hated parent, they may let their guard down and start to enjoy themselves. Then, almost as if they have realized that they are doing something "wrong," they will suddenly stiffen up and resume their expressions of withdrawal and animosity.

Another maneuver commonly seen in this situation is the child's claiming affection for the parent spoken to and hatred of the other and asking the loved parent to swear not to reveal the confessions to the other parent. And the same statements are made to the other parent with a similar extraction of a promise that the divulgences not be revealed to the absent parent. In this way these children "cover their tracks" and thereby avoid the disclosure of their schemes. Such children may find family interviews with therapists extremely anxiety provoking because of the fear that their manipulations and maneuvers will be divulged. The loved parent's proximity plays an important role regarding what the child will say to the hated one. The closer the loved parent, when the child is with the hated one, the greater the likelihood the hated parent will be denigrated. When seen alone in consultation, the child is likely to modify the litany in accordance with which parent is in the waiting room. Judges, lawyers, and mental health professionals who interview such children should recognize this important phenomenon.

The hatred of the parent often extends to include that parent's complete extended family. Cousins, aunts, uncles, and grandparents — with whom the child previously may have had loving relationships — are now viewed as similarly obnoxious. Grandparents, who previously had a loving and tender relationship with the child, now find themselves suddenly and inexplicably rejected. The child has no guilt over such rejection nor does the loved parent. Greeting cards are not reciprocated. Presents sent to the home are refused, remain unopened, or even destroyed (generally in the presence of the loved parent). When the hated parent's relatives call on the telephone, the child will respond with angry vilifications or quickly hang up on the caller. (These responses are more likely to occur if the loved parent is within hearing distance of the conversation.) With regard to the hatred of the relatives, the child is even less capable of providing justifications for the animosity. The rage of these children is so great that they become completely oblivious to the privations they are causing themselves. Again, the loved parent is typically unconcerned with the untoward psychological effects on the child of this rejection of the network of relatives who previously provided important psychological gratifications.

In family conferences, in which the children are seen together with both the loved and hated parent, the children reflexly take the position of the loved parent — sometimes even before the other has had the opportunity to present his (her) side of the argument. Even the loved parent may not present the argument as forcefully as the supporting child. These children may even refuse to accept evidence that is obvious proof of the hated parent's position. For example, one boy's mother claimed that her husband was giving her absolutely no money at all. When the father showed the boy canceled checks, signed by him and endorsed by the mother, the boy claimed that they were "forged." One girl claimed, after the death of her maternal grandfather from cancer, that it was her father who had murdered him. Although the mother herself considered the accusation preposterous, the child still persisted with the accusation. Commonly these children will accept as 100 percent valid the allegations of the loved parent against the hated one. One boy's mother claimed that her husband had beaten her on numerous occasions. The child presented this as one of the reasons why he hated his father. The father denied that he had ever laid a finger on the mother; in contrast, he claimed that the mother on a number of occasions had struck him. When I asked the child if he had ever *seen* his father hit his mother, he claimed that he had not, but that he believed his mother and insisted she would never lie to him. In this situation, as a result of an exhaustive evaluation, I concluded that the father's rendition was far more likely to have been valid.

Another symptom of the parental alienation syndrome is complete lack of ambivalence. All human relationships are ambivalent, and parent-child relationships are no exception. The concept of "mixed feelings" has no place in these children's scheme of things. The hated parent is "all bad" and the loved parent is "all good." Most children (normals as well as those with a wide variety of psychiatric problems), when asked to list both good and bad things about each parent, will generally be able to do so. When children with parental alienation syndrome are asked to provide the same lists, they will typically recite a long list of criticisms of the hated parent, but will not be able to think of one positive or redeeming personality trait. In contrast, they will provide only positive qualities for the preferred parent and claim to be unable to think of even one trait they dislike. The hated parent may have been deeply dedicated to the child's upbringing, and a strong bond may have been created over many years. The hated parent may produce photos that demonstrate clearly a joyful and deep relationship in which there was significant affection, tenderness, and mutual pleasure. But the memory of all these experiences appears to have been obliterated. When these children are shown photos of enjoyable events with the hated parent, they usually rationalize the experiences as having been forgotten, nonexistent, or feigned: "I really hated being with him then; I just smiled in the picture because he made me. He said he'd hit me if I didn't smile." "She used to beat me to make me go to the zoo with her." This element of complete lack of ambivalence is a typical manifestation of the parental alienation syndrome and should make one dubious about the validity of the professed animosity.

The child may exhibit a guiltless disregard for the feelings of the hated parent. There will be a complete absence of gratitude for gifts, support payments, and other manifestations of the hated parent's continued involvement and affection. Often these children will want to be certain the alienated parent continues to provide support payments, but at the same time adamantly refuse to visit. Commonly they will say that they *never* want to see the hated parent again, or not until their late teens or early twenties. To such a child I might say: "So you want your father to continue paying for all your food, clothing, rent, and education—even private high school and college—and yet you still don't want to see him at all, ever again. Is that right?" Such a child might respond: "That's right. He doesn't deserve to see me. He's mean and paying all that money is a good punishment for him."

Those who have never seen such children may consider this description a caricature. Those who have seen them will recognize the description immediately, although some children may not manifest all the symptoms. The parental alienation syndrome is becoming increasingly common, and there is good reason to predict that it will become even more prevalent if the recommendations presented below are not implemented.

Factors That Contribute to the Development of the Parental Alienation Syndrome

As mentioned, the parental alienation syndrome should not be viewed simply as due to *brainwashing*—the act of systematic programming of the child by one parent against the other, in a consciously planned endeavor. This is only one of four factors, each of which I will discuss separately.

Brainwashing. The brainwashing factor may be present to varying degrees. In some cases it may be minimal or even absent, and the disturbance results from one or more of the other contributing factors. More often, however, it is one of the predominant factors. I confine the word brainwashing to *conscious* acts of programming the child against the other parent. Most often the brainwashing is overt and obvious to the sensitive and astute examiner. The loved parent embarks upon an unrelenting campaign of denigration that may last for years. A mother, for example, whose divorce was the result of marital problems that contributed to her husband's seeking the affection of another woman, may continually vilify the father to her children with such terms as "adulterer," "philanderer," and "abandoner." Similarly, she may refer to the father's new woman friend as a "slut," "whore," and "home breaker." No attention is given to the problems in the marriage, especially this mother's problem(s), that may have contributed to the new involvement.

At times the criticisms may even be delusional, but the child is brought to believe entirely the validity of the accusations. The child may thereby come to view the hated parent as the incarnation of evil. A father, for example, may develop the delusion that his wife has been unfaithful to him and may even divorce her without any specific evidence for an affair. Innocent conversations with strange men are viewed as "proof" of her infidelity, and the children may come to view their mother as an adulteress. Often the infrequency of visits or lack of contact with the hated parent facilitates the child's accepting completely the loved parent's criticisms. There is little or no opportunity to correct the distortions by actual experiences.

A common form of criticism of the father is to complain about how little money he is giving. I am not referring here to situations in which the divorce has brought about some predictable privation. The healthy mother in such a situation recognizes that she and the children will not enjoy the same financial flexibility that they had prior to the separation. I am referring here to the use of the financial restrictions in the service of deprecating the father. A mother may complain so much about her financial restrictions that she will lead the children to believe that they may actually go without food, clothing, shelter, and that they may very well freeze and/or starve to death. I have seen cases in which extremely wealthy women utilized this maneuver, women who have been left with so much money that they will be comfortable for the rest of their lives. They may be spending thousands of dollars on extravagances, and yet the children may come to believe that because of their father's stinginess they are constantly on the verge of starvation.

There are mothers who, when talking to the children about their husbands having left the home, will make such statements as, "Your father's abandoned us." In most cases the father has left the mother and has not lost any affection for the children. Lumping the children together with herself (by using the word "us" rather than "me") promulgates the notion that they too have been rejected. In this way the mother contributes to the children's view of the father as reprehensible. The father in such situations may attempt (often unsuccessfully) to reassure the children that he has left the mother and not them, that he no longer loves the mother, but he still loves them.

Another way of brainwashing is to exaggerate a parent's minor psychological problems. The parent who may have drunk a little extra alcohol on occasion will gradually become spoken of as "an alcoholic." And the parent who may have experimented occasionally with drugs comes to be viewed as "a drug addict." Even though the accusing parent may have joined with the former spouse in such experimentation with drugs, the vilified parent is given the epithet. The deprecated parent might then be described in quite "colorful" terms: "He was dead drunk that night and he was literally out cold on the floor. We had to drag him to the car and dump him in the back seat." "The man was so stoned that he didn't have the faintest idea where he was and what he was doing." Often denial by the accused parent proves futile, especially if the accuser can provide concrete evidence such as a pipe used to smoke pot or a collection of bottles of liquor (which may be no more than the average person has in his or her home anyway).

There are parents who are quite creative in their brainwashing maneuvers. A father calls the home to speak to his son. The mother answers the telephone and happens to be in the son's room at the time. The father simply asks if he can speak with his son. The mother (with the boy right next to her) says nothing. Again, the father asks to speak with his son. More silence (during which the son is unable to hear his father's pleas for a response). Finally, the mother responds: "I'm glad he can't hear what you're saying right now" or "If he heard what you just said, I'm sure he would never speak with you again." When the father finally speaks with the boy and explains that he had said absolutely nothing that was critical, the boy may be incredulous. The result is that the father becomes very fearful of calling his son, lest he again be trapped in this way. A related maneuver is for the mother to say to the calling father (after a long period of stony silence during which the boy is within earshot of the mother and the father has made an innocuous statement): "That's *your* opinion. In *my* opinion he's a *very fine* boy." The implication here is that the father has made some scathing criticism and that the mother is defending the child.

Another mother greets her husband at the front door while their daughter is upstairs awaiting her father's visitation. Although the conversation is calm and unemotional, the mother suddenly dashes to the corner of the room, buries her head in her arms, and while cowering in the corner screams out, "No, no, no. don't hit me again." The girl comes running into the living room, and although she did not actually observe her father hit her mother, she believes her mother's claim that her father had just pulled himself back from beating her when he heard the girl coming down the stairs.

Selected use of pictures can also be used in the brainwashing process. There is hardly a child who hasn't at some time or other refused to be in a family picture. There is hardly a family who hasn't had the experience of cajoling the child to join them in the photograph. In many families a picture of the crying child will be taken, with a fond memory of the situation, the child's crying notwithstanding. Such a picture may be used by a brainwashing parent to convince the child that the other parent caused the child's grief and tears. The parent who is collecting evidence for litigation may be very quick to take pictures that could be interpreted as proof of the other parent's hostility toward the child. The healthy parent will argue with a child, scream once in a while, and make threatening gestures. If these can be caught on the camera they are considered to be good evidence for the parent's sadistic behavior toward the child.

Sarcasm is another way of getting across the message that the father is an undesirable character. A mother might say, "Isn't that wonderful, he's taking you to a ballgame." Although the words themselves are innocent enough, and might very well apply in a benevolent or noncharged situation, the sarcastic tonal quality says just the opposite. It implies: "After all these years he's finally gotten around to taking you to a ballgame" or "He really considers himself a big sport for parting with the few bucks he's spending to take you to a ballgame." Another mother says, in a singsong way, "Well, here he is again, your good ol' Daddy-O." Another says to her daughter, "So, the knight-in-shining-armor took his damsel to the movies." These comments are powerful forms of deprecation. If a therapist were to attempt to point out to such a mother how undermining these comments are, she might respond that she was "only kidding" and accuse the therapist of not having a good sense of humor.

A common maneuver used by these mothers is to instruct their children to tell their father that they are not at home when he calls. Or, they will tell them to give excuses like "She's in the bathroom" or "She's in the shower." These children are not only being taught to be deceitful, but they are being used as accomplices in the war between the parents. Of pertinence here is the message that the father is not an individual who is worthy of being treated with honesty and respect. Furthermore, there is the implication that he has objectionable qualities that warrant his being lied to and rejected. One mother told her children not to reveal the name and location of the day camp they were attending, and the children dutifully submitted to their mother's demand. When questioned in family session as to why she gave her children these instructions, she could only come up with a series of weak rationalizations: "He'll go to the camp and make trouble," "He'll embarrass them when he visits," and "I just get the feeling that it's not good for them for their father to know where they're going to camp." I knew the husband well enough to know that there was absolutely no justification for these concerns. Clearly, this mother was using the children as accomplices in her war and they were submitting.

There are a wide variety of other ways in which a mother may contribute to the children's alienation against their father. She may not forward to him copies of school reports. The implication here is that he is not interested in such material and that any comments he may make about them will be of little value to the child. Many go further and obstruct the father's attempt to obtain such material and may even inform the school that they, as the custodial parent, have every right to prevent the school from transmitting such material. She may refuse to allow the father to join with her in teacher's conferences and this may require the teacher to set up two separate meetings. When asked why she refuses to allow him to join her, the mother will often provide weak answers such as, "He'll disrupt the meeting," "I need all the time for myself," and "I just don't want to be in the same room with that man and that should be enough of an explanation." Of course, such mothers will have difficulties with school plays, concerts, and other presentations which are only given once. She may place the children in a very difficult position by stating that if the father attends she will not. Again, the implication is that even if the father is in the same auditorium with her, unpleasant and even terrible things are going to happen. And this position may be taken with regard to confirmations, Bar Mitzvahs, graduations, and family events to which both parents may be invited. These refusals also transmit the message that the father is somehow a noxious individual whose presence at any of these affairs is likely to ruin them.

A common way in which a parent will contribute to the alienation is to label as "harassment" the attempts by the hated parent to make contact with the children. The alienated parent expresses interest by telephone calls, attempts at visitation, the sending of presents, etc. These are termed "harassment" by the mother, and the children themselves come to view such overtures in the same vein. In frustration the father increases efforts in these areas, thereby increasing the likelihood that his attempts will be viewed as nuisances. A vicious cycle ensues in which the denigrated father increases his efforts, thereby increasing the likelihood that the approaches will be viewed as harassments. When such fathers call, the mother may respond with a quick statement which seemingly justifies hanging up on him immediately, without giving him any chance to respond or communicate with the children. Some of the more common putoffs utilized: "They're busy," "They're just ready to eat," "They're eating," "They're not done eating yet," "They're watching TV," "They're doing their homework and can't be disturbed," "They're playing with friends," and "They're getting ready to go to sleep." The father never seems to call at the right time. No matter what the children are doing, it serves as an excuse not to interrupt them. Every activity takes priority over speaking with the father. Related to this view of the calls as harassments, a mother may say to a calling father (with the child within earshot): "If you keep up this pressure to see him we're going to have one of those teen-age suicides on our hands." If this is said enough times the child then learns that this is a good way to avoid seeing his father. The next step then is for the child to threaten suicide if the father attempts to visit, to which the mother can then say to the father: "He keeps saying that he'll kill himself if he has to visit with you. Look what you've driven him to."

Subtle and often unconscious parental programming. The aforementioned attempts to denigrate a parent are conscious and deliberate. The brainwashing parent is well aware of what he (she) is doing. There are, however, other ways of programming children that can be equally if not more effective, but which do not involve the parent's actually recognizing what is going on. In this way the parent can profess innocence of brainwashing propensities. The motivations and mechanisms here are either unconscious (completely unavailable to conscious awareness) or subconscious (not easily available to conscious awareness).

There are many ways in which a parent may subtly and often unconsciously contribute to the alienation. A parent may profess to be a strong subscriber to the common advice: "Never criticize the other parent to the child." A mother may use this advice with comments such as: "There are things I could say about your father that would make your hair stand on end, but I'm not the kind of a person who criticizes a parent to his children." Such a comment engenders far more fear, distrust, and even hatred than would the presentation of an actual list of the father's alleged defects. A mother insists that the father park his car at a specific distance from the home and honk the horn, rather than ring the doorbell. She is implicitly saying to the child: "The person in that car is a dangerous and/or undesirable individual, someone whom I would not want to ring the doorbell of my house, let alone enter — even to say hello."

The parent who expresses neutrality regarding visitation ("I respect her decision regarding whether or not she wishes to visit with her father") is essentially communicating criticism of the father. The healthy parent appreciates how vital is the children's ongoing involvement with the noncustodial parent and encourages visitation, even when the child is "not in the mood." The healthy parent does not accept inconsequential and frivolous reasons for not visiting. Under the guise of neutrality, such a parent can engender and foster alienation. The "neutrality" essentially communicates to the child the message that the noncustodial parent cannot provide enough affection, attention, and other desirable input to make a missed visitation a loss of any consequence. Such a parent fails to appreciate that neutrality is as much a position in a conflict as overt support of either side.

Related to the neutrality maneuver is the parent who repeatedly insists that *the child* be the one to make the decision regarding visitation. Such a parent hammers away at the child with this principle. The child generally knows that the parent basically does not want the visitation, and so the child then professes the strong opinion that he or she does not wish to visit. Such a mother might say, after the child refuses: "I respect your strength in standing up for your rights." I once saw a mother in this category who went further and said, "If you don't want to visit with him, you can count on my full support. If we have to go to court to defend you we'll do it. I'm not going to let him push you around. You have your right to say no, and you can count on me to defend you." In extreme cases I have seen mothers who will actually hire an attorney to "protect" the child from this so-called coercing father who is insisting on visitation. Such mothers will give their children the impression that they would go to the Supreme Court if necessary in order to support them in "their" decision not to visit. And the more vociferous and determined the mothers become, the more adamant the children become in their refusal—refusal based not on the genuine desire not to see the father, but refusal based on the fear of not complying with their mothers' wish that they not visit. The mother and children then build together a stone wall of resistance against the father's overtures for involvement with the children.

One separated father calls, the mother answers, exchanges a few amenities, and then calls the child to the phone. Another mother answers and curtly says to the child, "It's your *father*" and stiffly gives the phone to the child—conveying the message that the caller is not a former husband, but a person who is so objectionable that the mother would not want in any way to be associated with him. The implication is that the caller is a possession of the child and is in no way related to her.

One mother encourages her child to visit with the father by saying, "You have to go see your father. If you don't he'll take us to court." Nothing is mentioned about the positive benefits to be derived by the child from seeing the father. The only reason to go is for them to protect *themselves* (". . . he'll take us to court") from the father's litigation. One mother, who had agreed to involve herself in court-appointed therapy in order to bring about a rapprochement between her two daughters and their father, told me early in the first session that her main purpose was to bring about such reconciliation. However, about ten minutes later she told me that she felt it was her obligation to help support her daughters' decisions not to see their father. In this case, there was absolutely no good reason for their not seeing their father, except that they were complying with their mother's subconscious wishes that they not do so.

There are mothers who use the "guilt trip" approach to programming their children against their husbands. For example, when the child wants to visit with the father during the scheduled visitation period, the mother might say, "How can you leave your poor old mother?" Not only is the child made to feel guilty about abandoning the mother, but in the ensuing discussion the father is also portrayed as an individual with little or no sensitivity to the mother's feelings. He has not only abandoned this poor helpless mother, but is now luring the children away, thereby increasing her loneliness. He comes to be viewed by the children as insensitive and cruel.

The children then, by exaggerating any of the father's weaknesses or deficiencies, can justify their not visiting with him and thereby lessen the guilt they feel over the abandonment of their mother.

The mother who moves to a distant city or state is essentially communicating to the children that distance from the father is not a consequential consideration. It is sometimes done with the implication that they are moving to bring about a cessation of the harassment and other indignities that they suffer while living close to the father. I am not referring here to situations in which such a move might be to the mother's benefit with regard to job opportunities or remarriage. Rather, I am referring to situations in which there is absolutely no reason for the move, other than to put distance between the children and their father. Sometimes parents will even litigate in order to gain permission to leave the state. However, the ostensible reasons are often unconvincing; the basic reason is to bring about a cessation of the parent-child relationship.

Another subtle maneuver commonly utilized by brainwashing parents relates to the psychological mechanism of doing and undoing. An example of this would be an individual who makes a racial slur, recognizes that the other person has been offended, and then retracts the statement by saying, "Oh, I didn't really mean it" or "I was only fooling." In the vast majority of cases the person so criticized does not "get the joke," the smiles and acceptance of the apology notwithstanding. Doing and undoing is not the same as never having done anything at all. A mother might angrily say, "*What* do you *mean* you're going to your father's house?" This may then be followed immediately with the statement, "Oh, what am I saying? That's wrong. I shouldn't have said that. I shouldn't discourage you from seeing your father. Forget I said that. Of course, it's okay for you to go to your father's house." The initial statement and the retraction, all taken together, are not the same as undiluted and unambivalent encouragement. The child gets the message that a strong part of the mother does not want the visitation. Some mothers may make such derogatory comments and then, when confronted with them later, claim that they were said at a time of extreme duress and that they were really not meant. One mother threatened her husband, as he left the home, "If you leave this marriage I vow to God that you'll never see your children again." She said this to her husband in front of their four children. In subsequent custody litigation she first denied to me that she had ever made the statement. When, however, in family session her husband and four children "refreshed her memory," she reluctantly admitted that she had made the statement. She then gave as her excuse that she was quite upset when her husband was leaving and she was thereby not responsible for her comment. She explained at length how, when people are upset, they will say all kinds of things that they don't really mean. Again, doing and undoing is not the same as never having done at all—and the children, at some level, recognize this.

One father, the owner of a large trucking company, dealt effectively with tough and often brutal truckers, union chiefs, and even underworld Mafia figures. He considered carrying a gun to be crucial for his survival as well as that of his company. A gun was viewed as standard professional equipment, like a doctor's stethoscope. He described numerous encounters with violent gangland figures. His fearlessness in these situations was remarkable. Yet, this same man claimed total impotence with regard to convincing his somewhat underweight and scrawny ten-year-old daughter to visit his former wife. His professions of helplessness were often quite convincing to his friends and relatives, and even when I pointed out to him the disparity between his ability to impose his opinion on people at work as compared to his home, he still claimed that he had absolutely no power over his child: "Doctor, I can't do a thing with her!"

One could argue that such subtle programming is extremely common in the divorce situation. I cannot deny this. However, in the parental alienation syndrome the child is *obsessed* with resentment above and beyond what might be expected in the usual divorce. It is the extent and depth of the alienation that differentiates the parental alienation syndrome from the mild alienation that is engendered in many divorces. In addition, there are other factors operative in producing the parental alienation syndrome that are not present in the common type of divorce programming—the most important of which are the presence of custody litigation and the threat of disruption of a strong parent-child (usually mother-child) bond.

Although the mothers in these situations may have a variety of motivations for programming their children against their fathers, the most common one relates to the old saying: "Hell hath no fury like a woman scorned." Actually, the original statement of William Congreve was: "Heaven has no rage, like love to hatred turned. Nor hell a fury, like a woman scorn'd" (*The Mourning Bride,* III, viii). Because these mothers are separated, and cannot retaliate directly against their husbands, they wreak vengeance by attempting to deprive their former spouses of their most treasured possessions, the children. And the brainwashing program is an attempt to achieve this goal. One of the reasons why such brainwashing is less common in fathers is that they, more often than mothers, have the opportunity to find new partners. Less frustrated, they are less angry and less in need of getting revenge.

It is important for the reader to appreciate that these mothers are far less loving of their children than their actions would suggest to the naive observer. Ostensibly, all their attempts to protect the child from harm by the dreaded parent are made in the service of their love of their children. Actually, the truly loving parent appreciates the importance of the non-custodial parent to the children and, with the rare exception of the genuinely abusing parent, facilitates all meaningful contact between the children and their father. These campaigns of denigration are not in the children's best interests and are in themselves manifestations of parental deficiency. More-over, these mothers exhibit the mechanism of reaction formation, in that their obsessive love of their children is often a cover-up for their underlying hostility. People who need to prove to themselves continuously that they *love* are often fighting underlying feelings of hate. On a few occasions, I have observed dramatic examples of this in my custody evaluations. In the midst of what could only be considered to be violent custodial conflicts—in which both parties were swept up in all-consuming anger—the mother would sud-denly state that she was giving up the custody conflict and handing the child over to the father.

In one such case, in the middle of a very heated session, the mother suddenly stated to the father: "Okay, if you want him that bad, take him." When I asked the mother if she was certain that this was her decision, she replied in the affirmative. I reemphasized that the implication of her statement was that the custody litigation should be discontinued and that I would therefore be writing a letter to the judge informing him that my services were no longer being enlisted because the mother had decided voluntarily to turn custody over to the father. At this point the mother's second husband leaned over and asked her if she appreciated the implica-tions of what she was saying. After two or three "jolts" by her new husband, the mother appeared to "sober up again" and stated, "Oh, I guess I didn't realize what I was saying. Of course, I love him very much." She then turned to her son and hugged him closely, but without any genuine expression of affection on her face. I believe that what happened here was an inexplicable relaxation of internal censorship that keeps unconscious processes relegated out of conscious awareness. My statement and that of her new husband served to "put things back in place" and she then proceeded with the litigation as viciously as ever. In short, we see another motivation for the obsessive affection that these mothers exhibit toward their children—an underlying rejection. And when these mothers "win," they not only win custody, but they win total alienation of their children from the hated spouse. The victory here results in psychological destruction of the children which, I believe, is what they basically want anyway. And they are dimly aware that their unrelenting litigation, indoctrination, and alienation will bring this about. In Chapter Nine I will discuss additional psychodynamic factors operative in these mothers, especially as they relate to the therapeutic approaches and the ways in which the courts should deal with them.

Factors arising within the child. Here, I refer to the factors that initially involve no active contribution on the part of the loved parent, conscious or unconscious, blatant or subtle. These are factors that originate within the child. Of course, a parent may use the child's contribution to promote the alienation, but it originates from psychopathological factors within the child.

The most important contributing factor relates to the fact that the child's basic psychological bond with the loved parent is stronger than with the hated parent. The campaign, then, is an attempt to maintain that tie, the disruption of which is threatened by the litigation. The aforementioned maneuvers utilized by mothers are also an attempt to maintain the integrity of this bond. (This point will be discussed in greater detail below.)

It is important also for the reader to appreciate that the weapons children use to support the mother's position are often naive and simplistic. Children lack the adult sophistication to provide themselves with credible and meaningful ammunition. Accordingly, to the outside observer the reasons given for the alienation will often seem frivolous. Unfortunately, the mother who welcomes the expression of such resentments and complaints will be gullible and accept with relish the most preposterous complaints. Unfortunately, attorneys and even judges are sometimes taken in by these children and do not frequently enough ask themselves the question: "Is this a justifiable reason for the child's never wanting to see the father again?" The inconsequential nature of the complaints and their absurdity are the hallmarks of the child's contribution to the development of the parental alienation syndrome.

Related to the aforementioned desire on the child's part to maintain the psychological bond with the preferred parent (usually the mother) is the fear of disruption of that bond. And there is also the fear of alienating the preferred parent. The hated parent is only ostensibly hated; there is still much love. But the loved parent is feared much more than loved. And it is this factor, more than any other, that contributes to the various symptoms discussed in this section. Generally, the fear is that of losing the love of the preferred parent. In the usual situation it is the father who has left the home. He has thereby provided for himself the reputation of being the rejecter and abandoner. No matter how justified his leaving the home, the children will generally view him as an abandoner. Most often the children subscribe to the dictum: "If you (father) really loved us you would tolerate the indignities and pains you suffer in your relationship with our mother." Having already been abandoned by one parent, the children are not going to risk abandonment by the second. Accordingly, they fear expressing resentment to the remaining parent (usually the mother) and will often reflexly take her position in any conflict with the father. This fear of the loss of mother's love is the most important factor in the development of the symptoms that I describe in this chapter. The parental alienation syndrome, however, provides a vehicle for expression of the anger felt toward the father because of his abandonment. This expression of resentment is supported by the mother, both overtly and covertly. It is part of the maneuver by which the children become willing weapons in the mother's hands, weapons that enable her to gratify her hostility through them.

A common factor that contributes to the obsessive hatred of the father is the utilization of the reaction formation mechanism. Obsessive hatred is often a thin disguise for deep love. This is especially the case when there is absolutely no reason to justify the preoccupation with the hated person's defects. True rejection is neutrality, when there is little if any thought of the person. The opposite of love is not hate, but indifference. Each time these children think about how much they hate their fathers, they are still thinking about them. Although the visual imagery may involve alienating fantasies, their fathers are still very much on their minds. The love, however, is expressed as hate in order to assuage the guilt they would feel about overt expression of affection for their fathers, especially in their mothers' presence. This guilt is often coupled with the aforementioned fear of their mothers' rejection if such expressions of affection for their fathers were to manifest themselves. One boy, when alone with me, stated: "I'm bad for wanting to visit with my father." This was a clear statement of guilt over his wish to visit with his father, his professions of hatred notwithstanding. This child was not born with the idea that it is bad to want to be with his father. Rather, he was programmed by his mother to be guilty over such thoughts and feelings.

There are situations in which factors operate with the result that the child will opt to support the parent with whom there is a weaker psychological bond or an unhealthy psychological bond. For example, a paranoid mother may be so successful in programming her child against the father that the child will take on her paranoid delusions. In such cases the child may exhibit morbid fear at the prospect of the father's coming to the home—lest the terrible consequences predicted by the mother be realized. Such children may even hide in closets and under the bed when the father comes to the home and visitation under such circumstances may be impossible.

Many of these children proudly state that their decision to reject their fathers is their own. They deny any contribution from their mothers. And the mothers often support this vehemently. In fact, the mothers will often state that they want the child to visit with the father and recognize the importance of such involvement. Yet, such a mother's every act indicates otherwise. Such children appreciate that, by stating that the decision is their own, they assuage mother's guilt and protect her from criticism. Such professions of independent thinking are supported by the mother, who will often praise these children for being the kinds of people who have a mind of their own and are forthright and brave enough to express overtly their opinions. As mentioned, in extreme cases such mothers will hire lawyers for the children and go to court in order to support what is ostensibly the child's own decision not to visit. The realities are that, with the exception of situations in which the father is indeed abusive, there is no good reason for a child's not wanting to have at least some contact with a father. Children are not born with genes that program them to reject a father. Such hatred and rejection are environmentally induced, and the most likely person to have brought about the alienation is the mother.

Situational factors. Often situational factors are conducive to the development of the disorder. By situational factors, I refer to external events that contribute to the development of the parental alienation syndrome — factors that abet the internal psychological processes in the parents and in the child. Most parents in a custody conflict know that time is on the side of the custodial parent. They appreciate that the longer the child remains with a particular parent, the greater the likelihood the child will resist moving to the home of the other. Even adults find change of domicile to be anxiety provoking. One way for a child to deal with this fear is to denigrate the noncustodial parent with criticisms that justify the child's remaining in the custodial home. For example, a mother dies and the maternal grandparents take over care of the child. Although at first the father may welcome their involvement, there are many cases on record of the maternal grandparents then litigating for the custody of the child. The child may then develop formidable resentments against the father in order to ensure that he or she will remain with the grandparents, the people whom the child has come to view as the preferable parents.

In one case I was involved with, two girls developed this disorder after their mother, with whom they were living, met a man who lived in Colorado. The mother then decided to move there with the two girls. The father brought the mother to court in an attempt to restrain her from moving out of the state of New Jersey with the children. Whereas previously there had been a good relationship with their father, the girls gradually developed increasing hatred of him, as their mother became progressively more deeply embroiled in the litigation. It was clear that the disorder would not have arisen had the mother not met a man who lived in Colorado, a man whom she wished to marry.

A common situation in which the child will develop complaints about the hated parent is one in which the child has observed a sibling being treated harshly and even being rejected for expressing affection for the hated parent. One boy I treated repeatedly observed his mother castigating his sister for her expressions of affection for their father. The sister was older and could withstand better the mother's vociferous denigration of her. The boy, however, was frightened by his mother's outbursts of rage toward his sister and was adamant in his refusal to see his father, claiming that he hated him, but only giving inconsequential reasons for his hostility. In this way he protected himself from his mother's animosity toward him. We see here clearly how his hatred of his father stemmed not so much from alienating qualities within the father, but from fear of the loss of his mother's affection.

One girl observed her mother making terrible threats to her older brother: "If you go to court and tell the judge that you want to live with your father, I'll have you put away as a psychotic. I'll have the child authorities put you away. You're crazy if you want to live with him." In this case the father was an unusually good parent, and the mother suffered with a moderately severe psychiatric disturbance. The older brother was strong enough to overtly express his preference for living with the father and appreciated that the mother had no power to unilaterally and perfunctorily have him incarcerated in a mental hospital. The younger sister, however, believed that this was a possibility and therefore told the judge that she wanted to live with her mother. Again, it was fear, not love of the mother, that brought about the child's professions of preference.

One boy repeatedly observed his father sadistically and mercilessly beating his mother. In order to protect himself from similar maltreatment, the boy professed deep affection for his father and hatred of his mother. The professions of love here stemmed from fear rather than from genuine feelings of affection. This phenomenon is generally referred to as "identification with the aggressor." It is based on the principle: "If you can't beat 'em, join 'em." Those who were knowledgeable about the father's brutal treatment of the mother expressed amazement that the child was obsessed with hatred of his mother and love of his father, and they were unable to understand why the boy kept pleading for the opportunity to live with his father. Another factor that may be operative in such situations is the child's model of what a loving relationship should be like. Love is viewed as manifesting itself by hostile interaction. Father demonstrates his "affection" for mother here by beating her. In order to be sure of obtaining this "love," the child opted to live with the hostile parent. This mechanism, of course, is central to *masochism* (Thompson 1959; Gardner 1970a, 1973a).

One 13-year-old girl's mother died in an automobile accident during the course of her parents' custody litigation. Specifically, she was killed en route home from a visit to her lawyer. Even prior to her mother's death, the girl had identified with and supported her mother's position and viewed her father as an abandoner. Her mother was supported in this regard by the maternal grandmother as well. At the time of the mother's death the girl manifested what I have described elsewhere (1979) as an "instantaneous identification" with her dead mother. This is one of the ways in which children (and even adults) may deal with the death of a parent. It is as if they are saying: "My parent isn't dead; he or she now resides within my own body." In the context of such immediate identification the child takes on many of the dead parent's personality traits, often almost overnight. And this is what occurred in this case. There was a very rapid maturational process in which the girl acquired many of the mannerisms of her mother. As part of this process she intensified her hatred of her father and even accused him of having caused the death of her mother: "If you hadn't treated my mother so badly, there wouldn't have been a breakup of the marriage, she wouldn't have had to go visit with her lawyer, and she wouldn't have been killed on the way home from his office." Although there were many other factors involved in her obsessive hatred and rejection of her father, this identification factor was an important one. Prior to her mother's death she had grudgingly and intermittently seen her father; after the death there was a total cessation of visitation. Interestingly, this identification process was supported by the maternal grandmother, who began to view the girl as the reincarnation of her dead daughter. And in the service of this process she supported the girl in her rejection of her father.

Concluding Comments

In this section I have focused primarily on the manifestations of the parental alienation syndrome and described contributing factors from four areas: (1) brainwashing, (2) subtle and often unconscious programming, (3) the child's contributions, and (4) situational factors. The main emphasis has been to describe the phenomenon of the parental alienation syndrome, but not to delve significantly into its underlying psychodynamics. I will discuss below in greater depth certain aspects of the programmer's psychodynamics, especially as they relate to therapeutic approaches and the ways in which the courts can deal with parents who contribute to the development and perpetuation of their children's parental alienation syndromes.

Lawyers and judges often ask examiners involved in custody evaluations whether a particular child has or has not been "brainwashed." Frequently, under cross-examination, they will request a yes or no answer. Under these circumstances I generally respond: "I cannot answer yes or no." To answer simply yes, I would only be providing a partially correct response and this would be a disservice to the brainwashing mother. The yes or no response does not give me the opportunity to describe the more complex factors, especially those originating within the child and the situation. Examiners are often asked, "With which parent does the child have a psychological bond?" Again, I usually refuse to answer this question. If I am given an opportunity to elaborate, I state that there is rarely a situation in which a child has a psychological bond with one parent and not with the other. Generally, the child has psychological bonds with both parents. What one really wants to know in custody evaluations is the parent with whom the child has the *stronger and/or healthier* psychological bond. And, if a stepparent is under consideration, one wants to know about the strength and nature of the psychological bond with the stepparent, as compared with each of the natural parents. The psychological bond consideration will be discussed in greater detail below.

Psychotherapeutic and Legal Approaches to the Three Types of Parental Alienation Syndrome Families

Families in which the children exhibit manifestations of the parental alienation syndrome can be divided into three categories: severe, moderate, and mild. Although there is actually a continuum, and many cases do not fit neatly into one of these categories, the differentiation is still useful — especially with regard to the therapeutic approaches. In each of the three categories not only are the children different, but the mothers as well. It is extremely important that evaluators determine the proper category if they are to provide the most judicious recommendations. In each category I will discuss the mothers, the children, and the appropriate therapeutic approaches. I will use the mother as the example of the preferred parent as this is so in the majority of cases; however, the same considerations apply to the father when he is the favored parent.

I wish to emphasize at this point that in many cases the therapy of these families is not possible without court support. Only the court has the power to order these mothers to stop their manipulations and maneuvering. And it is only the court that has the power to place the children in whichever-home would best suit their needs at the particular time. Therapists who embark upon the treatment of such families without such court backing are not likely to be successful. I cannot emphasize this point strongly enough.

Severe cases of the parental alienation syndrome. The *mothers* of these children are often fanatic. They will use every mechanism at their disposal (legal and illegal) to prevent visitation. They are obsessed with antagonism toward their husbands. In many cases they are paranoid. Sometimes the paranoid thoughts and feelings about the husband are isolated to him alone; in other cases this paranoia is just one example of many types of paranoid thinking. Often the paranoia did not exhibit itself prior to the breakup of the marriage and may be a manifestation of the psychiatric deterioration that frequently is seen in the context of divorce disputes, especially custody disputes. Central to the paranoid mechanism is projection. These mothers see in their husbands many noxious qualities that actually exist within themselves. By projecting these unacceptable qualities onto their husbands they can consider themselves innocent victims. When a sex-abuse allegation becomes part of the package (1987), they may be projecting their own sexual inclinations onto him. In the service of this goal they exaggerate and distort any comment the child makes that might justify the accusation. And this is not difficult to do because children normally will entertain sexual fantasies, often of the most bizarre form. I am in agreement with Freud that children are "polymorphous perverse" and they thereby provide these mothers with an ample supply of material to serve as nuclei for their projections and accusations.

Such mothers do not respond to logic, confrontations with reality, or appeals to reason. They will readily believe the most preposterous scenarios. Skilled mental health examiners who claim that there is no evidence for the accusation are dismissed as being against them, or as being paid off by the husband. And this is typical of paranoid thinking: it does not respond to logic and any confrontation that might shake the system is rationalized into the paranoid scenario. Even a court decision that the father is not guilty of the mother's allegations does not alter her beliefs or reduce her commitment to her scenarios of denigration. Energizing the rage is the "hell hath no fury like a woman scorned" phenomenon.

The *children* of these mothers are similarly fanatic. They have joined together with her in a *folie à deux* relationship in which they share her paranoid fantasies about the father. They may become panic-stricken over the prospect of visiting with their father. Their blood-curdling shrieks, panicked states, and hostility may be so severe that visitation is impossible. If placed in the father's home they may run away, become paralyzed with morbid fear, or be so destructive that removal becomes warranted. Unlike children in the moderate and mild categories, their panic and hostility may not be reduced in the father's home, even when separated for significant periods.

With regard to the *therapeutic approaches* in this category, traditional therapy for the mother is most often not possible. She is totally unreceptive to treatment and will consider a therapist who believes that her delusions are not warranted to be joining in with her husband. He thereby becomes incorporated into the paranoid system. A court order that she enter into treatment is futile. Judges are often naive with regard to their belief that one can order a person into treatment. This is an extension of their general view of the world that ordering people around is the best way to accomplish something. Most judges are aware that they cannot order an impotent husband to have an erection or a frigid wife to have an orgasm. Yet, they somehow believe that one can order someone to have conviction and commitment to therapy. Accordingly, the evaluator does well to discourage the court from such a misguided order.

Therapy for the children, as well, is most often not possible *while the children are still living in the mother's home.* No matter how many times a week they are seen, the therapeutic exposure represents only a small fraction of the total amount of time of exposure to the mother's denigrations of the father. There is a sick psychological bond here between the mother and children that is not going to be changed by therapy as long as the children remain living with the mother. While still in the mother's home the children are going to be exposed continually to the bombardment of denigration and other influences (overt and covert) that contribute to the perpetuation of the syndrome.

Accordingly, the first step toward treatment is *removal* of the children from the mother's home and placement in the home of the father, the allegedly hated parent. This may not be accomplished easily and the court might have to threaten sanctions and even jail if the mother does not comply. Following this transfer there must be a period of decompression and debriefing in which the mother has no opportunity at all for input to the children. The hope here is to give the children the opportunity to re-establish the relationship with the alienated father, without significant contamination of the process by the brainwashing mother. Even telephone calls must be strictly prohibited for at least a few weeks, and perhaps longer. Then, according to the therapist's judgment, slowly increasing contacts with the mother may be initiated, starting with monitored telephone calls. The danger here, however, is that these will be used as opportunities for programming the children.

Therefore, this period of slow and judicious renewal of contact between the children and the brainwashing parent must be monitored carefully so as to prevent a recurrence of the disorder. In some cases this may be successful, especially if the mother can see her way clear to entering into meaningful therapy (not often the case for mothers in this category). In these cases the children might ultimately be returned to the mother. However, if she still continues to alienate the children it may be necessary to assign primary custody to the father and allow a frequency of visitation that will be limited enough to protect them from significant reprogramming. In extreme cases, one may have to sever the children entirely from the mother for many months or even years. In such cases the children will at least be living with one parent who is healthy. The children will then be in a position to derive the benefits of placement with the father, continuing hostile attitudes toward him notwithstanding. However, my experience has been that in such cases the animosity toward the father gradually becomes reduced. In contrast, if the court is naive enough to allow the children to remain living with such a disturbed mother, then it is likely that there will be lifelong alienation from the father.

With regard to the individual therapeutic work with the *fathers,* my comments here refer to those fathers who have been good fathers, who have been significantly involved with their children, and in no way deserve animosity being vented upon them. The first step is to explain to them what is happening to their children and help them not to take so seriously the children's professions of hatred. The fathers must be helped to appreciate that a strong, healthy psychological bond has been formed with their children during their formative years and that the children's allegations of hatred are generally a facade. Accordingly, the fathers must be helped to develop a "thick skin." Some fathers become quite discouraged and think seriously about removing themselves entirely from their children, so pained are they by the rejections. Many will even have been given advice (sometimes by well-meaning therapists) to "respect" the children's desires not to see them. This is a grave mistake. Such removal will generally be detrimental to the children. The fathers must be encouraged to keep reaching out, keep telling the children how much they care for them, and divert the children's attention when they are involved in the denigration. At times, it is useful to encourage such fathers to say such things as: "You don't have to talk that way with me now, your mother's not around" and "I don't believe a word of what you're saying. You know and I know that we love one another deeply and that we've had great times together in the past and will have more great times in the future." As mentioned, in some cases permanent residence with the father may be the only viable option. In other cases varying degrees of visitation with the mother may be reasonable, and in some cases ultimate return to the mother (with liberal visitation to the father) may be possible.

Moderate cases of the parental alienation syndrome. The *mothers* of children in this category are not as fanatic as those in the more severe category, but are more disturbed than those in the mild category (who may not have a psychiatric disturbance). In these cases the rage-of-the-rejected-woman factor is more important than the paranoid projection contribution. They are able to make some differentiation between allegations that are preposterous and those that are not. There is still, however, a campaign of denigration and a significant desire to withhold the children from the father as a vengeance maneuver. They will find a wide variety of excuses to interfere with or circumvent visitation. They may be unreceptive to complying with court orders; however, they will often comply under great pressure, threats of sanctions and/or transfer of custody, etc. These mothers are less likely to be paranoid than those in the severe category. When a sex-abuse allegation is brought into the parental alienation syndrome, they will be able to differentiate between the children's preposterous claims and those that may have some validity. Whereas the mothers in the severe category have a sick psychological bond with the children (often a paranoid one), the mothers of children in this category are more likely to have a healthy psychological bond that is being compromised by their rage. The mothers in this category are more likely to have been good child rearers prior to the divorce. In contrast, the mothers in the severe category, even though not significantly disturbed prior to the separation, often have exhibited formidable impairments in child-rearing capacity prior to the separation. It is for these reasons that the mother can most often be allowed to remain the primary custodial parent and the combined efforts of the court and the therapist may be successful in enabling the children to resume normal visitation with the father.

The *children* in this category are less fanatic in their vilification of the father than those in the severe category, but more than those in the mild category. They, too, have their campaigns of deprecation of the father, but are much more likely to give up their scenarios when alone with him, especially for long periods. Once removed entirely from their mother's purview, the children generally quiet down, relax their guard, and involve themselves benevolently with their father. A younger child may often need the support of an older one to keep the campaign going. Under such circumstances the older child is serving as a mother surrogate during visitation. The primary motive for the children's scenarios is to maintain the healthy psychological bond with the mother.

With regard to the *therapy* for these families it is important that *one* therapist be utilized. This is not a situation in which mother should have her therapist, father his therapist, and the children their own. Such a therapeutic program, although seemingly respectful of each party's individual needs, is not likely to work for the treatment of families in which the children exhibit a parental alienation syndrome. Such fractionization reduces communication, sets up antagonistic subsystems within the family, and is thereby likely to intensify and promulgate the pathological interactions which contribute to the parental alienation syndrome. It is also important that the therapist be court ordered and have direct input to the judge. This can often be facilitated by the utilization of a guardian ad litem or a child advocate, who has the opportunity for direct communication with the court. The mother must know that any obstructionism on her part will be immediately reported to the judge, either by the therapist or through the guardian ad litem or child advocate. The court must be willing to impose sanctions such as fines or jail. The threat of loss of primary custody can also help such mothers "remember to cooperate."

If the mother has her own therapist a mutual admiration society may develop in which the therapist (consciously or unconsciously) becomes the mother's champion in the fight. Women in this category have a way of selecting therapists who will support their antagonism toward the father. Most often, the mother chooses a *woman* as a therapist—especially a woman who is herself antagonistic toward men. Typically, the mother's therapist has little, if any, contact with the father and so does not have the opportunity to hear his side of the story. When they do meet with him they typically will be hostile and unsympathetic. Accordingly, the mother and the therapist often develop a *folie à deux* relationship. Although the court may not wish to stop the mother from seeing this therapist, it does well to prohibit the children from being "treated" by her (as mentioned, rarely a man). Even if the court were to order the mother's therapist to stop treating her, it is likely that she would find another person who would support her position. And this is another reason why I generally do not recommend that the court order a cessation of the mother's treatment with the therapist with whom she is pathologically involved.

The court should order the mother to see the court's therapist, even though her cooperation is not likely to be significant and even though she may be influenced significantly by her own therapist. The court's therapist must have a thick skin and be able to tolerate the shrieks and claims of maltreatment that these children will provide. Doing what children profess they want is not always the same as doing what is best for them. Therapists of the persuasion that they must "respect" their child patients and accede to their wishes, will be doing these children a terrible disservice. These same therapists would not "respect" a child's wish not to have a polio shot, yet they will respect the child's wish not to see a father who shows no significant evidence for abuse, maltreatment, neglect, etc. The therapist does well to recall that prior to the separation the children were likely to have had a good, strong relationship with the father and that strong psychological ties must still be present. The therapist should view the children's professed animosity as superficial and as designed to ingratiate themselves to the mother. To take the allegations of maltreatment seriously is a terrible disservice to these children. It may contribute to an entrenchment of the parental alienation syndrome and may result in years of, if not lifelong, alienation.

Similarly, when a fabricated (as opposed to bona fide) sex-abuse allegation has been introduced, and if the therapist is convinced that it is false, then he (she) does well not to dwell on these allegations. Typically, over time such false allegations become elaborated and new allegations arise when the earlier ones do not work (1987). It is antitherapeutic to listen to these. Rather, it is therapeutic to say, "That didn't happen! So let's go on and talk about *real* things like your next visit with your father." The therapist must appreciate that the children *need* him to serve as an excuse for visiting with the father. When "forced" to visit with the father they can say to the mother that the therapist is mean, cruel, etc. and that they really do not want to see the father, but the therapist "makes them." And the judge should appreciate that he (she) too can serve this function for the children. With a court order, they can say to their mother, "I really hate my father, but that stupid judge is making me see him."

The therapist must also appreciate that older children may promulgate the mother's programming down to younger ones. And the older children are especially likely to do this during visits with the father. The mother thereby relies on her accomplice to "work over" the younger ones when in the enemy camp (the father's house). These older children may even mastermind "inside jobs" in the father's house. Accordingly, a "divide and conquer" approach sometimes is warranted. This is best accomplished by requiring the children to visit separately — or at least separate from the older sibling programmers — until they all have had the living experience (including the mother) that the terrible consequences of being alone with the father were not realized. For example, an older sister may be programming her two younger brothers into believing that the father is dangerous and/or noxious, when they themselves exhibit only mild manifestations of a parental alienation syndrome. When they visit with the father and relax their guard she may quickly remind them about the indignities they are likely to suffer under such circumstances. Structuring the visitations so that the sister visits separately from her brothers (at least for a time) is the most effective way of dealing with this kind of problem. This is a good example of an important aspect of the therapy of these families, namely, that less is done via the attempt to get people to gain insight and much more is accomplished by structuring situations and providing individuals with actual experiences.

Transition periods, that is the points when the children are transferred from mother to father, may be especially difficult for children with parental alienation syndrome. It is then (when both parents and the children are together) that the loyalty conflicts become most intense and the symptoms most severe. Accordingly, it is not a good idea to have the father pick up the children at the mother's home. In that setting—with the mother directly observing the children—they are most likely to resist going with their father and will predictably gain their mother's support (overt or covert) for their resistance. Alternative transitional arrangements must therefore be devised, arrangements that do not place the children in a situation in which they are with mother and father at the same time.

A good transition place is the therapist's office. The mother brings the children, spends some time with them and the therapist, and then goes home, leaving the children alone with the therapist. Subsequently the father comes, spends some time with the children and the therapist, and then takes them to his home. Or a truly impartial intermediary, with whom the children have a good relationship, can pick the children up at the mother's home and bring them to the father's home. A therapist, guardian *ad litem,* or child advocate can serve in this role.

Once the court has made a final decision that the children shall remain living with their mother, then the children are able to dispense with their scenarios of deprecation. This is a very important point. The children develop their campaigns of denigration in the desire to maintain the psychological bond with the mother. The custody litigation has threatened a disruption of this bond. Once the court has ruled that the children shall remain living primarily with their mother, they can relax and allow themselves to enjoy a more benevolent relationship with their father. In short, the court's order obviates the need for the symptoms and so they can be dispensed with.

I have been involved in a number of cases in which mothers in this category would suddenly decide that they wanted to move to another state. They suddenly become "homesick," after many years of comfortable adjustment in the state in which the children were raised. Some suddenly decided that they wanted to remove themselves (and children, of course) from the scene of the custody conflict (including the whole state) and "start all over" and/or "find themselves" at some remote place. A few claimed better job opportunities in another state. It would be an error for the examiner to take these arguments seriously. Rather, the court should be advised to inform the mother that she is free to leave the state at any time she wishes; however, she should understand that if she does so it will *not* be with the children. And such a position can be included in the evaluator's recommendations.

Whereas mothers in the severe category are not likely to be candidates for treatment, some mothers in the moderate category may indeed involve themselves meaningfully in the therapeutic process. I believe it is preferable for the court-ordered family therapist to work with the mother in dealing with her underlying problems. However, working with a separate therapist—who does not support her distortions—may be useful. It is crucial that the mother's therapist not be in the aforementioned category of person (more often a woman) who joins with the mother in her delusions about the father. Sometimes a central element in the mother's rage is the fact that the father has established a new relationship and she has not done so. Her jealousy is a contributing factor to her program of wreaking vengeance on her former husband by attempting to deprive him of his children, his most treasured possessions. Another factor that often contributes to the campaign of animosity is the mother's desire to maintain a relationship with her former husband. The tumultuous activity guarantees ongoing involvement, accusation and counteraccusation, attack and counterattack, and so on. Most people, when confronted with a choice between total abandonment and hostile involvement, would choose the acrimonious relationship. And these mothers demonstrate this point well. To the degree that one can help her "pick up the pieces of her life" and form new involvements and interests, one is likely to reduce the rage. The most therapeutic experience such a woman can have is meeting a new man with whom she becomes deeply involved and forming a strong relationship.

The therapeutic approach to the fathers in this category are similar to those utilized with fathers in the first category. One must explain to them what is happening and help them "thicken their skins." They must be helped not to take so seriously the children's vilifications. They must be helped to divert them to healthier interchanges and not dwell on whether a particular allegation is true or false. They must be helped to provide the children with healthy living experiences—which are the most effective antidotes to the delusions regarding his noxious and/or dangerous qualities.

When working individually with the children they must be discouraged from "buttering up" each parent and saying to each what they think that one wants to hear at the moment, regardless of the consequences. The therapist should express his incredulity over the children's vilification of the father. They should not take seriously the children's false allegations and quickly move on to other subjects. However, following visits with the father, they should emphasize to the children that their view of their father as an ogre was not realized during the visitation. In family sessions the therapist should "smoke out" the lies. This is much more likely to be done in family sessions than in individual sessions. The therapist does well to appreciate that as long as the litigation goes on direct work with the children will be difficult and complete alleviation of symptoms may not be possible. Accordingly, in communications to the judge the therapist should be ever reminding him (her) of the fact that the longer the litigation goes on the less the likelihood the treatment will be successful.

The therapist does well to try to find some healthy "insider" on the mother's side of the family. Sometimes the mother's mother and/or father can serve in this capacity. On occasion it might be the mother's brother or sister. Here, one is looking for a person who is aware that the mother is "going too far" with regard to the animosity that she has toward her husband and is fostering the children's alienation from him. If a good relationship existed between the father's parents and the mother's parents prior to the separation, the therapist might prevail upon the father's parents to speak with the mother's parents. Sometimes family meetings in which all four grandparents are present — with the mother and father — can be useful in this regard. The mother's mother can be a very powerful therapeutic ally if the therapist is able to enlist her services. I cannot emphasize strongly enough the importance of the therapist's attempting to find such an ally on the mother's side of the family. That individual can sometimes bring the mother to her senses and effectively prevail upon her to "loosen up" and appreciate how detrimental her maneuvers are to her children. Many parties who are appreciative of the mother's injudicious behavior take the position of "not wanting to get involved." The therapist does well to attempt to have access to such people and to impress upon them that their neutrality may be a terrible disservice to the children. I have no problem eliciting guilt in such individuals if it will serve the purpose of facilitating their involvement in the therapeutic process.

Not all therapists are suited to work with such families. As mentioned, they must have "thick skins" to tolerate the children's antics as they claim that they are being exposed to terrible traumas and indignities in their father's homes. They must also be people who are comfortable with taking a somewhat dictatorial position. And this is especially important in their relationship with the mothers of these children. The therapist must appreciate that more of the therapy relates to manipulating and structuring situations than providing people with insight. To the degree that the therapist can provide people with living experiences, to that degree will false perceptions be altered. Therapists with a strong orientation toward psychoanalytic inquiry are generally not qualified to conduct such treatment. I am a psychoanalyst myself and involve most of my adult patients in psychoanalytic therapy. However, when a parental alienation syndrome is present the therapeutic approach must *first* involve a significant degree of people manipulation (usually by court order) and structure before one can sit down and talk meaningfully with the parties involved. Moreover, therapists who accept as valid the patient's wishes (whether child or adult) and consider it therapeutically contraindicated to pressure or coerce a patient are also not candidates to serve such families. I too consider myself sensitive to the needs of my patients. As mentioned, doing what the patient *wants* and doing what the patient *needs* may be two entirely different things. It is for this reason that the courts play such an important role in the treatment of families in which a parental alienation syndrome is present. Without the therapist's having the court's power to bring about the various manipulations and structural changes, the therapy is not likely to be possible.

Mild cases of the parental alienation syndrome. The *mothers* of children in this category generally have a healthy psychological bond with the children. These mothers may recognize that gender egalitarianism in custody disputes is a disservice to children, but are healthy enough not to involve themselves in significant degrees of courtroom litigation in order to gain primary custody. These mothers recognize that alienation from the father is not in the best interests of their children and are willing to take a more conciliatory approach to the father's requests. They either go along with a joint custodial compromise or even allow (albeit reluctantly) the father to have sole custody with their having a liberal visitation program. Although these mothers believe it would be in the best interests of the children to remain with them, they recognize that protracted litigation is going to cause all family members to suffer more grief than an injudicious custody arrangement, namely, one in which the father has more involvement (either sole or joint custody) than they consider warranted. However, we may still see some manifestations of programming in these mothers in order to strengthen their positions. There is no paranoia here, but there is anger and there may be some desire for vengeance. The motive for programming the children, however, is less likely to be vengeance than it is merely to entrench their positions in an inegalitarian situation. Of the three categories of mothers, these mothers have generally been the most dedicated ones during the earliest years of their children's lives and have thereby developed the strongest and healthiest psychological bonds with them.

The *children* in this category also develop their own scenarios, again with the slight prodding of the mother. Here the children's primary motive is to strengthen the mother's position in the custody dispute in order to maintain the stronger healthy psychological bond that they have with their mothers.

These are the children who are most likely to be ambivalent about visitation and are most free to express affection for their fathers, even in their mothers' presence.

With regard to *therapy*, in most cases therapy is *not* necessary. What these children need is a final court order confirming that they will remain living primarily with their mother and there will be no threat of their being transferred to their father. This usually brings about a "cure" of the parental alienation syndrome. If the children need therapy it is for other things, possibly related to the divorce animosities.

Concluding comments regarding recommendations for families in which a parental alienation syndrome is present. My purpose in this section has been to provide mental health practitioners with guidelines for advising courts on how to deal with parental alienation children and their families. As mentioned, without proper placement of the child (for which a court order may be necessary), treatment may be futile. In the majority of cases of parental alienation syndrome, it is the mother who is favored and the father who is denigrated. However, there are certainly situations in which the mother is deprecated and the father favored. For simplicity of presentation, and because mothers are more often the favored parent, I have used her as the example of the preferred parent — but recognize that in some cases it is the father who is preferred and the one who may be programming the child and it is the mother who is the despised parent. In such cases the fathers should be divided into the aforementioned categories and given the same considerations as described for mothers.

I recognize that the division of these families into three categories is somewhat artificial. In reality, we have a continuum from very severe cases to very mild cases. However, the distinctions are valid and extremely important if one is to make proper therapeutic recommendations. It is especially vital for the examiner to make every attempt to differentiate between mothers in category one (severe) and those in category two (moderate). The former mothers are often so disturbed that custody should be transferred. The latter mothers, their antics notwithstanding, generally still serve better as the primary custodial parent.

Last, a special comment about the guardian *ad litem*. In most of the custody evaluations I conducted, I found the guardian ad litem to be useful. He (she) could generally be relied upon to assist in obtaining documents that a parent might have been hesitant to provide or to enlist the court's assistance in getting reluctant parents to cooperate in the evaluation. The guardian ad litem can be a powerful ally for therapists treating families in which a parental alienation syndrome is present. However, there is a definite risk in recommending that the court appoint such a person. A guardian ad litem who is not familiar with the causes, manifestations, and proper treatment of children in this category may prove a definite impediment in the course of treatment. The guardian ad litem generally takes pride in supporting the children's needs. Unfortunately, many are naive and reflexively support the children's positions. They may not appreciate that they are thereby promulgating the pathology. Some have great difficulty supporting coercive maneuvers (such as insisting that the children visit with a father who they profess they hate) because it goes so much against their traditional orientation to clients in which they often automatically align themselves with their client's cause. For guardians ad litem to effectively work with families of parental alienation syndrome children, they must accommodate themselves to this new orientation toward their clients. Accordingly, evaluators do well, when recommending a guardian ad litem, to impress upon the court the importance of securing an individual who is knowledgeable about the special approaches necessary to utilize when working with these families.

The Stronger, Healthy Psychological Bond Presumption

During the last few years, in association with my increasing involvement in child custody litigation, I have often had the thought that perhaps we should not have dispensed with the tender years presumption. If we are to consider the greatest good for the greatest number, I believe we probably would have done better to retain it. Of course, there would have been some children who would then have remained with the less preferable parent; however, many more children would have been spared the psychological traumas attendant to the implementation of the best interests of the child doctrine and the widespread enthusiasm for the joint custodial concept. There is no question that custody litigation has increased dramatically since the mid-1970s and there is no question, as well, that this increase has been the direct result of these two recent developments.

What should we do then? Go back to the old system? I think not. I believe that there is a middle path that should prove useful. To elaborate: First, the displacement of the tender years presumption with the best interests of the child philosophy was initiated primarily by men who claimed that the tender years presumption was intrinsically "sexist" because women are not necessarily preferable parents by virtue of the fact that they are female. State legislatures and the courts agreed. As a result, the best interests of the child doctrine has been uniformly equated with the notion that custody determinations should be "sex blind." Considerable difficulty has been caused, I believe, by fusing these two concepts. *It is extremely important that they be considered separately.* Everyone claims to be in support of doing what is in the best interests of the children. Everyone waves that banner: each parent, each attorney, the mental health professionals who testify, and certainly the judge. No one claims to be against children's best interests. The situation is analogous to the position politicians take with regard to their support for widows, orphans, the handicapped, and the poor. All politicians wave that banner. Even the suggestion that a politician might not be in strong support of these unfortunates would be met with denial, professions of incredulity, and righteous indignation.

With regard to all those who claim that the best interests of the child is their paramount consideration, one could argue that a wide variety of possible custodial arrangements could serve children's best interests. One could argue that automatic placement with the father serves their best interests, and this was certainly the case up until the early 20th century. Or one could claim that automatic preference for the mother serves the children best, and this was the case from the mid-1920s to the mid-1970s. One could argue that placing them with grandparents, uncles, aunts, or in foster homes, adoption agencies, or residential cottages might serve children's best interests. At this time, the prevailing notion is that sex-blind custody evaluations automatically serve children's best interests. Although it may be an unpopular thing to say at this time, I do not believe that sex-blind custody decisions necessarily serve the best interests of children. Somehow, the acceptance of the concept that fathers can be as paternal as mothers can be maternal was immediately linked with the concept that such egalitarianism serves the best interests of children. I do not accept this assumption of gender equality in child-rearing capacity and would go further and state that the younger the child, the less the likelihood that this assumption is valid. It follows then that I do not believe that sex-blind custody evaluations and decisions serve the best interests of children. I recognize that this is an unpopular position to take in the early 1990s, that it might appear to be very undemocratic and even sexist of me (here with the prejudice being against men), but it is the opinion that I have. My hope is that the reader will read on with some degree of receptivity and will come to the same conclusion.

To elaborate: No one can deny that men and women are different biologically. No one can deny, either, that it is the woman who bears the child and has within her the power to feed it with her own body (although she may choose not to do so). I believe that this biological difference cannot be disassociated from certain psychological factors that result in mothers' being more likely to be superior to fathers in their capacity to involve themselves with the newborn infant at the time of its birth. After all, it is the mother who carries the baby in her body for nine months. It is she who is continually aware of its presence. It is she who feels its kicks and its movements. It is she who is ever reminded of the pregnancy by formidable changes in her body and by the various symptomatic reminders of the pregnancy: nausea, vomiting, fatigue, discomfort during sleep, etc. Even the most dedicated fathers cannot have these experiences and the attendant strong psychological ties that they engender. The mother, as well, must suffer the pains of the infant's delivery. Even though the father may be present at the time of birth and an active participant in the process, the experience is still very much the mother's. And, as mentioned, it is the mother who may very well have the breast-feeding experience, something the father is not capable of enjoying. All these factors create a much higher likelihood that the mother—at the time of birth—will have a stronger psychological tie with the infant than will the father. This "up-front" programming places her in a superior position with regard to psychological bonding with the newborn infant at the time of birth. I believe that most individuals would agree that, if parents decided to separate at the time of birth and both were reasonably equal with regard to parenting capacity, the mother would be the preferable parent.

Some might argue that even if the aforementioned speculations are valid, the superiority stops at the time of birth and men are thereafter equal to women with regard to parenting capacity. Even here I am dubious. It is reasonable to assume that during the course of evolution there was a selective survival of women who were highly motivated child rearers on a genetic basis. Such women were more likely to seek men for the purposes of impregnation and more likely to be sought by men who desired children. Similarly, there was selective propagation of men who were skilled providers of food, clothing, shelter, and protection of women and children. Such men were more likely to be sought by women with high child-rearing drives. This assumption, of course, is based on the theory that there are genetic factors involved in such behavior. Women with weaker child-rearing drives were less likely to procreate, and men with less family provider and protective capacities were also at a disadvantage with regard to transmitting their genes to their progeny. They were less attractive to females as mates because they were less likely to fulfill these functions so vital to species survival. As weaker protectors they were less likely to survive in warfare and in fighting to protect their families from enemies.

Accordingly, although it may be the unpopular thing to say at the time of this writing (1990), I believe that the average woman today is more likely to be genetically programmed for child-rearing functions than the average man. Even if this speculation is true, one could argue that we are less beholden to our instincts than lower animals and that environmental influences enable us to modify these more primitive drives. I do not deny this, but agree only up to a point. There are limitations to which environment can modify heredity, especially in the short period of approximately 15 years since the tender years presumption was generally considered to be sexist. Environment modifies heredity primarily (and many would say exclusively) by the slow process of selective survival of those variants that are particularly capable of adapting to a specific environment. Accordingly, I believe that these genetic factors are still strong enough in today's parents to be given serious consideration when making custody decisions.

It would appear from the aforementioned comments that I am on the verge of recommending that we go back to the tender years presumption. This is not completely the case. *What I am recommending is that we give preference in custody disputes to the parent (regardless of sex) who has provided the greatest degree of healthy, child-rearing input during the children's formative years.* Because mothers today are still more often the primary childrearing parents, more mothers would be given parental preference in custody disputes adjudicated under this principle. If, however, in spite of the mother's superiority at the time of birth, it was the father who was the primary caretaker — especially during the early years of life — such a father might very well serve better as the preferable primary custodial parent. This presumption, too, is essentially sex blind (satisfying thereby present-day demands for gender egalitarianism) because it allows for the possibility that a father's input may outweigh the mother's in the formative years, even though he starts at a disadvantage. It utilizes primarily the *psychological bond* with the child as the primary consideration in custody evaluations. I would add, however, the important consideration that the longer the time span between infancy and the time of the custody evaluation and decision, the greater the likelihood that environmental factors will modify (strengthen or weaken) the psychological bonds that the child had with each parent during the earliest years.

I refer to this as the stronger, *healthy* psychological bond presumption, which, I believe, is the one that would serve the best interests of the child. It is important for the reader to appreciate that the parent who had the greater involvement with the child during infancy is the one more likely to have the stronger psychological bond. However, if the early parenting was not "good," then the bond that develops might be pathological. Accordingly, I am not referring here to any kind of psychological bond at all, but a *healthy* psychological bond. It is not a situation in which *any* psychological bond at all will do. A paranoid mother, who has so programmed her son that he too has developed paranoid feelings about his father, may have a strong psychological bond with her son, stronger than that which he has with his father. But this *folie à deux* is certainly not a healthy one and its presence is a strong argument for recommending the father as the primary custodial parent. It is for this reason that I refer to the presumption as the stronger, healthy psychological bond presumption. To clarify my position on these principles, I will first present a vignette that will serve as a basis for my subsequent comments.

Let us envision a situation in which a couple has one child, a boy. During the first four years of the child's life, the mother remains at home as the primary child rearer and the father is out of the house during the day as the breadwinner. When the child is 4 the mother takes a full-time job. During the day the child attends a nursery school and then stays with a woman in the neighborhood who cares for the children of working parents. At the end of the workday and over weekends both parents are involved equally in caring for the child. And the same situation prevails when the child enters elementary school. When the child is 7 the parents decide to separate. Each parent wants primary custody. The father claims that during the three years prior to the separation, he was as involved as the mother in the child's upbringing. And the mother does not deny this. The father's position is that the court should make its decision solely on the basis of parenting capacity—especially as demonstrated in the most recent three years of the child's life—and claims that any custody decision taking his gender into consideration is "sexist" and is an abrogation of his civil rights.

In the course of the litigation the child develops typical symptoms of the parental alienation syndrome. He becomes obsessed with hatred of his father, denies any benevolent involvement with him at any point in his life, and creates absurd scenarios to justify his animosity. In constrast, his mother becomes viewed by the boy as faultless and all-loving. I believe that in this situation the child's psychological bond is stronger with the mother, and the symptoms of alienation are created by him in an attempt to maintain that bond. Because the child's earliest involvement was stronger with the mother, residua of that tie are expressing themselves at the age of seven. If the father had been the primary caretaker during the first four years of the boy's life, and if then both mother and father shared equally in child-rearing involvement, I would predict that the child would develop symptoms of alienation from the mother, the parent with whom the psychological tie is weaker. Under such circumstances, I would recommend the father be designated the primary custodial parent.

In summary, the stronger, healthy psychological bond presumption is best stated as a three-step process:

1. Preference should be given to that parent (regardless of gender) with whom the child has developed the stronger, healthy psychological bond.

2. That parent (regardless of sex) who was the primary caretaker during the earliest years of the child's life is more likely to have developed the stronger, healthy psychological bond.

3. The longer the time-lag between the earliest years and the time of the custody evaluation or decision, the greater the likelihood other factors will operate that may tip the balance in either direction regarding parental capacity.

I believe that if courts were to utilize the stronger, healthy psychological bond presumption when making decisions about custody disputes there would be far fewer cases of the parental alienation syndrome. I do not believe that this would require any statutory changes in state legislatures, because the presumption fits well within the concept of the best interests of the child principle. I suspect that many "old fashioned" judges, who still subscribe to the tender years presumption, do so because of their appreciation of the importance of the psychological bond.

Concluding Comments

Another way in which therapists can help their patients prevent the development of psychopathology is to encourage them to mediate rather than litigate their divorce and custody disputes. Mediation is the sane way to deal with such disputes. Elsewhere (1986b, 1989), I have described in detail the mediation process. Proponents of mediation often have an uphill fight with certain segments of the legal profession, especially those who are hard-nosed litigators. These lawyers recognize that there is much more money to be made from protracted litigation than from mediation. However, these obstructions notwithstanding, I believe that mediation is making headway and will ultimately become the primary mode of custody dispute resolution. If, however, the parents cannot resolve their custody disputes by mediation, then they may have no choice but to resort to adversary litigation. In such cases, the therapist does well to encourage them to use the services of an impartial examiner, rather than a "hired gun" adversary mental health evaluator. Utilization of the former is more likely to protect the parents from the development of psychopathology; engagement of the latter will predictably protract the litigation and increase the likelihood of the development of psychopathology. Elsewhere (1986b, 1989), I describe in detail the optimum way for evaluators to conduct such examinations.

Last, because of space limitations, I have not discussed here the role of false sex-abuse accusations in the context of child custody disputes. Such an allegation has proved to be a very effective weapon for wreaking vengeance as well as removing the accused (most often the father) from involvement with the children. In the early 1980s courts were frequently taken in by such accusers. However, by the late 1980s judges were increasingly weary of these allegations and recognized that a high percentage of them were likely to be false. (False sex-abuse allegations in custody disputes should not be confused with sex-abuse allegations in the intrafamilial situation [incest] where there is a much higher percentage of sex-abuse allegations that prove to be valid.) Therapists do well to become familiar with the differentiation between bona fide and fabricated sex-abuse allegations (1987) in order to deal properly with their child patients who may be involved in such disputes. It is crucial that the therapist be certain that sex abuse has indeed taken place before embarking on a treatment program. All too often naive therapists will treat normal children, who are considered by naive and inexperienced evaluators to have been abused, much to the detriment of the child. Such "therapy" is likely to result in alienation from the alleged abuser that is totally unnecessary and other residual effects of the false accusation on the child's general psychological development. Elsewhere (1991) I have discussed this in the context of a broader hysteria regarding sex abuse that we have witnessed in recent years.

Chapter 15

CASE STUDY

Throughout this book I have provided clinical examples demonstrating specific techniques that I use in various situations. Here I present the full course of treatment of a child whose parents were separated. Although at the time of this writing they have not gotten legally divorced (and there is no reason to believe that they intend to in the immediate future), from the psychological standpoint they are very much divorced. As throughout this book, I present extensive verbatim clinical material in order to demonstrate exactly the techniques utilized. In addition, theoretical and analytic discussion is presented in order to make the material more meaningful.

Jack was referred at the age of nine-and-a-half because of difficulties in school and at home. His teacher described him as disruptive in the class-room. He would blurt out in the middle of lessons and showed no self-restraint. It was only in a one-to-one relationship that he would be calm enough to learn anything meaningful. Although he was in the fourth grade, his mathematics and reading were at the second grade level.

Both at home and in school he had difficulties relating to other children. His mother described him as "just not knowing how to be with other kids." He always wanted his way and had little knowledge of social amenities and consideration for others. Often he was scapegoated and would respond with primitive and misdirected outbursts.

Both parents were in their early fifties at the time of referral and had been married fifteen years. It was the first marriage for the mother and the second for the father. Jack had two older sisters, ages thirteen and eleven. Although the mother's pregnancy and delivery were normal, Jack was described as having been hyperactive since birth. His developmental milestones were normal. Since he began school he was always described as being hyperactive with a low frustration tolerance, and as exhibiting poor attention span, impulsivity, and hostile outbursts.

At age seven Jack was seen by a pediatric neurologist who found an impairment in the establishment of cerebral dominance, immature reproduction of Bender-Gestalt patterns, a significant cerebellar deficit manifested by finger to nose dysmetria and dysdiadokokinesis. The diagnosis was "minimal brain dysfunction, probably of prenatal etiology." Ritalin was prescribed but at the time of referral the dose levels had not been adequately adjusted.

When I first saw Jack I found him to be hyperactive and distractible. He spoke rapidly, often to the point of being incomprehensible. In addition to the problems mentioned, the mother described her husband as being progressively removed from the home. Although living in New Jersey, the father's business arrangements (by his own volition) involved his spending a significant amount of time in St. Louis. During the two years prior to referral, the amount of time the father spent in St. Louis had progressively increased so that by the time I first saw Jack the father was spending about 80 to 90 percent of his time away from the home. He professed no interest in or affection for Jack's mother and the whole family knew that he had a woman friend in St. Louis with whom he lived when he was not in New Jersey. Jack's mother stated that the only reason she did not get a divorce was that it would make her financial situation a much harder one. Being in her early fifties she did not see much of a prospect of her getting remarried and had decided to resign herself to the status quo.

During my initial evaluation I, too, found signs for a minimal brain dysfunction syndrome. However, I considered significant psychological problems to be present as well. In fact, I considered these the predominant difficulties. Jack harbored deep-seated feelings of resentment toward his father and was unable to overtly express them. His father, on those occasions when he would see Jack, would profess his love for him and would make many promises—most of which were not fulfilled. Yet Jack kept hoping that they would be realized and could not allow himself to fully appreciate the limitations of his father's involvement with him.

In the early weeks of treatment, Jack's medication regimen was adjusted and he was finally maintained on Ritalin, 10 mgm twice a day, and Mellaril,

20 mgm three times a day. He responded with a diminution in his hyperactivity and distractibility and improved his concentration in school. In addition, arrangements were made for him to be transferred to a special class for children with emotional problems. Although the school had a class for children with minimal brain dysfunction, both the school personnel and I agreed that Jack's psychological problems were more prominent than his organic problems and that he would fit better into the class for emotionally disturbed children. There he enjoyed greater individual attention with a teacher who was a most sensitive and sympathetic person. Fortunately, the teacher of this special class was a male and this, it was hoped, would also be salutary for Jack. Lastly, arrangements were made for Jack to be seen on a twice weekly basis, with his mother present during his sessions to participate as indicated.

During the first few months of treatment Jack spoke of his father in glowing terms and denied that any of his rejections, slights, hostilities, unkept promises, etc. in any way reflected lack of interest or affection on his father's part. Although his father had been repeatedly invited to meet with me as part of my routine evaluation, he continually made excuses to both Jack and his mother regarding calling me for an appointment. When he finally did call, it was to give me a reason why he was too busy to come; in addition, he tried to manipulate me regarding the payment of fees. Accordingly, Jack's mother decided to pay for the treatment out of her own personal savings, stating, "That's the way my husband is. He invariably tries to foul up every situation in which he involves himself."

During Jack's sixth session (second month of treatment) Jack began discussing his father's Christmas-New Year's vacation. The father had told the family that he would be staying home for two weeks. However, after one week he suddenly announced that he had to return to St. Louis for business purposes. Jack's mother was quite sure that the father was going back to St. Louis to be with his woman friend and that his business obligations did not require his premature return; Jack, however, insisted that his father be taken at his word. It was typical of Jack in such discussions never even to consider the possibility that his father was rejecting him and his family. During that session, he told this story:

> *Patient:* Once upon a time there was this kid. He was really a big brat, you know. He just went around like breaking windows for no reason. Like he would just go around and hit a kid for no reason. Like a new kid would come into his classroom and says—the new kid says, "Hi." He'd say "Ugh!" He was really nasty. He had no friends. Besides he was really tough. He'd just go around and like break the table for no reason or beat up a person for no reason, pull a fire alarm for the kicks. He felt really strong and think he'd make really a lot of friends, you know. And my

God, he'd just take a table and just break it.

Therapist: Hh hmm.

P: Throw a rock at the window. Break something. Let's say his friend had—he knew someone who had like a big $3,000 auto slot car with racing sets, a really elaborate one, you know. It has ten cars and tracks and you go whipping around the track, you know. He'd just break it. It was like $5,000. Break it.

T: Hh hmm.

P: Just for the fun of it, thinking he was really tough and strong, have some more friends. He went around school like a—he was picking on this—he was picking on this kid, you know.

T: Hh hmm.

P: The kid couldn't do anything. What did the kid do? Nothing.

T: Okay.

P: Then one day he was picking on a kid—the cops were, even—pulling fire alarms, breaking windows, and he [the boy he was picking on] said, "Hey kid, what's the idea of doing that?" You don't have any friends."

And he said, "Well, you have to be tough," and stuff like that.

And the friend said, "You have to learn how to be mature and polite. Why don't you speak to the polite old cop who said the same thing?"

And the teacher taught him that, told him that he went to the school principal, for a whole year, and like, I mean one day the cop said, "Look, you got to learn how to be mature and polite. You'll make more friends."

How's that one? Should I do some more?

T: Okay. Is that the end of it?

P: Hh hmm.

T: So what happens when the cop says you've got to be mature and polite so you'll have more friends? Then what happened?

P: Then he obeyed it.

T: Is that the end of the story?

P: Yeah, and the moral of the story is: You're going to have to learn one piece at a time. You have to learn everything one by one, step by step, and you'll be able to have more friends.

T: Hh hmm. Okay. Now it's my turn to tell a story.

In the beginning of the story the patient is clearly expressing some of the pent-up resentment he feels toward his father. In an orgy of hostility the boy destroys everything in sight. Almost overnight, with the helpful advice of a peer, "a polite cop," and the school principal the boy is suddenly transformed into a law-abiding citizen. However, the transcript does not convey the artificial quality with which the patient spoke as he described the advice given by these three individuals. There was a singsong manner which revealed the basic lack of conviction Jack had for these communications. I felt that the story was in the "snow job" category, and served the purposes of resistance rather than therapeutic progress. Sometimes it is difficult to differentiate between a story that has a healthy message and one whose messages are only ostensibly healthy. When the communications are made without conviction, in a rapid and slapdash manner, they are usually being made in the service of resistance—and this story is in that category. Accordingly, I responded with this story:

Therapist: Once upon a time there was a kid and this kid was really sad and it was really an unfortunate situation. He was going around breaking things up. He would break T.V. sets, break tables, throw rocks through windows, and when somebody said to him "Why are you doing all that?" he said, "Oh, no reason. It's just fun."

Now there's no such thing as no reason. This kid just didn't want to look at the reason and when everybody said to him "Why are you doing that? Why you doing that?" he said, "No reason. No reason." And the more he did it the more trouble he got into. They suspended him from school, the kids wouldn't play with him, and everytime he did these things he would say, "No reason."

Now the real reason was that this kid was very mad. He was very mad at his older brother, a teen-ager, who was doing a lot of things which were really getting him really angry, but he didn't want to admit that he was angry at his brother. He thought that it was terrible to be angry at his brother. He thought that if he got angry at his brother he'd even see less of his brother than he was seeing at that time. His brother was out doing a lot of things and didn't spend as much time with this boy.

Patient (interrupting): What did he do, like take heroin and stuff?

T: No, no. The brother didn't take heroin. The brother was just out with his friends.

P: He didn't take it. (Laughs)

T: But the brother wasn't a very good brother. The brother sometimes spent time with him, but most of the time the brother was out with his teen-age friends or his girl friends or things like that. And the brother just didn't want to spend too much time with this kid. And the boy was very angry at his brother but he thought that it was terrible to be angry at his brother, and he thought that if he told his brother how angry he was that terrible things would happen.

So he kept all his anger in and never told his brother. But what would happen is that he would fill up inside with all this anger and then he would go around with rocks breaking windows, beating up little kids, pulling fire alarms, and really getting into terrible trouble. So whenever people said "Why did you do it?" he said, "No reason, no reason at all." He was really scared to look at the real reason and so what happened was that as long as he kept trying to avoid—do you know what *avoid* means?

P: Yeah, not do anything, don't do anything. You can't help it.

T: What is *avoid*? I'm not clear what you're saying.

P: Like, um, he'd really try to avoid getting sick.

T: Getting sick?

P: Yeah, sick.

T: How's getting sick—where's getting sick fit into this?

P: I mean like if you can't help it you try—you don't try to get sick. You just try to be well as much as ou could.

T: You just try to what as much as you could?

P: Be well as much as you could.

T: What has that got to do with my story? Being sick and well?

P: You can avoid, like when you avoid it.

T: Well, I don't know what *avoid* . . . I don't know what you mean.

P: Try to stay away from it.

T: Okay! He tried to stay away from looking at what was going on between him and his brother, from seeing what was going on, and he kept making believe that there was no trouble between him and his brother, that he loved his brother, and that his brother loved him. And so he kept getting angry inside and he kept letting out the anger in such places as breaking windows and things like that.

And do you understand what this boy was doing?

P: Yeah.

T: What was he doing?

P: He just wasn't telling the reasons.

T: What were the reasons?

P: He was really mad, what he . . . (mumbles) . . . his anger.

T: What he *what* with his anger?

P: He just puffed up with it.

T: And did he let it out?

P: Nope.

T: Anywhere?

P: He just avoided stop getting angry.

T: At whom?

P: At people, everybody.

T: Okay. And what did he do with his anger instead? He didn't let it out at his brother. What did he do with it?

P: He let it out on his friends.

T: Right, on little kids or on breaking windows. And so he continued to get into trouble. So what finally happened with this boy?

P: He got heck!

T: He got in heck?

P: Yeah, always in heck.

T: And then what happened to him?

P: He got spanked and he got in really big trouble with the principal and by the cops.

T: What would have been better? What would have been better if he had done what?

P: If he didn't avoid the reason.

T: And what did he do?

P: Um, he kept. He avoid it. He avoid the reasons.

T: What would have been better for him to do? What should he do?

P: Take the anger and let it out on his brother.

T: Right. Very good. Now what would have happened if he told his brother how angry he was?

P: He'd be all right.

T: What would the brother have done?

P: Playing with him instead of with—one to one.

T: What would the older brother have done if the younger brother had told the older brother how angry he was?

P: Get mad and get mad at him.

T: And then what would have happened?

P: They'd break into a fight.

T: And then what would have happened?

P: It would be all right because.

T: Everything would be all right?

P: Yeah, because he wouldn't need to break windows and wouldn't have not gotten into any trouble.

T: Well, I'll tell you. Let me tell you how I end the story. You see, there are two possibilities. One, he tells the older brother how angry he is and the older brother spends more time with him or the older brother says, "Sorry, kid." He says, "Too bad you feel so bad but I'm not spending more time with you. You're a nice kid. I like you sometimes but I don't like to be around with you too much so you'll just have to take what you can get and stop knocking your brains out because you're not going to get more." Now if the kid got that answer what could he do?

P: He could get more friends.

T: Right! Absolutely right. He would get more friends and be with people who like him and people who want to spend more time with him.

Then he wouldn't be so angry. But he wouldn't be wasting his time trying to get friendship from a brother who only wants to give him a little bit and not trying to get more than a person can give.

And you know what the lessons of that story are? What are the lessons of that story?

P: You try—you don't avoid the reason. There's always a reason no matter what you do.

T: There's always a reason for everything. Right. There's no such thing as no reason. Right. That's one lesson.

P: I don't know . . . (mumbles) . . .

T: Pardon me.

P: I don't know what the other reason is.

T: Well, another lesson—let me ask you this. What did the boy learn about what you should do if you're angry at someone?

P: Take it out on the person you're angry at.

T: Rather than?

P: Taking it out on everybody else.

T: Right. And what did he learn about what could happen if you . . .

P (interrupting): The person you're mad at will leave you alone.

T: Wait. Say that again. What are the possibilities?

P: The person will be friends with you.

T: You mean you will get what you want?

P: Yeah, you'll get what you want.

T: Or?

P: He'll leave you alone.

T: And if he leaves you alone?

P: You won't have any trouble at the end.

T: I'm not clear about the second thing. When you say he'll leave you alone, could you be more specific? What do you mean by that?

P: Then he won't harm you anymore. You won't need to get angry at him.

T: Why won't he harm you anymore?

P: Just 'cause.

T: How come he won't harm you? Let's say the boy said to the teenage brother, "I'm angry at you because you don't want to spend more time with me." Now what could the teen-age brother say? What's one thing he could say?

P: . . . (mumbles) . . .

T: What's that? Say that again.

P: He says, "I don't want to spend more time with you."

T: Okay. Then what would the boy do?

P: He'd be all alone.

T: And what would the young boy do to make himself feel better?

P: Make more friends.

T: Right! Now suppose the teen-ager said, "You know, you're right. I haven't been spending enough time with you. I'll spend more." Then what would happen?

P: They'd be all right.

T: Right. Very good. Anything you want to say about this story? Did you like that story?

P: Hh humm.

T: What was the part you liked the most?

P: The one that was . . . (mumbles) . . . that was kind of funny.

T: The one that was *what*?

P: At the end.

T: Where?

P: Of the story you tell, like making more friends.

T: Oh, you liked that part about making friends best. Okay. Good. Okay. So that's the end of our program.

In my story the child, of course, represents the patient and the teen-age brother, his father. In the beginning, I tried to point out that there was a reason for the boy's antisocial behavior. I attempted thereby to counteract the seemingly spontaneous and unprovoked hostility of the boy in Jack's story. In the early phases of treatment it is important to emphasize to the patient that there are reasons for his behavior and this may be something that has never entered into his scheme of things.

It is of interest that when I described the older brother as "out doing a lot of things and didn't spend as much time with this boy," the patient immediately questioned whether the older brother was taking heroin. I considered this to reflect Jack's view that his father's involvement with his lady friend was, like heroin, an addiction that was more attractive to him than involvement with his own family.

In much of my story I tried to communicate to Jack the basic mechanisms of displaced anger and various factors that were contributing to his need to displace. The interchange between us regarding these various elements demonstrates well how difficult it may be to impart such communications to a deeply resistant child, especially in the early phases of treatment.

During the next two months, many of our discussions and therapeutic interchanges during games and play centered on Jack's relationship with his father. It was very difficult for Jack to accept his father's deficiencies in affection for him. He did ask his father to visit more; however, although promising to do so, the father never followed through. The patient frequently asked me to call his father and get him to have a conference with me and the rest of the family. His hopes were multiple: that I would get his father to spend more time with him; that I would get his father to love his mother more and live once again with the family; that I would encourage him to leave his woman friend; and that I might get him into treatment himself in order to more effectively bring about the changes. We discussed the fact that his father had not responded to my request—given both directly and through the patient's mother—that he visit me. However, I tried to impress upon Jack that, even were his father to come, it was not within my power to effect the changes Jack desired.

During Jack's fourth month in treatment (in his twenty-first session), Jack began talking about some of these issues. Sensing that the discussion might be worthy of our observing it afterwards on television, I suggested we talk with the television camera turned on. He agreed and this discussion ensued:

Therapist: Okay, today is February 20, 1973, and Jack and I are talking about some problems about his father. Now what were you saying about your father?

Patient: That he doesn't love me enough and he's supposed to love me.

T: And why do you say that?

P: Well, like he's never home. He's going out with a girl friend.

T: Hh hmm. And where is she?

P: She's in St. Louis, outside of it.

T: Hh hmm. All right. I agree with you. As I said, I believe that your father has less love for you than many other fathers have for their children.

P: Yes.

T: It's not that he doesn't love you at all because he does love you some because he comes to visit you once in a while.

P: Yeah, but he never comes enough. He's always going out with a girl friend.

T: Hh hmm.

P: He doesn't think, um, like he took me to Jamaica that's why I love him so much.

T: He took you to Jamaica.

P: Yeah. Have you ever been there?

T: No, I've never been there.

P: Are you ever going to go there?

T: I hope to go someday.

P: Do you know the places in Jamaica?

T: No, I don't know much about it. I know that it's nice there.

P: Name a city.

T: Pardon?

P: Name one city you know in Jamaica.

T: I know there's a city called Kingston. Isn't that the . . .

P (interrupts): Yeah, the capital. What's another city you know?

T: What's another city?

P: Guess. It starts with M.

T: I don't know. I haven't the faintest idea.

P: You say anything.

T: With M?

P: Yeah. It has a B. It has Bay.

T: Montego Bay?

P (yells): Heeeey!

T: Is that it?

P: Yeah. What are eight rivers? What's eight rivers?

T: Listen, you're changing the subject. I would like to get back to the . . . all right, I'll name one river—and then let's get back to the subject we were talking about.

P: Eight rivers. What's that in Spanish?

T: River—rio.

P: Yeah, and what's eight?

T: Eight? Ocho? Or something like that.

P: Yeah, that's it. Rio Ocho.

T: Rio Ocho. Okay, now . . .

P (interrupts): And we stayed in a hotel called La . . .

T (interrupting): Okay. I'm going to interrupt you now. Now the time that he took you to Jamaica . . .

P: I loved him.

T: Yes and it shows that he has some feelings for you and wanted to do something very nice with you.

P: Yes.

T: On the other hand, as you said, such things don't happen very often. In fact, they are very rare. So all things considered, he doesn't like you or love you very much. Right?

P: Right.

T: But he has *some* feelings for you because he does visit once in a while. Right?

P: Yeah, but like he'll never stay home. He's . . . (mumbles) . . .

T: He's what?

P: He's happy about the rocket. I'm getting a rocket license, you know.

T: All right. So that shows, that shows that there's some interest in you with this rocket license. Right. I would agree with that. Now the thing is this. Your main feelings about the situation with him are what? What are the main feelings you have?

P: He doesn't love me as much.

T: Uh huh. Okay. And what can you do about that?

P: Find a substitute. There's no substitute.

T: There's no substitute? What might be a substitute?

P: He doesn't come home every night like a father and uh . . .

T: That's right he doesn't.

P: He isn't married to my . . . (mumbles) . . . friend's wife.

T: What's that?

P: My friend is not my mom's wife.

T: Your friend is not your mom's wife?

P: Well, he isn't married to her.

T: Wait, I'm not—what friend are you talking about?

P: Any friend!

T: Is not your mom's wife?

P: Yeah, you can't. Wouldn't he be a little young to get married?

T: I don't know what you—oh, you mean the substitute. The substitute would not be your mother's husband you mean.

P: Yeah.

T: Right. But that doesn't mean that you can't have fun with a substitute. He doesn't have to be married to your mother.

P: Yes.

T: The thing is that that's one way of helping yourself feel better. Right?

P: Right.

T: By spending more time with other people, young and old.

P: Yes.

T: All right. What young people are you spending more time with now?

P: I don't want to mention the names on TV.

T: Okay, mention the first name.

P: Uh, uh, let's see, uh Okeo. He's Japanese.

T: Okeo. There's such a guy?

P: Okeo Sukiyaki.

T: Come on. Are you making . . .

P (interrupts): No, I'm not.

T: Who is that?

P: He's one of my friends. He's Japanese.

T: His name is Sukiyaki? Your mother is shaking her head.

P: Okeo. Yes he is, Mom.

T: It looks to me like you're making up some kind of a story.

P: It's Okeo. It's Okeo Okeaka.

T: Yeah, it sounds like some fishy name to me.

Patient's Mother: Sounds like he's trying to use some judo words.

P: That's not so.

T: Now, I know that you do have some friends though. Right?

P: Yeah. But they . . . (mumbles) . . .

T: None of them what?

P: They're not going to like me anymore because I'm rotten.

T: Why are you rotten?

P: Well, I never do anything right.

T: Like what, for instance, don't you do right?

P (laughs): Name one thing I do right, Ma.

T: No, I want you to.

P (shouting): I don't know what I do right but I do all the things wrong! Like I build . . . (mumbles) . . . wrong.

T: You build what wrong?

P: Models. I have the junkiest models built.

T: Do you think that has something to do with your father?

P: No, but like he's never home . . . (mumbles) . . .

T: Pardon me.

P: He's never home. He doesn't like—love the dog.

T: Uh huh.

P: He never comes home.

T: All right. What other things?

P: He doesn't come to take me to Judo or take me home.

T: That's right. That's very sad. But there's nothing you can do about it. Don't you know that? You can't change him.

P (crying): I know it.

T: He's not going to see you more. You have asked him. Haven't you?

P: Yes.

T: And he doesn't come around more. Does he?

P (crying): No.

T: Okay. Now I know that this makes you very sad and it's very upsetting to you.

P: Yes.

T: But it's not going to change.

P: Uh huh.

T: So the thing is what can you do? What can you do?

P: Just find a substitute.

T: All right. That's one thing. There's another thing about what your thoughts are about. What do you think this means that he doesn't want to spend much time with you?

P: He loves his girl friend more.

T: Well, that's possibly true that he loves her more. He loves her in a different way but he certainly wants to spend more time with her than with you.

P (crying bitterly): I know it. He doesn't love me.

T: He doesn't love you very much.

P: No, he doesn't.

T: What can you do?

P: I don't know.

T: Do you know what I think?

P: What?

T: I think that you think this means that there may be something wrong with you.

P: Yes. Can we finish it [the discussion] now? That's really all about my Dad . . . (mumbles) . . .

T: Pardon me.

P: That's all about my Dad.

T: No, no. I want to talk some more about this. No, I think there's more to talk about.

P: I got a headache, a fat headache.

T: Okay. Let's talk just a *few* more minutes about this now. Now what I want to know is this: What do you think this means about people liking you if your father doesn't love you very much?

P: I . . . (mumbles) . . .

T: You what?

P: I think cruddy things 'cause my Dad won't keep me.

T: Do you think you're cruddy?

P: No.

T: Do you think that no one can like you?

P: No.

T: I have a feeling you think that.

P (crying again): I don't!

T: What are the main feelings—you see you are crying now because your father doesn't love you very much. Right?

P: Yes, yes.

T: It means that something else must be going on. You must have some other thoughts about that.

P: I . . . (mumbles) . . .

T: You don't?

P: I do.

T: What are the other thoughts?

P: Like I . . . (mumbles) . . . birthday present.

T: Like what?

P: . . . (mumbles) . . . birthday present.

T (to mother): Do you understand what he is saying about birthday presents?

P: Yeah, and everytime he's never home.

T: Yeah, and what's this about birthday presents?

P: Like he never gave me them.

T: He never gets you birthday presents?

P: On my birthday. Like I get him birthday presents.

T: You get him birthday presents.

P: Yeah, but he doesn't get me—um, look I'm always nice to him. Like . . . (mumbles) . . .

T (to mother): What did he say?

Patient's Mother: He'd always help him fix the car.

P: Yeah, that's something.

T: Uh huh.

P's M: That's what he generally does when he's home—work on the car.

T: Uh huh.

P: And then he goes, "Get out of here you . . . I don't want to use the words, "jackass" or "stupid."

T: Hh hmm.

P: I want to do something. Should they—do they use someone to write, "Say what do you know, a talking baboon." [a retort used by a boy in one of my children's stories that the patient read] Would that be . . .

T: What are you—I'm not clear what you're saying.

P: Like, "What do you know, the first one I ever saw, a talking baboon." Wouldn't that be rude—kind of rude?

T: Oh, you mean the talking baboon thing from my book, from my story.

P: Yeah.

T: Would that be rude to say to him?

P: Yeah.

T: Yes, it would be. It's not the kind of thing that children can say to parents. You may think it and feel it.

P: What can I say back to him?

T: Do you think saying things back to him are going to make him love you?

P: No. But he insulted me, so I'm going to insult him!

T: Well, what kinds of insults does he make? What does he say?

P: "Stupid, damn dog."

T: He calls you a "stupid, damn dog?"

P: No. He says stupid non novel nnn ey ey eye uh. He says all right alja jub ey ey ey ugh!

T: All right. Look, there's no question that your father doesn't treat you well at times. The question is . . .

P (interrupts): He treats me sometimes well and sometimes . . .

T: The question is what other thoughts you have about this—what you think this means about the kind of person you are. If he calls you stupid and things, does this make you stupid?

P: No.

T: That's the important thing. If he doesn't love you very much does this make you the kind of person that no one else can love?

P: No.

T: I don't know if you believe that.

P: I do believe it.

T: What do you think it says about your father that he can't love his own kid too much? What do you think that says?

P: I don't know. He just doesn't.

T: What do you think it says about him? What do we learn about him when we know that?

P: I don't know. Let me ask you one question: What do we learn?

T: Now I want you to try to figure it out.

P: I can't!

T: Here you have a man who doesn't love his own child very much. What does that mean about him? What does that say about him? What can we learn about him from that?

P: That I'm going to have to try to find another substitute.

T: No, no, no. What can we learn about *him*? What does it mean about *him*?

P: I don't know.

T: What do you say about a man who can't love his children very much?

P: You never help him in anything. You never help him.

T (to Mother): What is he saying?

P's M: He's saying his father never—he's misunderstood your question.

T: Hh hmm.

P: He never helps me.

T: I'm saying this. Do you say that there's possibly something wrong with your father?

P: No.

T: Well, I think so. I think there's something wrong with a man who doesn't love his own children very much.

P: Yeah, you ought to go. You ought to get his number and call him.

T: And what should I say to him if I were to call him?

P: "Aw, come on. Why don't you come up to our house? My son's been asking for me to call you to come over here." Then he'll have a conference with you.

T: Well, I did invite him to come and he never made an appointment. You know that.

P: I know.

T: He called me a couple of times and he said he didn't have time to see me. What do you think about that?

P: He's lying.

T: What do you think . . .

P (interrupts): Don't you think he is lying Mom?

T: What do you think is the real truth?

P: He's going out with his girl friend.

T: And do you think that that's more important to him?

P: Yeah, probably.

T: Let's say he came here. What would you want me to tell him?

P: Why don't you love your son?

T: Do you think that could make him love you?

P: Then he could give me a sensible reason.

T: Well, do you—what do you think he would say?

P: I don't know.

T: I don't think he will be able to say very much. I don't think he knows himself. My guess is that he would say, "I do love him." Or he might say, "Well, that is as much as I love him." But I couldn't get him to love you.

P: Will you tell him to come here for a conference?

T: That won't get him to love you. You can't get anybody to love you by having a psychiatrist or some other person say, "Hey, you go love your son." It wouldn't work.

P: Well go, uh, like your need—tell him, "You need a psychiatrist. Your son goes to one."

T: I think that you're right. See, when you say your father needs a psychiatrist, I think you're right. There is something wrong with a person who can't love his own son very much.

P: Yes.

T: And such a person might be helped by a psychiatrist; however, your father doesn't want to see a psychiatrist and a psychiatrist can't help anybody who doesn't want to see him.

P: No.

T: Do you understand that?

P: Uh huh.

T: So the thing is that I think you have to realize that you're not going to change your father.

P: Yes, yes. It's correct.

T: Hh hmm. He's not going to change. He won't come to see me, even to talk about you.

P: Hh hmm.

T: And I don't think he's going to change.

P: Hhmm.

T: So what can you do?

P: Nothing.

T: Now the question I asked before is: you seem to feel very bad that he doesn't love you very much.

P: Hh hmm.

T: And I think you have certain thoughts about it which are making you feel worse and I would like to know what some of those other thoughts might be.

P: I don't know where to start.

T: What's the main thought I have? What's the main thing that I think?

P: That he doesn't love me as much.

T: Hh hmm. And what do you think that means to you?

P: . . . (mumbles) . . . that he isn't very nice.

T: Hh hmm. Is there something wrong with him?

P: No.

T: That's not what I said before.

P: Nothing's wrong with him. Well, something's wrong with him. I don't know!

T: Okay, but is something wrong with a man who can't love his son very much?

P: I don't know.

T: I think so. I think there's something wrong with him. I think he's to be pitied. Do you know what I mean by pitied?

P: No.

T: Feel sorry for him.

P: He should feel sorry for himself?

T: I think . . .

P (interrupts): He said he does.

T: Yeah, but people should be feeling sorry for him. He's missing out on something that's very pleasurable.

P: What is it?

T: The feeling of love for a son that he doesn't have.

P: Why don't you tell him to come see you? Maybe then he'll love me more.

T: I can't give that to somebody. I cannot make somebody love if they don't feel it.

P (turning toward Mother): Mom, could you—may I ask you something?

P's M: Yes, dear.

P: Can't you talk him into coming here?

P's M: Well, I can—you know what I can do. And that's all.

P: Yeah, what is it? What can you do?

P's M: I can ask him to come.

T: You see, your mother has asked him a couple of times.

P: Ask him again!

T: But you think if he comes here he's going to then love you.

P's M: That's not going to solve your problem.

T: He's not going to love you after he comes here.

P: I don't know.

T: He's not going to love you more. What do you think of that?

P: I don't know.

T: You see, you're hoping for something that can't happen.

P (crying): I know it.

T: You're hoping for something that can't happen.

P: I know that he'll never love me. (turns to mother) Mom, what's her name, does he love me more? Or less? Did he love me more? Does he love the girl friend more than me or does he love me more than his girl friend?

P's M: Well, Jack, I have to agree with Dr. Gardner that it's a different kind of love. But he doesn't love you enough to put you first.

P: Yes.

T: He loves you differently.

P: Yeah, if there was a fire and I was in it and his girl friend and like which would he probably get out first? Does he love me more than his girl friend?

T: He loves you in a different way but he wants to spend more time with his girl friend than with you and I don't think you're going to change that. And as long as you keep on trying to change that you're just going to feel more miserable.

P: Yes.

T: There's certain things you can't change.

P's M: Well, Jack, it's not your fault that your father doesn't love you; not for you to blame yourself. I get the feeling Jack blames himself.

T: Is that right? Do you think it's your fault?

P: No.

T: Uh huh. I think you're very sad about this but you keep making it worse by keeping and hoping that he'll love you more. And you would like for me to try to get him to love you more and you'd like your mother to try to do that, and we can't. No one can.

P: I know it.

T: But you act as if it's the end of your life. Is that right?

P: No.

T: Well, you're acting like it's the worst possible thing in the world. Hmm?

P: Right.

T: What do you think is going to happen to you as a result of this?

P: Nothing.

T: No, but you're acting as if something terrible will happen. What might happen because of this? What might happen?

P: They're going to divorce.

T: Maybe. And then?

P: They are going to definitely get a divorce.

T: And then what? Then what?

P: And then I'll never see him again.

T: You'll never see him again?

P: No.

T: I don't know about that. I think that even if your parents get a divorce, I think that your father will still . . .

P (interrupts): She'll never get married again, never.

T: Maybe your mother will. Maybe not. I think she would like to.

P (to Mother): Would you, Ma?

P's M: Yes, Jack, I would like to very much.

P: But you're never looking for someone to get married.

P's M: Honey, you don't shop in the supermarket for a husband.

T: It isn't very easy for a lady to find a husband when she's your mother's age.

P's M: I would love very much to give you a father.

T (to patient): What are you thinking right now?

P: I think that we'll find some father.

T: Maybe. But until that time comes—if it comes—you can't just sit around waiting and hoping for that.

P: . . . (mumbles) . . . it.

T: Hhmm?

P: I know it.

T: What's the main thing I'm saying to you? What am I saying to you?

P: I don't know.

T: Hhmm? What am I trying to say to you that might help you feel better?

P: That I should stop hoping for a dad.

T: That's right. Do you think you can do that?

P: No.

T: Hh hmm. Do you think you are going to continue hoping?

P: No.

T: What are you going to do?

P: Nothing. I'm just going to let him go if he wants to or not.

T: Hh hmm. You can't get him back.

P: I know it.

T: You can't get him back and the sooner you realize that the better off you'll be. Because if you're going to keep on trying and hoping and hoping and hoping you're just going to feel very very miserable.

P: Yes.

T: Because you'll be hoping for something that can't be. What do you think of that?

P: I think it's correct. Right?

T: Now it's hard to stop looking for something.

P: Yes.

T: But it can be done. People can realize that the battle's lost! Do you know what I mean?

P: Yeah.

T: You can give up on it.

P: Yeah! I don't want to watch this show because I feel so . . . (mumbles) . . .

T: Pardon me. You want to what?

P: I don't want to see the show.

T: You don't want to see this show?

P: Because I'll be embarrassed to see it.

T: You'll be embarrassed? All right, we'll turn it off in just a couple of minutes. What would be the main thing that would embarrass you?

P: Crying.

T: Do you think it's wrong to cry about a thing like this?

P: No.

T: I don't think there's anything to be embarrassed about.

P (crying): I'll be embarrassed myself!

T: You don't have to watch it if you don't want to.

P: I don't want to watch it.

T: Well, okay. You don't have to. You don't have to. The thing is that if you think you shouldn't be crying about something like this, I think you're making a mistake. I think that's wrong thinking. Crying helps you feel better, you know. It gets feelings off your chest. Right?

P: Right.

T: So crying serves a purpose and there's nothing to be embarrassed about with crying. I think it's very good that you can cry. It helps us feel better about things. What do you think about that?

P (crying): No so. I don't want to look at it anymore. I don't care at all. I got a headache!

T: Wait. What's the main thing you feel terrible about?

P: Crying.

T: And what's the next thing?

P: That's all.

T: Hh hmm. Before we stop I want to ask you if you could tell me the main things I've been trying to say to you.

P: That my father will never come back loving me again.

T: All right. That's one of the main things I'm trying to say. Now what are some of the other things we've said?

P: That's all, I guess . . . (mumbles) . . .

T: That's what?

P: That's all.

T: Well, I've said some other things that could help you feel better. I just didn't say that your father doesn't love you very much and that's it. I've said that, you know, the best thing you can do is to accept that and stop trying to fight it and change it.

P: I know.

T: Now what else have I said?

P: That's all.

T: Well, I said something about—what does this show about your father?

P: He doesn't love me.

T: What does it show about him as a person?

P: He don't love me very much, because he's supposed to love me.

T: And I said that it shows that there is something wrong with him.

P: Yeah.

T: Hh hmm. And that it's sad for a man like that and what did I say about . . .

P (interrupts): That's all.

T: . . . others loving you. What did I say about that?

P: Uh, because they [parents] don't love each other and everything like that is—doesn't mean that others can't love me.

T: That others can't. Right. And that others *can*. All right, look, let's stop here. All right?

P: Yes.

T: Okay.

P (crying to Mother): I feel terrible, Mommy.

P's M (placing arms around patient): It's all right.

The discussion was an extremely difficult one for Jack and the transcript does not convey the full impact of the feelings that were expressed during our conversation. On a few occasions the patient clearly asked to interrupt our discussion. At such points I was in definite conflict. On the one hand, I was sensitive to his pain and anxiety and wished to respond to his request that we do something else. On the other hand, I knew that something therapeutically important was taking place and that the expression of thoughts and feelings concerning his father were vital to his therapy. In such situations I generally try to continue the therapeutic activity and only discontinue it if a patient still requests that I do so. However, if he can be brought back into the activity and pushed through his anxiety, so to speak, he can continue to derive the therapeutic benefits. Accordingly, in this discussion, on those occasions when the patient did ask to go on to something else, I expressed sympathy for his feelings and urged him to continue. At each point he did so and, although he was upset by what we had spoken about, I was convinced that the discussion was most salutary. My subsequent experiences confirmed that my hunch was right; this interchange appears to have been a turning point in his treatment. Following it he was able to handle many aspects of his relationship with his father with greater competence and maturity. This is not to say that his problems with his father were completely alleviated; rather, this session represented a significant step toward that goal.

Two weeks later, I used Jack's twenty-fifth session for an interview at which Jack, his mother, his thirteen-year-old sister Gaye, and his twelve-year-old sister Lisa, were present. My main purpose in this interview was to learn more that might be useful to me in Jack's treatment. However, I had heard from the mother that Gaye and, to a lesser extent, Lisa were less suppressed than Jack in expressing their resentment to their father. My hope was that in such an interview their expression of anger toward their father might serve to catalyze Jack's.

During this family session Jack vacillated back and forth from such statements as "If I say something bad about my father, he'll puncture me like a bubble" and "I'm not going to fight back; I'll get into too much trouble," to such comments as "I know sometimes he doesn't care about me" and "I know he doesn't love me very much."

Both girls described Jack as not showing any anger toward his father. Gaye stated, "He [Jack] won't say anything bad about our father because he's afraid my father will stop loving him." Lisa said, "He [Jack] doesn't get mad

at my father." Both girls then described (with unusual psychological sensitivity) how Jack either turned his anger toward himself by blaming himself for
anything that went wrong between himself and his father or displaced it onto
their mother. Jack agreed that he tended to do this. In subsequent discussion
both girls described their mother as being passively accepting of her husband's hostility and as denying to Jack their father's maltreatment of her.
Gaye stated, "She [Jack's mother] is non-aggressive. She doesn't fight back."
Lisa stated, "He [Jack's father] say he won't send money and she [Jack's
mother] just listens and says nothing." The session ended with a discussion
about how Jack was modeling himself after his mother regarding passive acceptance of his father's maltreatment of the family. Although Jack was exposed to all these important insights about his situation, I did not get the
feeling that there was a significant amount of "sinking in."

In the next session, Jack's twenty-sixth, his mother described how she had
had a very strong reaction to the session with the three children. It made her
realize, more clearly than ever, how passively accepting she had been of her
husband's insensitivity to the family. However, she could not see her way
clear to do anything to change the family situation in that she did not feel
that either she or the children would be better off financially if she were to get
a divorce. And so, she was still going to resign herself to the status quo.

In this session I tried to elicit from Jack any insights he might have gained
from the previous sessions. Although there was some recollection of its main
points, I did not have the feeling that he was consciously moved by them.
However, the mother stated that Jack's teacher had been reporting improved
behavior in the classroom.

Two weeks later, during Jack's twenty-ninth session (and the end of his
fourth month of therapy), Jack told this story during the television game:

> *Patient:* Once upon a time there was a bank that was robbed in New
> York City. Well, they have a lot of crime. Well, and they suspected this
> man. They had no evidence. They suspected this man did it and this
> man was in St. Louis. They thought that the man was lying—during the
> bank robbery.
>
> *T:* You mean they thought that when he said he was in St. Louis they
> thought he was really in New York?
>
> *P:* Yeah.
>
> *T:* Hh hmm.
>
> *P:* And like this other crook and the crook did it. He had a police rec-
> ord of sniper . . .
>
> *T* (interrupts): You mean the real crook?
>
> *P:* Yeah, had a police record on snipers and stuff. Well, they took him
> to jail. They thought he was lying.

T: This man in St. Louis, not the real crook in New York.

P: Yeah. And they had no evidence they can do. They were doing the thing wrong . . . (mumbles) . . . doing it. And like then the real crook in New York showed up and they robbed the bank—and he robbed the bank and they described the guy [the N.Y. crook] and the guy [the St. Louis man] looked like him [the N.Y. crook], but he [the N.Y. crook] was a Negro and they forgot to say that he was a Negro—and he [the St. Louis man] was a white man. They thought . . .

T (interrupts): You're saying "he." Who was Negro? Who was white?

P: The real crook was a Negro and the man [in St. Louis] was white, and the chief of all the cops was colorblind.

T: The cops were colorblind and put the wrong guy in jail.

P: Yeah.

T: Okay. Go ahead.

P: And then they had a medicine to cure that and it cured it. And then they found the crook and they thought that he was really stealing. Then one day they caught the crook and they let the man in St. Louis go. . . . The moral of the story is: Don't do something until you're sure it's right.

T: Hh hmm.

P: That's the moral of the story.

T: Okay. Now it's my chance to tell a story.

In essence, the story is one of false accusation and imprisonment. A white man in St. Louis is falsely accused of committing a crime that took place in New York and is placed in jail. The crime was actually committed by a Negro man in New York—a man who already had a police record. Although the two men were of different races, they apparently had characteristics similar enough that a colorblind police captain could consider the innocent man to be the guilty one. In addition, those who told the police captain about the criminal "forgot to say that he was Negro."

I considered the two men to be symbolic of the patient's father. He did indeed lead a double life residing both in St. Louis and the New York City area. (The patient lived in a New Jersey suburb of New York City.) The father is seen as both guilty and innocent: a step forward from not seeing his father as guilty at all. However, there is great ambivalence regarding making any accusations of wrongdoing on his father's part. At one point he is falsely accused (thereby blameless); however, another facet of his father is the culprit. By making the culprit a Negro, however, rather than the man living in St. Louis, Jack strengthens the disguise and lessens the likelihood of conscious awareness of the crook's true identity, that is, the hostile facets of Jack's own father.

I considered the story to represent an advance in Jack's ability to see his father as something other than totally benevolent. Here, his father is split into innocent and malevolent facets. With this understanding of the story, I related mine:

> *Therapist:* Once upon a time there was a man in St. Louis, a black man, who did not commit a crime.
> *Patient:* Yeah.
> *T:* This man in New York, however, this white man, *did* commit the crime in New York. And so the man they suspected was this black man in St. Louis and they kept saying, "This white man could never commit a crime. A white man cannot commit a crime" and they kept denying that he would commit a crime and they kept trying to blame the guy in St. Louis. And they said, "He's the guy who committed the crime, whereas this white man in New York would never commit the crime."
> Well, so they took the black man, put him in jail, and let the white man go. Then the white man committed a crime—a second crime in New York—and by this time they had to admit that he indeed was the criminal.
> *P:* Yeah, what crime did he do?
> *T:* He robbed a bank.
> *P:* Oh.
> *T:* And then they realized that it wasn't colorblindness like when something was wrong with their eyes. It's just that they didn't want to accept the fact that somebody the same color as they were, somebody who looked like they looked, would commit a crime.
> *P:* Yeah, but can I tell you something?
> *T:* Yes.
> *P:* The cops—the police were prejudiced.
> *T:* Yes, they were prejudiced but they said, "Nobody like us would commit a crime." They just didn't want to accept the fact that a white man, somebody of their own color, their own kind, someone who was similar to them—it was almost like a member of the family one could say —that such a man could commit a crime. And they said, "It's got to be a stranger. Only the guys outside, guys way far away could commit crimes, but not anyone like us."
> And then when they caught the guy in the act, they had no choice but to change their ideas.
> And the lesson of that story is: Just because someone is like you, because he looks like you—he is the same skin color—he may live near you or he may be someone in your family or something like that, it doesn't mean that he's not capable of committing a crime. And if you're going to

blind yourself to the fact that such a person can, you may not only not stop the person who is committing the crime, but you may convict an innocent person. And you may blame a person who has nothing to do with it. You may blame an innocent person—somebody else who has nothing to do with the crime.

P: Are you going to save this story?

T: Pardon me.

P: Are you going to save this?

T: Do you want to save it?

P: Yeah.

T: Did you like this story?

P: Yup!

T: What is it about the story that you like?

P: Well, um, like stuff I dig, you know, like I didn't make it giving all the details and stuff.

T: Hh hmm. Do you think this story has anything to do with you?

P: No.

T: Not at all?

P: No, I wouldn't steal.

T: Hh hmm. And it had anything at all to do with you or anyone in your family?

P: Nothing at all.

T: What about blaming an innocent person for a crime?

P: I'd never blame an innocent person.

T: Hh hmm. I see. What about not blaming the right person and blaming the wrong person?

P: You're blaming wrong because you really should find out and get some more evidence.

T: Uh huh. I see. Okay. Let's stop here.

In my story I tried to effect a fusion of the good and bad father images. My main message is that even individuals who live in our own homes are capable of crimes. Although Jack consciously saw no relevance between my story and his own life situation, my hope was that at some level he would appreciate the significance of my message. My experience with the Mutual Storytelling Technique has been that such communications can be meaningfully received even though they are too anxiety-provoking to be appreciated in conscious awareness.

Jack's question about whether I was going to save the story relates to the patient's awareness that some of the videotaped stories are saved for teaching and publication purposes. I have found that this serves as an incentive for many children to take the game seriously and try to create rich and interesting stories.

One week later, during Jack's thirty-first session, he told this story:

> *Patient:* Once upon a time there was this man who was about forty years old and this—well, let's start it with this. This girl thought that . . . (mumbles) . . .
>
> *Therapist:* This girl thought that what?
>
> *P:* This girl thought that this man couldn't cook better than she could.
>
> *T:* Wait. This girl thought that this man could or could not cook well?
>
> *P:* Could not.
>
> *T:* This girl thought that this man could not cook better than she.
>
> *P:* Yeah. Of course, this woman was like twenty-nine and this man was old—in the forties.
>
> *T:* A real old guy, huh?
>
> *P:* Yeah.
>
> *T:* Okay.
>
> *P:* So one day this man said, "I'll challenge you to it."
> And they said, "We'll make a cake and someone will test it out."
> And this woman thought, you know, she could cook better than him, and men, you know—the best cooks in the world are men. And the man made a cake and which cake tasted better? The judge. And the judge said the man's cake tasted better.
> And the moral of the story is: Just because you're a woman doesn't mean that you can make so better than men.
>
> *T:* Just because you're a woman . . .
>
> *P* (interrupts): . . . doesn't mean that you can show better than a man.
>
> *T:* Think you can what?
>
> *P:* You can do things better that a woman do than a man.
>
> *T:* Okay.
>
> *P:* Your story.
>
> *T:* Okay.
>
> *P:* Are you going to save this story?
>
> *T:* We'll see. I think it's an excellent story. Now it's my chance.
>
> *P:* Hh hmm. Okay.

I considered the twenty-nine-year-old girl to represent Jack's mother and the man in his forties, Jack's father. The contest over who can bake a cake best symbolizes a contest over who can provide Jack with more love. Although the girl claims that she is the more loving, the father proves himself superior to her. The story represents some therapeutic regression on Jack's part, in that it reveals his denial of his father's deficits. Although this may be a source of disappointment and frustration for the therapist, it is an inevitable aspect of therapy. Anxiety-provoking communications are only slowly accepted and rejection of them, at times, is predictable. Accordingly, I responded with this story:

Therapist: Once upon a time there was a woman.

Patient: Yeah.

T: She was about twenty-nine years old.

P: Yeah.

T: And she was married to a guy who was very, very old, a guy around forty or so, a real old guy.

P: Hh hmm.

T: And they both liked to cook. And one day they were having an argument as to who was the better cook.

Now they had a boy and he always felt that no matter what his father did that that was great and that no matter what his mother did that was just okay. She was all right, but his father—he could not see anything wrong with his father. Anyway, so they had this contest and they baked these cakes—each of them baked a cake—everybody, all of the kids. . . . How many kids do you want to make in this family?

P: You know. I don't know.

T: How many do you want to make?

P: Ten, eleven, or twelve.

T: Okay, there were ten kids in this family, eleven kids in this family. So they baked the cake—each baked a cake—and they said, "Okay, kids, each person taste a cake and say whether he likes it—they didn't tell the kids which cake it was. You understand?

P: Hh hmm.

T: They just said, "Taste these two cakes and just say which one is the better. The kids were going to be the judges. So all of them tasted each cake and they each wrote down which cake they liked and the ten kids turned out to like the mother's cake best, and one kid liked the father's cake best. It seemed no matter—he sorted of sensed, he kind of knew which one was the father's cake and even though inside when he first tasted the cake he knew he was tasting his mother's cake, somehow he could not let himself say that it was the better cake. He really liked it but he just couldn't allow himself to say—couldn't just say that he liked the mother's cake better. He had to say that he liked the father's. Then he saw all the other kids and he said, "Aren't you scared to say that you don't like our father's cake?"

And they said, "No. The facts are that Father doesn't cook as well as Mommy. That's all, that he's not a good cook." The boy really knew that, but he was just scared to say it. So what do you think happened then?

P: He learned his lesson.

T: And what did he do after that? What was the lesson he learned?

P: That just because he's a man doesn't mean that he's better.

T: He also learned that if you don't like someone's cake you should say so. He was afraid terrible things would happen. He was afraid, for instance, if he told his father that he didn't like his cake the father might leave home, the father might beat him up, or the father might do terrible things. Now it so happens that in my story these parents subsequently got divorced, but this had nothing to do with the fact that the boy would say at times that he didn't like the father's cake, or even that the boy had the idea that if he told his father or if he criticized his father or something that his father would see him even less. And that was unfortunate because he had to hide things from himself in order to do that.

Okay. Do you know what the lesson of that story is?

P: It's your story . . . (mumbles) . . .

T: Pardon?

P: I said it's your story.

T: Well, the lesson is that you should try to see things as they really are and, for instance, if your father isn't as good a cook as your mother, you should say it. If he doesn't cook cakes as well as your mother, say it.

P: Yeah.

T: And this doesn't mean that he is going to like you any less if you tell him what's on your mind and tell him your true feelings. The end. You want to watch this.

P: Yeah.

In my story I attempted to assuage some of the guilt I knew Jack felt over hostile expression toward his father. The ten siblings, of course, represent his two sisters who are freer to express their hostility. The boy in my story inwardly agrees with his siblings but fears to express this. Hopefully, my story contributed to some alleviation of Jack's anxieties in this regard.

During the following week the patient's teacher reported continuing improvement in the classroom, both academically and in the behavioral area.

Two weeks later, at the beginning of his thirty-fifth session, Jack said that he wanted to talk about his father. After a few minutes, it became apparent that he was touching upon important considerations and I asked him if he would like to record the conversation on videotape. He readily agreed and this discussion (which will be interrupted intermittently for my comments) ensued:

Therapist: Good afternoon boys and girls, ladies and gentlemen. Today is Tuesday, the tenth of April, 1973, and our guest today and I are first going to have a little discussion to continue a talk we had just before the television program started. Now you said you wanted to talk about this on T.V. Right?

Patient: Yeah, about how my dad feels about sports and all my personal stuff.

T: Okay. Let's hear. Which do you want to talk about first?

P: Well, uh, the dog.

T: About the dog. Okay, what do you want to talk about your dog?

P: We didn't think it was a hot idea to get a dog . . . (mumbles) . . .

T: Your father didn't . . . try to speak very clearly. You tend to mumble sometimes.

P: My dad did not like the dog. He does not like the dog.

T: Okay.

P: And so like sometimes he pees in the house on like the furniture. This is . . . (crying).

T: What's the matter?

Patient's Mother: Why, he's done it once and he'd get banned from the house for two weeks.

T: The dog peed in the house once and he couldn't . . .

P (interrupts): Well, a couple of, maybe like once in a while, well like he only used to go to the bathroom he don't got time, like in the morning, like two o'clock in the morning he goes to the bathroom basement and he'd wake up two o'clock in the morning. You'd be pretty tired. You're really all fast asleep.

T: All right.

P: Well, my dad has not seen the dog pee in the house. He sees him pee in the—he sees dogshit.

T: Go ahead.

P: Dogshit in the basement and he gets mad.

T: That's not a word that you would use every day. You know that.

P: He sees "dog do" in the basement.

T: Okay. You know you're on television now. I think the sponsor might not be happy with your using that word. Huh?

P: (laughs)

T: They might take us off the air. So go ahead.

P: Yeah, well, he gets mad and says, "Don't let the dog pee. Clean up the mess." And I clean up the mess. Like he'd take care of the dog—he likes him now a little bit. He's liking him a little bit now.

T: Hh hmm.

P: Like let's say the dog was dying; he'd help him. He'd probably send him to the vet and stuff.

T: Hh hmm. Okay, but what is it you want to say about the dog with regard to your father? What's the main point?

P: He teaches him to bark. He teaches him to bark. You see, I . . . (mumbles) . . . this dog how to bark and he gives me all these—and he mumbles, you know. He's an easy type of person who puts himself first!

T: Your father?

P: Yeah. He puts himself first.

T: So what's this got to do with the dog. I'm not clear.

P: Well, he says like, "We'll have to get rid of that damn dog if he pees in the basement again."

T: Hh hmm.

P: You see, he's getting to like the dog more and more a little bit.

T: He's getting to like him more and more?

P: When he jumps up, he says, "Max, down!" (said in loud tone)

T: The dog's name is Max?

P: Yeah.

T: Well, I'm not clear. First you tell me that he wants to get rid of him. Then you tell me that he likes him more and more.

P: He likes him a little you know, he's—he wants—sometimes he doesn't like the dog. Sometimes he likes him. He's only bad—sometimes I take him on a walk and Dad wants to come, you know. He teaches him to heel, you know.

T: Well, I'm not clear what the problem is with regard to the dog.

P: Well, he thinks the dog—when he was a little boy he wanted a dog.

T: All right.

P: Our grandma likes Max, you know? Well, he got a little collie. There was a little dog. There was a little boy and a puppy. But he made him give it away. It was like—he had him for only three days.

T: Okay. You're still not coming to the point then.

P: If he really wants to do when he really wants a dog but when he gets older he says, "Ahhh." He wants a dog but when he gets one he—I told him, "You always wanted a dog didn't cha?" And then he gets mad! Then he gets mad when you get the dog.

T: And what does he do?

P: He loses his temper and that goddamn—and he says, "That darn dog isn't going to—I'm tired of living here and all this mumbling." Now that's the end of that discussion. All right? This part.

T: Okay, now wait a minute now. What's your question or—okay, your father mumbles about the dog, but what's your question or why do you bring this up?

P: Well, I just said. You know, you two [patient's mother and therapist] are always wondering about my father.

T: Hh hmm.

P: Well, I'm like just telling you my problems with him.

T: Okay, the problem with him is that he is always mumbling about the dog. Okay.

P: Yeah, like when the house is clean he always wants something to shout about. When the house is dirty he shouts about the house, but when the house is clean he shouts about the dog, and . . .

T (interrupts): Okay. Now . . .

P (interrupts): . . . when the basement's clean and the house is clean he doesn't know what he's going to shout about.

T: Okay. Now what do you think you can do about this?

P: Well, I don't know.

T: Hh hmm. Do you think there's anything you can do about it?

P: No, not really.

T: Tell me. How long has it been since your father has been home?

P: About a month.

T: Hh hmm. A month. So this really can't be too much of a complaint because your father's hardly around. Huh?

P: Like when he's home. Christmas Eve he was down in the basement fixing our furnace, you know?

T: Hh hmm.

P: You know?

T: Yeah.

P: And there was something . . . mumbles . . . like the water pump. Mom, what was he fixing?

P's M: The sump pump.

P: The sump pump. Well, he was talking and teaching me stuff. And he starts, "You'd better get that dog here." He said, "I'm tired of this darn dog!" And he says, "Put your nose to the floor and smell it. I'm gonna . . ." Well, fortunately I didn't do it.

T: Whose nose did he put . . .? He wanted *you* to put your nose to the floor?

P: Smell the "dog do." I didn't . . .

T (interrupts): He wanted you to do that?

P: Smell the floor!

T: Excuse me, you're not answering my question. Was it *you* or the *dog* he wanted to do this to?

P: He wanted *me* to do it. But like I thought it was meant to be—like when you receive something and it tastes bad like a—what would you say? Like let's say your wife cooked this chicken and it started to taste like wallpaper paste. You don't mean it tasted like wallpaper paste or, you know, library paste like corn flakes or something. I mean like that's what he means, like it usually means smelly. He loves me. He loves me enough not to think that I would do a stupid thing like that.

T: Well, you say that he loves you enough not to . . .

P (interrupts): . . . think I'd do a stupid thing like that.

T: Okay, but he asked you to do it. He asked you to smell the dogshit?

P: Well, see, like that smells like—let's say that you have wallpaper paste. He doesn't mean it. He just says, "Why don'tcha the thing like he usually . . . (mumbles) . . . don't do it.

T: Okay. Do you think he really wanted you to bend down and smell it?

P: No.

T: You mean he was just saying it as if it would be a . . .

P (interrupts): . . . kidding—well, not kidding, but he doesn't really mean it, but he . . .

T (interrupts): Okay, let's ask your mother whether she thought that he would really want you to lean down and smell it.

P's M: Yeah, he would be capable.

T: He would be capable of asking him actually to lean over and smell it?

P's M: When he's angry he always goes at something you like. He never expresses his anger at you. He's always threatened to do away with something.

T (to patient's mother): Okay. Were you there at the time?

P's M: No, I wasn't. I didn't know. This is the first time I ever heard of this.

T: Okay, but what do you think is the most likely thing that he was saying it . . .

P's M (interrupts): No, I think he meant it.

T: He meant that he would want him to . . .

P's M (interrupts): Yep, hh hmm.

T: . . . to bend down and smell it. Your mother said your father probably really wanted you . . .

P (interrupts): He really did, but I didn't do it.

T: Okay. The thing is just now you didn't want to really admit that he really wanted you to do it. You said that he was just saying it, just kidding.

P: I thought—at first I didn't. I'm not gonna smell a "dog do" for ten dollars!

T: Okay. But let me say something to you at this point. I think it's good that you're able to express and talk about some of the anger that you feel toward your father because there was a time when you wouldn't complain about anything about him. Is that right?

P: Yeah.

T: And I think now it's good that you can complain about certain things. I think that shows you're more comfortable with angry feelings toward him—which is good. However, what you've just said shows me that you're still a little afraid to see your father the way he really is.

P: I see him the way he really is!

T: Well . . .

P (interrupts): He doesn't love me so . . . (mumbles) . . .

T: He doesn't love you what?

P: He doesn't love me as much as he should. He loves me some. He loves me about 25 percent would you say?

T: Well, I can't give a percentage but considering that he doesn't come around very much but calls you . . .

P (interrupts): Like my aunt, like an aunt. My aunt lives in Mississippi. She likes—loves me.

T: Uh huh.

P: But you know Mississippi, flying on a . . . It costs a lot of money. 'Cause you don't get an airline ticket in a gumball machine.

T: Well, look I want to get back to—I want to get back to this question of your father and this whole business with the dog. So you see that your father's asking you to bend down and smell that "dog do" was really a kind of cruel thing. Right?

P: Right, but I wouldn't do it. If he told me—if he told me . . .

T (interrupts): Right. Would you say that's in the 25 percent love or the 75 percent unlove?

P: 75 percent unlove.

T: Right. I would agree. And the thing is: what can you do about when your father does come home and he complains a lot about the dog? What can you do?

P: Just ignore him.

T: That's about the only thing you can do.

P: I ignore his complaints. I try.

T: All right.

P: I think I do a good job of it.

T: Right. You can also not give him any excuses to complain. But you know your father is the kind of person who complains a lot. That would be in the 75 percent unlove part of him. Right?

P: Right.

T: Okay. Now it seems that he still lets you have the dog. He hasn't taken the dog away. Right?

P: No.

T: So what part would that be in then?

P: Like he—that's 25 percent love. He won't . . .

T (interrupts): Right. That's still in the 25 percent love. He lets you have the dog.

P: Yeah because like I didn't make him give up the car.

T: Yeah, well you can't really because you're a kid and he's the father.

P: . . . (mumbles) . . .

T: Excuse me. I want to interrupt you because I want to go on to the next point now. You were saying that there was another thing you wanted to talk about besides the dog. What was that?

P: This is part of it. Can I tell you something, like?

T: Go ahead.

P: Like, you see, my Dad knows that I really wanted a doggie. I love him and he loves me, you know. He's beginning to trust me a little bit though again like how would you like to take—He'd rip up your furniture at times. You really love those things and you let him rip things at times. So he still lets me have the dog.

T: Right. Right.

P: Well, he'd take care of the doggie if he was dying. He'd fit into it. Like let's say he was dying.

T: Yeah.

P: He'd probably help the dog like let's say take him to a vet, you know.

T: So what part would *that* put him in—the 25 percent love or the 75 percent . . .

P (interrupts): the 25 percent love.

T: That's part of the 25 percent love.

P: If Mom was dying Dad would help.

T: Okay.

P's M: May I say something about the dog?

T: Yeah.

P's M: It seems to be a bone of contention. We put off getting it for a long time and it's something that Jack wanted very very much. And his father threatened to leave home and never come back if we got the dog. He told Jack and his sisters wanted the dog too and naturally I wanted the dog.

T: Uh huh.

P's M: I wanted a dog that barks around here because I am alone in the house.

T: Yeah.

P's M: And I really wanted one for other reasons than just a pet. The first time that he came home and saw the dog he said to Jack, "Well, of course you know you've made me leave home forever."

T (to patient): Hh hmm. What do you think about that?

P: I think she's right. She needs a dog because there are other reasons for a dog.

T: Excuse me?

P's M: But he didn't do it. Of course, he said, "I'll never come back." Of course, he's been coming back.

T: But what do you think about what your father said when he saw the dog?

P: I think—like he said, "I don't want to come back with the dog."

T: But your mother said—what did your mother just say your father said when he first saw the dog?

P: I don't want to go home. Gaye said, "Hi. You want to take me to the movies or something?" Gaye said, "Like I don't want to help you with anything. We got the dog and the dog does not belong here."

T: But your mother said something about his saying, "I'm going to leave the house forever."

P: He said that but he comes back.

T: What do you think about his saying such a thing?

P: I think he's selfish and I um even think he's like doing that because like he didn't like us—just because he didn't like it and but I loved it. I loved him.

T: Do you think that's the reason he left the house because you got the dog? Do you think . . .

P (interrupts): No, Mom. He didn't love Mom so he left—kept going away and kept coming back.

T: Okay, so you think that was the real reason, that he didn't love your mother very much? Hh hmm?

P: He didn't love—like when they'd start eating—it was March 28th . . .

T (interrupts): Look, okay. I'm going to interrupt you again because you give a lot of details and we don't have all that time. What do you think about the fact that the real reason for his not coming home very often was that . . .

P (interrupts): . . . is Mom!

T (continuing): . . . is his relationship with your mother and *he* said that it was due to the fact that you bought a dog? What do you think about that?

P: It wasn't the dog's fault. He just didn't love my Mom anymore.

T: You got it.

P: Yeah.

T: What do you think about his blaming it on the dog? What do you think about that?

P: Oh, well, I think he was selfish and rude.

T: Hh hmm. Do you think he was mean?

P: Yeah.

T: Hh hmm. How did it make you feel?

P: Sad.

T: Hh hmm. Did it make you feel kind of bad about him or did it make you feel that you're responsible?

P: I think that I had a feeling that he was bad—bad, you know, that he was bad.

T: Or?

P: Wait. Let me tell you something. I don't like—I don't love this dog. I don't love him. I don't like him.

T: Okay, but my question to you is, do you think it really was your fault that he didn't come home because of the dog?

P: No, it was not my fault.

T: Right. Right. But it was mean of him to try to make you feel it was your fault. Huh?

P: Yup.

T: Put the blame on you. Hmm?

P: Yeah.

T: Where would you put that, 25 percent or 75 percent?

P: 75 percent hate.

T: Right. Now you said there was another point, another thing that you wanted to talk about.

P: Something else about the dog. Like Lisa and Gaye wanted a puppy and Mom wanted a puppy, and, you know, to play with. We, we—I could run around with him. Mom could keep—he could keep the house safe. It's like when you own a barking dog it keeps burglars away.

T: Hh hmm. It's a useful thing to have around. Right?

P: Yeah.

The above conversation reveals quite well that many of my therapeutic efforts were now bearing fruit. The patient was openly criticizing his father in a meaningful way. This was pointed out to him and he was complimented on his freedom to express his resentment. Such reinforcement is a vital point of the therapeutic process. Although I tried to direct the patient into a discussion of what he could *do* about his father's attitudes toward his dog, I was not too successful in this regard. Merely encouraging the expression of anger (or other suppressed and repressed feelings) is therapeutically beneficial as far as it goes; however, one must help the patient utilize these feelings in the service of problem solving. Otherwise, it becomes a situation of screaming into the wind.

In addition, I attempted during this discussion to help Jack more clearly appreciate his father's assets and liabilities. Although the father did many cruel things to Jack concerning the dog, there were also some benevolent attitudes as well. Although the 75 percent, 25 percent unlove quantification is certainly artificial, it can be helpful in helping patients more clearly view their parents. (Of course, other patients may have different percentages regarding their parents.) One of the most common problems that children of divorce have is their inability to see their parents as balanced human beings with both assets and liabilities. All too often they view them as either totally malevolent or totally benevolent. It is vital to the therapy of such children that they gain a more accurate view of their parents.

As I have mentioned previously, it is common for children of divorce to blame themselves for the disruption in the parents' relationship. Desire for the control of the uncontrollable and self-directed hostility are the most common elements in this mechanism. Generally, parents attempt to reassure the child that the separation was in no way his or her fault. However, on rare occasion a parent will actually tell the child that he was to blame for the separation. And Jack's father was one who did this. The therapist's job then becomes more difficult in that there has been actual parental accusation and confirmation of the patient's distorted thinking. In Jack's case, however, he appreciated the absurdity of his father's statement and he readily accepted his mother's and my refutations.

Lastly, the transcript well reveals how difficult it may be to communicate with some patients when they discuss anxiety-provoking material. Jack's teacher and school speech therapist did not consider him to have a speech problem. However, during sessions he would sometimes mumble inaudibly and at other times one could not understand what he was saying even though the words were clearly articulated. These were clear manifestations of anxiety and are easily seen in this transcript. They make the therapist's job much more difficult and as the child's situation improves, these anxiety manifestations generally recede.

T: Now I want to ask you something else. In the time we have left, let's switch. There was something else you wanted to talk about.

P: How about sports?

T: Okay. Let's talk about sports? Let's hear about that.

P: Well, he didn't—he um—well when I said, "Dad, you want to come over." When I was little he liked sailing and stuff. Like when I get up to see him well we liked throwing footballs and played catch. When I was four years old my Mom got me a ball and a bat.

T: Hh hmm.

P: And he's pitch to me and I'd try to underhit through him, because I liked baseball when I was a little boy.

T: Hh hmm.

P: I really liked it.

T: Go ahead.

P: And so like he pitched the ball underhand and I tried to hit the ball.

T: Hh hmm.

P: Well, one day like I asked him . . . (mumbles) . . . I liked football.

T: Go ahead.

P: I said, "Do you want to play touch football when you get home?" And he said, "Jack, I'm not a sports fan," he said, "like Joe Namath." And I said, "Would you like to be one?" and he said, "No." I said, "What team is Joe Namath on?" He said—he wouldn't even guess. Well, that's the way he is and like. . . . And then one day I would like to play bases and he'd say, "You know, I remember when I was on the Westwood Wolves, Westwood Wolves, Westwood Wolves. I used to hit every single ball. I used to bat one thousand!"

T: Is that what he said?

P: It was bragging.

T: Uh huh.

P: And that really got me mad.

T: Because?

P: Because like he was making—he was making fun of sports and something I liked.

T: Oh, you mean he really, he really wasn't—was there such a team as the Westwood Wolves?

P: No.

T: He was just making fun of it. What does he say about your interest in baseball?

P: Well, he sometimes—once in a while he goes to a ballgame with me and sometimes . . . (mumbles) . . .

T: Okay, when he goes to a ballgame with you do you have a good time?

P: Yeah. We went once to see a Yankee game together. We really went to only one ballgame. And he's come with me to my games many times.

T: Uh huh. Is there anything that happens at the time that you go to the ballgames with him that isn't fun?

P: They're fun. They're always fun.

T: Your mother is shaking her head. She seems to have something to say about this. What do you want to say?

P's M: I say that Jack you are deluding yourself. So far as I know he's only been to two or three Tiny Tim games and he hasn't stayed.

T: Tiny Tim games are what?

P's M: Baseball, when Jack was involved?

T: That's before the Little League?

P's M: Yeah. Tiny Tim. You see he's just graduated into the Little League.

T: I see. Go ahead.

P's M: This is for young ones. And he [Jack's father] has not shown any interest. He dropped him off and went home and on Saturdays usually there are fathers there. They're coaching or they're cheering the team on or something.

T: Uh huh.

P's M: And he simply hasn't the time to either spend at home or to be with Jack. I picked him up at the airport one day and took him over to one game. And it's true that he doesn't like sports.

T: Uh huh.

P's M: But he doesn't get involved in things. He doesn't realize the importance of his child.

T: I see. What is your mother saying? What is your mother saying?

P: That he doesn't want to be involved with anything. He doesn't want to be involved.

P's M: That's it.

T: Is that true?

P: Hh hmm.

T: Do you know what your mother meant when she said that you were deluding yourself?

P: I don't know what delute [sic] means.

T: Deluding means that you're fooling yourself, that you're trying to make yourself think that he's more involved in baseball than he really is. Even though you were complaining about his laughing at your sports you were saying, "Well, he takes me to baseball games" . . .

P (interrupts): Once!

T: Yeah, but that's the real truth, you know, that he hardly ever takes you, far less than the other fathers, and he doesn't seem to be interested in watching you play. Is that right?

P: Yeah.

T: What else can you tell me about that?

P: You know, you don't have to—well like—he doesn't have to make fun of me just because he doesn't like a sport. He just wants to make fun of it.

Once again, Jack began to complain about his father. Again this was a healthy step forward in that previously he had not felt so free to express his resentment. His criticisms of his father regarding the latter's lack of interest in playing ball with him were valid. However, in the midst of his complaining he began to describe an involvement on his father's part which was not valid. His mother immediately saw the distortions and pointed them out to him. This is another example of the value of the mother's presence in child therapy. Had she not been there, I would not have known what was reality and what was Jack's wish-fulfilling fantasy. Jack's problem in this area was primarily one of denying his father's deficits. Even in this session, where the main thrust of his conversation was toward accurately criticizing his father, his strong tendency to deny some of the latter's defects exhibited itself. This is an inevitable part of therapy—which is not a smooth upward course but rather a succession of advances and retrogressions. The advances must be reinforced and strengthened and the retrogressions identified and worked through. Parental cooperation can be most helpful in both the identifying and working through processes.

Having qualified Jack's father's antagonistic and disinterested attitudes toward Jack's sports involvements, I then introduced the question of what Jack could do about that:

> *Therapist:* Okay, what can you say to him?
> *Patient:* Well, if you don't want to—I don't know what I can say.
> *T:* Well, how do you feel when he makes fun of your baseball?
> *P:* Well, I feel sad. I feel like getting back at him.
> *T:* What do you feel like saying?
> *P:* I feel like saying, "When I was on the Tucson Toilets, I used to . . ."
> *T* (interrupts): In other words, are you saying to tell a joke back, like when he says "When I was on the Westwood Lions . . ." you say, "When I was on the Tucson Toilets . . ."? Is that it?
> *P:* Yeah, that's where he's from—from Tucson.
> *T:* He's from Tucson. I see. So you tell him a joke back about Tucson. He laughs at Westwood. You laugh at Tucson. Huh?
> *P:* Yeah.
> *T:* That's good. I think that's a good way of handling it.
> *P:* One night it was before my birthday . . .
> *T:* Hh hmm.
> *P:* Well, Dad was making fun, like he was Westwood Lions and I was sick of it! You know, it can be only funny once.
> *T:* Hh hmm.
> *P:* I could take it only once.
> *T:* Uh huh. Yeah.
> *P:* So one day I said, "Before you met your girl friend . . . (mumbles) . . .
> *T:* What did you say? I didn't understand what you said.
> *P:* I taught your girl friend how to fart.
> *T:* You said, "I taught your girl friend . . ."
> *P* (interrupts): . . . how to fart.
> *T:* You taught his girl friend how to fart. Is that what you're saying?
> *P:* No. I haven't seen her and anyway she looks . . .
> *T* (interrupts): I don't understand. Would you say it again? I can't understand.

P: I taught his girl friend how to fart.

T: I see. You taught your father's girl friend how to fart. Is that what you're saying?

P: Yeah.

T: Is that what you said to your father?

P: Just to get him mad.

T: Okay and what did . . .

P (interrupts): And he said, "Say it again, you spoiled brat!" He got mad at me.

T: Were you on the phone when you said this?

P: No, it was when he was at home.

T: Then what happened?

P: He got mad. "Say it again, you spoiled brat!"

T: Okay, then what happened?

P: Well, after we started to have a little race and I started . . . (mumbles) . . . I started to run, you know.

T: Then what happened?

P: He came and said, "Say it again, you spoiled brat!" He was strapping me with a belt.

T: He hit you with a belt?

P: Yeah.

T: Okay, so what did you learn from that?

P: I don't know.

T: Well, would you do that all over again?

P: No.

T: I don't think that's a good way of telling your father that you're angry—by calling his girl friend names.

P: Yeah, but he calls my dog names. I'm getting back at him.

T: That's not a good way to get back. That only makes things worse. I think that there are other things that you can do. What does he say about your dog?

P: Max—My father says he taught him how to bark. But a dog naturally learns how to bark.

T: Okay, so why do you think he's saying that he taught your dog how to bark?

P: Just to make fun of him.

T: To make fun of your dog and make fun of you? Is that what you're saying?

P: Yes, just to do something. He's always up to something.

T: So what can you say when he does that?

P: I just—would just say, "Come on. It's not funny anymore."

T: Right! Right! You just say, "It's not funny anymore" and some-

thing like that. Don't laugh at it or don't respond, or sometimes you can
ignore it as you said before. So what do you think things like that are in?
The 25 or the 75?

P: 75.

In response to my suggestion that Jack direct his attention to what he could
do about his father's attitudes toward Jack's interest in sports, Jack described
one appropriate and one inappropriate response. He was praised for his
"Tucson Toilets" response with its implication that if his father could make
fun of Jack's hometown, Westwood, then Jack could make fun of the father's
hometown, Tucson. However, his other comment about his having taught his
father's lady friend to fart was, although an age-appropriate response, one
that would probably alienate his father even more. Jack had to learn to differentiate between adaptive and maladaptive responses to his father and here
I attempted to help him acquire such differentiation.

Therapist: Yeah, 75. I agree. Well, listen, we have to stop our program today. I think that you're getting much better. I think that you're
talking about things that are very hard to discuss. When you first came
here it was very hard for you to talk about some of the angry feelings that
you've been having toward your father and it's not only important to talk
about them, but it's important to *do* something about them. Do you
know what I mean?

P: Yes.

T: And to decide what you can do and what you can't do. Do you understand?

P: Hh hmm.

T: How you can fight back and how you can't fight back, what you
should say and what you shouldn't say, and to know that your father has
some interest in you—you know, he calls once in a while—but that his
interest in you is not that deep, you know, not that great that he wants to
live in the same house with you.

P: Hh hmm.

T: Hmm?

P: Yes. He doesn't really want to live in the same house with Mom.

T: Right. And even more than that when he does come his interest in
you—you know his interest in you is not as great as other fathers—even
fathers who are divorced. Did you know that? Or fathers who aren't living in their house. Did you know that?

P: Yeah. Well, he's sort of like a ballplayer.

T: What do you mean?

P: Like he's always in St. Louis all the time, but a ballplayer travels

more. Like he's in New York for about three days—let's say a Yankee—
—then he's in Chicago and Detroit and Milwaukee and Oakland, you
know, things like that.

T: Hh hmm.

P: He's always traveling.

T: Hh hmm. Yeah. Why do you think he travels so much?

P: To see his girl friend.

T: Uh huh. That's one of the reasons. Any other reason?

P: He doesn't like home. He hates Westwood he says.

T: Hh hmm.

P: She thinks, um, he thinks St. Louis is safer than—I say—he says—

T: Wait. What is it?

P: He thinks St. Louis is safer than New York, and I say New York is
safer than St. Louis.

T: Hh hmm.

P: Because he lives both places both of the time.

T: Hh hmm.

P: He's been to both places.

T: Uh huh.

P: And I still think like like he's probably—I'm probably right because like St. Louis, that's a dangerous city. It's got a ballpark. You
can't go to either one. And like they're both dangerous, but New York's
dangerous—but the other one's Shea. Shea and Yankee's are
dangerous.

T: Well, I don't know which city is more dangerous.

P: I think St. Louis.

T: But it seems to me your father is doing something else there besides
just . . .

P (interrupts): I mean at the nighttime, at the nighttime New York is
sometimes dangerous.

T: But what is he doing there when he says St. Louis is safer? What is
he saying about you?

P: He's saying that he says that it doesn't, but he probably doesn't
know what he's talking about?

T: Well, I think that what he's doing is he's trying to compete with
you a little bit and trying to put you down a little bit. Yeah. I think he's
acting like a boy there, you know, saying, "My city's safer than your
city," or something like that. And that's the kind of thing that kids
might do but it's not the kind of thing that a father should be doing with
his son. You know what I mean?

P: Hh hmm.

T: And to me he's not acting, he's not acting his age there, and it
doesn't matter which city is safer or not safer, he shouldn't be competing

with you that way. Do you know what I mean?

P: Yeah.

T: And I think that's the kind of thing that is part of the 75 percent unlove part. You know?

P: Yeah.

T: It doesn't show great concern for you to try to knock down the city where you live. Do you know what I mean?

P: Yeah.

T: That's what I think it says. Okay, look, before we stop this program I'd like to know how you feel right now.

P: My father is making fun of the stuff I don't own—I own!

T: Yeah, how else do you feel?

P: That he don't love me as much as he should.

T: Anything else you feel?

P: That's all.

T: How do you feel about yourself right now?

P: Being brave.

T: You're being brave. Right. I think you're being very brave. Why are you being brave?

P: I'm seeing things that I should, really should.

T: Pardon me? Can you say that again?

P: I'm seeing things as they really are.

T: Right, and that's sometimes very hard to do, and I think you should be congratulated about talking about those things. (therapist shakes patient's hand)

P: Yeah, but like there's one thing, you're sometimes—like you said that you should see, you know it's the right idea that you should say that all people should see things as they really are.

T: Right. Right.

P: Well, you can't make all people see things as they really are.

T: It's harder to make some people than others. What do you think about you? How are you in that regard, about seeing things as they really are?

P: I don't know.

T: Are you a person that easily sees things or not?

P: Easily sees them as they really are.

T: Well, I think that you've changed. I think when you first came here it was very hard for you to see things as they really are, but I think now that you're seeing things much more clearly. Let's ask your mother what she thinks.

P's M: Yes, I do too.

T: I think so, and it's very hard to do that.

P's M: It takes a lot of courage.

T: It does. He is very brave. And I think that he's doing very well. Okay, let's stop the program.

There is little that I can add to the final phase of our interchange. The general feeling that all of us had was that something significant happened and that Jack had truly made progress.

Two and a half weeks later, during Jack's thirty-eighth session, he told a story about a man who lived in "cowboy times." This man was a compulsive gambler and although everyone warned him about the fact that he would ultimately lose all his money, he continued to gamble. The man ended up losing all his money. I considered this story to reflect Jack's awareness that trying to get deep affection from his father was a lost cause. Psychologically, the rewards of gambling are similar to love and affection from a significant figure. After a small investment on the gambler's part he hopes to be rewarded with a bonanza of money which, because it has the power to purchase material possessions, lends itself well to symbolizing the beneficence of love. I felt that this story revealed another step forward for Jack in that he was resigning himself to the fact that his attempts to extract affection from his father would not be effective; that he would be wasting his energy; and that he would only end up depleted of his own resources.

Two weeks later, during Jack's forty-first session, we played *The Talking, Feeling, and Doing Game.* Transcribed below are those responses and interchanges that I considered to be of therapeutic value in Jack's working through his problems.

Therapist: My card says: "What's the worst thing a child can say to his mother?"

If a mother says, "You never let me say what I feel," that's real bad.

My intent here was to lessen guilt over the expression of feelings.

Patient: My card says: "Tell a secret to someone." (comes over to me and whispers in my ear) "I like you."

The response was made with genuine affection and I considered it to be a manifestation of our good relationship.

P: "What's the worst thing a child can say to his father?" He can say, "I don't love you."

I considered this response to reflect a therapeutic advance. This response could not have been entertained in conscious awareness prior to the onset of treatment.

> *T:* "Make believe you're doing a sneaky thing."
> (I suddenly point to a corner of the room and shout) "Look over there!" (As the patient turns around to look in the direction I am pointing, I seize three of his reward chips. There is a playful interchange as he grabs them back.)

Such playful interchanges are vital in therapy and they entrench the child's gratifications from treatment and strengthen the therapeutic relationship. Not all therapy must directly concern itself with the narrowly therapeutic. Anything that strengthens the relationship may be salutary and this interchange is one demonstration of this.

> *T:* "What turns you off?"
> Kids who want to blind themselves to things that are going on around them.

The response was made in an attempt to lessen Jack's tendency to use the denial mechanism.

> *P:* "Make believe you're vomiting."
> (retches violently over the playing board.)
> *T* (after patient has finished retching): I'd appreciate your not vomiting on my game.

The patient responded with laughter to my comment. This is another example of the kind of humorous interchange that can enrich the therapy.

> *T:* "If you wrote a book about yourself, what title would give it?
> *Richard A. Gardner, M.D.—He Helps Kids See Things More Clearly.*

Again, this response was directed toward an alleviation of Jack's denial mechanism.

One week later, during his forty-second session, Jack's mother complained that she and his two sisters were quite upset with Jack's bad manners and habits. He would pick his nose openly and wipe his mucus on the furniture or make it into balls and throw them into the air. He would pass wind whenever he was so inclined without concerning himself with those who might be around. He had no hesitation passing gas at the dinner table or when there were visitors to the home. His table manners were atrocious. Jack refused to respond to his mother and sisters' attempts to control his alienating behavior and in session he stated that he just couldn't help it. However, it was clear that he was not making any attempt to inhibit himself.

Following the above discussion, we played the television program game. He told a story about a cow who lived in a corral. There, the animals were well fed until they were fat enough to be slaughtered. Recognizing his fate, the cow decides to escape from the farm. He sneaks into one of the farm trucks and then surreptitiously leaves it after the farmer has driven it into a nearby town. Ultimately, he gets to India where "cows run free" and he is treated royally. He never gets slaughtered and his life there is "nice and warm."

I considered Jack's story to be a reflection of his desire not to be inhibited in any way. The preceding discussion clearly was directed toward encouraging Jack to restrict himself and not indulge in his animal inclinations. In the story he was essentially saying: "I wish to be free of your absurd restrictions; I wish to be in a place where they would allow me every animal indulgence; becoming acculturated is to me like being slaughtered because it will rob me of my individuality and opportunity for antisocial acting out." With this understanding of Jack's story, I related mine:

Therapist: Once upon a time there was a cow and this cow lived on a farm. And he used to see that some of the cows were going to be sent to slaughter. Other cows, however, were not sent for slaughter. These cows were . . .

Patient (interrupts): . . . milk cows.

T: Milk cows. Right. And they stayed around the farm. And this cow used to sit around thinking, "It would be really great if I was in India because the people in India worship cows and I could walk around free and I wouldn't have to do anything. I could just do whatever I want whenever I want because the people in India worship cows . . ."

P (interrupts): Did your cow get slaughtered?

T: Well, the cow was destined to be slaughtered and the cow wanted to get out of it. He thought that maybe he could break out of the corral, break the fence, or break some of the trucks that they used to use to carry the cows from one place to the next and he found, however, that this wasn't very easy. In fact, it was impossible. The farmer was a pretty smart guy. The farmer had fences all around and he just couldn't break loose. And he was very sad because he wanted to go to India where everybody could treat him nicely and he could do what he wanted. In India he had heard that a cow could walk around. He could crap anywhere and on anybody he wanted and nobody would bother him.

P (laughing): Yeah.

T: Right. He could snort and shit and vomit and leave his saliva and snot anywhere he wanted and nobody would bother him. They thought he was a holy animal and everybody would worship him, and he'd be like a king of the world in India. But he wasn't in India. He happened to be on a farm right in New Jersey and he wasn't getting to India so quickly.

P: What town is he in?

T: I don't know. What town do you want to make him in?

P: Any town.

T: What town do you want to make it?

P: I don't know.

T: Let's make up—don't—I don't know.

P: I don't know.

T: Okay. All right. Look, it really doesn't matter which town. We'll make up a town. We'll call the town Golden Fence. Okay?

P: Yeah.

T: Golden Fence, New Jersey: that's what we'll call it. Anyway, when he found, you know, that that's where he had to be—in Golden Fence and that he couldn't go to India, then he was faced with a problem. Should he decide to do work around that farm, like this particular cow, I mean, he was a bull. Cows are female. Some of the cows would give milk and the bulls would have to do certain work also. They would have to mate with the female cows in order to produce more bulls and cows and sometimes they'd do some kind of work around the farm, pulling things and things like that.

Anyway, the farmer said to him, "Listen you're a lazy guy. You're not doing your job around here. Now either you'll do the work or you're destined to slaughter."

P (interrupts): I'd take the work.

T: Well, he realized that the third choice, which was to dream about going to India, was out, so he decided to do work around the farm, and he realized that it wasn't so bad. And the farmer also said to him, "Listen, you know, you've been kind of sloppy around here too."

The bull said, "Well, in India they let the cows shit wherever they want. They let them snort and anything else. The people think that their do-do is holy."

And the farmer said, "Well, that's India. That isn't here." He said, "Here you're a cow and we don't treat you that way. You're not a special privileged character or anything."

So the cow gradually got wise and realized that if he did some work around the place that he wouldn't get slaughtered. And he realized . . .

P (interrupts): Do you mean he worked?

T: Yeah. And he realized that you just can't walk around doing anything you want to do and expecting people to love you like they do in India. The end.

P: Amen.

T: Anything you want to say about this story?

P: Yeah. What's the moral?

T: What do you think the moral of that story is?

P: It's your story!

T: Okay, the moral is: If you want to get along in life you're going to have to follow certain rules and regulations. If you are a cow and you live in New Jersey, in a place like Golden Fence, New Jersey, you can't go to India and don't think you're going to go there and everybody is going to bow down and worship you and think you're the king of the world and let you do whatever you want. It's just not going to happen. And what's more, if you're living in New Jersey, you're going to have to follow certain rules and regulations or else you'll find yourself in serious trouble. The end.

P: Amen.

T: Okay? Do you want to watch that?

P: Yeah. I . . . (mumbles) . . .

T: What's that?

P: I want to watch my part first.

T: Yeah. You want to watch yourself?

P: Yeah.

T: Okay.

In my story the cow's (or more accurately, the bull's) fantasy that he can go to a world where there will be no restrictions on him is never fulfilled. In essence, I was telling Jack that his desire to live an unrestricted life cannot be realized. However, this does not mean that he will end up slaughtered, that is, he will be as good as dead. Restricting himself can result in a richer life; it does not mean his doom. I believed that Jack was perfectly capable of restricting himself from indulging in disgusting habits. The story, however, does not direct itself to the underlying hostility that is involved in these symptoms and the feelings of abandonment which foster his self-indulgent attitudes. As mentioned, stories that encourage self-control, although not "deep" and not directing themselves to underlying processes, can nevertheless be therapeutic. Conscious control is an intrinsic part of the treatment of most symptoms. In addition, my hope was that if Jack were able to control himself his life would be happier—and such better feelings generally serve as an antidote to the pathological processes that underlie symptoms. In this way, conscious control can play a role in reducing those factors that are at the basis of a patient's symptoms.

During the next session, Jack's forty-third, while playing *The Talking, Feeling, and Doing Game*, these interchanges took place:

Therapist: "What is the worst problem a person can have?"
The worst problem a person can have is trying to get someone to give more love and affection than that person can possibly give.

My attempt here was to communicate to Jack the futility of trying to extract more affection from his father than the latter was capable of giving.

T: "If you had to be changed into an animal, what animal would you choose? Why? Act like you're that animal."
I would want to be a lion. It doesn't let other animals take advantage of him. (roars like a lion)

My attempt here was to try to encourage Jack to assert himself against those who might take advantage of him. Again, my primary reference was to his father, who would often make promises that he would never fulfill and who would often not keep appointments.

Patient: "Of all the places in the world, where would you like to live the most? Why?
Jamaica and Virginia Beach. That's where my father took me.
T: I guess that's part of his 25 percent love.
P: (nods affirmatively)
T: "Act out what you would do if you found that you had magic powers."
I would give people the power to look at the unpleasant. Many people try to hide from that which is painful. They usually end up worse off because they don't solve the problem.

I was obviously attempting to deal with Jack's tendency to deny.

P: "What is the worst thing you can say to anyone?"
I hate you.
T: I think it's far worse to think that it's terrible to even think about hating anyone. There are some people who think that it's a terrible thing to even have thoughts of hating anybody. I don't agree with such people.

Here I was attempting to assuage some of Jack's guilt regarding the expression of hostility toward his father.

T: "Make up a lie."
Jack is not afraid to tell people when he is angry at them.
P (laughing): Oh, you're always saying things like that.

Again, I was trying to use a humorous communication in an attempt to assuage Jack's anger inhibition problem.

> *T:* "What is one of the stupidest things a person can do? Show someone doing that thing."
> Let a kid hit you and not fight back.

The response was designed to help Jack lessen his inhibition in asserting himself.

> *T:* "A child has something on his mind that he's afraid to tell his mother. What is it that he's scared to talk about?"
> I can't think of anything that a child should be afraid to tell his mother. I guess I just don't get a reward chip. A child should be able to tell his mother anything.

Jack was afraid to tell his mother about his hostile feelings toward his father and, to a lesser extent, toward her.

> *T:* "Say something funny."
> Jack never fights with his sisters.
> *P:* (laughs in response)

There was no psychological significance to my response other than to create an element of levity in an otherwise tense situation, the enjoyment of the game notwithstanding.

During Jack's forty-fifth session, he drew a picture of a tree. There were no leaves on it and nebulous black blotches could be seen as well. Jack said that the tree was the only one in the world that was left and that all the other trees had died. The black splotches were the ghosts of dead trees and they were surrounding the remaining live tree. He described the tree as feeling sad that all the other trees had died.

I considered the picture and its associations to reflect Jack's feelings that his father, in the psychological sense, was dead to him. His ghost, however, was still very much present, that is, his father still influenced him. On the one hand, the fantasy was positive in that it suggested resignation to his father's diminished interest in and affection for Jack. It also was a statement about the depth of the father's involvement, that is, it was limited and was only a "ghost" of what it might have been. In addition, the picture reflected Jack's feelings of loneliness associated with his acceptance of his father's limited environment with him.

In response, I told a story about a tree who thought that he was the only tree left in the world but that he soon came to realize that there were other trees on the other side of the mountain that he had not previously seen. In addition, I described how this tree dropped seeds into the ground, bringing about the growth of other trees to keep him company. In this way I hoped to provide Jack with the reassurance that there were other people in the world who could provide him with gratifications even though his father was significantly deficient in this regard.

Two weeks later, during Jack's forty-ninth session, we played a game similar to *Scrabble for Juniors*. In this game, however, the words on the board are similar to those used in *The Bag of Words Game* in that they tend to focus more specifically on issues that are likely to come up in a child's treatment. During play, this interchange took place:

> *Therapist:* Today is Thursday, the 14th of June, 1973, and Jack and I are playing the Storytelling Word Game. Jack has completed the word *nurse* and he's going to tell a story about a nurse.
>
> *Patient:* Once upon a time there was a nurse studying to be a nurse and she was in college and like she didn't study at all, you know. And then one day she asked her teacher—the teacher—that like she's going to college studying to be a nurse and says, "When will I be able to get a nurse's ... (mumbles) .. ?"
>
> "You won't be able to be a nurse because you're not—you don't study."
>
> And like she studied and became a nurse. And the moral of the story is: If you want to get a job you have to study hard.
>
> *T:* Hh hmm. So what finally happened to her?
>
> *P:* She became a nurse.
>
> *T:* Okay. Now it's my chance to tell a story.
>
> *P:* Yes.

The reality of Jack's life was that he was not applying himself diligently to his studies. As this story had a perfunctory quality having little to do with this reality, I considered it a put-on. He essentially was telling me what he suspected I wanted to hear. I therefore considered the story a resistance and responded with this story of my own:

> *T:* Once upon a time there was a nurse and she worked in a hospital. And one day, as she was making her afternoon rounds to give out medicine, she went into the room of a new patient and she said, "Here you are, Mr. Jones. Here's your pill."
>
> He said, "Get the hell out of this room!"

P: (laughs heartily)

T: And she said, "Mr. Jones, I have your medicine here. Your doctor says you must take this medicine."

"I don't want any of your goddamn medicine! Get the hell out of here!"

P: (still laughing)

T: "Mr. Jones, first of all, that's no way to talk to me. But even more important than that," she said, "if you don't take this medicine you're going to remain sick."

He said, "I don't give a damn! Get the hell out of here!" And he picked up his bedpan and he threw it right at the nurse. The thing clanged all over the floor and missed her head, fortunately.

P: (laughing hysterically)

T: She ran out of the room and she thought that there was something wrong with this guy. Anyway, they called the psychiatrist in and he saw the man, and he spoke to him and there was no reasoning with this guy. The psychiatrist tried to tell him that, "Look you're coming to the hospital in order to get treated. You're paying a lot of money for this room and here when they want to give you medicine you get obnoxious and you don't listen to what people are saying, and I think you're wasting your time here. Are you going to start taking your medicine to get better? Are you going to listen to what the doctor says or not?"

And the man says, "I don't care what you say. What do you know? You're only a psychiatrist. You don't know what you're talking about."

So the psychiatrist said, "Well, look, I don't know why you're staying here. I think you'd do better to stay home."

So the guy left the hospital and he didn't get his medicine. He wasn't treated and he didn't get better.

And the lesson of that story is: If you're coming to a doctor or going to a hospital and you don't listen to what the nurse and doctor say, there's no point in coming. The end.

P: . . . (mumbles) . . .

T: What did you say?

P: What happened to the guy after he came home from the hospital? What happened to him?

T: He remained sick.

P: Did he die or what happened to him?

T: Well, what do you think?

P: I don't know.

T: Well, this particular guy he remained sick for a long time.

P: What happened to him at the end?

T: And then finally he got wise and finally he realized that the doctors were right, that those people know what they're talking about, and that if they suggest that you do something that you're wisest in doing it. But if you don't then you remain sick. So he decided to take the medicine this time and he went back into the hospital, took the treatment, and got better. And that's what happened to him.

P: What did he have?

T: What did he have? I don't know. What do you want to make up? What kind of disease do you want to make up?

P: . . . (mumbles) . . .

T: What?

P: It's your story.

T: Well, let's think of it together. What kind of an illness do you think he had? (After long pause) Hhhmm?

P: I don't know.

T: I'll tell you what he had. He had ulcers in his stomach. Do you know what ulcers are?

P: Yeah, but they, yeah but that isn't a sickness.

T: Ulcers isn't a sickness? What is it? What do you call it if it's not a sickness? What is it?

P: Don't ask me!

T: Well, do you know what ulcers come from?

P: What?

T: Ulcers are an eating away of the inner walls of the stomach and it comes from worrying and tension and holding in feelings inside so that they don't come out, and it eats up your insides. Your stomach goes into knots and the acids get secreted and it's holding in your feelings. People who hold in their fears or their anger—they keep it all inside of them— and it eats up their stomach. And this guy not only needed medicine but he also needed advice on how to express his feelings and let out what was going on inside of him. (patient picks nose) Excuse me, that isn't very pretty—you picking your nose and rolling the snot into little balls.

P: That's my business!

P's M: No, it is not! No, it is not!

P (getting angry): But it's my business!

T: It's not your business. It's everybody else's business who has to watch you.

P: I can't stand Kleenex!

T: Well, it's disgusting. It's really disgusting.

P: Well, it's disgusting to blow your nose!

P's M: This is a great problem at home.

T: Yeah, very disgusting.

P's M: He does the same thing.

T: It's nauseating, really. Okay, anything you want to say about that story?

P: No. Is it time for us to quit?

T: It's time for us to start packing up. Yeah. Okay? Do you want to listen to the other part of it?

P: Yep.

T: Okay, let's turn it back.

In this interchange I tried to accomplish a number of things. First, I demonstrate quite dramatically that the person who refuses to cooperate in his treatment is not going to get better, and is going to continue suffering with his illness. The man in the hospital didn't take his pills, became obnoxious, threw the nurse out, did not listen to what the psychiatrist had to say, and so he continued being sick. The patient was clearly impressed by this. And the added dramatic elements enhanced his involvement in the story. He was somewhat worried about the sick man and wanted to know what ultimately happened to him. One could argue that I was being too harsh with Jack here and that I was feeding him very strong medicine. On the other hand, I believe that were I to have been more tender with him, I might not have gotten my message across. Often one cannot know in advance how forceful one must be when providing anxiety-provoking confrontations— either overtly or in symbolic form. I tend to try them out and rely on the patient's reaction as a barometer of whether he or she can handle them. To take too cautious a position in this regard may deprive patients of important information. Here Jack did not recoil, deny, or show other indications that my communications were producing excessive anxiety. Rather, he became swept up in the story and was receptive to its messages.

In my story the man decides to take the medicine and follow the doctor's recommendations. He goes back into the hospital and gets help. Here I was attempting to circumvent Jack's resistance as well as to increase his motivation to help himself. Rather than telling him directly that he was being resistive, I merely told him a story that points out the disadvantages of resistance and the benefits of cooperation.

Following the story the patient wanted to know what was wrong with the man. I usually try to get the child to provide answers to such questions in order to tap material that is meaningful to him. When Jack could not provide an answer, I decided to use a psychosomatic illness—one related to suppression and repression of feelings. Since one of the patient's problems was the repression of angry feelings that he felt toward his father, I chose ulcers and described how people get them when they keep their feelings inside.

At that point Jack became somewhat anxious, started picking his nose, rolling the mucus into little balls, and flipping them around the room. I immediately told Jack how nauseating a habit that was. His mother was sitting there and she too joined in. He got angry, said it was his business. I replied that it was the business as well of those who had to watch him. Although he was upset by this interchange, I believe that such confrontations are an important part of treatment and that we do our patients a disservice if we do not point out to them—in as benevolent a manner as possible—habits that are alienating to others. This is very much the job of the therapist. I am reminded at this point of the old Listerine advertisement that informs the reader that even his best friend won't tell him that he has bad breath. I believe that the therapist should be *better* than one's best friend. He should tell his patient that he has bad breath so that he'll do something about it: brush his teeth, buy Listerine, or what have you. If the therapist imparts such messages in a benevolent fashion the patient, although embarrassed, will often welcome the information. Even though I used words like *disgusting* and was somewhat stern with Jack here, I believe that my basic benevolence came through and that I was doing him a service by pointing this habit out— something that others might not have brought to his attention, having instead nothing to do with him.

Two days before Jack's fiftieth session, his father called after one month of silence. During this period the mother was of the opinion that he was in Europe with his girl friend and that calling long distance or writing would reveal his whereabouts. Jack was not at home when his father called and Jack was told that his father had promised to call again the next day. That night Jack had this dream:

> My friend and I were in a car. We had guns. There were some bad guys in a station wagon. The bad guys started to shoot at us so we shot back. I shot one of the bad guys and I think I killed him. I felt very guilty. I felt very bad. And then I woke up.

On the day following the dream (the day before his session), Jack's father called. Jack asked his father where he had been all this time and the father refused to answer the question. Jack replied, "Well, you could have at least sent a postcard." Again the father did not respond. After the conversation Jack had the thought, "I wish he'd go to hell."

Jack was very resistive to analyzing the dream. When I asked him who the bad man might represent, he came up with a few individuals, none of them his father. Finally I suggested that the man represented his father; this he vehemently denied. He insisted that although his father might be bad, he was certainly not a criminal, and that although he might be angry at his father, he certainly didn't wish him dead. It was only after a detailed discussion about how dreams tend to exaggerate and how small bits of anger, when repressed, can get built up into great rage that Jack agreed that the dream probably did reveal hostility toward his father.

I felt Jack's resistance to accepting his anger related to the one month's absence. Observing that his father could absent himself for such a long period of time confirmed for Jack the possibility that his father could conceivably abandon him entirely. Accordingly, he was even more fearful of expressing his hostility. It thereby built up into murderous rage, which was expressed in a dream. He could not allow that the anger was his because of its potential to alienate his father even further.

In spite of his resistance to analyzing the dream, I felt that the discussion had been therapeutic in that we were discussing the anger issue—a discussion which had a desensitizing and guilt-assuaging effect. In addition, the discussion was videotaped, affording Jack further exposure to my therapeutic messages.

During the weekend before his fifty-second session, Jack, his mother, and his two sisters went on a family outing. On the lake where they went boating, most of the children were accompanied by their fathers. Jack expressed resentment that his father was not there but did not get broken up about it. The mother described him as markedly improved regarding his father. She stated, "He's less frantic about his father; he's more relaxed about him; his father is less important to him now; he has less tension about his father; and he's far less uptight." She went on to describe how his more relaxed attitude about his father was only part of a more generalized decrease in his tension and hyperexcitability. Jack himself said, "I know my father doesn't love me very much and it doesn't bother me as much as it used to." In the session, as well, Jack appeared to be much less tense than he had been in the past.

Two sessions later Jack described the two dreams discussed in Chapter 3 (see Clinical Example: A mother helps analyze a boy's dream). As the reader may recall, Jack's behavior during the weekend prior to the dreams, as well as the dreams themselves, reflects some regression in his treatment. This is only to be expected. Treatment involves remissions and exacerbations as well as progress. Hopefully, the advances outweigh the retrogressions. It is easy for Jack to come to terms with his anger with his father and to resign himself to the latter's lack of interest when we discuss it in the session and when his father is not there. However, upon the actual appearance of his father, such resignation is a far more difficult thing; and his dreams reflect his temptation and feelings of frustration.

During his fifty-sixth session Jack related this dream:

> A boy was swimming in a pond with his dog. A cop came and said he was going to take the dog to a dog pound because the dog was swimming in the water and he wasn't supposed to. The boy was crying and arguing but the cop still said he was going to take the dog to the dog pound. I was watching this and then I went over to the cop. I started to argue with

him and tried to make him stop taking the dog away. I pushed him and the cop took me away too. ˙

I asked the patient who the cop might be and he did not know. His main comment about the cop was that he wasn't fair and that he treated both boys very badly. I then asked him if there was anyone he knew who was not fair to him and often treated him badly. He immediately replied that his father often treated him unfairly. He then described at length how his father would often yell at him when he had done nothing wrong. For example, when they would work on the car together his father would often scream at him for minor errors that he had no way of avoiding because of his ignorance of the particular procedure. In fact, Jack described how throughout his life his father would often scream at him for not knowing things that he had never learned. Rather than teaching him beforehand how to do the thing right, he would yell at Jack after he had made the inevitable mistake.

Jack realized that the dream related to his father. I considered the dream a step forward in his treatment in that it suggested that he was coming to terms with the malevolent aspects of his father's personality and was allowing himself to appreciate these, if only in the symbolic form of the dream. In addition, his receptivity to the dream analysis was also a sign of progress. Jack was becoming increasingly more receptive to dealing with such previously unacceptable material.

Immediately following the analysis of this dream, Jack described another that he had had on the same night:

I was getting a pair of glasses. They had wire frames. That's all there was to the dream.

Jack did not wear glasses. I considered the dream a reflection of his desire to see things more clearly and such an attitude as another manifestation of his progress in treatment. Jack himself was unable to come up with any specific meanings for the dream. However, when I suggested that perhaps he wanted to see things better and more clearly—things related to his problems —he agreed. He then quoted some statements of mine from *The Talking, Feeling, Doing Game* in which I had used the expression "seeing things as they really are." Jack said, "I guess I'm beginning to see things as they really are."

During his sixty-second session Jack described two dreams. The first occurred three days prior to the session:

I was with a famous baseball player and we were riding in an airplane. We landed in Boston. We went around town going to different ball parks.

I asked Jack how he felt during the dream and he replied that he enjoyed it. I considered the dream to have two possible interpretations. First, it could be a normal wish fulfilling dream that any boy of his age could have. Jack was very involved with baseball and it certainly would have been a treat for him to be with a famous baseball player. On the other hand, he expressed a certain amount of frustration that his father was not interested in taking him to baseball games and the famous baseball player might very well have stood for his father. In this case the dream would also be a wish fulfilling dream and would serve to compensate Jack for his father's deficiencies. Although the dream revealed continued cravings for an affectionate relationship with his father, of more importance was the clinical situation, in which he seemed to have gone a long way in coming to terms with his father's defects.

The second dream occurred the night before the session:

> I was at the high school in town and I met a kid there who I knew from Sunday school. We went to a harbor and saw a ship there and an ocean-liner and a fishing boat. The harbor was calm and like a lake.

Again I asked Jack how he felt during the dream and he replied that there were no special feelings. The general tone of the dream was one of calmness and pleasure. Again I considered it a normal dream, in which he experienced a pleasurable event with a peer, probably in gratification of a wish.

Both dreams were free of significant inner turmoil or frustration and reflected a generally more placid state of mind. This coincided with his clinical situation. In the session during which Jack related this dream, his speech was clearer than it had been for a long time and this I considered another manifestation of decreased tension. It is important to emphasize, however, that this session took place in mid-August, at a time when the patient was not in school and there were no significant pressures on him. This fact, while not discounting the importance of his improved attitude toward his father's rejection, must be considered a contributing factor in his improvement.

One month later, at the end of his tenth month of treatment and during his sixty-ninth session, Jack's mother described him as being generally much calmer at home and being able to involve himself in discussions about his father in a more rational and less tense manner. She described his frustration tolerance as being greater and his relationships with peers as being markedly improved. In the sessions, as well, Jack appeared far more relaxed to me. In this session he described a dream which occurred three nights previously, in which Jack and two of his pals went to a football game. He described his feelings in the dream as pleasurable and stated that that was the whole dream. He recognized the dream as a fulfillment of his wishes to attend a football game—wishes that were particularly frustrated by his father's lack of interest in taking him to sporting events. However, he was able to discuss the dream without the degree of agitation and denial that was characteristic of such discussions in the early phases of his treatment.

During the next session, two days later, Jack's mother described a conversation with his teacher. (Jack had started the fifth grade two weeks previously and this was the first teacher's report.) The teacher described Jack as having markedly improved in the social area. He was now consistently accepted by his classmates and was showing much greater social restraint and awareness. His sportsmanship in games had improved and he was now being asked to join in, whereas previously his participation was only unenthusiastically agreed to by the boys. He was also functioning academically at the fifth grade level.

I considered his social improvement to be specifically related to the extensive use of *The Talking, Feeling, and Doing Game* during the previous two or three months. In this period Jack was not enthusiastic about telling stories, either on television or with various word games. He found *The Talking, Feeling, and Doing Game* quite enjoyable and it was in this context that I transmitted most of my therapeutic communications.

However, his teacher described a persistence of his poor attention span, sloppy work habits, and difficulties in following directions. Although I considered psychogenic elements to be contributing to these remaining symptoms, I felt that his basic organic problem was certainly operative. In essence, I felt that there had been a marked diminution of Jack's psychogenic difficulties and that the organic substrate was exhibiting itself unbeclouded by significant psychogenic pathology. Because of the marked clinical improvement, I decided to reduce the frequency of Jack's sessions to one per week. At that time his chemotherapeutic regimen was: Mellaril, 30 mg twice a day and Ritalin, 40 mg twice a day.

During the next five months Jack had his ups and downs. At times he was receptive to discussing his difficulties with his father; at other times he was particularly unreceptive. Generally this was a period of irritability and difficulty in adhering to classroom routine. I considered the hyperactivity and distractibility associated with Jack's organic problem to be playing a significant role in his classroom difficulties.

During Jack's eighty-eighth session, at the end of his fifteenth month of treatment, we played *The Talking, Feeling, and Doing Game*. I present here some excerpts from that game with associated interpretations of our interchanges.

> *Therapist:* My question is "What's the worst thing that ever happened to you?"
> Well, I would say that one of the worst things that ever happened to me occurred when I was a teen-ager. There was a girl in my class in high

school whom I liked very much. I guess at that time I would say that I loved her. And I thought about nothing else but this girl, and I kept thinking about her and I stopped studying. All I could do was walk around and think about her and I don't think she cared for me too much. She wanted to be friendly with me, but she didn't like me anywhere near as much as I liked her. And I met her around June or so or May. I really got hooked on her and started thinking about her all the time, and she didn't treat me very nicely. And it wasn't until the end of August that she sent me a very painful letter in which she spoke about how much she didn't like me. And I discussed this with a friend of mine and he kind of knocked sense into my head and told me that I was crazy if I answered that letter. And after that it was hard, but I didn't answer it and I stopped seeing her and I gradually got over it. But it was very painful to me and it was too bad that I didn't realize that it was a foolish thing . . .

Patient (interrupting): I got the message.

T: What's the message?

P: Like, you loved the girl so much, but she didn't love you!

T: Right. And so what do you do in such a situation?

P: Just ignore her.

T: Hhmm. Okay. Do I get a chip for that?

P: Um, no.

T: How come?

P: You wear glasses.

T: What's that got to do with getting a chip?

P: You can't see very well. It might be bad, you know.

T: I'm not clear what you're saying.

P: If you wear glasses you might have a foul eyesight, you know.

T: If I wear glasses I have bad eyesight and then what?

P: Even with your glasses on, you might have bad eyesight.

T: Yeah, and then what might I do?

P: You might then misread the cards.

T: And then what?

P: And then you, you like get, you get [the playing card] *Good Luck, You Get an Extra Turn*. That's why.

T: Oh, so what's this got to do with my not getting a chip for this card?

P: If you've got bad eyesight you might misread it. It might say, it might say, "What's the best thing that happened to you?"

T: What would be the best thing?

P: I don't know.

T: I don't understand this.

P: When I came into your room the first day.

T: Yeah. That's the best thing?

P: Yeah.

T: Well, that was one of the good things, but you were talking about my glasses and my eyesight.

P: There might be a little something wrong with it, you know.

T: But you wouldn't want me to see the cards clearly. Is that it? Is that what you're saying?

P: You might not see the cards clearing—clearly.

T: And what might happen if I don't see the cards clearly?

P: You might misread it.

T: And then what would happen?

P: You wouldn't get a chip? It might be a different one.

T: Oh, I see, so that if I have poor eyesight I wouldn't get a chip and then you would win the game. Is that it?

P: Yeah.

T: I see. But maybe you wouldn't want me to read cards like that one. Maybe you didn't like that card that I just answered. Huh? What do you think about that? Do you think that maybe you didn't like that answer?

P: No.

T: Huh?

P: Yeah, I liked it.

T: What was the main point that I was making in that answer?

P: You loved the girl and the girl didn't love you.

T: And so what do you do in those circumstances?

P: I don't know.

T: Well, what should you do?

P: Don't let it bother you.

T: Uh huh. Try to get wise, not trying to get something . . .

P (interrupts): Yeah, yeah, yeah, yeah, yeah! (throws dice)

T: Okay. Good.

In my initial response to the card I related a real incident that occurred during my high school days. There are those who believe that the therapist should strictly refrain from revealing things about his personal life to his patients. They hold that the therapist should be a blank screen upon which the patient can project and that such revelations can only contaminate treatment. In addition, they claim that the patient is not coming to hear about the therapist but, rather, that he is coming to talk about himself.

I believe that such personal revelations, *judiciously utilized*, can be therapeutic. I do not agree that they must necessarily be antithetical to the purposes of treatment. The "blank screen" concept certainly has merit, as does the warning that the therapist should not use the patient's time talking about himself because he may thereby be neglecting his patient. However, I believe that there are times when such revelations can be therapeutic.

Generally, we encourage our patients to express themselves and to free themselves from the inhibitions that impede them in this regard. However, the therapist often does not serve as a good model in this regard. In such extreme cases as classical psychoanalysis or strict forms of nondirective therapy, the therapist may never reveal his own feelings. He thereby serves as a poor model for his patients in this area regardless of what other benefits they may derive from the treatment. No matter how we may try to avoid it, our patients, I believe, still use us as a model for their behavior. Hopefully, the qualities they emulate in us and introduce into their own life patterns will serve them well. Accordingly, the therapist does well, at appropriate times, to exhibit emotions in order to help his patient do so as well. The crucial problem is that of when it is appropriate for him to do so and when it is not. I believe that it would be inappropriate to contrive situations in order to provide the therapist with a justification for such emotional expression. The contrived and artificial quality of such expressions could not but be sensed by the patient and they would, therefore, engender disbelief and even distrust. Also, it would be inappropriate if the therapist's revelations contained significant neurotic material. These can be injurious to the patient and may tend to involve him in the therapist's neuroses. Revelations can be appropriate when they serve to encourage healthy adaptations by the patient. In addition, they tend to lessen the idolization of the therapist that so often occurs when he does not reveal much about himself. Revealing, on occasion, one's own deficiencies and problem areas can make the patient feel less unworthy when he compares himself to the therapist. All too often the patient has a view of the therapist as a perfectly healthy human being, while viewing himself, by comparison, as loathesome and animallike. The therapist's judicious revelation of some of his own deficiencies—at the right time and at the right place in treatment—tends to lessen this antitherapeutic and esteem-lowering disparity.

Such revelations can also be therapeutic when they serve to communicate a message that would be healthy for the patient to incorporate. Like the responding story, they can transmit important therapeutic messages in a way that does not produce significant anxiety. Like the self-created story, the patient need not focus on his own deficiencies; rather he is talking about the defects and the problems of other people, whether they be in the therapist's self-created story or in his relating an event from his own life.

In general, the therapist should reveal an incident in which he demonstrates a deficiency on his part: this rather than a situation similar—except for his better handling of it—to one faced by his patient. The latter type of revelation tends to lower the patient's self-esteem, where the former does not.

I believe that my responding revelation of the incident that occurred when I was a teen-ager was of therapeutic benefit to the patient. While talking about my own experience, I was really encouraging him to take a more realistic attitude toward his father. By my relating the course of events that led to my own resolution to discontinue trying to get affection from someone who was not going to provide it, I was encouraging him to act similarly with his father. At the same time, I revealed to him that I too am susceptible to such problems; I hoped thereby to lessen that antitherapeutic idolization so frequently occurring in treatment.

At the end of my revelation the patient sharply stated, "I got the message." It was clear that he did not wish to discuss the matter further, but I encouraged him to do so. As I have mentioned, I respect the patient's anxieties and resistances but usually try to push him a little bit further in the hope that he will go on toward deeper exploration. However, I do not push hard, and if after one or two attempts there is still resistance and anxiety, I am most respectful of the patient's desire to direct himself to other areas. The patient did respond by revealing further evidence of his having understood my message.

He then said, apparently out of context, "You wear glasses." Because it was so much out of context I felt that such a statement warranted further inquiry; I suspected that it had particular meaning to the patient. In the ensuing discussion it became apparent that Jack would have preferred that I not be able to see the game cards well. Then I might not be able to read clearly the card that provided me an extra turn. I felt that he was in this way expressing some hostility he felt toward me. This hostility might have been redirected from his father or it might have been related to my giving him a message not particularly palatable, in that it encouraged his giving up his futile quest for more affection from his father. In addition, if I could not see well I might read the card incorrectly and think that it was the one that asked the question: "What's the *best* thing that happened to you?" In this way I would once again avoid providing him with the anxiety-provoking response.

Although at the end of our discussion the patient denied that his thoughts about my eyeglasses related in any way to these speculations, he did close with a restatement of his understanding of the fundamental messages I was trying to communicate. However, at the end, he quickly interrupted my final reiteration of the message and threw the dice in order to take his turn. Recognizing this as his final refusal to discuss the matter further, I allowed him to continue.

Soon after, the following interchange took place:

> *T:* Okay, my card says, "Make believe a piece of paper just blew in the window. Something is written on it. Make up what is said on the paper."

It says on the paper, "If at first you don't succeed, try, try again. If after that you still don't succeed, forget it. Don't make a big fool of yourself." That's what it says on the paper. What do you think of that?

P (laughing): That's a good one.

T: Okay.

My response is a quote from W. C. Fields, who is alleged to have made the statement. In my *The Boys and Girls Book about Divorce* (Gardner, 1970b, 1971a) I have elaborated on this message and made it into a chapter entitled "Fields' Rule." The message here is essentially a reiteration of my previously described experience with my teen-age girl friend. This time, however, the patient did not resist the message and stated with enthusiasm, "That's a good one."

Following the patient's taking a card, this interchange took place:

P: "Tell a secret to someone." (whispers something to therapist)

T: You what?

P: (whispers again into therapist's ear)

T: You do, huh? You make those funny phone calls. Does your mother know about it?

P: (continues to whisper)

T: I shouldn't say anything about it?

P: No.

T (whispering): Okay. Well, we'll keep it a secret, but I'll tell you you shouldn't make too many of those because it really bothers people. Would you like to be bugged that way?

P: It would be a riot. I've never received one.

T: I think once in a while it's okay, but if you did it too much I think you're going to get in trouble.

P: Yeah.

T: Okay.

The patient whispered about how he and a few friends had made some "funny" phone calls. Although an age-appropriate prank, I felt that mild discouragement was warranted; however, I did not wish to make the patient feel excessively guilty over this common form of misbehavior and so my criticisms were only lightly made. To have refrained from any criticism would have been antitherapeutic, in my opinion, in that it could have served to foster inappropriate behavior. In addition, I tried to help the patient appreciate the effects of such antics on the recipient by asking him, "Would you like to be bugged that way?" Like most children, Jack needed some further enhancement of his sensitivity to the feelings of others and encouragement to project himself into another person's position. Such a quality is vital if one is to get along well with other individuals.

Subsequently, the following interchange took place:

T: My card says, "Sing your favorite song."

P: Aw, it's going to be those national songs. (The patient is referring here to "America, the Beautiful," which I had sung in response to this card on a previous occasion.)

T: A national song. Do you know my favorite song already?

P: Yeah.

T: What's my favorite song?

P (starts singing): "A red purple star, da, da, da, da, da." (sung to the melody of "America, the Beautiful")

T: All right. "America, the Beautiful." Why do I like that song?

P: I like to make up my favorite song with lots of . . . (mumbles) . . .

T: Is what?

P: That's the . . . (mumbles) . . . right now.

T: What's . . .

P: . . . (mumbles) . . .

T (interrupting): Excuse me. I do not understand what you are saying. Now speak clearly. What is your favorite song?

P: I don't know. "I Got Superstition" or something like that.

T: Superstition?

P (begins singing): "Superstition, da, da, da." I can't sing it really well.

T: Okay. You want to know, okay, on my card was my favorite song. Now you know my favorite song.

P: Yeah.

T: It's "America, the Beautiful." Right? (patient nods affirmatively) Right? (begins singing) "Oh, beautiful" (I have to sing part of it to get my chip) "Oh beautiful for spacious skies, for amber waves of grain." Do you know that?

P: Yeah.

T: Now do you remember why I said it was my favorite song the last time I got this card?

P: I don't know. Maybe because (in sing-song manner) it's a . . . (mumbles) . . . of your country.

T: It's a what?

P: It's, it's your country.

T: It's my country.

P (in annoyed or impatient tone): You like your country.

T: But I said something very more specific. What about this country that makes me like that song?

P (yawning): It's—I don't know. It's the country you live in.

T: Yeah, but it doesn't necessarily mean that I have to love every part of it, you know.

P: I know.

T: You see, I have mixed feelings about America. There are lots of things in it that are very good. There are lots of things in it that I don't like. However, one thing that it has is that it does give many people an opportunity to be things, and to progress and advance, and to get things in life. But you usually have to work for it, you know. It doesn't happen. It's not given to you. The people who first came here thought there might be gold in the streets or something like that and that isn't so. But it does give you a chance, if you are willing to work for something to get a lot of good things in life.

I interrupt the sequence at this point in order to better facilitate its analysis.

When a patient recalls my response to a previous card, I generally ask what his recollection is. The information so gained can tell me whether my response was meaningful to him, whether the message had sunk in, and whether he had distorted it. Like practically everything that happens in therapy, the patient's productions can serve as a point of departure for therapeutically meaningful interchanges. In this case I could not learn very much about Jack's reactions to my previous responses to the card. He somewhat sarcastically and mockingly criticized my liking the song, but gave no further information.

He then spoke about his favorite song, the title of which, I gathered, contained the word "superstition." I surmised that this was a popular rock song but did not have the feeling that an inquiry regarding his favorite song would be productive. At times a child will answer my card and I will use this as an opportunity for further discussion and exploration. The purpose of the game is not to stick to its rules, but rather to utilize it in the service of catalyzing and encouraging therapeutic interchanges. But here, I felt his interruption was a digression in the service of his resisting my singing my song and then discussing its implications. Accordingly, I proceeded to bring him back to my song. First, I sang the first few lines—ostensibly to warrant my getting a chip, but actually to bring him away from what I considered to be a digression in the service of resistance.

After singing my refrain I once again tried to get him to recall what I had said when I had gotten that card a few weeks previously. Jack then made comments regarding the relationship of the song to my liking my country. I then used this as a point of departure to discuss the mixed feelings I have about America. However, in discussing my ambivalence about America, I was really talking about ambivalence in all human relationships—especially the one between Jack and his father. In addition, I used the song as an opportunity to talk about the fact that in the United States there are opportunities for advancement for those who are willing to work. The child with minimal brain dysfunction must work harder than the normal child to achieve the same academic goals and it therefore behooves the therapist to be a strong adherent to the work ethic.

Our interchange then continued:

> P (suddenly switching the subject entirely): Who did you vote for in the presidential election?
> T: Last time? (referring to 1972)
> P: Yeah.

I interrupt the sequence again because of the importance of the issue raised by the patient's question. Generally, therapists are advised to refrain from answering questions of such a personal nature. Rather, they are advised to explore in depth the reasons for the patient's question. Such inquiries are often quite revealing and can be of the utmost significance. However, the advantages of such an inquiry notwithstanding, there are times when it is appropriate to answer the question directly. Although analysis of the patient's reasons for asking the question may be compromised significantly if it takes place after the question has been answered, there are times when such analytic desiderata must be sacrificed because of the overriding value of an immediate answer.

One reason for providing an immediate answer exists when the patient is unreceptive to such analysis. Although some of the previous transcriptions of Jack's therapy clearly reveal a receptivity to such inquiry, he was, for the most part, unreceptive to analytic investigation. In this session, particularly, he was especially resistive. In addition, I immediately recognized the value of an answer because it readily provided me with a point of departure for a communication of what I considered a valuable message.

In spite of the reasons for providing Jack with an immediate response, I probably would have done well to have still tried to elicit an answer from him before offering mine. Accordingly, my immediately answering was an error (its therapeutic benefits notwithstanding) and was caused by my impulsively grabbing on to the opportunity to use the question for therapeutic purposes. I could still have used it as I had *after* I had tried to use his answer.

> T: Well, I voted for McGovern, but I really wasn't very happy voting for him because I didn't want to vote for Nixon, but it wasn't a very happy choice. Sometimes in life you have to make a choice between two

unpleasant alternatives. Do you know what that means? Like it's not really great, but you have to choose between one unpleasant thing and another unpleasant thing. Do you know what's like that?

P: Yeah.

T: What's like that? Name another thing that's like that.

P: Like uh, like if it's between like—let's say you have—you um uh have to give up one of your kids has to die.

T: Well, uh, that's a very unusual kind of decision that people have to make.

P: But I, I, I want—would you save my life? Would you try to save my life?

T: You mean your life and a choice between two unpleasant alternatives?

P: Like let's say—let's say, it was between your—naturally you—wouldn't you understand that it was a difference between like your kids had to ask which they wanted to live—the mother or this, er, you? Would you want them to say your mother?

T: Now look. That's a kind of situation . . .

P (interrupts): Let's leave them and say the mother. Wouldn't you understand?

T: I've never personally come across a situation where there was an alternative between a mother or a child living. I mean that hardly ever happens. But I could think of something that's very much closer and real, and that is let's say, for example, in a divorce. The people who live together have to make a decision between living together and being unhappy or splitting up and being unhappy. But if they split up they may be a little happier, but there are all kinds of problems when they split up.

P: But I think Mom—I don't think Mom and Dad should divorce because if she, she should take or stick—I think she should stick because she she's going to end up . . . (mumbles) . . . if she does.

T: She's going to end up a wallflower? Is that what you said?

P: We . . . we . . . welfare!

T: On welfare. Oh, on welfare! I see.

P: We might be living in the poor section of town.

T: Well, I don't think that's likely.

P: . . . (mumbles) . . .

T: But what I was saying was that when the parents split up they know that it's going to be an unhappy time for the children and they usually don't want to hurt the children. They usually love the children or at least love them a certain amount, maybe not completely.

P: Yes.

T: And they know that there's a choice between staying together and being unhappy or at least one of the people is unhappy, or splitting up and causing unhappiness for the children. And usually they don't want to cause that unhappiness for the children, but they do. And that's the kind of thing where they have to choose between two things, both of which are unpleasant. That's like choosing between McGovern or Nixon —two unpleasant alternatives—and, you know, as I saw it. Do you have any unpleasant choices to make in your life?

P: No.

T: None at all?

P: No.

T: How about with your father?

P (in loud voice): Ah, let's get on with the game!

T: You don't want to talk about that? Okay. I get a chip for that. Right?

P: Right.

T: Okay.

As can be seen, I used the election issue and the conflict which the voting caused me to serve as the opportunity to introduce the issue of ambivalence, or, more particularly, the issue of making a choice between unpleasant alternatives. I tried to point out the relationship between the situation I was in when I had to choose between two men, both of whom I had misgivings about with regard to their ability to function as president, and the situation Jack's parents were in regarding the decision to divorce. In both situations the individuals are placed in the position of choosing between unpleasant alternatives. In the context of the divorce decision I tried to communicate to Jack that his parents (especially his father) were hesitant to make a final decision because of the pain and discomfort it would cause their children.

The examples that Jack provided for choices between unpleasant alternatives were indeed morbid: choosing between the lives of two children or between the lives of a mother and her child. These considerations were followed by Jack's expressing the fear that his mother would end up on welfare. Accordingly, I considered them to be statements about Jack's fears that the separation of his parents would result in his starvation and possibly even his death. In addition, he understood my question about choosing between unpleasant alternatives to mean that one of the alternatives might be the actual starvation or death of one of the individuals concerned. Accordingly, I reassured him that the death of a child in such situations was something that I had never personally encountered. In addition, I also tried to assuage his anxiety about his mother's going on welfare. This, too, was an extremely remote possibility.

In response to a subsequent card, the following interchange took place:

T: Okay, what does your card say?

P: "Make believe that you're looking into a crystal ball that can show anything that's happening anywhere in the whole world. What do you see?"

T: You're looking into a crystal ball that can show anything that's happening anywhere in the whole world. What do you see?

P: Nixon being kicked out of office.

T: Okay, if that's what you see. Why would you want him kicked out?

P: Um, because I don't like him.

T: Why not?

P: He started the energy crisis.

T: He started it? You really feel he started the whole energy crisis?

P: Yep!

T: What else?

P: ... (mumbles) ...

T: Pardon me.

P: President Nixon tried to ... (mumbles) ...

T: Would you please try to speak clearly. I can't understand you.

P: The U.S. Government. He tried to show that he wasn't using gas by not taking a plane to San Clemente.

T: Uh huh. Right. Okay. So you don't think very much of him. Right?

P: Ya.

T: I'm going to ask you a hard question. I want you to say three good things about President Nixon.

P: He loves the country.

T: All right.

P: He stopped the war.

T: Okay.

P: And, he stopped, he, he finished the Watergate hearings.

T: Did he finish the Watergate hearings?

P: Yeah, they're not on TV, you know. Because I was missing a lot of good shows with that dumb Watergate.

T: Okay, but that's a bad thing about Nixon. Let's see, you say that he started the Watergate hearings?

P: He ended the Watergate.

T (interrupts): Oh, that was because he ended the Watergate hearings so that you could see some of your old TV programs.

P: Yeah.

T: Why do you think I asked you to say three good things about him? What was my reason for doing that?

P: I don't know.

T: Well, my reason was to try to show you that no matter how bad a person is, usually they're a mixture of good and bad. And there are lots of things that most people think are pretty bad about Nixon, but there are some good things about him too. Everybody is a mixed bag, you know?

P: (nods affirmatively)

T: Okay. You get a chip. Okay.

Again, using President Nixon as a father figure, I introduced the subject of ambivalence. At the time of this interchange (February, 1974) President Nixon's popularity was at such a low ebb that he lent himself well to being symbolized by patients as the incarnation of all that was evil. By asking the patient to name three good things about President Nixon, I was helping him gain a more balanced view of the President and, by implication, a more balanced view of his father.

Subsequently, the following interchange took place:

T: What does your card say?

P: "Tease someone."

T: Go ahead.

P: Uh, you don't have—you're not wearing sneakers. Ha, ha, ha, ha, ha.

T: I'm not wearing sneakers?

P: No.

T: What's so—what kind of a tease is that?

P: It just is.

T: Hh hmm. Okay. Anything else you want to tease me about other than sneakers?

P: Yeah. Gray hair, gray hair, glasses!

T: Glasses! What's so funny about . . .

P (interrupts): Funny clothes, funny clothes.

T: What's so funny about glasses?

P: It just is.

T: Well, I don't know. I'm very happy that I wear glasses because, you know, without them I couldn't see too well.

P: What's the problem with you? What's your eyesight?

T: It's pretty bad—about 20/400.

P: What is it—I mean like uh—what's your eye problem? Is it blurry or what?

T: No, I'm nearsighted. I'm nearsighted. I can see things very close, but when it gets any distance I have trouble. Let me tell you something.

P: What?

T: With my glasses I can see 20/20 or practically 20/20. I can see things very clearly and I think it is very important to see clearly. What do you think?

P: Yeah.

T: I think some people have a problem. They don't want to look at things clearly. They think they're better off not looking at things clearly and denying the unpleasant, whereas . . .

P (interrupts): Yeah, I get the message.

T: You get the message?

P: I do.

T: Okay. Do you do anything like that?

P: No. (throws dice in order to proceed with the game)

T: Okay. Wait a minute. Let me get my chip. Okay.

The patient's "Tease someone" card provided him with an opportunity to release hostility toward me. One cannot consider such hostility to be highly motivated by unconscious anger because the card itself requests a hostile act toward someone. However, at this point I felt that the card served Jack as an opportunity to release anger displaced toward me but primarily harbored toward his father. At first he teased me about my not wearing sneakers. I suspected that this comment related to the fact that boys his age wore sneakers and men my age generally did not. I felt he was lording over me the fact that he was a member of a group to which I did not belong.

His second tease was directed at my gray hair. Here he was putting me down because of my age and was hoping to make me feel bad because I was getting older. He then went on to tease me about the fact that I have to wear glasses and that my clothes were "funny." I suspected that these hostile comments were in part displacements of anger he felt toward his father and in part related to some of the anger he felt toward me for having discussed anxiety-provoking material concerning his relationship with his father. Because he was at a point of significant resistance regarding these important issues, I decided to focus on his comments about my wearing glasses in the hope that it would produce a discussion about the value of seeing things clearly. When Jack did appreciate what I was driving at in my discussion about the use of glasses in clarifying things, he abruptly interrupted me, threw the dice, and indicated strongly that he wished to proceed with the game. I agreed to go along with him in this regard because I felt that he did sense what I was driving at and that he was not receptive to further discussion of the issue.

Subsequently, the following interchange took place:

T: What does the card say?

P: "What frightens you the most?"

T: What frightens you the most? Okay.

P: Being stabbed or something.

T: Uh huh. Is that something that you think is likely going to happen to you?

P: No. But it frightens me. All right. (pointing to therapist) Get the chip! Get the . . .

T (interrupts): Wait a minute. I want to ask you about that. Hold on a second. That has never happened to you.

P: No.

T: No one has tried to stab you, but you have a feeling. Now what would you do if someone came up and tried to stab you?

P: I don't know. I'd give him anything he wants.

T: Hh hmm. All right. Let's say he was—that's one possibility. That would be wise—to give him anything he wants. Let's say that he was somebody you thought you might have a chance of fighting. What would you do then?

P: I'd fight him and I'd go.

T: Uh huh.

P (thrusting fist forward): And I'd go boom!

T: Okay. So sometimes if there's a danger, like somebody trying to stab you, you try to fight him. And sometimes you know it's wiser to . . .

P (interrupts): What happens if you were driving in the nighttime and you saw a stabbing in an alley. What would you do?

T: Stabbing in an alley?

P: Like in New York City or somewhere.

T: Well, I'll tell you. I think there are two possibilities: one, that I would try to intervene and help the person, and the other is that I would call the police. It depends upon how I felt and what the situation was.

P: Like my sister's friend—she doesn't live here anymore—was driving through the slums of Minneapolis. It was the nighttime. They looked in an alley. They saw a stabbing.

T: Hmm. What did they do?

P: They called—they got the police. It was nighttime.

T: Well, it's pretty sad and I think one has to try to avoid trouble, but one has to try to fight trouble if you possibly can. You've got to size up the situation and see whether it's one in which you can fight or one in which you have to give up and accept the fact that you can't fight it and . . .

P (interrupts): Yeah—yeah, I get the message.

T: Okay. All right. Look we have to stop here today. Let's count up and see how many chips we each have.

> *T:* Okay. Let's say good-bye. So long.
> *P:* So long, folks!
> *T:* Okay.

Although the patient had never actually been in danger of being stabbed, he was, in a sense, "stabbed in the back" by his father's disloyalty. After emphasizing the point that he had never in fact been exposed to such a danger, I then encouraged a discussion centering on the issue of how one handles a hostile individual. In essence, I encouraged him to fight when appropriate and when there was the possibility of a favorable outcome, and I also encouraged him to leave the situation in which there was little, if any, possibility of his being successful. In essence, I was speaking about his relationship with his father and encouraging him to take a more realistic attitude.

At the end of Jack's nineteenth month of therapy, during his one hundred and second session, his mother described significant improvement in the classroom. He was less disruptive and was getting along much better with his classmates. Whereas previously his coordination deficits resulted in his being laughed at by his classmates, he was now accepted by them. This was partly due to the physical improvement and partly related to his better relationship with them. The following interchanges took place as we played *Scrabble for Juniors*.

> *T:* Okay, you finished the word *seal*, for which you get one reward chip. If you can say anything at all about the word *seal* you get a second chip.
> *P:* Once upon a time there was a seal . . .
> *T* (interrupts): No, no, no. That's a story. First, just say anything at all about the word *seal*—just a statement about the word *seal*.
> *P:* The seal is an animal that lives in the cold.
> *T:* Okay, you get one for that. Now, can you tell a story about the word *seal*?
> *P:* Once upon a time there was an Eskimo hunter who was going to catch a seal and there was a couple of the seals. This one seal said, "I'm too smart for that guy." And like he um uh—so he put some bait, you know, kind of like fishing, you know, fish and he got the bait and he caught the seal, and the seal was, you know, he killed the seal or put him in a zoo, more or less, put him in the zoo.
> And in the zoo he didn't have as much fun. He was in the zoo, you know, bored.
> *T:* Hh hmm.
> *P:* He couldn't catch his own fish and stuff so he was bored. That's where I quit. That's my story.

T: That's the whole story. Lesson?

P: That don't think you're so smart on catching in traps.

T: Don't think you're so smart . . . ?

P: Don't think—don't be so sure in traps.

T: Can you be a little bit more specific?

P: Like um don't . . . that's what I really mean . . . don't uh . . .

T: Don't what?

P: Just because you see a little piece of bait lying out you don't just get it.

T: Hh hmm.

P: Because it might be led to a trap.

T: Hh hmm. Okay, you take two chips.

P: I got two chips already.

T: You got one for completing the word *seal* and saying seals live in the cold. Take two more for the story. Okay.

I considered the seal to represent the patient and the Eskimo trapper those around him whom he considers malevolent. There is a healthy element in the story in that the seal's wise guy attitude is being criticized. However, the seal does get caught and this, I believe, is a statement of the patient's feeling that he is somewhat helpless to protect himself from those who would be malevolent to him. Being put in the zoo symbolizes, I believe, the patient's feeling that he is entrapped by overwhelming forces.

With this understanding of the patient's story, I related mine:

T: Now wait a minute. It's my chance to tell a story now. Okay, you want to wait.

P (proceeding with the game): Yeah.

T: Just hold up. Now I tell a story about the word *seal* and I can get two chips for it. Once upon a time . . . actually you get one for getting the word, one for saying something about it, and two for the story. Okay?

P (nods affirmatively)

T: Now I go. I get two if I can tell a story.

Once upon a time there was a seal and this seal lived up North where it was cold and there were Eskimos who were constantly trying to capture seals. So this seal's mother and father said to him, "Now listen, you know the Eskimos are out to catch us and we have to be very careful. We have to watch out for their traps and watch out for their bait."

Well, this seal was kind of a wise guy and he said, "Ahhh, I don't have to watch out for their bait. I don't have to watch out for their traps. I don't have to watch out. Nothing is going to happen to me."

So whereas the other seals listened very carefully to their teachers and their mothers and fathers regarding the kinds of traps the Eskimos used and the kinds of bait that they used, this seal didn't. And sure enough one day he got caught in a trap, but fortunately only his fin got caught. He was able to pull himself out of it and he got away. And he had his fin, his little paw—I don't know what they call them—the seals have little flappers, his flapper was . . . (to patient's mother) What do they call it?

P's M: Flipper.

T: Flipper. His flipper had a little piece of flesh nipped off, but otherwise he was all right. And he came back to his parents and he was bleeding, leaving a kind of trail of blood, but they managed to fix him up.

And for the rest of his life he remembered that little experience and every time he looked at his flipper and saw the scars there it reminded him to be careful. And, of course, after that he learned very much about the kinds of traps that Eskimos have and how to avoid them.

And what do you think the lesson of that story is?

P: It's your story, not mine.

T: Okay, the lesson of that story is that often it pays to learn about the things that can be useful to you in life and they can often save you a lot of trouble. The end.

P: You can . . . on his flipper. Nothing was . . . nothing was . . . he didn't have anything cut off.

T: No, no. Just a . . .

P (interrupts): . . . scar.

T: A scar and a little piece of tissue was taken out, but the scar filled that up. Okay, I get two chips.

In my story I confirmed the healthy element in Jack's story by stressing the inappropriateness of the wise guy attitude. However, in my story the seal, although scarred, learns that one can avoid certain dangers by considering their possibility in advance. The scar serves as an everpresent reminder of his trauma and helps him remember to avoid difficulties throughout the rest of his life. My main message here, of course, was that one need not be helpless with regard to dangers that may be present; one has within himself the power to avoid them if one wishes to attend to them. I was referring here not only to the patient's classroom difficulties, but to his problems with his father as well.

Subsequently, the following interchanges took place:

T: Okay, you completed the word *cat*. Wait, you get one chip for the word *cat*.

P: A cat is an animal. It's a smaller animal related to the lion.

T: Okay, now you get . . .

P (interrupts): Then there's tigers; zee, um, chet . . . cheetahs and jaguars are all cats.

T: All right, now if you can tell a story about the word *cat* you get two more.

P: Once upon a time there was a cat and the cat really liked these people, you know. They didn't think—they didn't like him, you know. They . . .

T (interrupts): Wait. The cat liked the people, these people?

P: Yeah.

T: Go ahead.

P: And it kept on . . . (mumbles) . . .

T: What?

P: And the cat didn't like the people . . . the cat liked the people, you know. The people didn't like the cat and the cat's an old bugger.

T: Wait. The cat liked the people, but the people didn't like the cat.

P: Yeah.

T: Okay.

P: And um they'd tell the cat, "Get lost, you old cat." The cat came back the very next day. The cat would not stay away. Hey, that rhymes!

T: Okay, go ahead.

P: And they did it again. They kept on doing it and doing it because the cat like was abandoned and he wanted someone to own him, you know, love him.

T: Hh hmm.

P: And the cat . . . they'd kick it out and it kept on doing it and this cat came back (sings) the very next day. The cat would not stay away.

T: Okay.

P: And um so the cat . . . so the cat foretold them, "Don't think that . . ." the cat . . . well, they looked around the place where there were rats, you know, rats and mice.

T: Yeah, I'm not clear. What's that about rats and mice?

P: Well, the people lived around a place where there were rats and mice and stuff.

T: Yeah.

P: And the cat killed them all, you know.

T: Yeah.

P: The cat was hanging around and when the cat wasn't hanging around there weren't any mice, so they decided, "Hey, that cat's really helpful. He gets rid of the rodents and stuff." So they got the cat and the moral of the story is like you don't just kick around someone because you don't like them, like they might be very useful and they like you. That's the moral of the story.

T: Hh hmm. Okay. Okay. You get two for that. That was a very good story.

I considered the cat to represent the patient himself and the owner, his father. At first, Jack is abandoned; however, when he proves that he has a worthwhile skill he is then reaccepted into the household. The story reveals the patient's lingering feelings of rejection; however, it also reveals his appreciation that one way that one can counteract rejection is to exhibit useful and ingratiating qualities. The fantasy, therefore, is a reflection of a healthy adaptation. However, it does reveal the fact that Jack has not given up completely his hope of regaining his father's affection. With this understanding of the patient's story, I related mine:

> *T:* Okay, now it's time for me to tell my story. Once upon a time there was a cat and he lived with this man and this man decided that he didn't like this cat too much. The cat was all right in some ways, but he decided that he didn't want him. So he told the cat to leave. And the cat went out and he was very unhappy. He said, "Aw, come on, let me come back and live with you."
> The man said, "Ah, you're no use."
> And the cat said, "I'll show you. I'll show you that I can be useful. You don't like me anymore and you won't let me live with you anymore. Okay, we'll see."
> Anyway, the cat went to a nearby house and there were some people there who were really having a lot of trouble with mice and rats and things like that. And he said to them, "You know, I can be very helpful to you in killing off these mice and rats."
> And they said, "You can? Would you come to live with us?"
> And he said, "You people look like you'll appreciate me," so he went to live with these other people and he was very useful, and they gave him a good home, they gave him good food, and they gave him a good place to sleep.
> And then the other man that he had left realized that he had made a mistake in sending this cat off, but it was too late. The cat had already lived with these other people, but he saw his first owner once in a while. He would see the old owner once in a while and the old owner realized that he had made a big mistake in sending this cat off, but it was too late. The cat had another home. And the cat realized a very important lesson, which was what?
> *P:* It's your story!
> *T:* Okay, the lesson is that if someone doesn't like you or, you know, may like you very little, it doesn't mean that no one else in the whole world will not like you. There are always other people in the world who can appreciate the good things in you. The end.
> Anything you want to say about that story?

P: (nods negatively)
T: Okay.

Whereas in Jack's story reconciliation with his father is accomplished, in my story there is no such reconciliation. To foster hopes of such reconciliation would have been unrealistic because of the long period of time that the patient had been separated from his father and the fact that there was absolutely no reason to believe that the father was going to return to the home. However, I did emphasizes the ingratiating qualities that the patient possessed so as to reinforce this element from his story.

More significantly, however, in my story the cat finds love and affection in another home, while still maintaining some relationship with the previous owner. My attempt here was to help Jack appreciate that others can show him affection in compensation for the deprivations he suffers in his relationship with his father. This need not mean, however, that he has to break off completely his relationship with his father; rather, he can maintain gratifying relationships with a number of individuals.

During his twenty-second month of treatment Jack entered a regular sixth-grade class on a trial basis. In the ensuing months Jack had his ups and downs. This was related to his difficulties not so much with his father (these had reduced significantly) as with a certain boy whose taunts Jack did not have the self-control to ignore. Accordingly, Jack had at times to be returned to his special class.

At the end of his second year of treatment, during his one hundred eighteenth session, Jack's mother reported that his father had been home for a few days. She described Jack as having coped. She described him as having resigned himself to the fact that his father would neither share his interest in sports nor take him to sporting events. And rather than brooding over this, as he had done in the past, Jack had gone to a local high school football game with some friends and appeared to have enjoyed himself.

The mother also stated that for the first time Jack's father was really hearing what Jack was saying to him. She described her husband as feeling more guilty over his rejection of the children, and this guilt, she felt, was the result of Jack's calm statements about his father's neglect—this, rather than angry outbursts, displacement, and acting out. Accordingly, she described less tension in the house during the father's visit.

During the next month things did not go well for Jack and he had to spend much time in his class for emotionally disturbed children. One factor in his difficulties was his continuing inability to stay away from the boy who was teasing him. In addition, his special education teacher was taking a very relaxed attitude toward Jack's not doing his assignments and was not making appropriate demands upon him. I spoke to the teacher, strongly recommending that he take a "hard line," and in the ensuing weeks Jack shaped up considerably.

In his twenty-seventh month of therapy Jack was spending just about all of his time back in his regular sixth-grade class and was doing grade level work. He had learned to ignore his tormentor as well. Accordingly, I was able to cut his sessions down to once every other week.

During the next two months things continued to go well for Jack. He remained in his regular sixth-grade class and was able to discontinue entirely the visits to his special class. His impulse control also remained fairly good and he was able to restrain himself when confronted by teasers. Needless to say, taunting was significantly reduced. At home he was much more manageable and when his father visited he did not get unduly frustrated; rather, he accepted his father's deficiencies with healthy resignation and equanimity. (Incidentally, at no time did I ever see Jack's father. Early in treatment, he had turned down my invitation to meet with me and I never heard from him afterward. I suspect, however, that he basically approved of Jack's seeing me, because he never criticized me to Jack. Without this tacit support my work would have been much harder; however, had I had his more active cooperation, it would have been much easier.) Jack was also getting along better with neighborhood children and was doing well in scouting. Accordingly, treatment was terminated in his one hundred thirty-first session, in his twenty-ninth month of treatment.

As with most patients, the word *cure* would not be applicable to Jack's status at the time of discharge. The basic organic substrate was still present. His Ritalin had been discontinued six months previously, when it began to excite rather than quiet him. He continued taking Mellaril twice a day and was being maintained on that medication by his pediatrician at the time of discharge. Having spent two years in a special education class, Jack had lost time in certain academic areas, and so, although generally functioning at sixth-grade level, the question arose as to whether he would be able to go on in six months to the more rigorous seventh grade in his local junior high school. As his termination occurred in March, a final decision was put off till June.

In a follow-up telephone conversation eight months after termination, Jack's mother reported that he was holding quite well the gains he had made in his relationship with his father. At school it was felt that he had done well enough academically to enter a regular seventh-grade class (although some supplementary tutoring was being given). He had gained the reputation among school personnel as one of the more successful "special ed" students. With peers he was having his ups and downs, but had done well at summer camp.

CONCLUDING COMMENTS

This book was written in the hope that it might play some part, however small, in reducing the untoward psychological sequelae that children of divorce may suffer. Although divorce does not necessarily cause psychopathological reactions in the child, stresses and traumas occurring before, during, and after the separation are potential sources of difficulty. Throughout the book I have discussed in detail many of the specific ways in which the child can acquire such maladaptive reactions and have attempted to describe approaches that may be successful in their prevention and treatment.

As is to be expected, children of divorce do not fare as well as those who grow up in intact homes. Among the most dire statistics confirming this are those of Dorpat et al. (1965), who found that 50 percent of 114 completed adult suicides and 63.9 percent of 121 attempted suicides occurred in people who came from broken homes. (Dorpat does not differentiate homes broken by parental separation from those broken by parental death.) Children of divorce are likely to be less trusting of human relationships and to look upon them as unstable and capricious. When older, they may eschew marriage altogether in order to avoid what they may consider a form of enslavement or a relationship doomed to failure. If married they may feel insecure in the relationship. Some, having observed the detrimental effects of their own parents' fighting, may vow not to fight at all. Such repression and suppression, of course, merely substitute one form of pathology for another. Or, modeling themselves after their parents, they may enter into marriages characterized by violence. Divorce is more likely in the marriages of those whose parents were divorced. Divorce is much more in their scheme of things and there is less family discouragement of this method of dealing with marital difficulties. The more divorce in the family history, the greater likelihood there is that younger married people will resort to it when things become difficult. Divorced parents who try to discourage their children from getting divorced are like smoking parents who try to discourage their children from smoking.

There are some children, however, who appear to have learned from their parents' mistakes. They grow up avoiding involvement in the kinds of pathological relationships that contributed to the deterioration of their parents' marriages. The more information youngsters are provided about the reasons for the breakup of their parents, the greater the likelihood they will be able to avoid making the same mistakes. Because children identify so with their parents, such rejection of the parental model is neither common nor easily accomplished. However, recognition of the pathological parental patterns can occur—especially in a therapeutic setting. Because of the great benefits to be derived by such youngsters from such awareness, this has been one of the main themes of this book. Hopefully, the many therapeutic recommendations presented will help reduce the number of those carrying into adult life problems that originated in association with their parents' divorces.

My focus in this book has been on the family elements contributing to the psychopathological reactions of children of divorce. I am, however, aware that social and cultural factors also contribute to these difficulties. Such problems are often the final result of a whole series of environmental factors. One way of understanding the reasons for divorce is to look into the reasons for marriage. If these are weak or maladaptive, the marriage is bound to be unstable and the likelihood of marital discontent and divorce great.

In the United States there is only one acceptable reason for getting married, namely, love. People get married because they find that they experience certain euphoric feelings when thinking about or in the presence of a specific person of the opposite sex. A delusion is quickly formed that the particular party is the only one in the whole world capable of inducing this particular state of elation. In addition, they believe that these euphoric feelings can last throughout their lives even though they have never personally observed any-one—except on the movie or television screen—who has sustained this state beyond a few years.

I believe that an important contributing factor to the development of these feelings of romantic love is the need to provide oneself with a narcotic. Like the narcotic, it produces a pleasurable sensation and thereby provides enjoy-ment as an antidote to the pains and discomforts one would feel if he were to view reality more clearly. In addition, like the narcotic, it desensitizes one to pain. There are many painful affects associated with the prospect of mar-riage. One is committing oneself to a lifelong arrangement—a decision that cannot but be extremely anxiety provoking. The prospect of living for the rest of one's life with the same human being cannot but make an intelligent and sensitive human being shudder. Romantic love is an extremely potent tran-quilizer for the treatment of such anxieties. It serves also to assist the indi-vidual in denying deficiencies in the partner that may be obvious to anyone else. The lover, who believes that the feelings he experiences are engendered by the other party, is deluding himself; they are self-induced and the other party serves merely as a catalyst.

I do not wish the reader to conclude from this somewhat cynical descrip-tion of what I consider to be one element in romantic love (specifically, that element that enables individuals to get married) that I am totally condemning the phenomenon. I believe that in moderation it is an enriching experience and makes life more meaningful. It is only when it is used to excess, when people are so blinded by it that they enter into self-destructive involvements, that I consider it pathological. Unfortunately, the disease appears to be widespread among youth, although I suspect that in recent years there may have been some diminution in the propensity of young people to become ad-dicted. The "tell it like it is" philosophy may very well lessen the tendency of younger people to enter this self-induced delusional state.

Just as love is the only acceptable reason for getting married, one of the more common reasons for getting divorced is: "We are no longer in love." A marriage based on the hope that a narcotic will continue to exert its euphoric effects is doomed from the outset. As every medical student learns (and as every addict well knows) the euphoric effect of narcotics ultimately wears off.

I agree with Kubie (1956) that romantic love can also serve as a reaction-formation to underlying anger. He states that the romantic Western tradition "rationalizes and beatifies a neurotic state of obsessional infatuation.... It is an obsessional state which, like all obsessions, is in part driven by uncon-scious anger." All human relationships are ambivalent and there is no reason why the one between two young people should be any different. If young people are led to believe that only positive, warm, and loving feelings should exist between them if they are to have a solid basis for their marriage, then they will mobilize neurotic mechanisms to deal with the hostile feelings that arise in any relationship. In romantic love such angry feelings are dealt with by denial, repression, and reaction-formation. The obsessive love is only a cover-up for the angry feelings that must exist in any real relationship. We cannot satisfy one another's desires all the time; the frustrations that ultimately result in all close human encounters must produce resentments. If young people can be helped to recognize unrealistic expectations in themselves, they may have less of a need to use romantic love as a narcotic.

I believe that romantic love should be used like the occasional drink: it lifts our spirits and desensitizes us to some of our pains and frustrations. To be chronically inebriated cannot but cause us difficulties, as we remove ourselves totally from the real world.

Another common reason for getting married is that marriage is supposed to enhance one's personal happiness. Whatever miseries one may have (and each person has his own collection) marriage may be looked upon as the panacea. Ackerman (1958) states, "Marriage is approached as a potential cure for whatever psychic ills a man may suffer." Those who look upon marriage as a potential source of happiness generally subscribe to the view that it is within the capability of human beings to attain a state of happiness. Thomas Jefferson was wise enough to appreciate the fallacy of such a notion. In the Declaration of Independence he guaranteed us only "Life, Liberty, and the Pursuit of Happiness." He was wise enough to appreciate that no one can be guaranteed a state of happiness, because life is such that we will inevitably have our moments of unhappiness.

Those who look upon marriage as a source of happiness become disillusioned when it fails to provide them this expected state and they divorce because they are no longer happy. Hunt (1966) states it well: "the wide use of divorce today is not a sign of a diminished desire to be married, but of an increased desire to be happily married."

We are very much a youth-worshiping culture. There was a time when aged people were revered for their experience and were not considered ugly. Today we farm them out to nursing homes to spend their last years watching television. The youth culture reigns and beauty reigns supreme. The mass media contribute significantly to this mystique, as do advertisers, manufacturers, and salesmen. Many consider themselves the object of envy because of the beautiful partner they have acquired. Their esteem, then, is dependent upon the maintenance of the physical attractiveness of the partner. A marriage based on the hope that such beauty will persist is inevitably doomed.

Many consider the ideal marriage to be one in which the two individuals enjoy doing together most of the important activities of their lives. "Togetherness" appears to be the ideal to be achieved. The individuals live together, sleep together, raise children together, and socialize as "a couple." Invitations are invariably addressed to "Mr. & Mrs." Saturday night invitations are responded to with "We can't make it this week. How about next week?" I often refer to this as The Siamese Twin Theory of Marriage. No other human relationship makes such demands. No other human relationship requires such a degree of unified activity between two people. To the degree that the couple (that word again) subscribes to this theory, to that degree will they suffer mounting resentments and a desire for "freedom."

In recent years, with increasing awareness of this source of frustration and difficulty in marriage, many have become "more liberated" and each has done his or her "thing." I believe that this is a healthy trend. However, there are still certain problems that have yet to be solved. Most will agree that greater opportunity for a variety of separate experiences is salutary for a marriage. When such experiences, however, include extramarital sex, many would say that things have gone too far. Some hold that jealousy over a partner's involvement in extramarital sex is intrinsic to and inevitable in a close human relationship. They believe that the closer the relationship the more pained one will be in such a situation. Others hold that such jealousy is socially conditioned and that the mature individual feels no such jealousy and places no such restrictions on a partner. I tend to agree with the former position and believe that anyone who experiences no untoward reaction to a partner's extramarital involvement has a somewhat superficial relationship. I do not claim that I have come to a final answer. I only present this as one of the problems that one must deal with in deciding how much variety and independent experience is tolerable in a marriage. Obviously, the conflicts surrounding this issue contribute to marital dissatisfaction and divorce.

In recent years we have witnessed a greater incidence of marriage between persons of different cultures, classes, races, religions, and creeds. Montagu (1956) holds that such marriages are less stable than those between individuals of the same ethnic background. And this he considers to be one of the factors contributing to our rising divorce rate.

Epstein (1974) considers the recent emphasis on individual self-fulfillment to be an important factor in marital disillusionment and frustration. He considers ours to be an extremely egotistical society in which each individual is urged to "do his own thing" and satisfy himself to the greatest degree possible. Individuals are led to believe that they are not getting their share of the joys of life and often leave their marriages in the hope they will find it elsewhere. I would add to this the effects of the mass media on engendering practically limitless cravings in all of us. Bombardment with images of countless objects and experiences, only a small fraction of which we can possibly acquire, must produce in us frustrations that are probably not present in those who lead a less complicated and more limited existence.

The Women's Liberation movement has contributed (and is still doing so) to the lessening of many prejudices that were deeply entrenched in our social structure. One of the outgrowths of this movement has been increasing dissatisfaction on the part of many women with domestic life. Many have become freer to express their basic dissatisfaction with the childbearing and child rearing role and have abandoned it entirely.

The weakening of organized religion has certainly contributed to an increase in the divorce rate. Fewer people remain in unhappy marriages because of religious restrictions and fewer feel guilty over breaking them when dissolving their marriages.

The passage of no-fault divorce laws has also contributed significantly to the rising divorce rate. As I have mentioned, the notion that divorce should be granted only if one party has committed a "crime" such as adultery, drug addiction, or alcoholism, is a legacy of the past. Although the passage of no-fault divorce laws is certainly a sign of progress and has eased the suffering of many, I am not convinced that these laws are an unmixed blessing. Since they make it so easy for people to dissolve a marriage, there are many who are unwilling to suffer what I would consider to be the usual frustrations and resentments intrinsic to the institution. Accordingly, a separation and divorce may be misguided and, if children are involved, even more damage is done. There is no question that many marriages that would have survived fairly successfully in former days, when there were more stringent divorce laws, have been dissolved under the new laws, to the detriment of all concerned. I am not suggesting repeal of these new laws, however; they have still done much more good than harm.

I have focused thus far on the social and cultural factors that contribute to marital difficulties and divorce. I have not mentioned the individual neurotic factors that often play such a vital role in marital discontent. In what I call the Some-Enchanted-Evening-Across-a-Crowded-Room Theory of Marriage two individuals decide to marry because they are simultaneously stricken (as if by lightning) by an intense craving to be with one another at all times and to share their lives together in every minute aspect. I also refer to this as the Viral Disease Theory of Marriage in that the euphoric state appears to come from without, not, as is the case, from within. As the two individuals run, trip, stumble, and climb over all those who stand between them in their mad pursuit to embrace one another, they are ostensibly exhibiting intense feelings of affection. But contributing to this strange attraction, in addition to feelings of romantic love, are neurotic factors. The lovers gravitate toward one another because of a dovetailing of their neurotic needs. (This is not to say that healthy needs are not also being complemented in marital relationships; but when there is frenzy I tend to see the pathological.)

Kubie (1956) holds that many neurotic difficulties between married people result from the discrepancy between each partner's conscious and unconscious wishes from the other. A man may unconsciously want his wife to be a mother and she, in turn, may unconsciously want her husband to be a father. Although each may profess a desire for an egalitarian relationship, these basic unconscious needs cause them difficulties as each becomes frustrated with the other. Ackerman (1958) considers the desire to assuage neurotic anxiety to be an important element in many sick marriages. An impotent man, for example, may marry a woman who is frigid and thereby protect himself from the anxieties he would experience with a woman of stronger sexual interest. His frigid wife, as well, may have chosen her husband because of her appreciation of his sexual inhibition. As long as both parties avoid anxiety-provoking involvements the marriage appears stable. When, however, one of the partners becomes healthier and no longer avoids the anxiety-provoking situation, the neurotic equilibrium is disrupted and the marriage may dissolve.

There are many changes taking place in the world today that may ultimately reverse the trend toward more divorces. Some of these changes should lessen the likelihood of unsound marriages ever occurring. The recent trend in premarital cohabitation is probably reducing the number of unwise marriages. The greater freedom for premarital sexual experience makes it less likely that people today are going to marry primarily for sexual gratification. The greater availability of contraceptive devices and the relaxing of restrictions on their use make it more likely that people will have premarital sex (and therefore not marry for sex) and less likely that unmarried women will get pregnant (and therefore marry for this reason). The widespread legalization of abortion also makes it less likely that people will get married because the woman is pregnant. The lessened stigma of unwed motherhood, also, is probably bringing about fewer injudicious marriages.

There are, however, other changes that I think could be instituted that would work toward the goal of reducing the frequency of unfortunate marriages. At the present time, in most educational systems, courses in family living and family psychology are usually minor courses, sometimes still taught by the gymnasium teacher, and they are not given the distinction of such major courses as history, mathematics, science, and English. Accordingly, students tend to take them less seriously. I believe that family living and family psychology are the most important courses a youngster can take. I believe that they should be major courses from the sixth grade on and if a youngster fails such a course, he should have to repeat it just as he would one of the traditional major courses.

Another change that I think might also reduce the high divorce rate would be the establishment of a mandatory waiting period between the time one gets a marriage license and the time one is permitted to marry. Presently one can usually get married within a few days of making the decision; divorces, by contrast, even with no-fault divorce laws, can take many months and even years to get. I think that three to six months would be optimal. The mandatory "cooling off" period would be waived only if the couple could prove that they had been living together during the prescribed period or if the woman were pregnant. Of course, there are loopholes in such a system. A woman could bring a pregnant friend's urine for testing and use that to prove that she is pregnant. And one could get a false statement from a landlord. However, in spite of its possible circumvention, the principle is still a valid one and I think it could be effective in reducing the divorce rate.

Lastly, I am in agreement with Kardiner (1968), who views monogamous marriage as the best arrangement for the healthy psychological development of the children—the frustrations and restrictions it causes the parents notwithstanding. There is nothing new in the alternative life-styles that people are talking so much about today. There is no arrangement that people today can conceive of that hasn't been tried hundreds of times over in mankind's history. Polygamy, polyandry, group marriages, homosexual marriages, single parenthood, and communal life have all been tried many times. It appears that children do best when they grow up in a home where there is one recognized mother and one recognized father, each of whom has established a close relationship with the child. Such children are most likely to perpetuate their heritage and build upon it. Children of other arrangements, with rare exception, are more likely to be lost in history.

BIBLIOGRAPHY

Ackerman, N.W. (1958). *The Psychodynamics of Family Life*. New York: Basic Books.

Ames, L.B. (1966). Children's stories. *Genetic Psychology Monographs* 73: 336-396.

Arnstein, H.S. (1962). *What to Tell Your Child*. New York: Bobbs-Merril.

Bazelon, D. L. (1974). The perils of wizardry. *The American Journal of Psychiatry,* 131:1317–1322.

Beck, A.T. (1974). Depressive neurosis. In *American Handbook of Psychiatry*, 2nd edition, ed. S. Arieti, vol. 3, pp. 61-90. New York: Basic Books.

Beres, D. (1958). Vicissitudes of superego precursors in childhood. *Psychoanalytic Study of the Child*, 13:324-351.

Bergler, E. (1948). *Divorce Won't Help*. New York: Harper & Brothers.

Bieber, I. (1962). *Homosexuality: A Psychoanalytic Study*. New York: Basic Books.

———— (1974). The psychodynamics and treatment of male homosexuality. Lecture to the New Jersey Psychiatric Association and the Academy of Psychoanalysis of New Jersey, October 9, 1974.

Blake, N.M. (1962). *The Road to Reno: A History of Divorce in the United States*. New York: Macmillan.

Bowlby, J. (1951). *Maternal Care and Mental Health*. Geneva: World Health Organization.

Breuer, J. and Freud, S. (1895). *Studies on Hysteria*. New York: Basic Books, 1957.

Carter, H. and Glick, P. (1970). *Marriage and Divorce: A Social and Economic Study*. Cambridge: Harvard University Press.

Crumley, F.E. and Blumenthal, R.S. (1973). Children's reactions to temporary loss of a father. *American Journal of Psychiatry* 130:778-782.

Despert, L.F. (1953). *Children of Divorce*. Garden City, New York: Dolphin Books.

Deutsch, H. (1937). Absence of grief. *Psychoanalytic Quarterly* 6:12-22.

Diagnostic and Statistical Manual of Mental Disorders (DSM-II). Washington, D.C.: American Psychiatric Association.

Dorpat, T.I., Jackson, J.K., and Ripley, H.S. (1965). Broken homes and attempted suicide. *Archives of General Psychiatry* 12:213-216.

Epstein, J. (1974). *Divorced in America*. New York: E.P. Dutton.

Erikson, E. (1963). *Childhood and Society*. New York: W.W. Norton.

Forer, L. G. (1975). *The Death of the Law*. New York: David McKay

Freud, A. and Burlingham, D.T. (1944a). *War and Children*. New York: International Universities Press.

_____ (1944b). *Infants without Families*. New York: International Universities Press.

Freud, S. (1909). A phobia in a five-year-old boy. In *Collected Papers*, vol. 3, pp. 149-289. New York: Basic Books, 1959.

_____ (1924). The passing of the Oedipus complex. In *Collected Papers*, vol. 2, pp. 269-276. New York: Basic Books, 1959.

_____ (1917). Mourning and melancholia. In *Collected Papers*, vol. 3, pp. 152-170. New York: Basic Books, 1959.

Forrest, T. (1966). Paternal roots of female character development, *Contemporary Psychoanalysis* 3:21-38.

Frohlich, N. (1971). *Making the Best of It*. New York: Harper and Row.

Fromm, E. (1948). The Oedipus complex and the Oedipus myth. In *The Science and Culture Series*, vol. 5, *The Family: Its Function and Destiny*, ed. R.N. Anshen. New York: Harper and Brothers.

Furman, R.A. (1964). Death of a six-year-old's mother during his analysis. *Psychoanalytic Study of the Child* 19:377-397.

Gardner, G.E. (1956). Separation of the parents and the emotional life of the child. *Mental Hygiene* 40:53-64.

Gardner, R.A. (1969a). The guilt reaction of parents of children with severe physical disease. *American Journal of Psychiatry* 126:636-644.

_____ (1969b). Guilt, Job, and J.B. *Medical Opinion and Review* 5 (2): 146-155.

_____ (1970a). The use of guilt as a defense against anxiety. *The Psychoanalytic Review* 57:124-136.

_____ (1970b). *The Boys and Girls about Divorce*. New York: Jason Aronson.

_____ (1971a). *The Boys and Girls Book about Divorce*. New York: Bantam.

_____ (1971b). *Therapeutic Communication with Children: The Mutual Storytelling Technique*. New York: Jason Aronson.

_____ (1971c). A proposed scale for the determination of maternal feeling. *Psychiatric Quarterly* 45 (1): 23-34.

_____ (1972a). *Dr. Gardner's Stories about the Real World*. Englewood Cliffs, N.J.: Prentice-Hall.

_____ (1972b). Little Hans—the most famous boy in the child psychotherapy literature. *International Journal of Child Psychotherapy* 1 (4): 24-50.

_____ (1973a). *Understanding Children*. New York: Jason Aronson.

_____ (1973b). Women's lib., sex role development, and children's play. *Medical Aspects of Human Sexuality* 2 (1): 7-12.

_____ (1974). Divorce: from the man's view. *The Single Parent* 17 (9): 5-10, 38.

_____ (1974a). *Dr. Gardner's Fairy Tales for Today's Children*. Englewood Cliffs, N.J. Prentice-Hall.

_____ (1974b). Psychological aspects of divorce. In *American Handbook of Psychiatry*, ed. S. Arieti, 2nd edition, vol. 1, pp. 496-512. New York: Basic Books.

_____ (1975). *Psychotherapeutic Approaches to the Resistant Child*. New York: Jason Aronson.

_____ (1977). *The Parents Book about Divorce*. New York: Doubleday.

_____ (1979). *The Parents Book About Divorce* (paperback edition). New York: Bantam Books, Inc.

_____ (1985). *Separation Anxiety Disorder: Psychodynamics and Psychotherapy*. Cresskill, N.J.: Creative Therapeutics.

_____ (1986a). *The Psychotherapeutic Techniques of Richard A. Gardner*. Cresskill, N.J.: Creative Therapeutics.

_____ (1986b). *Child Custody Litigation: A Guide for Parents and Mental Health Professionals*. Cresskill, N.J.: Creative Therapeutics.

_____ (1987). *The Parental Alienation Syndrome and the Differentiation Between Fabricated and Genuine Child Sex Abuse*. Cresskill, N.J.: Creative Therapeutics.

_____ (1988). *Psychotherapy with Adolescents*. Cresskill, N.J.: Creative Therapeutics.

_____ (1989). *Family Evaluation in Child Custody Mediation, Arbitration, and Litigation*. Cresskill, N.J.: Creative Therapeutics.

_____ (1991). *Sex Abuse Hysteria: Salem Witch Trials Revisited*. Cresskill, N.J.: Creative Therapeutics.

Gauthier, Y. (1965). The mourning reaction of a ten-and-a-half-year old boy. *Psychoanalytic Study of the Child* 20:481-494.

Gettleman, S. and Markowitz, J. (1974). *The Courage to Divorce*. New York: Simon and Schuster.

Glieberman, H. A. (1975). *Confessions of a Divorce Lawyer*. Chicago: Henry Regnery Co.

Glueck, E. and Glueck, S. (1950). *Unraveling Juvenile Delinquency*. Cambridge, Mass.: Harvard University Press.

_____ (1952). *Delinquents in the Making*. New York: Harper and Row.

Goldstein, J., Freud, A., and Solnit, A.J. (1973). *Beyond the Best Interests of the Child*. New York: The Free Press.

Goode, W.J. (1956). *Women in Divorce*. New York: The Free Press.

Gregory, I. (1965a). Anterospective data following childhood loss of a parent: I. Delinquency and high school dropout. *Archives of General Psychiatry* 13:99-109.

_____ (1965b). Anterospective data following loss of a parent: II. Pathology, performance and potential among college students. *Archives of General Psychiatry* 13:110-120.

Grollman, E.A. (1969). *Explaining Divorce to Children*. Boston: Beacon Press.

Hetherington, E.M. (1973). Girls without fathers. *Psychology Today* 6 (9): 46-52.

Hunt, M. (1966). *The World of the Formerly Married*. New York: McGraw-Hill.

Johnson, A. (1949). Sanctions for superego lacunae of adolescents. In *Searchlights on Delinquency*, ed. K.R. Eissler, pp. 225-245. New York: International Universities Press.

_____ (1959). Juvenile delinquency. In *American Handbook of Psychiatry*, ed. S. Arieti, vol. 1, pp. 840-865. New York: Basic Books.

Kanner, L. (1957). *Child Psychiatry*. Springfield, Ill.: Charles C Thomas.

Kardiner, A. (1968). A psychological understanding of monogamy. In *The Marriage Relationship*, ed. S. Rosenbaum and I. Alger. New York: Basic Books.

Keiser, S. (1953). A manifest Oedipus complex in an adolescent girl. *Psychoanalytic Study of the Child* 8: 99-107.

Kliman, G. (1968). *Psychological Emergencies of Childhood*. New York: Grune & Stratton.

Kling, S.G. (1967). *The Complete Guide to Divorce*. New York: Simon and Schuster.

Kritzberg, N. (1966). A new verbal projective test for the expansion of the projective aspects of the clinical interview. *Acta Paedopsychiatrica* 33 (2): 48-62.

Kubie, L.S. (1964). The challenge of divorce. *Journal of Nervous and Mental Diseases* 138:511-512.

Landis, J.T. (1960). The trauma of children when parents divorce. *Marriage and Family Living* 22: 7-13.

Lindsely, B. C. (1976). Custody proceedings: battlefield or peace conference. *Bulletin of the American Academy of Psychiatry and the Law,* 4(2):127-131.

McDermott, J.F. (1968). Parental divorce in early childhood. *American Journal of Psychiatry* 124:1424-1432.

———— (1970). Divorce and its psychiatric sequelae in childhood. *Archives of General Psychiatry* 23:421-427.

McDermott, J.F., Bolman, W.M. et al. (1973). The concept of child advocacy. *American Journal of Psychiatry* 130: 1203-1206.

Mahler, M.S. and Rabinovitch, R. (1956). The effects of marital conflict on child development. In *Neurotic Interaction in Marriage*, ed. V.W. Eisenstein, pp. 44-56. New York: Basic Books.

Malmquist, C.P. (1968). Conscience development. *Psychoanalytic Study of the Child* 23: 301-331.

Meiss, M.L. (1952). The oedipal problem of a fatherless child. *Psychoanalytic Study of the Child* 7: 216-229.

Monahan, T.P. (1958). The changing nature and instability of remarriages. Eugenics Quarterly 5: 73-85.

Montagu, M.F.A. (1956). Marriage—A cultural perspective. In *Neurotic Interaction in Marriage*, ed. V.W. Eisenstein, pp. 3-10. New York: Basic Books.

Morrison, J.R. (1974). Parental divorce as a factor in childhood psychiatric illness. *Comprehensive Psychiatry* 15 (2): 95-102.

Neubauer, P.B. (1960). The one parent child and his oedipal development. *Psychoanalytic Study of the Child* 15: 286-309.

Nizer, L. (1968), *My Life in Court*. New York: Pyramid Publications.

Nye, I.F. (1957). Child adjustment in broken and in unhappy unbroken homes. *Marriage and Family Living* 19: 356-361.

Piers, G. and Singer, M. B. (1953). *Shame and Guilt*. Springfield, Ill.: Charles C Thomas.

Pitcher, E.G. and Prelinger, E. (1963). *Children Tell Stories: An Analysis of Fantasy*. New York: International Universities Press.

Plateris, A.A. (1967). Divorce statistics analysis: United States—1963. Public Health Service Publication 1000, Series 21, No. 13. U.S. Government Printing Office, Washington, D.C.

Polatin, P. and Philtine, E.C. (1964). *Marriage in the Modern World*. Philadelphia: Lippincott.

―――― (1974). Divorce: from the man's view. *The Single Parent* 17 (9): 5-10, 38.

Robins, L.N. (1966). *Deviant Children Grown Up*. Baltimore: Williams and Wilkins.

Scharl, A. (1961). Regression and restitution in object loss. *Psychoanalytic Study of the Child* 16: 471-480.

Schwartz, A.C. (1968). Reflections on divorce and remarriage. *Social Casework* 49: 213-217.

Shambaugh, B. (1961). A study of loss reactions in a seven-year-old. *Psychoanalytic Study of the Child* 16: 510-527.

Short, J.F. (1966). Juvenile delinquency: the social-cultural context. In *Review of Child Development Research*, ed. L.N.W. Hoffman and M.L. Hoffman, vol. 2. New York: Russell Sage Foundation.

Sopkin, C. (1974). The roughest divorce lawyers in town. *New York* 7 (44): 52-56.

Stone, I. (1971). *The Passions of the Mind*. New York: Signet.

Strupp, H.H. (1975). Psychoanalysis, "focal psychotherapy," and the nature of the therapeutic influence. *Archives of General Psychiatry* 32: 127-135.

Sugar, Max (1970). Children of divorce. *Pediatrics* 46: 588-595.

Sullivan, H.S. (1953). *The Interpersonal Theory of Psychiatry*. New York: W.W. Norton.

Trunnell, T.L. (1968). The absent father's children's emotional disturbances. *Archives of General Psychiatry* 19: 180-188.

Thompson, C. (1959). The interpersonal approach to the clinical problems of masochism. In: *Individual and Family Dynamics,* ed. J. Masserman. New York: Grune & Stratton.

Wallerstein, J. S. and Kelly, J. B. (1980). *Surviving the Breakup*. New York: Basic Books.

Watson, A. S. (1969). The children of Armageddon: problems of custody following divorce. *Syracuse Law Review,* 21:55–86.

Weiss, P. S. (1975). *Marital Separation*. New York: Basic Books.

Weinstein, A.S. and Moskowitz, J.A. (1972). "Let no man put asunder." *New York State Journal of Medicine* 72:2347-2349.

Westman, J.C. (1972). Effect of divorce on a child's personality. *Medical Aspects of Human Sexuality*, January, 1972.

Westman, J.C., Cline, D.W. et al. (1970). Role of child psychiatry in divorce. *Archives of General Psychiatry* 23: 416-420.

Whitaker, C.A. and Miller, M.H. (1969). A reevaluation of "psychiatric help" when divorce impends. *American Journal of Psychiatry* 126: 611-618.

Wolfenstein, M. (1966). How is mourning possible? *Psychoanalytic Study of the Child* 21:93-123.

Wylie, H. and Degado, R. (1959). A pattern of mother-son relationship involving the absence of the father. *American Journal of Orthopsychiatry* 29: 644-649.

INDEX